Y0-BDX-716

Peace and War

Peace and War
A Guide to Bibliographies

Berenice A. Carroll, Clinton F. Fink, and Jane E. Mohraz

With Foreword by
Michael Keresztesi

ABC-Clio, Inc.

Santa Barbara, California

Oxford, England

©1983 by Berenice A. Carroll, Clinton F. Fink, and Jane E. Mohraz

All rights reserved. No part of this publication may be reproduced, stored in a retrieval system, or transmitted, in any form or by any means, electronic, mechanical, photocopying, recording, or otherwise, except for the inclusion of brief quotations in a review, without prior permission in writing from the publishers.

Preparation of this volume was made possible by a grant from the Research Materials Program of the National Endowment for the Humanities, an independent federal agency.

Library of Congress Cataloging in Publication Data
Carroll, Berenice A.
  Peace and war.

  (War/peace bibliography series)
  Bibliography: p.
  Includes indexes.
  1. Peace—Bibliography. 2. War—Bibliography.
I. Fink, Clinton F. II. Mohraz, Jane E. III. Title.
IV. Series.
Z6464.Z9C55 [JX1952]   016.3271'72   81-4980
ISBN 0-87436-322-5   AACR2

10 9 8 7 6 5 4 3 2 1

ABC-Clio, Inc.
2040 Alameda Padre Serra, Box 4397
Santa Barbara, California 93103

Clio Press Ltd.
55 St. Thomas Street
Oxford, OX1 1JG, England

Manufactured in the United States of America

8 3 4 3 6 6

LIBRARY
ALMA COLLEGE
ALMA, MICHIGAN

The War/Peace Bibliography Series

Richard Dean Burns, Editor

This series has been developed in cooperation with the Center for the Study of Armament and Disarmament, California State University, Los Angeles.

#1 *Songs of Protest, War and Peace*
A Bibliography and Discography
R. SERGE DENISOFF

#2 *Warfare in Primitive Societies*
A Bibliography
WILLIAM TULIO DIVALE

#3 *The Vietnam Conflict*
Its Geographical Dimensions,
Political Traumas and Military
Developments
MILTON LEITENBERG AND
RICHARD DEAN BURNS

#4 *The Arab-Israeli Conflict*
A Historical, Political, Social, and
Military Bibliography
RONALD M. DEVORE

#5 *Modern Revolutions and
Revolutionists*
A Bibliography
ROBERT BLACKEY

#6 *Arms Control and Disarmament*
A Bibliography
RICHARD DEAN BURNS

#7 *The United States in World War I*
A Selected Bibliography
RONALD SCHAFFER

#8 *Uncertain Judgment*
A Bibliography of War Crimes Trials
JOHN R. LEWIS

#9 *The Soviet Navy, 1941–1978*
A Guide to Sources in English
MYRON J. SMITH, JR.

#10 *The Soviet Air and Strategic Rocket
Forces, 1939–1980*
A Guide to Sources in English
MYRON J. SMITH, JR.

#11 *The Soviet Army, 1939–1980*
A Guide to Sources in English
MYRON J. SMITH, JR.

#12 *The Secret Wars*
A Guide to Sources in English
Volume I: Intelligence, Propaganda
and Psychological Warfare,
Resistance Movements, and Secret
Operations, 1939–1945
MYRON J. SMITH, JR.

The War/Peace Bibliography Series

With this bibliographical series, the Center for the Study of Armament and Disarmament, California State University, Los Angeles, seeks to promote a wider understanding of martial violence and the alternatives to its employment. The Center, which was formed by concerned faculty and students in 1962-63, has as its primary objective the stimulation of intelligent discussion of war/peace issues. More precisely, the Center has undertaken two essential functions: (1) to collect and catalogue materials bearing on war/peace issues; and (2) to aid faculty, students, and the public in their individual and collective probing of the historical, political, economic, philosophical, technical, and psychological facets of these fundamental problems.

This bibliography series is, obviously, one tool with which we may more effectively approach our task. Each issue in this series is intended to provide a comprehensive "working," rather than definitive, bibliography on a relatively narrow theme within the spectrum of war/peace studies. While we hope this series will prove to be a useful tool, we also solicit your comments regarding its format, contents, and topics.

RICHARD DEAN BURNS
Series Editor

Contents

Part III: War

Foreword

The literature on peace and war has been accumulating for centuries at an accelerating rate, reflecting the persistent concerns of individuals, organizations, and official bodies. The richness and diversity of forms that characterize the literary terrain of peace research reflect the vitality with which these concerns have sought expression in societal action, governmental measures, and international arrangements. Concurrently with the proliferation of writing and publishing on the subject of peace and war, countless attempts have been made to bring this rising tide of materials under some degree of bibliographic control for optimum use in study, research, teaching, or contemplation. The number and variety of bibliographic artifacts that have appeared over the past century to facilitate access to the subject literature has increased to the point of constituting in itself a distinct literary medium of considerable proportion and complexity in need of a bibliographic organization of its own.

Thus, from a historical vantage point, publication of the present work must be considered a significant event in the annals of peace research. Aiming to identify, describe, and organize the hitherto unsorted multitude of bibliographic works in the field, the compilers have opened up broad vistas for research and analysis. No bibliographic instrument of comparable chronological and topical scope has been constructed so far. The end product of a broad-gauge inventorial effort, this guide well meets the needs of scholars, writers, librarians, international policymakers, educators, and students in their quest for pertinent documentary and literary resources. Beyond being an efficient finding tool, a time-saver and reliable guidepost, the present work is also capable of serving as a point of departure for new inquiries and investigations, thus fostering progress in peace research.

Bringing organization into the bibliographic realm of a disciplinary domain also involves imposing order and structure indirectly upon its literature. The quality of a subject bibliography reveals itself through the concepts that determine the field's epistemological boundaries and the categorization of the pertinent subject matter, and through the logical coherence and empirical viability of the classification scheme used to structure the field. One of the main virtues of the work at hand is that the principles underlying its organization were developed from the perspectives of subject specialists and professional researchers who have worked in the field for many years. They have contributed creatively to its substantive literature. From under their expert hands a map of the frontiers of peace research clearly emerges, offering orientation for both sophisticated and lay users.

The meticulous and abundantly informative annotations encompassing the quantity, quality, format, chronological origin, and provenance of the literature in each bibliography make this guide an exceptional research aid. For social science scholarship, its value is further enhanced because the mass of bibliographic data displayed in the entries was processed by computer. This method makes possible many different approaches to the material through tabulation of the data by a variety of facets of the bibliographies cited. The computer can produce listings ordered by title, year, place of publication, language, or chronological range of works enumerated in the bibliographies, as well as by publisher, and the title of the journal in which a given bibliography appeared.

The electronic sorting of bibliographic data by so many variables is an innovation. It paves the way for anatomical explorations not only into the nature of the literature on peace and war but into the life processes and destiny of peace research itself. Out of these explorations, some of which are now under way, new insights may be gained that can illuminate hitherto obscure historical, political, economic, sociological, psychological, and cultural phenomena.

Clearly, this work transcends the purely inventorial functions of traditional bibliographic guides. It is itself a document, a resource to be studied and analyzed, mining its rich layers of information for the advancement of knowledge.

MICHAEL KERESZTESI
Wayne State University
President, Association for the
Bibliography of History

Acknowledgments

This project has extended over a number of years and the authors have many persons to thank for their assistance in various aspects of the work. Although it is impossible to name all those we have talked with, learned from, and relied upon in various ways, we wish to name here and give warm thanks to those who have been most directly helpful to this project.

In particular, we would like to thank those who served as research assistants: Miriam Lowinger, Gautam Sen, and Leslie Moch; those who assisted us in entering data and struggling with the vagaries of the computer: Roberta Klein, Heidi Epp, Lin Rowley, John Resman, Roberta Owen, Kathleen Goodwin, Phyllis Barkhurst, Kim Tingley, Frances Au, David Carroll, and Malcolm Carroll; those who assisted in preparation of the manuscript through various editorial, clerical, and secretarial tasks: Roberta Owen, Helen K. Curley, Mary J. Stone, Angie Dey, Ellen Ozur, Patricia Dinota, Irene Salazar, Malcolm Carroll, David Carroll, Stephanie Maggs, and Katherine Maggs; and those who provided assistance with translations and editorial tasks in languages other than English: Heidi Epp, Mary J. Stone, Roberta Owen, Chris Jocius, Sharon Bickel, and Robert Carroll.

We would also like to thank colleagues who served as consultants or advisers: Michael Keresztesi, Sandi E. Cooper, Richard Dean Burns, Blanche W. Cook, Warren Kuehl, and Charles Chatfield; Scott Preece and Martha Williams of the Information Retrieval Research Laboratory, UIUC; Marion M. Carter and Nancy Morrison of the Social Sciences Quantitative Laboratory, UIUC; Peggy Lowry of the Research Services Office, UIUC; and other members of the UIUC secretarial and administrative staff who assisted in technical and budgetary tasks. Thanks are also gratefully offered to Yvette Scheven of the University of Illinois Library, Bernice Nichols of the Swarthmore College Peace Collection, and other librarians and archivists who assisted us at the various libraries and collections we have visited or worked at for extended periods, including the libraries of the University of Illinois at Urbana-Champaign, the University of Michigan at Ann Arbor, and the University of Maryland at College Park; the New York Public Library, the Hoover Library of War, Revolution and Peace, and the Stanford University Library; the British Library (London), the Bibliothèque Historique de la Ville de Paris and the Bibliothèque Nationale (Paris); and the Library of Congress.

Finally, we acknowledge with gratitude the support and assistance of the Research Materials Program of the National Endowment for the Humanities and the Research Board of the University of Illinois at Urbana-Champaign.

Introduction

This volume is an annotated guide to bibliographies on peace and war published from 1785 through 1980. The guide encompasses bibliographies published as separate books, articles, and pamphlets; bibliographies appearing as sections of nonbibliographic works (including articles, books, pamphlets, yearbooks, and other works); and some unpublished bibliographies available in the Library of Congress or in other libraries. It draws together materials from numerous fields and disciplines, including the humanities, the social sciences, the professions, and the natural sciences.

This bibliography is unique in that it combines several special characteristics: 1) it is the first to provide comprehensive coverage of bibliographies on questions relating to peace and war; 2) it has extensive annotations; 3) it has a detailed subject index in addition to a general classificatory scheme; 4) within the main subject categories, it is arranged chronologically, for those interested either in the history of the field or in locating the most recent materials. These features make accessible both to scholars and to the public a body of bibliographic information heretofore retrievable only through long and laborious searches in widely scattered sources and locations.

Any person concerned with the question of peace, whether scholar, scientist, humanist, educator, professional, public servant, or other interested person, will find appropriate and valuable resources here. Since many of the materials listed in the bibliographies are directed to general audiences or compiled by organizations dedicated to working with the public, the guide should be useful not only to academics in the fields of peace research, peace studies, and related areas, but also to study groups, religious groups, public action organizations, and government agencies.

Background and Previous Bibliographic Aids

This guide grew out of an ongoing study of the history of peace research and peace theory since 1800. In 1975, under a grant from the National Endowment for the Humanities, Berenice A. Carroll and Clinton F. Fink undertook to develop a bibliography of peace theory and peace research for the period 1800 to 1945. In the early stages of that project, it became clear that there was no adequate guide to the large number of existing bibliographies on the problems of peace and war. Carroll and Fink undertook to provide such a guide, under continuing support from the National Endowment for the Humanities. Jane E. Mohraz joined the project in 1976, first as research assistant and later as co-author.

The previous bibliographic aids available include general bibliographic resources; guides to bibliographies in the fields of political science, international relations, and national security affairs; and specialized bibliographies on war and peace which include sections listing other bibliographies. All of these resources have been consulted in the preparation of this volume, and all of the disciplinary and specialized bibliographies we used are included and described in this guide. Details concerning our main sources, search methods, and the limits of our search are provided below.

Several previously existing bibliographic aids contain lists of 50 or more relevant bibliographies, but all have marked limitations. Since 1964 *Peace Research Abstracts Journal* (item No. 553 in this guide) has published a section on bibliographies that is limited mainly to separately published bibliographic works appearing since 1945. Several bibliographies in the fields of political science and international relations are worthy of note. Eric H. Boehm's *Bibliographies on International Relations and World Affairs* (1965, our item No. 218) lists only relevant periodicals that regularly contain bibliographic information, whether in the form of book reviews, abstracts, or book lists. The Universal Reference System's *Bibliography of Bibliographies in Political Science, Government, and Public Policy* (1968, item No. 108) is an annotated listing of bibliographies, organized by accession numbers and indexed with a chronological listing of authors and titles under main subject heads, including "war," "peace," and "arms control and disarmament." There is considerable overlap in individual items on these lists, however, and the total number of pertinent items is clearly far smaller than the number encompassed in the present guide. A few subject bibliographies which focus specifically on peace and war include lists of 40 to 100 bibliographies: Florence Brewer Boeckel, *Between War and Peace: A handbook for peace workers* (1928, item No. 27); Blanche W. Cook, *Bibliography on Peace Research in History* (1969, item No. 686); Gerta Scharffenorth and Wolfgang Huber et al., *Neue Bibliographie zur Friedensforschung* (1973, item No. 977); Lalit K. Aggarwal, *Peace Science: A bibliography* (1974, item No. 980); and Elise Boulding, J. Robert Passmore, and Robert Scott Gassler, *Bibliography on World Conflict and Peace* (1979, item No. 130). Each of these bibliographies may list, for reasons explained below under "Main Sources and Search Methods," some individual bibliographies not encompassed in the present guide. Nevertheless, this guide is far more comprehensive and more extensively annotated and subject-indexed than any previous aid providing access to bibliographies in its field.

Scope

The table of contents and the subject index clearly indicate the scope of this guide. In general, Part I contains bibliographies of the broadest and most general scope concerning both peace and war or on topics that bridge both areas, such as international relations, religion, or social movements in their relation to peace and war. Part II covers bibliographies focusing mainly on peace, the peace movement, and related topics. Part III contains bibliographies focusing on war and its various aspects, causes, and consequences.

One of our principles has been to cover works of general application rather than bibliographies that focus on particular wars or conflicts. While bibliographies that focus on or contain sections on particular wars or conflicts are cited here and listed in the subject index, they do not constitute main subject categories except for the two world wars (Section 26). Another principle we followed was to emphasize works most directly concerned with the goals of abolishing the war system and establishing a peaceful world society. Consequently, bibliographies dealing with military science, military strategy, deterrence policies, and similar topics have not been specifically sought but are included if they appeared in our primary sources. The scope of materials covered is also defined in part by the extent of our searches, as explained further below.

Among the 1398 entries in this volume, there are items published in 30 countries and over 15 languages. Aside from those items that appeared in journals, and a few for which we do not have publisher information, approximately 71 percent of the items listed were published in the United States; about 11 percent appeared in the United Kingdom, Canada, and Australia; about 15 percent in Western Europe and Scandinavia; and about 3 percent in countries of Eastern Europe, Latin America, Asia, and the Near East. In chronological scope, fully one-third of the entries appeared in the decade 1936-1945, about one-third since 1945, and about one-third prior to 1936 (but only 23 of the bibliographies listed were published prior to 1900). In geographical focus, most of the entries cover materials concerned mainly with the United States and Western Europe, but many also cover materials relating to other countries and geographic regions, which are listed in the subject index.

Arrangement of the Guide

The entries in this guide are arranged under 34 main subject categories. These categories emerged from an analysis of the contents of the bibliographies rather than from an a priori division and reflect the concerns of the compilers of bibliographies on peace and war in the periods covered. Thus, for example, in our searches we found too few entries focusing primarily on race or on imperialism to justify establishing either of these as a major category, though these topics appeared as sections of many larger bibliographies and today would be regarded as important in the study of peace and war. The subject index provides a more detailed picture of the specific topics covered in the bibliographies.

Within each main subject category, entries are listed chronologically by publication date, then alphabetically by author within each year. Each entry appears under only one subject category in the main text of the guide, although many of the bibliographies have a wider scope and might appropriately be listed under other subject heads as well; such other appropriate subject headings are indicated in the subject index. In some cases the classification may differ substantially from what one might expect based on the title of the work; our classification is based on examination of the actual content of the bibliography itself, which is often more general than the title of the work in which it appears. An exception to this rule is the case of publication lists of peace organizations, which are usually entered under "Peace Movement—Publication Lists" rather than under the main subject emphasis of the works listed; the subjects covered by these works are indicated in the subject index.

Form of Citation

A uniform format for the bibliographic data has been followed. In general, we have followed the *Chicago Manual of Style,* with certain modifications appropriate to this guide or necessitated by the constraints of computerization. A sample citation is:

> **11**   JX1908.U5,v.3
> Levermore, Charles H[erbert].
>
> "Suggestions for the study of international relations." *World Peace Foundation Pamphlet Series,* 3, 11, Part 2 (November, 1913). 28 pp.

We have provided Library of Congress call numbers when available. These appear at the upper right of the entry on the item number line. In some cases we provide call numbers for other libraries. In the case of the British Library, for example, the call number reads "BL: 11904.66.60." See the list of symbols and abbreviations below.

Users of the guide may wish to note certain practices followed in the citations:

1. Book and journal titles are underlined in main citations, but titles of other editions, reprints, and works mentioned in annotations are not underlined.

2. Titles of pamphlets, typed or mimeographed reading lists, reports, and unpublished dissertations are not underlined or set off by quotation marks.

3. Titles of articles or chapters are set off by quotation marks; however, descriptive headings (such as Bibliography, References) are not.

4. Information provided by the compilers as a result of examining an item or consulting other sources of information is provided in brackets.

5. Translations of titles, publishers, and other bibliographical information are set off by a slash mark if given in the original; translations of titles supplied by the compilers are set off by brackets.

6. Place of publication in foreign countries has been anglicized. Multiple publishers or places of publication are separated by slash marks.

Annotations

Approximately two-thirds of the bibliographies covered by this guide were examined directly by the compilers and annotated as to length, scope, and content. For example, the annotation of the Levermore entry (see the sample citation above) reads:

> 262 items, 1884–1913. English; also French, German (6), Italian (2), Dutch (1), Danish (1), Swedish (1). Many items have brief critical and/ or descriptive annotations; introduction (2 pp.) plus introductions (in outline form) to each section.
>
> Periodicals and other publications of peace and international relations organizations (51), relation of war to civilization (44), influence

of democracy on international relations (43), international influence of religion in theory and practice (19), historical and critical discussion of arbitration (25), work of existing international organizations and associations (28), world organization and the attainment of peace and justice (52).

This illustrates the types of information provided, as follows:

1. *Number of items.* In general, the number given is by exact count. In the case of very large bibliographies, the number is sometimes estimated from a sample of pages; this is so stated in the annotation. In some cases of bibliographic essays or bibliographic footnotes where the items do not appear in lists, the number of items is omitted.

2. *Chronological scope of items.* This usually states the earliest and latest year of items listed. For very large bibliographies, approximate dates are given.

3. *Language scope.* Here we give first the main language or languages of the bibliography, including any language which constitutes 20 percent or more of the titles in the bibliography, listed in order of relative frequency. Next we list secondary languages (following the word "also") in order of frequency. If there are fewer than ten items for a given language, the exact number appears in parentheses. In large bibliographies with numerous languages, we may restrict ourselves to general comments such as "other western languages" or "other eastern languages."

4. *Format.* Here we indicate the proportion of items annotated (if any), using the following terms: "a few" (less than 10 percent), "some" (10 to 40 percent), "many" (40 to 80 percent), "most" (more than 80 percent), "all" (100 percent); we note further the length of the annotations ("brief," "medium-length," or "abstract-length") and the type of annotations ("descriptive," "critical," or a combination thereof). If items are discussed in text or footnotes, this information is specified. Next we note the presence and length of any introduction, preface, foreword, or section introductions; the presence of a table of contents; the presence and nature of indexes (subject index, author index, or combined subject/ author index); and the presence and nature of any appendices.

5. *Content (scope of materials and subjects).* This section of the annotation describes the kinds of materials listed in the bibliography (e.g., books, pamphlets, articles, documents, reports) and the subjects treated. Where the kinds of materials are not specified, the reader may assume that the materials are generally mixed and that the bibliography is not divided by type of material. The subject scope of the bibliography is conveyed either by brief description of the more frequently occurring topics or, where there are internal subject headings within the bibliography, by specifying these headings and the number of items under each head (in parentheses). In a few cases where the title and subtitle of an item are fully descriptive of the contents, the content annotation is omitted.

Items we have not examined or have not verified, are indicated by the mark " < " following the item number. In these cases, the data in the citation are as given in the source and no annotations are provided. In a few cases, efforts to secure rare items produced no result; we have indicated this with the notation "apparently unavailable."

Indexes

We have provided both an author index and a subject index. The author index contains all authors, co-authors, editors, and compilers of bibliographies included in the guide. Authors or editors of works in which the cited bibliographies appear are also included in the index, but authors of introductions to such works who may be noted in the item descriptions are excluded.

The subject index is composed of about 1800 index categories that emerged from the items contained in the bibliographies. With the exception of the entries not examined by us, the subject indexing is based on direct assessment of the contents of each entry. *It should be noted that the subject indexing for a given entry is likely to be more detailed than the description of contents in the annotation.* Individuals' names appear in the subject index if there is an entire bibliography, a section of a bibliography, or a substantial number of items in a bibliography dealing with them or their works but not if they appear only occasionally or only as authors of works within a subject bibliography. Geographical indexing has not been done systematically, but countries or regions were included in the index if they appeared in a bibliography as a section containing four or more items or constituted a significant subject emphasis. The 34 main subject heads under which the entries have been arranged are included in the subject index; where these are broader than other appropriate subject categories in the index, the entry has been indexed also under the latter.

Computerization of the bibliography has made possible a number of indexes that have not been published in this volume due to limitations of space. These additional indexes, which are available for consultation from the compilers, include an author and title index; a title index; a chronological index (year, author, and title); an index of publishers, place of publication, and series; and a subject, author, and title index.

Main Sources and Search Methods

The main initial bibliographic sources used in the preparation of this guide were Theodore Besterman, *A World Bibliography of Bibliographies: And of bibliographical catalogues, calendars, abstracts, digests, indexes, and the like,* 4 volumes, Lausanne: Societas Bibliographica, 1965 (4th ed., revised and greatly enlarged throughout); and *Bibliographic Index: A cumulative bibliography of bibliographies,* vols. 1-17, (1937–1977), New York: H. W. Wilson, 1945–1978. From these sources, we took all items listed under subject headings beginning with the words "peace" and "war" (including, for example, "peace plans" and "war—effects of"). We also searched the card catalog of the Library of Congress, to December 1975, for items under "peace—bibliography," "peace—bibliography—catalogs," and "war—bibliography."

These three sources contain a total of 697 entries under the indicated subject headings. Of these, 85 are duplicate entries, leaving a primary list of 612 bibliographies on war and peace. Virtually all of the latter are included in this guide; we excluded only a very small number that are no longer available or that after inspection proved inappropriate in content. It is therefore unnecessary for the researcher to have further recourse to these sources for the years indicated.

The main initial sources had several notable limitations. *Bibliographic Index* does not cover items published before 1937, and the other two do not include bibliographies appearing as sections of nonbibliographic works. Given these limitations, and the absence of other comparable sources to fill in these gaps, we decided to search the bibliographies in our primary list for additional relevant bibliographies in the field, especially for the period before 1937.

A systematic search through about 500 of the bibliographies in our primary list yielded a secondary list of nearly 1500 new items. Approximately half of these have been included in the present volume. We excluded some bibliographies that were only marginally useful for study of peace and war; others were excluded to avoid overweighting the guide with bibliographies in particular areas, such as international law, military science, or specific wars and conflicts. Many, unfortunately, had to be excluded mainly for lack of time and resources. We hope to include the most relevant of these in future editions of the guide.

In addition to these systematic searches, we drew on a variety of other sources to identify approximately 100 additional bibliographies included in this volume. These sources included visits to a number of libraries and archives in the United States and abroad; our own past and current research and editorial experience; and the advice of consultants, colleagues, librarians, and archivists. The libraries visited and the consultants and others who have been especially helpful are named in the acknowledgments.

The limits of time and resources placed restraints on the extent of our searches. Resources permitting, the guide could be more comprehensive with additional systematic searches in other general bibliographic sources and in bibliographies included here but not drawn from our primary list (and therefore not encompassed in our systematic secondary search). A search under additional subject headings, such as "pacifism," "militarism," "racism," "imperialism," "nonviolence," "world government," would also augment the guide. All these topics appeared frequently in the sources used, and there might be much duplication of items already included here; nevertheless, a more exhaustive search under such headings would undoubtedly produce many valuable new items. We hope that such searches may be possible in the future.

Symbols and Abbreviations

BL	British Library (London)
BN	Bibliothèque Nationale (Paris)
CST	Stanford University Library
CST-H	Hoover Institute Library
DLC-DB	Library of Congress, Division of Bibliography
IU	University of Illinois Library
IaU	University of Iowa Library
MII	Harvard University Library
MiU	University of Michigan Library
NN	New York Public Library
NNC	Columbia University Library
PPL	Peace Palace Library (The Hague)
PSC-PC	Swarthmore College Peace Collection
<	Item not examined or not verified.

Part I: Peace and War

PART I: PEACE AND WAR

INTRODUCTION

    The bibliographies in Part I are those that we judged to
have about equal emphasis on peace and war, or that it seemed
best to subsume under a single heading with equal relevance to
peace or war.

    The 130 items listed in Section 1 (Peace and War--General)
are the most general bibliographies in the field, having the same
subject scope as the entire guide. Perhaps the best
introductions to the literature through the early twentieth
century are the annotated lists found in Sturge et al. (No. 7)
and Levermore (No. 11), and the syllabus by Jordan and Krehbiel
(No. 9). For later periods, especially valuable introductions
for students and the general reader are provided by Johnsen (No.
26), Boeckel (No. 27), de Ligt (No. 45), Talbott (No. 55), Jacobs
and DeBoer (No. 65), Cheever and Haviland (No. 87), McNeil
(No. 96), Starke (No. 107), Pickus and Woito (No. 113), Nesbitt
(No. 118), and Beitz and Herman (No. 124). Perhaps the most
interesting and informative introduction to the field, however,
is the illustrated catalogue of the works reprinted in the
Garland Library of War and Peace (Cook, Chatfield, and Cooper,
No. 114). For those who wish more comprehensive subject guides
to the whole range of literature on peace and war, see the
bibliographies by Kunz (No. 22), Aufricht (No. 74), Universal
Reference System (No. 108), Medling (No. 117), and Boulding,
Passmore, and Gassler (No. 130).

    Section 2 (Peace and War--U.S. Policy) lists 55
bibliographies that focus more narrowly on United States policies
regarding peace and war. The inclusion here of such a large
section focusing on the diplomatic history and foreign policy of
the United States reflects the considerable attention given to

the U.S. in our sources. But this list can in no way be regarded
as a comprehensive guide to bibliographies on American foreign
policy, since that was not the focus of our literature search.
Indeed, few of the works listed here deal with the whole range of
relevant issues, and those which do are limited to particular
historical periods. Of those which we have examined, Foster (No.
131) covers work appearing from 1835 to 1906, Johnsen (No. 153)
is limited to the four years 1936-1939, and Hallgren (No. 144),
Bailey (No. 170), and Davis (No. 176) cover periods of various
lengths beginning with World War I. Most of the remaining items
deal with more limited topics, such as neutrality, the Monroe
Doctrine, the Cold War, the Cuban missile crisis, American
policies during the two world wars, or proposals for a Department
of Peace.

Like the section on U.S. policy, Section 3 (International
Relations) makes no claim to comprehensive coverage of
bibliographies in the field of international relations. Many of
the 47 items included here focus on relatively narrow topics such
as the Aaland Islands dispute, sovereignty over the polar
regions, the impact of foreign investments, Soviet foreign
relations, or relations between the United States and Latin
America. However, a number of substantial bibliographies
providing a broad overview of international relations literature
are also included, notably those by Moon and Townsend (No. 192),
Buell (No. 195), Elovainio and Lehtinen (No. 212), Roberts (No.
217), DeGrazia (No. 227), Dexter (No. 229), and Larson (No. 230).
For students, teachers, and others wishing to do research on
international relations, helpful guidance through the maze of
reference tools is provided by Zawodny (No. 223), Holler
(No. 231), and LaBarr and Singer (No. 232).

Section 4 (International Law) gives only a small sample
(60 items) of the large number of extant bibliographies on
international law. The earliest entry in the present volume
appears here (No. 233, Ompteda, published in 1785), and several
entries date from the nineteenth century, suggesting that the
need for bibliographies was felt much earlier in the field of
international law than in other fields represented here. The
reader should note that the works we cite that include the most
extensive international law bibliographies are not listed in this
section, because they are too general in scope. These are the
various printed catalogues of the Peace Palace Library (items No.
16, 23, 24, 30, 33, 36, 48, 49, 88, and 100). Bibliographies
focusing mainly on the legal aspects of war, war crimes, and war
crimes trials are also not listed in this section, but rather in
the last two sections of the guide (items No. 1341-1398). For
the most part the bibliographies in Section 4 cover special
topics in the field, such as arbitration, international courts,
codification of international law, the Drago Doctrine, or
maritime law. A useful brief general bibliography for works up
to 1945 is Scanlon (No. 278). Brownlie (No. 287) provides much
more extensive coverage through 1961. For more recent

bibliographies, the reader may wish to consult the <u>Bibliographic</u> <u>Index</u> under "international law," a heading we did not consult in the compilation of this guide.

Of the 90 items in Section 5 (Armament and Disarmament), the majority deal with disarmament, arms control, and arms limitation, while relatively few deal with weapons and the munitions industry. The best guide to the vast literature on disarmament and arms control through 1977 is Burns (No. 374), which contains useful introductory essays to the various sections of the book. For the earlier disarmament literature through 1931, the annotated bibliography by the League of Nations Library (No. 310) is especially valuable. Control of nuclear weapons is the subject of an extensive annotated bibliography by the Mid-West Debate Bureau (No. 348). Of several items dealing with the arms trade, those by Matthews (No. 312) and Johnsen (314) are useful for the first third of the twentieth century, while the arms traffic sections in Burns (No. 374) and SIPRI (No. 381) cover the more recent period. Excellent guides to various special topics may be found in the recent series of bibliographies published by the Center for the Study of Armament and Disarmament (items No. 366-370, 372, 373, 375, 379, 382).

Section 6 (Militarism and the Military) includes among its 44 items a small sample of bibliographies on military sciences, war gaming, and strategic analysis (e.g.. Cockle, No. 384; Ellinger and Rosinski, No. 399; Dennis, No. 401; Riley and Young, No. 403; Sztarski, No. 407; Deutsche Gesellschaft für auswärtige Politik, No. 409; and Hart and Hart, No. 426). However, the main emphasis is on sociological and political analyses of militarism and military institutions. For the period before World War II, the bibliographies by the Library of Congress (No. 385), Mannheim (No. 396), and Herring (No. 397) are especially valuable. After World War II, the focus shifts to analyses of the military-industrial complex, which is well-covered by Pilisuk and Hayden (No. 411), Stackhouse (No. 419), and Meeker (No. 423). Finally, a valuable guide to the literature on conscription is that by Anderson and Bloom (No. 425).

The relation of religious groups, ideas, and institutions to questions of peace and war is covered in Section 7 (Religion, Peace, and War). All 34 items in this section deal with Christian perspectives, but Harris (No. 455) also lists works on Jewish theology. For coverage of other religious traditions in relation to war and peace, some of the entries listed under "Pacifism, Nonviolence, Conscientious Objection" (Section 17) are helpful. The best introductions to the literature in this section are probably those of Potter (No. 454) and Marrin (No. 458).

The 16 items listed in Section 8 (Women, Peace, and War) reflect a predominant concern with the economic impact of war on women, especially through their movement into industrial jobs

during World War I (see Nims, No. 463) and World War II (see
Hellman, No. 466). The more general question of mobilizing women
for war is covered by Rupp (No. 472). Matthews (No. 464) and
Degen (No. 465) deal with women's opposition to war and their
peace movement activities. For a brief introduction to the
literature on this whole topic, see Kusnerz (No. 471). The
brevity of this section should not be taken as indicative of the
relative importance of the topic, and numerous bibliographies
listed in other sections of this guide include substantial
numbers of items on women and peace or women and war (see these
categories in the subject index).

Section 9 (Social Movements and Other Political Topics)
lists 39 bibliographies covering diverse topics. Two items
briefly cover social movements in general (Wilson and Johnsen,
No. 481; Johnsen, No. 484), while Neumann (No. 501) provides
extensive coverage of numerous movements. Others deal with
various specific movements such as socialism (Independent Labor
Party, No. 485; Egbert, Persons, and Basset, No. 506), the
cooperative movement (Co-operative Union, No. 499), and
communalism (Webber, No. 510). Several extensive bibliographies
on nationalism also appear here (Dominian, No. 478; Pinson, No.
489; Deutsch, No. 508; Deutsch and Merritt, No. 515). The
remaining bibliographies in this section deal with a variety of
topics not easily subsumed under a single heading.

Twenty-eight bibliographies are cited in Section 10
(Creative Literature, Drama, Arts), providing lists and some
critical commentary on creative work relating to war and peace.
The only comprehensive coverage of creative literature in this
area is the 1930 bibliography by Nitchie et al., (No. 519), which
includes 888 items published between 1870 and 1930. Others are
more specialized, covering such topics as children's books on
goodwill and international understanding (Nos. 516-518), war
poets (Blunden, No. 534), the American novel in World War I
(Cooperman, No. 536), antiwar plays (Federal Theatre Project,
Nos. 522-524), and peace plays (Bates, No. 525). Several items
deal with music, the most comprehensive being the bibliography
and discography of American war, peace, and protest songs by
Denisoff (No. 540). Dougall (No. 538) provides a fairly recent
film guide to materials on peace and war. No separate
bibliographies on art appear in this section, but materials
relating to art and literature can be found in the more general
bibliographies in this guide by consulting the subject index.
For example, substantial sections on creative literature and the
arts appear in major bibliographies by Jordan and Krehbiel (No.
9), Haass et al. (No. 583), Moch (No. 644), La Fontaine (No.
645), and the Nobel Institute Catalogue (No. 648).

The final section in Part I (11. Bibliographic Periodicals)
lists 13 periodicals whose main content is bibliographic
information. The most important of these is the Peace Research
Abstracts Journal (Newcombe and Newcombe, No. 553). It is by far

the most comprehensive current multidisciplinary index to peace
research literature since 1945. No single source covers the
period before 1945, although the monthly bulletins issued by the
American Association for International Conciliation (No. 544) and
by the National Council for Prevention of War (No. 545) each
attempted to cover, in a more limited way, the same range of
literature for the periods 1908-1913 and 1923-1932 respectively.
Eighty-three journals that include important sections of
abstracts, book reviews, or current literature references are
listed in Boehm's annotated directory of bibliographies on
international relations (No. 218).

Peace and War--General

1 <

Dunant, Henri.

Bibliothèque Internationale Universelle [Universal
International Library].
Paris, 1867. 3 pp.

2   AP2.A6,v.11

Will, Thomas E.

Bibliography on peace and war in "The abolition of war."
Arena (Boston), 11, 61 (December, 1894): 138-144.

   249 items, 1643-[1894]. English.

   Books, pamphlets, and reports on peace (95) and the moral
   aspects of war (41); current periodical literature (113) on
   international arbitration, causes and prevention of war,
   peace societies, and international organization.

3 <

Bureau International Permanent de la Paix, à Berne.

Ouvrages en Dépôt [Works on Deposit].
Berne: [Bureau International Permanent de la Paix], 1896. 1 p.

4 <

Bureau International Permanent de la Paix, à Berne.

Catalogue d´Ouvrages sur la Paix et la Guerre, Classés dans la
Bibliothèque du Bureau International à Berne, Juin 1900
[Catalogue of Works on Peace and War, Classified in the Library
of the International Peace Bureau at Berne, June 1900].
Berne: Walchli et Hauri, 1900. 19 pp.
Another edition, March 1901, 22 pp.

Peace and War--General

5   H1.P8,v.15

Robinson, Edward Van Dyke.

Brief bibliography of war in "War and economics in history and
theory."
Political Science Quarterly, 15, 4 (December, 1900): 623-628.
Reprinted in Carver, Thomas H. [ed.], Sociology and Social
Process: A handbook for students of sociology, Boston, [1905],
pp. 133-173.

   219 items, 1310-1900 (many items, some going back to
   ancient Greece, are undated). English, French, German; also
   Latin, Italian (6), Spanish (2).

   Theoretical and historical works on the social, political,
   and economic aspects of war and peace, the history of wars,
   the causes and effects of war, international law, peace
   theory, and proposals for universal peace.

6 <

Perris, H. S.

Bibliography.
In The Cult of the Rifle and the Cult of the Peace.
London: Clarke, 1907. pp. 43-46.

7   Z6464.Z9L6

Sturge, Charles, T. P. Newman, O. R. Hobson, and M. L. Cooke
(comps.).

"The best hundred books on peace and war [4 lists]."
In A Library of Peace and War, with an introduction by Francis
W. Hirst.
London: Speaker, 1907. pp. 7-30, 31-38, 39-49, 50-57.

   400 items, 1350-1907. English; also French, German (6), Latin
   (2). All items in List I have brief to abstract-length
   critical and descriptive annotations and many of the items in
   the other lists have brief descriptive annotations;
   introduction (4 pp.), plus brief introductions to Lists I and
   III; author index.

   Four lists submitted to a prize contest sponsored by the
   Speaker Publishing Company. List I--works of reference (3),
   general statements of the case against war and for possible
   substitutes (15), defenses of war (10), war as it is (11),
   war from religious and ethical standpoints (13), commercial

Peace and War--General

and financial aspects (6), modern developments and tendencies
in their bearing on the question of peace (6), international
law (3), specific proposals for restricting or abolishing
war, practical applications of such proposals, and criticism
thereon (24), biographies dealing largely with the question
[of peace] (3), miscellaneous (6); List II--general (16), the
duel (2), jurisprudence (2), federation (12), international
law (5), international arbitration (4), political economy of
war (9), war and Christianity or morals (11), imperialism and
patriotism (4), war in the light of evolution (6), realities
of war (7), history (5), poetry (4), novels and stories (13);
List III--has no subdivision but covers almost the same
topics as above (100); List IV--general and legal (81),
fiction (4), general foreign-language works (12), foreign-
language fiction (3).

8   JX1938.P52

Perris, G. H.

Note on books.
In his A Short History of War and Peace.
New York/London: Henry Holt/Williams and Norgate (Home
University Library of Modern Knowledge, No. 4), 1911.
pp. 253-254.

    48 items (no dates given). English; also French (6), German
    (1). All items are discussed in the note.

    Brief bibliographic essay covering works on military history,
    international law, effects of war and antiwar novels.

9   IU: 341.6J76s

Jordan, David Starr and Edward Benjamin Krehbiel.

References [31 lists]; Peace periodicals; Pamphlets, fiction,
and the like.
In their Syllabus of Lectures on International Conciliation:
Given at Leland Stanford Junior University.
Boston: World Peace Foundation, 1912. pp. 15-16, 23, 27, 31,
37, 42-43, 47-48, 51-52, 62, 65, 67, 71, 74, 76, 80, 84, 86,
96, 106-107, 114, 117, 120, 124, 129, 132, 139, 147-148, 156,
158, 161-162, 166, 179, 180.

    700 items, 1801-1912 (some items undated). English; also
    French, German, Latin, Dutch (1), Japanese (1), other Western
    European languages. A few items have brief descriptive
    annotations.

Peace and War--General

   Books, pamphlets, and articles on history of warfare, the
   economic, social, demographic, medical, moral, and legal
   aspects of war, peace theory, peace movement, international
   relations, international arbitration, the first and second
   Hague conferences, international courts, international law,
   internationalism, world federation, peace education; peace
   periodicals; fiction.

   10   JX1963.M16

Maciejewski, Casimir.

Bibliographie.
In his La Guerre [War]: Ses causes et les moyens de la prévenir
[Its causes and the means of preventing it].
Paris: M. Giard and E. Brière, 1912. pp. [89]-91.

   37 items, 1795-1912. French; also German (5), Polish (5),
   English (5).

   Books and journal articles on peace plans, the Hague
   conferences, peace theory, international arbitration,
   disarmament, causes and prevention of war.

   11   JX1908.U5,v.3

Levermore, Charles H[erbert].

"Suggestions for the study of international relations."
World Peace Foundation Pamphlet Series, 3, 11, Part 2 (November,
1913): 28 pp.

   262 items, 1884-1913. English; also French, German (6),
   Italian (2), Dutch (1), Danish (1), Swedish (1). Many items
   have brief critical and/or descriptive annotations;
   introduction (2 pp.) plus introductions (in outline form) to
   each section.

   Periodicals and other publications of peace and international
   relations organizations (51), relation of war to civilization
   (44), influence of democracy on international relations (43),
   international influence of religion in theory and practice
   (19), historical and critical discussion of arbitration (25),
   work of existing international organizations and associations
   (28), world organization and the attainment of peace with
   justice (52).

Peace and War--General

12   JX1904.P4,1914

[Huntsman, M. H. (comp.)].

"Publications of the National Peace Council; Pacifist press
directory; Bibliography."
In National Peace Council (London), Peace Year Book, 1914.
London: National Peace Council, 1914. pp. 131-133, 206-208,
208-214.

   145 items, [1913]. English. A few items have brief
   descriptive annotations.

   Publications of the NPC (57); pacifist press directory (28);
   armaments (12), Germany (11), recent wars and punitive
   expeditions (11), general list of recent books (26).

13   JX1904.P4,1915

[Huntsman, M. H. (comp.)].

"Publications of the National Peace Council; Pacifist press
directory; Bibliography."
In National Peace Council (London), Peace Year Book, 1915.
London: National Peace Council, 1915. pp. 94-97, 115-116,
117-124.

   236 items, [1914]. English.

   Publications of the NPC (58), pacifist press directory (30),
   bibliography [on the war] (148).

14   JX3275.P5

Plater, Charles (ed.).

"Bibliography of peace and war."
In his A Primer of Peace and War: The principles of
international morality, edited for the Catholic Social Guild.
New York/London: P. J. Kenedy and Sons/P. S. King and Son,
1915. pp. 266-274.

   145 items, 1584-1915 (many items undated). English, Latin;
   also French (7), German (1). Some items have brief
   descriptive and/or critical annotations; introduction (1
   paragraph).

   Theoretical works on war and peace from historical,
   political, philosophical, religious, and legal perspectives.

Peace and War--General

15   Z6464.Z9M4,1916

Mez, John [Richard].

Peace Literature of the War: Material for the study of
international polity.
New York: American Association for International Conciliation
(International Conciliation, Special Bulletin), January, 1916.
23 pp.

  165 items, 1913-1915. English; also German (3), French (1).
  Most items have brief to abstract-length critical or
  descriptive annotations; introduction (2 pp.); appended list
  of new peace organizations formed during the war.

  Books (38), fiction and drama (7), periodicals and magazines
  (7), pamphlets (113) on the causes and prevention of war,
  internationalism, world government, international
  organization, etc.

16   Z6464.Z9H3

Molhuysen, P[hilip] C[hristiaan] and E[lsa] R[achel] Oppenheim.

Catalogue [de la] Bibliothèque du Palais de la Paix.
Leiden: A. W. Sijthoff, 1916. xlv pp. + 1576 col.

  Approximately 10,000 items (estimated from a sample of
  pages), 1523-1916. German, French, Dutch; also English,
  Latin, Spanish, Italian, Greek, other Western and Eastern
  European languages (relative frequency of languages estimated
  from a sample of pages). Preface (2 pp.); table of contents;
  subject index; author/title index.

  Catalog arranged by subjects, mainly law, politics,
  diplomacy, history, and geography. About half of the items
  are listed under international law, which includes a section
  of about 327 items on the peace movement, disarmament, peace
  conferences, the Peace Palace, and militarism.

17   JX1904.P4,1916

[National Peace Council (London)].

"Official publications on the war; Publications of the National
Peace Council; Pacifist press directory; Bibliography."
In its Peace Year Book, 1916.

Peace and War--General

London: National Peace Council, 1916. pp. 1-2, 85-87, 94-96,
96-98.

  157 items, [1915]. English.

  Official publications on the war (22), publications of the
  NPC (54), pacifist press directory (35), bibliography (46).

18   JX1937.R4

Reely, Mary Katharine (comp.).

Bibliography, to July, 1914; Bibliography, July, 1914 to
December 1915.
In her Selected Articles on World Peace: Including
international arbitration and disarmament.
White Plains/New York: H. W. Wilson (Debaters´ Handbook
Series), 1916 (2nd and enl. ed.). pp. [xv]-xxv; [xxvi]-xxxiv.
First edition, 1914, pp. [xv]-xxv.

  303 items, 1823-1915. English. A few items have brief
  descriptive annotations.

  General references (38), affirmative references (172), and
  negative references (93) relating to the resolution "That in
  the settlement of international disputes, law can and should
  be substituted for armed force." These books, pamphlets, and
  magazine articles are particularly concerned with arbitration
  and disarmament but also include other topics.

19   JX1904.P4,1917

[National Peace Council (London)].

"Some official publications during 1916; Pacifist press
directory; Bibliography, 1916-17."
In its Peace Year Book, 1917.
London: National Peace Council, 1917. pp. 1-3, 80-82, 82-84.

  114 items, 1916-1917. English.

  Official publications, 1916 (25), pacifist press directory
  (34), bibliography, 1916-1917 (55).

Peace and War--General

20   JX1904.P4,1918

[Huntsman, M. H. (comp.)].

"Pacifist Press Directory; Bibliography, 1917-18."
In National Peace Council (London), Peace Year Book, 1918.
London: National Peace Council, 1918. pp. 119-121, 121-123.

   91 items, 1917-1918. English.

   Pacifist press directory (33), bibliography, 1917-1918 (58).

21   JX1904.P42,1919-20

[Huntsman, M. H. (comp.)].

"Bibliography."
In National Peace Council (London), 1919-1920 Supplement to the
1918 International Peace Year Book.
London: National Peace Council, 1920. pp. 26-31.

   112 items, [1918-1919]. English. Some items have brief
   descriptive annotations.

   Mostly works on World War I, with some general works on peace
   problems.

22   Z6207.E8K9

Kunz, Josef L.

Bibliographie der Kriegsliteratur [Bibliography of War
Literature]: Politik, Geschichte, Philosophie, Völkerrecht,
Friedensfrage [Politics, history, philosophy, international
law, and the peace question], im Auftrage der österreichischen
Völkerbundliga (Wien).
Berlin: Hans Robert Engelmann, 1920. 101 pp.

   1565 items, 1815-1920. German, French; also English, Italian,
   Dutch, Swedish (4), Danish (3), other Eastern and Western
   European languages. Introduction (2 pp.); most sections also
   have brief introductions.

   Bibliographies (10), documents (72), speeches (20), works on
   the period preceding World War I (143), outbreak of the war
   (70), the question of guilt (31), biographies and memoirs
   (47), particular problem areas and nationalities (197),
   political history of the war (141), the Russian Revolution
   and Bolshevism (71), economic warfare (45), socialism and
   social democracy (35), press and propaganda (68), the

Peace and War--General

   nationalities principle (24), philosophy and sociology of
   war, militarism, and imperialism (77), international law
   (77), the peace question: pacifism, Wilson, the Pope, and
   peace (119), war and peace aims of the countries (96),
   arbitration and the League of Nations (102), postwar
   problems, peace in the East, and the Paris Peace Treaties
   (120).

23   Z6464.Z9H3,Suppl.

Molhuysen, P[hilip] C[hristiaan] and D. Albers.

Premier Supplément du Catalogue (1916) [de la] Bibliothèque du
Palais de la Paix.
Leiden: A. W. Sijthoff, 1922. xlv pp. + 1042 col.

   Approximately 10,200 items (estimated from a sample of
   pages), 1567-1921. German, French, Dutch; also English,
   Latin, Spanish, Italian Greek, other Western and Eastern
   European languages (relative frequency of languages estimated
   from a sample of pages). Preface (1 paragraph); table of
   contents; subject index.

   Supplement arranged by subjects, following same scheme as the
   original 1916 catalog, covering mainly law, politics,
   diplomacy, history, and geography. Nearly half of the items
   are listed under international law, which includes a section
   of about 294 items on the peace movement, disarmament, peace
   congresses and conferences, the Peace Palace, and militarism.

24   Z6464.Z9H3,Index1922

Bibliothèque du Palais de la Paix.

Index Alphabétique du Catalogue (1916) et du Supplément (1922)
[de la] Bibliothèque du Palais de la Paix.
Leiden: A. W. Sijthoff, 1922. 790 col.

25   BR115.P4D3

Davis, Jerome and Ray B. Chamberlin.

"Bibliography on war and the peace movement."
In their Christian Fellowship among the Nations: A discussion
course which will help groups of young people and adults to do
straight thinking on our greatest problem.
Boston/Chicago: Pilgrim Press, 1925. pp. 114-116.

Peace and War--General

   73 items, 1910-1924. English. A list of peace organizations
   precedes the bibliography.

   Books and pamphlets on the history of the peace movement (8),
   war and human nature (5), war and Christianity (12),
   economics and war (11), women and war (1), the last war and
   the next war (9), the world today (16), world organization
   (7), fiction (4).

26   JX1937.J6

Johnsen, Julia E. (comp.).

Bibliography.
In her Selected Articles on War--Cause and Cure.
New York/London: H. W. Wilson/Sir Isaac Pitman and Sons (The
Handbook Series), October, 1926. pp. [xi]-lxiv.

   589 items, 1899-1926 (most items published after 1916).
   English. A few items have brief descriptive annotations;
   explanatory note (2 pp.).

   Bibliographies (9), books, pamphlets, documents, and magazine
   and journal articles on war and peace in general (202),
   causes of war (95), and cures for war (283). The list is
   designed to give a cross-sectional view of the literature on
   the nature of war and means of peace.

27   JX1952.B55

Boeckel, Florence Brewer.

Bibliography.
In her Between War and Peace: A handbook for peace workers.
New York: Macmillan, October, 1928. pp. [513]-553.

   515 items, 1911-1928. English. Introduction (1 p.) plus
   introductory comments to each major section.

   Comprehensive bibliographies on special subjects (70), books
   for the general reader classified according to various phases
   of the peace movement (343), periodicals focusing on world
   peace problems (22), publications of organizations interested
   in international relations and world peace (16), yearbooks
   (6), children's books on subjects relating to peace (58).
   Each of the subdivisions is broken down into many
   subcategories, e.g., education and peace, women and peace,
   problems of war and peace, famous peace documents, fiction,
   war debts, and international relations.

Peace and War--General

28   Z6464.Z9I7

International Conciliation.

List of Documents, April 1907-February 1929.
Worcester, Mass.: Carnegie Endowment for International Peace,
Division of Intercourse and Education, February, 1929. 22 pp.
Other editions appeared in December 1930, September 1935, and
January 1937.

  293 items, 1907-1929. English. Introduction (1 p.).

  Lists 247 numbered bulletins and 46 special bulletins.
  Numbers 1-199 were published by the American Association for
  International Conciliation. Covers a wide range of topics
  including international relations, international
  organization, international law, U.S. foreign policy,
  armament and disarmament, the causes and prevention of war,
  conditions of peace, the peace movement, World War I, League
  of Nations, international cooperation, and peace plans.

29   Z1009.N27,no.21

Huntsman, M. H. (comp.).

The Prevention of War: A selected list of books compiled by
Miss M. H. Huntsman and printed for the National Council for
Prevention of War, 39 Victoria Street, London S.W.1.
London: National Book Council (Book List No. 21), December,
1930 (3rd ed.). 4 pp.
First edition, May, 1926, 3 pp.; second edition, June, 1928,
4 pp.

  160 items, 1911-1930. English.

  Books on the general and historical aspects of war and peace
  (26), the nature, causes, and prevention of war (16),
  international law, courts of justice, and arbitration (14),
  religious and ethical questions (16), armament and
  disarmament (14), economics (7), League of Nations (16),
  education and juveniles (23), war letters, autobiographies,
  and novels (28).

Peace and War--General

30   Z6464.Z9H3,Suppl.1929

Ter Meulen, J[acob] and A[rnoldus] Lysen.

Deuxième Supplément (1929) au Catalogue (1916) [de la]
Bibliothèque du Palais de la Paix.
Leiden: A. W. Sijthoff, 1930. xx pp. + 1553 col.

   Approximately 15,000 items (estimated from a sample of
   pages), 1512-1928. German, French, Dutch; also English,
   Latin, Spanish, Italian, Greek, other Western and Eastern
   European languages (relative frequency of languages estimated
   from a sample of pages). Preface (2 pp.); table of contents;
   subject index.

   Second supplement arranged by subjects, following same scheme
   as the original 1916 catalog and the 1922 supplement,
   covering mainly law, politics, diplomacy, history, and
   geography. About half of the items are listed under
   international law, which includes a section of about 740
   items on the peace movement, projects of international
   organization, armament and disarmament, peace conferences,
   the Peace Palace, and militarism.

31   JX1904.P4,1931

National Council for Prevention of War (London).

"Peace press directory for Great Britain; List of recent
pamphlets and leaflets dealing with peace and war."
In its Peace Year Book, 1931.
London: National Council for Prevention of War, 1931. pp. 132,
133-135.

   98 items, [1930]. English.

   Peace periodicals (29) and pamphlets and leaflets on
   arbitration and the World Court (6), armaments and
   disarmament (10), international security (5), economics (3),
   education (18), outlawry of war (4), religion (5), and
   miscellaneous subjects relating to peace and war (18).

32   JX1904.P4,1932

[National Peace Council (London)].

"List of recent pamphlets and leaflets dealing with peace and
war; Peace press directory."

Peace and War--General

In its Peace Year Book, 1932.
London: National Peace Council, 1932. pp. 169-172, 173.

   104 items, [1931]. English.

   Pamphlets and leaflets on arbitration and the World Court
   (4), disarmament (48), international security (6), education
   (7), economic (2), religious (6), miscellaneous (14); current
   periodicals (17).

33   Z6464.Z9H3,Index1929

[Ter Meulen, Jacob and Arnoldus Lysen (comps.)].

Index Alphabétique par Noms d´Auteurs ou Mots d´Ordre du
Catalogue (1916) et des Suppléments (1922 et 1929) [de la
Bibliothèque du Palais de la Paix].
Leiden: A. W. Sijthoff, 1932. 1466 col.

34 <

Hindmarsh, Albert E.

Bibliography.
In his Force in Peace: Force short of war in international
relations.
Cambridge, Mass.: Harvard University Press, 1933. pp. [231]-242.

35   Z6463.F73

Langer, William L. and Hamilton Fish Armstrong.

"War, peace, security and disarmament."
In their Foreign Affairs Bibliography: A selected and annotated
list of books on international relations, 1919-1932.
New York/London: Harper and Brothers, for the Council on
Foreign Relations, 1933. pp. 67-86.

   238 items, 1922-1932. English, French; also German, Italian
   (6), Spanish (2), Russian (1). All items have brief
   descriptive and/or critical annotations; preface to entire
   bibliography (2 pp.); author index for entire bibliography.

   Books and articles on war, modern warfare, air warfare,
   chemical warfare, peace theory, international arbitration,
   the outlawry of war, treaties and pacts, disarmament,
   security, naval disarmament conferences.

Peace and War--General

36   Z6464.Z9H3,Index1933

[Lysen, Arnoldus (comp.)].

Index Sommaire par Ordre Alphabétique des Matières du Catalogue
(1916) et des Suppléments (1922 et 1929) [de la Bibliothèque du
Palais de la Paix]/Concise Alphabetical Subject Index to the
Catalogue (1916) and to the Supplements (1922 and 1929) [of the
Peace Palace Library].
Leiden: A. W. Sijthoff, 1933. 76 col./80 col.

37 <

Folliet, J.

Bibliographie [after each chapter].
In Morale Internationale.
[Paris]: Bloud et Gay, (Biblioth. Cath. des Sc. rel.), 1935.

38   JX1952.W7

Wright, Quincy.

List of books and articles.
In his The Causes of War and the Conditions of Peace.
London/New York/Toronto: Longmans, Green (Publications of the
Graduate Institute of International Studies, Geneva,
Switzerland/ Institut Universitaire de Hautes Etudes
Internationales, Genève, Suisse, No. 14), 1935. pp. 126-139.

   331 items, 1838-1935. English; also French, German (8),
   Italian (1), Swedish (1). Introduction (2 paragraphs).

   Books and articles on the study of war, international law,
   international relations, the psychological, social, and
   economic aspects of war, the history of war and warfare, ways
   to attain peace, international arbitration, and theories of
   war, peace, and social interaction.

39   JX1953,L33

Lash, Joseph P. and James A[rthur] Wechsler.

A selected bibliography.
In their War, Our Heritage, with an introduction by Bruce
Bliven.

Peace and War--General

New York: International Publishers, 1936. pp. 158-159.

  29 items, 1931-1936. English.

  Books on the causes and prevention of war, the peace
  movement, militarism in education, and the relation of
  socialism to war and peace.

40   Z1009.N27,no.21A

National Peace Council (London).

International Affairs: A selected list of books, complementary
to No. 21 Prevention of War, compiled by the National Peace
Council, 39 Victoria Street, London S.W. 1, for distribution by
the National Book Council (with a few exceptions, all the books
mentioned have been published since the last edition of No. 21
in December, 1930).
London: National Book Council (Book List No. 21A), January,
1936 (4th ed.). 8 pp.

  293 items, 1911-1936. English.

  General (54), historical (22), international law,
  arbitration, etc. (11), religious and ethical (26),
  armaments, disarmament, and security (52), economic (37),
  League of Nations (22), educational and juvenile (16), Europe
  (20), Near and Far East (21), reference (12). For list No. 21
  see item No. 29, above.

41   JX1952.A79

Atkinson, Henry A[very].

Bibliography.
In his Prelude to Peace: A realistic view of international
relations.
New York/London: Harper and Brothers, 1937. pp. 211-213.

  76 items, 1926-1936 (no dates given for books). English; also
  French (2).

  Books, pamphlets, and articles on causes and prevention of
  war, economics of war and peace, religious approaches,
  nationalism, imperialism, League of Nations, peace education,
  disarmament, U.S. foreign policy.

Peace and War--General

42   JX4508.B33

Ballis, William.

Bibliography.
In his The Legal Position of War: Changes in its practice and
theory from Plato to Vattel.
The Hague: Martinus Nijhoff, 1937. pp. 174-184.
Reprinted, New York: Garland (Garland Library of War and
Peace), 1973.

   192 items, 1504-1936. English; also French, German, Latin,
   Spanish (1).

   Sources (46), books (101), and articles (45) on international
   law, the history of political theory, and international
   relations.

43   U21.E55

Engelbrecht, H[elmuth] C[arol].

Notes and references.
In his Revolt against War, with a foreword by Robert S. Lynd.
New York: Dodd, Mead, 1937. pp. 337-353.

   351 items, 1900-1937. English; also German, French, Italian
   (8), Dutch (2), Norwegian (2). Footnote format, arranged by
   chapters.

   Books, articles, and newspaper coverage on causes of war,
   religion and war, medical aspects of war, military law,
   propaganda, psychological effects of war, effects of war in
   general, conditions of achieving peace, militarism, pacifism,
   conscription, conscientious objectors, armament and
   disarmament, history of wars, war and crime, munitions
   industry, war toys, imperialism, nationalism, international
   law and organization.

44   PSC-PC

Fenwick, Charles G[hequiere].

Suggested readings for further study.
In his A Primer of Peace.
Washington, D.C.: Catholic Association for International Peace,
1937. pp. 56-58.

   58 items, 1913-1937. English.

Peace and War--General

   Pamphlets, articles, and books on causes and prevention of
   war, peace theory, international law, international
   organization, and disarmament, especially from a Catholic
   viewpoint.

45   JX1952.L3652

Ligt, Bart[hélemy] de.

Bibliography.
In his The Conquest of Violence: An essay on war and
revolution, with an introduction by Aldous Huxley (translated
by Honor Tracy from the French text, revised and enlarged by
the author).
London: Routledge, 1937. pp. 289-296.
Also published in New York: E.P. Dutton, 1938. Reprinted, New
York/London: Garland (Garland Library of War and Peace), 1972.

   186 items, 1877-1937. English, French; also German, Dutch.

   Books and pamphlets on social change, revolutionary
   movements, violence and nonviolence, pacifism, various
   aspects of war, the lives of political activists, and
   theoretical works on revolution, socialism, anarchism,
   politics, ethics, war, and peace.

46   Z732.M74,v.12

[Minnesota Department of Education, Library Division].

"Inexpensive peace material for all libraries."
Library Notes and News, 12, 1 (March, 1937): 12.

   20 items, 1934-1936. English. Introduction (one paragraph).

   Books (10) and pamphlets (10) on the causes and prevention of
   war, conditions of peace.

47   JX1904.P4,1937

[National Peace Council (London)].

"Bibliographies--the year's books (1936), the year's pamphlets
(1936), League of Nations publications, government
publications, posters, peace plays; Peace press directory."
In its Peace Year Book, 1937.
London: National Peace Council, 1937. pp. 385-401, 402-403.

Peace and War--General

428 items, 1936. English.

Books and pamphlets on Africa and Abyssinia (23), armament
and disarmament (21), air warfare and civil aviation (10),
democracy and dictatorship (5), economics (33), Europe (12),
Germany (30), League of Nations (28), Japan and the Far East
(11), Spain (7), U.S. (14), security and sanctions (32),
pacifism (33), religion (15), miscellaneous (86), League of
Nations publications (13), government publications (14),
posters (10), peace plays (8); peace periodicals (23).

48   Z6464.Z9H3,Suppl.1937

Ter Meulen, J[acob] and A[rnoldus] Lysen.

Troisième Supplément (1937): (Acquisitions 1928/1929-1936) [du]
Catalogue de la Bibliothèque du Palais de la Paix; Droit,
Relations Internationales, Histoire/Third Supplement (1937):
(Acquisitions 1928/1929-1936) [of the] Catalogue of the Peace
Palace Library; Law, International Relations, History.
Leiden: A. W. Sijthoff, 1937. xix pp. + 2743 col.

21,729 items (number of items estimated from a sample of
pages), 1490-1936. French, English, German; also Spanish,
Italian, Dutch, Latin, Hungarian, other Eastern and Western
European languages (relative frequency of languages estimated
from a sample of pages). Preface (2 pp.); table of contents;
subject index (all in French and English).

Third supplement arranged by subjects, following same scheme
as the original 1916 catalog and the 1922 and 1929
supplements, covering mainly law, politics, diplomacy,
history, and geography. About 40 percent of the items are
listed under international law, which includes a section of
about 1630 items on the peace movement, projects of
international organization, armament and disarmament, the
Hague conferences, the Peace Palace, and militarism.

49   Z6464.Z9H3,Suppl.1937,Index

[Ter Meulen, Jacob and Arnoldus Lysen (eds.)].

Index Alphabétique par Noms Propres du Troisième Supplément
(1937); (Acquisitions: 1928/1929-1936) [du] Catalogue de la
Bibliothèque du Palais de la Paix; Droit, Relations
Internationales, Histoires/Alphabetical Index of Proper Names
to the Third Supplement (1937); (Acquisitions: 1928/1929-1936)
[of the] Catalogue of the Peace Palace Library; Law,
International Relations, History.

Peace and War--General

Leiden: A. W. Sijthoff, 1937. 79 pp.

50   H62.A1S6,v.1

Thomas, Harrison C.

"Materials on peace [bibliographic essay]."
Social Education(New York), _, 9 (December, 1937): 629-632.

   20 items, [1937] (no dates given). English. All items are
   cited and discussed in text, some of them also listed in
   footnotes.

   Suggests periodicals and a few books dealing with
   international relations and war/peace problems that would be
   useful for high school classes.

51   JC362.W3

Watkins, Arthur Charles.

Important books, pamphlets, and materials for teachers and for
school libraries.
In his America Stands for Pacific Means: A book for boys and
girls on the principles and practice of social cooperation.
Washington, D.C.: National Capital Press, 1937. pp. 122-123.

   19 items, 1928-1937. English. All items have brief
   descriptive and/or critical annotations.

   Paris Pact (3), international relations (10), the conference
   method (6).

52   Z732.M74

[Minnesota Department of Education, Library Division].

"Peace or war?"
Library Notes and News, 12, 5 (March, 1938): 165-168.

   93 items, 1932-1937. English. Some items have brief
   critical and/or descriptive annotations.

   Ways to peace (15), roads to war (29), what price war? (5),
   understanding and prevention (10), Civil War [U.S.] in
   fiction (16), World War [I] in fiction (18).

Peace and War--General

53   JX1904.P4,1938

[National Peace Council (London)].

"Bibliographies--the year´s books (1937), League of Nations
publications, government publications, the year´s pamphlets and
leaflets (1937), posters; Exhibitions, films, plays, etc. for
local use; Peace press directory."
In its Peace Year Book, 1938.
London: National Peace Council, 1938. pp. 300-323, 324-346,
348-349.

    717 items, 1932-1937. English.

    Books, pamphlets, and leaflets on Abyssinia (6), armaments,
    air warfare etc. (61), collective security (15), economic and
    colonial questions (34), democracy, fascism, and civil
    liberties (13), Europe (10), Far East (22), Germany (25),
    India (21), international law and relations (12), pacifism
    (45), Palestine (6), Spain (49), U.S.A. (11), U.S.S.R. (15),
    League of Nations publications (34), imperial and foreign
    affairs (9), education (6), League of Nations (8),
    miscellaneous (89), posters (34); exhibitions, films, plays,
    etc. (168); peace press directory (24).

54   L11.C53,v.12

Syracuse Peace Council (comp.).

"Books on peace for senior-high libraries."
Clearing House (New York), 12, 8 (April, 1938): 460.

    39 items, 1926-1937. English.

    Books on peace and the negative aspects of war.

55   JX1963.T28

Talbott, E[verett] Guy.

Bibliography [9 lists]; Periodicals dealing with peace.
In his Essential Conditions of Peace.
Gardena, Calif.: Institute Press, 1938. pp. 13, 15, 20, 25, 27,
33, 45, 48, 55, 67.

    90 items, 1916-1937. English.

    Short lists of books on alternative approaches to peace (9),
    the inevitability of war (10), substitutes for war (8),

Peace and War--General

   trends toward war (11), formulas for peace (6), causes of war
   (8), U.S. neutrality (6), U.S. foreign relations (5),
   citizens´ promotion of peace (6), public opinion (7); peace
   periodicals (14).

56   JX1952.T57

Tobenkin, Elias.

Bibliography.
In his The Peoples Want Peace.
New York: G. P. Putnam´s Sons, 1938. pp. 225-232.

   107 items, 1899-1936. English, German; also Russian, French
   (6), Italian (3), Norwegian (2), Polish (1), Danish (1),
   Swedish (1).

   General works (40) on the causes and prevention of war and on
   conditions of peace; other works on special conditions and
   problems in particular countries--Denmark (8), Norway (6),
   Sweden (5), Austria (2), Czechoslovakia (5), Germany (6),
   Italy (2), Poland (5), U.S.S.R. (7), China (4), Japan and
   Japanese-Russian relations (12), Manchuria (5).

57   HB195.V6

Vogt, Johan.

Litteraturfortegnelse [Literature list].
In his Mens Våpnene Hviler [While Weapons Rest]: Krigsførsel og
nøitralitet i støpeskjeen [Warfare and neutrality in the
crucible].
Oslo: H. Aschehoug (W. Nygaard), 1938. pp. 145-152.

   43 items, 1910-1938. German, English; also Danish (4), French
   (4), Norwegian (4), Dutch (1), Swedish (1). Most items have
   brief annotations in Norwegian.

   Selected books on war economy, international crises,
   international political economy, neutrality, and other
   topics; memoirs of military and civilian leaders.

58   Z7164.L1M5

[Black, Henry, et al.].

"International relations and war."

Peace and War--General

In his A Basic List of Books and Pamphlets for a Labor School
Library.
Mena, Ark.: Commonwealth College Library (Bulletin No. 3),
February, 1939. pp. 23-25. (mimeo).

   38 items, 1925-1938. English. The bibliography as a whole
   has a foreword (2 pp.); table of contents; author index;
   subject index.

   Books on international politics (especially in the Far East),
   imperialism, armaments, and economic aspects of war. Other
   sections of this bibliography contain works on labor in
   politics, fascism, the Soviet Union, race relations, and
   other topics.

59   JX1904.P4,1939

[National Peace Council (London)].

"The year´s books; The year´s pamphlets and leaflets; League of
Nations publications; Government publications; Memoranda; Peace
press directory; Posters."
In its Peace Year Book, 1939.
London: National Peace Council, 1939. pp. 119-123, 130-142,
143-145, 146-149, 150-151, 152-153, 154.

   777 items, 1938-1939. English.

   Books and pamphlets on Africa (10), armaments and air raid
   precautions (25), collective security (18), economic and
   colonial questions, imperialism, etc. (46), conscription and
   national service (6), democracy, fascism, and civil liberties
   (26), education (5), Czechoslovakia (24), Europe (12), Far
   East (38), Germany (36), Spain (36), U.S.A. (16), U.S.S.R.
   (7), Italy and the Mediterranean (9), India (6), Palestine
   (7), international law and relations (15), League of Nations
   (4), pacifism (49), refugees (13), miscellaneous on war and
   peace (157); League of Nations publications (74); government
   publications (48); memoranda (31); peace press directory
   (26); posters (33).

60   U21.R39

Richardson, Lewis F.

References.
In his Generalized Foreign Politics: A study in group
psychology.

Peace and War--General

Cambridge: Cambridge University Press (The British Journal of
Psychology Monograph Supplements, 23), 1939. pp. 88-89.

   53 items, 1879-1939. English; also French (2).

   Works on mathematics, meteorology, armament statistics,
   mathematical studies of war, and approaches to peace.

61   Z733.S815S7

Almond, Nina [Elizabeth] and H. H. Fisher.

Special Collections in the Hoover Library on War, Revolution,
and Peace, with a foreword by Herbert Hoover.
Stanford: Stanford University, 1940. 111 pp.

   273 items (collections, no dates given). English, Russian; also
   German, Italian, Polish, Hungarian, French, other eastern and
   western languages. All items have brief to abstract-length
   descriptive annotations; introduction (9 pp.); foreword (3
   pp.); table of contents; subject/author index.

   An informal guide to the Hoover Library's special collections
   of official documents and publications, files of
   organizations, private papers of public figures, and
   miscellaneous materials relating to war (particularly World
   War I) and the problems of peace. International collections
   (33), multinational collections (22), national and regional
   collections (218).

62   H83.A72

Arnold, Joseph Irvin.

Interesting books to read in "War and peace: The 20th
challenge."
In his Challenges to American Youth.
New York/San Francisco/Evanston: Row, Peterson, 1940. pp.
486-487.

   27 items, 1933-1938. English.

   Books on foreign policy, international relations, peace,
   and war.

Peace and War--General

63   BR115.W2C6

Corkey, Robert.

[Bibliographical footnotes].
In his War, Pacifism and Peace: A study in ultimate war aims,
for peace-lovers in Britain and America.
London: Society for Promoting Christian Knowledge, [1940].
171 pp.

  90 items (no dates given). Items are discussed in text and
  notes.

  Works cited in chapters on the church at the crossroads (6),
  moral authority (13), defective theories of good and evil
  (4), conditions of peace (19), why the League failed (16),
  the doctrines of pacifism (14), the judgment of the church in
  the past (12), and the shadow of things to come (6).

64   JX1953.C58

[Haile, Pennington].

Bibliographies [7 lists]; General reading list.
In his A Study of the Organization of Peace: Based upon the
preliminary report of the Commission to Study the Organization
of Peace.
New York: Commission to Study the Organization of Peace,
November, 1940. pp. 17, 18, 19, 20, 21, 25, 29; 29-32.
An earlier version of this bibliography appeared in Haile's
Study Outline on the Organization of Peace, New York:
Commission to Study the Organization of Peace, January, 1940,
pp. 26-31.

  130 items, 1929-1940. English.

  The world today (6), the world we want (5), the nature of
  peace (4), the nation-state (2), the nature of federation
  (3), building peace (7), problems confronting the United
  States (31); general reading list on war and peace (72).

65   JX1961.U6N33

Jacobs, Ida T. and John J. DeBoer (eds.).

"Selected best books for secondary schools."
In their Educating for Peace: A report of the Committee on
International Relations of the National Council of Teachers of
English.

Peace and War--General

New York/London: D. Appleton-Century, for the National Council
of Teachers of English (English Monograph No. 9), 1940.
pp. 243-269.

   415 items, 1883-1940. English. Some items have brief
   descriptive and/or critical annotations.

   The Pacific area--China, Japan, Philippines, Russia (34);
   Great Britain in the twentieth century--political background,
   relations with Ireland, foreign policy, evolution of the
   empire, India (25); Germany (10), Finland (1), Italy (3),
   Spain (2), newspapers and public opinion (4), the Pacific
   area (5), international relations (18), additional
   bibliography (19), children's books on Latin America (17),
   children's books on history and travel (2); touring Europe
   with Oliver Hazard Perry--England, France, Holland, Italy,
   Norway, Poland, Ireland, Switzerland, Sweden, Russia,
   Scotland (98); a list of World Affairs Pamphlets (13),
   Foreign Policy Reports (33), study packets (11), tests (3),
   headline books (6), world affairs pamphlets (3), public
   policy pamphlets (7), suggestions for classroom libraries,
   eleventh and twelfth years (20), plays and pageants (61),
   some plays selected for the peace play tournament (20).

66   HM106.M8

Mühlmann, Wilhelm Emil.

Anmerkungen.
In his Krieg und Frieden [War and Peace]: Ein Leitfaden der
politischen Ethnologie, mit Berücksichtigung völkerkundlichen
und geschichtlichen Stoffes [A guide to political ethnology
considering anthropological and historical materials].
Heidelberg: Carl Winter (Kulturgeschichtliche Bibliothek, Neue
Folge, Zweite Reihe/Lehrbucher, Band 2), 1940. pp. 220-240.

   296 items, 1744-1939. German, English, French; also Dutch
   (1). Endnote format, organized by chapters.

   Books, articles, and reports on the history, ethnology, and
   anthropology of war and warfare and on peaceful customs and
   forms of social organization. Includes some general works on
   the theory and sociology of war and numerous references for
   individual cultures, both western and nonwestern.

Peace and War--General

67   JX1904.P4,1940

[National Peace Council (London)].

"The year´s books; The year´s pamphlets and leaflets; League of
Nations publications; Peace press directory."
In its Peace Year Book, Supplement for 1940.
London: National Peace Council, 1940. pp. 37-42, 43-50, 51,
52-53.

   326 items, 1938-1940. English; also French (1).

   Books, pamphlets, and leaflets on armaments (7), collective
   security (4), colonialism, imperialism and economic questions
   (12), Czechoslovakia (7), democracy, fascism, and civil
   liberties (13), Europe (11), Far East (6), federal union (8),
   Germany (35), international law and relations (8), pacifism
   (42), war (9), Italy (2), Palestine (7), Spain (1), U.S.S.R.
   (4), peace terms and war aims (15), conscription and national
   service (14), miscellaneous (73); League of Nations
   publications (19); peace press directory (29).

68   JX1961.U6N33

Row, William H.

Bibliography in "A unit on world peace."
In Jacobs, Ida T. and John J. DeBoer, Educating for Peace: A
report of the Committee on International Relations of the
National Council of Teachers of English.
New York/London: D. Appleton-Century, for the National Council
of Teachers of English (English Monograph No. 9), 1940.
pp. 168-170.

   33 items, 1927-1939. English.

   Causes of war (7), effects of war (4), World War I
   reparations and debts (3), prevention of international war
   (3), League of Nations (2), the World Court (2),
   international law (1), Germany (3), Central Europe (2), Japan
   and China (2), Italy and the fascist movement (2), Russia
   (2).

69   Z6204.I6

Iowa State College, Library Staff (comps.), with the assistance
of Department of History and Government.

Peace and War--General

Education for Victory and for Permanent Security through World
Peace [bibliographic essay].
Ames: Iowa State College Library, 1941 (prelim. ed.). 28 pp.
(mimeo).

   127 items, 1912-1941. English. Some items mentioned and
   discussed in text, others listed with brief to medium-length
   descriptive and/or critical annotations throughout the text;
   introduction (2 pp.).

   Books on Nazism (20), international relations (11), civilian
   morale (13), industrial cooperation and control of strikes
   (8), control of inflation (5), public information and
   education (7), preparations for peace (14), South America and
   hemisphere relations (13), war in the Pacific (16), U.S.
   armed forces (12); pamphlet series (8).

70   JX1904.P4,1941

[National Peace Council (London)].

"Bibliographies--the year's books in 1940, the year's pamphlets
and leaflets in 1940, League of Nations publications, a press
directory."
In its Peace Year Book: Supplement for 1941.
London: National Peace Council, 1941. pp. 31-59.

   633 items, 1940-1940. English.

   Books, pamphlets, and leaflets on collective security (9),
   colonies and imperialism (10), conscription (8), democracy
   and dictatorship (12), economic questions (16), Europe (16),
   Far East (9), federation (22), Germany (41), India (16),
   international relations (12), Middle East (7), pacifism (51),
   refugees, etc. (4), religions (32), Scandinavia, U.S.S.R.,
   etc. (16), U.S. (12), the war (47), war aims and peace terms
   (57), miscellaneous (60); League of Nations publications
   (30); press directory (47).

71   JX1255.B7,1942

Brown, William.

Bibliography.
In his War and the Psychological Conditions of Peace.
London: Adam and Charles Black, 1942 (2nd and enl. ed.).
p. 144.
First published as War and Peace: Essays in Psychological
Analysis, 1939.

Peace and War--General

32 items, 1910-1942. English; also German (3).

Books on political theory, fascism, and the psychological
causes of war.

72   JX1954.C5722

[Haile, Pennington].

References [11 lists]; General bibliography.
In his Study Courses on Immediate Postwar Problems: With study
questions and suggested references (Based upon the second
report, "The Transitional Period," of the Commission to Study
the Organization of Peace).
New York: Commission to Study the Organization of Peace, April,
1942. pp. 8-9, 15, 18, 19, 21, 22-23, 24, 25, 26-27, 32, 36,
37-39.

106 items, 1931-1942. English.

Pamphlets (65) and books (41) on the causes of World War II,
the League of Nations, enforcement of peace, economic aspects
of war and peace, postwar problems, conditions of peace,
postwar planning, nationalism, the effects of war, U.S.
foreign policy, and world order.

73   JX1904.P4,1942

[National Peace Council (London)].

"Books and pamphlets, March 1941-May 1942; League of Nations
publications; Memoranda and special reports (in stencilled
form), issued by the National Peace Council between June, 1940
and May, 1942; A press directory."
In its Peace and Reconstruction Year Book, 1942.
London: National Peace Council, 1942. pp. 37-59, 60-61, 62-63,
64-67.

587 items, 1940-1942. English.

Books and pamphlets on fundamental principles of peace,
democracy and dictatorship, pacifism, etc. (86), political
and constitutional issues, League of Nations, federation,
etc. (28), economic and social issues (37), colonial
questions, future of imperialism, mandates, etc. (17),
general topics (62), the U.S. and Anglo-American relations,
Latin America (28), the U.S.S.R. and Anglo-Soviet relations
(27), the British Commonwealth of Nations (15), India (15),
the Far East (19), Europe (43), Germany (27), refugee
questions (6), blockade and food relief (14), the war (17),

Peace and War--General

miscellaneous (34); League of Nations publications (13);
publications of the International Labor Office (13);
memoranda and special reports issued by the National Peace
Council (9); press directory (77).

74   Z6207.W81A8

Aufricht, Hans.

War, Peace and Reconstruction: A classified bibliography.
New York: Commission to Study the Organization of Peace,
[1943]. 52 pp.
An earlier edition, entitled "General bibliography on
international organization and post-war reconstruction,"
appeared in the Bulletin of the Commission to Study the
Organization of Peace, Vol. 2, Nos. 5 and 6 (May-June, 1942),
pp. 1-28; and Vol. 3, Nos. 1 and 2 (January-February, 1943),
pp. 20-24 (Supplement).

  2155 items, 1898-1943. English; also French, German. A few
  items have abstract-length descriptive annotations; foreword
  (1 p.); table of contents.

  Background material (242), war (202), international
  organization (122), international administration (127),
  pacific settlement of disputes (68), security and sanctions
  (67), federations (117), regionalism (288), economic
  reconstruction (249), political ideologies, public opinion
  and propaganda, education (185), religion (72), postwar
  reconstruction (416). Each of these 12 main headings is
  further divided into several subtopics, making a total of
  about 70 subject headings.

75 <

New York State Library, Reference Section.

Peace or War? A suggested reading list relating not to
particular wars nor to particular peace settlements but to all
war, past and future, and to the hope of future peace.
Albany: New York State Library, Reference Section, 1943. 6 pp.

  Apparently unavailable; not located through interlibrary
  loan.

Peace and War--General

76   JX1904.P4,1944

[National Peace Council (London)].

"Books, June 1942-December 1943; Pamphlets and leaflets . . . ;
League of Nations publications; Publications of the
International Labour Office; A press directory."
In its Peace and Reconstruction Year Book, 1944.
London: National Peace Council, 1944. pp. 38-48, 49-60, 61,
62-63, 64-68.

   582 items, 1942-1943. English.

   Fundamental principles (93), political and constitutional
   issues (45), economic and social issues (85), colonial
   questions (13), the British Commonwealth of Nations (4), U.S.
   and Anglo-American relations (38), U.S.S.R. and Anglo-Soviet
   relations (25), India (35), Far East (22), Europe and
   European countries (32), Germany (32), the Jewish question
   (18), relief and rehabilitation (20), civil liberties and
   conscription (11), miscellaneous (10); League of Nations
   publications (16), publications of the International Labour
   Office (24), press directory (59).

77 <

[Foreign Affairs Outlines].

Bibliography in "Education for victory."
In special issue, Building the Peace.
Foreign Affairs Outlines, 3 (April 3, 1945): 10-11.

78   Z6463.F73

Woolbert, Robert Gale.

"War, peace, security and disarmament."
In his Foreign Affairs Bibliography: A selected and annotated
list of books on international relations, 1932-1942.
New York/London: Harper and Brothers, for the Council on
Foreign Relations, 1945. pp. 99-119.

   278 items, 1931-1942. English; also French, German, Italian
   (4), Danish (2), Russian (2), Spanish (2), other European and
   oriental languages. All items have brief descriptive and/or
   critical annotations; introduction to whole work (2 pp.);
   table of contents.

   General works on war (27), general strategy of modern warfare
   (28), techniques and tactics (27), aerial warfare (29), naval

Peace and War--General

    warfare (19), chemical warfare (8), propaganda and espionage
(9), the armaments industry (13), peace (36), peaceful change
and arbitration (13), pacifism (13), security and disarmament
(6), security (22), disarmament (28).

79   JX1952.K5

Knudson, Albert C[ornelius].

A brief bibliography.
In his The Philosophy of War and Peace.
New York/Nashville: Abingdon-Cokesbury Press, 1947.
pp. 211-215.

    45 items, 1886-1946. English; also German (1).

    Books on peace plans, international relations, causes of war,
international law, conditions of peace, the relationship
between Christianity and war and peace, and peace theory.

80   JF51.M4,1947

Magruder, Frank Abbott.

Bibliography [6 lists].
In his National Governments and International Relations.
Boston/etc.: Allyn and Bacon, 1947 (new ed.). pp. 542, 557,
570, 594, 610-611, 624.
First edition, 1929. Revised edition, 1943.

    91 items, 1934-1946. English.

    Lists of references following chapters on international law
(9), causes of international wars (16), effects of
international wars (9), proposed methods of preventing
international wars (20), the United Nations (19), the need
for world federation (18).

81   JX1391.M6

Morgenthau, Hans J[oachim].

Bibliography.
In his Politics among Nations: The struggle for power and
peace.
New York: Alfred A. Knopf, 1948. pp. 473-489.
Later editions appeared in 1954, 1960, 1967, and 1973.

Peace and War--General

    361 items, 1748-1948. English; also French, German.
    Introduction (1 paragraph).

    Periodicals (13); general treatises on international politics
    (24), understanding international politics and the problems
    of international peace (7), international politics as a
    struggle for power (52), national power (53), limitation of
    international power and the balance of power (31),
    international morality and world public opinion (22),
    international law (31), world politics in the mid-twentieth
    century (27), peace through limitation (58), peace through
    transformation (24), peace through accommodation (19).

82   JX1308.W58

Wittmann, Erno.

Books consulted.
In his History: A guide to peace.
New York: Columbia University Press, 1948. pp. 379-393.

    349 items, 1701-1946. English; also German, French, Latin
    (2), Spanish (1).

    Books and articles on world history, political theory,
    diplomacy and diplomatic history, foreign policy,
    international relations, and causes of war.

83 <

Davis, Francis.

"Peace and war: a short bibliography."
Blackfriars (Oxford, now London), 30 (December, 1949): 599.

84   JX4511.G7

Grob, Fritz.

Bibliography.
In his The Relativity of War and Peace: A study in law,
history, and politics, with a foreword by Roscoe Pound.
New Haven/London: Yale University Press/Geoffrey Cumberlege,
Oxford University Press, 1949. pp. 333-349.

    201 items, 1754-1946. English, French; also German, Italian
    (7), Latin (1). Introduction (1 paragraph).

Peace and War--General

Books and journal articles (135) and official documents (66)
on international law, the Hague peace conferences,
neutrality, social and political history, definitions of war,
war termination, treaties, foreign policy, intervention,
international relations, and diplomacy.

85   PSC-PC; also IU: f355.
                                        0213B63P,1979

Bofman, Albert.

Peace and Militarization: A survey of current documents and
reports, produced especially for Mid-Century Peace Conference,
with an introduction by Kermit Eby.
Chicago: Committee Against Militarization (List No. 1), May,
1950. [vi] + 78 pp. (mimeo).

    1923 items, 1860-1950. English. Some items have brief
    descriptive and/or critical annotations; introduction (2 pp.)
    plus introductions to main sections; table of contents;
    statistical summary of militarization of U.S.A.; materials on
    the Committee Against Militarization; advertisements.

    U.S. government publications--compulsory military service
    (40), civil defense plan (6), bills to create a department of
    peace, international peace gardens, etc. (45), militarism,
    America's biggest industry, expands (personnel, 174;
    construction, 208), U.S. military expansion (international
    agreements, 40; after World War II, 42; miscellaneous, 30),
    1950 military establishment appropriation (43), North
    Atlantic Treaty, military assistance program (49), Cold War
    and restrictions on free movement of persons by U.S.A. (58),
    foreign aid (45), State Department and international
    organizations (56), miscellaneous (105); publications of
    information offices of foreign governments and United Nations
    (160); publications of nongovernmental organizations--peace
    organizations (276), other organizations (323), political
    parties (23), anticonscription and other groups (16);
    selected books on peace and militarization--examined and
    recommended by the compiler (113), not examined but likely to
    be of interest (68); the garrison state--important articles
    (3).

86   HM51.S68

Speier, Hans.

[Bibliographical] Notes.
In his Social Order and the Risks of War: Papers in political
sociology.

Peace and War--General

New York: George W. Stewart (Library of Policy Sciences), 1952.
pp. 457-497.

    593 items, 1602-1950. German, English; also French, Norwegian
    (1). Endnote format, some items are critically discussed in
    the notes.

    Notes organized by chapters; about half deal with social
    order and the rest with such topics as the sociology of war,
    warfare, militarism, class structure and total war, treachery
    in war, public opinion, diplomacy, and National Socialism.

87   JX1954.C465

Cheever, Daniel S. and H[enry] Field Haviland, Jr.

Suggestions for further reading [26 lists].
In their Organizing for Peace: International organization in
world affairs.
Boston/New York/etc.: Houghton Mifflin (Riverside Press), 1954.
pp. 16-17, 42-43, 70-72, 108-109, 131, 157-158, 186, 225-226,
277-280, 299-300, 330-331, 352-353, 396-397, 424-425, 470-471,
506, 525-526, 569-570, 597-598, 623-624, 669-670, 687, 709-710,
785-787, 812-813, 842-844.

    739 items, 1911-1954. English.

    Books, articles, and documents on causes of war, war and
    society, international law, international organization,
    United Nations, peace conferences, U.S. foreign policy,
    League of Nations, peacemaking, various agencies of the
    United Nations, international arbitration, International
    Court of Justice, peace organizations, atomic energy for
    military use, disarmament, international control of atomic
    energy, world order, international politics, refugees and
    human rights, colonialism, economic development, European
    integration, and other topics.

88   Z6464.Z9H32,v.1-6

[Landheer, B., J. L. F. Van Essen, and W. S. Russer (eds.)].

Catalogue de la Bibliothèque du Palais de la Paix:
Supplément[s] 1937-1952, I-VI/Catalogue of the Peace Palace
Library: Supplement[s] 1937-1952, [Vols.] I-VI.
The Hague: Bibliothèque du Palais de la Paix/Library of the
Palace of Peace, 1954 to 1963. 1093 pp.

Peace and War--General

    Follows the same classification scheme as the earlier
    catalogues of the Peace Palace Library. (See Nos. 16, 23,
    24, 30, 33, 36, 48, and 49, above, and 100, below.)

89   Z6461.B4

Beardsley, Seymour W. and Alvin G. Edgell.

Human relations in international affairs: A guide to
significant interpretation and research.
Washington, D.C.: Public Affairs Press, in cooperation with the
American Friends Service Committee, 1956. vi + 40 pp.

    117 items, 1941-1956. English. All items have medium- to
    abstract-length descriptive and critical annotations;
    introduction (4 pp.); topical cross-reference guide; a short
    selected bibliography; pertinent periodicals.

    Books on psychological, sociological, and anthropological
    aspects of international relations.

90

Centre d´Etudes Sociologiques.

Bibliography.
In International Sociological Association, et al., The Nature
of Conflict: Studies on the sociological aspects of
international tensions.
Paris: UNESCO (Tensions and Technology Series), 1957.
pp. 225-310.

    1160 items, 1918-1954 (most items published after 1940).
    English; also French, German, Russian, Spanish, Norwegian,
    other Western European languages. Some items have brief to
    abstract-length descriptive annotations.

    Books and journal articles on sociology and the
    psychosociology of intergroup conflicts (394), international
    relations (370), racial conflicts and colonialism (288),
    class conflict involving industry and agriculture (93);
    papers from 1954 American Sociological Meeting (15).

Peace and War--General

91   JX1308.W3

Waltz, Kenneth N.

Bibliography.
In his Man, the State and War: A theoretical analysis, with a
foreword by William T. R. Fox.
New York/London: Columbia University Press (Topical Studies in
International Relations, No. 2), 1959. pp. 239-251.

   240 items, 1798-1957. English; also French (6), German (4).

   Books and articles on international relations, causes of war,
   social and political aspects of war, theory of war,
   sociological studies, nationalism, political philosophy, and
   peace theory.

92   U21.B623

Bouthoul, Gaston.

Bibliography.
In his War, translated by Sylvia and George Lesson.
New York: Walker, 1962. pp. 142-144.

   43 items, 1902-1961. English; also French (1).

   Books on political philosophy, peace theory, causes and
   effects of war, nuclear weapons, and disarmament.

93   HN51.J6,v.18(2)

Deutsch, Morton.

References in "Psychological alternatives to war."
Journal of Social Issues, 18, 2 (1962): 118-119.

   26 items, 1911-1961. English.

   Articles on psychological approaches in the study of war and
   peace and sociopsychological theories of cooperation,
   competition, conformity, bargaining, and trust.

Peace and War--General

94   Z6464.Z9N55

Newcombe, Hanna (comp.).

Bibliography on War and Peace.
Dundas, Ontario: Canadian Peace Research Institute (Peace
Research Abstracts), August, 1963. 19 pp. (mimeo).

  531 items, 1923-1963 (most items published after 1945).
  English; also French (1). Introduction (2 paragraphs).

  Mostly books, monographs, and pamphlets on peace theory and
  peace research; conditions conducive to peace; the arms race,
  arms control, disarmament, and deterrence; national defense,
  foreign policy, and international relations; the U.N. and
  NATO; and the study of war and conflict, particularly the
  Cold War and nuclear warfare.

95

Kahn, Robert L. and Elise Boulding (eds.).

Selected bibliography and references.
In their Power and Conflict in Organizations.
New York: Basic Books, 1964. pp. 158-166.

96   HM36.5.M25

McNeil, Elton B[urbank] (ed.).

References [13 lists by various authors].
In his The Nature of Human Conflict.
Englewood Cliffs, N.J.: Prentice-Hall, 1965. pp. 13, 38-41,
61-63, 89-90, 114-115, 134-138, 153-154, 170-171, 225-226,
248-249, 271-273, 290-292, 315.

  358 items, 1871-1964. English; also German (4), French (1).

  References to articles entitled the nature of social science
  and human conflict (9), the nature of aggression (57), the
  psychology of human conflict (28), the social psychology of
  human conflict (30), the sociology of human conflict (29),
  the anthropology of human conflict (77), the political
  science of human conflict (19), the history of human conflict
  (14), game theory and human conflict (5), world law and human
  conflict (26), systems theory and human conflict (32),
  decision-making theory and human conflict (29), the future of
  human conflict (3).

Peace and War--General

97   BT 736.2.S7

Strijd, Kr.

Literatuur.
In his 52 vragen over oorlog en vrede [52 Questions about War
and Peace].
Amsterdam: W. Ten Have (Christen-zijn in internationale
verhoudingen, Carillon-Reeks No. 52), 1965. pp. 166-173.

   167 items, 1926-1965. Dutch, English; also German, French.
   Introduction (1 paragraph).

   General political, military situation (16), nuclear armament
   (14), on the reality of war (16), disarmament (9), Soviet
   Russia (10), China (10), Cuba (5), Africa (5), Christian
   faith, ecumenical movement, churches, etc. (14), Roman
   Catholic publications (11), nonpacifist publications (10),
   pacifist publications (31), new [nonviolent] preparedness
   (16).

98   L11.E29,v.30

Tedeschi, James T.

Bibliography in "A peace issues course."
Educational Forum, 30, 1 (November, 1965): 86-87.

   38 items, 1954-1964. English.

   Books, articles, reports, and pamphlets on disarmament, the
   arms race, foreign affairs, international relations, the Cold
   War, and conditions conducive to peace.

99   U21.W7,1965

Wright, Quincy.

"Select bibliography on war, 1945-64."
In his A Study of War: Second edition, with a commentary on war
since 1942.
Chicago/London: University of Chicago Press, 1965 (2nd ed.).
pp. 1564-1577.

   283 items, 1945-1964. English. Introduction (3 pp.).

   Books on psychology and propaganda (49), technology and
   armament (54), politics and diplomacy (61), international
   organization and the United Nations (29), international law

Peace and War--General

and ethics (57), population, trade, and economic development
(33).

100 <   Z6464.Z9H32,Suppl.1966,Index

[Landheer, B., J. L. F. Van Essen, and W. S. Russer (eds.)].

Index: Suppléments 1937-1952, I-VI [de la] Catalogue de la
Bibliothèque du Palais de la Paix.
The Hague: Bibliothèque du Palais de la Paix/Library of the
Palace of Peace, 1966. 80 pp.

101   JX1963.L27

[Landsforbundet Aldrig Mere Krig].

Literaturfortegnelse [Literature list].
In its Aldrig Mere Krig [No More War].
[Copenhagen]: Borgens Forlag, 1966. pp. 151-152.

  40 items (no dates given). Danish.

  Books and pamphlets on the causes and prevention of war,
  nuclear weapons, nonviolence, pacifism, and the peace movement.
  Publication information not given.

102

Martin, David A.

List of sources.
In his Pacifism: An historical and sociological study.
New York: Schocken Books, 1966. pp. 225-242.

  345 items, 1899-1963. English; also French (1).

  The break with nature (15), Catholic compromise and sectarian
  rejection (29), a pilot study (25), old and new dissent (22),
  the Labour Party and the ILP (71), pacifism and the
  intelligentsia (73), dissent and the establishment (35),
  sect, order, and cult (21), pacifism in the United States
  (12), unclassified and general sources (14), articles (15),
  theses (13).

Peace and War--General

103   BR115.A8502

O´Brien, William V[incent].

Bibliography.
In his Nuclear War, Deterrence and Morality.
Westminster/New York/Glen Rock/etc. Newman Press, 1967.
pp. 111-120.

   156 items, 1919-1967. English; also French (8), German (3).

   Books, articles, and pamphlets on just war theory, morality,
   and nuclear war (51), pacifist thoughts on morality and
   nuclear war (21), arms control, disarmament, and national
   security policy (46), international relations theory,
   international law, organization, and morality (21), Communist
   thoughts on defense, arms control, and disarmament (5), Cuban
   Missile Crisis (2), Hiroshima and Nagasaki (6), effects of
   nuclear explosions (4).

104   JX1901.J6,v.12

[Converse, Elizabeth].

"Author index, 1957-1968 (Volumes I through XII)."
Journal of Conflict Resolution, 12, 4 (December, 1968):
[533]-550.

   An alphabetic list of authors with article titles, dates,
   volume and page references, and cross-references for
   additional authors.

105   Z6464.W3E9

[Everts, Philip P. (comp.)].

Boeken over oorlog en vrede [Books on War and Peace].
Utrecht/Voorburg: Katholiek Bibliotheek- en Lectuurcentrum
IDIL/Protestantse Stichting tot Bevordering van het
Bibliotheekwezen en de Lectuurvoorlichting in Nederland,
[1968]. 20 pp.

   85 items, 1960-1968 (most items undated). Dutch.
   Bibliographic essay format, all items are discussed in the
   text; introduction (1 p.); author/title index.

   General works (8), polemological studies (12), nuclear
   weapons (8), spreading of nuclear weapons (3), international
   problems (7), armament and disarmament (7); religious and
   ethical discussions--from Protestant circles (10), from

Peace and War--General

Catholic circles (4), other (1); education and instruction
(5); miscellaneous (9); periodicals (11).

106   JX1901.J6,v.12

Fink, Clinton F[rederick].

References in "Some conceptual difficulties in the theory of
social conflict."
Journal of Conflict Resolution, 12, 4 (December, 1968):
456-460.

125 items, 1883-1967. English; also German (1), French (1).

Books and articles on the theory of social conflict, types of
conflict, competition, and other social antagonisms ranging
from interpersonal to international levels, including
philosophical works and those from social and behavioral
sciences.

107   JX1952.S77

Starke, J. G.

Bibliography.
In his An Introduction to the Science of Peace (Irenology).
Leiden: A. W. Sijthoff (International Series of Studies on
Sociological Problems), 1968. pp. 204-207.

71 items, 1919-1966. English; also French (6), German (2).

Books on peace theory, peace research, conditions of peace,
causes and effects of war, international relations,
international law, world order, theories of conflict, and
disarmament.

108   Z7161.A1U6

Universal Reference System.

Bibliography of Bibliographies in Political Science,
Government, and Public Policy: An annotated and intensively
indexed compilation of significant books, pamphlets, and
articles, selected and processed by the Universal Reference
System. Prepared under the direction of Alfred DeGrazia,
general editor, et al.
Princeton: Princeton Research Publishing (Political Science,
Government, and Public Policy Series, Vol. 3), 1968.
xix + 927 pp.

Peace and War--General

   Annotated listing of bibliographies organized by accession
   numbers; indexed with a chronological listing of authors and
   titles under main subject heads.

   109   Z6464.Z9T6

World Without War Council.

To End War: An annotated bibliography and 1968 literature
catalogue.
Berkeley, Calif.: World Without War Council of Northern
California, 1968. 48 pp.

   306 items, 1940-1968. English. All items have brief
   descriptive and/or critical annotations; introduction (1 p.);
   table of contents.

   Books, pamphlets, monographs, and reports on nonviolence
   (26), crisis problems and area studies (31), moral,
   religious, and philosophical issues and attitudes (23),
   conscientious objection (19), international organization and
   world law (40), world development and world community (28),
   disarmament problems and approaches (26), the Communist
   nations (24), United States foreign policy (17), war,
   weapons, and strategy (23), social research and analysis
   (19), the peace effort (17), peace education with children
   (13).

   110   U21.2.C7

Ginsberg, Robert (ed.).

"A bibliography of the philosophy of war in the atomic age."
In his The Critique of War: Contemporary philosophical
explorations.
Chicago: Henry Regnery, 1969. pp. 345-353.

   147 items, 1940-1969. English.

   Books and articles on theories of war and peace, causes of
   war, conditions of peace, pacifism, nonviolence, world order,
   world government, and the relationship between religion, war,
   and peace.

Peace and War--General

111   JX1395.S4

Senghaas, Dieter.

Literaturverzeichnis [Literature list].
In his Abschreckung und Frieden [Deterrence and Peace]: Studien
zur Kritik organisierter Friedlosigkeit [Critical studies on
organized peacelessness].
Frankfurt am Main: Europäische Verlagsanstalt (Kritische
Studien zur Politikwissenschaft), 1969. pp. 295-316.

   533 items, 1912-1969. English, German; also French.
   Introduction (1 paragraph).

   Books and articles on U.S. foreign policy, international
   relations, nuclear weapons, arms control, national security,
   strategy, disarmament, military science, war theory,
   aggression, deterrence, and international conflict.

112   JX1901.J6,v.14

Goldstein, Joel W.

Bibliography in "The psychology of conflict and international
relations: A course plan and bibliography."
Journal of Conflict Resolution, 14, 1 (March, 1970): 116-120.

113   Z6464.Z9P5

Pickus, Robert and Robert Woito.

Bibliography [13 lists]; War/peace periodicals.
In their To End War: An introduction; ideas, books,
organizations, work that can help (prepared for those who wish
to aid in work to end war).
New York/Evanston/London: Harper and Row (Perennial Library),
1970 (rev. ed.). pp. 9-15, 22-29, 36-48, 56-66, 74-85, 92-102,
108-118, 124-136, 141-147, 154-164, 173-185, 189-203, 249-257;
296-308.
First edition, Berkeley, Calif.: World Without War Council,
1970.

   723 items, 1939-1971. English. All items have brief to
   abstract-length descriptive and/or critical annotations; list
   of peace organizations appended.

   Books and pamphlets on the causes and nature of war (34),
   disarmament (34), world development and world community (63),
   international organization and world law (57), the U.S. and
   international relations (55), communist nations and

Peace and War--General

international relations (57), area studies, crisis problems,
and issues (57), moral and religious thought on war (69),
conscientious objection and the draft (33), nonviolent
approach to social change (57), political processes and the
peace effort (61), peace research (50), peace education (37);
peace periodicals (60).

114

Cook, Blanche Wiesen, Charles Chatfield, and Sandi Cooper
(eds.).

The Garland Library of War and Peace: A collection of 360
titles bound in 328 volumes, with an introduction by Merle
Curti.
New York: Garland, 1971. 136 pp.

362 items, 1464-1971. English; also French, German. Most
items have brief descriptive and/or critical annotations;
preface (1 p.); introduction (2 pp.) plus brief introductions
(1-2 paragraphs) to some of the sections; table of contents;
author index.

Catalogue of the reprint series, with numerous illustrations;
sections on peace proposals (38), history and problems of the
organized peace movement (32), biographies and memoirs of
peace leaders (16), character, causes, and political economy
of war (72), labor, socialism, and war (25), arms control and
limitation (28), international arbitration (34),
international law (24), Kellogg Pact and outlawry of war (7),
nonresistance and nonviolence (24), conscription and
conscientious objection (25), religious and ethical positions
on war (14), the artist on war (9), and documentary
anthologies (14).

115 <   Z6204.S72

Glazier, Kenneth M. and James R. Hobson.

International and English-language Collections: A survey of
holdings at the Hoover Institution on War, Revolution and
Peace.
Stanford: Stanford University, Hoover Institution on War,
Revolution and Peace (Hoover Institution Survey of Holdings,
3), [1971]. 20 pp.

Peace and War--General

116 <   JX1395.S362

Lepawsky, Albert, Edward H. Buehrig, and Harold D[wight]
Lasswell (eds.).

[Bibliographies by various authors].
In their The Search for World Order: Studies by students and
colleagues of Quincy Wright.
New York: Appleton-Century-Crofts, [1971].

117   Z6461.M38

Medling, Margaret (comp.).

The Eagle and the Dove: Selected titles on war and peace.
St. Louis: St. Louis University, Pius XII Library, 1971. 41 pp.
A revised and enlarged edition compiled by Marilyn Huxford and
Sandra Schelling appeared under the title "Perspectives on War
and Peace in a Changing World: A select bibliography," St.
Louis: St. Louis University, Pius XII Memorial Library
(Publication No. 10), 172 pp., 1975.

   629 items, 1910-1971. English. Table of contents; author
   index.

   Books arranged under 39 subject headings relating to war and
   peace, including armament and disarmament, international
   relations, international law, U.S. foreign policy, pacifism,
   and political dissent.

118   U21.2.N48

Nesbitt, William A.

Bibliography [17 lists].
In his Teaching about War and War Prevention.
New York: Foreign Policy Association (New Dimensions Series),
1971. pp. 5-6, 19-20, 28-29, 37, 55-56, 68, 78-79, 86, 92-93,
104, 106-107, 108, 109-110, 111-112, 114, 133-134, 164-166.

   143 items, 1958-1971. English. Some items have brief
   descriptive and/or critical annotations.

   General (7), conflicts, violence, and war (9), man as the
   cause (5), psychological factors (7), nation states as the
   cause (14), understanding the international system (9), the
   military system and arms (11), usefulness of war (4), the
   possibilities of large scale war (11), examining proposals
   for changes in the current system (36), proposals for system
   change (16), units and courses on war and peace (14).

Peace and War--General

119

Stinnes, Manfred.

Bibliography.
In his Peace Movement and Peace Research Theory: The case of
Western Europe. Unpublished M.A. thesis,
University of Minnesota, March, 1971. pp. [150-159].
(typescript).

   134 items, 1912-1971. English, German; also Dutch (1), French
   (1), Norwegian (1).

   Books (86) and articles (48) on peace research, nonviolence,
   economic consequences of disarmament, concepts of war,
   deterrence, arms control, and theories of war and peace.

120 <

Kinton, Jack F.

Sociology of War and Peace and the Military Institution.
Mt. Pleasant, Iowa: Social Science and Sociological Resources,
1972. 5 pp.

   Apparently unavailable; not located through interlibrary
   loan.

121   HV8138.P7

Prassel, Frank Richard.

Bibliography.
In his The Western Peace Officer: A legacy of law and order.
Norman: University of Oklahoma Press, 1972. pp. 291-320.

   491 items, 1847-1969. English.

   Personal interviews and correspondence (19), archival
   materials (80), theses and dissertations (20), government
   documents (61), cases (77), constitutional materials (15),
   statutory materials (40), newspapers (27), general works
   (71), periodical articles (81) on the western law enforcement
   officer and U.S. frontier history.

Peace and War--General

122   JX1291.R86

Russett, Bruce M. (ed.).

Bibliography.
In his Peace, War, and Numbers.
Beverly Hills/London: Sage, 1972. pp. 321-335.

   295 items, 1880-1973. English; also German (2), Norwegian
   (1).

   Books and articles on international relations, the causes of
   war, patterns of conflict, quantitative methods, peace theory
   and peace research, social science theories and methods.

123 <

[Beiträge zur Konfliktforschung].

[Bibliography of peace and conflict research--in German].
Beiträge zur Konfliktforschung, 3 (1973): 141.

124   JX1937.B43

Beitz, Charles R. and Theodore Herman (eds.).

Suggestions for further reading [11 lists].
In their Peace and War, with a foreword by Alan Geyer.
San Francisco: W. H. Freeman (A Project of the Institute for
World Order), 1973. pp. 6, 34, 72-73, 111, 137-143, 150-151,
217, 240-241, 274, 310-315, 344.

   316 items, 1932-1972. English.

   Books and articles on the morality of war (9), war as a means
   for achieving social justice (10), war and deterrence as
   instruments of diplomacy (16), war as an expression of human
   nature (7), human violence (101), world government (8),
   reforming the state system (9), regions and the future of the
   global system (22), domestic change and world peace (6), Is
   there a military-industrial complex that prevents peace?
   (121), civilian defense and nonviolence (7).

Peace and War--General

125

Beitz, Charles R., A. Michael Washburn, and Thomas G. Weiss (eds.).

Peace Studies: College courses on peace and world order.
New York: Institute for World Order, for the Consortium on Peace Research, Education and Development, May, 1973. 145 pp.

  1803 items, 1923-1972 (many items undated). English; also
  Spanish, Italian (1), Portuguese(1). Introduction (2 pp.);
  table of contents.

  Reading lists for courses on conflict, revolution, peace,
  world order, world politics, development and justice in the
  Third World, future studies, social criticism and individual
  change, and the U.S. context.

126   U21.2.B35

Blainey, Geoffrey.

Select bibliography.
In his The Causes of War.
New York: Free Press, 1973. pp. 264-273.

  232 items, 1810-1970. English. A few items have brief
  descriptive annotations; introduction (2 paragraphs).

  Mostly books on political, diplomatic, military, and economic
  history; some peace theory, theories of war causation, and
  general social, economic, and political theory.

127 <

Weber, Paul J.

Psychologies of Human Aggression and Their Implications for
Public Policy: A bibliographical discussion.
Monticello, Ill.: Council of Planning Librarians (Exchange
Bibliography No. 515), 1974. 41 pp.

128

Wehr, Paul.

Bibliography.

Peace and War--General

In his Conflict Regulation.
Washington, D.C.: American Association for the Advancement of
Science (AAAS Study Guides on Contemporary Problems, No. 7),
[1975] (test ed.). pp. 174-190.

   172 items, 1905-1974. English; also Danish (1). Many items
   have brief critical annotations.

   Conflict analysis (61), conflict regulation (67), self-
   limiting conflict processes (19), active learning (14),
   listing of peace and peace-oriented journals and newsletters
   (25).

129

Wehr, Paul and [A.] Michael Washburn.

Bibliography.
In their Peace and World Order Systems: Teaching and research.
Beverly Hills/London: Sage (Sage Library of Social Research,
Vol. 25), 1976. pp. 119-146.

   422 items, 1946-1976. English. Most items have brief to
   medium-length descriptive or critical annotations.

   Dimensions of the emerging global system--trends, structures,
   values, transnationalism, interdependence (41); problems in
   peace and world order studies--the depletion of resources and
   the limits to growth (34), the energy and food crises of the
   mid-1970s (34), the growing gap between rich and poor and
   future directions for development strategy (34), war and war
   prevention (59); the dynamics of conflict, conflict
   resolution, and conflict regulation (39); the study of
   nonviolence--resistance, direct action, and defense (32); the
   future in peace and world order studies--forecasting,
   planning and design methods (17), alternative visions and
   preferred worlds (36); theories, strategies, and techniques
   of social change (31); peace education and research--history,
   evaluation techniques, resource materials (65).

130   MiU: Z6464.Z9B681,1979

Boulding, Elise, J. Robert Passmore, and Robert Scott Gassler
(comps.).

Bibliography on World Conflict and Peace: Second Edition.
Boulder, Colo.: Westview Press (Westview Special Studies in
Peace, Conflict, and Conflict Resolution), 1979. xxx + 168 pp.

Peace and War--General

First edition in pamphlet form compiled by Elise Boulding and
J. Robert Passmore with the assistance of Maureen Carson, Bill
Ferrall, Dorothy Carson, and Judy Fukuhara. Boulder, Colo.:
Institute of Behavioral Science, for the American Sociological
Association Committee on the Sociology of World Conflicts and
the Consortium on Peace Research, Education and Development,
August, 1974, 70 pp.

   Approximately 2335 items, 1814-1978 (most items 1945-1978).
   English; also French (8), German (1), Spanish (1).
   Introduction (9 pp.); table of contents; subject guide. Items
   listed alphabetically within categories by types of
   materials; the main subject emphases of books and articles
   are indicated in marginal labels, following the subject
   guide.

   Books and articles (approximately 1135), collections,
   annuals, and series (31), periodicals (82), and
   bibliographies (86) covering a broad range of subjects
   relating to world conflict, armament and disarmament,
   nonviolent action, and peace research.

Peace and War--U.S. Policy

131   JX1705.F7

Foster, John W.

Bibliography: List of titles of books referred to in this
volume.
In his The Practice of Diplomacy: As illustrated in the foreign
relations of the United States.
Boston/New York: Houghton Mifflin, 1906. pp. [385]-388.

   92 items, 1835 - 1906. English.

   Books, periodicals, reports, documents, letters, and
   reference works on diplomatic history, biography and
   international law.

132   JX1416.U7

Usher, Roland G.

Bibliography.
In his Pan-Americanism: A forecast of the inevitable clash
between the United States and Europe's victor.
New York: Century, 1915. pp. 443-459.

   75 items, 1865 - 1915. English; also Spanish (8), French (5),
   German (1). Many items have brief critical annotations;
   introduction (6 pp.).

   Books and articles on the history, foreign policy, and
   diplomacy of the U.S., Britain, Japan, and Latin America,
   with attention to sea power, geopolitics, imperialism, and
   international politics. Divided into sections on United
   States (36), Latin America (22), and Pan-Americanism (17).

133 <

Berdahl, Clarence A.

Bibliography.
In his War Powers of the Executive in the United States.
Urbana: University of Illinois (University of Illinois Studies
in the Social Sciences, Vol. 9, Nos. 1-2), 1920. pp. 271-281.

Peace and War--U.S. Policy

134 <

[Carnegie Endowment for International Peace, Library].

Monroe Doctrine.
Washington, D.C.: Carnegie Endowment for International Peace,
Library (Miscellaneous Reading List No. 16), 1921. (mimeo).

135 <

[Carnegie Endowment for International Peace, Library].

Participation of the U.S. in International Affairs.
Washington, D.C.: Carnegie Endowment for International Peace,
Library (Miscellaneous Reading List No. 17), 1923. (mimeo).

136 <

[Carnegie Endowment for International Peace, Library].

Some American Statesmen and World Peace.
Washington, D.C.: Carnegie Endowment for International Peace,
Library (Miscellaneous Reading List No. 50), 1933. (mimeo).

137 <

Emeny, Brooks.

Bibliography.
In his The Strategy of Raw Materials: A study of America in
peace and war.
New York: Macmillan, 1934. pp. 189-195.

138 <

Phelps, Edith M. (ed.).

Bibliography in "Armed intervention for protection of American
interests abroad."
In her University Debaters' Annual, 1933-1934.
New York: H. W. Wilson, 1934. pp. 97-103.

Peace and War--U.S. Policy

139   PN4181.U5

[Johnsen, Julia E. (comp.)].

Bibliography: "Japan and naval parity."
In Phelps, Edith M. (ed.), University Debaters´ Annual:
Constructive and rebuttal speeches delivered in debates of
American colleges and universities during the college year,
1934-1935 [Vol. 21].
New York: H. W. Wilson, September, 1935. pp. [445]-450.

   108 items, 1921 - 1935. English.

   Books and pamphlets (17) and periodicals (91) on
   diplomatic/military relations between U.S. and Japan relevant
   to the debate resolution "That the United States should grant
   naval parity to Japan."

140   Z6464.A1C3,no.5a

Matthews, Mary Alice (comp.).

Neutrality and American Policy on Neutrality: With select
references on contraband of war, embargo on arms, and freedom
of the seas.
Washington, D.C.: Carnegie Endowment for International Peace,
Library (Brief Reference List No. 5), March 28, 1935. 11 pp.
(mimeo).

   137 items, 1866 - 1935. English; also French (9), German (3).
   Some items have brief descriptive annotations.

   Books, journal articles, pamphlets, official documents,
   reports, and presidential addresses on U.S. neutrality policy
   during World War I and the reconsideration of neutrality in
   light of the Kellogg Pact, current international and maritime
   law, the legal rights and obligations of neutrals, the
   munitions industry, the effect of arms embargoes, and the
   issue of freedom of the seas.

141   Z6461.C29,no.5

Matthews, Mary Alice (comp.).

The Monroe Doctrine: With special reference to its modern
aspects.
Washington, D.C.: Carnegie Endowment for International Peace,
Library (Select Bibliographies, No. 5), July 9, 1936. 15 pp.
(mimeo).

Peace and War--U.S. Policy

   154 items, 1886 - 1936. English; also Spanish, French (8),
   German (1). Some items have brief descriptive annotations.

   Bibliographies (5), books, and articles on the Monroe
   Doctrine, its development and applications, and its impact on
   U.S. foreign relations, especially with Europe, Latin
   America, and the League of Nations.

   142   Z6464.A1C3,no.5b

Matthews, Mary Alice (comp.).

Neutrality and American Policy on Neutrality: With select
references on contraband of war, embargo on arms, and freedom
of the seas.
Washington, D.C.: Carnegie Endowment for International Peace,
Library (Brief Reference List No. 5), December 18, 1936
(supplement). 9 pp. (mimeo).

   106 items, 1933 - 1936. English; also French (3). Some items
   have brief descriptive annotations.

   Bibliographies and debates (6), books, periodical articles,
   and congressional reports (100) on legislation concerning
   American neutrality, U.S. foreign policy, the prevention of
   war, and the maintenance of peace.

   143   Z6461.C29,no.6

Matthews, M[ary] Alice (comp.).

The Department of State: With supplement concerning treaties
between the United States and other powers.
Washington, D.C.: Carnegie Endowment for International Peace,
Library (Select Bibliographies, No. 6), July 15, 1936. 9 pp.
(mimeo).

   108 items, 1862 - 1936. English. Some items have brief
   descriptive annotations.

   Books, articles, and official documents on the history,
   policies, activities, and functions of the U.S. Department of
   State; list of proposed and/or ratified treaties of the U.S.

Peace and War--U.S. Policy

144   UA23.H35

Hallgren, Mauritz A.

Bibliography.
In his The Tragic Fallacy: A study of America's war policies.
New York/London: Alfred A. Knopf, 1937. pp. 445-452.

   135 items, 1916 - 1937. English; also German (1), French (1),
   Swedish (1).

   Books, articles, pamphlets, official documents, and reports
   on U.S. defense policy, naval history, American foreign
   policy, arbitration, international law, international
   relations, and disarmament.

145 <

[Carnegie Endowment for International Peace, Library].

Peace Department.
Washington, D.C.: Carnegie Endowment for International Peace,
Library (Miscellaneous Reading List No. 59), 1938. (mimeo).

146   UA23.E43

Eliot, George Fielding.

Selected bibliography.
In his The Ramparts We Watch: A study of the problems of
American national defense.
New York: Reynal and Hitchcock, 1938. pp. 361-362.

   24 items (no dates given). English.

   Books on strategy, land, air and naval warfare, U.S. foreign
   policy, and national defense.

147 <

Johnsen, Julia E. (comp.).

Bibliography.
In her United States Foreign Policy: Isolation or alliance.
New York: H. W. Wilson (The Reference Shelf, Vol. 12, No. 6),
1938. pp. 281-307.

Peace and War--U.S. Policy

148 <

[Matthews, Mary Alice (comp.)].

Naval Policy of the United States.
Washington, D.C.: Carnegie Endowment for International Peace,
Library (Brief Reference List No. 10), 1938. 3 pp.

149   Z6464.N4C3

Matthews, M[ary] Alice (comp.).

Neutrality: Select list of references on neutrality and the
policy of the United States in the World War and postwar
periods.
Washington, D.C.: Carnegie Endowment for International Peace,
Library (Reading List No. 37), September 26, 1938. 36 pp.

   455 items, 1866 - 1938. English; also French, German, Spanish
   (1). Some items have brief descriptive annotations; table of
   contents; author index.

   Bibliographies (8), general, historical, and legal works
   (143), neutrality in World War I (30), American policy in the
   postwar period (274).

150   DLC-DB

Baden, Anne L. (comp.), under the direction of Florence S.
Hellman.

List of Speeches, Addresses, Etc., on Neutrality as Printed in
the Congressional Record, 1937-1939.
[Washington, D.C.]: Library of Congress, Division of
Bibliography, October 28, 1939. 42 pp. (mimeo).

   647 items, 1937 - 1939. English. A few items have brief
   descriptive annotations.

   Speeches, editorials, articles in the 75th (92) and 76th
   (555) Congresses on U.S. neutrality, foreign policy, and
   various proposals for embargoes.

Peace and War--U.S. Policy

151   DLC-DB

Fuller, Grace Hadley (comp.), under the direction of Florence
S. Hellman.

American National Defense: A list of recent references
(supplementary to typewritten list of June 1936).
Washington, D.C.: Library of Congress, Division of
Bibliography, October 3, 1939. 42 pp. (mimeo).

   543 items, 1935 - 1939. English. A few items have brief
   descriptive annotations.

   Books, articles, and government documents on national defense
   policy, the pros and cons of specific defense plans, and
   military and industrial preparations for war.

152 <

Hellman, F[lorence} S.

A List of Recent References on Neutrality.
Washington, D.C.: Library of Congress, Division of
Bibliography, 1939. 19 pp. (mimeo).

153   E744.J64

Johnsen, Julia E. (ed. and comp.).

Bibliography.
In her The United States and War.
New York: H. W. Wilson (The Reference Shelf, Vol. 12, No. 8),
1939. pp. 153-179.

   475 items, 1936 - 1939. English. Some items have brief
   descriptive annotations or excerpts.

   Books, pamphlets, and periodical articles on general U.S.
  ˙ foreign policy (180), neutrality (46), the war referendum
   (11), Nazism´s peril to religion (22), national defense
   (158), China and Japan (58).

154   Z6461.C29,no.5,suppl.

Matthews, Mary Alice (comp.).

The Monroe Doctrine: With special reference to its modern
aspects.

Peace and War--U.S. Policy

Washington, D.C.: Carnegie Endowment for International Peace,
Library (Select Bibliographies, No. 5, Supplement), April 18,
1939. 2 pp. (mimeo).

   24 items, 1931 - 1939. English; also French (4), Spanish (1).

   Books and articles on the Monroe Doctrine as it affects U.S.
   relations with Europe, Latin America, Canada, Japan, and the
   League of Nations.

155   Z6464.A1C3,no.14

Matthews, M[ary] Alice (comp.).

Isolation and Economic Nationalism.
Washington, D.C.: Carnegie Endowment for International Peace,
Library (Brief Reference List No. 14), January 21, 1939. 5 pp.
(mimeo).

   54 items, 1898 - 1938. English. Some items have brief
   descriptive annotations.

   Periodical articles, books, and speeches on U.S. foreign
   policy, economic nationalism, and the shortcomings of
   isolationism.

156   Z6464.A1C3,no.13

Matthews, M[ary] Alice (comp.).

The Prevention of War: With special reference to "Keeping
America out of war."
Washington, D.C.: Carnegie Endowment for International Peace,
Library (Brief Reference List No. 13), January 18, 1939. 6 pp.
(mimeo).

   82 items, 1923 - 1939. English. A few items have brief
   descriptive annotations.

   Books, pamphlets, bibliographies, and articles on neutrality,
   war prevention, peaceful change, war resistance, conditions
   of peace, and keeping the U.S. out of World War II.

Peace and War--U.S. Policy

157 <

Peterson, Horace C.

Bibliography.
In his Propaganda for War: The campaign against American
neutrality, 1914-1917.
Norman: University of Oklahoma Press, 1939. pp. 343-352.

158   DLC-DB

Conover, Helen F. (comp.), under the direction of Florence
S. Hellman.

Western Hemisphere Defense: A brief list of references.
Washington, D.C.: Library of Congress, Division of
Bibliography, November 6, 1940. 15 pp. (mimeo).

   159 items, 1937 - 1940. English.

   Books and articles on American defense policy, armament,
   analysis of Monroe Doctrine, Canadian defense problems.

159   E743.C25,1940

Hubbard, Ursula P[halla] (ed.).

Selected references [9 lists]; Getting information.
In her Handbook for Discussion Leaders: America's problems as
affected by international relations, with a foreword by
Nicholas Murray Butler.
New York: Carnegie Endowment for International Peace, Division
of Intercourse and Education, April, 1940. pp. 13, 20, 27, 36,
54-56, 65, 76-77, 85-88, 99-100, 105-113.

   263 items, 1921 - 1940. English. A few items have brief
   descriptive or critical annotations.

   Books, pamphlets, and articles on foreign trade (24),
   agriculture (12), health (7), general economic problems (16),
   the International Labor Organization (10), the cooperative
   movement (11), American youth (11), the organization of peace
   (15), U.S. foreign policy (7), South America and Pan-American
   relations (46), aspects of democracy (8), discussion methods
   (12); official publications (5), periodicals (38), list of
   organizations concerned with peace and international
   organization (41).

Peace and War--U.S. Policy

160   E743.C25,1940a

Hubbard, Ursula P[halla] (ed.).

Supplementary reading list (to November, 1940).
In her Handbook for Discussion Leaders: America´s problems as
affected by international relations, with a foreword by
Nicholas Murray Butler.
New York: Carnegie Endowment for International Peace, Division
of Intercourse and Education, December, 1940 (2nd printing).
pp. 116-138.

   274 items, 1926 - 1940. English. Some items have brief
   descriptive or critical annotations; introduction (1 p.);
   list of peace and foreign affairs organizations.

   This shrinking world and what it means to America (10),
   understanding foreign trade (12), the U.S. farmer´s stake in
   world peace (14), health care as an international problem
   (5), social and economic justice--within America (20), the
   International Labor Organization (10), the cooperative
   movement (25), American youth (29), organization of peace
   (15) problems of the western world (55), can we the people
   solve our problems? (14), U.S. foreign policy and war in
   Europe and Asia (35), national defense and conscription (19),
   refugees and aliens (11).

161   PN4181.U5,1939/40

[Johnsen, Julia E. and Alberta Worthington (comps.)].

Bibliography: "The neutrality policy of the United States."
In Phelps, Edith M. (ed.), University Debaters´ Annual:
Constructive and rebuttal speeches delivered in debates of
American colleges and universities during the college year
1939-1940, [Vol. 26].
New York: H. W. Wilson, August, 1940. pp. 180-188.

   148 items, 1923 - 1940. English.

   Books and pamphlets (24) and articles (124) on the question
   of U.S. neutrality posture, effects of war on U.S. economy,
   U.S. foreign relations, foreign trade of the U.S., American
   defense policy, U.S. effort to remain peaceful.

Peace and War--U.S. Policy

162   PN4181.U5,1939/1940

[Johnsen, Julia E. and Alberta Worthington (comps.)].

Bibliography: "Shall the United States enter the war?"
In Phelps, Edith M. (ed.), University Debaters´ Annual:
Constructive and rebuttal speeches delivered in debates of
American colleges and universities during the college year
1939-1940, [Vol. 26].
New York: H. W. Wilson, August, 1940. pp. 87-95.

  139 items, 1933 - 1940. English.

  Books and pamphlets (30), articles (109) on the analysis of
  U.S. foreign policy and domestic public opinion as to whether
  U.S. should be a participant in the Second World War.

163   H35.I6,v.21

Nichols, Egbert Ray (ed.).

"Bibliography: Aid to the allies."
In his Intercollegiate Debates: Yearbook of college debating,
Vol. 21.
New York: Noble and Noble, 1940. pp. 233-234.

  34 items, 1921 - 1940. English.

  Books and pamphlets (12) and magazine and periodical articles
  (20) on the causes of war, economic aspects of war, and U.S.
  policy during World War II.

164   H35.I6,v.21

Nichols, Egbert Ray (ed.).

Bibliography: "International federal union of democracies."
In his Intercollegiate Debates: Yearbook of college debating,
Vol. 21.
New York: Noble and Noble, 1940, p. 192.

  14 items, 1939 - 1940. English.

  Books, pamphlets, and magazine articles related to the debate
  resolution "That the United States should join a federal
  union of world democracies."

Peace and War--U.S. Policy

165   H35.I6,v.21

Nichols, Egbert Ray (ed.).

Bibliography: "Isolation from countries at war."
In his Intercollegiate Debates: Yearbook of college debating,
Vol. 21.
New York: Noble and Noble, 1940, pp. 153-156.

   77 items, 1925 - 1940. English.

   Books, pamphlets, magazine and journal articles relevant to
   the debate question "American isolation from countries
   outside the Western Hemisphere engaged in civil or
   international conflict."

166   HD171.A1A3,v.4

Shaw, Ralph R.

"Books on peace and war."
Land Policy Review, 4, 7 (July, 1941): 42-45.

   23 items, 1939 - 1941. English. Introduction (3 pp.).

   Publications referred to in the text (14), supplementary
   readings (9) on social and economic effects of World War II
   and postwar planning in the U.S.

167   LA246.A35,1942

[Douglass, Harl R., et al. (eds.)].

"Bibliography of teaching materials and aids on education and
the national emergency (for administrators, teachers, and
pupils)."
In Colorado Schools in the Emergency, foreword by Inez Johnson
Lewis.
[Denver]: State of Colorado, Department of Education, [1942].
pp. [43]-51.

   145 items, 1940 - 1942. English.

   Education for civic and economic intelligence in defense
   times (29), health and physical education (13), vocational
   and military education (18), education for patriotism, unity,
   and developing appreciation of what we defend--civilian
   morale (8), education for world peace, international
   relations, postwar problems and reconstruction (24), support
   and defense of the school program during the war (9),

Peace and War--U.S. Policy

comprehensive and miscellaneous suggestions to schools--home
economics, guidance, mathematics, radio, films, etc. (44).

168 <

Inter-Allied Information Center.

Research and Post-war Planning in the U.S.A.: Bibliography,
Parts I-IX.
New York: [Inter-Allied Information Center], February, 1942 to
June, 1943.

169   D825.N47,no.1

Sturmthal, Adolf.

Bibliography.
In his A Survey of Literature on Postwar Reconstruction.
New York: New York University (Institute on Postwar
Reconstruction, Series of Publications, No. 1), May, 1943.
pp. 95-100.

  105 items, 1933 - 1942. English.

  Books and articles on the economic aspects of postwar
  reconstruction.

170   D643.A7B3

Bailey, Thomas A[ndrew].

Bibliographical notes.
In his Woodrow Wilson and the Lost Peace.
New York: Macmillan, 1944. pp. 326-370.
Reprinted, Chicago: Quadrangle Paperbacks, 1963.

  149 items, 1917 - 1944. English; also German (2). Essay form,
  all items are critically discussed in the text.

  Books, articles, and bibliographies on diplomatic history of
  the United States, neutrality, war aims of the United States,
  propaganda and public opinion, American diplomacy during
  World War I, the 1918 election campaign, the Paris Peace
  Conference, U.S. peace documents, biographies and papers of
  national leaders, the peace settlement, international
  relations, peace proposals, peace negotiations, treaties, the
  League of Nations, peacemaking, the mandate system,
  reparations, the issue of race equality, the protests filed
  by the Germans at Versailles, and national minorities.

Peace and War--U.S. Policy

171   E179.H22,1947

Hamlin, C[harles] H[unter].

Bibliography [8 lists].
In his The War Myth in United States History.
Wilson, N.C.: Atlantic Christian College, October 1, 1946 [2nd
ed.]. pp. 9, 20, 28, 32, 39, 48, 57, 77.
First edition, with introduction by Charles F. Dole, New York:
Vanguard Press and Association to Abolish War, 1927. First
edition reprinted in Charles Hunter Hamlin, Propaganda and Myth
in Time of War, with a new introduction and epilogue by Charles
Chatfield, New York/London: Garland (Garland Library of War and
Peace), 1973.

   77 items (no dates given for most items). English; also German
   (1).

   Books and a few articles on causes of war, political and
   military history of the U.S., and pacifist critiques of U.S.
   policy.

172   LC6301.N43,v.28

[Rankin, E. R. (comp.)].

Bibliography.
In his special issue, What Is the Responsibility of the United
States in World Affairs? (High School World Peace Study and
Speaking Program, 1948-49).
University of North Carolina Extension Bulletin, 28, 2
(November, 1948): [55]-59.

   122 items, 1944 - 1948. English. Introduction (2 pp.).

   Books, articles, and films on the United Nations, world
   government, U.S. foreign policy, and conditions of peace.

173   LC6301.N43,v.29

Rankin, E. R. (comp.).

Bibliography.
In his special issue, Building World Peace in the Atomic Age:
What are the responsibilities of the United States in the
United Nations and in the Atlantic Pact? (High School World
Peace Study and Speaking Program, Peace Handbook 1949-50).

Peace and War--U.S. Policy

University of North Carolina Extension Bulletin, 29, 2
(November, 1949): [52]-55.

  85 items, 1945 - 1947. English. Introduction (1 p.).

  Books, articles, and films on the United Nations, world
  government, U.S. foreign policy, conditions of peace, and the
  NATO Pact.

174   LC6301.N43,v.30

Rankin, E. R. (comp.).

Bibliography.
In his special issue, How Can We Help to Build World Peace in
the Atomic Age? (High School World Peace Study and Speaking
Program, Peace Handbook 1950-51).
University of North Carolina Extension Bulletin, 30, 2
(November, 1950): [56]-59.

  80 items, 1945 - 1950. English. Introduction (1 p.).

  Books, articles, and films on the United Nations, world
  government, U.S. foreign policy, and international relations.

175   LC6301.N43,v.31

Rankin, E. R. (comp.).

Bibliography.
In his special issue, Building World Peace: What is the
responsibility of the United States in the light of Communist
aggression? (High School World Peace Study and Speaking
Program, Peace Handbook 1951-52).
University of North Carolina Extension Bulletin, 31, 2
(November, 1951): 65-68.

  64 items, 1945 - 1951. English. Introduction (2 pp.).

  Books, articles, and films on U.S. foreign policy, world
  federation, United Nations.

176   JX1952.D385

Davis, Jerome.

Suggestions for study and bibliography.

Peace and War--U.S. Policy

In his Peace, War and You, with an introduction by Clarence
E. Pickett.
New York: Henry Schuman, 1952. pp. 267-279.

   159 items, 1917 - 1951. English.

   American people's objectives in international affairs (13),
   foreign policy and objectives (40), failure of U.S. foreign
   policy (54), an alternative program (52). Appended list of
   peace organizations.

177 <   Z7405.P8U48

Knezo, Genevieve Johanna (comp.).

Science, Technology, and American Diplomacy: A selected,
annotated bibliography of articles, books, documents,
periodicals, and reference guides (prepared for the
Subcommittee on National Security Policy and Scientific
Development of the Committee on Foreign Affairs, U.S. House of
Representatives, by the Science Policy Research and Foreign
Affairs Divisions, Legislative Reference Service, Library of
Congress).
Washington, D.C.: U.S. Government Printing Office, 1970. 69 pp.

178 <

Rodberg, Leonard S. and Derek Shearer (eds.).

Research guide and bibliography.
In their The Pentagon Watchers.
Garden City, N.Y.: Doubleday, 1970.

179   JX1573.H35,1970

Grech, Anthony P.

"Expansion of the Viet Nam War into Cambodia: Selected
bibliography."
In Fox, Donald T. (ed.), The Cambodian Incursion . . . Legal
Issues: Proceedings of the Fifteenth Hammarskjöld Forum, May
28, 1970.
Dobbs Ferry, N.Y.: Oceana, for the Association of the Bar of
the City of New York, 1971. pp. 79-89.

   224 items, 1863 - 1970. English; also French (7), Spanish (1),
   German (1).

Peace and War--U.S. Policy

General (64), constitutional aspects (97), and international
legal aspects (63).

180   Z6465.U5D63

Doenecke, Justus D.

The Literature of Isolationism: A guide to non-interventionist
scholarship, 1930-1972.
Colorado Springs: Ralph Myles, 1972. 89 pp.

English. Table of contents; preface (3 pp.); author/subject
index; essay format.

Extensive bibliographic essay divided into chapters on
theory, the interwar years, movements and leaders
(isolationist and pacifist organizations, senators,
congressmen, scholars, publicists, and other opinion
leaders), the politics of war and bipartisanship, opposition
to consensus politics, the revival of "isolationism,"
manuscripts and oral history projects (Middle West, West
Coast, East Coast, South), bibliographies, and books of the
interwar period.

181 <   Z1361.D4G73

Greenwood, John (comp.), with the advisement of Robin Higham.

American Defense Policy since 1945: A preliminary bibliography,
edited by Geoffrey Kemp, Clark Murdock, and Frank L. Simonie.
Lawrence: University Press of Kansas, for the National Security
Education Program (National Security Studies Series; Kansas
State University Library Bibliography Series, No. 11), 1973.
xv + 317 pp.

182   KF5060.J38,Law

Javits, Jacob K[oppell], with Don Kellerman.

Bibliography.
In their Who Makes War: The President versus Congress, with
forewords by Barbara W. Tuchman and Alexander M. Bickel.
New York: William Morrow, 1973. pp. 275-292.

414 items, 1797 - 1973. English. Introduction (1 paragraph).

Mainly historical works on the U.S. Congress, the presidency,
and foreign policy.

Peace and War--U.S. Policy

183   Z7165.E8K5

Kitter, Audrey (comp.).

The U.S. and the EEC: American reaction to and involvement in
the "Common Market" [a bibliography].
Los Angeles: California State University at Los Angeles, Center
for the Study of Armament and Disarmament (Political Issues
Series, Vol. 2, No. 7), August, 1973. 62 pp.

   729 items, 1916 - 1973. English. Introduction (5 pp.); table
   of contents.

   Magazine and journal articles, books, and reports on early
   U.S. reactions (31), the U.S. and EEC in the 1960s and 1970s
   (88), overall economic relations (64), American business
   relations (77), industry (27), agriculture (24), "chicken
   war" (7), financial matters (23), balance of payments (6),
   dollar and loan problems (11), banking problems (4), legal
   difficulties with EEC (20), antitrust aspects (19), U.S.
   foreign policy and the EEC (71), European integration (41),
   Atlantic Alliance (60), Anglo-American involvement (9),
   treaties (14), U.S. trade and the EEC (95), General Agreement
   on Tariff and Trade (14), the "Kennedy round" (24).

184   JX560.E23

Eagleton, Thomas F.

Bibliography.
In his War and Presidential Power: A chronicle of congressional
surrender.
New York: Liveright, 1974. pp. 226-232.

   83 items, 1950 - 1974. English.

   Books, articles, and government publications on
   constitutional, legal, and political aspects of warmaking
   powers in the United States, with special emphasis on
   disputed legality of the Vietnam War.

185

Gillingham, Arthur and Barry Roseman (comps.).

The Cuban Missile Crisis: A selected bibliography.
Los Angeles: California State University at Los Angeles, Center
for the Study of Armament and Disarmament (Political Issues
Series, Vol. 2, No. 6), 1976. 34 pp.

Peace and War--U.S. Policy

450 items, 1936 - 1975. English; also Spanish, French (7),
German (5), Portuguese (3), Russian (3), Italian (1).
Introduction (2 pp.); table of contents.

Bibliography (14), chronologies (8), documentary collections
(11), events of 1962 encompassing American decision making
and Soviet decision making along with legal and other related
analysis concerning the crisis (239), background to the
crisis (178).

International Relations

186 <

[Carnegie Endowment for International Peace, Library].

Balance of Power.
Washington, D.C.: Carnegie Endowment for International Peace,
Library (Miscellaneous Reading List No. 3), 1921. (mimeo).

187 <

[Carnegie Endowment for International Peace, Library].

Treaties and Conventions.
Washington, D.C.: Carnegie Endowment for International Peace,
Library (Miscellaneous Reading List No. 29), 1921. (mimeo).

188 <

[Carnegie Endowment for International Peace, Library].

Aaland Islands.
Washington, D.C.: Carnegie Endowment for International Peace,
Library (Miscellaneous Reading List No. 1), 1922. (mimeo).

189 <

[Carnegie Endowment for International Peace, Library].

Spheres of Influence and Interest.
Washington, D.C.: Carnegie Endowment for International Peace,
Library (Miscellaneous Reading List No. 27), 1923. (mimeo).

190   HC54.V5

Viallate, Achille.

Bibliography.
In his Economic Imperialism and International Relations during
the Last Fifty Years.
New York: Macmillan (The Institute of Politics Publications,
Williams College, Williamstown, Mass.), 1923. pp. 171-173.

International Relations

     51 items, 1898 - 1921. English, French.

     Works on international relations, economic development of
     modern states, imperialism, and conditions of peace.

191 <

Earle, Edward Mead, with the collaboration of Florence
Billings.

Problems of the Near East.
New York: Carnegie Endowment for International Peace (Division
of Intercourse and Education, International Relations Clubs,
Bibliography Series, No. 2), 1924.

192   JX1311.M7

Moon, Parker Thomas [with the assistance of Mary Evelyn
Townsend].

General bibliography.
In his Syllabus on International Relations.
New York: Macmillan, for the Institute of International
Education, 1925. pp. 239-276.

     996 items, 1858 - 1924. English; also French, German, Italian
     (8), Spanish (6), Portuguese (2). Introduction (1 paragraph).

     Books and reference works on world politics, foreign policy,
     diplomacy, imperialism, the history of international
     relations, war, militarism, nationalism, world economic
     problems, international organization, and political, social,
     and economic history.

193 <

[Carnegie Endowment for International Peace, Library].

Recent Publications in International Relations.
Washington, D.C.: Carnegie Endowment for International Peace,
Library (Reading List No. 7), 1926. (mimeo).

194   Z881.N52A35

Newark Public Library (comp.).

Aids to International Understanding: A book list with notes.

International Relations

Madison, N.J.: New Jersey Federation of Women's Clubs,
Committee on International Relations, [1928]. 16 pp.

  283 items, 1906 - 1927. English. Most items have brief
descriptive or critical annotations; introduction (1
paragraph); author index.

  General readings (12), U.S. history and foreign relations
(12), European history, economics (14), Near East (8), Far
East (6), international relations (26), League of Nations
(5), World Court (4), causes and prevention of war (11),
racial and national backgrounds in Asia, Africa, South
America, and Europe (185).

195   JX3110.B8I5

Buell, Raymond Leslie.

Bibliography; Supplementary bibliography of books, 1925-1929.
In his International Relations.
New York: Henry Holt (American Political Science Series), 1929
(rev.ed.). pp. 775-813, 815-820.
First edition, 1925.

  1350 items, 1852 - 1929. English; also French, German, Spanish,
Italian (4), Esperanto (1), Norwegian (1).

  Books, articles, and pamphlets on international relations,
nationalism, the problem of racial and ethnic minorities,
race relations, internationalism, the International Labor
Organization, immigrant labor, imperialism, colonialism, the
mandate system, alliances and federations, treaties, foreign
policy, diplomacy, the costs and causes of war, armament,
arbitration, international conferences, international law,
and the League of Nations. Organized by chapters of the text.

196   JX1311.B6

Bowman, Isaiah.

"Books on international relations."
In his International Relations.
Chicago: American Library Association (Reading with a Purpose,
No. 60), September, 1930. pp. 34-51.

  5 items, 1928 - 1930. English. All items are critically and
extensively discussed in the text.

International Relations

Books on international affairs, foreign policy, the League of
Nations, and problems of war and peace, particularly as they
relate to the U.S.

197   IU: 379.1705H1G,v.7

McNutt, Russell T.

References in "Education for world citizenship."
High School Teacher (Blanchester, Ohio), 7, 10 (December, 1931):
369, 377.

55 items (no dates given). English. Introduction (1
paragraph).

Books and journals relating to international relations,
imperialism, foreign policy, causes of war, and international
law for high school students.

198 <

[Carnegie Endowment for International Peace, Library].

The Economic Boycott.
Washington, D.C.: Carnegie Endowment for International Peace,
Library (Miscellaneous Reading List No. 44), 1932. (mimeo).

199 <

[Carnegie Endowment for International Peace, Library].

Sovereignty over the Polar Regions.
Washington, D.C.: Carnegie Endowment for International Peace,
Library (Miscellaneous Reading List No. 45), 1932. (mimeo).

200 <

[Carnegie Endowment for International Peace, Library].

World Politics, Economic and Social Conditions.
Washington, D.C.: Carnegie Endowment for International Peace,
Library (Miscellaneous Reading List No. 42), 1932. (mimeo).

International Relations

201   Z1361.R4C3

Matthews, Mary Alice (comp.).

Intellectual and Cultural Relations between the United States
and Latin America: Select list of books, pamphlets, and
periodical articles, with annotations.
Washington, D.C.: Carnegie Endowment for International Peace,
Library (Reading List No. 35), June 1, 1935. 16 pp.

  176 items, 1893 - 1935. English; also Spanish (6). Many items
  have brief descriptive and/or critical annotations; list of
  addresses of organizations mentioned in this bibliography;
  list of other bibliographies (18) published by the CEIP
  appended.

  Works on intellectual cooperation among universities,
  schools, student clubs, scientific and technical
  organizations, cultural organizations, and regional
  international organizations; research on intercultural
  relations.

202   Z6461.C29,no.4

Matthews, Mary Alice (comp.).

Diplomacy: Select list of works in English on diplomacy,
diplomatic and consular practice, and foreign office
organization.
Washington, D.C.: Carnegie Endowment for International Peace,
Library (Select Bibliographies, No. 4), March 5, 1936. 7 pp.
(mimeo).

  71 items, 1813 - 1936. English. Some items have brief
  descriptive annotations; definitions of diplomacy by three
  great Americans; list of other bibliographies (9) published
  by the CEIP appended.

  Mostly books on diplomatic history and prodecures.

203   DU29.T3

Talbott, E[verett] Guy.

Bibliography.
In his Peace in the Pacific.
Gardena, Calif.: Institute Press, 1936. pp. 46-47.

  28 items, 1933 - 1936. English.

International Relations

    Periodicals (6) and books (22) on socioeconomic conditions,
    foreign policy, and the causes of conflict in the Far East.

204   D421.H5

Hinton, Harold B.

Bibliography.
In his America Gropes for Peace.
Richmond/Atlanta/Dallas/New York/Chicago: Johnson, 1937.
pp. 205-207.

    39 items, 1929 - 1937. English.

    Books on United States foreign policy, neutrality, and
    presidential controls (15), foreign relations, peace efforts,
    and internal political situations in Europe (14), and the Far
    East (10).

205 <

Matthews, Mary Alice (comp.).

Intervention, with Special Reference to Protection of Foreign
Loans and Investments.
Washington, D.C.: Carnegie Endowment for International Peace,
Library (Reading List No. 18), December 21, 1938 (rev. ed.).
(mimeo).
First edition, 1927.

206   Z6464.A1C3,no.12

Matthews, M[ary] Alice (comp.).

Anglo-American Alliance, with Some Recent References on Anglo-
American Relations.
Washington, D.C.: Carnegie Endowment for International Peace,
Library (Brief Reference List No. 12). September 13, 1938.
5 pp. (mimeo).

    60 items, 1917 - 1938. English. Many items have brief
    descriptive annotations.

    Journal articles, speeches, and essays on Anglo-American
    relations, alliance treaties, and U.S. foreign policy.

International Relations

207   HF499.F4,1940

Feis, Herbert.

Bibliography.
In his The Changing Pattern of International Economic Affairs.
New York/London: Harper and Brothers, 1940. pp. 131-132.

    28 items, 1927 - 1940. English.

    Books and articles on international trade, international
    economic relations, and U.S. foreign policy.

208 <

Carnegie Endowment for International Peace, Library.

Foreign Investments: Their effect upon international relations.
[Washington, D.C.: Carnegie Endowment for International Peace]
(Special Bibliographies, No. 1), September 15, 1941. 44 pp.

209

Ragatz, Lowell Joseph (comp.).

The Literature of European Imperialism, 1815-1939: A
bibliography.
Washington, D.C.: Paul Pearlman, 1947 (3rd rev. printing). iii
+ 153 pp.
First edition, 1944.

210

Perry, Stewart E.

"An annotated bibliography on game theory from the standpoint
of a student of international relations."
Bulletin of the Research Exchange on the Prevention of War, 4,
1 (January, 1956): 9-11.

211 <

Meacham, Stewart.

Bibliography.
In his Labor and the Cold War.

International Relations

Philadelphia: American Friends Service Committee, Peace
Education Program, 1959.

212   MiU: Z6461.E48

Elovainio, Mauri K. and Rauno Lehtinen.

A Bibliography on International Relations: Literature published
in Denmark, Finland, Norway, and Sweden, 1945-1960.
Stockholm: Utrikespolitiska Institutet (Swedish Institute of
International Affairs)/Nordiska Sammarbetskommitten för
Internationell Politik, [1960]. [viii] + 200 pp.

  2584 items, 1945 - 1960. Swedish, Danish, Finnish, Norwegian
  (an English translation is given for each title). Preface
  (1 p.); table of contents; author index.

  Bibliographies and works of reference (8), books, articles,
  and documents on teaching methods and research techniques
  (6), general theoretical studies (25); international
  organizations and administration--legal framework (139), the
  international community (19), the United Nations (231), the
  United Nations specialized agencies (97), the tasks of the
  international organizations (202), other international
  organizations (274), nongovernmental organizations (12);
  international politics--foreign policy: general aspects of
  international life (13), the history of international
  politics (437), specific states in international affairs
  (886), problems of international politics (235).

213 <

European Community Information Service.

A Selected Bibliography on European Integration.
Washington, D.C.: [European Community Information Service],
March, 1961.

214   E173.C15,v.69

Burr, Robert N.

Bibliography.
In his The Stillborn Panama Congress: Power politics and
Chilean-Colombian relations during the War of the Pacific.
Berkeley/Los Angeles: University of California Press
(University of California Publications in History, Vol. 69),
1962. pp. 137-140.

International Relations

    87 items, 1865 - 1959. Spanish, English. Introduction
    (1 paragraph).

    Document collections on constitutions of Latin American
    countries, diplomatic correspondence (21), government
    publications on foreign relations (9), books, articles, and
    pamphlets on history, international politics, and economic
    affairs of Latin American countries (57).

215 <

Moussa, Farag.

Diplomatie Contemporaine [Contemporary Diplomacy]: Guide
bibliographique [Bibliographic guide].
Geneva: Centre Européen de la Dotation Carnegie pour la Paix
Internationale, 1964. 199 pp.

216 <   Z7401.R4

Rettig, Richard A.

Bibliography on Science and World Affairs.
Washington, D.C.: U.S. Department of State, for the Foreign
Service Institute, 1964. 179 pp.

217 <

Roberts, Henry L.

Foreign Affairs Bibliography: A selected and annotated list of
books on international relations, 1952-62.
New York: Harper and Row, for the Council on Foreign Relations,
Spring, 1964.

218   Z1002.B65

Boehm, Eric H. (ed.).

Bibliographies on International Relations and World Affairs: An
annotated directory.
Santa Barbara, Calif.: Clio Press, for the American
Bibliographical Center (Bibliography and Reference Series,
No. 2), 1965. ii + 33 pp.

    83 items, 1890 - 1965. English; also French (2), German (2).
    All items have abstract-length annotations; introduction (8
    pp.); table of contents; title index and negative list;

International Relations

   summary of listings.

   An alphabetical list of periodicals in publication as of
   1965, that regularly include bibliographic information in the
   form of reviews, book lists, abstracts, accessions lists,
   etc., in the field of international relations and world
   affairs.

   219 <

   Crawford, Elisabeth T.

   The Social Sciences in International and Military Policy: An
   analytic bibliography.
   Washington, D.C.: Bureau of Social Science Research, 1965.

   220 <

   Hammond, Thomas T.

   Bibliography of Soviet Foreign Relations and World Communism.
   Princeton: Princeton University Press, 1965. 1240 pp.

   [7000 items. 30 languages. Annotated].

   221

   Angell, Robert C.

   "The sociology of international relations: A trend report and
   bibliography."
   Current Sociology, 14, 1 (1966): 5-62.

   448 items, 1944 - 1965. English; also French (26), Spanish
   (18), German (11), Russian (4), Italian (3), Polish (3),
   Norwegian (2), other Western and Eastern European languages.
   Some items have brief descriptive and critical annotations.

   Books and journal articles on sociological approaches to
   international relations, the international system, conflict,
   conflict resolution, international communications, foreign
   policy, regional groupings, the effects of transnational
   experiences, the U.N., and war and peace in general.

International Relations

222   HM36.5.N4,v.1

Nerlich, Uwe (ed.).

Literaturhinweise [3 lists].
In his Krieg und Frieden in industriellen Zeitalter [War and
Peace in the Industrial Age]: Beiträge der Sozialwissenschaft I
[Contributions to social science I].
Gutersloh: C. Bertelsmann (Krieg und Frieden: Beiträge zu
Grundproblemen der internationalen Politik, Band 6), 1966.
pp. 234-239, 380-381, 420-421.

　　These lists are the references to German translations of
　　chapters from Quincy Wright´s The Study of International
　　Relations (1955) and Herbert Kelman´s International Behavior
　　(1965).

223   Z6461.Z3

Zawodny, J[anusz] K.

Guide to the Study of International Relations.
San Francisco: Chandler (Chandler Publications in Political
Science), 1966. xii + 151 pp.

　　514 items, 1809 - 1964. English; also French, German (9),
　　Spanish (2), Italian (1). All items have brief to abstract-
　　length descriptive annotations; preface (1 p.) plus
　　introductions to some sections; table of contents;
　　author/title index.

　　A guide to abstracts (12), United States government archives
　　(5), atlases (7), behavioral sciences: sources relevant to
　　international relations (14), bibliographies (55),
　　biographies (27), book reviews (7), collections and libraries
　　(12), dictionaries (6), dissertation lists (6), documents
　　(44), encyclopedias (6), guides to films (11), guides to
　　literature (11), institutions in the field of international
　　relations (6), international conferences and congresses (3),
　　international law (22), international organizations (57),
　　interviews and oral histories (2), newspapers (13),
　　periodicals (101), research in progress (5), statistics and
　　other quantitative data (16), surveys of world events (23),
　　treaty collections (15), and yearbooks (28).

International Relations

224 <

Ditmas, E. M. R. (ed.).

Consolidated Index to the Survey of International Affairs,
1920-1938, and Documents on International Affairs, 1928-1938.
London: Oxford University Press, 1967.

225 <

Trask, David, Michael Meyer, and Roger Trask (eds.).

A Bibliography of United States--Latin American Relations since
1810: A selected list of 11,000 published references from the
beginning of the Latin American independence movement.
Lincoln: University of Nebraska Press, 1968.

226

Crawford, Elisabeth T. and Albert D. Biderman (eds.).

Bibliographic appendix.
In their Social Scientists and International Affairs: A case
for a sociology of social science.
New York/etc.: John Wiley and Sons, 1969. pp. 285-328.

   Most items have medium-length descriptive annotations;
   introduction (2 pp.) plus introductory paragraphs for each of
   five sections; author index.

227 <

DeGrazia, Alfred (ed.).

The Universal Reference System, Political Science, Government,
Public Policy Series, Vol. 1, International Affairs.
Princeton: Princeton Research Publishing, 1969. 1206 pp.

228   JC361.B45

Belfiglio, Valentine J.

Bibliography.
In his The United States and World Peace.
Berkeley, Calif.: McCutchan, 1971. pp. 71-74.

   68 items, 1893 - 1970. English.

International Relations

   Books on political theory, theories of international
   relations, and international law.

   229 <

   Dexter, Byron (ed.).

   The Foreign Affairs 50-Year Bibliography: New evaluations of
   significant books on international relations.
   New York: Bowker, for the Council on Foreign Relations, 1972.
   936 pp.

   230

   Larson, Arthur D.

   National Security Affairs: A guide to information sources, with
   a foreword by Paul Wasserman.
   Detroit: Gale Research, 1973. 411 pp.

      4200 items, 1945 - 1973 (most items published after 1958).
      English. Introduction (11 pp.) plus introductions (1
      paragraph) to each section; key-word index.

      The bibliography is organized into seven parts, with
      subdivisions and subject categories. Parts I-IV include
      books, articles, and documents on the world setting of
      national security (1267), U.S. national security affairs
      (1529), national security and domestic affairs of other
      nations (446), theory, research, concepts, and teaching in
      national security affairs, including conflict and conflict
      resolution, games, game theory, and simulation (391); Part V
      includes bibliographies, handbooks, dictionaries, and other
      reference materials (189); Part VI provides information on
      periodicals relevant to national security affairs (65); Part
      VII describes national security affairs research and
      education organizations and their publications and libraries
      in the U.S. and other countries (313).

   231   MiU: Z7161.H74,v.4,1975

   Holler, Frederick L.

   The Information Sources of Political Science, Vol. 4:
   International relations and organizations; Comparative and area
   studies.
   Santa Barbara, Calif./Oxford: ABC-Clio, 1975 (2nd ed.).
   xxxv + 123 + [41] pp.

International Relations

232   Z6461.L3

LaBarr, Dorothy F. and J[oel] David Singer.

The Study of International Politics: A guide to the sources for
the student, teacher, and researcher.
Santa Barbara, Calif./Oxford: Clio Books, 1976. xix + 211 pp.

International Law

233 <   Z6461.056

Ompteda, Diedrich Heinrich Ludwig von.

Litteratur des gesammten sowohl natürlichen als positiven
Völkerrechts [Literature of the Whole Natural and Positive
International Law]: Nebst vorangeschickter Abhandlung von dem
Umfange des gesammten sowohl natürlichen als positiven
Völkerrechts, und Ankündigung eines zu bearbeitenden
vollständigen Systems desselben [Including introductory
discussion of the scope of the entire natural and positive
international law, and announcement of a forthcoming complete
system of the same] (2 Theile in I).
Regensburg: J. L. Montags sel. Erben, 1785. 672 pp.

234 <   Z6461.056,3.th.

Kamptz, Karl [Cristoph] Albert [Heinrich] von.

Literatur des gesammten, sowohl natürlichen als positiven
Völkerrechts III [Literature of the Whole Natural and Positive
International Law III]: Neue Literatur der Völkerrechts seit
dem Jahre 1784; als Ergänzung und Fortsetzung des Werks des
Gesandten von Ompteda [New Literature of international law
since the year 1784; as a supplement and continuation of the
work of ambassador von Ompteda].
Berlin: Duncker und Humblot, 1817. xxii + 384 pp.

235 <

Lorimer, James.

Bibliography.
In his The Institutes of the Law of Nations: A treatise of the
jural relations of separate political communities . . . , Vol.
II.
Edinburgh/London: W. Blackwood, 1883 to 1884. pp. 590-594.

International Law

236 <

Rivier, Alphonse [Pierre Octave].

Note sur la Littérature du Droit des Gens avant la Publication
du Jus Belli ac Pacis de Grotius (1625) [Note on the Literature
of International Law before the Publication of Grotius' Law of
War and Peace (1625)].
Brussels: [Académie Royale de Belgique], 1883. 74 pp.
First published in Bulletin de l'Académie Royale de Belgique,
3me série, Vol. 6, Nos. 9-10, 1883.

237 <   JX2458.E3,1887

Davis, George B[reckenridge].

List of authorities.
In his Outlines of International Law: With an account of its
origin and sources and of its historical development.
New York: Harper and Brothers, 1887. pp. xix-xxiv.
New revised edition entitled The Elements of International Law,
1900. Third edition, 1908. Fourth edition revised by Gordon E.
Sherman, 1916.

238 <

Kamarovski, L.

Obzor Sovremennoy Literatouri po Mejdounarodnomou Pravou
[Review of Current Literature on International Law].
Moscow: Manontov, 1887. xlv + 354 pp.

239

Rivier, Alphonse [Pierre Octave].

[Bibliography].
In his Programme d'un Cours de Droit des Gens, pour Servir à
l'Etude Privée et aux Leçons Universitaires [Programme of a
Course in International Law, for Use in Private Study and in
University Lectures].
Brussels: G. Mayolez, 1889. pp. 14-26.

International Law

240 <   Z6451.J96

Stoerk, Felix.

Die Litteratur des Internationalen Rechts, 1884 bis 1894 [The
Literature of International Law, 1884 to 1894].
Leipzig: J. C. Hinrichs, 1896. 40 pp.
Reprinted from Juristischer Litteraturbericht . . . (Leipzig),
pp. 327-366, 1896.

241 <

[Dalmau y Olivart, Ramón, Marquis de].

Catalogue d´une Bibliothèque de Droit International et Sciences
Auxiliaires [Catalogue of a Library of International Law and
Auxiliary Sciences]: Brouillon de la table systématique des
fiches [Rough draft of the systematic table of entries].
Paris/Leipzig: Pedone/Brockhaus, 1899. xxiv + 406 pp.
Volume 2, entitled Catalogue de ma bibliothèque . . . ,
xxiv + 296 pp., 1907. Second edition, 1905-1910. Supplement,
1912.

242 <

[New York Public Library].

"List of books on international arbitration, etc."
New York Public Library, Monthly Bulletin of Additions
(October, 1905).

243 <

Moore, J. B.

Authorities in "History and digest of international
arbitrations."
House Miscellaneous Documents (56th Congress, 1st and 2nd
sessions), 128-132 (1906): lxxxiii-xcviii.

244   JX4494.H7

Hogan, Albert E[dmond].

Bibliography.
In his Pacific Blockade.
Oxford: Clarendon Press, 1908. pp. [7]-10.

International Law

58 items, 1855 - 1907. French, English, German; also Italian
(1), Spanish (1). A few items have brief descriptive or
critical annotations.

Books and articles on international law, maritime law, and
the history of pacific blockade. Brief bibliographies of
documents and other works are also provided as footnotes to
separate accounts of specific occurrences from Greece (1827)
to Venezuela (1902-1903) in Part II of the text.

245   JX1393.D8M7

Moulin, H[enri]-A[lexis].

Bibliographie.
In his La Doctrine de Drago [The Drago Doctrine].
Paris: A. Pedone (Questions de Droit des Gens et de Politique
Internationale), 1908. pp. 361-368.

117 items, 1865 - 1907. French, English; also German, Spanish,
Italian (5). Introduction (1 paragraph) plus an introductory
paragraph for each section.

Works on international relations and international law,
especially dealing with the Drago Doctrine against forcible
collection of interstate debts, particularly by European
states against South American states.

246   Z881.U5

[United States] Library of Congress, [Division of Bibliography]
(comp.), under the direction of Appleton Prentiss Clark Griffin
and [William Adams Slade].

List of References on International Arbitration.
Washington, D.C.: U.S. Government Printing Office, 1908.
151 pp.

Approximately 1000 items, 1832 - 1908. English, French; also
German, Italian, Spanish. Some items have annotations, of
varying length; subject and author indexes. Books are listed
alphabetically by author, periodical articles and government
documents listed chronologically.

Books, articles, and documents on international arbitration,
the Hague conferences, international law, limitation of
armaments, international finance, the French occupation of
Mexico (1861-1867), the Venezuela case (1902-1903), the Santo
Domingo question (1904-1905), and general questions of war
and peace.

International Law

247 <   JX1916.W55,v.2

Wehberg, H[ans].

Bibliography.
In his The Problem of an International Court of Justice,
translated by Charles G. Fenwick.
Oxford/London/New York/etc.: Clarendon Press/Humphrey Milford,
for the Carnegie Endowment for International Peace, Division of
International Law (Work of the Hague, Vol. 2), 1918. pp. xiii-
xxxiii.

248   IU: 341G91pu,no.8

Bellot, Hugh H. L.

Bibliography in "Introduction."
In Grotius Society, Texts Illustrating the Constitution of the
Supreme Court of the United States and the Permanent Court of
International Justice.
London: Sweet and Maxwell (The Grotius Society Publications,
Texts for Students of International Relations, No. 8), 1921.
pp. 38-39.

   16 items, 1908 - 1921. English.

   Writings on the U.S. Supreme Court, the Permanent Court of
   International Justice, and the judicial settlement of
   disputes within the Pan American Union.

249 <   JX4481.S8

Stowell, Ellery [Cory].

Bibliography.
In his Intervention in International Law.
Washington, D.C.: J. Byrne, 1921. pp. 459-540.

250 <

[Carnegie Endowment for International Peace, Library].

Permanent Court of International Justice.
Washington, D.C.: Carnegie Endowment for International Peace,
Library (Miscellaneous Reading List No. 21), 1923. (mimeo).
Other editions, 1924 and 1925.

International Law

251 <

[Carnegie Endowment for International Peace, Library].

Protocol for Pacific Settlement of International Disputes.
Geneva: Carnegie Endowment for International Peace, Library
(Miscellaneous Reading List No. 23), 1924. (mimeo).

252 <

[Matthews, Mary Alice (comp.)].

The Hague Permanent Court of International Justice.
Washington, D.C.: Carnegie Endowment for International Peace,
Library (Reading List No. 6), August 15, 1926. (mimeo).

253 <

[Matthews, Mary Alice (comp.)].

The Hague Permanent Court of International Justice, Supplement.
Washington, D.C.: Carnegie Endowment for International Peace,
Library (Reading List No. 6, Supplement), October 25, 1927.
(mimeo).

254 <

Matthews, M[ary] Alice (comp.).

Extraterritoriality.
Washington, D.C.: Carnegie Endowment for International Peace,
Library (Reading List No. 9), 1927. (mimeo).

255 <

Matthews, M[ary] Alice (comp.).

Central American Court of Justice.
Washington, D.C.: Carnegie Endowment for International Peace,
Library (Reading List No. 24), 1928. (mimeo).

International Law

    256 <

    Matthews, M[ary] Alice (comp.).

    International Arbitration.
    Washington, D.C.: Carnegie Endowment for International Peace,
    Library (Reading List No. 21), 1928. 14 pp. (mimeo).

    257 <

    [Carnegie Endowment for International Peace, Library].

    Codification of International Law.
    Washington, D.C.: Carnegie Endowment for International Peace,
    Library (Miscellaneous Reading List No. 34), 1930. (mimeo).
    An earlier list with same title appeared as Miscellaneous
    Reading List No. 6, 1923. (mimeo).

    258 <

    [Carnegie Endowment for International Peace, Library].

    Permanent Court of Arbitration.
    Washington, D.C.: Carnegie Endowment for International Peace,
    Library (Miscellaneous Reading List No. 33), 1930. (mimeo).
    An earlier bibliography with same title appeared as
    Miscellaneous Reading List No. 20, 1924. (mimeo).

    259 <

    Matthews, Mary Alice (comp.).

    The Permanent Court of International Justice and the Relation
    of the United States to the Court: Select list of books,
    pamphlets, and periodical articles.
    Washington, D.C.: Carnegie Endowment for International Peace,
    Library (Reading List No. 28), June 12, 1930. 17 pp. (mimeo).

    260 <

    [Carnegie Endowment for International Peace, Library].

    Bibliographies and Catalogs of International Law.
    Washington, D.C.: Carnegie Endowment for International Peace,
    Library (Miscellaneous Reading List No. 36), 1931. (mimeo).

International Law

261 <

[Carnegie Endowment for International Peace, Library].

References on Arbitral Procedure.
Washington, D.C.: Carnegie Endowment for International Peace,
Library (Miscellaneous Reading List No. 39), 1931. (mimeo).

262 <

Matthews, Mary Alice (comp.).

The Permanent Court of Arbitration: Select list of references
on arbitrations before the Hague tribunals and the
international commissions of inquiry, 1902-1928.
Washington, D.C.: Carnegie Endowment for International Peace,
Library (Reading List No. 30), March 9, 1931. 29 pp. (mimeo).

263 <

[Carnegie Endowment for International Peace, Library].

Self-defense in International Law.
Washington, D.C.: Carnegie Endowment for International Peace,
Library (Miscellaneous Reading List No. 47), 1933. (mimeo).

264   Z6461.C29,no.2

Matthews, M[ary] Alice (comp.).

The American Institute of International Law and the
Codification of International Law.
Washington, D.C.: Carnegie Endowment for International Peace,
Library (Select Bibliographies, No. 2), July 28, 1933. 17 pp.
(mimeo).

  167 items, 1912 - 1932. English, Spanish, French; also
  Portuguese (5), Italian (1). Many items have brief to medium-
  length descriptive annotations; introductory note (1
  paragraph).

  Official (46) and unofficial (98) publications on the Pan-
  American congresses on international law, 1915-1927; official
  (8) and unofficial (15) publications on the codification of
  international law.

International Law

265   Z6461.C29,no.1

Matthews, M[ary] Alice (comp.).

The International Commission of Jurists (Rio de Janeiro) and
the Codification of International Law.
Washington, D.C.: Carnegie Endowment for International Peace,
Library (Select Bibliographies, No. 1), May 23, 1933. 8 pp.
(mimeo).

   72 items, 1912 - 1928. English, Spanish; also French,
   Portuguese. Many items have brief descriptive annotations.

   Official (3) and unofficial (14) publications on codification
   of international law; official (20) and unofficial (35)
   publications on various conferences and commissions.

266   Z6464.R3C3,1933

Matthews, M[ary] Alice (comp.).

Recognition in International Law, with Special Reference to
Russia.
Washington, D.C.: Carnegie Endowment for International Peace,
Library (Reading List No. 11), March 23, 1933 (rev. ed.). 6 pp.
(mimeo).
First edition, 1927.

   81 items, 1906 - 1933. English; also French (6). Some items
   have brief descriptive annotations; list of other
   bibliographies (7) published by the CEIP appended.

   General works on diplomatic recognition (18), recognition of
   Soviet Russia (57), and debates (6).

267 <

Matthews, Mary Alice (comp.).

Codification of International Law.
Washington, D.C.: Carnegie Endowment for International Peace,
Library (Miscellaneous Reading List No. 51), 1934. (mimeo).

International Law

268   JX74.H3,v.59

McNair, Arnold D.

Bibliography in "Les effets de la guerre sur les traités [The
effects of war on treaties]."
Recueil des Cours, Académie de Droit International de la Haye,
59 (1937): 584.

   19 items, 1917 - 1936. English, French.

   Books and articles on effects of war, treaties and
   international law.

269 <

Przic, Ilija A.

Bibliographie Yougoslave de Droit International [Yugoslav
Bibliography of International Law] (1930-1936).
Belgrade/Paris: Editions Internationales, 1937. 74 pp.
Reprinted from Annuaire de l´Association Yougoslave de Droit
International, III, 1937.

270   JX5268.F7

Frasconà, Joseph L[ohengrin].

Bibliography.
In his Visit, Search, and Seizure on the High Seas: A proposed
convention of international law on the regulation of this
belligerent right.
New York: J. L. Frasconà, 1938. pp. 147-153.

   114 items, 1854 - 1934. English; also French (2).

   Books, journal articles, codifications, conventions,
   conferences, and cases on international law, neutrality,
   prize law, and naval warfare.

271   JX5212.G4,v.1

Genet, Raoul.

Index bibliographique général.
In his Précis de Droit Maritime pour le Temps de Guerre
[Summary of Maritime Law for Wartime, Vol. 1].

International Law

Paris: E. Muller (Collection de la Revue Internationale
Française du Droit des Gens, No. 1), [1938]. pp. ix-xv.

  145 items, 1616 - 1936. French; also Italian (9), Latin (3),
  Spanish (1).

  Books and articles on maritime law, the history of
  international law, and naval warfare.

272   JX5135.F5S35

Schödensack, Hellmut.

Schrifttum [Literature].
In his Der Flaggenmissbrauch im Landkriege [The Misuse of Flags
in Land Warfare].
Berlin: Franz Vahlen (Wehrrechtliche Abhandlungen, No. 7),
1938. pp. 40-44.

  115 items, 1864 - 1937. German, English, French; also Latin
  (2).

  Despite the book title, this bibliography contains mainly
  books, articles, texts, and official publications of a
  general nature concerning international law, the laws of war,
  neutrality, the Hague conferences, and treaties.

273 <

[Carnegie Endowment for International Peace, Library].

Natural Law as a Basis for Positive Law.
Washington, D.C.: Carnegie Endowment for International Peace,
Library (Miscellaneous Reading List No. 62), 1939. (mimeo).

274   Z6464.A1C3,no.18

Matthews, M[ary] Alice (comp.).

The Arctic and Antarctic Regions: With special reference to
territorial claims.
Washington, D.C.: Carnegie Endowment for International Peace,
Library (Brief Reference List No. 18), August 22, 1940. 3 pp.
(mimeo).

  43 items, 1906 - 1940. English; also French (5), Spanish (1).
  A few items have brief descriptive annotations.

International Law

   Articles and a few books concerning jurisdiction over the
   polar areas.

275 <

Menzel, Eberhard.

Die völkerrechtlichen Dissertationen [Dissertations on
International Law] 1933-1939 [Beiheft zur Zeitschrift fur
Völkerrecht xxv].
Berlin: Duncker und Humblot, 1941. 64 pp.

   German, Austrian, and Swiss dissertations.

276 <

Feilchenfeld, Ernst Hermann.

Bibliography.
In his The International Economic Law of Belligerent
Occupation.
Washington, D.C.: [Carnegie Endowment for International Peace]
(Monograph Series, No. 6), 1942.

277   JX4003.V6

Vonlanthen, Albert.

Literaturverzeichnis [Literature list].
In his Die völkerrechtliche Selbstbehauptung des Staates [The
Self-assertion of States in International Law].
Freiburg, Switzerland: Paulusdruckerei, 1944. pp. xv-xxii.

   218 items, 1586 - 1937. German, French; also Latin (5), Italian
   (1).

   Books, articles, and texts on international law,
   intervention, humanitarian intervention, laws of war,
   emergency, self-defense, colonialism, coercion, community,
   philosophy of law, juridical equality of states, treaties,
   natural law, dissolution of treaties, rebus sic stantibus,
   scholasticism and Thomism, and other topics.

International Law

278   Z6461.C29,no.3a

Scanlon, Helen Lawrence (comp.).

International Law: A selective list of works in English on
public international law.
Washington, D.C.: Carnegie Endowment for International Peace,
Library (Select Bibliographies, No. 3), February 15, 1946 (rev.
ed.). 20 pp. (mimeo).
First edition, compiled by Mary Alice Matthews, 1936. 21 pp.
(mimeo).

  192 items, 1795 - 1945. English; also Latin, French (1), Czech
  (1). Some items have brief descriptive annotations;
  introduction (1 paragraph); table of contents.

  Bibliographies and indexes (12), general treatises and
  collections (118), particular treatments (38), cases (24) of
  international law.

279 <

Stone, Julius.

[Bibliographic footnotes].
In his Legal Controls of International Conflict.
London/New York: Stevens/Rinehart, 1954. 851 pp.

280 <

Sukijasovic, Miodrag.

Bibliography of Selected Articles on International Law.
Belgrade: Institut za Medjunarodnu Politiku i Privredu, 1957.

281 <

Sukijasovic, M[iodrag] and O. Racic.

Bibliography of Selected Articles on International Law.
Belgrade: Institut za Medjunarodnu Politiku i Privredu, 1958.

International Law

282 <

Pindic, D[imitrije] and D. Janca.

Bibliography of Selected Articles on International Law.
Belgrade: Institut za Medjunarodnu Politiku i Privredu, 1959.

283 <

Janca, D. and D. Milic.

Bibliography of Selected Articles on International Law.
Belgrade: Institut za Medjunarodnu Politiku i Privredu, 1960.

284 <

Mitrovic, Tomislav.

Bibliography of Selected Articles on International Law.
Belgrade: Institut za Medjunarodnu Politiku i Privredu, 1961.

285 <

Sukovic, O. and A. Djordjevic.

Bibliography of Selected Articles on International Law.
Belgrade: Institut za Medjunarodnu Politiku i Privredu, 1962.

286   JX5244.M6B6

Bock, Ingeborg.

Literaturverzeichnis [Literature list].
In Die Entwicklung des Minenrechts von 1900 bis 1960 [The
Development of Maritime Law on the Use of Mines from 1900-
1960].
Hamburg: Universität Hamburg, Forschungsstelle für Völkerrecht
und ausländisches öffentliches Recht (Hektographierte
Veröffentlichungen . . . No. 40). 1963. pp. 357-392.

   316 items, 1880 - 1961. German, English, French; also Italian
   (5), Spanish (1).

   Books, journal articles, treatises, lectures, and official
   documents (298) on jurisprudence, international law and its
   codification, naval warfare, maritime law, blockades,
   contraband of war, neutrality, the Hague conferences, and
   U.S. foreign policy; list of periodicals (18).

International Law

287   JX4511.B77

Brownlie, Ian.

"Table of cases (. . . with references to law reports or other
sources) . . . ; Table of documents . . . ; Bibliography of
books and articles on the law relating to the use of force by
states [12 tables and lists]."
In his International Law and the Use of Force by States.
Oxford: Clarendon Press, 1963. pp. 437-519.

   1153 items, 1812 - 1961. English, French; also German, Italian,
   Spanish, Russian (9), Dutch (8), Polish (6). Some items have
   brief critical or descriptive annotations; introductory note
   to the main biblography (1 p.).

   Extensive bibliography of books and articles on international
   law, its history, legal and philosophical aspects of war and
   other uses of force, intervention, "just wars," conquest,
   treaties, war crimes, crimes against peace, peacemaking, etc.
   (921); table of documents (105); ten short lists of general
   reference works, official sources, and selected works on
   special topics such as rights and duties of states, law of
   the seas, international criminal jurisdiction, League of
   Nations Covenant, United Nations Charter; list of
   periodicals; references to sources for cases.

288 <

Sukijasovic, M[iodrag] and O. Racic.

Bibliography of Selected Articles on International Law.
Belgrade: Institut za Medjunarodnu Politiku i Privredu, 1963.

289 <

Pindic, Dimitrije.

Bibliography of Selected Articles on International Law.
Belgrade: Institut za Medjunarodnu Politiku i Privredu, 1964.

290 <

Pindic, D[imitrije] and P. Davinic.

Bibliography of Selected Articles on International Law.

International Law

Belgrade: Institut za Medjunarodnu Politiku i Privredu, 1965.

291 <   Z6461.R3

Rauschning, Dietrich.

Bibliographie des deutschen Schrifttums zum Völkerrecht, 1945-
64 [Bibliography of German literature on International Law,
1945-64].
Hamburg: Hansischer Gildenverlag, for the Institut für
Internationales Recht an der Universität Kiel, 1966.
xi + 569 pp.

292 <

Robinson, J.

International Law and Organization: General sources of
information.
Leiden: A. W. Sijthoff, 1967. 560 pp.

Armament and Disarmament

293 <   UA647.S18

Salvador, Gabriel.

De l´Agitation pour la Défense Nationale en Angleterre [On the
Agitation for National Defense in England]: Examen critique des
principaux documents publiés sur cette question [Critical
examination of the principal documents published on this
question].
Paris: J. Corréard, 1848. iv + 351 pp.

294   DLC-DB

[United States Library of Congress, Division of Bibliography].

List of References on the Nationalization (or Government
Monopoly) of the Manufacture of Arms and Munitions.
[Washington, D.C.]: Library of Congress, Division of
Bibliography, January 24, 1917. 5 pp. (typescript).
Original edition, February 10, 1915, 2 pp.

   64 items, 1894 - 1916. English.

   Articles, reports, and congressional speeches on the pros and
   cons of government manufacture of armor plating for defense
   needs and governmental intervention in the munitions
   industry.

295

[Carnegie Endowment for International Peace, Library].

"Disarmament and cost of armament and war: List of references
prepared in the Library of the Carnegie Endowment for
International Peace."
Advocate of Peace, 83, 5 (May, 1921): 198-199.
A mimeographed list entitled "Disarmament" (Miscellaneous
Reading List No. 10) also appeared in 1921; another edition in
1925.

   92 items, 1899 - 1921. English.

   Books, pamphlets, official reports, and periodical articles
   on disarmament, arms limitation, the cost of armament and

Armament and Disarmament

   war, world peace, and international arbitration.

   296   Z6464.D6B7

[McCarthy, Michael (comp.)].

Disarmament and Substitutes for War: Selected references to
books and periodicals in the Public Library of the City of
Boston.
Boston: Trustees [of the Boston Public Library] (Brief Reading
Lists, No. 21), November, 1921. 17 pp.

   221 items, 1822 - 1921. English; also French, German (5),
   Spanish (3). A few items have brief descriptive annotations;
   table of contents.

   Disarmament (110), international arbitration (72), Central
   American Court of Justice (7), Congress of Nations (1),
   International Court of Justice (12), League of Nations, 1919
   (4), Peace Conference, The Hague, 1899 and 1907 (6),
   Permanent Court of Arbitration, The Hague (4), Permanent
   Court of International Justice (5).

   297   DLC-DB

[United States Library of Congress, Division of Bibliography].

Brief Select List of References on Disarmament.
[Washington, D.C.]: Library of Congress, Division of
Bibliography, August 10, 1921. 5 pp. (typescript).

   56 items, 1899 - 1921. English; also French (2). Some items
   have brief descriptive annotations.

   Magazine articles and congressional reports and speeches on
   disarmament, costs of war, arms limitation, U.S. and British
   naval policy, international law, and the control of
   armaments.

   298   IU: 327C21i,no.12

Wright, Quincy.

[Bibliographic footnotes]; Readings [9 lists].
In his Limitation of Armament.
New York: Institute of International Education (International
Relations Clubs, Syllabus No. 12), November, 1921. 39 pp.

Armament and Disarmament

299   DLC-DB

[United States Library of Congress, Division of Bibliography].

Brief List of References on War Devices of Use in Peace.
[Washington, D.C.]: Library of Congress, Division of
Bibliography, May 31, 1923. 3 pp. (typescript).

  26 items, 1917 - 1922. English. A few items have brief
  descriptive annotations.

  Mostly magazine articles on technological and economic
  aspects of converting war materials (swords) into peaceful
  uses (plowshares).

300   H69.W6,1923

Wilson, Justina Leavitt and Julia E. Johnsen (comps.).

"Disarmament."
In their Questions of the Hour: Social, economic, industrial;
study outlines.
New York: H. W. Wilson (The Reference Shelf, Vol. 1, No. 9),
April, 1923 (2nd ed., rev. and enl.). pp. 35-36.

  25 items (no dates given). English.

  American national defense (14), the case for disarmament and
  the underlying causes and future trend of war (11).

301 <

Matthews, M[ary] Alice (comp.).

Traffic in Arms and Munitions of War.
Washington, D.C.: Carnegie Endowment for International Peace,
Library (Reading List No. 17), October 5, 1927. (mimeo).
Revised edition, 1935, 10 pp.

302 <

Smith, Rennie.

Bibliography.
In his General Disarmament or War?
[London]: Allen and Unwin, for the National Council for
Prevention of War, 1927.

Armament and Disarmament

303 <

Shillock, John C.

Bibliography.
In his The Post-war Movements to Reduce Naval Armaments.
International Conciliation, No. 245 (December, 1928): 91-92.

304   DLC-DB

Hellman, Florence S. (comp.), under the direction of William
Adams Slade.

Disarmament, with Special Reference to Naval Limitation: A
bibliographical list.
[Washington, D.C.]: Library of Congress, Division of
Bibliography, December 11, 1929. 40 pp. (mimeo).
Original edition 21 pp., May 19, 1927.

  476 items, 1908 - 1929. English; also French, German, Italian
  (2), Norwegian (2). Some items have brief descriptive
  annotations.

  Bibliographies (9), books (98), and periodical articles (369)
  on armament statistics, pros and cons of disarmament,
  disarmament proposals, freedom of the seas.

305 <

Matthews, M[ary] Alice (comp.).

Disarmament: A select list of recent publications.
Washington, D.C.: Carnegie Endowment for International Peace,
Library (Reading List No. 23), November 4, 1929 (rev. ed.).
(mimeo).

306   DLC-DB

[United States Library of Congress, Division of Bibliography].

Conference on the Limitation of Naval Armaments, Geneva, 1927:
(The three-power naval conference: a bibliographical list).
[Washington, D.C.]: Library of Congress, Division of
Bibliography, December 16, 1929. 11 pp. (typescript).

  140 items, 1926 - 1929. English; also French, German (2),
  Italian (2). A few items have brief descriptive annotations.

Armament and Disarmament

Journal and newspaper articles, reports, and speeches on the
Anglo-American-Japanese Naval Conference on arms limitation
at Geneva in 1927, U.S. naval policy, and general problems of
disarmament.

307   DLC-DB

[United States Library of Congress, Division of Bibliography].

The League of Nations and Disarmament: A bibliographical list.
[Washington, D.C.]: Library of Congress, Division of
Bibliography, December 18, 1929. 18 pp. (mimeo).

178 items, 1921 - 1929. English, French; also German (1),
Italian (1). A few items have brief descriptive annotations.

Official League of Nations publications (60), books (34), and
articles (84) on arbitration, security, disarmament, and
peaceful settlement of international disputes.

308   DLC-DB

[United States Library of Congress, Division of Bibliography].

Russia's Disarmament Proposals: A bibliographical list.
Washington, D.C.: Library of Congress, Division of
Bibliography, December 18, 1929. 6 pp. (typescript).

55 items, 1926 - 1929. English; also French (8), German (3),
Russian (3). Some items have brief descriptive annotations.

Articles and official reports and documents on Soviet
disarmament proposals and reactions to them.

309   JX1974.J6

Johnsen, Julia E. (comp.).

Bibliography.
In her Disarmament.
New York: H. W. Wilson (The Reference Shelf, Vol. 6, No. 6),
February, 1930. pp. [23]-40.

275 items, 1928 - 1929 (one item published in 1921). English.
A few items have brief descriptive annotations; some comments
on bibliography in introduction to the book.

Bibliographies (2), general references (197), affirmative
references (45), and negative references (31) relating to the

Armament and Disarmament

debate question "The nation should adopt a plan of complete
disarmament, excepting such forces as are needed for police
purposes." Most items are magazine and newspaper articles.

310   Z6464.D6

League of Nations, Library.

Annotated Bibliography on Disarmament and Military Questions.
Geneva: League of Nations, Publications Department, 1931.
163 pp.

613 items, 1869 - 1931. English, French; also German, Italian,
Spanish (9), Polish (5), Russian (4), other Eastern and
Western European languages. Most items have brief to medium-
length descriptive annotations; preface (1 p.); introduction
(2 pp.); author/subject index; user´s guide to the League of
Nations Library; price list of publications of the
Disarmament Section.

Major subject categories in two main sections: Armed Forces--
general (34), organization of defensive forces (105),
military aviation and its regulation (30), chemical warfare
and the movement for its suppression (26), supervision of the
trade and private manufacture of arms and ammunition and
implements of war (20), the laws of warfare and their
evolution (42); Disarmament--and the League of Nations (204),
outside the League of Nations (31), naval (68), and security
(60), from the economic point of view (32), and the general
disarmament movement (11).

311   Z6464.D6C2

Matthews, Mary Alice (comp.).

Disarmament and Security: Select list of recent books,
pamphlets and periodical articles.
Washington, D.C.: Carnegie Endowment for International Peace,
Library (Reading List No. 32), August 31, 1931. 31 pp.

439 items, 1912 - 1931. English; also French, German. Some
items have brief descriptive annotations; address list of
organizations mentioned in bibliography.

Books and pamphlets (192) and periodical articles (247) on
security, disarmament, naval power of nations, peace
treaties, reduction of arms, arms trade, League of Nations,
political aspects of war, defense policy, peace
organizations, public opinion, international law,
international relations, world order.

Armament and Disarmament

312   Z6724.M9C3

Matthews, Mary Alice (comp.).

Traffic in Arms, Munitions, and Implements of War and Control
of Their Manufacture: Select list of books, pamphlets, and
periodical articles with annotations.
Washington, D.C.: Carnegie Endowment for International Peace,
Library (Reading List No. 34), April 6, 1933. 22 pp.

   256 items, 1872 - 1933. English; also French, German (8),
   Italian (1), Spanish (1). Some items have brief descriptive
   annotations; appended list of other bibliographies (7)
   published by the CEIP.

   Works on arms traffic, arms control, disarmament, munitions
   industry, and arms embargo.

313   DLC-DB

Hellman, Florence S. (comp.).

Disarmament, with Special Reference to Naval Limitation: A list
of recent references.
[Washington, D.C.]: Library of Congress, Division of
Bibliography, December 15, 1934. 42 pp. (mimeo).

   483 items, 1929 - 1934. English; also French, German (10),
   Italian (9), Spanish (3). A few items have brief descriptive
   annotations; author index.

   Bibliographies (7), books and pamphlets (124), articles (254)
   and speeches from the Congressional Record (98) on armament
   statistics, pros and cons of disarmament, disarmament
   conferences and plans, and U.S. naval policy.

314   JX5390.J6

Johnsen, Julia E. (comp.).

Bibliography.
In her International Traffic in Arms and Munitions.
New York: H. W. Wilson (The Reference Shelf, Vol. 9, No. 9),
November, 1934. pp. [27]-48.

   313 items, 1912 - 1934. English. A few items have brief
   descriptive annotations; some comments on bibliography in
   introduction to the book.

Armament and Disarmament

Bibliographies (5), general references (174), affirmative references (104), and negative references (30), all relating to the debate question "Nations should agree to prevent the international shipment of arms and ammunition."

315   UF530.S4

Seldes, George.

Bibliography.
In his Iron, Blood and Profits: An exposure of the worldwide munitions racket.
New York/London: Harper and Brothers, 1934. pp. 329-332.

143 items, 1900 - 1933 (most items undated). English; also French, German (6).

Books and reports relating to war in general, the munitions industry, armament and disarmament, economic aspects of war, causes of war, and arms trade.

316   DLC-DB

[United States Library of Congress, Division of Bibliography].

A List of Recent References on Traffic in Arms, Munitions and Implements of War and Control of Their Manufacture.
[Washington, D.C.]: Library of Congress, Division of Bibliography, [1934]. 11 pp. (typescript).

121 items, 1932 - 1934. English; also French (3), German (2). A few items have brief descriptive annotations.

Magazine and journal articles and hearings on the manufacture of armaments and control of their production and distribution.

317 <

National Council for Prevention of War (Washington).

Literature on the Munitions Industry Available through the . . . Council.
Washington, D.C.: [National Council for Prevention of War], 1935. 2 pp. (mimeo).

Armament and Disarmament

318   DLC-DB

[United States Library of Congress, Division of Bibliography].

Selected List of Recent References on American National
Defense.
[Washington, D.C.]: Library of Congress, Division of
Bibliography, June 16, 1936. 18 pp. (typescript).

   239 items, 1926 - 1936. English; also French (1). A few items
   have brief descriptive annotations.

   Bibliographies (3), books, magazine articles, and official
   reports (172), and speeches in congress (64) on national
   defense, armament, disarmament, munitions, U.S. military
   strength, industrial mobilization, the economic aspects of
   war, militarism, and the prevention of war.

319   Z7409.L86,no.292

London Science Museum, Science Library.

Books and Pamphlets, Published since 1919, on Chemical Warfare
and Defense.
London: Science Museum (Science Library Bibliographical Series,
No. 292), January 23, 1937. 5 pp.

   90 items, 1919 - 1936. German, French, Italian; also English,
   Spanish (3).

   Books, articles, and government publications on chemical
   weapons, chemical warfare, medical aspects, and civil
   defense.

320   Z7409.L86,no.342

London Science Museum, Science Library.

Books and Pamphlets, Published since 1919, on Chemical Warfare
and Defense (Supplement to No. 292).
London: Science Museum (Science Library Bibliographical Series,
No. 342), August 31, 1937. 2 pp.

   30 items, 1925 - 1937. English, German; also French (4),
   Italian (2), Spanish (1).

   Emphasis on medical aspects, air raid precautions.

Armament and Disarmament

321   JX1953.J65

Johnsen, Julia E. (comp.).

Bibliography.
In her Peace and Rearmament.
New York: H. W. Wilson (The Reference Shelf, Vol. 11, No. 8),
September, 1938. pp. 29-48.

  304 items, 1917 - 1938. English. A few items have descriptive
  annotations.

  Bibliographies (8), general references (175), affirmative
  references (42), and negative references (79) relating to
  whether the United States should rearm; includes books,
  pamphlets, documents, magazine and journal articles on the
  causes and prevention of war, relations between military
  preparations, war, and peace, national defense, collective
  security, armament, disarmament, rearmament, the arms race,
  U.S. foreign policy, and the peace movement.

322   UG630.S59

Spaight, J[ames] M[olony].

[Bibliographic footnotes].
In his Air Power in the Next War.
London: G. Bles, 1938. ix + 181 pp.

  A few items in footnotes scattered throughout the text.

323 <

Tiffen, Charles.

Bibliography.
In his Course aux Armements et Finances Publiques [Armaments
Race and Public Finance].
Paris: Librairie Générale de Droit et de Jurisprudence, 1938.
pp. 263-265.

324 <

Fuller, Grace H[adley] (comp.).

A Selected List of References on the Expansion of the U.S.
Navy, 1933-1939.

Armament and Disarmament

Washington, D.C.: [Library of Congress, Division of
Bibliography], December, 1939. 34 pp. (mimeo).

325   Z7409.L86,no.500

London Science Museum, Science Library.

Books on Chemical Warfare: Supplement to Nos. 292 and 342.
London: Science Museum (Science Library Bibliographical Series,
No. 500), October 2, 1939. 2 pp.

   29 items, 1937 - 1939. English, German (9); also French (4),
   Italian (3).

   Updates the 1937 bibliography with additional general works
   and works on technical and medical aspects, civil defense
   measures.

326   DK266.M24,1940

Mahaney, Wilbur Lee, Jr.

Bibliography.
In his The Soviet Union, the League of Nations and Disarmament:
1917-1935 (Ph.D. dissertation, Political Science, University of
Pennsylvania).
Philadelphia: University of Pennsylvania, 1940. pp. 196-199.

   99 items, 1918 - 1938. English; also French (7).

   Books (59), League of Nations documents (10), newspapers
   (14), and miscellaneous documents (16) on disarmament,
   international relations, the Russian Revolution, the Soviet
   Union, fascism, Nazism, and international conferences.

327 <

Atwater, Elton.

Bibliography.
In his American Regulation of Arms Exports.
Washington, D.C.: [Carnegie Endowment for International Peace]
(Monograph Series, No. 4), 1941.

Armament and Disarmament

328   VA61.K3,1942

Katz, Mitchell D., Jr., Herbert C. Lee, and Edwin L. Levy, Jr.

Bibliography.
In their Our Fighting Ships.
New York/London: Harper and Brothers, 1942 (1st ed.). p. 90.

  26 items, 1897 - 1941. English.

  Mostly books on the U.S. navy and warships.

329   JX1974.T3

Tate, Merze.

Bibliography.
In her The Disarmament Illusion: The movement for a limitation
of armaments to 1907, with a foreword by Bernice Brown
Cronkhite.
New York: Macmillan, for the Bureau of International Research,
Harvard University and Radcliffe College, 1942. pp. 365-378.

  207 items, 1632 - 1941 (most items published after 1890).
  English; also French, German, Spanish (1). Introduction (1
  paragraph).

  General treatises (18), official documents (16), semiofficial publications (3), international law documents (6),
  international law journals (3), projects and proposals (12),
  reports on the Inter-Parliamentary Union, Lake Mohonk
  Conference, Socialist Congress, and peace congresses (14),
  autobiographies and memoirs (8), correspondence, addresses,
  and writings (12), biographies (19), miscellaneous secondary
  treatises and material (67), periodicals (21), and newspaper
  articles (8) on armament and disarmament, international law
  and arbitration, international relations, peace plans and
  congresses, theories on peace and war, and European and
  American history.

330   Z1007.B94

Beers, Henry P.

"Bibliography of publications containing lists or other data
pertaining to United States naval vessels: [Part I]; Part II."
Bulletin of Bibliography, 18, 7 (May-August, 1945): 160-163;
8 (September-December, 1945): 182-184.

Armament and Disarmament

    97 items, 1636 - 1920. English. Some items have brief to
    medium-length descriptive and/or critical annotations.

331   Z6461.C29,no.15

Scanlon, Helen Lawrence (comp.).

Security in the Atomic Age; International Control of the Bomb:
An annotated bibliography with supplementary list of
documentary materials on national problems of control.
Washington, D.C.: Carnegie Endowment for International Peace,
Library (Select Bibliographies, No. 15), April 12, 1946. 20 pp.
(mimeo).

    203 items, 1945 - 1946. English. Many items have brief
    descriptive annotations.

    Magazine articles, pamphlets, speeches, and reports on the
    political implications of nuclear weapons, the need for world
    government, and various proposals for the international
    control of atomic energy (185); supplementary list of
    documentary material on national problems of control (18).

332 <

Tate, Merze.

Bibliography.
In her The United States and Armaments.
Cambridge, Mass.: Harvard University Press, 1948.

333 <

United States Atomic Energy Commission.

Civil Defense and Atomic Warfare: A selected reading list.
Washington, D.C.: U.S. Government Printing Office, 1953.

334   IU: 327.73B937a

Burns, Richard Dean.

Bibliography.
In his American Statesmanship and the London Naval Disarmament
Conference of 1930. Unpublished M.A. thesis, History,
University of Illinois, 1958. pp. 132-138.

Armament and Disarmament

   76 items, 1908 - 1956 (most items published after 1929).
   English.

   Memoirs, diaries, and collected papers (13), newspaper and
   journal articles (42), and books (21) on the London Naval
   Conference, British, French, and (primarily) U.S. foreign
   policy, and U.S. diplomatic history.

   335 <

   Collart, Yves.

   Disarmament: A study guide and bibliography on the efforts of
   the United Nations.
   The Hague: M[artinus] Nijhoff, for the World Federation of
   United Nations Associations, 1958. 110 pp.

   336 <

   United States Library of Congress, Legislative Reference
   Service.

   Controlling the Further Development of Nuclear Weapons: A
   collection of excerpts and a bibliography.
   Washington, D.C.: U.S. Government Printing Office, 1958.

   337 <

   National Committee for a Sane Nuclear Policy.

   Bibliography on Nuclear Weapons, Disarmament and Peace.
   New York: [National Committee for a Sane Nuclear Policy], 1959.
   3 pp.

   338 <

   Friends Committee on National Legislation.

   Some Published Materials on the Economics of Disarmament.
   Washington, D.C.: Friends Committee on National Legislation,
   1960. 5 pp.

Armament and Disarmament

339 <

Wright, Christopher.

"Selected critical bibliography [on arms control]."
Daedalus, 89 (1960): 1055-1070.

340 <

United States Department of State.

A Basic Bibliography: Disarmament, arms control and national
security.
[Washington, D.C.: U.S. Department of State] (Publication No.
7193), June, 1961.

341 <

Harrison, Stanley.

Selected Bibliography on Arms Control.
Washington, D.C.: Institute for Defense Analyses, Weapons
Systems Evaluation Division, May 1, 1962. 30 pp.

342 <

Crum, Norman J.

Arms Control Guide (Annotated Bibliography).
Santa Barbara, Calif.: General Electric (TEMPO-SP-215),
January 1, 1963. pp. 1-129.

343 <

Student Peace Union.

Bibliography on Issues of Peace and Disarmament.
Chicago: [Student Peace Union], April, 1963.

344 <

United States Department of State, External Research Staff.

Studies in Progress or Recently Completed: Arms control and
disarmament (annotated bibliography).

Armament and Disarmament

[Washington, D.C.]: U.S. Department of State, Bureau of
Intelligence and Research, May, 1963. 62 pp.

345 <

[Current History].

"Readings on weapons control and disarmament."
Current History (August, 1964): 109-110.

346 <

Driver, Christopher.

Bibliography.
In his The Disarmers: A study in protest.
London: Hodder and Stoughton, 1964.

347 <

Holsti, J. J.

Soviet Strategy and Disarmament Policy: A bibliography.
Kjeller, Norway: Norwegian Defence Research Establishment,
1964.

348   JX1974.M48

Mid-West Debate Bureau.

"Bibliography; Affirmative rebuttal file; Negative rebuttal
file."
In its Control of Weapons and World Peace: What policy for
control of weapons systems would best insure the prospects for
world peace? (Debate Handbook).
Normal, Ill.: Mid-West Debate Bureau, 1964. pp. 37-64, 131-194,
195-258.

   1840 items, 1939 - 1964. English. All of the items in the
   rebuttal files have brief to abstract-length descriptive
   annotations, the rest are unannotated; introductions (1
   paragraph each) to the articles and files.

   Pamphlets (68), books (74), magazine articles (1128),
   affirmative rebuttal file (275), and negative rebuttal file
   (295) relevant to the question "Resolved that nuclear weapons
   should be controlled by an international organization."

Armament and Disarmament

349 <   JX1975.A1U52,no.22

United States Arms Control and Disarmament Agency.

A Brief Bibliography, Arms Control and Disarmament.
[Washington, D.C.: U.S. Arms Control and Disarmament Agency
(Publication 22)], [1964]. 33 pp.

350

Waskow, Arthur (ed.).

Suggestions for additional reading [bibliographic essay].
In his The Debate over Thermonuclear Strategy.
Boston/etc.: D. C. Heath (Problems in American Civilization),
1964. pp. 113-114.

351 <

Clemens, Walter C., Jr. (comp.).

Soviet Disarmament Policy, 1917-1963: An annotated bibliography
of Soviet and western sources.
Stanford: Stanford University, Hoover Institution on War,
Revolution and Peace (Hoover Institution Bibliographical
Series, No. 22), 1965. 151 pp.

352   V750.C68

Cowburn, Philip.

Bibliography.
In his The Warship in History.
New York: Macmillan, 1965. pp. 352-357.

  95 items, 1894 - 1963. English. Introduction (1 paragraph).

  Books and a few articles on warships in general (13), ships
  in the ancient world (7), the Viking ship (4), the English
  warship before 1600 (10), galleys, galleasses, and galleons
  (3), northWestern European warships in the seventeenth
  century (7), the British navy in the eighteenth century (9),
  the American navy in the days of sail (3), the nineteenth
  century revolution (14), early submarines, destroyers and
  cruisers (3), the twentieth century battleship (12), the
  submarine in war (6), and the aircraft carrier (4).

Armament and Disarmament

353

[Moskowitz, Harry and Jack Roberts (comps.)].

U.S. Security, Arms Control, and Disarmament, 1961-1965.
Washington, D.C.: U.S. Department of Defense, Office, Deputy
Assistant Secretary, Arms Control; and Office, Assistant
Secretary, International Security Affairs, February, 1965.
vii + 140 pp.

   679 items, 1961 - 1965. English. Most items have brief to
   abstract-length descriptive annotations; introduction (1 p.);
   table of contents; nine appendices.

   National interests, arms control, and disarmament: the global
   spectrum (299); arms control and disarmament: means, methods,
   trends, and developments (186); nuclear energy and weapons
   (38); outer space (22); peace and war (50); source materials
   for research and reference (84).

354 <   JX1974.7.W3

Walch, John W.

"[A bibliography of recent materials on nuclear weapons
control]."
In his Supplement on Weapons Control.
Portland, Maine: [J. W. Walch], [1965].

355

Watson, Lorna.

References; Bibliography.
In her History of Disarmament Negotiations.
Peace Research Reviews, 1, 2 (April, 1967): 85-98, 99-107.

356 <

United Nations, Secretariat.

Disarmament: A select bibliography, 1962-1967.
New York: United Nations (Dag Hammarskjöld Library,
Bibliographical Series, No. 12; United Nations Document
ST/LIB/Ser. B12), 1968 (rev. and enl. ed.). xi + 38 pp.
Originally published as Disarmament: A select bibliography,
1962-1964, New York: United Nations (Document ST/LIB/15),
1965, 85 pp.

Armament and Disarmament

357

Frank, Lewis A.

Selected bibliography.
In his The Arms Trade in International Relations.
New York/Washington/London: Frederick A. Praeger (Praeger
Special Studies in International Politics and Public Affairs),
1969. pp. 259-266.

358   V750.M32

Macintyre, Donald and Basil W. Bathe.

Bibliography.
In their Man-of-War: A history of the combat vessel, with a
preface by Edward L. Beach.
New York/Toronto: McGraw-Hill, 1969. pp. 262-263.

   169 items, 1670 - 1968. English; also Danish, French, Italian,
   German (8), Dutch (8), Swedish (7), Spanish (6).

   Books, periodicals, and reference works on naval history and
   the development of warships from 4000 B.C. to the present.

359 <   Z1035.C5,v.6

Oboler, Eli M.

"World disarmament: A selected reading list."
Choice, 6 (July/August, 1969): 630-632.

360 <

Heurlin, Bertel (comp.).

Bibliography.
In his Disarmament [Kildesamling], Udg. i samarb. med Unesco-
Skoleprojekt.
Copenhagen: Gyldendal, 1970. pp. 180-182.

Armament and Disarmament

361   JX1907.C33

Kemp, Geoffrey.

[Bibliographic footnotes]; Selected bibliography.
In his Arms Traffic and Third World Conflicts.
International Conciliation, No. 577 (March, 1970): 5-71, 75-76.

   42 items, 1950 - 1970. English.

   Bibliographic footnotes (30) on arms trade, foreign aid,
   military expenditures, and arms control; selected
   bibliography (12) of books and articles on cost of war,
   economics of defense in nuclear age, international relations,
   national security, conflict analysis.

362 <

Melman, Seymour (ed.).

Bibliography.
In his The Defense Economy: Conversion of industries and
occupations to civilian needs.
New York: Frederick A. Praeger, 1970.

363 <

Sica, Geraldine P.

"A Preliminary bibliography of studies of the economic effects
of defense policies and expenditures."
In Melman, Seymour (ed.), The Defense Economy.
New York: Praeger. 1970.
Bibliography appeared originally as a pamphlet, McLean,
Virginia: Research Analysis Corporation (AD679038), October,
1968.

364 <   UA840.I55,v.1

Wasan, R. P.

"Chemical and biological warfare: A select bibliography."
Institute for Defence Studies and Analyses, New Delhi, 2
(January, 1970): 365-378.

Armament and Disarmament

365 <

Kodzic, Petar.

Military Effort and Arms of Developing Countries: A select
annotated bibliography.
Ljubljana, Yugoslavia: University of Ljubljana, Co-operation
with Developing Countries Research Center, 1971. [61] pp.

366   JX1974.7.M42

Meeker, Thomas A. (comp.).

SALT: An alternative to the Soviet-American arms race (a
selected list of research-study materials designed to acquaint
the student with the operatives of the Soviet-American
disarmament dialogue).
Los Angeles: California State University at Los Angeles, Center
for the Study of Armament and Disarmament, Bibliographic
Reference Service (Classroom Study Series [Political Issues
Series], Vol. 1, No. 1), 1972. 33 pp.

    225 items, 1956 - 1972. English. Introduction (3 pp.); each
    section and subsection also has an introductory paragraph;
    table of contents.

    Journal and magazine articles, books, papers, and govermental
    reports on SALT, encompassing strategic, political, and
    international viewpoints (139); background information on
    arms control, nuclear strategy, and weaponry (86).

367   MiU: Z6464.D6B97

Burns, Richard Dean (comp.).

Inspection, Verification, Control and Supervision in Arms
Control and Disarmament [a bibliography].
Los Angeles: California State University at Los Angeles, Center
for the Study of Armament and Disarmament (Political Issues
Series/Classroom Study Series, Vol. 2, No. 4), 1973. 60 pp.

    535 items, 1916 - 1975. English; also French (7), German (5).
    Introduction (5 pp.); each section also has an introductory
    paragraph; table of contents.

    Articles, official documents, papers, speeches, and books on
    historical and contemporary inspection issues (58),
    inspection techniques (99), verification procedures (37),
    international supervision (93), compliance and evasion (5),
    special issues (35), inspection of arms control arrangements

Armament and Disarmament

(148).

368   Z6464.D6P37

Parker, Jerry and Thomas A. Meeker (comps.).

SALT II: A selected research bibliography.
Los Angeles: California State University at Los Angeles, Center
for the Study of Armament and Disarmament (Political Issues
Series, Vol. 2, No. 8), 1973. xv + 36 pp.

369   Z7165.U5R63

Roswell, Judith (comp.).

Arms Control, Disarmament, and Economic Planning: A list of
sources, with an introduction by Dennis Ray.
Los Angeles: California State University at Los Angeles, Center
for the Study of Armament and Disarmament (Political Issues
Series, Vol. 2, No. 3), 1973. 26 pp.

  295 items, 1957 - 1973. English. Introduction (3 pp.); the
  first section and subsections also have introductory
  paragraphs; table of contents.

  Articles, books, pamphlets, papers, and reports on the
  economic consequences of disarmament (115), problems and
  plans for conversion (46), studies and publications of the
  U.S. Arms Control and Disarmament Agency (35), defense
  economics (22), impact of defense spending (18), cost of
  armaments (10), civilian-military relations (13), military-
  industrial complex (22), arms control and disarmament (14).

370

Robinson, Julian Perry.

Chemical/Biological Warfare: An introduction and a
bibliography.
Los Angeles: California State University at Los Angeles, Center
for the Study of Armament and Disarmament (Political Issues
Series, Vol. 3, No. 2), 1974. 34 pp.
Revised and updated edition, prepared by Richard Dean Burns,
appeared as Political Issues Series, Vol. 6, No. 2, 1979,
49 pp., 387 items.

  339 items, 1920 - 1974. English. A few items have brief
  descriptive annotations; introduction (9 pp.) plus an
  introductory paragraph in each section; table of contents.

Armament and Disarmament

   General studies on chemical and biological warfare (48),
   technological and medical aspects of CBW (40), use of CB
   weapons in the past (56), chemical/biological warfare in
   contemporary military and strategic theory (23), national CBW
   policies and postures (37), the propriety of special
   restraints on CBW (40), CBW and international law (13),
   chemical/biological disarmament (26), current issues (56).

   371 <

   Rosenblad, Esbjörn.

   Prohibited Weapons: Treaties and bibliography.
   Stockholm: Kungliga Biblioteket (Dok. och data, 6), 1974.
   48 + 2 pp.

   372

   Westing, Arthur H. (comp.).

   Herbicides as Weapons: A bibliography.
   Los Angeles: California State University at Los Angeles, Center
   for the Study of Armament and Disarmament (Political Issues
   Series, Vol. 3, No. 1), 1974. 36 pp.

      294 items, 1955 - 1974. English. Introduction (2 pp.); table
      of contents.

      Books, articles, and government reports on biological,
      chemical, bacteriological, and radiological warfare
      (particularly as applied in the Vietnam War), effects on the
      environment and human life, and the issue of war crimes and
      atrocities.

   373

   Cahn, Anne H. (comp.).

   Lasers: For war and peace [a bibliography].
   Los Angeles: California State University at Los Angeles, Center
   for the Study of Armament and Disarmament (Political Issues
   Series, Vol. 3, No. 3), 1975. 24 pp.

      236 items, 1955 - 1975. English. Introduction (2 pp.); table
      of contents.

      General background (43), military interests and activities
      (146), plasma thermonuclear possibilities (27), laser funding
      (11), congressional concern (9), laser journals (6).

Armament and Disarmament

374   Z6464.D6B87

Burns, Richard Dean.

Arms Control and Disarmament: A bibliography.
Santa Barbara, Calif./Oxford: ABC-Clio (War/Peace Bibliography
Series, No. 6), 1977. xvi + 430 pp.

  8847 items. Introduction (7 pp.) plus introductory essays for
  each of 13 chapters; table of contents; subject index; author
  index.

  Books, articles, pamphlets, and other materials grouped under
  the following main headings: research resources and arms
  control and disarmament organizations; introduction to arms
  control and disarmament issues; historical surveys and
  contemporary views; League of Nations and United Nations;
  inspection, verification and supervision; special issues--
  economic consequences of disarmament, negotiations, science
  and technology, bureaucratic politics and the military-
  industrial complex, legal and psychological dimensions;
  limitation of weapons and personnel; the SALT era (1969-
  1976); demilitarization, denuclearization, and
  neutralization; regulating and outlawing weapons and war;
  controlling arms manufacture and traffic; controlling nuclear
  proliferation; rules of war and stabilizing of the
  international environment.

375   MiU: Z6464.D6R54

Ridgeway, Susan (comp.).

NPT: Current Issues in Nuclear Proliferation: A selected
bibliography.
Los Angeles: California State University at Los Angeles, Center
for the Study of Armament and Disarmament (Political Issues
Series, Vol. 5, No. 1), 1977. x + 57 pp.

  517 items, 1961 - 1977. English. Introduction (4 pp.);
  sections also have brief introductions; table of contents.

  Resource documents (21), origins of the NPT (17),
  proliferation issues (71), arms control and nonproliferation
  (11), the Nonproliferation Treaty (13), the Nonproliferation
  Treaty Review Conference of 1975 (17), safeguards (32),
  terrorism (7), the Threshold Test Ban Treaty of 1974 and
  Peaceful Nuclear Explosion Treaty of 1976 (16), Comprehensive
  Test Ban Treaty (22), nuclear free zones (15), nuclear energy
  (39), nuclear export policy (30), breeder reactors (8),
  peaceful nuclear explosions (22), worldwide view of

Armament and Disarmament

    proliferation: Europe (14), France (9), West Germany (6),
    Middle East (12), Israel (10), South Africa (19), Asia (11),
    Australia (4), India (33), Pakistan (4)), Japan (18), China
    (8), Latin America (10), Brazil (13), Argentina (5).

    376 <   Z6464.D6R43,1978

    [Graham, Thomas W. and Ridgely C. Evers (comps.)].

    Bibliography: Nuclear Proliferation, prepared for the
    Subcommittee on Energy, Nuclear Proliferation, and Federal
    Services of the Committee on Governmental Affairs, United
    States Senate, and the Committee on International Relations and
    Committee on Science and Technology, U.S. House of
    Representatives, by the Environment and Natural Resources
    Policy Division, Congressional Research Service, The Library of
    Congress.
    Washington, D.C.: U.S. Government Printing Office, 1978.
    x + 159 pp.

    377   H62.U475,no.39IU: 300Un2r,v.39

    UNESCO (United Nations Educational, Scientific and Cultural
    Organization).

    Annotated bibliography.
    In its Review of Research Trends and an Annotated Bibliography:
    Social and economic consequences of the arms race and of
    disarmament (prepared under the auspices of the International
    Peace Research Association by the International Institute for
    Peace, Vienna, the Arbeitsgruppe Rustung und Unterentwicklung,
    Hamburg, and the Tampere Peace Research Institute, Tampere).
    Paris: UNESCO (Reports and Papers in the Social Sciences, No.
    39), 1978. pp. 23-44.

      178 items, 1961 - 1977. English; also German, Russian, 11 other
      Eastern and Western European languages. All items have
      medium- to abstract-length descriptive annotations. Appended
      lists of military periodicals and other journals relevant to
      the bibliographies, and reference books.

      Books, articles, and pamphlets on the military establishment,
      military industry, and society (35); arms race, disarmament,
      and the economy (48); arms trade and military assistance--
      international and national implications (40); military
      regimes in the Third World and their impact on society (15);
      military research and development and its impact on
      scientific institutions (17); consequences of the arms race
      for the international system and its processes (23).

Armament and Disarmament

378 <   JX1977.A2,ST/LIB/SER.B/26

United Nations, Dag Hammarskjöld Library.

Disarmament/Désarmement: A select bibliography, 1973-1977/
Bibliographie sélective, 1973-1977.
New York: United Nations (Bibliographical Series, Dag
Hammarskjöld Library, No. 26; United Nations Document
ST/LIB/SER.B/26), 1978. xii + 139 pp.

379

Burns, Richard Dean and Susan Hoffman Hutson (comps.).

The SALT Era: A selected bibliography.
Los Angeles: California State University at Los Angeles, Center
for the Study of Armament and Disarmament (Political Issues
Series, Vol. 6, No. 1), 1979 (rev. ed.). ix + 59 pp.

   526 items, 1963 - 1979. English; also German (4). Many
   sections have brief introductions (1-2 paragraphs); table of
   contents.

   Background (30), SALT I (140), SALT II (161), SALT III (6),
   SALT and related issues: U.S. views (15), Soviet views (31),
   Europe and SALT (16), China and SALT (19), other issues
   (108).

380 <   Z6465.G7L56,1979

Lloyd, Lorna and Nicholas A. Sims.

British Writing on Disarmament from 1914 to 1978: A
bibliography.
London/New York: Frances Pinter/Nichols, 1979. 117 pp.

381   IU: UA10.I55,1979

Stockholm International Peace Research Institute.

References [15 lists].
In its World Armaments and Disarmament: SIPRI Yearbook 1979.
London/New York: Taylor and Francis/Crane, Russak, 1979.
pp. 20, 32, 64, 70, 187-188, 303-304, 328, 380-387, 417-420,
449-452, 461-462, 486-489, 520-523, 662, 679-680.

   463 items, 1955 - 1979 (most items are post-1972). English;
   also German (3), Swedish (2), French (1).

Armament and Disarmament

References at end of introduction (3) and of chapters on
world military expenditures (6), world arms production (2),
world arms trade (20), military use of outer space (32),
nuclear power and nuclear proliferation (8), expansion of
naval forces (116), command and control of sea-based nuclear
deterrent (45), strategic antisubmarine warfare (32),
prohibition of inhumane and indiscriminate weapons (14),
stockpiles of chemical weapons and their destruction (51),
the U.N. Special Session on Disarmament (96), confidence-
building in Europe (2), NGOs and disarmament (36). Similar
lists of references can be found in previous SIPRI yearbooks,
beginning in 1969.

382

Ball, Nicole and Milton Leitenberg.

A selected bibliography.
In their Disarmament, Development, and Their Interrelationship:
A critical essay and selected bibliography.
Los Angeles: California State University at Los Angeles, Center
for the Study of Armament and Disarmament (Political Issues
Series, Vol. 6, No. 3), 1980. pp. 30-42.

130 items, 1965 - 1978. English; also German (1).
Introductory essay (20 pp.) with reference notes (8 pp.);
table of contents.

U.N. resolutions and reports (8), U.S. government reports and
documents (9), articles and books on arms, militaries, and
development (113).

Militarism and the Military

383   Z671.L7,v.23

[DuVal, R. J. (comp.)].

"Books relating to warfare."
Library Journal, 23, 5 (May, 1898): 191-194.

   149 items, 1863-1898. English. Some items have brief
   descriptive and/or critical annotations; introduction (1 p.).

   Books on the technical aspects of warfare, armament, strategy
   and tactics, and defense policies.

384   Z6725.G7C6

Cockle, Maurice J. D.

A Bibliography of English Military Books up to 1642 and of
Contemporary Foreign Works, with an introductory note by
Charles Oman (edited by H.D. Cockle).
London: Simpkin, Marshall, Hamilton, Kent, 1900. xl + 268 pp.

   632 items, 431 B.C.-1657. Italian, English; also Latin,
   French, Spanish, German, Dutch (4), Portuguese (4). Most
   items have brief to abstract-length descriptive and/or
   critical annotations; introduction (4 pp.); preface (19 pp.);
   author/subject index.

   Bibliography of military books in English (166) and foreign
   languages (466) divided into subtopics dealing with such
   subjects as military history, military strategy and
   techniques, warfare, armaments, pyrotechnics, military
   training, castrametation (camp layout) and fortification,
   medical care, topography, and military law.

385   DLC-DB

[United States Library of Congress, Division of Bibliography].

List of References on Militarism.
[Washington, D.C.]: Library of Congress, Division of
Bibliography, November 5, 1915. 11 pp. (typescript).

Militarism and the Military

    162 items, 1864-1915. English; also French, German (2). A
    few items have brief descriptive annotations.

    Books (46) and magazine and journal articles (116) on the
    history of war and militarism, arguments for and against
    militarism, causes and costs of war, and the burden of
    armaments.

    386 <

Index Medicus.

War Supplement: A classified record of literature on military
medicine and surgery, 1914-1917.
Washington, D.C.: Carnegie Institution of Washington, 1918.
260 pp.

    387   DLC-DB

[United States Library of Congress, Division of Bibliography].

List of References on Voluntary Enlistment in the Army.
[Washington, D.C.]: Library of Congress, Division of
Bibliography, November 26, 1920. 4 pp. (typescript).

    40 items, 1903-1920. English.

    Mostly magazine articles, official reports, and speeches
    concerning the debate over the volunteer system versus
    conscription.

    388 <

[Carnegie Endowment for International Peace, Library].

Compulsory Military Training.
Washington, D.C.: Carnegie Endowment for International Peace,
Library (Miscellaneous Reading List No. 7), [1923]. (mimeo).

    389   HN51.W6,v.9

[The World Tomorrow].

"A reading list on militarism."
The World Tomorrow, 9, 5 (October, 1926): 173.

    22 items (no dates given). English.

Militarism and the Military

Books on military training and the causes, consequences, and prevention of war.

390   UA23.J55,1928

Johnsen, Julia E. (comp.).

Bibliography.
In her Selected Articles on National Defense.
New York: H. W. Wilson (Handbook Series, Ser. II, Vol. 6),
December, 1928. pp. xxxix-lxxxii.
Original edition, New York: H. W. Wilson (Debaters' Handbook
Series), 1920, pp. [xxxi]-lx.

  662 items, 1919-1928. English. A few items have brief
  descriptive annotations.

  Bibliographies (10), general references (131), army (40),
  military training (16), industrial mobilization (23),
  universal draft (24), chemical warfare (26), arms traffic
  (14), navy (171), disarmament (57), military aeronautics
  (37), organizations (13).

391 <

Cochenhausen, F. von (ed.).

[Classified bibliography].
In his Die Wehrwissenschaften der Gegenwart [Current Military
Sciences].
Berlin: Junker und Dünnhaupt, 1934.

392   U104.G6

Golub', P. (comp.).

Lenin o Voine i Armii [Lenin on War and the Army]:
Predmetno-tematicheskii ukazatel' [Subject index].
Leningrad: Voenno-politicheskáia Akademiia RKKA im. Tolmacheva
[Tolmachev Military-Political Academy of the Worker-Peasant Red
Army], 1934. 252 pp.

  No dates given. Russian. All items have brief descriptive
  annotations; introduction (2 pp.).

  Primary and secondary material on Lenin's views on war, the
  army, militarism, imperialism, and related topics.

Militarism and the Military

393   MH: Ital 98.29

Rysky, Carlo de.

Bibliografia.
In his I Problemi della Guerra Moderna e la Politica Militare
dell'Italia [The Problems of Modern War and the Military
Politics of Italy].
Milan/Varese: Instituto Editoriale Cisalpino, 1939.
pp. 323-326.

  63 items (no dates given). Italian; also French.

  Books on militarism, military strategy and tactics,
  imperialism, and the history and effects of war.

394 <

[Carnegie Endowment for International Peace, Library].

Military Occupation.
Washington, D.C.: Carnegie Endowment for International Peace,
Library (Miscellaneous Reading List No. 65), 1940. (mimeo).

395 <   '   DLC-DB

Fuller, G[race] H[adley] (comp.).

German Militarism: A selected list of recent writings.
Washington, D.C.: Library of Congress, Division of
Bibliography, August 2, 1940. 27 pp. (typescript).

396   CB425.M36,1940

Mannheim, Karl.

Bibliography: "Military methods and the application of power as
social techniques."
In his Man and Society in an Age of Reconstruction: Studies in
modern social structure.
New York: Harcourt, Brace, 1940. pp. 407-411.

  88 items, 1900-1939. English, German; also French (5),
  Italian (2).

  The principle of power (19), some concrete forms of social
  pressure (14), modern warfare and the totalitarian war (34),
  psychological aspects of modern militarism and morale (21).

Militarism and the Military

397   UA23.H46

Herring, [Edward] Pendleton.

Bibliography.
In his The Impact of War: Our American democracy under arms.
New York/Toronto: Farrar and Rinehart, 1941. pp. 285-294.

103 items, 1880-1941. English. Most items have brief
descriptive and/or critical annotations; introduction (1 p.).

Books, articles, and official reports on military history of
the United States, civil-military relations, U.S. militia,
politics of national defense, military policy, mobilization,
and the effects of warmaking and militarism.

398   U102.C663,1942a

[Blatto, Oete].

Nota bibliografica.
In Clausewitz, [Karl] von, La Guerra (Vom Kriege) [On War]:
Pagine scelte [Selected pages], con introduzione a cura di Oete
Blatto.
Florence: Felice le Monnier (Biblioteca degli Scrittori
Militari, Sezione Straniera, [Vol.] 2), 1942. pp. xix-xx.

28 items, 1796-1935. German, French; also Italian (5).

Works by Clausewitz (6), translated works (3), selections
(2), biographical and critical works (17).

399   Z6835.U5E4

Ellinger, Werner B. and Herbert Rosinski.

Sea Power in the Pacific, 1936-1941: A selected bibliography of
books, periodical articles, and maps from the end of the London
Naval Conference to the beginning of the war in the Pacific,
with an introduction by Edward Mead Earle.
Princeton/London: Princeton University Press/Humphrey Milford,
Oxford University Press, 1942. xiv + 80 pp.

705 items, 1936-1941 (a few items published before 1936).
English; also German, French, Dutch (7), Italian (3). Many
items have brief descriptive annotations; introduction
(2 pages); table of contents; author index.

Militarism and the Military

   Statistical handbooks, treatises, articles, bibliographies,
   books, maps, and official documents on naval ratios and
   maritime power (44), naval geography of the Pacific Ocean
   (44), problems of sea power and naval strategy in the Pacific
   area (512); list of periodicals (105). Emphasis is placed on
   factual information, naval strategy, and materials having
   particular relevance to World War II.

400   U102.R9

Rysky, Carlo de.

Bibliografia.
In his La Guerra Moderna [Modern War]: Problemi, preparazione,
condotta politica e militare, il nuovo imperialismo italiano
[Problems, preparations, political and military conduct, the
new Italian imperialism].
Milan/Messina: Giuseppe Principato, 1942. pp. 459-462.

   83 items (no dates given). Italian; also French, German (1).

   Books, almanacs, and yearbooks on modern warfare, militarism,
   military strategy and tactics, military history, the history
   of specific wars, and Italian imperialism.

401   Z881.M6318A,v.14

[Dennis, Willard Kelso (comp.)].

"Books on modern military science."
About Books (at the Olin Library, Wesleyan University,
Middletown, Conn.), 14, 1-2 (September-December, 1943): 9-11.

   79 items, 1897-1942. English. Introduction (1 paragraph).

   Books on warfare, battles, military science, strategy and
   tactics.

402   Z881.N6Br2,v.20

Foster, Jeannette H. (comp.).

"For the armchair strategist."
New York Public Library, Branch Library Book News, 20, 7
(September, 1943): 102.

   16 items (no dates given, presumably 1943). English. All
   items have brief descriptive annotations.

Militarism and the Military

   Books on military strategy and tactics.

403   Z6724.S8R5

Riley, Vera and John P[arke] Young.

Bibliography on War Gaming.
Chevy Chase, Md.: Johns Hopkins University, Operations Research
Office (B[ibliographic] R[eference] S[eries], 7), April 1,
1957. 94 pp.

   375 items. 1824-1957. English; also German, French, Spanish
   (2), Serbian (1). Some items have brief to abstract-length
   descriptive and/or critical annotations; introduction
   (9 pp.).

   Board games (41), map maneuvers (59), field exercises (33),
   sand table games (24), other types (30), theoretical games
   (117), air war games (29), land war games (17), sea war games
   (8), gaming devices (9), economic and industrial gaming (8).

404   UA23.J3

Janowitz, Morris.

Notes to chapters [6 lists]; Selected bibliography.
In his Sociology and the Military Establishment, with a
foreword by Leonard S. Cottrell, Jr.
New York: Russell Sage Foundation, 1959. pp. 23-24, 42-43,
62-63, 81-82, 95, 106, 109-112.
Revised edition, in collaboration with Roger Little, 1965.

   140 items, 1920-1958. English. A few of the items are
   critically discussed in the notes.

   Books and articles on military structure, organization,
   leadership and personnel, military sociology, psychology and
   psychiatry, civil-military relations, militarism, civilian
   attitudes toward the military, guerrilla warfare and other
   topics.

405   JX1901.J6,v.4

Brody, Richard A.

"Deterrence Strategies: An annotated bibliography."
Journal of Conflict Resolution, 4, 4 (December, 1960): 443-457.

Militarism and the Military

406 <

United States Naval War College.

Directive for Strategic Study [bibliography].
August 31, 1962. 162 pp.

407   HD20.S94

Sztarski, M[arian] R[yszard].

Literatura.
In his Wojsko a Badania Operacji [Army and Operations
Research].
Warsaw: Wydawnictwo Ministerstwa Obrony Narodowej, 1963. pp.
277-282.

  84 items, 1916-1962. English, Polish; also Russian, French,
  German (3), Spanish (1).

  Books, reports, articles, and monographs on the theory and
  practice of operations research, strategic analysis, military
  strategy and tactics, and game theory; list of periodicals.

408

Lissak, Moshe.

Selected literature of revolutions and coups d´état in the
developing nations.
In Janowitz, Morris (ed.), The New Military: Changing patterns
of organization.
New York: W. W. Norton, 1964. pp. 339-362.

  132 items, 1927-1964 (most items published after 1940).
  English; also French (5). All items have medium-length
  descriptive annotations; introduction (5 pp.).

  Books and articles on the role of the military in developing
  countries.

409   U162.S615

Deutsche Gesellschaft für auswärtige Politik,
Forschungsinstitut (comp.).

Militarism and the Military

Bibliographie.
In Sokolowski, W[asiliĭ] D[anilovich] (ed.), Militär-strategie
[Military Strategy] (Deutsche Übersetzung aus dem Russischen
der zweiten verbesserten und ergänzten Auflage [German
translation from the Russian of the second improved and
enlarged edition], translated by Werner Meermann, I. W. Lomow,
and Hermann Hackenberg).
Frauenfeld, Switzerland: Huber, 1965. pp. 543-567.

   281 items, 1955-1964. English, German; also Russian, French
   (2), Swedish (1), Norwegian (1). Some items have brief
   descriptive annotations.

   Soviet and non-Soviet sources on the adaptation of Soviet
   military strategy to the missile age (36), present
   controversies concerning Soviet strategy (51), relationship
   between political and military leadership in the Soviet Union
   (22), relative military strength of the West and East (37),
   long-term Soviet technical and strategic options [economic
   factors] (36), Soviet military strategy and foreign policy
   (48), military problems of the eastern bloc (19), the
   Sokolovsky strategy (17); bibliographies (15).

410 <

Einaudi, L. and H. Goldhamer.

An Annotated Bibliography of Latin American Military Journals.
Santa Monica, Calif.: RAND Corporation (RAND Report RM-4890-
RC), December, 1965. 89 pp.

411   HN51.J6,v.21(3)

Pilisuk, Marc and Thomas Hayden.

References in "Is there a military industrial complex which
prevents peace? Consensus and countervailing power in
pluralistic systems."
Journal of Social Issues, 21, 3 (July, 1965): 113-117.

   106 items, 1948-1965. English.

   Books, articles, and governmental reports on political,
   economic, and military elites, the formulation of U.S. public
   policy, armament and disarmament, and political, social, and
   economic theory.

Militarism and the Military

412 <   U21.5.R5

Riddleberger, Peter B.

Military Roles in Developing Countries: An inventory of past
research and analysis.
Washington, D.C.: American University (Special Operations
Research Office, Task Role Research Memorandum 65-2), 1965.
182 pp.

413 <

Ziegler, Rolf.

"Ausgewählte Literatur zur Militärsoziologie [Selected
literature on military sociology]."
In Koenig, René et al. (eds.), Beiträge zur Militärsoziologie
[Contributions to Military Sociology].
Cologne/Opladen: West Deutscher Verlag, 1968. pp. 327-357.

414 <   E181.M55,v.33

Birkos, Alexander S.

"A bibliographical introduction to foreign military
periodicals."
Military Affairs, 33 (December, 1969): 393-396.

415 <

Bergatt, B.

"Ausgewählte neuere Literatur zum Militär in Afrika [Selected
recent literature on the military in Africa]."
Afrika Spectrum, 1 (1971): 78-88.

416 <

Hausrath, Alfred Hartmann.

[Bibliography].
In his Venture Simulation in War, Business, and Politics.
New York: McGraw-Hill, 1971. pp. 321-375.

Militarism and the Military

417 <

Larson, Arthur D. (comp.).

Civil-Military Relations and Militarism: A classified
bibliography covering the United States and other nations of
the world.
Manhattan: Kansas State University Library (Bibliography
Series, No. 9), 1971. 113 pp.

418   HC110.D4M42

Melman, Seymour (ed.).

Bibliography.
In his The War Economy of the United States: Readings on
military industry and economy.
New York: St. Martin's Press, 1971. pp. 243-244.

   43 items, 1962-1971. English. A few items have brief
   descriptive annotations; introduction (1 paragraph).

   Bibliographies (5), the scale of military economy (3), the
   military industrial firm (12), economic consequences of
   military industry (6), conversion from military to civilian
   economy (17).

419   HN65.S7

Stackhouse, Max L.

Selected bibliography.
In his The Ethics of Necropolis: An essay on the military-
industrial complex and the quest for a just peace.
Boston: Beacon Press, 1971. pp. 138-145.

   118 items, 1899-1970. English.

   Books and journal articles on the military-industrial
   complex, U.S. defense and foreign policy, militarism, and
   the moral aspects of war.

420   U21.2.C53

Clarke, Robin.

Sources.

Militarism and the Military

In his The Science of War and Peace.
New York/St. Louis/etc.: McGraw-Hill, 1972. pp. 320-335.

   335 items, 1842-1970. English; also German (1).

   Books, articles, pamphlets, reports, and speeches arranged by
   chapters on the war explosion (8), the nuclear future (35),
   missiles and the moon (44), military control of the oceans
   (41), the environment wreckers (38), science in the warfare
   state (38), psychology of aggression (31), the natural
   history of war (40), the science of conflict (31), revolution
   and change (20), the technology explosion (9).

421 <

Featherstone, Donald F.

[Bibliography].
In his War Games through the Ages, 3000 B.C. to 1500 A.D.
London: S. Paul, September, 1972. pp. 278-286.

422 <   U21.5.L35

Lang, Kurt.

Military Institutions and the Sociology of War: A review of the
literature with annotated bibliography.
Beverly Hills, Calif.: Sage, 1972. 337 pp.

423   Z7165.U5M35

Meeker, Thomas A. (comp.).

The Military-Industrial Complex: A source guide to the issues
of defense spending and policy control.
Los Angeles: California State University at Los Angeles, Center
for the Study of Armament and Disarmament (Political Issues
Series/Classroom Study Series, Vol. 2, No. 2), 1973. 23 pp.

   257 items, 1866-1973. English. Introduction (2 pp.); each
   section and subsection also has an introductory paragraph;
   table of contents.

   Journal and magazine articles, books, and congressional
   hearings on the current issue of the military-industrial
   complex (83), arms trade (6), the "complex" in historical
   perspective (59), civil-military relations (23), defense
   economics (54), and militarism (28); unpublished
   dissertations (4).

Militarism and the Military

424

Mantell, David Mark and Marc Pilisuk (eds.).

References [several lists by various authors].
In their special issue, Soldiers in and after Vietnam.
Journal of Social Issues, 31, 4 (Fall, 1975): 1-195.

425

Anderson, Martin and Valerie Bloom (comps. and eds.).

Conscription: A select and annotated bibliography.
Stanford: Stanford University, Hoover Institution Press, 1976.
xvii + 453 pp.

   1385 items 1819-1975 (most items published after 1900).
   English. All items have brief to abstract-length descriptive
   annotations; preface (2 pp.); introduction (6 pp.); author
   index; title index.

   Books, unpublished manuscripts, articles, pamphlets,
   reprints, speeches, government documents, and bibliographies
   on the historical development of conscription, the legal,
   philosophical, economic, and racial aspects of conscription,
   all-volunteer armed force, the selective service system,
   national guard and reserves, military training, and universal
   national service. Special emphasis is given to the United
   States, but there are two separate chapters on England and
   other foreign countries.

426 <

Hart, Basil Liddell and Adrian Liddell Hart (eds.).

[Bibliography].
In their The Sword and the Pen: Selections from the world´s
greatest military writings.
New York: Crowell, 1976. pp. 275-280.

Religion, Peace, and War

427   IU: 341G91pu,no.4

Society of Friends (London), Literature Committee.

Bibliography.
In [Grotius Society], Quakers and Peace, with an introduction
and notes by G.W. Knowles.
London: Sweet and Maxwell (The Grotius Society Publications,
Texts for Students of International Relations, No. 4), 1927.
pp. 15-18.

  57 items, 1907-1927. English.

  Books and pamphlets on the history of Quakerism (17),
  Quakerism in theory and practice (29), and biographies of
  Quakers (11).

428 <

Matthews, M[ary] Alice (comp.).

War and Religion.
Washington, D.C.: Carnegie Endowment for International Peace,
Library (Reading List No. 14), 1933 (rev. ed.). 7 pp.
First edition, May 11, 1927. (mimeo).

429 <   BR115.W2R37

Regout, Robert [Hubert Willem].

Notice bibliographique.
In La Doctrine de la Guerre Juste, de Saint Augustin à Nos
Jours [The Just War Doctrine from St. Augustine to Our Times]:
D´après les théologiens et les canonistes catholiques
[According to Catholic theologians and canonists].
Paris: A. Pedone, 1935.

Religion, Peace, and War

430 <

[Women´s International League for Peace and Freedom].

World Citizenship and the Religious Program: A bibliography of
suggested material.
Philadelphia: Women´s International League for Peace and
Freedom, 1937.

431   BX865.A4,1938

La Brière, Yves de and P. M. Colbach (trans. and eds.).

Bibliographie.
In their La Patrie et la Paix [The Fatherland and Peace]:
Textes pontificaux, traduits et commentés [Pontifical texts,
translated and annotated].
Paris: Desclée de Brouwer (Cathedra Petri), 1938. pp. [447]-
449.

   39 items, 1916-1937. French; also Latin (1).

   Works on nationalism and patriotism (7), the Catholic Church
   and peace (8), war (10), and the Catholic Church and
   international organization (14).

432   BR115.W2S3

Scott-Craig, T[homas] S[tevenson] K[irkpatrick].

Bibliography.
In his Christian Attitudes to War and Peace: A study of the
four main types.
London/Edinburgh: Oliver and Boyd, 1938. pp. 175-178.

   49 items, 1883-1937. English, German; also French (3), Latin
   (1).

   Books on the theological underpinnings of the Christian
   church´s positions on peace and war, the church´s relation to
   the state, and pacifism.

433   BV630.W3

Wallace, James.

Bibliography [2 lists].

Religion, Peace, and War

In his Fundamentals of Christian Statesmanship: A study of the
Bible from the standpoint of politics and the state.
New York/London/Edinburgh: Fleming H. Revell, 1939. pp. 306-
307, 347-348.

   66 items, 1903-1938. English.

   Books on Christian ethics and the relationship between
   Christianity and the state, with special reference to peace
   and war.

434   HN51.S45,v.6

Bainton, Roland H. and Robert L. Calhoun.

Suggested reading in "Christian conscience and the state."
Social Action, 6, 8 (October 15, 1940): 42.

   11 items, 1932-1940. English. Some items have brief
   descriptive and/or critical annotations.

435 <

Bell, G. K. A.

Bibliography.
In his Christianity and World Order.
Harmondsworth, England: Penguin Books, 1940. pp. 155-156.

436   U21.R87,1940

Ryan, John K[enneth].

Bibliography.
In his Modern War and Basic Ethics.
Milwaukee: Bruce, 1940. pp. 134-140.
First edition published as Ph.D. dissertation, Washington,
D.C.: Catholic University of America, 1933.

   145 items, 1582-1940. English; also Latin, French, German.

   The scholastic doctrine (55); on modern war (74); reviews
   (16).

Religion, Peace, and War

437 <

Terlin, Rose.

The Christian Basis of a New Society [a study outline].
Washington, D.C.: World´s Young Women´s Christian Association,
1942.

438   BX850.A48

Koenig, Harry C. (ed.).

Bibliography.
In his Principles for Peace: Selections from papal documents,
Leo XIII to Pius XII, with preface by Samuel A. Stritch.
Washington, D.C.: National Catholic Welfare Conference, 1943.
pp. 821-827.

   114 items, 1844-1943. English, Latin; also French (7),
   Italian (5), German (2), Spanish (1).

   Official documents, books, periodicals, and newspapers on the
   Catholic Church´s appeals for peace, the history of the
   church and the papacy, and the church in international
   affairs.

439   BR115.P4Y6,1943

Yoder, Edward, in collaboration with Jesse W. Hoover and
Harold S. Bender.

"A short bibliography on nonresistance."
In their Must Christians Fight: A scriptural inquiry.
Akron, Pa.: Mennonite Central Committee, 1943 (2nd ed.).
[p. 69.]

   21 items, 1920-1943. English; also German (1).

   Books and pamphlets on the Mennonites´ views on
   noncooperation, nonresistance, peace principles, and war
   and the Christian conscience.

440   BR115.W2N35

MacArthur, Kathleen W.

Bibliography in "The Christian and war."

Religion, Peace, and War

In Limbert, Paul et al., Christians Face War.
New York: Association Press, for the National Intercollegiate
Christian Council, 1944. pp. 23-24.

    32 items, 1925-1944. English.

    Books (10), pamphlets (6), and articles (16) on Christianity,
    Christian ethics and war, and pacifism.

441   BR115.P4N6,1944

Nolde, O[tto] Frederick.

References.
In his Christian World Action: The Christian citizen builds for
tomorrow.
Philadelphia: Muhlenberg Press, March, 1944 (rev. ed.). pp.
137-140.
First edition, 1942. Second edition, September, 1943, pp. 124-
127.

    37 items, 1925-1944. English. A few items have brief
    descriptive annotations.

    Books and pamphlets on the role of the Christian church in
    effecting peace and on the social, political, and economic
    aspects of peace from a Christian perspective.

442   BR115.W2N35

Wygal, Winnifred and Winburn T. Thomas.

Bibliography in "The power of nonviolent good will."
In Limbert, Paul et al., Christians Face War.
New York: Association Press, for the National Intercollegiate
Christian Council, 1944. p. 43.

    19 items, 1899-1944. English.

    Books, articles, and pamphlets on the relationship between
    Christianity and war in the classical and early Christian
    period (7), Middle Ages (2), modern period (10).

Religion, Peace, and War

443   HN51.S45,v.11

Bainton, Roland H.

Literature in "The churches and war: Historic attitudes toward
Christian participation."
Social Action, 11, 1 (January 15, 1945): 70-71.

   61 items, 1888-1944. English; also German, French (8). Some
   items have brief descriptive annotations.

   Surveys (2), general works (7), Hebrew and classical (4), New
   Testament (2), early church (6), Christian Roman Empire (5),
   Middle Ages (9), Renaissance and Reformation (7), modern
   peace churches (4), North American wars (7), American peace
   movement (3), conscience (1), pacifism and nonpacifism (4).

444   Z6207.W81L3

Landis, Benson Y[oung] and Inez M. Cavert (comps.).

Church Literature on Post-war Planning: Selected references.
New York: Inter-Council Committee on Postwar Planning, June,
1945. 31 pp.

   286 items, 1939-1945. English. Most items have brief
   descriptive annotations; introduction (1 p.).

   Church literature (200), supplementary materials (86) on
   Catholic and Protestant associations for international peace,
   peace proposals, world society, messages of peace from the
   Pope, world order, social welfare programs, the role of the
   churches in reconstruction, demobilization, rehabilitation of
   veterans, and various commissions and organizations studying
   peace.

445   BX961.P4N4

Neill, Thomas P[atrick].

A note on books; Footnotes.
In his Weapons for Peace.
Milwaukee: Bruce, 1945. pp. 221-224, 225-229.

   193 items, 1768-1944. English; also Latin, German, French
   (5), Italian (2). Bibliographic essay critically discusses
   some items; footnotes arranged by chapter, with brief
   critical comments on a few items.

Religion, Peace, and War

   Books, papal encyclicals, periodicals, pamphlets, articles,
   and other materials on European social and political history,
   Catholic views on social and political problems, the
   principles and conditions of peace, political and democratic
   theory, National Socialism and fascism, peace theory, and
   related topics.

446 <

Lasserre, Jean.

Bibliography.
In his La Guerre et l'Evangile [War and the Gospel], preface by
Henri Roser.
Paris: La Réconciliation, 1953. pp. 249-253.

447   U22.N3

Brown, Noel J.

"The moral problem of modern warfare: A bibliography."
In Nagle, William J. (ed.), Morality and Modern Warfare: The
state of the question.
Baltimore: Helicon Press, 1960. pp. 151-168.

   421 items, 1939-1960. English; also German, French, Spanish
   (4), Italian (3), Portuguese (1). Introduction (1 paragraph).

   Periodical articles (204), books and pamphlets (159) and
   select continental publications (58) on nuclear warfare,
   control of the atomic bomb, nuclear energy and its control,
   arms control, deterrence, the moral aspects of war, the
   prevention of war, attitudes toward war, the notion of just
   war, the relationship between Christianity and war and peace,
   science and war, and pacifism.

448   JX4512.C6

Coste, René.

Bibliographie.
In his Le Problème du Droit de Guerre dans la Pensée de Pie XII
[The Problem of the Law of War in the Thought of Pius XII].
Paris: Aubier (Théologie: Etudes Publiées sous la direction de
la Faculté de Théologie S.J. de Lyon-Fourvière, 51), 1962. pp.
508-517.

   226 items, 1858-1961. French; also Italian, English (9),
   German (9), Latin (9), Spanish (3).

Religion, Peace, and War

Books, articles, and official documents on international law,
the Catholic Church's positions on war and peace, concepts of
war, just war, moral aspects of war, conscientious objection,
pacifism, National Socialism, war crimes, legal aspects of
war, and the history of war.

449   B765.T54T6

Tooke, Joan D.

Bibliography.
In her The Just War in Aquinas and Grotius, with a foreword by
W. L. Mascall.
London: S.P.C.K. [Society for Promoting Christian Knowledge],
1965. pp. 315-321.

169 items, 1869-1964. English; also French (8), German (5),
Latin (2), Italian (1).

Books (129) and pamphlets (40) on Christian views on war and
peace, political theory, peace theory, international law,
European history, the Middle Ages, the moral aspects of war,
pacifism, and the philosophy of peace.

450 <

Hormann, Karl.

Bibliography.
In his Peace and Modern War in the Judgment of the Church,
translated by Caroline Hemesath.
Westminster, Md.: Newman Press, 1966.

451   BT736.4.E44

Emeis, Dieter.

Kleiner Literaturhinweis; Quellenverzeichnis [Short list of
suggested readings; list of sources].
In his Zum Frieden Erziehen [Educate for Peace]: Ein
Arbeitsbuch [A workbook].
Munich: J. Pfeiffer (Pfeiffer-Werkbücher, No. 71), 1968. pp.
266-267, 267-271.

49 items, 1951-1968. German.

List of sources credited, including publishers,
organizations, and individuals; also a brief list of
additional references. The two lists together contain books,

Religion, Peace, and War

pamphlets, articles, prayers, documents, and bibliographies
concerning peace, peace education, peace theory and theology,
religion and war, and peace research.

452   HJ2305.K3

Kaufman, Donald D.

Bibliography.
In his What Belongs to Caesar? A discussion on the Christian's
response to payment of war taxes, with an introduction by
Howard H. Charles.
Scottsdale, Pa.: Herald Press, 1969. pp. 105-122.

  355 items, 1888-1969. English.

  Books and pamphlets (196) and periodical articles (159) on
  Christian attitudes toward war, the relationship between the
  church and the state, the Mennonites and their antiwar
  activities, pacifism, civil disobedience, and the tax
  resistance movement and its opponents.

453   Z7853.093

Overbeeke, Addy P. van (comp.).

Gereformeerden over het oorlogsvraagstuk [Calvinists on the
Problem of War]: Bibliografisch overzicht van het denken van
Gereformeerden over de problemen van oorlog en vrede in de
jaren 1953-1968 [Bibliographic survey of Calvinist thought on
problems of war and peace in the years 1953-1968]. 51 pp.
Amsterdam: [Addy P. van Overbeeke], 1969. (mimeo).

  302 items, 1953-1968. Dutch; also English (2). Introduction
  (7 pp.); table of contents; author index.

  Publications of the General Synod of the Reformed Church in
  the Netherlands (12), independent Calvinist publications
  (14), discussion in Calvinist circles (125), contributions of
  Calvinist writers to the discussion in other circles (116),
  list of periodicals in which the articles appear (35).

454   BT736.2.P63

Potter, Ralph B.

Notes; Bibliographical essay.

Religion, Peace, and War

In his War and Moral Discourse.
Richmond, Va.: John Knox Press, 1969. pp. 79-85, 87-123.

   166 items, 1853-1968. English. Most items are discussed in
   text.

   Notes list books and articles dealing with Christianity and
   war, ethics, international law (41); bibliographical essay
   deals with books and articles on Christian attitudes toward
   war, war crimes, international law, social teachings of the
   Christian churches, pacifism, peacemaking, peace missions,
   Christian faith and nuclear warfare, moral aspects of war
   (125).

455   BS680.P4H37

Harris, Douglas J[ames].

Bibliography.
In his Shalom! The biblical concept of peace.
Grand Rapids, Mich.: Baker Book House, 1970. pp. 65-73.

   164 items, 1660-1967. English; also German (6), Latin (2),
   Dutch (1).

   Books, articles, and pamphlets on Jewish and Christian
   theology and ethics, the relationship between religion and
   attitudes toward war and peace, pacifism, moral and spiritual
   bases for peace, and various concepts of peace.

456 <

Poppe, K. H., et al.

[Bibliography (several lists)].
In Deschner, Karlheinz (ed.), Kirche und Krieg [Church and
War]: Der christliche Weg zum ewigen Leben [The Christian way
to eternal life].
Stuttgart: Gunther, 1970.

457 <

Hammer, Karl.

[Bibliography].
In his Deutsche Kriegstheologie [German war theology] (1870-
1918).
Munich: Kösel, 1971. pp. 346-369.

Religion, Peace, and War

458   BT736.2.M375

Marrin, Albert (ed.).

Suggested additional readings.
In his War and the Christian Conscience: From Augustine to
Martin Luther King, Jr.
Chicago: Henry Regnery, 1971. pp. 335-342.

   83 items, 1915-1968. English. Many items have brief
   descriptive and/or critical annotations; introduction (1
   paragraph).

   General books on war, the state, and religion (24), pacifism
   and peace movements (16), sectarian Christianity and the
   social gospel movement (14), conscientious objection and the
   draft (4), warfare since 1945 (16), Vietnam War (6);
   periodicals (3).

459

Russell, Elbert W.

References.
In his Christianity and Militarism.
Peace Research Reviews 4, 3 (November, 1971): 70-77.

460   Z7845.1.S95

Swinne, Axel Hilmar (comp.).

Bibliographia Irenica, 1500-1970: Internationale Bibliographie
zur Friedenswissenschaft; kirchliche und politische Einigungs-
und Friedensbestrebungen, Oekumene und Völkerverständigung
[International bibliography of peace studies; religious and
political efforts for unity and peace, ecumenicism, and
international understanding], mit faksimiles [with facsimiles].
Hildesheim: Gerstenberg (Studia Irenica, No. 10), 1977. xxvi +
319 pp.

   2061 items, 1500-1970.

Women, Peace, and War

461 <

Russell Sage Foundation.

[Bibliography].
In its Women in Industry in War Time.
[Russell Sage Foundation] Library Bulletin, No. 26 (December, 1917).

462 <

Johnson, Ethel M.

[Bibliography] in "Women: War time occupations and employment."
Special Libraries, 9 (January-February, 1918).

463   Z6207.E8U45

Nims, Marion R.

Woman in the War: A bibliography, with a foreword by Ida M. Tarbell.
Washington, D.C.: [U.S.] Government Printing Office, 1918.
77 pp.

   1190 items, 1915-1918 (four earlier citations, one dated
   1866). English; also French, German (9), Italian (1). Some
   items have brief descriptive annotations; foreword (1 p.);
   table of contents.

   Books, pamphlets, and periodical articles on the conditions,
   activities, and needs of American and European women during
   World War I. This was prepared for the Woman's Committee of
   the Council for National Defense in the U.S. and focuses
   primarily on economic issues.

Women, Peace, and War

464   Z6464.A1C3,no.9

Matthews, M[ary] Alice (comp.).

Women in Peace Work.
Washington, D.C.: Carnegie Endowment for International Peace,
Library (Brief Reference List No. 9), April 10, 1937. 8 pp.
(mimeo).

   113 items, 1845-1937. English; also French (5), German (1).
   Some items have brief descriptive annotations.

   Women's activity in the peace movement, influence on national
   policies, disarmament efforts.

465   H31.J6,ser.57,no.3

Degen, Marie Louise.

Bibliography.
In her The History of the Woman's Peace Party.
Baltimore: Johns Hopkins Press (Johns Hopkins University
Studies in Historical and Political Science, Series 57, No. 3),
1939. pp. 253-256.

   87 items, 1904-1939. English.

   Manuscript collection (1), government publications (2),
   official pamphlets and reports of the Woman's Peace Party
   (22), pamphlets and reports issued by other organizations
   (3), autobiographies and memoirs (11), special works and
   biographies (15), periodical articles (28), newspapers (5).

466   DLC-DB

Hellman, Florence S. (comp.).

Women's Part in World War II: A list of references.
Washington, D.C.: Library of Congress, Division of
Bibliography, May 19, 1942. 84 pp. (mimeo).

   748 items, 1936-1942. English; also German, French (6),
   Italian (4), Spanish (1). Some items have brief descriptive
   annotations; table of contents; subject/author index.

   General works on women and war (20), women's wartime
   activities in the U.S. (270), Great Britain (240), and other
   European, Asian, and American countries (218).

Women, Peace, and War

467   JX1952.P35

Cohen, J[ohn].

References in "Women in peace and war."
In Pear, Tom Hatherly (ed.), Psychological Factors of Peace and
War.
London/New York: Hutchinson/Philosophical Library, 1950.
pp. 109-110.
Reprinted, Freeport, New York: Books for Libraries Press (Essay
Index Reprint Series), 1971.

   22 items, 1901-1948. English.

   Books and journal articles including anthropological,
   psychological, historical, and sociological studies of women
   in society, government, and war.

468   HQ1121.B36

Beard, Mary R[itter].

An illustrative bibliography.
In her Woman as Force in History: A study in traditions and
realities.
New York/London: Collier Books/Collier-Macmillan, 1962. pp.
341-369.
Original hardcover edition, New York: Macmillan, 1946.

   469 items, 1539-1945. English; also French, German, Latin
   (5), Italian (1). Some items have brief descriptive
   annotations; introduction (2 pp.), introductory paragraphs in
   some sections.

   General works (40), autobiographies, diaries, journals (20),
   art (8), business (15), economy (26), education (16),
   government and politics (71), law (13), letters (23),
   medieval affairs (4), medicine and nursing (7), monasticism
   (3), novels (16), peace (14), philosophy (22), pioneers as
   migrants (6), primitives (21), religion (42), the Renaissance
   (25), revolutionists (17), salons (17), science (10), war
   (33).

469   MiU: HQ1627.H62

Heymann, Lida Gustava, in collaboration with Anita Augspurg.

Literaturhinweise.

Women, Peace, and War

In their Erlebtes-Erschautes [Lived and Seen]: Deutsche
Frauen Kämpfen für Freiheit, Recht, und Frieden, 1850-1940
[German women struggle for freedom, justice, and peace, 1850-
1940], edited by Margit Twellmann.
Meisenheim am Glan: Anton Hain, 1972. p. 311.

   12 items, 1895-1933. German.

   Books and journals on the women´s movement, women and
   politics, and the Women´s International League for Peace and
   Freedom.

470   HQ1154.B7

Boulding, Elise.

Bibliography.
In her Women in the Twentieth Century World.
New York, etc.: John Wiley and Sons, Halsted Press Division,
for Sage Publications, 1977. pp. 245-252.

   170 items, 1893-1976. English; also Norwegian (1), German
   (1), Dutch (1), French (1).

   Books, pamphlets, articles, papers, and reports on women´s
   history; peasant societies, agriculture, and economic
   development; and women in relation to these topics.

471

Kusnerz, Peggy Ann (comp.).

"The role of women in conflict and peace: A bibliography."
In McGuigan, Dorothy G. (ed.), The Role of Women in Conflict
and Peace.
Ann Arbor: University of Michigan, Center for Continuing
Education of Women, 1977. pp. 87-91.

   64 items, 1917-1976. English; also French (1).

   Works by and about women, war, aggression, peace, and
   nonviolence.

Women, Peace, and War

472   D810.W7R8

Rupp, Leila J.

Selected bibliography.
In her Mobilizing Women for War: German and American
propaganda, 1939-1945.
Princeton: Princeton University Press, 1978. pp. 189-237.

   736 items, 1907-1976. English, German.

   Archival sources (9); published documents, speeches,
   statistical sources (12); newspapers, periodicals (21);
   books, articles, pamphlets, dissertations (504); secondary
   sources (190).

473   HQ1236.W65,1979

Berkin, Carol R. and Clara M. Lovett (eds.).

Annotated bibliography.
In their Women, War, and Revolution.
New York/London: Holmes and Meier, 1980. pp. 285-297.

   191 items, 1848-1979. English; also French (8). Some items
   have brief to medium-length descriptive and/or critical
   annotations; introduction (1 p.).

   Bibliographic guides (12); general works (20); books,
   articles, and pamphlets on Asia and Australia (17); Europe
   (36); Latin America (11); United States and Canada: American
   revolution (31), Civil War (11), World War I (20), World War
   II (33).

474   HQ1236.W65,1979

Rupp, Leila J.

Suggestions for further reading in "´I don´t call that
Volksgemeinschaft´: Women, class, and war in Nazi Germany."
In Berkin, Carol R. and Clara M. Lovett (eds.), Women, War, and
Revolution.
New York/London: Holmes and Meier, 1980. p. 53.

   Brief bibliographic essay on women in Nazi Germany.

Women, Peace, and War

475   HQ1236.W65,1979

Skold, Karen Beck.

Suggestions for further reading in "The job he left behind:
American women in the shipyards during World War II."
In Berkin, Carol R. and Clara M. Lovett (eds.), Women, War, and
Revolution.
New York/London: Holmes and Meier, 1980. pp. 73-75.

   14 items, 1972-1979. English. All items have abstract-
   length descriptive and critical annotations.

   Books and articles on women and the economy during and after
   World War II.

476   HQ1236.W65,1979

Steinson, Barbara J.

Suggestions for further reading in "´The mother half of
humanity´: American women in the peace and preparedness
movements in World War I."
In Berkin, Carol R. and Clara M. Lovett (eds.), Women, War, and
Revolution.
New York/London: Holmes and Meier, 1980. pp. 281-284.

   Bibliographic essay on women and the peace movement in World
   War I.

Social Movements and Other Political Topics

477   Z7161.M13

McCulloch, J[ohn] R[amsay].

The Literature of Political Economy: A classified catalogue of
select publications in the different departments of that
science, with historical, critical, and biographical notices.
London: Longman, Brown, Green, and Longmans, 1845. xv + 407 pp.
Reprinted, London: London School of Economics and Political
Science (Series of Reprints of Scarce Works on Political
Economy, No. 5), 1938.

478   Z6466.Z9W83,v.1

Dominian, Leon.

Selected bibliography in "The nationality map of Europe."
A League of Nations, 1, 2 (December, 1917): 82-93.

   183 items, 1860-1917 (one item published in 1816). English,
   French; also Italian, German, Spanish (4), Rumanian (2), Dutch
   (1), Eastern European languages. All items have brief
   descriptive and/or critical annotations.

   Books, articles, and maps relating to European ethnic,
   national, and linguistic groupings and problems.

479   Z7164.I8B7

[Boston Public Library].

Problems of Peace, Racial and Territorial: Selected references
to recent books and magazines in the Public Library of the City
of Boston.
Boston: Trustees [of the Boston Public Library] (Brief Reading
Lists, No. 8), January, 1919. 36 pp.

   363 items, 1841-1918. English, French, German; also Italian,
   Portuguese (1), Lithuanian (1). A few items have brief
   descriptive annotations; subject index.

   General (32), Northern Europe (31), Eastern Europe (58),
   Western Europe (53), the Balkans (35), Near East (56), Jews
   (10), colonies (88).

Social Movements and Other Political Topics

480 <

[Carnegie Endowment for International Peace, Library].

German Political Theory.
Washington, D.C.: Carnegie Endowment for International Peace,
Library (Miscellaneous Reading List No. 13), 1920. (mimeo).

481   H69.W6,1923

Wilson, Justina Leavitt and Julia E. Johnsen (comps.).

"Modern social movements."
In their Questions of the Hour: Social, economic, industrial;
study outlines.
New York: H. W. Wilson (The Reference Shelf, Vol. 1, No. 9),
April, 1923 (2nd ed., rev. and enl.). pp. 28-29.

   25 items (no dates given). English.

   Cooperative movement (3), Labor party (3), syndicalism (4),
   anarchism (2), Bolshevism (3), co-partnership (2), national
   industrial councils (3), guild socialism (2), Plumb Plan (3).

482 <   HD9560.5.L4,1924

L´Espagnol de la Tramerye, Pierre.

Bibliography.
In his The World Struggle for Oil, translated from the French
by C. Leonard Leese.
New York: Alfred A. Knopf, 1924. pp. 251-253.

483   JX1908.U52,v.8,no.1

Buell, Raymond Leslie.

"Problems of the pacific: A brief bibliography (prepared for the
American Group of the Institute of Pacific Relations)."
World Peace Foundation Pamphlets, 8, 1 (1925): 1-34.

   132 items, 1898-1925. English. Most items have brief
   descriptive and/or critical annotations; introduction (1 p.).

   Books, handbooks, and official publications on peoples of the
   Pacific (43), political relations of the countries of the
   Pacific (15), problems of imperialism in the Pacific (23),
   commercial and industrial problems of the Pacific (7),

Social Movements and Other Political Topics

problems of population and emigration (8), treatment of
Orientals in western countries (8), interracial cooperation
(13), religions and cultural contacts in the Pacific (9),
naval and strategic problems of the Pacific (6).

484   H69.J6,1927

Johnsen, Julia E. (comp.).

"Modern social movements."
In her Questions of the Hour.
New York: H. W. Wilson (The Reference Shelf, Vol. 4, No. 10),
April, 1927 [3rd ed.]. pp. 48-49.

20 items, 1922-1925 (most items undated). English.

Socialism (4), Bolshevism (4) syndicalism (6), guild
socialism (3), anarchism (3). Items differ substantially from
items listed in the second edition (No. 481, above).

485   Z1009.N27,no.38

[Independent Labour Party Literature Department (comp.)].

Socialism: A selected list of books obtainable from the
Independent Labour Party Literature Department, 14, Great
George St., Westminster, London, S.W.1, or any bookseller.
London: National Book Council (Book List No. 38), May, 1929
(3rd ed.). 2 pp.
First edition appeared June, 1926.

64 items, 1889-1929 (most items undated). English.

British expositions of socialist theory (17), Marxism (6),
history (6), reports (3), biography (14), socialistic novels
(5), municipal socialism (2), state control and trading (6),
antisocialism (5).

486 <

[Carnegie Endowment for International Peace, Library].

Individualism and the State.
Washington, D.C.: Carnegie Endowment for International Peace,
Library (Miscellaneous Reading List No. 49), 1933. (mimeo).

Social Movements and Other Political Topics

487 <

[Carnegie Endowment for International Peace, Library].

Nationalism and Internationalism.
Washington, D.C.: Carnegie Endowment for International Peace,
Library (Miscellaneous Reading List No. 48), 1933. (mimeo).

488 <

Hodgson, J. G.

Bibliography.
In Economic Nationalism.
New York: [H. W. Wilson] (The Reference Shelf, Vol. 9, No. 1),
1933. pp. 25-44.

489   Z7164.N2P6

Pinson, Koppel S.

A Bibliographical Introduction to Nationalism, with a foreword
by Carlton J.H. Hayes.
New York: Columbia University Press, 1935. [vii + 71 pp.]

   431 items, 1882-1934. English, German; also French. All
   items have brief to abstract-length descriptive and critical
   annotations; preface (2 pp.); table of contents; author
   index.

   The entire bibliography is devoted to the study of
   nationalism and is divided into theoretical and analytical
   studies, historical and regional studies. The theoretical
   and analytic studies include books and journal articles
   dealing with the concept of nationalism (56) and the
   theoretical relationship between nationalism and psychology
   (10), race (7), religion (5), language (4), politics (11),
   economic affairs (11), socialism and communism (6), education
   and propaganda (5), national minorities and national autonomy
   (8). The historical and regional studies focus on nationalism
   in the ancient and medieval worlds (6), in various countries
   in the western world (248), in the Orient (32), and among the
   Jews (22).

Social Movements and Other Political Topics

490   Z6464.A1C3,no.8

Matthews, M[ary] Alice (comp.).

Danube Economic Union (Proposed).
Washington, D.C.: Carnegie Endowment for International Peace,
Library (Brief Reference List No. 8), August 11, 1936. 2 pp.
(mimeo).

    24 items, 1928-1935. English, French. Many items have brief
    descriptive annotations.

    Journal articles and memoranda on the economic reconstruction
    of Central and Eastern Europe and the Danubian plan for
    economic restoration.

491   Z6464.A1C3,no.7

Matthews, M[ary] Alice (comp.).

National Self-determination and Plebiscites.
Washington, D.C.: Carnegie Endowment for International Peace,
Library (Brief Reference List No. 7), August 6, 1936. 5 pp.
(mimeo).

    58 items, 1871-1935. English; also French, German (4),
    Spanish (1). Some items have brief descriptive annotations.

    Magazine and journal articles, documents, and a few books on
    national minorities, plebiscites, the conditions of peace,
    and the concept of national self-determination.

492   HD82.M33

MacKenzie, Findlay (ed.).

Bibliography.
In his Planned Society, Yesterday, Today, Tomorrow: A symposium
by 35 economists, sociologists and statesmen, with a foreword
by Lewis Mumford.
New York: Prentice-Hall, 1937. pp. 939-977.

    732 items, 1920-1937. English; also French (1).

    Books, conference papers, reports, pamphlets, and articles on
    economic and social planning between World Wars I and II,
    covering such areas as agriculture, political economy, trade,
    business, finance, industrial relations, employment, wages,
    pricing, distribution, social security, national defense,
    politics, and the nature of capitalism and socialism,

Social Movements and Other Political Topics

   particularly in the U.S., Germany, Italy, Great Britain, and
   the Soviet Union.

493 <   JC481.F55

Florinsky, Michael T.

Bibliography.
In his Fascism and National Socialism: A study of the economic
and social policies of the totalitarian state.
New York: Macmillan, 1938. pp. 277-283.

494   Z6461.C29,no.8

Matthews, M[ary] Alice (comp.).

Federalism: Select list of references on federal government,
regionalism, etc., and notable examples of federations and
unions of states.
Washington, D.C.: Carnegie Endowment for International Peace,
Library (Select Bibliographies, No. 8), March 15, 1938. 11 pp.
(mimeo).

   119 items, 1826-1937. English; also Spanish, French, German
   (4). Some items have brief descriptive annotations; table of
   contents.

   Books, articles, and official documents on federalism and
   regionalism (26), the federation of specific countries (83),
   and other unions of states (10).

495   Z6464.A1C3,no.2

Matthews, M[ary] Alice (comp.).

Interstate Compacts.
Washington, D.C.: Carnegie Endowment for International Peace,
Library (Brief Reference List No. 2), November 30, 1938 (rev.
ed.). 8 pp. (mimeo).
First edition, October 17, 1934, 3 pp.; earlier revised edition,
September 20, 1935, 4 pp.; supplement to revised edition,
February 16, 1938, 2 pp.

   102 items, 1909-1938. English. A few items have brief
   descriptive annotations.

   Articles, reports, and official documents on interstate
   compacts in the U.S. concerning transportation, labor,
   industries, crime, and property.

Social Movements and Other Political Topics

496   HB75.S5

Silberner, Edmund.

Bibliographie.
In his La Guerre dans la Pensée Economique du XVIe au XVIIIe
Siècle [War in Economic Thought from the 16th to the 18th
Century], avec une préface par William E. Rappard.
Paris: Sirey (Etudes sur l´Histoire des Théories Economiques,
Vol. 7), 1939. pp. 271-294.
Reprinted, with a new introduction by Dennis Sherman, New York:
Garland (Library of War and Peace), 1972.

   488 items, 1516-1938. French; also English, German, Italian,
   Dutch (1). Introduction (2 pp.).

   Books and articles on eighteenth- and nineteenth-century
   international trade, commerce, political economy,
   mercantilism, usury, political theory, and peace theory.

497   Z6464.A1C3,no.17

Matthews, M[ary] Alice (comp.).

Democracy in America.
Washington, D.C.: Carnegie Endowment for International Peace,
Library (Brief Reference List No. 17), February 27, 1940. 7 pp.
(mimeo).

   90 items, 1931-1940. English. Some items have brief
   descriptive annotations.

   Books, articles, and addresses on the theory and practice of
   democracy in the U.S., competing political ideologies, the
   relationship between education and democracy, and U.S.
   history.

498   HD82.M8

Munk, Frank.

Bibliography.
In his The Economics of Force.
New York: George W. Stewart, 1940. pp. 245-249.

   66 items, 1912-1940. English.

   Books on political economy, economic planning, socialism,
   capitalism, National Socialism, fascism, political theory,
   and conditions of peace.

Social Movements and Other Political Topics

499   Z1009.N27,no.8

Co-operative Union Limited (comp.).

Co-operation: A selected list of books compiled and printed by
the Co-operative Union Limited, Holyoake House, Hanover Street,
Manchester 4.
London: National Book Council (Book List No. 8), April, 1941
(6th ed.).
First edition, Works on Cooperation, [1926], 4 pp. Third to
fifth editions, August, 1928; July, 1933; May, 1937.

   133 items, 1893-1941. English.

   Administration (16), agriculture (13), biography (9), history
   of cooperation in Britain (32), theory (27), cooperation
   abroad (21), yearbooks and reports (11), periodicals (4).

500 <

Huntington, Thomas W[aterman].

Morale in the Democracies: Dynamic documentation.
Boston: [T. W. Huntington] (Chronological Bulletin No. 1),
February 3, 1941. 5 pp.

501   JC481.N37

Neumann, Sigmund.

Bibliography.
In his Permanent Revolution: The total state in a world at war.
New York/London: Harper and Brothers, 1942. pp. 313-375.
Reprinted as Permanent Revolution: Totalitarianism in the age
of international civil war, 1965.

   1063 items, 1853-1942. English; also German, French, Italian
   (9), Spanish (1). Bibliography is partly in the form of a
   bibliographic essay, with introductions to each section and
   critical comments scattered throughout the list; organized by
   chapters.

   Books, articles, and periodicals on the history and
   development of modern dictatorships, democratic and
   dictatorial leadership, the emerging masses, the theory and
   process of revolution and social movements, the Industrial
   Revolution, the social basis of fascism, the nature of modern

Social Movements and Other Political Topics

    party systems and the one-party state, institutions and
    instruments for controlling the masses, totalitarianism,
    generational analysis, the background of World War II,
    National Socialism and the challenge to democracy.

502   IU: A900N42t

[New York Public Library, Readers´ Advisers (comps.)].

Together We Stand: A list of books on the United Nations.
New York: New York Public Library, 1942. [16 pp.].

    88 items, 1923-1942. English. All items have brief
    descriptive and/or critical annotations; introduction (1 p.).

    Books about the countries allied against the Axis in World
    War II.

503 <   HF1545.T4

Tenenbaum, Edward.

Bibliographical footnotes.
In his National Socialism vs. International Capitalism.
New Haven: Yale University Press, 1942.

504 <

Conover, Helen F.; under the direction of Florence S. Hellman.

Soviet Russia: A selected list of recent references.
Washington, D.C.: [Library of Congress, Division of
Bibliography], 1943. 85 pp.

505   H31.P7

Lasswell, Harold D[wight] and Howard H. Cummings.

Bibliography [2 lists].
In their Public Opinion in War and Peace: How Americans make up
their minds.
Washington, D.C.: National Council for the Social Studies and
National Association of Secondary-School Principals (Problems
in American Life, Unit Number 14), 1943. pp.46-50, 67-68.

    70 items, 1905-1942. English. Some items have brief
    descriptive and/or critical annotations.

Social Movements and Other Political Topics

   Books and articles on public opinion, propaganda, social
   psychology.

506

Egbert, Donald, Stow Persons, and T. D. Seymour Basset.

Socialism and American Life: Volume 2, bibliography--
descriptive and critical.
Princeton/London: Princeton University Press/Oxford University
Press, 1952. xiv + 575 pp.

507   HX545.D7

Drachkovitch, Milorad M.

Bibliographie.
In his Les Socialismes Français et Allemand et le Problème de
la Guerre, 1870-1914 [French and German Socialism and the
Problem of War, 1870-1914].
Geneva: E. Droz (Etudes d'Histoire Economique, Politique et
Sociale, 3), 1953. pp. 355-362.

   277 items, 1828-1950. French; also German, English (1).

   Books, documents, and journal articles on socialist theories,
   socialist congresses, the history of socialism, social
   democratic movements in France and Germany, international
   socialist movements, social and political history of France
   and Germany, labor movements, critiques of Marxism, and
   political theory.

508 <

Deutsch, Karl W.

An Interdisciplinary Bibliography on Nationalism, 1935-1953.
Cambridge, Mass.: Massachusetts Institute of Technology, 1956.
165 pp.

509

Dahrendorf, Ralf.

Bibliography.
In his Class and Class Conflict in Industrial Society
(translated, revised, and expanded by the author).

Social Movements and Other Political Topics

Stanford: Stanford University Press, 1959. pp. 319-328.
First published as Soziale Klassen und Klassenkonflikt in der
industriellen Gesellschaft, 1957.

510   HX653.W4

Webber, Everett.

Bibliography.
In his Escape to Utopia: The communal movement in America.
New York: Hastings House, 1959. pp. 421-435.

   209 items, 1781-1954. English. Some items have brief
   critical annotations; some sections have introductory
   paragraphs.

   Books and magazine articles on the social, economic, and
   religious backgrounds out of which communitarianism developed
   and studies of the movement as a whole.

511 <

[World Without War Council].

Select Bibliography on Civil Disobedience and the American
Democratic Tradition.
[Berkeley, Calif.]: World Without War Council, 1964. 5 pp.

512 <

Ekman, Russell.

A Bibliography on Revolution.
[Berkeley, Calif.]: World Without War Council, 1968. 11 pp.

513   U22.3.B7

Meyers, Samuel M. and Albert D. Biderman.

Bibliography.
In their Mass Behavior in Battle and Captivity: The Communist
Soldier in the Korean War, with a foreword by Morris Janowitz.
Chicago/London: University of Chicago Press, 1968. pp. 367-370.

   65 items, 1944-1965. English.

Social Movements and Other Political Topics

Books and articles on Chinese and Soviet Communism, the
Chinese Communist revolution, Chinese social and political
history, brainwashing, and Korean prisoners of war.

514 <

Cremer, Peter.

The Legitimation of Governments: An annotated bibliography.
[Berkeley, Calif.]: World Without War Council, 1969. 6 pp.

515 <   Z7164.N2D43

Deutsch, Karl W. and Richard L. Merritt.

Nationalism and National Development: An interdisciplinary
bibliography.
Cambridge, Mass.: MIT Press, 1970. 519 pp.

Creative Literature, Drama, Arts

516

Boeckel, Florence Brewer (comp.).

A list of books.
In her Across Borderlines.
Washington, D.C.: National Council for Prevention of War (Books
of Goodwill, Vol. 2), 1926. pp. 147-151.

  126 items (no dates given). English.

  Children's books depicting life on earth (2), life in
  different countries of the world (54), adventures in everyday
  life (33), modern war (12), and efforts to free the world
  from war (5); a list of courses on peace (6), addresses of
  organizations that provide materials on the problems of world
  peace (11), periodicals devoted to articles on world peace
  (3).

517   JX1953.B545

Boeckel, Florence Brewer (comp.).

Books to read.
In her Through the Gateway.
Washington, D.C.: National Council for Prevention of War (Books
of Goodwill, Vol. 1), 1926. pp. 114-118.

  125 items (no dates given). English.

  Children's books depicting life on earth (15), how people
  live in other countries of the world (55), heroes of
  peacetime (8), the quest for peace and its heroes (23);
  magazines from all around the world (4) and addresses of
  publishers of books, pamphlets, and plays of all nations
  (20).

518   PN6014.M15

McSkimmon, Mary and Carol Della Chiesa (comps.).

Suggestions for further reading.

Creative Literature, Drama, Arts

In their This Interlocking World: Compiled from the literatures
of many lands.
Boston/New York/etc.: Allyn and Bacon, 1929. pp. 242-248.

   108 items (no dates given). English.

   Books for children, mostly fictional works and biographies,
   intended to acquaint them with the world and its people.

519   Z6464.29N7

Nitchie, Elizabeth, Jane F[aulkner] Goodloe, Marion E[msley]
Hawes, and Grace L. McCann (comps.).

Pens for Ploughshares: A bibliography of creative literature
that encourages world peace.
Boston: F. W. Faxon (Useful Reference Series, No. 40), 1930.
106 pp.

   888 items, 1870-1930. German, English; also French, Russian,
   Swedish, Czech (8), other Western and Eastern European
   languages. Most items have brief to medium-length critical
   and/or descriptive annotations; foreword (6 pp.) and
   prefatory notes (1-3 pp.) for English, French, German, and
   Russian sections.

   British and American fiction (104), drama (45), poetry (60),
   personal narratives, essays, etc. (26); French fiction (84),
   drama (20), poems (18), diaries, letters, personal narratives
   (25), essays (12); Italian literature (15); Spanish
   literature (5); German fiction (158), drama (94), poetry
   (47), essays, personal narratives, diaries, letters (81);
   Dutch literature (3); Danish and Norwegian literature (11);
   Swedish literature (22); Russian fiction (25) and nonfiction
   (15); Czech literature (8); Hungarian literature (2); Polish
   literature (8).

520   HQ750.A2P3,v.6

Child Study Association of America, Children´s Book Committee
(comp.).

"Books that portray other lands sympathetically."
Parents´ Magazine, [6] (July, 1931): 61.

   18 items (no dates given). English. All items have brief
   descriptive and critical annotations.

   Children´s stories and picture books intended to promote
   international understanding.

Creative Literature, Drama, Arts

521 <

Barns, Florence E[lberta].

Bibliographies.
In her Drama as a Key to International Understanding.
Washington, D.C.: American Association of University Women,
[1934]. 26 + 3 pp.

522 <

Federal Theatre Project.

. . . Anti-war Plays, Foreign and Anglo-Jewish Lists . . .
[New York: National Service Bureau] (Publication No. 28),
October, 1937. 54 pp. (mimeo).

  Includes brief synopsis of each play.

523 <

Federal Theatre Project.

. . . Anti-war Plays, Royalty List . . .
New York: National Service Bureau (Publication No. 31),
November, 1937. 36 pp. (mimeo).

524 <

Federal Theatre Project.

. . . Anti-war Plays for Community Theatres . . .
[New York: National Service Bureau (Publication No. 32)], 1937.
87 pp. (mimeo).

  Includes brief synopsis of each play.

525   PN1880.B34

Bates, Esther Willard.

Bibliography: "Peace plays."
In her The Church Play and Its Production.
Boston: Walter H. Baker, 1938. pp. 294-300.

  57 items (no dates given). English. All items have brief
  descriptive and/or critical annotations.

Creative Literature, Drama, Arts

    Antiwar dramas, comedies, satires, fantasies, tragedies,
    melodramas, and pageants.

526   PR471.M8

Muir, Edwin.

"War books."
In his The Present Age from 1914.
London: Cresset Press (Introductions to English Literature,
Vol. 5), 1939. pp. 301-302.
Reprinted, New York: McBride, 1940.

    21 items, 1914-1937. English. Many items have brief
    critical annotations; introduction (1 paragraph).

    Poetry (5), prose (16).

527   PT405.P4

Pfeiler, William K[arl].

Bibliography.
In his War and the German Mind: The testimony of men of fiction
who fought at the front, with a foreword by George N. Shuster.
New York: Columbia University Press, 1941. pp. 323-332.

    155 items, 1915-1941. German, English; also French (1).

    List of German fiction, letters, and diaries (111) dealing
    with the background of World War II and the war experience of
    both soldiers and civilians; works (44) commenting on the
    problem of war and German war literature.

528   RC321.J7

Stone, James.

Bibliography in "War music and war psychology in the Civil War."
Journal of Abnormal and Social Psychology, 36 (October, 1941):
559-560.

    27 items, 1861-1933. English.

    Spirituals, patriotic music, drum taps, English folk songs,
    soldiers' letters and diaries, and journal articles on music
    and its relation to war.

Creative Literature, Drama, Arts

529   M1629.D7,1942

Dolph, Edward Arthur.

Bibliography.
In his "Sound Off!" Soldier songs from the Revolution to World
War II.
New York/Toronto: Farrar and Rinehart, 1942 [2nd ed.].
pp. 613-615.
First edition, 1929.

   76 items, 1798-1942 (many items undated). English. A few
   items have brief descriptive annotations; introduction
   (2 paragraphs).

   Songbooks of World War I (9), Spanish-American War (3), Civil
   War (22), Mexican War (5), War of 1812 (6), Revolutionary War
   (8), general (23).

530   PT5488.P4D3

Daniëls, Fr[anciscus Antonius Maria] (ed.).

Bij de inleiding; Bij de gedichten.
In his Het lied van den vrede [The Song of Peace]: Een bundel
gedichten voor onzen tijd [a collection of poems for our time].
Naarden: Uitgeverij "In Den Toren," [1945]. pp. 158-159,
160-163.

   112 items, 1630-1939. Dutch; also Latin (9).

   Contains about 30 references in notes to the introduction,
   and a list of 82 published sources from which the poems in
   this collection were drawn.

531   Z6464.Z9L4

[Bobovich, E. S. and M. V. Rebok (comps.)].

Khudozhestvennaia Literatura v Bor'be za Mir [Creative
Literature in the Struggle for Peace]: Rekomendatel'nii
ukazatel' literatury [List of recommended literature].
Leningrad: Publichnaia Biblioteka im. M. E. Saltykova-
Shchredina [Saltykov-Shchredin Library], 1951. 52 pp.

   248 items, 1947-1951. Russian (in Cyrillic alphabet). Most
   items have brief to medium-length descriptive annotations;
   foreword (2 pp.); table of contents; author/title index.

Creative Literature, Drama, Arts

Poems, novels, stories, plays, etc., in the struggle for
peace, grouped under several headings: the great Stalin (33),
Soviet writers (22), Soviet Army (9), work of the Soviet
people (15), friends and enemies (57), literature of people's
democratic countries (29), People's Republic of China (7),
Korean People's Democratic Republic (4), German People's
Democratic Republic (10), progressive writers of capitalistic
countries (41), anthologies (9), reviews (12).

532   PR531.L3

Langsam, G[ert] Geoffrey.

Bibliography.
In his Martial Books and Tudor Verse (Ph.D. dissertation,
Philosophy, Columbia University).
New York: Columbia University (King's Crown Press), 1951.
pp. 199-207.

196 items, 1539-1946. English; also German (2).
Introduction (1 paragraph).

Books and pamphlets on military subjects (92), plays
mentioned (29), other primary (26) and secondary sources
(49).

533   Z6464.Z9S65

[Vulcheva, Aneliya Khristova, et al. (comps.)].

Pisateli Poluchili Mezhdunarodni Nagradi za Mir [Writers Who
Have Received the International Peace Prize].
Sofia: Durzhavna Biblioteka "Vasil Kolarev," 1956. 120 pp.

Brief bio-bibliographic essay about each of 25 writers, plus
a list of works (novels, plays, poetry, essays, speeches,
etc.) by each writer and literature about the writer. In
Bulgarian.

534   PR604.B6

Blunden, Edmund [Charles].

"War poets 1914-1918: A select bibliography."
In his War Poets 1914-1918.
London: Longmans, Green, for the British Council and the
National Book League (Bibliographical Series of Supplements to
"British Book News" on Writers and Their Work, No. 100), 1958.
pp. 40-43.

Creative Literature, Drama, Arts

  Reprinted with additions to bibliography, London: Longmans,
  Green, 1964.

    61 items, 1912-1956. English. Introductory note (1
    paragraph).

    Lists works of 19 poets, including Rupert Brooke, Siegfried
    Sassoon, Wilfred Owen, and others.

  535   ML3551.H35

  Heaps, Willard A[llison] and Porter W[arrington] Heaps.

  Bibliography.
  In their The Singing Sixties: The spirit of Civil War days
  drawn from the music of the times.
  Norman: University of Oklahoma Press, 1960. pp. 399-401.

    31 items, 1863-1957. English. Introduction (1 paragraph).

    Songbooks (13) and poems and songs (18) containing war songs
    and patriotic poems from the sixteenth to the twentieth
    century.

  536   PS221.C63

  Cooperman, Stanley.

  Selected bibliography.
  In his World War I and the American Novel.
  Baltimore: Johns Hopkins Press, 1967. pp. 243-251.

    321 items, 1914-1966. English.

    Creative literature written in the period of World War I,
    literary criticism of war literature, and general works on
    war and U.S. political and social history.

  537   PN6110.W28R6,1967

  Roscher, Achim (ed.).

  Verzeichnis der Dichter und Quellennachweis [List of poets and
  sources].
  In his Tränen und Rosen [Tears and Roses]: Krieg und Frieden in
  Gedichten aus fünf Jahrtausenden [War and peace in poems from
  five millennia].

Creative Literature, Drama, Arts

Berlin: Verlag der Nation, 1967 (2nd rev. and enl. ed.).
pp. 513-530.

326 items, 1817-1967. German.

Works of poetry and lyrics, listed by poet´s name, from
ancient Sumer, China, and Greece to the modern world. Poetry
of many nations, almost all under German titles, in editions
published in Germany. List of illustrations: antiwar art by
Durer, Picasso, Kollwitz, and others.

538 <   U21.2.D58

Dougall, Lucy.

The War/Peace Film Guide.
Berkeley, Calif.: Inter-Council Publications Committee, for the
World Without War Council of Greater Seattle, 1970. [50 pp.]

539

Roemer, Kenneth M.

"American utopian literature (1888-1900): An annotated
bibliography."
American Literary Realism, 4, 3 (Summer, 1971): 227-254.

540   ML128.W2D5

Denisoff, R. Serge.

Songs of Protest, War and Peace: A bibliography and
discography.
Santa Barbara, Calif./Oxford: ABC-Clio (War/Peace Bibliography
Series, [No. 1]), 1973 (rev. ed.). xvi + 70 pp.
First published as American Protest Songs of War and Peace: A
selected bibliography and discography, Los Angeles: California
State College (Center for the Study of Armament and
Disarmament, Bibliography Series, No. 1), 1970, 15 pp.
(offset).

1187 items, 1915-1970. English. Introduction (7 pp.); table
of contents; subject/author index.

Books (154) and periodical articles (390) analyzing songs of
protest, war, and peace, songbooks (72), selected propaganda
songs in Communist Party publications from 1932 to 1949 (75),
songs of war and peace from 1950 to 1964 (68), selected songs
of war and peace from 1962 to 1972 (137), selected

Creative Literature, Drama, Arts

    discography of American protest songs (136), selected
    discography of patriotic country and western songs (63),
    country music and patriotic songs (43), and literature on the
    radical right's attack on protest songs (49).

541 <

Aichinger, Peter.

[Bibliography].
In his American Soldier in Fiction: A history of attitudes
toward warfare and the military establishment.
Ames: Iowa State University Press, 1975. pp. 117-118, 131-138.

542 <

Smith, Julian.

[Bibliography].
In his Looking Away: Hollywood and Vietnam.
New York: Scribner's, 1975. pp. 223-228.

543 <

Jones, Peter G.

[Bibliographies].
In his War and the Novelist: Appraising the American war novel,
with a foreword by M. L. Rosenthal.
Columbia: University of Missouri Press, 1976. pp. 239-246,
246-256.

Bibliographic Periodicals

544

[American Association for International Conciliation].

Monthly Bulletin of Books, Pamphlets, and Magazine Articles
Dealing with international Relations.
New York: Association for International Conciliation, 1908 to
1913.

  3868 items, 1908-1913. English; also German, French. Most
  items have brief descriptive and/or critical annotations.

  Appeared as an unbound pamphlet for most months between April
  1908 and July 1913; covered current literature on a wide
  range of peace movement and international relations topics.

545   Z6463.I59

[Webster, Mary Phillips and Isabelle Kendig-Gill (eds.)].

International Affairs as Presented in Recent Periodicals, Books
and Pamphlets, No. 1-107 [monthly, title varies].
Washington, D.C.: National Council for Prevention of War, 1923
to 1932. 1048 pp. (mimeo).

  Approximately 30,100 items, 1923-1932. English.

  Issues No. 1-6 were edited by Isabelle Kendig-Gill, research
  secretary for the National Council for Prevention of War.
  Issue No. 1 was entitled "Magazine Articles Dealing with
  Questions of War and Peace." Issues No. 2-14 were entitled
  "International Relations as Presented in Fifty Leading
  Periodicals." Issues No. 88-107 were entitled "A Selected
  List of Recent Articles on International Affairs." Each
  issue classified the items under several subject headings,
  which varied from month to month, but usually included
  sections on general international relations, international
  organization and the League of Nations, armament and
  disarmament, the peace movement, women in public affairs,
  race relations, world economics and finance, current
  problems, international cooperation, U.S. foreign relations,
  and international relations of particular countries or
  regions.

Bibliographic Periodicals

546 <   Z7163.B936

Office de Documentation Internationale Contemporaine,
International Institute of Intellectual Co-operation, and
European Center Carnegie Endowment for International Peace.

Bulletin Bibliographique de Documentation Internationale
Contemporaine/Bibliographical Bulletin on International
Affairs, Vol. 1-3, 4-10.
Paris: Les Presses Universitaires de France, 1926 to 1928,
1929 to 1935.

547   Z6472.L43

League of Nations.

Monthly/Periodical List of Publications Recently Issued:
Supplements Nos. 1-19 to 1927 catalog.
Boston: World Peace Foundation, 1927 to 1929. 8-16 pp. per
issue.

   English; also French.

548 <

League of Nations, Library.

Monthly List of Books Catalogued in the Library of the League
of Nations.
Geneva: League of Nations, 1928--.

549   Z6463.I61,no.1-[25]

World Peace Foundation.

International Book News, No. 1 to No. [25].
Boston: World Peace Foundation, January, 1928 to May, 1934
(published occasionally).

   Approximately 3811 items, 1919-1934. English; also French,
   German (3), Spanish (1). Many items have brief descriptive
   annotations.

   Each issue lists books, pamphlets, articles, series, and
   documents published by various official and semiofficial
   international organizations on such topics as arbitration,
   armament and disarmament, international law, the Permanent
   Court of International Justice, League of Nations,

Bibliographic Periodicals

     international relations, world economics, international trade
     and finance, industry and workers´ conditions, agriculture,
     national resources, health, child welfare, slavery, refugees,
     reparations, mandates, peace organizations, international
     transportation, and the social, economic, and political
     conditions in various countries.

550 <

League of Nations, Library.

Monthly List of Selected Articles.
Geneva: League of Nations, 1929--.

551 <

[Société des Nations, Bibliothèque/League of Nations, Library].

Liste Bimensuelle d´Articles Sélectionnés/Fortnightly List of
Selected Articles.
Geneva: [Société des Nations, Bibliothèque/League of Nations,
Library], 1929--.

552   JX1975.A1C8386,v.1-7

[Leonard, L. Larry (ed.)].

Current Thought on Peace and War: A world affairs digest of
literature and research in progress on current international
issues, Vol. 1-7 (Quarterly, 1960; semiannual or annual,
1961-1968).
New York: Institute for International Order/ Current Thought,
Inc., 1960 to 1968.

553   JX1901.P38

[Newcombe, Alan G. and Hanna Newcombe (eds.)].

Peace Research Abstracts Journal (An offical publication of the
International Peace Research Association, published with
assistance from UNESCO; monthly).
Clarkson, Ontario: Canadian Peace Research Institute, June,
1964 to 1976.
Beginning with Volume 14, published at Dundas, Ontario: Peace
Research Institute, 1977--.

     Annual volumes average nearly 9000 items each, covering the
     period since 1945. Includes both published and unpublished

Bibliographic Periodicals

works as well as speeches and work in progress. Most titles
and all abstracts are given in English, but the coverage is
worldwide. Items are numbered in a single series and listed
under ten major subject headings: I--the military situation;
II--limitation of arms; III--tension and conflict; IV--
ideology and issues; V--international institutions and
regional alliances; VI--nations and national policies; VII--
pairs of countries and crisis areas; VIII--international law,
economics and diplomacy; IX--decision making and
communications; X--methods and miscellaneous. Includes
author and subject indexes, the latter based on numerous
subcategories grouped under each of the ten major headings.
A revised coding manual is issued every few years.

554   JX1974.A1A7

United States Library of Congress, Reference Department, Arms
Control and Disarmament Bibliography Section.

Arms Control and Disarmament: A quarterly bibliography with
abstracts and annotations [Vol. 1-8].
Washington, D.C.: U.S. Government Printing Office, 1964 to
1973.

14,558 items, 1964-1972.

555

Newcombe, Alan G. and Hanna Newcombe (eds.).

Peace Research Reviews (bimonthly).
Clarkson, Ontario: Canadian Peace Research Institute, 1967--.

Each issue contains one or more review articles and a
bibliography on a special topic in the field covered by Peace
Research Abstracts Journal.

556 <   Z6274.H6W36

Militärgeschichtliches Forschungsamt.

War and Society Newsletter: A bibliographical survey (beginning
with Vol. 3, 1975, appears as supplement to
Militärgeschichtliche Mitteilungen, No. 17--; [semiannual]).
Karlsruhe: Militärgeschichtliches Forschungsamt, 1973--.

Part II: Peace

Part II : Peace

PART II: PEACE

INTRODUCTION

      Part II presents bibliographies emphasizing peace topics,
divided into twelve sections. The first (Section 12.
Peace--General) contains 87 general bibliographies listing works
relating to ideas of peace, conditions conducive to peace,
efforts to ensure peace (e.g., international arbitration,
conferences and congresses, internationalism, disarmament), basic
social, political, and economic problems that threaten peace,
reconstruction efforts, and postwar planning. Two early
bibliographies, La Fontaine (No. 558) and Gordon (No. 564)
provide fairly comprehensive coverage of peace topics through the
nineteenth century. Materials on ideas for the preservation of
peace can be found in Marygrove College (No. 612), covering plans
from ancient Greek civilization through World War II, and
Zampaglione (No. 639), concentrating on ancient ideas. Hicks
(No. 567) is an early annotated bibliography on internationalism,
while Kuehl (No. 643) is more recent and certainly the most
comprehensive bibliography on internationalism. Flenley (No.
611) is probably the best overall bibliography on reconstruction
efforts and postwar planning for the World War II period. The
National Peace Council bibliographies from 1912 through 1957
cited in this section contain materials relating to world
affairs, the social, political, and economic conditions in
various countries, and miscellaneous topics concerning peace,
while Acts for Peace (No. 634) provides more recent coverage of
materials on the politics of peace.

      The next section (13. Peace Movement--General) presents 49
bibliographies that include materials on the history, aims, and
methods of the peace movement, national and international efforts
of specific groups (e.g., women, labor, socialist, religious,
business) in promoting peace, militarist and imperialist
arguments against the peace movement, and a wide range of peace
movement activities and concerns. Ter Meulen (Nos. 666 and 669)
is an extensive two-part bibliography on the peace movement and a
broad range of peace and war related topics from the late
fifteenth century through the nineteenth century. International
in scope, La Fontaine (No. 645), Nobel Institute (No. 648), and
Fried (No. 650) are the best overall bibliographies on the peace
movement through the early twentieth century. Two shorter
bibliographies (Allen, No. 659, and Davis, No. 660) are useful,

193

the former because its citations on the peace movement and
theories of peace and war from 1774 to 1930 are topically
arranged and the latter because it concentrates on the period
before and after World War I. Matthews' three bibliographies
(Nos. 655, 671, and 673) are especially good on the period
between World War I and II, though they do contain earlier
materials as well. More contemporary bibliographies offering a
broad sweep of peace activities up through the 1960s are Miller
(No. 680), Reconciliation Library (No. 681), and Cook (No. 686).
Cook is particularly useful for its international coverage of a
wide range of subjects, including the antiwar movement of the
1960s. Four fairly recent bibliographies are good on the
American peace movement: Marchand (No. 689) dealing with the
period from 1898 to 1918, DeBenedetti (No. 691) focusing on the
period from 1905 to 1929, Chatfield (No. 688) covering the period
from 1914 to 1941, and Wittner (No. 687) concentrating on the
period from 1941 to 1960.

Section 14 (Peace Movement--Publication Lists) contains 14
publication lists of various national and international peace
organizations, some in existence since the early nineteenth
century. It should be pointed out that this section does not
cover material on peace organizations per se; rather, it focuses
on their publishing activities. Materials on the peace
organizations, other than their publishing activities, can be
found in the index under the organization's name or under such
headings as: Peace Movement--General; World Order, World Society,
World Government; and International Organization.

Section 15 (Peace Movement--Individuals) contains 34
bibliographies listing biographies and writings of a number of
individuals who have made theoretical or practical contributions
to peace efforts, as well as critical commentary on their works.
This section does not provide comprehensive coverage of either
individuals who have been active in the peace movement or their
works, since it is limited only to those bibliographies that
appeared in our sources.

Section 16 (Peace Movement--Special Topics) pertains to the
literature on more specific international peace efforts,
primarily during the 1930s and 1940s, including the youth
movement, Roerich peace movement, peace Sunday, and peace
gardens. Nearly half the 12 citations relate to the
international youth movements, which were directly or indirectly
involved with world peace.

The 36 items in Section 17 (Pacifism, Nonviolence,
Conscientious Objection) focus rather specifically on these three
subjects but also include materials on related topics, such as
war resistance, civil disobedience, social reform, conscription,
and militarism. Matthews (No. 761) provides a brief but
well-rounded early bibliography covering the major subjects.
Probably the most comprehensive bibliographies on these topics

are Comité "Pax" (No. 677) and Cook (No. 686), both found in
Section 13, above (Peace Movement--General). The best overall
bibliography on pacifism is Hyatt (No. 784). Those by Brock
(Nos. 778 and 782) are excellent on, respectively, American and
European pacifism up to World War I. The most general
bibliography on nonviolence is Carter (No. 780). Gregg (No. 768)
is a good source for materials through World War II, while Stiehm
(No. 785) focuses on the more contemporary literature on
nonviolent resistance. Blumberg (No. 779) is an excellent
annotated list of serials dealing with issues relating to
nonviolence. Lamkin (No. 786) probably provides the best overall
coverage of conscientious objection through the 1970´s. An
earlier but useful bibliography with a Quaker focus is Hall (No.
757). A good annotated bibliography on conscientious objection
and related topics is Doty (No. 770), though it only covers
materials through 1954.

Section 18 (Peace Conferences and Peacemaking) provides
bibliographies relating to specific peace treaties and peace
conferences (especially the Paris Peace Conference and the Hague
conferences) and more general works on peace negotiations, war
termination, and peace settlements. There is a heavy emphasis on
the Paris Peace Conference (approximately half of the 21 items in
this section) and World War I. Probably the best introductions
to these materials are Almond and Lutz (No. 795), which is
annotated, and Marston (No. 804). Two general bibliographies on
war termination and peace settlements with an historical
perspective are Iklé (No. 807) and Randle (No. 808).

Section 19 (Peace Plans) presents 15 bibliographies on
proposals and plans for ensuring world peace, the history of
schemes for world organization, and peace aims promulgated in the
course of particular wars. The bibliographies only cover
materials published through World War II. Good historical
coverage of peace projects and schemes of world organization for
the preservation of peace are, chronologically, Hicks (No. 811),
Matthews (No. 813), and Hemleben (No. 821). Johnsen (No. 823) is
an excellent bibliography on peace plans during World War II,
while Brodie (No. 817) is useful because it is annotated.

Section 20 (World Order, World Society, World Government)
includes 29 bibliographies on regional and world federation to
ensure world order (especially see Scanlon, No. 835 and Johnsen,
No. 837, in addition to Matthews, Nos. 494 and 495 in Section 9,
Social Movements and Other Political Topics), internationalism as
a basis for world society and world government (see Baden, No.
831), world government from legal, constitutional, political,
economic, and philosophical points of view (especially see
Ishida, No. 849), and postwar planning for world order (see
Johnsen, Nos. 841 and 842). It also includes more specialized
bibliographies on such topics as international police (Scanlon,
No. 845) and constitutions designed to promote world peace
(Harrod, No. 850). The majority of the bibliographies in this
section focus on the period of World War II.

Section 21 (International Organization) provides 63
bibliographies on the history, activities, and publications of
various international organizations (including the League of
Nations, Pan American Union, and the United Nations) and on
international organization in general. There are also more
specialized bibliographies on such topics as international
cooperation (Richardson et al., No. 859, which has 970 items
focusing on the early twentieth century), intellectual
cooperation (U.S. Library of Congress, No. 884), collective
security (Matthews, No. 879), and particular peacekeeping efforts
(Taylor et al., No. 910). Though there is no comprehensive
bibliography on the United Nations listed, there are several
bibliographies on the League of Nations worth noting: Société des
Nations, No. 866; Carroll, No. 869; Breycha-Vauthier, No. 877;
and Aufricht, No. 894. There is also a good bibliography on the
Red Cross (Knitel, No. 907). Hicks (No. 858) is an early but
good annotated bibliography covering materials on international
organization from 1601 through 1918. The most comprehensive
bibliographies on international institutions and international
organization are those by Speeckaert (Nos. 899 and 904). More
recent bibliographies on international organization are Haas (No.
915) and Atherton (No. 916).

The 41 bibliographies in Section 22 (Peace Education) are
heavily concentrated in the two decades from 1924 to 1944, a time
when the output of publications related to peace education had
grown enormously. The central concern of peace educators in that
period, education for "international understanding,"
"international friendship," "world goodwill," and
"worldmindedness," is reflected in most of the bibliographies
cited here. A few items focus on the numerous efforts at
revising school textbooks (see especially Matthews, No. 924, and
UNESCO, No. 950). Several others provide lists of recommended
books and other teaching materials designed to promote
international understanding and attitudes conducive to peace.
For the period before 1940, the most extensive lists are
Lobingier and Lobingier (No. 923), Kiely (No. 942), and Wilson
(No. 944); for the era of the United Nations, extensive lists are
found in Rosenhaupt (No. 949), American Friends Service Committee
(No. 952), and especially Flynn (No. 953). Several other
bibliographies in this section cover both the above kinds of
materials and works on other aspects including the philosophy and
methods of peace education. Hansen (No. 921) and White (No. 948)
provide extensive lists on peace education in the United States
during the 1920s; King (No. 934) and Matthews (Nos. 937 and 946)
cover somewhat longer time periods; and Fink (No. 957) provides a
brief (55 items) birdseye view of the development of peace
education from 1815 to 1976. Numerous bibliographies in other
sections of this guide list substantial numbers of items on peace
education, international education, international understanding,
and related topics (see the subject index). Noteworthy among
these are Boeckel (No. 27), Jacobs and DeBoer (No. 65), Boulding
et al. (No. 130), Boeckel (Nos. 516-517), Haass et al. (No. 583),

La Fontaine (No. 645), Nobel Institute (No. 648), and
Scharffenorth et al. (No. 977).

Section 23 (Peace Research) presents 26 bibliographies
listing works relating to the definition of peace research,
philosophical and methodological issues concerning the study of
peace and conflict, and peace research centers and projects. The
bibliography providing the best coverage of materials on peace
research is Scharffenorth et al. (No. 977), which lists 3778
items published between 1894 and 1974. Durkee (No. 982) is
particularly useful for materials on the definitions and
objectives of peace research from 1936 to 1975, while Aggarwal
(No. 980) has 651 items on the issues and methodology of peace
research from 1923 to 1973. Van Den Dungen (No. 983) provides a
brief list of references pertinent to the development of peace
science since 1815.

Peace--General

557   BL: 11904.bb.60.(2)

[Sothern, W. A. (comp.)].

A Handy Reference List: Books, pamphlets, articles, leaflets,
etc., relating to international peace and arbitration.
London: International Abitration and Peace Association, 1888.
8 pp.
First published as "The literature of war, peace, and
arbitration," Concord, May 16, 1888.

   291 items, 1816 - 1888. English; also French, German (1),
   Italian (1).

   General works relating to peace, war, and international law
   (200); publications of La Société Française des Amis de la
   Paix, Paris (15) and of the Ligue Internationale de la Paix
   et de la Liberté, Geneva (8); miscellaneous French works (8);
   publications of the Peace Society, London (60).

558   Z6464.Z9L16

La Fontaine, H[enri].

Essai de Bibliographie de la Paix.
Brussels: Th. Lombaerts, 1891. 25 pp.

   463 items, 1712 - 1891. French; also English, Italian, Dutch,
   German, Danish (3), Spanish (3), Swedish (2), Latin (1).
   Introduction (3 pp.); table of contents.

   General works on peace and war, international law,
   international arbitration (283), items in almanacs (77),
   arbitration (3), contests and prizes (6), interparliamentary
   conferences (2), peace congresses and meetings (50),
   federation of peace societies (1), parliamentary declarations
   (7), journals and anthologies (29), peace societies (2),
   bibliographies (3). This bibliography contains many items on
   international law and arbitration that are not included in La
   Fontaine's 1904 bibliography on the peace movement.

Peace--General

559   JX1930.U58,1891

Universal Peace Congress, Third (Rome, 1891).

"Publications et ouvrages manuscrits envoyés en hommage au
Congrès [Publications and manuscript works sent in honor of the
Congress]."
In its Troisième Congrès International de la Paix [Third
International Peace Congress], Rome, Novembre 1891 (aux soins
de MM. le Prof. Cesare Facelli et l'Avocat Antonio Teso, du
Comité Romain de la Paix).
Rome: Unione Cooperativa Editrice, 1892. pp. 189-198.

   71 items, 1867 - 1891. French, Italian, English; also German
   (2), Spanish (1), Esperanto (1).

   Books, pamphlets, and manuscripts dealing with peace
   education, peace leaders, international law, international
   arbitration, international organization, free trade,
   conditions of peace, and various questions of interest to the
   Congress.

560 <

[Salem Public Library].

"Reading list on peace."
Salem Public Library Bulletin (October, 1904).

561 <

Buffalo Public Library.

The World's Peace: A short reading list in celebration of the
meeting of the Russian and Japanese Peace Commission.
Buffalo, N.Y.: Buffalo Public Library, 1905.

562 <

[New York Public Library].

"List of books on peace."
New York Public Library, Monthly Bulletin of Additions (May,
1906).

Peace--General

563   JX1965.P612

Pictet, Jeanne.

Appendice bibliographique.
In her Le Rôle de la Femme dans la Paix Universelle [Woman's
Role in Universal Peace].
Lausanne: F. Rouge, 1907. [p. 56].

  15 items, 1902 - 1907. French. Introduction (1 paragraph).

  Books on peace theory, the effects of war, the Hague
  conferences, international arbitration; peace periodicals.

564   Z6464.Z9B8

[Gordon, Alys M. (comp.)].

International Peace: A list of books with references to
periodicals in the Brooklyn Public Library.
Brooklyn, N.Y.: Brooklyn Public Library, 1908. 53 pp.

  504 items, 1625 - 1908. English. Most items have brief
  descriptive annotations; introduction (1 paragraph); appended
  chronological list of 12 peace societies and congresses.

  Bibliographies (19), books (103), and magazine articles (382)
  on the causes and effects of war, war prevention,
  international law, world federation, international
  arbitration, internationalism, disarmament, militarism, the
  peace movement, conditions of peace, peace plans, and related
  topics.

565 <

[Independent].

"Book list No. 10: Peace."
Independent (April 18, 1908).

566   JX1904.P4,1912

[Huntsman, M. H. (comp.)].

"Publications of the National Peace Council; Pacifist press
directory; Bibliography."
In National Peace Council (London), Peace Year Book, 1912.

Peace--General

London: National Peace Council, 1912. pp. 138-139, 179-180,
181-194.
An earlier edition appeared in the Peace Year Book, 1910, also
reprinted as a pamphlet entitled "Peace Bibliography," London:
National Peace Council [1910], 10 pp. Another edition appeared
in the Peace Year Book, 1911, pp. 178-190, 216-217.

   235 items, [1760 - 1911]. English; also French.

   Publications of the NPC (25); pacifist press directory (18);
   arbitration (10), armaments (12), biography (13), capture of
   private property at sea (16), Christianity and peace (13),
   commerce and peace (4), congresses (9), conscription (17),
   education (12), fiction (13), general (20), Hague Conference
   (8), history (12), imperialism (10), international law (15),
   patriotism (8).

567   Z6464.Z9H6

Hicks, Frederick C.

"Internationalism: A selected list of books, pamphlets and
periodicals."
International Conciliation, No. 64 (March, 1913): 30 pp.

   89 items, 1892 - 1912. English; also French, German (4),
   Italian (1). Most items have brief to medium-length critical
   and/or descriptive annotations, some excerpts; preface
   (2 pp.); table of contents; appended list of publications of
   the American Association for International Conciliation.

   Bibliographies (6), general works (13), racial adjustment
   (5), economics (7), international law (20), biographical
   works (4), fiction (5), yearbooks (6), periodicals (12),
   pamphlets (11).

568   JX1904.P4,1913

[Huntsman, M. H. (comp.)].

"Publications of the National Peace Council; Pacifist press
directory; Bibliography."
In National Peace Council (London), Peace Year Book, 1913.
London: National Peace Council, 1913. pp. 165-167, 208-210,
211-219.

   190 items, [1912]. English; also French.

   Publications of the NPC (49); pacifist press directory (22);
   arbitration (7), armaments (5), biography (5), capture of

Peace--General

    private property at sea (10), Christianity and peace (7),
    congresses, yearbooks, and other reports (13), conscription
    and compulsory military service (14), fiction (5), general
    (15), Germany (9), Hague Conference (5), history (9),
    international law (10), patriotism (5).

569 <

Moody, Katharine T. (comp.).

"A list of books on international peace and arbitration."
St. Louis Public Library Monthly Bulletin, 2 (New Series)
(1913): 102-105.

570 <   PPL

Vies, A. B. van der.

Nederlandsche Bibliographie over het Vredesvraagstuk
[Netherlands Bibliography on the Peace Question].
The Hague: Algemeene Nederlandsche Bond "Vrede Door Recht"
(Publicatie, No. 1), 1913. 31 pp.

571   Z6464.Z9R8

Root, Robert Cromwell (comp.).

Bibliographies on International Peace Topics.
[Los Angeles/Berkeley: California Peace Societies], June, 1914.
16 pp.

    159 items, 1904 - 1914 (many items undated). English.

    Growth of the peace movement (12), success of arbitration or
    the victories of peace (10), the value of the Hague
    conferences (13), international courts as a remedy for war
    (8), the interdependence of nations (12), the federation of
    the world (15), industrial peace (11), American-Japanese
    relations (15), the economic waste of war (12), relation of
    trusts or vested interests to war scares (12), socialism's
    battle against war (5), union labor's opposition to war (5),
    war and "race degeneracy" (6), popular fallacies concerning
    war (8), peace work in schools and colleges (8), war the
    enemy of Christianity (7).

Peace--General

572   JX1953.B5

Bigelow, John.

Bibliography.
In his World Peace: How war cannot be abolished; how it may be
abolished.
New York: Mitchell Kennerley, 1916. pp. 266-274.

   118 items, 1795 - 1915. English, French; also German (7).

   Illusion of pacifism (43), arbitration (19), a world
   judiciary, a league of peace (28), a world people (15), a
   world state (13).

573 <

National Board for Historical Service.

Peace and Reconstruction: Preliminary bibliography.
World Peace Foundation Pamphlets, 2, special number (1919).

574   JX1904.P4,1921

[National Peace Council (London)].

"Pacifist and internationalist press directory."
In its Peace Year Book, 1921.
London: National Peace Council, 1921. pp. 89-92.

   61 items, [1920]. English; also other Western European
   languages.

575 <

[Carnegie Endowment for International Peace, Library].

World Peace.
Washington, D.C.: Carnegie Endowment for International Peace,
Library (Miscellaneous Reading List No. 30), 1923.

576 <

[Carnegie Endowment for International Peace, Library].

Peace at Any Price.

Peace--General

Washington, D.C.: Carnegie Endowment for International Peace,
Library (Miscellaneous Reading List No. 19), 1927. (mimeo).

577 <

Matthews, M[ary] Alice (comp.).

Outlawry of War.
Washington, D.C.: Carnegie Endowment for International Peace,
Library (Reading List No. 20), 1927. (mimeo).

578   JX1904.P4,1927

National Council for Prevention of War (London).

"Bibliography."
In its Peace Year Book, 1927.
London: National Council for Prevention of War, 1927.
pp. 85-90.

   63 items, [1926]. English.

   Books and pamphlets of general international interest (37),
   international law and courts of justice (8), history (14),
   economics (4).

579   Z1219.P98,v.116

American Library Association and World Peace Foundation
(comps.).

"International cooperation for peace: A book list for the tenth
anniversary of the League of Nations."
Publishers' Weekly, 116, 26 (December 28, 1929): 2910-2913.

   50 items, 1921 - 1929. English. All items have brief
   descriptive and/or critical annotations; introduction
   (1 paragraph).

   Books on international relations, European history, and
   institutions and ways to promote peace, including the League
   of Nations, international law, diplomacy, and the Paris Peace
   Pact (Kellogg Pact).

Peace--General

580 <

Matthews, M[ary] Alice (comp.).   ,

Multilateral Treaty for Renunciation of War.
Washington, D.C.: Carnegie Endowment for International Peace,
Library (Reading List No. 26), 1929. (mimeo).

581   JX1904.P4,1929

National Council for Prevention of War (London).

"Peace press directory for Great Britain; List of recent
pamphlets and leaflets dealing with peace and war."
In its Peace Year Book, 1929.
London: National Council for Prevention of War, 1929.
pp. 113-114, 114-116.

   106 items, [1928]. English.

   Peace press directory (27); arbitration and the World Court
   (10), armament and disarmament (16), economics (1), education
   (10), outlawry of war (7), religion (9), miscellaneous (26).

582   JX1953.B546

Boeckel, Florence Brewer.

"A selected list of books and pamphlets on peace."
In her The Turn toward Peace.
New York: Friendship Press, 1930. pp. [195]-203.

   145 items, 1915 - 1930. English.

   Arranged according to sections and topics in the book:
   general history (3), international relations (5), foreign
   relations of the U.S. (1), peace and war (5), the world today
   (4), war today (7), arbitration and conciliation (8), the
   World Court and the League of Nations (16), nationalistic
   policies (15), the menace of armaments (9), the organized
   peace movement (20), what you can do for peace (48),
   bibliographies and reference (4). List of peace organizations
   appended.

Peace--General

583   JC362.D7,1931 or JX1963.
                                     D685,1931

Haass, Adalia, Grace Lefler, Marian Gwinn, and Mildred Berrier
(eds.).

"Selected books, plays, poems, and orations suitable for the
promotion of international understanding."
In Dowling, Evaline (comp. and ed.), World Friendship: A series
of articles written by some teachers in the Los Angeles schools
and by a few others who are likewise interested in the
education of youth.
Los Angeles: Los Angeles City School District, Committee on
World Friendship, 1931 (3rd ed.). pp. [251]-270.
First edition, 1927. Second edition, 1928.

    665 items, 1925 - 1931 (the children's books are undated).
    English. A few items have brief descriptive and/or critical
    annotations.

    Books, articles, plays, poems, and orations on international
    cooperation, disarmament, League of Nations, peace, treaties,
    World Court, and international understanding in the
    elementary schools and high schools all over the world.

584 <

International Institute of Intellectual Co-operation.

Bibliography.
In its International Understanding through Youth: Interchanges
and travel of school pupils.
Paris: [International Institute of Intellectual Co-operation]
(International Co-operation Series), 1933. pp. 195-200.

585   JX1904.P4,1933

[National Peace Council (London)].

"Bibliography--the year's pamphlets (1932); Peace press
directory."
In its Peace Year Book, 1933.
London: National Peace Council, 1933. pp. 272-275, 276.

    99 items, 1932. English.

    Pamphlets on disarmament (29), India (10), League of Nations
    (9), religious aspects (5), Sino-Japanese dispute (4),
    traffic in arms (3), miscellaneous (22); press directory
    (17).

Peace--General

586 <   JX68.H28

Harley, John Eugene.

Bibliographies.
In his Documentary Textbook on International Relations: A text
and reference study emphasizing official documents and
materials relating to world peace and international cooperation.
Los Angeles: Suttonhouse (University of Southern California,
School of Research Series, No. 3), 1934. pp. 801-840.

587   JX1904.P4,1934

[National Peace Council (London)].

"Bibliographies--the year´s pamphlets (1933), the year´s books
(1933), peace plays and pageants, special reports and memoranda
issued by the National Peace Council in 1933; Peace press
directory."
In its Peace Year Book, 1934.
London: National Peace Council, 1934. pp. 259-270, 272.

  303 items, 1933. English.

  Pamphlets and books on disarmament (14), education(6),
  Germany (29), League of Nations (34), religious (11), slavery
  (6), traffic in arms (6), miscellaneous (78), economics and
  finance (20), Europe (5), peace plays and pageants (60),
  Geneva Disarmament Conference (7), international security
  (7); peace periodicals (20).

588 <

Matthews, Mary Alice (comp.).

Labor and World Peace.
Washington, D.C.: Carnegie Endowment for International Peace,
Library (Reading List No. 8), September, 1935 (rev. ed.). 8 pp.
(mimeo).
First edition, January 18, 1927.

Peace--General

589   JX1904.P4,1935

[National Peace Council (London)].

"The year´s books and pamphlets, 1934; Posters; Peace plays and
pageants; Peace press directory."
In its Peace Year Book, 1935.
London: National Peace Council, 1935. pp. 279-296, 297.

   434 items, 1934. English.

   Books and pamphlets on armaments and disarmament (31),
   Christianity and peace (24), democracy and dictatorship (32),
   economics and finance (26), Europe (10), Far East (12),
   education (5), Germany (42), India (12), League of Nations
   (25), religious (6), Saar (5), sanctions and security (21),
   trade in arms (20), miscellaneous (115); peace plays and
   pageants (22); special reports and memoranda (7); peace press
   directory (19).

590   Z6464.Z9B5

Boeckel, Florence Brewer (comp.).

Fifty Books on Peace Questions.
Washington, D.C.: National Council for Prevention of War,
November, 1936. 10 pp. (mimeo).

   57 items, 1926 - 1936. English. Most items have descriptive
   and/or critical annotations.

   General (13), democracy and peace (4), neutrality (4), trade
   (6), national defense policies (2), Far East (4), Latin
   America (2), League of Nations and the Kellogg Pact (8),
   munitions industry (5), peace movement (5), periodical
   publications of the National Council for the Prevention of
   War (4).

591   JX1904.P4,1936

[National Peace Council (London)].

"The year´s books and pamphlets, 1935; Important articles,
documents, etc., 1935; Peace plays; Peace press directory."
In its Peace Yearbook, 1936.
London: National Peace Council, 1936. pp. 328-350, 352-353.

   443 items, 1935. English.

Peace--General

    Books and pamphlets on Africa (8), Abyssinia (7), armament
    and disarmament (20), democracy and dictatorship (14),
    Christianity, pacifism, and peace (30), economics and finance
    (24), education (4), Europe (9), Germany (26), imperial
    questions (7), India (4), international law (6), League of
    Nations (42), Near and Far East (6), Pacific affairs (10),
    sanctions and security (14), trade in arms (6), general and
    miscellaneous (79); articles (92); peace plays (8); special
    reports and memoranda (6); peace press directory (21).

    592 <

[Société des Nations, Bibliothèque/League of Nations, Library].
Liste d´Ouvrages sur les Changements Pacifiques Catalogués à la
Bibliothèque de la Société des Nations/List of Works on
Peaceful Change Catalogued in the Library of the League of
Nations.
Geneva: [Société des Nations, Bibliothèque/League of Nations,
Library] (Listes Bibliographiques/Miscellaneous Bibliographies,
[No.] 6), 1936 (édition provisoire). (mimeo).

    593   JX1975.A574,1937

Akhavi, (Ali Akbar).

Bibliographie.
In his L´Echec de la S.D.N. dans l´Organisation Pratique de la
Paix [The Failure of the League of Nations in the Practical
Organization of Peace]: Ses causes, son avenir [Its causes, its
future].
Paris: Recueil Sirey, 1937. pp. 213-214.
Original edition, L´organisation pratique de la paix (Thèse
pour le doctorat en droit . . . 19 décembre 1936 . . . ,
Université de Paris), Paris: Les Presses Modernes, 1936,
pp. 213-214.

    34 items (no dates given). French, English; also German (2).

    Books on international law, international organization, the
    economic aspects of war, internationalism, pacifism, and
    peace theory.

Peace--General

594   JX1963.P74

Potter, Pitman B.

Suggested readings.
In his Collective Security and Peaceful Change.
Chicago: University of Chicago Press (Public Policy Pamphlet
No. 24), 1937. pp. 37-38.

   13 items, 1927 - 1937. English. All items have brief critical
   annotations.

   Books on international organization, collective security, and
   sanctions.

595   H69.T6,v.3

[New York Public Library, Readers´ Advisers].

Selected bibliography.
In McCormick, Ann O´Hare, et al., special issue, Is There a Way
to World Peace?
Bulletin of America´s Town Meeting of the Air, 3, 23 (April 11,
1938): 4.

   9 items, 1934 - 1938. English. Most items have brief
   descriptive annotations.

   Short list of books on peace and international relations.

596 <

[Carnegie Endowment for International Peace, Library].

Peaceful Change.
Washington, D.C.: Carnegie Endowment for International Peace,
Library (Miscellaneous Reading List No. 61), 1939. (mimeo).

597 <   JX1963.P34,1939a

[Peace Pledge Union].

Book list.
In its Peace Service Handbook: A guide suggesting some of the
ways by which the people of Britain can help their country and
the world to live at peace.
London: Peace Pledge Union, June, 1939. (2nd ed.). pp. 46-47.
First edition, May, 1939.

Peace--General

598   H62.A1S6,v.3

Winter, Carl G.

"A unit on peace" [bibliographic essay].
Social Education (New York), 3, 1 (January, 1939): 33-36.

   21 items, 1925 - 1938. English. All items are listed and
   briefly discussed in text, pp. 33-34.

   Works on armaments, international relations, peace plans, and
   the peace movement, used in classes for high school seniors.

599   PN4181.U5,1939/40

[Johnsen, Julia E. and Alberta Worthington (comps.)].

Bibliography: "The basis of a lasting peace."
In Phelps, Edith M. (ed.), University Debaters´ Annual:
Constructive and rebuttal speeches delivered in debates of
American colleges and universities during the college year
1939-1940 [Vol.26].
New York: H. W. Wilson, August, 1940. pp. 42-50.

   148 items, 1924 - 1940. English.

   Books, pamphlets (49), periodical articles and speeches (99)
   on alternative approaches to peace and world order.

600   JX1963.C68

[Shotwell, James Thomson, et al.].

References.
In their Which Way to Lasting Peace? A series of radio
broadcasts over the network of the Columbia Broadcasting
System, in cooperation with the Commission to Study the
Organization of Peace.
New York: Commission to Study the Organization of Peace,
[1940]. Inside back cover.

   14 items, 1936 - 1940. English.

   Pamphlets (9) and books (5) on world organization, U.S.
   foreign policy, and international cooperation.

Peace--General

601   Z6207.W81C3

Canadian Institute of International Affairs.

Post-war Reconstruction Studies: Bibliography.
[Toronto]: Canadian Institute of International Affairs
(No. 64-300), December 22, 1941. 9 pp. (mimeo).

   95 items, 1934 - 1941 (no dates given for pamphlet
   references). English. Most items have brief descriptive and
   critical annotations.

   Pamphlets, books, and articles published in North America and
   Great Britain dealing with the possible problems of
   reconstruction in the post-World War II period.

602 <

[Commission on World Peace].

Bibliography.
In its When Hostilities Cease: Addresses and findings of the
exploratory conference on the basis of a just and enduring
peace, Chicago Temple, 1941.
Chicago: Commission on World Peace, 1941. pp. 125-127.

603   D816.C58

[Dulles, John Foster, et al.].

Bibliography.
In their A Just and Durable Peace: Data material and discussion
questions.
New York: Federal Council of the Churches of Christ in America,
Commission to Study the Bases of a Just and Durable Peace,
[1941]. pp. 62-[65].

   31 items, 1935 - 1941. English. All items have brief to
   abstract-length descriptive and/or critical annotations.

   Books and pamphlets on world order, Christianity's
   contribution to world peace, and international organization.

Peace--General

604   JX1961.F8S6

Souleyman, Elizabeth V.

Bibliography.
In her The Vision of World Peace in Seventeenth and Eighteenth-
Century France.
New York: G. P. Putnam's Sons, 1941. pp. 211-224.
Also published as Ph.D. dissertation, Columbia University,
1940.

   244 items, 1559 - 1938. French, English; also German.

   Primary (114) and secondary (130) sources on the political
   and social conditions of peace, international organization,
   political theory, and political history.

605   Z6207.W81C3,suppl.no.1

Canadian Institute of International Affairs.

Post-war Reconstruction Studies: Supplement No. 1 to
bibliography of December 22, 1941.
[Toronto]: Canadian Institute of International Affairs
(No. 98-300), February 27, 1942. 8 pp. (mimeo).

   55 items, 1941 - 1942. English. All items have brief
   descriptive annotations.

   Periodical articles, pamphlets, and books published in North
   America and Great Britain dealing with post-World War II
   reconstruction problems, particularly as they relate to
   international organization and the Canadian, British, and
   U.S. economies.

606   Z6207.W81C3,suppl.no.2

Canadian Institute of International Affairs.

Post-war Reconstruction Studies: Supplement No. 2 to
bibliography of December 22, 1941.
[Toronto]: Canadian Institute of International Affairs
(No. 135-300), May 22, 1942. 9 + 2 pp. (mimeo).

   68 items, 1941 - 1942. English. All items have brief
   descriptive annotations.

   Periodical articles, books, and pamphlets published in North
   America and Great Britain dealing with the problems of post-

Peace--General

World War II reconstruction, particularly as they relate to
European federation and the economy.

607   PN4177.D4,v.16

Foulkes, William R. (ed.).

"Current books on world problems."
Debaters' Digest, 16, 7 (October, 1942): 53.

32 items (no dates given). English.

Books on the U.S. role in world affairs, international
relations, international organization, world order,
peacemaking, the conditions of peace, and peace theory.

608   Z1231.P2P3,v.3-4

Pamphleteer Monthly.

"Post-war planning."
Pamphleteer Monthly (New York), 3, 2 (June, 1942): 3-10.

130 items, 1940 - 1942. English. A compilation of pamphlet
titles listed in previous issues of this journal, beginning
with the May, 1940 issue. All items have brief descriptive
annotations; introduction (1 paragraph).

Pamphlets on postwar planning and reconstruction in the areas
of defense, employment, business, social security,
government, economic development, and international
organization.

609   IU: A940.93144D48p

Detroit Public Library.

Peace and the Post-war World [a bibliography].
[Detroit]: Detroit Public Library, 1943. [10 pp.].

53 items, 1941 - 1942. English. All items have brief
descriptive and/or critical annotations.

Shadow of the past (6), the object of war in peace (14),
blueprints for a new world (16), future of the United States
(9), spiritual imperatives for peace (8). Deals mainly with
the conditions conducive to peace.

Peace--General

610   D816.5.F393

Federal Council of the Churches of Christ in America,
Commission on a Just and Durable Peace.

"Bibliography."
In its Six Pillars of Peace: A study guide based on "A
Statement of Political Propositions".
New York: Federal Council of the Churches of Christ in America,
Commission on a Just and Durable Peace, 1943. pp. 83-85.

   56 items (no dates given). English. Some items have brief
   descriptive and/or critical annotations.

   Books (20) and pamphlets (36) on the basis and organization
   of peace.

611   Z6207.W81F58

Flenley, R[alph].

Post-war Problems, a Reading List: A select bibliography on
post-war settlement and reconstruction.
Toronto: Canadian Institute of International Affairs, April,
1943. 62 pp.

   964 items, 1937 - 1943. English. Many items have brief
   descriptive and/or critical annotations; preface (1 p.);
   table of contents.

   Reference works and organizations (99), official documents
   and speeches (33), peace settlement and immediate problems
   (32), reconstruction and peace aims (97), international
   organization and cooperation (122), economic principles,
   problems, and proposals (132), social and cultural problems
   and policies (79), particular countries and regions (370).

612   JX1954.M36

Marygrove College (Detroit).

Bibliography.
In its Quest of the Centuries: Peace.
Detroit: Marygrove College, 1943. pp. 76-82.

   530 items, 1713 - 1943. English; also French, Latin (5),
   Italian (3), German (1). Explanation of bibliography
   (1 paragraph) in introduction to the text.

Peace--General

Papal documents (14) and references (516) on plans for the
preservation of peace from the time of the Greeks to the
present, history of the peace movement, peace theory,
international relations, and international organization, with
emphasis on Catholic perspectives.

613   JK1108.A35,no.24

Wiley, Evelyn.

Selected references.
In her Major Efforts to Assure World Peace, 1918-1939
(Representative views on their defects).
Washington, D.C.: Library of Congress, Legislative Reference
Service (Public Affairs Bulletin No. 24), August, 1943.
pp. 27-32. (mimeo).

109 items, 1918 - 1943. English. Introduction (1 paragraph).

Books and articles on peace plans, the United States and the
League of Nations, the Permanent Court of International
Justice, peace treaties, international law, international
relations, and international organization.

614   HD7091.P54

Pink, Louis H[eaton].

Bibliography.
In his Freedom from Fear: The interrelation of domestic and
international programs, with a foreword by Owen D. Young.
New York/London: Harper and Brothers, 1944 (1st ed.).
pp. 239-241.

46 items, 1798 - 1943. English.

Books on domestic social and economic programs (including
social security and national health insurance) conducive to
peace and on diplomatic history, the U.S.S.R., conditions of
peace, and peace plans.

615   Z1219.P98,v.147

[Council on Books in Wartime, Library Committee].

This is your peace [Book list] in "Books play a part at San
Francisco Conference."

Peace--General

Publishers' Weekly, 147, 18 (May 5, 1945): 1825-1826.
Also published in a six-page folder as its May 1945 booklist by
The Library Committee of the Council on Books in Wartime.

   27 items, 1944 - 1945. English. All items have brief
   descriptive and/or critical annotations; introduction (3 pp.)
   includes mention of a number of other current books not in
   the booklist.

   Books on peace plans, world order, world government, economic
   aspects of peace, U.S. role in peacemaking, science and
   peace.

616   Z881.S2M

[Langpaap, Frances K., Dolores Cadell, and Rose Suttey
(comps.)].

"Peace plans--new and old [and 11 more lists]."
In their special issue, United Nations Conference on
International Organization, San Francisco, April, 1945.
San Francisco Public Library Monthly Bulletin, 45, 4 (April,
1945): 29-36.

   227 items, 1899 - 1945. English. Most items have brief
   descriptive and/or critical annotations; introduction (1 p.);
   list of signatories and adherents to U.N. Declaration of
   1942.

   Peace plans, old and new (28), postwar worlds (30),
   international relations (34), global geography and politics
   (16), international commerce (14), economics (30), building
   the peace (14), Dumbarton Oaks (6), Bretton Woods (12),
   United Nations (8), world organization (21); periodicals
   (14).

617   D825.M24

MacLean, Donald A[lexander].

Bibliography.
In his A Dynamic World Order, with prefaces by Cardinal
Villeneuve and Joseph Husslein and a foreword by Will Lissner.
Milwaukee: Bruce (Science and Culture Series), 1945. pp. 215-
229.

   302 items, 1888 - 1944. English; also French, Latin, German
   (6), Italian (2), Spanish (1).

Peace--General

   Papal encyclicals and other Christian sources on peace and
   international order (20), books and articles on Nazism,
   Fascism, "Nipponism," and Marxism (11), and a wide range of
   specialized and general works (262) on ethical, religious,
   economic, political, social, legal, and ideological aspects
   of establishing world peace.

618   Z881.N6B8,v.23

Kingery, Robert E.

"Roads to peace [a selected book list]."
New York Public Library, Branch Library Book News, 23, 7
(September, 1946): 100-102.

   26 items, 1944 - 1946. English. All items have brief
   descriptive and/or critical annotations; introduction to each
   section (1 paragraph).

   Books on the fundamental conditions of peace (6), peace plans
   (7), concepts of federated Europe (3), United Nations (6),
   and world government (6).

619   JX1904.P4,1946

[National Peace Council (London)].

"Books published in 1944 and 1945; Pamphlets and leaflets
. . . ; Press directory, a selected list."
In its Peace and Reconstruction Year Book, 1946.
London: National Peace Council, 1946. pp. 32-45, 46-61, 62-66.

   715 items, 1944 - 1945. English.

   Books, pamphlets, and leaflets on basic issues and principles
   (76), political and constitutional issues (95), economic and
   social issues (56), British Commonwealth and colonial
   questions (48),S.A. and Anglo-American relations (25),
   U.S.S.R. and Anglo-Soviet relations (25), India (19), Far East
   (26), Europe and European countries (89), Germany (57),
   relief and rehabilitation (11), refugee and Jewish questions
   (12), relief and reconstruction (19), civil liberties,
   conscription, etc. (10), miscellaneous (48); press directory
   (99).

Peace--General

620   JX1904.P4,1947

[National Peace Council (London)].

"Books on peace and international affairs published in Great
Britain in 1946, a selected list; Pamphlets . . . ; British
official documents on international affairs for 1946;
Periodicals on peace and international affairs published in
Great Britain, a selected list."
In its Peace Year Book, 1947.
London: National Peace Council, 1947. pp. 60-67, 68-71, 72-78,
79-81.

   381 items, 1946. English.

   Books, pamphlets, and leaflets on fundamental principles
   (30), history, politics and economics (37), toward a world
   order (21), science and atomic energy (17), pacifism (4),
   Britain, the empire and the colonies (10), America (9),
   Europe--general (7), Western Europe (16), Germany and Austria
   (26), U.S.S.R. and Eastern Europe (29), the Middle East and
   Africa (15), Palestine, the Middle East, and the Jewish
   problem (8), India and the Far East (20), miscellaneous (5);
   British official documents on international affairs for 1946
   (79); periodicals on peace and international affairs (38).

621   CB425.M56

[Kingsley, Marion M. (comp.)].

"Educational materials on war and ways to peace."
In Moore, Harry H[ascall] (ed.), Survival or Suicide: A summons
to old and young to build a united, peaceful world.
New York: Harper and Brothers, 1948. pp. 185-191.

   46 items, 1945 - 1947. English. Some items have brief
   descriptive and critical annotations.

   Books (17), pamphlets (13), periodicals (16) emphasizing
   atomic energy and weapons, world government, international
   organization, and the United Nations.

622   CB425.M56

Moore, Harry H[ascall] (ed.).

References.
In his Survival or Suicide: A summons to old and young to build
a united, peaceful world.

Peace--General

New York: Harper and Brothers, 1948. pp. 195-202.

Approximately 60 items, 1944 - 1948. English. Endnote format.

Articles, books, memoranda, statistical sources, news items
and letters, cited as references for chapters, dealing with a
variety of international, political, and economic problems
including atomic energy, public expenditures, population,
hunger, the U.S.S.R., air power, racism, and United Nations
agencies. Appended list of voluntary organizations promoting
world peace.

623   JX1904.P4,1948

[National Peace Council (London)].

"Books on peace and world affairs published in Great Britain in
1947, a selected list; Pamphlets . . . ; British official
documents on international affairs for 1945; Periodicals . . ."
In its Peace Year Book, 1948.
London: National Peace Council, 1948. pp. 70-75, 75-78, 79-84,
84-86.

156 items, 1947. English.

Books and pamphlets on fundamental principles (28), history,
politics, and economics (10), world order (8), pacifism and
conscription (4), Europe and European union (12), atomic
energy (6), commonwealth and colonial affairs (7), Germany
and Austria (19), U.S.S.R. (19), U.S.A. and the Americas
(10), Middle and Near East, Palestine (17), Asia and Africa
(11), India and the Far East (4), reference (4),
miscellaneous (10); British official documents (56); British
periodicals (36).

624   Z881.N5Li

Newark Public Library.

The United Nations Builds for Peace: A selected reading list.
Newark, N.J.: Newark Public Library, March, 1948. 4 pp.

39 items, 1945 - 1948. English. Most items have brief
descriptive and/or critical annotations.

Books and pamphlets on a troubled world (17), atomic energy
(3), human rights (3), world federation (6), and the U.N.
(10).

Peace--General

625   JX1904.P4,1949

[National Peace Council (London)].

"Books on peace and world affairs published in Great Britain in
1948, a selected list; Pamphlets on peace and world affairs,
1948 to spring 1949, a selected list; A selected list of
British official documents on world affairs published in 1948;
Periodicals on international affairs published in Great
Britain, a selected list."
In its Peace Year Book, 1949.
London: National Peace Council, Summer, 1949. pp. 80-87, 87-92,
93-97, 97-99.

   361 items, 1948 - 1949. English.

   Books and pamphlets on fundamental issues and world order
   (34), history, politics, and economics (26), Europe, world
   government, and western union (37), Commonwealth and colonial
   affairs (22), Germany and Austria (9), U.S.S.R. (33), U.S.
   (18), Middle East (5), Asia and Africa (19), U.N. (28),
   pacifism and conscription (11), atomic energy (3),
   miscellaneous (32); British official documents on world
   affairs (44); British periodicals (40).

626

[Busse, Nataliya].

Kakvo da Chetem v´v Vr´zka s Borbata za Mir [What to Read in
Connection with the Struggle for Peace]: Prepor´chitelna
bibliografiya [Selected bibliography].
Sofia: Bŭlgarski Bibliografski Institut Elin Pelin, 1950.
61 pp.

   103 items, 1949 - 1950. Bulgarian (in Cyrillic alphabet).
   Most items have brief to medium-length annotations; preface
   (2 pp.); introduction (25 pp.); table of contents;
   author/subject index; appended list of publications of the
   Bulgarian Bibliographic Institute.

627   Z6464.Z9M63

[Lukicheva, T. S. (comp.)].

Na Strazhe Mira [To Guard Peace].
Moscow: Publichnaia Biblioteka im. V. I. Lenina, Nauchno-
metodicheskii Kabinet Bibliotekovediniia [Lenin Public Library,

Peace--General

Scientific-Methodological Office of Library Science], 1951.
24 pp.

628   JX1904.P4,1951

[National Peace Council (London)].

"Books on world affairs published in Great Britain, 1949-50, a
selected list; Pamphlets . . . ; Films, selected lists;
Periodicals . . ."
In its Peace Year Book, 1951: Festival edition.
London: National Peace Council, 1951. pp. 61-70, 72-78, 79-83,
86-88.

  432 items, 1949 - 1950. English.

  Books and pamphlets on fundamental issues, world order, world
  government, and federalism (45), history, politics, and
  economics (25), Great Britain, the Commonwealth, and colonial
  affairs (30), Europe, western union, etc. (36), Germany (12),
  U.S.S.R. (43), U.S. (25), Middle and Near East (5), Africa
  (13), Asia (32), U.N. (27), pacifism and conscription (18),
  atomic energy (6), miscellaneous (29); films (46); British
  periodicals (40).

629   JX1904.P4,1953

[National Peace Council (London)].

"Books and pamphlets, a selected list; Periodicals on peace and
world affairs."
In its Peace Year Book, 1953.
London: National Peace Council, 1953. pp. 22-30, 34-35.

  237 items, 1952. English.

  Books and pamphlets on fundamental issues and world order
  (25), history, politics, and economics (19), United Nations
  (18), armaments and rearmament (11), pacifism and
  conscription (15), Europe, western union, etc. (19), Great
  Britain, the Commonwealth, and colonies (10), U.S. (9), U.S.
  S.R. (30), Near and Middle East (7), Africa (13), Asia and
  the Far East (34), miscellaneous (6); British periodicals
  (21).

Peace--General

630   JX1952.R36

Raumer, Kurt von.

Schrifttum [Literature].
In his Ewiger Friede [Eternal Peace]: Friedensrufe und
Friedenspläne seit der Renaissance [Peace demands and peace
plans since the Renaissance].
Freiburg/Munich: Karl Alber (Orbis Academicus, Geschichte der
politischen Ideen in Dokumenten und Darstellungen), 1953. pp.
498-505.

   159 items plus additional citations in notes, 1503 - 1953.
   German, French, Latin; also English, Italian, Dutch.
   Bibliographic essay (154 items with critical remarks),
   followed by chapter footnotes (24 pp.) and textual notes
   (9 pp.) containing additional references.

   Books, articles, bibliographies, reference works, and
   critical editions of texts concerning the history of ideas
   of peace, pacifism, internationalism, and the lives of major
   proponents of peace from Erasmus to Gentz.

631   JX1904.P4,1954

[National Peace Council (London)].

"Books and pamphlets published in Great Britain, 1953, a
selected list; Periodicals and news sheets."
In its Peace Year Book, 1954.
London: National Peace Council, 1954. pp. 28-37, 39-45.

   346 items, 1953. English; also French, Italian (3), German (3),
   Swedish (2), Spanish (1), Dutch (1).

   Books and pamphlets on fundamental issues and world order
   (16), history, politics, and economics (28), United Nations
   (16), armaments and disarmament (4), pacifism and
   conscription (8), Europe, western union, etc. (46), Great
   Britain, Commonwealth, and colonies (9), U.S.A. (8), U.S.S.R.
   (24), Near and Middle East (9), Africa (21), Asia and the Far
   East (26), miscellaneous (16); periodicals and news sheets
   (115). List of peace organizations appended.

Peace--General

632   JX1904.P4,1955

[National Peace Council (London)].

"Books and pamphlets published in Great Britain, 1954, a
selected list; Periodicals and news sheets."
In its Peace Year Book, 1955.
London: National Peace Council, 1955. pp. 25-34, 36-45.

   361 items, 1954. English; also German, French, Norwegian (4),
   Swedish (3), Italian (3), other Western European languages.

   Books and pamphlets on fundamental issues and world order
   (27), history, politics, and economics (31), United Nations
   (7), armaments and disarmament (12), pacifism and
   conscription (8), Europe, western union, etc. (20), Great
   Britain, the Commonwealth and colonies (13), U.S.A. (14), U.
   S.S.R. (21), Near and Middle East (10), Africa (15), Asia and
   the Far East (22), miscellaneous (7); periodicals and news
   sheets arranged by country (154). List of peace organizations
   appended.

633   JX1904.P4,1957

[National Peace Council (London)].

"Books [and] pamphlets published in Great Britain, 1955-6, a
selected list; Periodicals and news sheets."
In its Peace Year Book, 1957.
London: National Peace Council, 1957. pp. 27-37, 39-47.

   340 items, 1955 - 1956. English; also German, French,
   Swedish(4), Italian (3), Norwegian (3), other Western
   European languages.

   Books and pamphlets on fundamental issues and world order
   (22), history, politics, and economics (23), United Nations
   (9), armaments and disarmament (7), pacifism and conscription
   (7), Europe and European countries (16), Britain, the
   Commonwealth and colonies (11), U.S.A. (11), U.S.S.R. (17),
   Near and Middle East (12), Africa (33), Asia and the Far East
   (24), miscellaneous (8); periodicals and news sheets arranged
   by country (140). List of peace organizations appended.

Peace--General

634   CSt-H: S.P.U.S.A.

[Acts for Peace].

Literature List.
Berkeley, Calif.: Acts for Peace, 1960. 28 pp. (mimeo).

   336 items, 1942 - 1960. English. Most items have brief
   descriptive and/or critical annotations; introduction
   (1 paragraph); table of contents.

   The politics of peace (28), United Nations and growth toward
   world law (49), challenge of world economic and social
   development (15), ending the arms race (22), civil defense
   (8), economics of peace (6), tension areas (3), the Communist
   world (14), defense in the nuclear age (26), militarism and
   conscription (11), conscientious objection to war (25),
   nonviolent resistance as an alternative to war (29), social
   responsibility in science (9), Gandhi and contemporary
   pacifist thought (13), religious pacifism (26), the church
   and peace (21), philosophical and political work (12),
   miscellaneous (19).

635 <

Acts for Peace.

Ideas and Information on Peace and World Affairs.
[Berkeley, Calif.]: Acts for Peace, 1961. 13 pp.

   Apparently unavailable; not located through interlibrary
   loan.

636   JX1954.P45

Pereña [Vicente], Luciano.

Bibliografia.
In his En la Frontera de la Paz [On the Frontier of Peace].
Madrid: Editorial Católica (Colección Cristianismo y Mundo,
No. 9), 1961. pp. 215-248.

   824 items, 1935 - 1959. Spanish, French; also Italian, English,
   German, Latin, Dutch (4), Portuguese (3). Introduction
   (1 p.).

   Works by the Catholic hierarchy and by Catholic thinkers on
   systematization of Christian thought about war and peace
   (105), the nature of peace (164), international man (193),

Peace--General

   brotherhood of nations (79), international law (97), war
   against hunger (60), turn toward Christian morality (126).

637 <

Union of International Associations.

"[Bibliography of studies on international cooperation]."
Journal of International Associations (Brussels), (January,
1965).

638

Sorokin, Pitirim A[leksandrovich].

[Bibliographic] notes.
In his The Ways and Power of Love.
Chicago: Henry Regnery (Gateway Edition), 1967. pp. [285]-313.
First edition, Boston: Beacon Press, 1954.

639   JX1941.Z35

Zampaglione, Gerardo.
Bibliografia
In his L´Idea della Pace nel Mondo Antico [The Idea of Peace in
the Ancient World].
Turin: ERI-Edizioni Rai Radiotelevisione Italiana (Saggi, 52),
1967. pp. 453-480.

   910 items, 1824 - 1964. French, German, English; also Italian,
   other Western European languages. Introduction (1 p.).

   Books on peace and war in general (56), the idea of peace in
   Greek civilization (412), peace in Roman thought and in later
   Hellenistic speculation (193), peace in the Old Testament
   (65), and peace in Christian doctrine (184). Each of these
   sections is further subdivided.

640   JX1952.H452

Herman, Sondra R.

Bibliography.
In her Eleven against War: Studies in American internationalist
thought, 1898-1921.
Stanford: Stanford University, Hoover Institution Press, 1969.
pp. 230-258.

Peace--General

Works by and about Elihu Root, Nicholas Murray Butler, Josiah
Royce, Jane Addams, Thorstein Veblen, Woodrow Wilson, and
others on peace and internationalism; secondary sources on
the peace movement, the League of Nations, social reform, and
social, economic, and political theory.

641 <

[Publishers for Peace].

"Peace: A Publishers for Peace bibliography."
Library Journal (October 15, 1970).

642   JX1903.J6

Barsegov, Yuri and Rustem Khairov.

References in "A study of the problems of peace."
Journal of Peace Research, 10, 1,2 (1973): 79-80.

  62 items, 1919 - 1971. English; also Spanish (1), French (1).

  Mostly books on social and political theory, peace theory,
  and social psychology.

643

Kuehl, Warren F. (comp.).

Internationalism: A selected list of research-study materials
to provide students with information on the historical
evolution of an idea and an ideal.
Los Angeles: California State University at Los Angeles, Center
for the Study of Armament and Disarmament (Political Issues
Series, Vol. 3, No. 4), 1975. 42 pp.

  273 items, 1840 - 1974. English. Introduction (3 pp.); each
  section also has an introductory paragraph; table of
  contents.

  Books, articles, and documentary materials on the political
  organization of the world (163), peaceful resolution of
  disputes (44), community internationalists (34), new
  internationalism (24), and bibliographies (8).

Peace Movement--General

644   BN: 8° Q.Pièce.2398

[Moch, Gaston (comp.)].

Catalogue de l´Exposition de la Paix [Catalogue of the Peace
Exhibit]: Organisée par le Bureau International Permanent de la
Paix dans le Palais des Congrès et de l´Economie Social
(section Suisse) à Paris (Exposition Universelle de 1900)
[Organized by the Permanent International Peace Bureau in the
Palace of Congresses and of Social Economy (Swiss section) at
Paris (Universal Exhibition of 1900)].
Berne: Büchler, 1900. pp. 4-28.

   476 items, 1867 - 1900. French; also English, German, Italian,
   Swedish, Danish (4), other Western and Eastern European
   languages. Preface (2 pp.); table of contents;
   author/organization index.

   Works on the organization, history, and bibliography of the
   peace movement (95), periodicals published by peace societies
   (49), peace and antiwar propaganda (74), documents and
   various objects of the general peace movement and of peace
   societies (13), history and theory of international law and
   international arbitration (68), the [first] Hague Conference
   (8), war and armaments (75); works and documents on past wars
   (11), creative literature, poetry, anthologies, and art (46),
   instructional materials (10), biographies (3), South African
   (Boer) War (12), miscellaneous (12).

645   Z6464.Z9L17

La Fontaine, Henri.

Bibliographie de la Paix et de l´Arbitrage Internationale, Tome
Premier [Bibliography of Peace and International Arbitration,
Volume One]: Mouvement pacifique [Peace movement].
Monaco/Paris/Vienna/Brussels/Zurich: Institut International de
la Paix/Bureau Bibliographique Parisien/Secrétariat de
l´Institut International de Bibliographie/Institut
International de Bibliographie/Concilium Bibliographicum
(Publications de l´Institut International de la Paix, No. 1),
1904. xii + 280 pp.

   2218 items, 1430 - 1903. French, German; also English, Italian,
   Dutch, Danish, Norwegian, other Western and Eastern European

Peace Movement--General

languages. Preface (5 pp.); outline of the subject
classification; author index; subject index.

The first major bibliography on peace and the peace movement,
developed as part of the Bibliographia Universalis, a
collection of over 40 volumes on many subjects published by
the Institut International de Bibliographie. General works on
peace and war (1113), periodicals (54), conferences,
associations, expositions, etc. (411), anthologies (20),
histories of the peace movement (25), the peace movement in
various countries (31), the peace movement in various forms,
including architecture, design, painting, photography, music,
literature, and theater (255), the peace movement in its
various aspects: bibliography, the press, morality, religion,
social science, politics, economics, working classes,
socialism, law, education, feminism, biographies (309).

646   Z6464.Z9N6

Association de la Paix par le Droit.

Réglement et Catalogue de la Bibliothèque Circulante [Rules and
Catalogue of the Circulating Library].
Nimes: Association de la Paix par le Droit, Bibliothèque
Pédagogique, [1905]. 30 pp.

566 items, 1859 - 1904. French; also English, Italian, German,
Dutch (4), Spanish (3), Danish (1), Latin (1), Polish (1).
Rules of the library; outline of the subject classification.

General works on peace and war (59), war (45), pacifist
propaganda (84), peace societies and organizations (47),
peace congresses and conferences (38), the reduction of
armaments (26), expectations of a European conflagration (9),
colonization (10), international politics, peace, and
arbitration (127), political and social economy (50), novels,
poetry, and drama on peace and war (31), pacifism in the
schools (11), almanacs (10), periodicals (19).

647   JX1908.W55M43

Mead, Edwin D[oak].

The Literature of the Peace Movement [bibliographic essay].
Boston: International School of Peace, 1909. 14 pp.
First published in the Chautauquan, May, 1909. Reprinted, World
Peace Foundation Pamphlet Series, 1910-1911, Vol. 1 (unnumbered
pamphlet); and WPF Pamphlet Series, 1912, Vol. 2 (7, Part 4,
October).

Peace Movement--General

32 items, 1795 - 1909. English. All items are discussed in
the text.

Major philosophical works on peace, sermons, peace plans, and
works on international law and arbitration.

648   Z6466.082

[Norske Nobelinstitutt].

Bibliographie du Mouvement de la Paix [Bibliography of the
Peace Movement]: Littérature pacifiste dans la Bibliothèque de
l'Institut Nobel Norvégien [Pacifist literature in the Library
of the Norwegian Nobel Institute] (Catalogue de la Bibliothèque
de l'Institut Nobel Norvégien: I, Littérature pacifiste).
Kristiania/Paris/Munich and Leipzig/London/The Hague/New York:
H. Aschehoug (W. Nygaard)/Félix Alcan/Duncker und
Humblot/Williams and Norgate/Martinus Nijhoff/G. P. Putnam's
Sons, 1912. xi pp. + 226 col. + pp. 227-239.

2735 items, 1523 - 1912. French, English, German; also Italian,
Norwegian, Swedish, Danish, Dutch, other western languages.
Introduction (4 pp.); outline of subject classifications;
table of contents; subject index; author index.

Bibliography (15), manuals (9), history of the idea of peace
(122), universal federation and internationalism (103),
patriotism (35), philosophy of peace and war (74), general
works on peace and war (57), collections (23), essays,
pamphlets (586), sermons (74), conferences, lectures (85),
addresses, petitions, letters, demonstrations, etc. (48),
periodicals (85), Interparliamentary Union (133), Nobel
Committee of the Norwegian Parliament (32), International
Peace Institute, Monaco (3), Bureau International Permanent
de la Paix, Berne (32), international associations for peace
(53), national peace societies (224), universal peace
congresses (75), national peace congresses (47), museums and
expositions (9), history of the peace movement (52),
biographies of pacifists (97), peace and religious beliefs
(174), Quakers and peace (55), economic and social questions
and peace (113), peace and education (95), women and peace
(27), fine arts (painting, music) and peace (33), literary
works with pacifist tendencies (165).

Peace Movement--General

649   JX1904.A44

[Bureau International Permanent de la Paix, à Berne].

Publications périodiques reçues par le Bureau (1912);
Bibliographie [Periodical publications received by the Bureau
(1912); Bibliography].
In its Annuaire du Mouvement Pacifiste pour l´Année 1913
[Yearbook of the Peace Movement for the Year 1913].
Berne: Bureau International Permanent de la Paix, 1913.
pp. 210-225; 226-277.

   846 items, 1813 - 1912. English, French, German; also Dutch,
   Italian, other Western and Eastern European languages. A few
   items have brief descriptive annotations.

   Mostly peace periodicals received by the Bureau from Germany
   (9), Belgium (7), Denmark (2), Spain (2), France (19),
   Britain (9), Hungary (1), Italy (8), Norway (1), Netherlands
   (1), Poland (1), Rumania (1), Sweden (1), Switzerland (8),
   Turkey (1), U.S. (5), Central America (1), Mexico (1),
   Australia (3), Canada (1), and Japan (3); works published by
   the Bureau (36); and German (112), American (152), British
   (226), French (111), Dutch (47), Italian (26), and
   Scandinavian (51) works on the history, aims and methods of
   the peace movement and on the whole spectrum of problems of
   war and peace.

650   JX1905.F7,1911a

Fried, Alfred Hermann.

"Führer durch die pazifistische Literatur [Guide to pacifist
literature]."
In his Handbuch der Friedensbewegung, zweiter Teil [Handbook of
the Peace Movement Part Two]: Geschichte, Umfang und
Organisation der Friedensbewegung [History, extent, and
organization of the peace movement].
Berlin/Leipzig: Friedens-Warte, 1913 (Zweite, gänzlich
umgearbeitete, erweiterte Auflage). pp. [423]-462.
Reprinted, with a new introduction by Daniel Gasman, New
York/London: Garland (Library of War and Peace), 1972.

   305 items, 1846 - 1912. German, French; also English, Italian
   (4), Dutch (2), Japanese (1), Esperanto (1), other Eastern
   and Western European languages. Most items have brief
   descriptive annotations; table of contents.

   Periodicals--pacifist journals (33), yearbooks and almanacs
   (11), scientific journals for international law and
   international organization (7), periodicals that have ceased

Peace Movement--General

publication (10), pamphlet series (7); books and pamphlets--
bibliography (8), introduction to the peace movement (21),
the work at the Hague (25), arbitration (24), various
questions of international law (8), armaments and economy
(25), international organization, internationalism, etc.
(20), sociology, biology, philosophy (19), history of the
peace movement (26), organizations and congresses (19),
education and Christianity (9), Germany and France (9),
descriptions of war (7), miscellaneous (13), arguments
against the peace movement (4).

651   JX1908.U5,v.3

[World Peace Foundation].

"The international library: The most important series of books
on the peace movement."
World Peace Foundation Pamphlet Series, 3, 5, Part 2 (May, 1913):
2-7.

  21 items (no dates given). English. All items have medium- to
  abstract-length descriptive and critical annotations.

  Books and speeches on opposition to war, peace projects, the
  peace movement, international understanding, Hague
  conferences, international arbitration, and theories of war
  and peace.

652   DLC-DB

[United States Library of Congress, Division of Bibliography].

Brief List of References on International Conciliation and
Peace.
[Washington, D.C.]: Library of Congress, Division of
Bibliography, December 16, 1914. 2 pp. (typescript).

  17 items, 1909 - 1914. English.

  Books and pamphlets on international arbitration, the peace
  movement, and disarmament. Appended list of peace societies
  that distribute free pamphlets.

Peace Movement--General

653   Z7164.I8H6

Hicks, Frederick C.

Internationalism: A list of current periodicals selected and
annotated.
New York: American Association for International Conciliation
(International Conciliation, Special Bulletin), May, 1915.
19 pp.

   49 items (no dates given, periodicals current in 1915, some
   began publication before 1850). English, French; also German
   (7), Italian (2), Dutch (1), Russian (1), Japanese (1). Most
   items have brief to medium-length descriptive annotations;
   prefatory note (2 pp.); table of contents.

   Pacifist periodicals (18), periodicals on international
   understanding (17), and periodicals on international law
   (14).

654   Z6464.Z9M4,1915

Mez, John [Richard].

The War and Peace Problem: Material for the study of
international polity.
New York: Carnegie Endowment for International Peace, Division
of Intercourse and Education, February, 1915. 12 pp.

   50 items, 1890 - 1915. English; also German (6), French (3).
   Most items have brief to abstract-length descriptive and/or
   critical annotations.

   Modern pacifism (25), some famous books on the peace movement
   (9), the opposite (militarist and imperialist) point of view
   (7), periodicals (5), additional sources (4).

655   Z6464.Z9C3

[Matthews, Mary Alice (comp.)].

Peace and the Peace Movement: Select list of references
prepared by the librarian of the Carnegie Endowment for
International Peace.
Washington, D.C.: Carnegie Endowment for International Peace,
Library (Miscellaneous Reading List No. 18), August 12, 1924.
28 pp. (mimeo).

   323 items, 1736 - 1924. English; also French (17), German (8).
   Some items have brief descriptive annotations; table of

Peace Movement--General

contents.

General works on peace (222), bibliographies (14),
collections of essays, poetry, and quotations (15), peace
pageants (5), materials on peace movements (29), and early
peace projects (38).

656   H69.J6,1927

Johnsen, Julia E. (comp.).

"Internationalism."
In her Questions of the Hour.
New York: H. W. Wilson (The Reference Shelf, Vol. 4, No. 10),
April, 1927 [3rd ed.]. pp. 29-31.

   38 items (no dates given). English.

   Internationalism and the rights and duties of nations (5),
   rise and progress of the peace movement (5), some essentials
   and influences tending to lasting peace (6), League of
   Nations (5), World Court (6), cancellation of the allied debt
   (6), recognition of Soviet Russia (6).

657   Z6466.Z9W8

World Peace Foundation (comp.).

International Relations Publications: Available from a group of
American organizations.
Boston: World Peace Foundation, [1927]. 71 pp.

   472 items, 1897 - 1927. English. Most items have brief
   descriptive annotations; introduction (1 p.); subject index;
   appended list of peace organizations.

   Pamphlets and some books on a wide range of peace movement
   and international relations topics, grouped under about 75
   subject headings including arbitration (10), armament problem
   (13), peace classics (13), Permanent Court of International
   Justice (21), education (14), League of Nations (32), peace
   organizations (38), outlawry of war (16), peace advocates
   (6), history of peace movement (7), programs for meetings
   (7), and the world war (10).

Peace Movement--General

658   JX1961.U6C8

Curti, Merle E[ugene].

Bibliography.
In his The American Peace Crusade, 1815-1860.
Durham: Duke University Press, 1929. pp. [230]-241.
Reprinted, New York/London: Garland (Library of War and Peace),
1971.

   151 items, 1809 - 1926. English; also French (14). Some items
   have medium-length critical annotations.

   Manuscript materials (10), peace periodicals (9), government
   documents (4), pamphlets, tracts, and addresses (43),
   autobiographies and memoirs (14), treatises (34), secondary
   books (24), and articles (3) on the American peace movement
   from 1815 to 1860.

659   JX1952.A65

Allen, Devere.

References.
In his The Fight for Peace.
New York: Macmillan, 1930. pp. 701-716.
Reprinted, with a new introduction by Charles Chatfield, New
York: Garland (Library of War and Peace), 1971; also New York:
Jerome S. Ozer (Peace Movement in America Series), 1972.

   Approximately 511 items, 1774 - 1930. English. Endnote
   format, some items are critically discussed; introduction
   (1 p.).

   Books, tracts, speeches, pamphlets, newspaper, magazine, and
   journal articles on the history of peace movements and
   theories of peace and war.

660   HM66.D11

Davis, Jerome.

Bibliography in "The peace movement."
In his Contemporary Social Movements.
New York/London: Century (The Century Social Science Series),
1930. pp. 859-868.

   290 items, 1907 - 1930. English.

Peace Movement--General

    War (28), the peace movement (94), the League of Nations
    (14), the World Court (6), outlawry of war (4), policies of
    the United States (49), fiction on war (28), drama (19),
    periodicals (23), organization publications (13),
    organizations (12).

661   JX1948.G7

Phelps [Grant], Christina.

Selected bibliography.
In her The Anglo-American Peace Movement in the Mid-nineteenth
Century (Ph.D. dissertation, Faculty of Political Science,
Columbia University).
New York: Columbia University Press (Studies in History,
Economics, and Public Law), 1930. pp. 214-223
Reprinted, New York: Garland (Library of War and Peace), 1972.

    244 items, 1641 - 1929. English; also French, Latin (3),
    Italian (2).

    General bibliographies of peace literature (8), primary
    sources (98), secondary sources (99), American periodicals
    (10), and British periodicals (29) covering the whole range
    of peace movement activities and concerns.

662   Z6464.Z9A38

Wilson, E[dward] Raymond and Elsie Lowenberg.

Preliminary Study of Current Literature Dealing with Peace or
International Relations: Pamphlets and study courses
(preliminary report--not for publication or quotation).
New York: American Community, in cooperation with 53
organizations, March 3, 1930. 34 pp. (mimeo).

    433 items (no dates given).

    References listed in tables xv-xviii, appended to content
    analysis of the items, including pamphlets (285), study
    courses and outlines (64), bibliographies (39), and
    periodicals and bulletins (45).

Peace Movement--General

663   JX1938.B4

Beales, A[rthur] C. F.

Bibliography.
In his The History of Peace: A short account of the organised
movements for international peace.
New York: Lincoln MacVeagh, Dial Press, 1931. pp. 335-344.
Reprinted, New York: Garland (Library of War and Peace), 1972.

  270 items, 1823 - 1930. English; also French, German, Dutch
  (1).

  Bibliographies, statistics, etc. (7), works on the period to
  1815 (18), newspapers and periodicals (16), works by peace
  advocates (50), congress and conference reports (15),
  yearbooks, etc. (6), biographies of peace advocates (40),
  aspects of the peace movement (45), international arbitration
  (26), twentieth-century peace questions (33), miscellaneous
  (14).

664 <

Galpin, William F.

Bibliography.
In his Pioneering for Peace: A study of American peace efforts
to 1846.
Syracuse, N.Y.: Bardeen Press, 1933. pp. 217-233.

665 <

Angell, Norman.

Bibliography in "Peace movements."
In Encyclopedia of the Social Sciences, Vol. 12.
New York: Macmillan, 1934. pp. 41-47.

666   Z6464.Z9H43

[Ter Meulen, Jacob (ed.)].

Bibliographie du Mouvement de la Paix avant 1899/Bibliography
of the Peace Movement before 1899 (Listes
provisoires/Provisional Lists), [1778-1898].
The Hague: Bibliothèque du Palais de la Paix/Library of the
Palace of Peace, [1934]. 124 columns in 4-column galleys.

Peace Movement--General

3536 items, 1778 - 1898. English, French, German; also Italian,
Dutch, Swedish, Danish, Norwegian, other Western and Eastern
European languages.

Books, pamphlets, periodicals, and articles on the peace
movement and a wide range of war/peace topics, arranged
chronologically. The number of items is inflated by
repetition of periodical titles for each year of publication.

667   Z6464.Z9H43,Index

[Ter Meulen, Jacob (ed.)].

Bibliographie du Mouvement de la Paix pour la Période 1776-
1898: Index alphabétique des noms propres/Bibliography of the
Peace Movement for the Period 1776-1898: Alphabetic index of
names.
[The Hague: Bibliothèque du Palais de la Paix/Library of the
Palace of Peace], 1934. 7 pp.

668   JX1961.U6C83

Curti, Merle [Eugene].

[Bibliographic] Notes.
In his Peace or War: The American struggle, 1636-1936.
New York: W. W. Norton, 1936. pp. 313-358.

1692 - 1935 (mainly late nineteenth and early twentieth
century materials). Endnote format, listing sources by
chapter, page, and line of text.

Books, articles, letters, documents, reports, periodicals,
and histories of the peace movement in the United States,
England, and Europe.

669   Z6464.Z9H43

Ter Meulen, Jacob (ed.), with the collaboration of J.
Huizinga and G. Berlage.

Bibliographie du Mouvement de la Paix avant 1899 (Listes
Provisoires)/Bibliography of the Peace Movement before 1899
(Provisional Lists); Période/Period: 1480-1776.
The Hague: Bibliothèque du Palais de la Paix/Library of the
Palace of Peace, 1936. 24 pp.
Also published as: Bibliographie der Friedensbewegung für die
Periode 1480-1776, Friedens-Warte, 1936, v. 36, pp. 82-89,
149-161 (JX1903.F7,v.36).

Peace Movement--General

466 items, 1480 - 1776. Latin, French; also German, English,
Dutch, Italian (9), Swedish (3), other western and eastern
European languages. List arranged chronologically; author
index.

Includes various editions and translations of many of the
works cited. Covers early peace plans and works on the causes
and effects of war, the nature and conditions of peace,
religion and peace, and creative literature on war and peace.

670   L11.N15,v.27

Farley, Belmont.

[Bibliography] "The road to peace."
Journal of the National Education Association, 27, 5 (May, 1938):
A97-A98.

19 items, 1905 - 1936. English. Some items have brief
descriptive annotations; introduction (1 paragraph).

Books on the history of the peace movement, international
organization, history of war and peace, and the Hague
conferences.

671   Z6464.Z9C46,1938

Matthews, Mary Alice (comp.).

Peace Forces of Today: Select list of recent books and articles
on various aspects of the peace movement, with annotations.
Washington, D.C.: Carnegie Endowment for International Peace,
Library (Reading List No. 27), May 20, 1938 (rev. ed.). 54 pp.
Earlier editions of Reading List No. 27 appeared in 1930 and
1934.

640 items, 1893 - 1938. English; also French The 1930 edition
contained 508 items, 1909-1930, in 35 pp. The 1934 edition
contained 411 items, 1907-1934, in 33 pp. Some items have
brief descriptive and/or critical annotations; table of
contents; author index; list of bibliographies (34) compiled
in the library of the CEIP.

General works (54), communications and transit (28),
economics and finance (53), fine arts and recreation (37),
intellectual cooperation (58), inter-American relations (43),
international organization (36), language and literature
(22), law and legislation (48), League of Nations (13),
military, naval, and air policies (29), peace movement (33),
philosophy and religion (29), political institutions (17),

Peace Movement--General

public opinion and the press (24), science and technology
(12), social institutions (19), women in peace work (21),
youth movement (30). The 1930 and 1934 editions of this
bibliography were similar in format and content but contained
a substantial number of different items, with a slightly
different scheme of organization, including sections such as
"Disarmament and Security" and "Politics and Government,"
references on special topics such as reparations, and address
lists of peace organizations.

672   UB342.U5F72

French, Paul Comly.

Bibliography.
In his We Won't Murder: Being the story of men who followed
their conscientious scruples and helped give life to democracy.
New York: Hastings House, 1940. pp. 181-189.
Reprinted, New York: Jerome S. Ozer (The Peace Movement in
America: A Facsimile Reprint Collection), 1972.

   145 items, 1885 - 1940. English. Introduction (1 paragraph).

   Books (79), articles (25), pamphlets and leaflets (36), and
   miscellaneous material (5) on pacifism, the peace movement,
   the causes and prevention of war, and various approaches to
   peace.

673   Z6464.Z9C47

Matthews, Mary Alice (comp.).

The Peace Movement: Select list of references on the work of
national and international organizations for the advancement of
peace; with special attention to the movement in the United
States.
Washington, D.C.: Carnegie Endowment for International Peace,
Library (Reading List No. 39), October 15, 1940. 67 pp.

   751 items, 1870 - 1940. English; also French, German (5),
   Spanish (4), Danish (1), Swedish (1). Some items have brief
   descriptive annotations; explanatory notes (1 p.); table of
   contents; subject/author index.

   Bibliographies (7), general works (232), lists and
   descriptions of international organizations (171), national
   peace organizations (131), organizations having peace or
   international relations committees (95), miscellaneous
   organizations promoting international understanding (67),
   peace periodicals (48).

Peace Movement--General

674   BX7641.5.P35H2

American Friends Service Committee, Peace Section.

For further reading [5 lists]; Periodicals.
In its Handbook for Peacemakers.
Philadelphia: American Friends Service Committee, October,
1942. pp. 7, 14, 18, 19, 22, 23-24. (mimeo).

  67 items, 1930 - 1942. English.

  Books and pamphlets on postwar planning and reconstruction,
  Christianity and peace, war resistance, nonviolence, peace
  education, community services and peace, conscientious
  objectors, pacifism, world order and community cooperation;
  list of peace periodicals and peace organizations.

675   Z733.S97B85,v.45

Brinton, Ellen Starr and Hiram Doty (comps.), with the
assistance of Gladys Hill.

Guide to the Swarthmore College Peace Collection: A memorial to
Jane Addams (Peace Collection Publication No. 1).
Swarthmore College Bulletin, 45, 4 (1947): 1-72.

  311 items (collections), 1675 - 1947. English; also French,
  German, Dutch, other Eastern and Western European languages.
  Most items have brief to abstract-length descriptive
  annotations; foreword (2 pp.); table of contents;
  subject/author index.

  Lists and describes the various document collections in the
  SCPC as of 1947; includes records from various individuals
  and organizations in several countries who were primarily
  interested in the promotion of peace or whose work was
  closely related to the peace movement; also includes special
  collections of attacks on the peace movement, books,
  cartoons, church and religious peace material, international
  languages, peace plays, peace posters, peace seals, stamps
  and covers, periodicals, paintings by Benjamin West on Penn´s
  peace treaty with the Indians, and youth peace materials.

Peace Movement--General

676   Z733.S97B85,v.46

[Brinton, Ellen Starr (comp.)].

"Current peace periodicals."
In Swarthmore College Peace Collection: A memorial to Jane
Addams (Peace Collection Bulletin No. 2),
Swarthmore College Bulletin, 46, 3 (September, 1949): 8-16.

   91 items (no dates given). English; also French, German (9),
   Swedish (5), Danish (4), Spanish (4), other Western and
   Eastern European languages. Some items have brief descriptive
   annotations; introduction (1 paragraph).

   Lists peace periodicals published in various countries of the
   world. Periodicals are arranged alphabetically by country of
   publication.

677   BL: 7960.g.3.

Comité "Pax".

Construisons la Paix [Let´s Build Peace]: Catalogue de
l´exposition de livres, autographes, affiches, médailles et
documents divers, organisée par le Comité "Pax" pendant la
quinzaine de la paix, du 12 au 26 juin 1949, en la Maison de la
Paix à Bruxelles [Catalog of the exposition of books,
autographs, posters, medals, and miscellaneous documents,
organized by the "Pax" Committee during the fortnight of peace,
from June 12 to 26, 1949, in the House of Peace in Brussels].
Brussels: Comité "Pax," 1949. 10 pp.

   472 items, 1509 - 1946. French; also English, German, Dutch,
   Swedish (1).

   Precursors (8), pacifist associations and congresses from the
   beginning of the nineteenth century (33), Tolstoy and Henri
   Ner (26), works on peace to the end of the nineteenth century
   (20), some pacifist associations of the nineteenth century
   (21), Nobel prize, international groups (40), the world city,
   the Mundaneum, some great pacifists (29), pre-World War I,
   antimilitarism, foundations in the U.S.A. (30), pacifism
   during World War I (39), the beginning of the "interwar
   period" (30), India and nonviolence (43), conscientious
   objection (55), the church and peace (27), peace and
   education (8), the campaign against the arms merchants (28),
   before and after the [1932] disarmament conference (35).

Peace Movement--General

678 <   BL: 11927.R.18.

[Academia Republicii Populare Romîne, Biblioteca].

Lupta Pentru Apărarea Păcii [Struggle in the Defense of Peace]:
Indrumare bibliographică [Bibliographic guide].
Bucharest: Academia Republicii Populare Romîne, Biblioteca,
1950. vi + 231 pp.

679 <   Z6464.Z9P6

Polónyi, Péter and Maria Szántó.

Tiz Eves a Békemozgalom [Ten Years of the Peace Movement]:
Bibliográfiai tájékoztatás a békevilágmozgalom és a
világifjúsági találkozók magyarnyelvii irodalmáról
[Bibliographic information on the peacetime movement and the
Hungarian writers of the World Youth Festival].
Budapest: Fővárosi Szabó Ervin Könyvtár, 1959. 82 pp.

680   Z6464.Z9M5

Miller, William Robert (comp. and ed.).

Bibliography of Books on War, Pacifism, Nonviolence and Related
Studies.
Nyack, New York: Fellowship of Reconciliation, 1960. v + 30 pp.
(mimeo).
Revised edition with addenda and author index, 1961, v + 37 pp.
A third edition, revised and updated, was published in Peter
Mayer (ed.), The Pacifist Conscience, New York: Holt, Rinehart,
and Winston, 1966, pp. 440-472.

    516 + 38 items, 1846 - 1961. English. Some items (select list
    and list of periodicals) have brief descriptive annotations;
    foreword (1 p.); table of contents; postscripts about library
    research sources, the Fellowship of Reconciliation, and the
    pamphlet series of the Pacifist Research Bureau (2 pp.);
    author index (2nd edition only).

    Select list (51), pacifist living (34), challenge of ethics
    (11), problems of war and peace (93), meaning and dimensions
    of active love (10), discipleship and commitment resources
    (15), Christianity and society (28), social power and human
    nature (23), nationalism (5), "man" and state (13), U.S.
    foreign policy (8), the good society and social revolution
    (29), disarmament and international order (24), war and
    militarism (22), conscientious objection to war (24), nuclear
    energy and explosions (11), wars of our time (14), population
    and resources (11), communism in the world conflict (32), the

Peace Movement--General

Negro in America (26), emergent Africa (7), current
periodicals (10); addenda (2nd edition, 38 items). The
edition published in 1966 follows a somewhat different scheme
of organization and contains many new items published in the
intervening years. The first part of this edition is a
"Select List" of 55 items recommended by members of a
Bibliography Committee.

681   Z921.L6165

Reconciliation Library (London).

Catalogue 1962-1963.
London: International Fellowship of Reconciliation, 1963.
56 pp.

1012 items, 1887 - 1961. English; also German, French, Dutch
(3), Spanish (2), Swedish (1), Italian (1), Norwegian (1).
Introduction (1 p.); table of contents.

Historic and current literature on "Reconciliation" and peace
through the Christian ideal of love and nonviolence: general
and reference works (51), philosophy (125), religion and
theology (211), social sciences (37), political science (27),
colonial policy (15), international affairs (75), socialism
(21), law (144), war (53), social relief and welfare (10),
military and naval technology (7), literature (32), history
(107), and biography (97).

682   JX1907.I5,1963

Wilcox, Laird M. (ed.).

Periodicals.
In Wilkie, Lloyd and Laird M. Wilcox (eds.), International
Peace/Disarmament Directory.
York, Pa.: Lloyd Wilkie, Fall, 1963 (3rd ed.). pp. 67-92.

448 items (no dates given). English; also French, German, Dutch
(6), other European and oriental languages. Introduction
(1 paragraph).

List of periodicals that contain materials on peace and
disarmament, appended to a list of organizations interested
in peace and disarmament.

Peace Movement--General

683

Weinberg, Arthur and Lila Weinberg (eds.).

Selected bibliography; Sources.
In their Instead of Violence: Writings by the great advocates
of peace and nonviolence throughout history.
Boston: Beacon Press, 1965. pp. 475-483, 484-486.

684   HX243.B83

Bünger, Siegfried.

Quellen- und Literaturverzeichnis [Sources and literature
list].
In his Die sozialistische Antikriegsbewegung in
Grossbritannien, 1914-1917 [The Socialist Antiwar Movement in
Great Britain, 1914-1917].
Berlin: Deutscher Verlag der Wissenschaften (Schriftenreihe des
Instituts für Allgemeine Geschichte an der Humboldt-Universität
Berlin, Vol. 10), 1967. pp. 199-205.

   280 items, 1900 - 1966. English; also German, French (3),
   Russian (3).

   Journals, newspapers, reports, memoranda, documents,
   yearbooks, articles, and books on socialism and its
   relationship to war and peace, socialist theories, trade
   unionism, the labor movement, pacifism, imperialism,
   internationalism, memoirs and biographies of socialists,
   socialist opposition to war, and the history of the peace
   movement.

685 <

Willoughby, George.

Select Bibliography on the History of the American Peace
Movement.
Philadelphia: American Friends Service Committee, 1967.

686   Z6464.Z9C7

Cook, Blanche Wiesen (ed.).

Bibliography on Peace Research in History, with a preface by
Charles A. Barker.

Peace Movement--General

Santa Barbara, Calif.: ABC-Clio (Bibliography and Reference
Series, No. 11), 1969. v + 72 pp.

   1129 items, 1848 - 1969. English; also French, German, Dutch
   (2), Spanish (1), various Eastern European languages. Some
   items have brief descriptive and/or critical annotations;
   introduction (1 p.); table of contents; author index.

   Manuscript sources (21), bibliographical aids and
   organizations providing materials for the peace researcher
   (128), journals of peace research and related subjects (61),
   church history and religious pacifism (91), pacifism,
   antimilitarism, and nonviolence (193), arbitration,
   internationalism, and world law (183), histories of peace
   organizations (41), autobiographies, memoirs, and biographies
   of leaders in peace movements (141), politics and propaganda
   of peace and war (181), contemporary peacekeeping operations
   and studies in disarmament (63), works on Vietnam (26).

687

Wittner, Lawrence S.

Bibliography.
In his Rebels against War: The American peace movement, 1941-
1960.
New York/London: Columbia University Press (Contemporary
American History Series), 1969. pp. 287-328.

   907 items, 1923 - 1968. English.

   Manuscript collections (15), public documents (18), books and
   pamphlets (388), articles and periodicals (462), unpublished
   material (17), and personal communications (7) on the history
   of peace movement organizations, individuals, and activities
   in the United States, primarily during the period from 1930
   to 1960.

688

Chatfield, Charles.

Bibliographical notes.
In his For Peace and Justice: Pacifism in America, 1914-1941.
Knoxville: University of Tennessee Press, 1971. pp. 345-369.

   Manuscript sources, interviews and oral memoirs, periodicals,
   annual reports, memoirs, autobiographies, and secondary
   sources on peace leaders, pacifism, and the peace movement in
   the U.S.

Peace Movement--General

689   JX1961.U6M37

Marchand, C. Roland.

Bibliography; Bibliographical essay.
In his The American Peace Movement and Social Reform, 1898-
1918.
Princeton: Princeton University Press, 1972. pp. 391-395,
395-422.

   405 items, 1880 - 1971. English. Most items are critically
   discussed in the bibliographic essay.

   Lists of manuscript collections (50), materials from the
   history project of Columbia University (6), dissertations and
   theses (30); bibliographical essay includes general works on
   the peace movement, 1898-1918 (25), specific American peace
   societies and organizations (26), courts, lawyers, and judges
   on international law (26), businesspeople and the peace
   movement (10), peace through research foundations (18), peace
   organizations´ responses to World War I (22); women and the
   peace movement (38), social reformers (38), labor (59), the
   role of churches in the peace movement (46), and general
   studies of the progressive era (11).

690

Chickering, Roger.

Bibliography.
In his Imperial Germany and a World Without War: The peace
movement and German society, 1892-1914.
Princeton: Princeton University Press, 1975. pp. 421-466.

   Bibliographical aids, documents, journals, newspapers,
   yearbooks, protocols, memoirs, diaries, and secondary sources
   on the history of the international peace movement with
   special emphasis on the German peace movement, pacifism,
   peace congresses, peace societies, and the relationship
   between the German peace movement and Germany´s political
   culture.

Peace Movement--General

691   JX1961.U6D4

DeBenedetti, Charles.

Bibliographical essay.
In his Origins of the Modern American Peace Movement, 1915-
1929.
Millwood, N.Y.: KTO Press (KTO Studies in American History),
1978. pp. 253-267.

   323 items, 1917 - 1977. English. List of manuscript
   collections (65), followed by a discussion in essay format of
   books, articles, and periodicals (258).

692   JX1961.U6D42

DeBenedetti, Charles.

Bibliographical essay; Notes.
In his The Peace Reform in American History.
Bloomington: Indiana University Press, 1980. pp. 201-202,
203-226.

   22 items plus numerous uncounted items in notes, 1794 - 1978.
   English. Bibliographic essay (2 pp.); other references in
   endnote format.

   Books, articles, and dissertations on pacifism and the peace
   movement in American history.

Peace Movement--Publication Lists

693 <

[Peace Society (London)].

Catalogue of Peace Tracts.
London: Dyer Brothers, 1891. 16 pp.

694 <

Peace Society (London).

Select List of Publications, 1905.
London: Peace Society, 1905. 8 pp.

695   Z6464.Z9A4 or microfilm
                                 32500Z

American Peace Society.

Publications of the American Peace Society; Publications for
Sale by the American Peace Society.
Washington, D.C.: American Peace Society, [1916]. 2 pp.
An earlier edition, 1908, 4 pp.

   149 items, 1893 - 1916 (most items undated). English.

   Pamphlets, reports, and books on a wide variety of peace
   movement topics.

696   Z6464.Z9C2

[Carnegie Endowment for International Peace].

Publications of the Carnegie Endowment for International Peace,
with a List of Depository Libraries and Institutions.
Washington, D.C.: Carnegie Endowment for International Peace
[List No. 9], August 1, 1920. 48 pp.

   335 items, 1907 - 1920. English; also Latin, French (9),
   Spanish (2). Introduction (1 p.).

   Publications of the secretary's office (11), division of
   intercourse and education (17), division of economics and

Peace Movement--Publication Lists

history (9), economic studies of the war (26), division of
international law (28), pamphlet series, division of
international law (33), classics of international law (12),
Bibliothèque Internationale de Droit des Gens (4),
publications of American Institute of International Law (7),
publications of the American Association for International
Conciliation (188); list of depository libraries and
institutions of the endowment.

697   Z6466.Z9W83

World Peace Foundation.

World Peace Foundation Publications.
Boston: World Peace Foundation, 1924. 5 pp.
Another edition, 1932, 4 pp.

106 items, 1845 - 1923. English; also French (3), German (1).
A few items have brief descriptive annotations; appended
price list and order form.

Armaments (9), arbitration (4), Europe (4), European War
(14), The Hague (9), peace work and peace workers (6),
reparation (1), World Court (4), world organization (8),
World Peace Foundation (11), League to Enforce Peace (3),
Pan-American affairs (7), bibliographies (2), peace essays
(2), international relations (10), international unions (3),
League of Nations (9).

698   Z6464.Z9C2

[Carnegie Endowment for International Peace].

Publications [of the] Carnegie Endowment for International
Peace, with a foreword by Joseph E. Johnson.
New York: Carnegie Endowment for International Peace, Autumn,
1950. vi + 64 pp.
Earlier editions appeared in 1920, 1948, etc. Lists of the
Endowment´s publications also appeared in various editions of
its Yearbook and its Annual Report, including those for 1941-
1948.

683 items, 1911 - 1950. English; also Latin, Spanish, French
(9), German (2). Foreword (2 pp.); table of contents.

War and peace (154), armament control (11), international
organization and administration (121), law (131),
international economic relations (61), education (10), work
of the Carnegie Endowment (7), Western Hemisphere (70),
Europe (63), Middle East and Africa (10), Asia (27);

Peace Movement--Publication Lists

   bibliographies (18).

   699 <

[Carnegie Endowment for International Peace].

Complete Catalogue of Publications: 1953, 1954, 1955, 1957,
1960-61, 1964-1965, 1966-67 Supplement.
New York: Carnegie Endowment for International Peace, 1953 to
1967.

   700 <

[Fellowship of Reconciliation].

"Catalogue: F.O.R. peace publications."
Fellowship (February, 1964).

   701 <

[American Pax Association].

[Pax Bibliography].
Peace, 3 (Spring/Summer, 1967): 3-38.

   702   JX1963.G2513

Galtung, Johan.

Publicaties van het International Peace Research Institute te
Oslo [Publications of the International Peace Research
Institute at Oslo].
In his Polemologie [Polemology]: Vraagstukken van oorlog en
vrede [Questions of war and peace], met een voorwoord van
B.V.A. Roling.
Amsterdam: Polak and Van Gennep (Kritiese Biblioteek), 1968.
pp. 74-82.
First published in his Fredsforskning, Oslo: Pax Forlag, 1967,
pp. 99-110.

   109 items, 1959 - 1968. English; also Norwegian (9), Spanish
   (3), Italian (2), German (1).

   Articles and papers on general theories of conflict (8),
   social aspects of technical assistance (10),
   institutionalized conflict resolution (2), personal contact
   in conflict situations (2), peaceful uses of military
   resources (3), cultural conflict and social change (5),

Peace Movement--Publication Lists

causes and consequences of racial conflict (2), causes and
consequences of ethnic conflict (1), intrasystem conflicts
(1), rank conflicts in stratified systems (1), armament,
disarmament, and the balance of power (6), intrasocial
consequences of peace and war (3), modern diplomacy (3), news
communication (2), Peace Corps (1), public opinion and
international relations (5), international peacekeeping
forces (4), international "man" (2), foreign policy decision
making (2), nonmilitary power (5), the structure of the world
community (12), supranational integration patterns (8), peace
research (7), peace organizations (2), the image of peace
(7), miscellaneous (2); the monograph series (3).

703 <

World Law Fund.

1968/69 Catalogue: War prevention and world order.
New York: World Law Fund, 1969. 24 pp.

704 <

Atomic Bomb Casualty Commission.

Bibliography of Published Papers of the Atomic Bomb Casualty
Commission, 1970.
Hiroshima/Nagasaki: Atomic Bomb Casualty Commission (ABCC
Technical Report Series), 1970. 6 pp.

705   Z6464.C27

Hannigan, Jane A. (comp.).

Publications of the Carnegie Endowment for International Peace
1910-1967 Including International Conciliation 1924-1967.
New York: Carnegie Endowment for International Peace, 1971.
229 pp.

1474 items, 1910 - 1967. English; also French, German, Spanish,
Swedish, other Western and Eastern European languages.
Preface (2 pp.); author index; subject index.

Peace Movement--Publication Lists

706 <

[Peace Pledge Union].

"Publications of the Peace Pledge Union."
Peace and Conflict Research Programme Newsletter (University
of Lancaster, U.K.), 1, 1 (March, 1971): 22-26.

Peace Movement--Individuals

707 <

Peignot, Gabriel.

Recherches Historiques, Littéraires et Bibliographiques sur la
Vie et les Ouvrages de M. de La Harpe [Historical, Literary,
and Bibliographical Studies on the Life and Works of Mr. de la
Harpe].
Dijon, 1820.

708 <

[Sellon, Jean Jacques de].

Liste Raisonnée des Ecrits Publiés par le Comte (Jean Jacques)
de Sellon, Fondateur de la Société de la Paix de Genève
[Analytical List of Writings Published by Count (Jean Jacques)
de Sellon, Founder of the Geneva Peace Society].
Geneva: [Société de la Paix de Genève], 1836

709 <

Goumy, Edouard.

[Bibliographical information].
In his Etude sur la Vie et les Ecrits de L'Abbé de Saint-Pierre
[Study of the Life and Writings of the Abbé de Saint-Pierre].
Paris: Bourdier, 1859.

710   Z6464.Z9F8

[Fried, Alfred Hermann].

Verzeichnis von 1000 Zeitungs-Artikeln Alfred H. Fried's zur
Friedensbewegung (bis März 1908) [List of 1000 newspaper
articles by Alfred H. Fried on the peace movement (through
March, 1908)]: Nach Materien geordnet, mit bibliographischen
Nachweisen und zum Teil mit kurzen Inhaltsandeutungen versehen
[Organized by subject, with bibliographic data and partly
provided with brief annotations].
Berlin: "Friedens-Warte," 1908. 80 pp.

Peace Movement--Individuals

1000 items, 1892 - 1908. German; also Italian (9), French (4),
English (4). Many items have brief descriptive annotations;
introduction (4 pp.); table of contents; list of Fried's
books (43) on the peace movement.

List of articles by Fried appearing in 95 newspapers and
magazines, dealing with the Hague conferences,
internationalism, pacifism, peace congresses (1894-1907), and
various aspects of the international peace movement.

711   IU: B.C348d

Drouet, Joseph.

Bibliographie.
In his L'Abbé de Saint-Pierre: L'homme et l'oeuvre [The man and
his work].
Paris: Librairie Ancienne Honoré Champion, 1912. pp. [371]-383.

204 items, 1695 - 1911. French. Introduction (1 paragraph).

Chronological list of the works of the Abbé de Saint-Pierre
(146); list of principal authors and documents consulted or
cited in the course of this work--manuscripts (11) and
printed works (47) on Saint-Pierre, his predecessors and
contemporaries, including works and letters by Rousseau,
Voltaire, and several women such as Elizabeth of Orleans.

712   DLC-DB

[United States Library of Congress, Division of Bibliography].

List of References on William Howard Taft's Plan for
International Peace.
[Washington, D.C.]: Library of Congress, Division of
Bibliography, November 11, 1915. 2 pp. (typescript).

13 items, 1909 - 1914. English.

Addresses, articles, and a book by President William Howard
Taft presenting his proposals for peace through international
arbitration; articles (5) commenting on Taft's proposals.

Peace Movement--Individuals

713   IU: 341G91pu,no.1

Corbett, Percy Ellwood.

Bibliography in "Introduction."
In [Grotius Society], Erasmus´ Institutio Principis Christiani:
Chapters III-XI, translated by Percy Ellwood Corbett.
London: Sweet and Maxwell (The Grotius Society Publications,
Texts for Students of International Relations, No. 1), 1921.
p. 17.

   14 items, 1540 - 1917. English; also Latin (3), French (3),
   German (1).

   Erasmus´ works, biographies and commentaries on Erasmus,
   books on international law, arbitration, and tribunals.

714   DC122.5.S8

Ogg, David.

Bibliography in "Introduction."
In [Grotius Society], Sully´s Grand Design of Henry IV: From
the memoirs of Maximilien de Béthune, duc de Sully (1559-1641).
London: Sweet and Maxwell (The Grotius Society Publications,
Texts for Students of International Relations, No. 2), 1921.
pp. 15-16.

   15 items, 1638 - 1917. French, German. Introduction
   (1 paragraph).

   Memoirs and monographs of the Duke of Sully and several
   general reference works.

715 <

[Carnegie Endowment for International Peace, Library].

Hugo Grotius.
Washington, D.C.: Carnegie Endowment for International Peace,
Library (Miscellaneous Reading List No. 14), 1922. (mimeo).

716   IU: 341G91pu,no.3

Knight, W. S. M.

Bibliography in "Introduction."

Peace Movement--Individuals

In [Grotius Society], Hugonis Grotii De Jure Belli Ac Pacis;
Libri Tres: Selections, translated by W. S. M. Knight.
London: Sweet and Maxwell (The Grotius Society Publications,
Texts for Students of International Relations, No. 3), 1922.
pp. 25-26.

   26 items, 1625 - 1922. English, French, Latin.

   Grotius' works, translations, critical commentary on his
   work, and biographies of Grotius.

717   B2382.A5B7

Pereire, Alfred.

Notice bibliographique.
In Saint-Simon, Comte Claude Henri, L'Oeuvre d'Henri de Saint-
Simon [The Works of Henri de Saint-Simon]: Textes choisis
[Selected texts], avec une introduction par C. Bouglé.
Paris: Félix Alcan, 1925. pp. [xxv]-xxxii.

   50 items, 1803 - 1925. French; also English (1), German (1).
   Two brief lists appended to a brief bibliographic essay (5
   pp.).

   Works by Saint-Simon (20) and about Saint-Simon and Saint-
   Simonism (30).

718   Z8370.M59

Ter Meulen, Jacob.

Concise Bibliography of Hugo Grotius: Preceded by an abridged
genealogy by Jhr. E. A. van Beresteyn, LL.D., and a sketch of
Grotius' life, adopted from the catalogue of the Grotius
exhibition, The Hague, 1925.
Leiden: A. W. Sijthoff, for the Library of the Palace of Peace,
1925. 88 pp.

   850 items, 1609 - 1925. Latin, Dutch; also English, French,
   German, Danish (3), Portuguese (2), other eastern and western
   languages. Preface (2 pp.); subject index; author index.

   Works by Grotius--political writings and works on
   international law (191), juridical works (45), historical
   works (35), theological works (167), poetical works and poems
   (110), philological and literary works (43), works on natural
   science and philosophy (7), collected and separate letters
   (48); works concerning Hugo Grotius--bibliographies and
   catalogues (5), editions of letters to Grotius (10), general

Peace Movement--Individuals

biographies (22), trial of Grotius (16), Grotius' escape
(11), other writings on Grotius' life (35), writings on his
political and juridical doctrines, including international
law (51), Grotius as theologian (29), Grotius as man of
letters, historian, and economist (10), commemorations (15).
There follows a list of Grotius' works in chronological order
of the first editions (92).

719 <

Terasaki, Taro.

Bibliographie.
In his William Penn et la Paix [William Penn and Peace] . . .
Paris: A. Pedone, 1926. pp. [159]-163.

720   JX1946.K3

Buckland, Jessie H.

Bibliography in "Introduction."
In [Grotius Society], Kant's Perpetual Peace: A philosophical
proposal, translated by Helen O'Brien.
London: Sweet and Maxwell (The Grotius Society Publications,
Texts for Students of International Relations, No. 7), 1927.
pp. 17-18.

  20 items, 1795 - 1925. English, German; also French (1).

  Kant's works, translations, and analyses of his works and
  life.

721   IU: 341G91pu,no.6

Colombos, C. John.

Bibliography in "Introduction."
In [Grotius Society], Jeremy Bentham's Plan for an Universal
and Perpetual Peace.
London: Sweet and Maxwell (The Grotius Society Publications,
Texts for Students of International Relations, No. 6), 1927.
pp. 9-10.

  19 items, 1838 - 1913. English; also French (3), German (3),
  Spanish (1).

  Bentham's works, translations, and critical and historical
  works about Bentham.

Peace Movement--Individuals

722   Z6464.Z9J6,1927

Jordan, David Starr.

For International Peace: List of books, reviews, and other
articles in the interest of peace, friendship, and
understanding between nations by David Starr Jordan, 1898 to
1927.
Stanford: Stanford University Press, 1927. 24 pp.
First edition (1898-1925), 1925, 30 pp.

   472 items, 1898 - 1927. English; also French (5), German (3),
   Spanish (2), Japanese (1). A few items have brief descriptive
   annotations; prefatory note; list of towns in which addresses
   on international relations and world peace were delivered,
   1908-1925.

   A chronological list of printed works by Jordan from the
   onset of the Spanish-American War in 1898 through February,
   1927. Covers such topics as U.S. imperialism, negative
   eugenic effects of war, international relations, economic and
   other causes and effects of war, World War I, peace
   education, conditions of peace, peacemaking, peace plans,
   peace theory, Japan in world politics, militarism, and
   international organization.

723 <

[Carnegie Endowment for International Peace, Library].

Bibliography of the Writings of James Brown Scott.
Washington, D.C.: Carnegie Endowment for International Peace,
Library, 1928.

724 <

[Carnegie Endowment for International Peace, Library].

Edward Gaylord Bourne.
Washington, D.C.: Carnegie Endowment for International Peace,
Library (Miscellaneous Reading List No. 32), 1928.

Peace Movement--Individuals

725 <

[Carnegie Endowment for International Peace, Library].

Bibliography of the Writings of James Brown Scott: Supplement.
Washington, D.C.: Carnegie Endowment for International Peace,
Library, 1932.

726   JC223.B5K3

Kayser, Elmer Louis.

Bibliography.
In his The Grand Social Enterprise: A study of Jeremy Bentham
in his relation to liberal nationalism (Ph.D. dissertation,
Political Science, Columbia University).
New York: Columbia University Press, 1932. pp. 94-103.

   207 items, 1778 - 1931. English; also French, Spanish (6),
   German (5), Italian (3), Russian (1), other Romance languages
   (2).

   Works by Bentham, books cited in the text, and books on
   Bentham and his times.

727   PN35.I6,v.5,no.5

Huggard, William Allen.

[Bibliographic footnotes] in "Emerson and the problem of war
and peace."
(Ph.D. dissertation, English, State University of Iowa, April
1938).
University of Iowa Humanistic Studies, 5, 5 (1938): 1-76.

   72 items, 1817 - 1935. English; also French (5), German (1).
   Many items are discussed critically in the footnotes.

   Writings about and by Ralph Waldo Emerson, history of the
   peace movement, and peace plans.

728   JX1946.S37,1939

Collinet, Paul.

Bibliography in "Introduction."
In Saint-Pierre, C[harles François] I[renée] Castel, Abbé de,
St. Pierre; Scheme for Lasting Peace: Selections from the
second edition of the Abrégé du Projet de Paix Perpétuelle,

Peace Movement--Individuals

translated by H. Hale Bellot.
London: Peace Book Company (Peace Classics, Vol. 5), 1939.
pp. 11-13.
Reprint of Grotius Society edition, 1927.

    21 items, 1712 - 1920. French, English; also German (1).
    Introduction (1 paragraph).

    Works of Saint-Pierre in the original (6), in translation
    (1), principal biographies (3), historical works (5), and
    critical works (6).

729   Z8818.1.B5

Shotwell, James Thomson.

Bibliography, 1904-1941.
[New York: Columbia University, for the Carnegie Endowment for
International Peace, [1942]. 22 pp. (mimeo).

    411 items, 1904 - 1942. English; also German (8), French (7).
    Introduction (1 paragraph).

    Works by Shotwell including edited volumes and series (7),
    books (12), articles and addresses (392).

730 <   IU: 051J0

Polinger, E. H.

[Bibliographic footnotes] in "Saint-Simon, the utopian
precursor of the League of Nations."
Journal of the History of Ideas, 4 (October, 1943): 475-483.

731   JX1908.U6C35,no.33

Koenig, Harry C. (comp.).

Bibliography.
In his A Papal Peace Mosaic, 1878-1944: Excerpts from the
messages of Popes Leo XIII, Pius X, Benedict XV, Pius XI, and
Pius XII.
Washington, D.C.: Catholic Association for International Peace
(Pamphlet No. 33), 1944. p. 59.

    20 items, 1903 - 1944. English.

Peace Movement--Individuals

Books and documents on the Catholic Church, peace and
international order, including letters, encyclicals, and
speeches of the popes from Leo XIII to Pius XII.

732 <

Ter Meulen, Jacob.

Bibliographie des Ecrits Imprimés de Hugo Grotius [Bibliography
of the Printed Writings of Hugo Grotius].
The Hague: M[artinus] Nijhoff, 1950.

733 <

Fischer, Louis.

Sources and bibliography.
In his The Life of Mahatma Gandhi.
London: Cape, 1951. pp. 545-584.

734 <

Hays, Alice Newman.

David Starr Jordan: A bibliography of his writings, 1871-1931.
Stanford: Stanford University Press, 1952.

735 <

[Carnegie Endowment for International Peace].

Bibliography, 1915-1957: Quincy Wright.
New York: Carnegie Endowment for International Peace, 1957.

736   JX1901.J6,v.1

Richardson, Stephen A.

"A bibliography of Lewis Fry Richardson's studies of the
causation of wars with a view to their avoidance."
Journal of Conflict Resolution, 1, 3 (September, 1957):
305-307.

Peace Movement--Individuals

737   JX1901.J6,v.14

Fink, Clinton F[rederick] and Christopher Wright.

Selected bibliography in "Quincy Wright on war and peace: A
statistical overview and selected bibliography."
Journal of Conflict Resolution, 14, 4 (December, 1970):
548-554.

   147 items, 1916 - 1970. English. Introduction (6 pp.).

   Books (21) and articles (126) by Quincy Wright on
   international law, causes of war, United Nations and
   international law, international relations, legal problems in
   war, peacemaking, effects of nuclear weapons, world
   government, disarmament, peace treaties. Items selected from
   1100-item bibliography of Wright's works.

738   JX1962.A2085

[Skarprud, Elsa (comp.)].

Nobels Fredspris [The Nobel Peace Prize]: Et utvalg litteratur
om prisvinnerne [And selected literature on the prize winners].
Oslo: Nobelinstituttets bibliotek, 1970. 22 pp. (mimeo).

   263 items, 1897 - 1969. Swedish, English; also Norwegian,
   French, German, Danish (6), Dutch (3), Italian (1).
   Introduction (1 paragraph); subject index.

   A chronology of 53 Nobel Peace Prize winners from 1901 to
   1960, listing a few biographical or testimonial works about
   each recipient.

739 <   JX1953.B17

Randall, Mercedes M. (ed.).

Bibliography.
In her Beyond Nationalism: The social thought of Emily Greene
Balch.
New York: Twayne Publishers, 1972. pp. 243-249.

Peace Movement--Individuals

740

Van Den Dungen, Peter.

A Bibliography of the Pacifist Writings of Jean de Bloch.
London: Housmans, 1977. 28 pp.

  199 items, 1894 - 1972 (only a few items published after
  1916). English, German, French; also Dutch (9), Italian (4),
  Swedish (3), Danish (1), Hebrew (1), Spanish (1).
  Introduction (4 pp.); table of contents; author index.

  Lists books, pamphlets, and articles by Bloch (87), and three
  categories of secondary literature: biographical and general
  (43), book reviews and comments (44), and the International
  Museum of War and Peace (25).

Peace Movement--Special Topics

741 <

Peace Society (London).

Peace Sunday, December 18th, 1904: Leaflets, pamphlets,
sermons.
London: Peace Society, 1904. 2 pp.

742 <

Peace Society (London).

Peace Sunday Literature, 1905.
London: Peace Society, 1905. 2 pp.

743   DLC-DB

[United States Library of Congress, Division of Bibliography].

Renunciation of War: A bibliographical list.
[Washington, D.C.]: Library of Congress, Division of
Bibliography, September 20, 1928. 10 pp. (typescript).

   143 items, 1927 - 1928. English; also French (5).

   Articles and editorials in magazines, newspapers, and
   journals, texts of treaty proposals and diplomatic notes
   relating to outlawry of war, prevention or renunciation of
   war, peace proposals, and the Kellogg Peace Pact.

744 <

Warren, Gertrude L.

Selected list of references.
In her Youth Movements Abroad.
Washington, D.C.: U.S. Department of Agriculture (U.S.
Department of Agriculture, Extension Service Circular 211),
[1935]. pp. 13-19.

Peace Movement--Special Topics

745   NN: YAMp.v.315

Cardiff Public Library.

The Peace Movement in Wales: List of publications in the
Cardiff Public Library (International Peace Congress, Cardiff,
June 12-19, 1936).
Cardiff, Wales: Cardiff Public Library, 1936. 8 pp.

   71 items, 1846 - 1936. English, Welsh.

   Peace Society (29), League of Nations (33), League of Nations
   Union, Welsh National Council (9).

746   Z7164.Y8S4

Schnapper, M[orris] B[artel].

Youth Faces War and Fascism: An annotated bibliography.
New York: American League Against War and Fascism, National
Youth Committee, [1937]. 18 pp. (mimeo).

   252 items, 1912 - 1937. English. Some items have brief
   descriptive annotations and/or excerpts; introduction (1 p.).

   General--peace (49), militarization (11), ROTC (37),
   education and war (23), students against war (18), the CCC
   [Civilian Conservation Corps] (19), Boy Scouts of America
   (13), the DAR (7), the American Legion (17), professional
   patriots--their stand (14), professional patriots--youth
   replies (11), army and navy (12), youth in fascist Italy (9),
   youth in Nazi Germany (12).

747 <

[Carnegie Endowment for International Peace, Library].

Peace Gardens.
Washington, D.C.: Carnegie Endowment for International Peace,
Library (Miscellaneous Reading List No. 55), 1938. (mimeo).

748   Z7164.Y8C2,1940

Matthews, Mary Alice (comp.).

The Youth Movement: List of works on the youth movement; with
selected references on student societies; and some account of
youth-serving organizations.

Peace Movement--Special Topics

Washington, D.C.: Carnegie Endowment for International Peace,
Library (Reading List No. 19), February 15, 1940 (rev. ed.).
13 pp. (mimeo).
First published as The Youth Movement (Reading List No. 19),
December 1, 1927, 2 pp. (mimeo). (The 1927 edition lists many
items not included in the 1940 edition.) Another bibliography
with the same title appeared in 1927 as Miscellaneous Reading
List No. 31. An 8 pp. (mimeo) edition was published in 1934.

   122 items, 1923 - 1940. English; also French (1). Many items
   have brief descriptive and/or critical annotations; table of
   contents; author/subject index.

   Bibliographies (7), general works on the youth movement (32),
   youth movements abroad (29), youth and world peace (18),
   student societies (18), youth-serving organizations (18).

749   N8750.R62

[Roerich Pact and Banner of Peace Committee].

Bibliography.
In its The Roerich Pact and the Banner of Peace.
New York: Roerich Pact and Banner of Peace Committee, 1947.
pp. 48-61.

   278 items, 1898 - 1944. English; also Russian, French,
   Lithuanian, Polish (9), Latvian (6), other eastern and
   western languages.

   Magazine and journal articles on the Roerich Pact, the Banner
   of Peace, and the Roerich peace movement.

750   Z6464.Z9M6

[Zakharevich, P. B. (comp.)].

Molodezh´ v Bor´be za Mir [Youth in the Struggle for Peace]:
Kratkiĭ rekomendatel´niĭ ukazatel´ literatury [A short list of
recommended literature].
Moscow: Publichnaĭa Biblioteka im. V. I. Lenina [Lenin Public
Library], 1951. 41 pp.

   91 items, 1920 - 1951. Russian (in Cyrillic alphabet). Most
   items have abstract-length descriptive annotations; foreword
   (1 p.); table of contents; author index.

   Lenin and Stalin on the problem of Komsomol and youth in the
   building of communism (8), the Soviet Union in the vanguard
   of the struggle for peace (37), the international youth

Peace Movement--Special Topics

movement in the struggle for peace (36), creative literature
(10).

751

[Busse, Nataliya and M. Mineva (comps.)].

Mladezhta v Borbata za Mir [Youth in the Struggle for Peace]:
Prepor´chitelna bibliografiya [Selected bibliography].
Sofia: Bŭlgarski Bibliografski Institut Elin Pelin, 1952.
16 pp.

  61 items, 1948 - 1952. Bulgarian (in Cyrillic alphabet). Most
  items have brief to medium-length descriptive annotations.

752   Z6464.Z9B86

Fővárosi Szabó Ervin Könyvtár.

A Népek Bécsi Békekongresszusától a Béke-világtanács Budapesti
Üléséig/From the Vienna Congress of the Peoples for Peace to
the Session of the World Peace Council in Budapest: Válogatott
folyóiratcikk bibliográfia a békeharcról, 1952 december 12-1953
junius 1/Bibliography of selected articles on the fight for
peace (December 12, 1952 to June 1, 1953) [titles and entries
also in Russian, French and German].
Budapest: Fővárosi Szabó Ervin Könyvtár, 1953. 29 pp. (mimeo).

  148 items, 1953. Hungarian, Russian, English; also French,
  German.

  Mostly magazine and journal articles on the Congress of the
  Peoples for Peace held in Vienna in 1952, peace negotiations
  during the Korean War, war crimes, the relationship between
  socialism, the Communist Party, the trade union movements,
  and peace; list of journals.

Pacifism, Nonviolence, Conscientious Objection

753   DLC-DB

[United States Library of Congress, Division of Bibliography].

List of References on Conscientious Objectors.
[Washington, D.C.]: Library of Congress, Division of
Bibliography, June 27, 1917. 3 pp. (typescript).

  27 items, 1916 - 1917. English.

  Magazine articles and parliamentary debates on conscientious
  objectors, especially in Britain.

754 <

Floyd, William.

Bibliography.
In his War Resistance.
New York: Arbitrator Press, [1931]. p. 40.

755   UB342.U5W7

Wright, Edward Needles.

Bibliography.
In his Conscientious Objectors in the Civil War (Ph.D. thesis,
University of Pennsylvania).
Philadelphia: University of Pennsylvania Press, 1931.
pp. 240-262.

  182 items, 1811 - 1930. English.

  Minutes of meetings (6), personal collections (3), government
  documents (24), religious documents (7), newspapers and
  periodicals (13), pamphlets (8), personalia (21), and books
  (100) on conscientious objection, conscription in various
  states, the treatment of conscientious objectors, and the
  history of various religious denominations (e.g., Mennonites,
  Quakers, Brethren, Moravians) out of which conscientious
  objectors emerged.

Pacifism, Nonviolence, Conscientious Objection

756   PN4181.U5

[Johnsen, Julia E. (comp.)].

Bibliography: "Pacifism the highest form of patriotism."
In Phelps, Edith M. (ed.), University Debaters' Annual:
Constructive and rebuttal speeches delivered in debates of
  American colleges and universities during the college year,
1934-1935 [Vol. 21].
New York: H. W. Wilson, September, 1935. pp. 403-408.

  110 items, 1928 - 1935. English.

  Books and pamphlets (20), periodicals (90) on pros and cons
  of pacifism and patriotism and the relationship between them.

757   BX7675.H3

Hall, Willis H.

Bibliography.
In his Quaker International Work in Europe since 1914 (Doctoral
thesis, Political Science, Université de Genève).
Chambéry (Savoie), France: Imprimeries Réunies, 1938.
pp. 297-310.

  453 items, 1672 - 1938. English.

  Manuscript sources (129), printed sources (148), books (81),
  pamphlets (37), and periodicals (58) on conscientious
  objection, disarmament, militarism, peace theory, Quaker
  publications, etc.

758 <   Z1009.N27,no.152

[Peace Pledge Union].

The Theory and Practice of Pacifism.
London: National Book Council (Book List No. 152), 1938. 2 pp.

759   UB341.F7

American Friends Service Committee, Peace Section, et al.

What to read.
In their Pacifist Handbook: Questions and answers concerning
the pacifist in wartime, prepared as a basis for study and
discussion.

Pacifism, Nonviolence, Conscientious Objection

[Philadelphia]: Fellowship of Reconciliation, 1939. pp. 47-48.

   54 items, 1918 - 1939. English.

   Books, articles, and magazines on the conscientious objector,
   pacifism, nonviolence, and the relationship between
   Christianity and war and peace.

760   BX7624.P36,no.5

Gregg, Richard B[artlett].

[Bibliographic footnotes].
In his A Pacifist Program: In time of war, threatened war, or
fascism.
[Wallingford, Pa.]: Pendle Hill (Pamphlet No. 5), April, 1939.
61 pp.

   90 items, 1895 - 1938. English.

761   IU: A341.6C21r,no.12

Matthews, M[ary] Alice (comp.).

Conscientious Objectors and War Resisters.
Washington, D.C.: Carnegie Endowment for International Peace,
Library (Reading List No. 12), November 28, 1939 (rev. ed.).
8 pp. (mimeo).
First edition published in 1927.

   89 items, 1894 - 1939. English; also French (2), German (1).
   Many items have brief descriptive annotations.

   Books, articles, and official reports on pacifism, war
   resistance, nonviolence, conscription, conscientious
   objectors, and the renunciation of war.

762   UB341.J6,1940a

American Friends Service Committee, Peace Section, Joint
Committee on The Conscientious Objector and Joint Committee on
The Conscientious Objector, Women's International League for
Peace and Freedom.

Bibliography.
In their What about the Conscientious Objector? A supplement to
the Pacifist Handbook.

Pacifism, Nonviolence, Conscientious Objection

Philadelphia: American Friends Service Committee, Peace
Section/Women's International League for Peace and Freedom,
National Literature Department, November, 1940 (rev. ed.).
pp. 86-98.

  63 items, 1919 - 1940. English. All items have brief to
  abstract-length descriptive and/or critical annotations.

  Brief, inexpensive, general works (9), personal experiences
  of conscientious objectors (4), government and the
  conscientious objector (7), religious groups and the
  conscientious objector (11), toward a solution (10), poetry
  (2), fiction (6), plays (14).

763   JX1953.M85

Muste, A[braham] J[ohn].

Selected bibliography.
In his Non-violence in an Aggressive World.
New York/London: Harper and Brothers, 1940. pp. 204-205.
Reprinted, New York: Jerome S. Ozer (The Peace Movement in
America: A Facsimile Reprint Collection), 1972.

  22 items, 1928 - 1939. English.

  Books and periodicals on nonviolence, pacifism, and
  religious approaches to war and peace.

764   JX1953.P2

[Wilson, Edward Raymond, et al. (eds.)].

For further reading [14 lists].
In their Pacifist Living--Today and Tomorrow: A brief
exploration of pacifism under conscription, in time of war, and
in post-war reconstruction.
Philadelphia/Wallingford: American Friends Service Committee,
Peace Section/Pendle Hill, 1941. pp. 10, 13, 16, 17, 18, 24,
25, 27, 28, 32, 36, 53, 62, 80.
Reprinted, with a new introduction by Mulford Q. Sibley, New
York: Garland (Library of War and Peace), 1972 (JX 1953,S54).

  81 items, 1919 - 1941. English. A few items have brief
  descriptive annotations.

  Brief lists of pamphlets and articles on areas of concern to
  pacifists: refugees, inter-American relations, U.S. foreign
  policy, peace education, civil liberties, race relations,

Pacifism, Nonviolence, Conscientious Objection

anti-Semitism, conscientious objectors, conscription, world
order, and pacifist programs.

765   BX7635.A1A25,no.189; also
                                           BX7748.W2F7

Friends World Committee for Consultation (American Section),
Peace Commission.

Bibliography [12 lists].
In its Peace Study Outline: Problems of applied pacifism.
Philadelphia: Friends World Committee for Consultation, [1942].
pp. 12, 15, 20, 25, 31, 38, 43, 52, 58, 66, 72, 79.

   74 items (no dates given). English.

   Historical background (12), religious basis (4), pacifism and
   the individual (5), the individual and the community (4),
   peace, law, and government (8), social ills and ideological
   answers (7), the Quaker group contribution (5), positive
   world cooperation (8), problems of world government (4),
   Quakerism and the world community (4), politics (7),
   education (6).

766   Z6464.Z9P3

Pacifist Research Bureau.

Five Foot Shelf of Pacifist Literature.
Philadelphia: Pacifist Research Bureau, 1942. 7 pp.

   76 items, 1920 - 1942. English. All items have brief
   descriptive and/or critical annotations; introduction
   (2 paragraphs).

   Essential books (20), additional books (30), pamphlets (26).

767   Z6464.Z9W3

[War Resisters League].

Literature List.
New York: War Resisters League, Literature Department, [1943].
5 pp. (folder).

   176 items (no dates given). English. A few items have brief
   descriptive and/or critical annotations; price list and order
   form.

Pacifism, Nonviolence, Conscientious Objection

Mostly pamphlet material, including publications of the War
Resisters League (31), War Resisters International (10), and
publications from other sources on conscientious objectors
and conscription (24), pacifism and religion (45), peace now
pleas and postwar plans (29), forerunner material for high
school age youth (6), miscellaneous war/peace topics (19),
and periodicals of interest to pacifists (12).

768   HM278.G7,1959

Gregg, Richard B[artlett].

[Bibliographic] Notes by chapters.
In his The Power of Non-violence, with an introduction by Rufus
M. Jones.
New York: Fellowship Publications, 1944 (new [rev.] ed.).
pp. 213-247.
Original edition, London/Philadelphia: J.P. Lippincott, 1935,
pp. 295-348. Second revised edition, with a foreword by Martin
Luther King, Jr., Nyack, N.Y.: Fellowship Publications, 1959,
pp. 176-187.

211 items, 1880 - 1943. English. Many items discussed in
footnotes, arranged by chapters at end of book.

Modern examples of nonviolent resistance (40), moral jiu-
jitsu (17), what happens (18), utilizing emotional energy
(6), how is mass nonviolence possible (16), the working of
mass nonviolent resistance (28), an effective substitute for
war (7), nonviolence and the state (38), persuasion (28), the
need for training (6), training (7).

769 <

Hayes, Denis.

Bibliography.
In his Challenge of Conscience: The story of the conscientious
objectors of 1939-1949, with a foreword by Fenner Brockway.
London: Allen and Unwin, 1949. pp. 393-394.

770   Z6464.W3D6

Doty, Hi[ram] (comp.).

Bibliography of Conscientious Objection to War: A selected list
of 173 titles, annotated, with a logical index, and with notes
on additional sources.

Pacifism, Nonviolence, Conscientious Objection

Philadelphia: Central Committee for Conscientious Objectors,
1954. 24 pp.
An earlier edition entitled Conscientious objection to war: A
selected bibliography, [Norma Jacob and Caleb Foote, (comps.)],
appeared in mimeographed form in 1949.

   173 items, 1777 - 1954. English. All items have brief
   descriptive and/or critical annotations; preface (1 p.);
   table of contents.

   Books, articles, and pamphlets (162), periodicals (11) on
   religious pacifism, conscientious objection, nonviolence,
   socialist opposition to war, the history of the peace
   movement, noncooperation, nonresistance, and civil
   disobedience.

771 <

Lyttle, Bradford.

Bibliography.
In his National Defense through Non-violent Resistance.
Chicago: Fred Steib, 1958. pp. 65-69.

772 <

Prosad, Devi.

Non-violence and Peacemaking: A bibliography.
London: Commonweal Trust, for War Resisters International,
1963.

773 <

Miller, William Robert.

[Annotated bibliography].
In his Nonviolence: A Christian interpretation.
New York: Association Press, 1964.

774 <

[Verband der Kriegsdienstverweigerer, Dokumentationsabteilung].

Bibliography on Non-violence.
Ahrensburg, West Germany: Verband der Kriegsdienstverweigerer,
1965. (mimeo).

Pacifism, Nonviolence, Conscientious Objection

775   Z6464.Z9R67

Roth, H. [O].

Pacifism in New Zealand: A bibliography.
Auckland: University of Auckland, Library (Bibliographical
Bulletin 3), 1966. 10 pp.

  166 items, 1899 - 1965. English. Introduction (1 p.).

  Pamphlets, journal and newspaper articles, papers, speeches,
  correspondence, and a few books and dissertations on the
  South African War (6), arguments for and against conscription
  (47), conscientious objection during World War I (27),
  arguments against war and fascism (19), conscientious
  objection during World War II (25), conscription and nuclear
  war (42).

776 <

Westow, Theodore L.

"The argument about pacifism: A critical survey of English
studies."
In Bockle, Franz (ed.), War, Poverty, Freedom: A Chrisrian
response.
Glen Rock, N.J.: Paulist Press (Concilium 15), 1966.
pp. 105-118.

777 <

Blumberg, Herbert H.

"A guide to organizations, books and periodicals concerned with
non-violence."
Sociological Inquiry, 38 (1968): 77-93.

778   JX1944.B75

Brock, Peter.

Bibliography.
In his Pacifism in the United States: From the colonial era to
the First World War.
Princeton: Princeton University Press, 1968. pp. 949-983.

  829 items, 1694 - 1968. English; also German (17), French (1).

Pacifism, Nonviolence, Conscientious Objection

> Primary (467) and secondary (362) sources on the theory and
> practice of American pacifism, pacifist groups, sects, and
> individuals, and the history of the American peace movement.

779

Blumberg, Herbert H.

"An annotated bibliography of serials concerned with the
non-violent protest movement."
Sociological Abstracts, 17 (July-August, 1969): xxi-xlx [sic].

> 185 items, 1828 - 1968. English; also Hindi (4), French (1),
> Italian (1). Many items have brief descriptive annotations;
> introduction (2 pp.).

> Periodicals and newsletters of organizations devoted to
> nonviolent and radical protest. The serials focus on such
> topics as pacifism, conscientious objection, war resistance,
> direct action, arms control and disarmament, race relations,
> student protests, the antiwar movement, social
> and revolutionary movements in general, socialism, international
> relations, peace research, and theories concerning both war
> and peace.

780   HM278.C35

Carter, April, David Hoggett, and Adam Roberts.

Non-violent Action: A selected bibliography.
London/Haverford, Pa.: Housmans/Haverford College, Center for
Nonviolent Conflict Resolution, June, 1970 (rev. and enl. ed.).
83 pp.
First published as Non-violent Action: Theory and practice--a
selected bibliography, London: Housmans, 1966. 48 pp.

> 407 items, 1895 - 1970. English; also French (1). Most items
> have brief descriptive annotations; introduction (6 pp.) plus
> brief introductions (1-2 paragraphs) to some of the
> subsections; table of contents; author index.

> General titles on nonviolent action (33), specific methods of
> nonviolent action (15), cases of resistance involving use of
> nonviolent action (267), practical aspects of nonviolent
> action (12), nonviolent action in international relations
> (35), aspects of nonviolent social order (45).

Pacifism, Nonviolence, Conscientious Objection

781   HM278.S447

Sharp, Gene.

Selected further readings.
In his Exploring Nonviolent Alternatives.
Boston: Porter Sargent (Extending Horizons Books), 1970.
pp. 133-159.

   220 items, 1906 - 1970. English.

   Books, articles, and pamphlets on the technique of nonviolent
   action (60); "human nature," social conflict, and the
   elimination of war (12); cases of nonviolent action (143);
   pacifism (5).

782

Brock, Peter.

Bibliographical notes; Bibliographical postscript.
In his Pacifism in Europe to 1914.
Princeton: Princeton University Press, 1972. pp. 505-541,
542-544.

   426 items, 1662 - 1971. Essay format.

   General works (14), the early church (27), the Czech Brethren
   and their forerunners (32), the Anabaptists (64), the Polish
   Antitrinitarians (14), the Mennonites (78), British Quakerism
   (84), non-Quaker pacifism in nineteenth-century Britain (55),
   Russian sectarian pacifism and Tolstoy (41), miscellaneous
   nineteenth-century pacifist sects on the European continent
   (17); postscript (16).

783

Gujarat Vidyapith, Peace Research Centre.

"Bibliography on peace research."
In its Perspectives of Peace Research (based on the proceedings
of the Seminar on Concept, Methodology and Areas of Peace
Research in India, held on 7, 8, 9, August, 1972 at Peace
Research Centre, Gujarat Vidyapith, Ahmedabad-14).
Ahmedabad: Gujarat Vidyapith, August, 1972. pp. 131-163.

   257 items, 1912 - 1972. English.

   Bibliography and journals (12), civil disobedience (8),

Pacifism, Nonviolence, Conscientious Objection

    disarmament (16), international organizations (16),
    nonviolence (45), pacifism (141), satyagraha (19).

784   Z6464.Z9H94

Hyatt, John (comp.).

Pacifism: A selected bibliography.
London: Housmans, August, 1972. 52 pp.

    511 items, 1823 - 1972. English. Many items have brief
    descriptive and/or critical annotations; introduction
    (2 pp.); table of contents; subject/author index.

    Books and pamphlets on the history of the peace movement and
    pacifism (46), pacifists in World War I (28), pacifists in
    World War II (14), Christianity and pacifism (51), pacifism
    in action (39), pacifist writings (208), writings on pacifism
    (16), biography and autobiography (69), bibliographies on
    pacifism and nonviolence, reading lists, booklists,
    suppliers, and libraries (40).

785

Stiehm, Judith.

Selected bibliography.
In her Nonviolent Power: Active and passive resistance in
America.
Lexington, Mass./Toronto/London: D. C. Heath, 1972.
pp. 118-128.

    256 items, 1839 - 1971 (most items published after 1960).
    English. Introduction (1 paragraph).

    Books, pamphlets, articles, and journals on nonviolent
    resistance (141), subjects related to nonviolent resistance
    (56), civil disobedience or conscientious objection (25), and
    recent books related to nonviolent resistance (34).

786

Lamkin, David (comp.).

The "Amnesty" Issue and Conscientious Objection: A selected
bibliography, with an introduction by Charles Chatfield.
Los Angeles: California State University at Los Angeles, Center
for the Study of Armament and Disarmament (Political Issues
Series, Vol. 2, No. 5), 1973. 42 pp.

Pacifism, Nonviolence, Conscientious Objection

456 items, 1789 - 1974. English. Introduction (15 pp.); table of contents.

Magazine and journal articles, books, films, dissertations, and pamphlets on the amnesty issue (145), background material on conscientious objection (182), current problems (39), legal discussion of problems (15), "supreme being belief" problem (20), atheists as conscientious objectors (7), selective conscientious objection (39), and draft information for conscientious objectors (9).

787

McNitt, William (comp.).

Bibliography of Resources on the History of Pacifism and Conscientious Objection in the Michigan Historical Collections. Ann Arbor: University of Michigan (Bentley Historical Library, Michigan Historical Collections, Bibliographical Series, No. 1), December, 1973. 13 pp.

37 items (collections), 1898 - 1973. English. All items have brief to abstract-length descriptive annotations; introduction (2 pp.).

Papers, reports, records, newspaper clippings, letters, photographs, speeches, newsletters, magazines, leaflets, and pamphlets concerning the peace movement, activities of various peace organizations, student protests, antiwar efforts, the labor movement, social reform, pacifism, and conscientious objection.

788   JC328.3.S45,1973

Sharp, Gene, with the editorial assistance of Marina Finkelstein.

Bibliography.
In his The Politics of Nonviolent Action.
Boston: Porter Sargent (Extending Horizons Books), 1973.
pp. 819-840.

Peace Conferences and Peacemaking

789   Z881.B75BM,v.10

Boston Public Library.

"The Hague Conference and international arbitration [brief
reading list]."
Monthly Bulletin of Books Added to the Public Library of the
City of Boston, 10, 12 (December, 1905): 439-442.

   80 items, 1795 - 1905. English, French; also German (3),
   Spanish (1). A few items have brief descriptive annotations;
   introduction (1 paragraph).

   Books, reports, documents relating to international
   arbitration, disarmament, the amelioration or abolition of
   war, the Hague Conference, European federation, and various
   peace conferences and congresses.

790 <

Matthews, M[ary] Alice (comp.).

Locarno Treaties.
Washington, D.C.: Carnegie Endowment for International Peace,
Library (Reading List No. 4), 1925. (mimeo).
Another edition, 1926.

791   IU: A940.91.L536,no.1

Stanford University, Hoover War Library.

A Catalogue of Paris Peace Conference Delegation Propaganda in
the Hoover War Library.
Stanford: Stanford University Press (Hoover War Library
Bibliographical Series, I), 1926. 96 pp.

   Introductory note (2 pp.); table of contents.

   Documents presented to the conference and distributed by the
   various delegations to the public, grouped by country.

Peace Conferences and Peacemaking

792   D1.J6,v.1

Binkley, Robert C.

"Ten years of peace conference history [review article with
bibliographical footnotes]."
Journal of Modern History, 1, 4 (December, 1929): 607-629.

   40 items, 1919 - 1929. English; also German (5), Italian (5),
   French (4). All items are critically discussed in the text.

   Books, memoirs, reports, and documents on the Paris Peace
   Conference and the Versailles Treaty. See also Paul Birdsall,
   "The second decade of peace conference history" (1939),
   No. 797, below.

793 <

Phelps, Edith M. (ed.).

"The Pact of Paris [debate and bibliography]."
In her University Debaters Annual, 1928-1929.
New York: H. W. Wilson, 1929.

794 <

[Carnegie Endowment for International Peace, Library].

The Revision of the Peace Treaties.
Washington, D.C.: Carnegie Endowment for International Peace,
Library (Miscellaneous Reading List No. 40), 1932. (mimeo).

795   Z6207.E8A4

Almond, Nina [Elizabeth] and Ralph Haswell Lutz.

An Introduction to a Bibliography of the Paris Peace
Conference: Collections of sources, archive publications, and
source books.
Stanford/London: Stanford University Press/Humphrey Milford,
Oxford University Press (Hoover War Library Bibliographical
Series, 2), 1935. 32 pp.

   123 items, 1918 - 1932. English; also French, German, Bulgarian
   (1), Hungarian (1). Many items have brief to abstract-length
   descriptive annotations; foreword (1 p.); table of contents;
   author index.

Peace Conferences and Peacemaking

    Armistice materials (12), preconference materials (5),
    conference materials (99), materials on relief operations in
    Europe during the conference period (7).

796   D651.I7A8

Albrecht-Carrié, René.

Bibliography.
In his Italy at the Paris Peace Conference.
New York: Columbia University Press, for the Carnegie Endowment
for International Peace (The Paris Peace Conference--History
and Documents), 1938. pp. 533-541.
Reprinted, Hamden, Conn.: Archon Books, 1966.

    163 items, 1911 - 1937. Italian, English; also French, German
    (6), Serbo-Croation (1).

    Memoirs, diaries, official documents, reports, memoranda, and
    secondary sources on the Paris Peace Conference from the
    Italian perspective, the Adriatic question, and Italian
    foreign policy.

797   D1.J6,v.11

Birdsall, Paul.

"The second decade of peace conference history"
[bibliographical article].
Journal of Modern History, 11, 3 (September, 1939): 362-378.

    41 items, 1918 - 1939. English; also French (5), German (3),
    Italian (2). Footnote format, all items are listed and
    discussed in text and notes.

    Bibliographies, documents, and works on the Paris Peace
    Conference of 1919. This article is a sequel to Robert C.
    Binkley's "Ten years of peace conference history" (1929),
    No. 792, above.

798   Z6464.A1C3,no.16

Matthews, M[ary] Alice (comp.).

Third Hague Peace Conference: List of references on proposals
and programs for a third conference as recommended by the
Second International Peace Conference, 1907.

Peace Conferences and Peacemaking

Washington, D.C.: Carnegie Endowment for International Peace,
Library (Brief Reference List No. 16), April 27, 1939. 5 pp.
(mimeo).

52 items, 1907 - 1939. English; also French, Dutch (3), German
(2). Some items have brief descriptive annotations.

Newspaper and journal articles, official documents, reports,
and pamphlets on plans for convening the Third Hague Peace
Conference for strengthening international law.

799   D643.A7M57

Moulin, Léo.

Bibliographie sommaire.
In his Du Traité de Versailles à l´Europe d´Aujourd´hui, 1919-
1939 [From the Versailles Treaty to Today´s Europe, 1919-1939].
Brussels: Centrale d´Education Ouvrière, 1939. pp. 177-184.

158 items, 1914 - 1939. French; also English, Italian, German
(5).

Memoirs, diaries, and secondary sources on the Paris Peace
Conference (1919), the Adriatic question, peacemaking, peace
negotiations, the political and economic aspects of peace,
international relations, Italian foreign policy, national
minorities, and the history of war.

800   CSt-H: D644.B638

Blanchard, M[argaret] Gertrude.

Bibliography.
In her The Role of the Foreign Press at the Paris Peace
Conference. Unpublished M.A. thesis, History,
Stanford University, March 25, 1941. pp. 108-109. (typescript).

22 items, 1918 - 1940. English.

Books (11), documents (4), and journals (7) on the Paris
Peace Conference and the role of the press in the
deliberations.

Peace Conferences and Peacemaking

801   D643.A7L83,1941a

Luckau, Alma [Maria].

Bibliography.
In her The German Delegation at the Paris Peace Conference,
with a foreword by James T. Shotwell.
New York: Columbia University Press, for the Carnegie Endowment
for International Peace, Division of Economics and History (The
Paris Peace Conference--History and Documents), 1941.
pp. 499-504.
Also appeared without documents as Ph.D. dissertation, Columbia
University, 1941.

  121 items, 1918 - 1940. German, English; also French (9).

  Published and unpublished documents, memoirs, diaries, and
  secondary sources on the Paris Peace Conference (1919), the
  social and economic history of World War I, war aims, peace
  proposals, and prominent political and military figures.

802   D651.H7D4

Deák, Francis.

Bibliography.
In his Hungary at the Paris Peace Conference: The diplomatic
history of the Treaty of Trianon, with a foreword by James T.
Shotwell.
New York: Columbia University Press, for the Carnegie Endowment
for International Peace, Division of Economics and History (The
Paris Peace Conference--History and Documents), 1942.
pp. 563-567.

  81 items, 1920 - 1939. English; also French, German (3).

  Documents of the Paris Peace Conference (21), government
  publications (15), unofficial documentation (4), general
  works and memoirs (34), articles (7).

803   D643.A7J4

Jessop, T[homas] E[dmund].

Books for further reading.
In his The Treaty of Versailles: Was it just?
London/Edinburgh/Paris/Melbourne/Toronto/New York: Thomas
Nelson and Sons, 1942. pp. 163-164.

Peace Conferences and Peacemaking

28 items, 1919 - 1942. English.

General (12), text of treaty (3), the war (1), the eastern
frontiers (1), the German colonies (4), reparations (4),
disarmament (2), war criminals (1).

804   D645.M387

Marston, F[rank] S[wain].

Bibliography.
In his The Peace Conference of 1919: Organization and
procedure.
London/New York/Toronto: Oxford University Press, under the
auspices of the Royal Institute of International Affairs, 1944.
pp. 247-253.

147 items, 1918 - 1944. English; also French (7), Italian (2),
German (2).

Documents (25), diaries and correspondence (8), preconference
works (20), the conference (40) bibliographical works (3),
list of works quoted (51).

805   JX1392.5.T5,1945a

Thomson, David, E. Meyer, and A. Briggs.

Select bibliography.
In their Patterns of Peacemaking.
New York: Oxford University Press (International Library of
Sociology and Social Reconstruction), 1945. pp. 388-390.

63 items, 1910 - 1944. English; also French (1). All items
are grouped under brief descriptive notes; introduction
(1 paragraph).

Books (51), pamphlets and periodicals (12) on peacemaking,
international relations, and international organization.

806   Z6463.F73

Woolbert, Robert Gale.

"The peace negotiations."
In his Foreign Affairs Bibliography: A selected and annotated
list of books on international relations, 1932-1942.

Peace Conferences and Peacemaking

New York/London: Harper and Brothers, for the Council on
Foreign Relations, 1945. pp. 126-129.

   39 items, 1932 - 1942. English, German, French; also Italian
   (1), Hungarian (1). All items have brief descriptive and/or
   critical annotations; introduction to whole work (2 pp.);
   table of contents.

   The Paris Peace Conference and treaties (22), criticism and
   proposals for revision (17).

807   U21.2.I36

Iklé, Fred Charles.

"Bibliography on the termination of wars."
In his Every War Must End.
New York/London: Columbia University Press, 1971. pp. 151-153.

   46 items, 1916 - 1968. English; also French (4), German (3),
   Japanese (1). Introduction (1 paragraph).

   Books and articles on war termination, peace treaties, and
   diplomatic history.

808   JX5166.R35

Randle, Robert F., [with the assistance of Jeffrey Golden].

Bibliography.
In his The Origins of Peace: A study of peacemaking and the
structure of peace settlements.
New York/London: Free Press/Collier-Macmillan (Institute of War
and Peace Studies Series), 1973. pp. 517-535.

   395 items, 1668 - 1971. English, French; also German, Spanish,
   Italian (4), Latin (1).

   Works dealing with termination of wars and peacemaking (21),
   collections containing treaties of peace and related
   agreements (23), historical works dealing with the peace
   settlements in numerous wars (through the Korean War)
   considered in the text (351).

Peace Conferences and Peacemaking

809 <

[International Peace Academy].

Bibliography on Multilateral Negotiations and Third-party
Roles.
[New York: International Peace Academy], 1980. 23 pp.

Divided into six sections: general studies on international
negotiation, the art of negotiation, third-party roles,
negotiation and simulation, audiovisual sources, the
application of negotiation.

Peace Plans

810   JX1963.L22

Scott, James Brown.

Footnotes in "Introduction."
In Ladd, William, An Essay on a Congress of Nations for the
Adjustment of International Disputes without Resort to Arms
(reprinted from the original edition of 1840).
New York: Oxford University Press, for the Carnegie Endowment
for International Peace, Division of International Law, 1916.
pp. iii-xlv.

   27 items, 1713 - 1915. English, French; also German (3).

   References deal mainly with early peace projects.

811   Z673.A54P

Hicks, Frederick C.

"The literature of abortive schemes of world organization."
In American Library Institute, The American Library Institute:
Papers and proceedings, 1919.
Chicago: [American Library Association], 1920. pp. 160-178.

   135 items, 1516 - 1919. English, French; also German, Latin,
   Dutch (3), Spanish (1). Some items are discussed in a
   bibliographic essay, followed by a chronological list of
   works in which a few items have brief descriptive
   annotations.

   Original works published between 1516 and 1840, with selected
   critical editions and works of commentary published through
   1919. Projects, schemes, and visions of world organization
   and preservation of peace, which taken as a whole trace the
   development of ideas of peace and internationalism.

812 <

Fagley, Richard M.

Books and pamphlets for further reading.

Peace Plans

In his Proposed Roads to Peace.
Boston/Chicago: Pilgrim Press (Adult Education Series), [1935].

813   Z6464.Z9C48

Matthews, M[ary] Alice (comp.).

Peace Projects: Select list of references on plans for the
preservation of peace from medieval times to the present day.
Washington, D.C.: Carnegie Endowment for International Peace,
Library (Reading List No. 36), March 4, 1936. 60 pp.

    532 items, 1468 - 1935. English; also French, German, Latin,
    Spanish (8), Dutch (2). Most items have brief descriptive
    annotations; table of contents; author/subject index.

    General works (36), individual projects before 1800 (160),
    individual projects of the nineteenth century (83),
    individual projects of the twentieth century (158), select
    list of projects of societies, organizations, international
    conferences, and governments (95). General works include
    bibliographies, histories, and studies that analyze two or
    more projects; individual projects cite original texts,
    English translations, secondary works, and biographies of
    authors of some of the projects.

814   JX1938.M3

Marriott, Sir John A[rthur] R[ansome].

Appendix: Short list of books.
In his Commonwealth or Anarchy? A survey of projects of peace
from the sixteenth to the twentieth century.
London: Philip Allan (Quality House), 1937. pp. 220-222.

    65 items, 1859 - 1936. English; also French (4). Introduction
    (1 paragraph).

    Books on peace plans, political philosophy, international
    relations, and diplomatic history.

815   D410.U7,no.87

Knox, Frank, Walter H. C. Laves, and William H. Spencer.

Suggested readings in "After the next armistice--what? (a
radio discussion)."

Peace Plans

University of Chicago Round Table, No. 87 (November 12, 1939):
22.

  10 items, 1938 - 1939. English.

  Articles and a book on conditions for peace.

816   H69.T6,v.5

[Town Hall (comp.)].

Selected bibliography.
In Hindus, Maurice et al., special issue, What Kind of Peace
Can Europe Make?
Town Meeting, 5, 8 (December 4, 1939): 34.

  11 items, 1939. English. All items have brief descriptive
  annotations; introduction (1 paragraph).

  Current articles (8), pamphlets (1), books (2) on peace
  plans.

817   Z6207.W8B7,1942

Brodie, Fawn M.

Peace Aims and Post-war Planning: A bibliography selected and
annotated.
Boston: World Peace Foundation, July, 1942. 53 pp.

  250 items, 1939 - 1942. English. All items have brief to
  medium-length descriptive and/or critical annotations;
  preface (1 p.); table of contents.

  Books, pamphlets, and articles on postwar reconstruction,
  world order, international organization, and plans for
  ensuring world peace.

818 <

Library of International Relations.

Reading Suggestions on Post War Peace Plans.
Chicago: [Library of International Relations], February, 1942.
4 pp.

Peace Plans

819 <

United States Library of Congress, Legislative Reference
Service.

Post-war Planning and Reconstruction (April 1941-March 1942):
Selected and annotated bibliography on post-war plans and
problems.
Washington, D.C.: Library of Congress, [Legislative Reference
Service] (Bibliographies of the World at War, No. 10), 1942.
181 pp. (mimeo).

820 <

United States Library of Congress, Legislative Reference
Service.

Selected References on Post-war Planning.
Washington, D.C.: [Library of Congress, Legislative Reference
Service], September, 1942. 11 pp. (mimeo).

821   JX1938.H43

Hemleben, Sylvester John.

Bibliography.
In his Plans for World Peace through Six Centuries.
Chicago: University of Chicago Press, 1943. pp. 195-222.
Reprinted, with a new introduction by Walter F. Bense, New
York/London: Garland (Library of War and Peace), 1972.

   414 items, 1623 - 1941. English; also French, German, Latin
   (7), Spanish (1). Bibliographical note (2 pp.) in
   introduction to the text.

   Books and pamphlets (343), articles (71) on peace plans,
   peace theory, and international organization.

822   Z6464.Z9H65

Hirsch, Rudolf (comp.).

Plans for the Organization of International Peace, 1306-1789: A
list of thirty-six peace proposals.
New York: New York Public Library, 1943. 14 pp.

   46 items, 1306 - 1943. French, Latin, English; also German (8),
   Italian (1). Many items have brief annotations in English;
   introduction (3 pp.).

Peace Plans

    References (10), list of proposals for the organization of a
    lasting peace (36).

    823   JC362.J62

    Johnsen, Julia E. (comp.).

    Bibliography.
    In her World Peace Plans.
    New York: H. W. Wilson (The Reference Shelf, Vol. 16, No. 5),
    August, 1943. pp. 250-281.

        568 items, 1941 - 1943. English. A few items have brief
        descriptive annotations.

        Bibliographies (16), books, pamphlets, magazine and journal
        articles on general plans for peace (319), Atlantic Charter
        (11), Churchill plan (8), Culbertson plan (10), Hoover plan
        (7), Stassen plan (7), Streit plan (10), economic problems
        (70), freedom of the air (18), regionalism and its problems
        (44), Pacific and the Far East (29), Pan-Americanism (9),
        and world police (10).

    824   PN4181.U5

    [Johnsen, Julia E. and Alberta Worthington (comps.)].

    Bibliography: "World peace settlement."
    In Phelps, Edith M. (ed.), University Debaters´ Annual:
    Constructive and rebuttal speeches delivered in debates of
    American colleges and universities during the college year
    1944-1945 [Vol. 31].
    New York: H. W. Wilson, October, 1945. pp. 67-76.

        152 items, 1943 - 1945. English.

        Books and pamphlets (39), and periodical articles (113) on
        post-war planning, international organization, war and peace
        aims, proposals for world government, conditions of peace,
        and peace plans.

World Order, World Society, World Government

825 <

Trueblood, Benjamin F.

Bibliography.
In his The Federation of the World.
Boston/New York: Houghton Mifflin, 1899 (2nd ed.). pp. 1-9.
Third edition, 1907.

826 <

Duras, Victor Hugo.

Bibliography.
In his Universal Peace: Universal peace by international
government.
New York: Broadway, 1908. pp. 185-186.

827   IU: 341.6W881

Fabian Research Department, International Agreements Committee.

A select bibliography in "Part III, Articles suggested for
adoption by an international conference at the termination of
the present war."
In Woolf, L[eonard] S. International Government: Two reports
. . . together with a project by a Fabian committee for a
supernational authority that will prevent war, with an
introduction by Bernard Shaw.
New York: Brentano's, 1916. pp. 411-412.

  18 items, 1623 - 1913. English; also French (1). Essay
  format.

  Books and articles on peace plans, the Hague conferences,
  legislative control of foreign policy, and international
  relations.

World Order, World Society, World Government

828   Z8091.21.B8,v.10

Rockwood, E. Ruth.

"International government and the League to Enforce Peace: A
bibliography."
Bulletin of Bibliography (Boston), 10, 2 (April, 1918): 30-34.

   204 items, 1904 - 1918. English; also French (3), German (1).
   Table of contents.

   Bibliographies (3), internationalism (13), international
   arbitration (24), Hague and other conferences (5),
   international law (20), international courts (13),
   international government (11), conditions of lasting peace
   (20), League to Enforce Peace (53), other proposed
   international organizations (32), organizations to promote
   peace (10).

829   JX1995.H88

Hudson, Manley O.

Readings [on lectures I-IV].
In his Current International Co-operation: Calcutta University
readership lectures, 1927.
Calcutta: Calcutta University, 1927. pp. 29, 72-73, 110-111,
149.

   27 items, 1916 - 1926. English.

   Books and articles on the formation of an international
   society, international governments, world order,
   international organization, League of Nations, the Permanent
   Court of International Justice, and international law.

830 <

McMullen, Laura W. (ed.).

Selected bibliography [at the end of each chapter].
In her Building the World Society: A handbook of international
relations.
New York: McGraw-Hill (Whittlesey House), 1931.

World Order, World Society, World Government

831   DLC-DB

Baden, Anne L. (comp.), under the direction of Florence S.
Hellman.

Selected List of Recent Writings on Internationalism (Super-
state).
[Washington, D.C.]: Library of Congress, Division of
Bibliography, August 8, 1933. 30 pp. (mimeo).

  329 items, 1915 - 1933. English; also French (4), German (4),
  Italian (1), Norwegian (1). Some items have brief descriptive
  annotations.

  Bibliographies (7), books and pamphlets (175), articles in
  periodicals (147) dealing with world unity, internationalism,
  nationalism, peace education, world society, world
  government, and international relations.

832 <

Schwarzenberger, Georg.

Bibliography.
In his The League of Nations and World Order: A treatise on the
principle of universality in the theory and practice of the
League of Nations.
London: Constable (The New Commonwealth Institute Monographs,
Series A, No. 3), 1936. pp. 182-191.

833 <

Lyons, Jacob G. (comp.).

Union Now: A bibliograpy on the federal union of nations
(preliminary report of the Research Committee).
Washington, D.C.: Washington Association for Union Now,
Research Committee, 1940. 12 pp.

834   JC357.M3,1940

Mackay, R[onald] W[illiam] G[ordon].

Short reading list; Bibliography.
In his Federal Europe: Being the case for European federation
together with a draft constitution of a United States of
Europe, with a foreword by Norman Angell.

World Order, World Society, World Government

London: Michael Joseph, 1940. pp. 311-312, 313-316.
Revised lists appear in his Peace Aims and the New Order:
Outlining the case for European federation together with a
draft constitution of a United States of Europe, with a
foreword by Norman Angell, New York: Dodd, Mead and Co., 1941,
pp. 297-298, 299-302.

   88 items, 1917 - 1939. English.

   Books and pamphlets on causes of war, political theory, world
   order, peace aims, international affairs, the theory and
   practice of democracy, imperialism, and capitalism.

835   Z6461.C29,no.10

Scanlon, Helen L[awrence] (comp.), under the direction of M[ary]
Alice Matthews.

The New World Order: Select list of references on regional and
world federation; together with some special plans for world
order after the war.
Washington, D.C.: Carnegie Endowment for International Peace,
Library (Select Bibliographies, No. 10), December 12, 1940.
17 pp. (mimeo).

   221 items, 1917 - 1940. English; also French (7), German (1).
   Many items have brief descriptive annotations; table of
   contents.

   Bibliographies (8), periodicals (10), books, pamphlets, and
   magazine articles (203) on various proposals for the
   organization of peace following World War II, especially
   those for world federation, inter-American league of nations,
   European federation, Atlantic union, and a reorganized League
   of Nations.

836   E744.H43,no.32

Dean, Vera Micheles.

Suggested reading.
In her The Struggle for World Order.
New York: Foreign Policy Association (Headline Books, No. 32),
November, 1941. pp. 95-96.

   17 items, 1939 - 1941. English. All items have brief critical
   annotations.

   Books on various plans for world order from the Congress of
   Vienna to postwar planning in the early years of World

World Order, World Society, World Government

War II, including Hitler´s "new order," proposals for peace
in the Far East, and a number of British and American
proposals.

837   JC362.J6

Johnsen, Julia E. (comp.).

Bibliography.
In her International Federation of Democracies (Proposed).
New York: H. W. Wilson (The Reference Shelf, Vol. 14, No. 8),
April, 1941. pp. [239]-263.

  476 items, 1917 - 1941. English.

  Bibliographies (8), books, pamphlets, magazine and journal
  articles on world order (129), federation of democracies
  (133), regional federation (98), Pan-Americanism (39), Asia
  (9), world organization (36), the League of Nations (11), and
  international police (13).

838   JX1908.U6C35,no.29

O´Donnell, Charles (ed.).

Bibliography.
In his The World Society: A joint report.
Washington, D.C.: Catholic Association for International Peace
(Pamphlet No. 29), 1941. pp. 47-48.

  22 items, 1926 - 1941. English.

  Moral bases of world society (6), nationalism in world
  society (3), the economics of world society (6), social and
  cultural aspects of world society (2), world society and a
  commonwealth of nations (5).

839   PN4177.D4,v.16

Foulkes, William R. (ed.).

"Abstracted references [on world organization]."
Debaters´ Digest, 16, 6 (September, 1942): 31-44.

  226 items, 1939 - 1942. English. All items have abstract-
  length descriptive annotations; introduction (1 paragraph).

  Articles on various plans for regional and world federation,
  the relationship between democracy and peace, peacemaking,
  conditions conducive to peace, reasons for the failure to

World Order, World Society, World Government

achieve permanent peace, international organization,
reconstruction, nationalism, isolationism and U.S. foreign
policy.

840   PN4177.D4,v.16

Foulkes, William R. (ed.).

"Books; Pamphlets; Magazines [on world organization]."
Debaters´ Digest, 16, 9 (December, 1942): 69-72.

   73 items, 1941 - 1942 (no dates given for the books and
   pamphlets). English. All of the magazine articles have brief
   to abstract-length descriptive and/or critical annotations
   while the rest are not annotated.

   Books (18), pamphlets (31), magazine articles (26) on peace
   plans, the United Nations, world organization, religion and
   peace, and postwar planning and reconstruction.

841   D825.J64

Johnsen, Julia E. (comp.).

Bibliography.
In her The "Eight Points" of Post-war World Reorganization.
New York: H. W. Wilson (The Reference Shelf, Vol. 15, No. 5),
March, 1942. pp. [103]-126.

   362 items, 1940 - 1942. English.

   Bibliographies (2), books, pamphlets, magazine and journal
   articles on world order (49), Axis war aims (37), Allied aims
   and principles (62), the eight-point program (61),
   international federation (69), Anglo-American union (48),
   regional organization and problems (34).

842   D825.J643

Johnsen, Julia E. (comp.).

Bibliography.
In her Plans for a Post-war World.
New York: H. W. Wilson (The Reference Shelf Vol. 16, No. 2),
September, 1942. pp. [213]-238.

   390 items, 1941 - 1942. English. A few items have brief
   descriptive annotations; appended list of organizations
   working for postwar plans.

World Order, World Society, World Government

Bibliographies (14), books, pamphlets, magazine and journal
articles on postwar planning and world order (189), the
Atlantic Charter (19), the democracies and the U.N. (32),
regional problems (34), reconstruction in Europe (40),
religious statements on reconstruction and peace (27),
economic problems (35).

843   D443.K2

Lengyel, Emil.

Bibliography in "Peace planning."
In Kalijarvi, Thorsten V., et al., Modern World Politics.
New York: Crowell, 1942. pp. 816-818.

29 items, 1936 - 1942. English. Many items have brief
descriptive and/or critical annotations.

Books (15), articles, booklets, pamphlets (14), on world
order, international organization, and such related issues as
colonialism, economic aspects of peace, postwar
reconstruction, and American isolationism.

844   H1.I65,v.1

Denicke, George.

"Recent trends in the literature of postwar planning."
International Postwar Problems, 1, 4 (September, 1944):
560-573.

15 items, 1942 - 1944. English. Bibliographic essay, many
items are critically discussed in the text.

Books on world order, international organization, and
conditions conducive to peace.

845   Z6461.C29,no.7a

Scanlon, Helen Lawrence (comp.).

International Police: Proposals for cooperative defense through
the use of international armies, navies, and air forces.
Washington, D.C.: Carnegie Endowment for International Peace,
Library (Select Bibliographies, No. 7), May 15, 1944 (rev.
ed.). 18 pp. (mimeo).
Original edition, compiled by Mary Alice Matthews, March 29,
1937. 9 pp.

World Order, World Society, World Government

   189 items, 1915 - 1944. English; also French (3). Some items
   have brief descriptive annotations.

   Bibliographies (5), books, pamphlets, and magazine articles
   (184) on proposals for international police forces,
   disarmament and arms control, and critiques of those
   proposals.

   846   LC6301.N43,v.26

   Levering, S[amuel] R.

   References for further information in "World government, the
   path to peace."
   In special issue, High School World Peace Speaking Program on
   the topic "Is world government the path to peace?"
   University of North Carolina Extension Bulletin, 26, 4 (October,
   1946): 23-24.

     21 items, 1945 - 1946 (most are undated). English.

     Mostly popular magazine articles on world government, the
     United Nations, international organization for peace, and the
     balance of power.

   847 <   JX1977.J6

   Johnsen, Julia E. (comp.).

   Bibliography.
   In her United Nations or World Government.
   New York: H. W. Wilson (The Reference Shelf), 1947.
   pp. 241-285.

   848   LC6301.N43,v.27

   [Rankin, E. R. (comp.)].

   Bibliography.
   In special issue, How Can the United Nations Be Strengthened?
   (High School World Peace Study and Speaking Program, 1947-48).
   University of North Carolina Extension Bulletin, 27, 3 (October,
   1947): 53-59.

     113 items, 1943 - 1947 (most items published in 1947).
     English. Introduction (2 pp).

     Book, articles, and films on the United Nations, world
     government, and the conditions of peace.

World Order, World Society, World Government

849

Ishida, Gladys.

"World government bibliography."
Common Cause, 3, 4 (November, 1949): 212-219.

   125 items, 1948 - 1949. English. Many items have brief
   descriptive and critical annotations; introduction (1
   paragraph).

   Books and articles (published in the U.S.) on the problem of
   and prospects for world government from legal,
   constitutional, political, economic, and philosophical points
   of view.

850   JX1901.C68,v.3

Harrod, Elizabeth B.

"An analytic bibliography of world constitutional drafts:
Part[s] I, II, III."
Common Cause, 3, 6,7,9 (January, February, April, 1950):
325-331, 384-388, 496-500.

   32 items, 1940 - 1949. English; also French (3), Italian (1).
   Most items have medium- to abstract-length descriptive
   annotations; introduction to Part I (1 paragraph).

   Articles, pamphlets, manuscripts, and a few books on various
   constitutions, specific plans for world government, and
   proposals for changing the United Nations.

851 <   Z6464.Z9W55

Williams, Stillman P.

Toward a Genuine World Security System: An annotated
bibliography for layman and scholar.
[Washington, D.C.]: United World Federalists, [1964]. 65 pp.

852   JX1974.G67

Green, Lucile [Wolfe] and Esther Yudell (eds.).

Bibliography: Sources and complete texts of material used in
this book; Suggested readings.

World Order, World Society, World Government

In their The Worried Woman´s Guide to Peace through World Law.
Piedmont, Calif.: N. California Women for Peace, Committee on
World Law, 1965. pp. 96, 97-98.

   31 items, 1905 - 1964. English. A few items have descriptive
   annotations.

   Pamphlets, speeches, monographs, and journals on a world
   constitution, world federation, international organization
   and law.

853

Newcombe, Hanna.

References.
In her Alternative Approaches to World Government, II.
Peace Research Reviews, 5, 3 (February, 1974): 77-94.
An earlier edition appeared in Peace Research Reviews, 1,
1 (January, 1967).

   179 items, 1893 - 1972. (Most items 1944-1972). English; also
   French (2), German (1).

   Books, articles, pamphlets, and documents on mundialization,
   world peace, world law, world government, the United Nations,
   and peace theory.

International Organization

854   DLC-DB

[United States Library of Congress, Division of Bibliography].

List of References on a League to Enforce Peace.
[Washington, D.C.]: Library of Congress, Division of
Bibliography, December 14, 1916. 3 pp. (typescript).

   33 items, 1910 - 1916. English.

   Books, articles, and reports on international organization,
   proposals for a league of nations, international arbitration,
   and the role of force in the maintenance of peace.

855   Z6466.Z9W83,v.1

[World Peace Foundation].

"Books on a League of Nations."
A League of Nations, 1, 1 (October, 1917): 51-53.

   18 items, 1914 - 1917. English; also French (3), German (1),
   Dutch (1). Most items have brief descriptive annotations.

   Books, proceedings, and speeches on a league of nations,
   peacemaking, proposals to enforce peace, the conditions of
   peace, and world governments.

856   Z6466.Z9W83,v.1

[World Peace Foundation].

"Books on a League of Nations: [Supplement]."
A League of Nations, 1, 6 (August, 1918): 343-344.

   22 items, 1915 - 1918. English; also French (2), Italian (2),
   German (1), Dutch(1). A few items have brief descriptive
   annotations.

   Books, articles, reports, addresses, and journals on a league
   of nations, internationalism, international organization, and
   peace plans.

International Organization

857   Z7164.L4B7

[Boston Public Library].

A League of Nations: Selected references to recent books and
magazines in the Public Library of the City of Boston.
Boston: Trustees [of the Boston Public Library] (Brief Reading
Lists, No. 7), March, 1919 (3rd ed.). 26 pp.

   397 items, 1899 - 1919. English; also Russian (2), Italian (1),
   French (1). A few items have brief descriptive annotations.

   Books, articles, debates (389), periodicals (1), and
   bibliographies (7) on various proposals and plans for setting
   up a league of nations to ensure a durable peace.

858   Z6474.A51,no.134

Hicks, Frederick C.

"International Organization: An annotated reading list."
International Conciliation, No. 134 (January, 1919): 67-115.

   190 items, 1601 - 1918. English; also French, Spanish (2).
   Most items have brief to abstract-length descriptive and
   critical annotations; introduction (1 p.); table of contents;
   appended list of publications of the Carnegie Endowment for
   International Peace.

   Books and articles on the state (6), sovereignty (6),
   equality (6), nationality (9), sanctions for international
   law (4), balance of power (6), early proposals for
   international organization (10), argument for a new world
   polity (18), international congresses, commissions and unions
   (7), Hague conferences (6), Permanent Court of Arbitration
   (4), court of arbitral justice (33), international prize
   court and the international naval conference (6), Central
   American court of justice (3), codification of international
   law (5), recent proposals and discussions of international
   organization (61).

859   Z673.A54P

Richardson, Ernest Cushing, Reginald H. Lawrence, and Ralph E.
Kent.

"The literature of international cooperation."

International Organization

In American Library Institute, The American Library Institute:
Papers and proceedings, 1919.
Chicago: [American Library Association], 1920. pp. 41-159.

   970 items, 1843 - 1919 (only 11 items before 1900). English;
   also French, Spanish (2). Most items have brief to medium-
   length descriptive and/or critical annotations; introduction
   (1 paragraph).

   Mostly articles but some books on plans for a league of
   nations and a "world commonwealth."

860 <

[Carnegie Endowment for International Peace, Library].

League of Nations.
Washington, D.C.: Carnegie Endowment for International Peace,
Library (Miscellaneous Reading List No. 15), 1922.
Other editions, 1923 and 1924.

861   H69.W6,1923

Wilson, Justina Leavitt and Julia E. Johnsen (comps.).

"Internationalism."
In their Questions of the Hour: Social, economic, industrial;
study outlines.
New York: H. W. Wilson (The Reference Shelf, Vol. 1, No. 9),
April, 1923 (2nd ed., rev. and enl.). pp. 33-34.

   27 items, 1919 - 1922. English.

   History, achievements, and opposition to League of Nations
   (17); history and controversy over cancellation of the Allied
   war debt (10).

862   Z6472.L43,1927

[League of Nations, Publications Department].

Publications Issued by the League of Nations.
Boston: World Peace Foundation, [November 1, [1927]. 160 pp.
Another edition, [October 31], 1929, 239 pp.

   English, French; also German (2).

International Organization

863 <

Harrison, A. W.

List of books [at the end of chapters].
In Christianity and the League of Nations.
[London]: Epworth Press, 1928.

864   Z1009.N27,no.102

League of Nations, Publications Department.

League of Nations (Official Publications): A selected list of
books prepared by the League of Nations, Publications
Department, Geneva.
London: National Book Council (Book List No. 102), September,
1928. 11 pp.

   74 items, 1920 - 1928. English; also French (1). Most items
   have brief descriptive annotations.

   Covenant (1), monthly summary of the League of Nations (1),
   special cases of protection of minorities (1), economics and
   finance (17), health (7), social questions (4), legal
   questions (5), mandates (2), political questions (7),
   communications and transit (6), disarmament (3),
   international cooperation (2), international bureaux (1),
   publications prepared by the information section (17).

865   JX3160.P6

Potter, Pitman B.

Bibliography.
In his An Introduction to the Study of International
Organization.
New York: Century (The Century Political Science Series), 1928
(3rd ed., completely rev. and enl.). pp. 561-576.
First edition, 1922. Second edition, [1925].

   354 items, 1726 - 1926. English; also French, German, Italian
   (1). Introduction (1 p.).

   Books, articles, journals, and documents on international
   law, diplomacy, international relations, international
   politics, treaties and negotiations, alliances, arbitration,
   peace conferences, international administration,
   international organization, and the League of Nations.

International Organization

866   Z6473.L43

Société des Nations, Bibliothèque/League of Nations, Library.

Ouvrages sur l'Activité de la Société des Nations Catalogués à
la Bibliothèque du Secrétariat/Books on the Work of the League
of Nations Catalogued in the Library of the Secretariat.
Geneva: [Société des Nations, Service des Publications/League
of Nations, Publications Department], 1928. viii/viii + 274 pp.

  2364 items, 1804 - 1927. English, French, German; also Italian,
  Spanish, Dutch, Polish, Danish, other Eastern and Western
  European languages. Preface (2 pp.); table of contents;
  subject/author index.

  Books and pamphlets on the origin of the League of Nations
  and its wide range of activities, particularly with respect
  to international cooperation, disarmament, international law,
  education, churches, women, reconstruction, refugees, social
  welfare, international politics, mandates, minorities,
  health, intellectual cooperation, labor, membership, and
  societies formed for its support. The bibliography is
  subdivided by issue areas and by country.

867 <

Matthews, M[ary] Alice (comp.).

International American Conferences.
Washington, D.C.: Carnegie Endowment for International Peace,
Library (Reading List No. 25), 1929. (mimeo).
An earlier edition appeared August 8, 1928.

868   Z6472.A1L4

Société des Nations, Bibliothèque/League of Nations, Library.

Guide Sommaire des Publications de la Société des Nations/Brief
Guide to League of Nations Publications.
Geneva: League of Nations, Publications Department, 1929.
32 pp.

  25 items, 1920 - 1928. French, English. All items have
  abstract-length descriptive annotations; preface (1
  paragraph) and introductions to each section; complete French
  text followed by complete English text.

  Lists League of Nations publications in various categories:
  those published regularly several times a year, those that

International Organization

    appeared continuously but not at fixed intervals, and
    nonperiodical publications.

869   Z6471.A1WS,suppl.

Carroll, Marie J.

Key to League of Nations Documents Placed on Public Sale, 1920-
1929, with a foreword by T. P. Sevensma.
Boston: World Peace Foundation, 1930. 340 pp.
Another edition in 4 volumes covering the period 1920-1933,
Boston: World Peace Foundation, 1934; a fifth volume, covering
the period 1934-1936, New York: Columbia University Press,
1937.

    Approximately 2900 items, 1920 - 1929. English; also French.
    Introduction (6 pp.); table of contents; list of
    abbreviations used in official numbers on League of Nations
    documents; list of League meetings and conferences with
    references to documentation; chart on League organization;
    index of official numbers and series of League publications
    numbers.

    Lists periodicals, official documents, reports, articles,
    pamphlets, and books by the League of Nations on statutes and
    proceedings of the League, administrative commissions,
    minorities, economic and financial issues, health, social
    questions, legal questions, mandates, slavery, political
    section, communications and transit, disarmament, financial
    administration, drug traffic, intellectual cooperation,
    international bureaus, refugees, general questions,
    information section, and the library.

870 <

League of Nations, Secretariat.

Bibliography.
In its Ten Years of World Co-operation.
[Geneva]: League of Nations, Secretariat, 1930. pp. 431-460.

871 <

[Carnegie Endowment for International Peace, Library].

International Agencies for Peace.
Washington, D.C.: Carnegie Endowment for International Peace,
Library (Miscellaneous Reading List No. 43), 1932. (mimeo).

International Organization

872 <

League of Nations Association, Educational Committee.

A Study Course on the League of Nations, with foreword by Mary
E. Woolley.
New York: [League of Nations Association, Educational
Committee], 1932. 68 pp.

873   Z6475.C8C3,1935

Matthews, Mary Alice (comp.).

The League of Nations Covenant: Select references to books and
articles on the Covenant and its revision, with annotations.
Washington, D.C.: Carnegie Endowment for International Peace,
Library (Reading List No. 1), April 24, 1935 (rev. ed.). 18 pp.
(mimeo).
First published as Reading List No. 1, 1926. Another edition,
Reading List No. 1a, appeared in 1928.

   206 items, 1919 - 1935. English, French; also German, Italian
   (2), Spanish (1). Some items have brief descriptive
   annotations or excerpts; table of contents; appended list of
   other bibliographies (18) published by the CEIP.

   General works (88), texts of the Covenant (4), special
   articles of the Covenant (95), the Covenant and the Kellogg
   Pact (19).

874   Z1009.N27,no.12

League of Nations Union (comp.).

League of Nations: A selected list of books compiled by The
League of Nations Union, 15 Grosvenor Crescent, London
S.W.1. . .
London: National Book Council (Book List No. 12), May, 1936
(5th ed.). 4 pp.
Third edition, February, 1930; fourth edition, July, 1931.

   150 items, 1911 - 1936. English; also French (3).

   General (39), historical background (11), junior books (6),
   International Labor Office (7), Covenant (5), economic work
   (8), social and humanitarian work (13), League of Nations and
   British Empire (2), international law (6), Permanent Court of
   International Justice (5), mandates (7), minorities (11),
   arbitration, security, and disarmament including the Kellogg

International Organization

   Pact (21), protocol (2), Anglo-American relations and the
   freedom of of the seas (7).

875   JX1963.W82

Wright, Louise Leonard.

References.
In her Toward a Collective Peace System.
Washington, D.C.: National League of Women Voters, 1937.
pp. 55-58.

   77 items, 1925 - 1937. English. Introduction (1 paragraph)
   including a list of organizations producing materials on
   foreign policy and international cooperation.

   General (33), peaceful change (13), disarmament (8),
   sanctions (8), neutrality (15).

876   Z6464.A1C3,no.11a

Matthews, M[ary] Alice (comp.).

League of American Nations.
Washington, D.C.: Carnegie Endowment for International Peace,
Library (Brief Reference List No. 11), October 31, 1938
(rev. ed.). 4 pp. (mimeo).

Original edition, September 9, 1938, 3 pp.

   29 items, 1864 - 1938. English, Spanish; also French, German
   (1). Many items have brief descriptive annotations.

   Periodical articles, speeches, books, and official documents
   on inter-American relations, Pan American Union, regionalism,
   and the League of American Nations.

877   Z6473.B84

Breycha-Vauthier, A. C. de.

Sources of Information: A handbook on the publications of the
League of Nations, with a preface by James T. Shotwell.
London/New York: George Allen and Unwin/Columbia University
Press, 1939 (English ed.). 118 pp.
Original edition in German, 1934. Other editions in Czech
(1936), Russian (1937), and French (1937).

   574 items, 1926 - 1938. English; also French, German (6),
   Danish (3), Italian (2), Dutch (1), Eastern European

International Organization

   languages. Introduction (1 p.); table of contents; subject
   index.

   Books, documents, reports, articles published by the League
   of Nations up to December 1, 1938, on economics, transport,
   health, social and humanitarian work, intellectual
   cooperation, legal questions, mandates, political activities,
   limitation of armaments and security.

878 <

Matthews, Mary Alice (comp.).

League of Nations.
Washington, D.C.: Carnegie Endowment for International Peace,
Library (Brief Reference List No. 11), March 17, 1939 (2nd rev.
ed.). (mimeo).

879   Z6464.A1C3,no.15

Matthews, M[ary] Alice (comp.).

Collective Security.
Washington, D.C.: Carnegie Endowment for International Peace,
Library (Brief Reference List No. 15), April 20, 1939. 5 pp.
(mimeo).

   71 items, 1928 - 1939. English; also French (3). A few items
   have brief descriptive annotations.

   Books, articles, and pamphlets on efforts to enforce peace
   and achieve security by collective action, the legal, social,
   and political aspects of security, and the League of Nations
   effort for world cooperation.

880   F1034.B4,v.2

Carter, Gwendolen M.

Reading list in "Consider the record: Canada and the League of
Nations."
Behind the Headlines, 2, 6 (May 1, 1942): [25].

   12 items, 1930 - 1942. English. Most items have brief
   descriptive annotations.

   Books on Canada's position on the League.

International Organization

881

Lerner, Max, Edna Lerner, and Herbert J. Abraham.

Bibliography [2 lists].
In their International Organization After the War: Roads to
world security.
Washington, D.C.: National Council for the Social Studies and
National Association of Secondary-School Principals (Problems
in American Life, Unit Number 15), 1943. pp. 36-38, 53-56.

  115 items, 1939 - 1943. English. A few items have brief
  descriptive annotations.

  Books and pamphlets on world order, conditions of peace,
  postwar planning and reconstruction, international
  organization, and the United Nations.

882   JX1954.A5

[American Historical Association, Historical Service Board].

Suggestions for further reading.
In its Can We Prevent Future Wars?
Washington, D.C.: [U.S.] War Department (Education Manual
EM 12, GI Roundtable Series), August 19, 1944. pp. 27-28.

  12 items, 1935 - 1943. English.

  Books on collective security and international organization.

883 <

Aufricht, Hans.

World Organization: An annotated bibliography.
New York: Woodrow Wilson Foundation, January, 1945 (4th rev.
ed.). 16 pp.
Another edition, July, 1943.

884   Z6475.I5U5

[United States Library of Congress, General Reference and
Bibliography Division].

The League of Nations Intellectual Co-operation Program: A list
of references.

International Organization

Washington, D.C.: Library of Congress, General Reference and
Bibliography Division, 1945. 20 pp.

  136 items, 1920 - 1941. English; also French, Italian (1).
  Many items have brief to abstract-length descriptive
  annotations; subject index.

  The League of Nations intellectual cooperation program (66),
  references in the League of Nations official journal (70).

885 <

Bentwich, Norman.

Bibliography.
In his From Geneva to San Francisco: An account of the
international organisation of the new order.
London: Gollancz, 1946. pp. 110-111.

886   Z6461.C29,no.16

Scanlon, Helen Lawrence (comp.).

The United Nations: A selected list of materials on the
organization and functions of the United Nations, for the use
of teachers, students and discussion leaders.
Washington, D.C.: Carnegie Endowment for International Peace,
Library (Select Bibliographies, No. 16), June 10, 1946. 10 pp.
(mimeo).

  87 items, 1945 - 1946. English. Some items have brief
  descriptive annotations.

  Pamphlets, articles, official documents, and a few books on
  the United Nations (40), General Assembly (10), Economic and
  Social Council (8), Trusteeship Council (7), Security Council
  (6), International Court of Justice (12); periodicals (4).

887   JX1904.P4,1947

[National Peace Council (London)].

Selected list[s] of publications in "The United Nations."
In its Peace Year Book, 1947.
London: National Peace Council, 1947. pp. 85-90.

  46 items, 1944 - 1946. English.

International Organization

    Official documents, books, pamphlets, and periodicals by and
    about the United Nations (23) and some of the agencies
    connected with the U.N. (23).

    888

    Scanlon, Helen Lawrence (comp.).

    International Organization, with Emphasis on the United
    Nations: A guide to published sources of documentation,
    bibliographies, and general information.
    Washington, D.C.: Carnegie Endowment for International Peace,
    Library (Memoranda Series, No. 4), August 25, 1947. 8 pp.
    (mimeo).

        76 items, 1945 - 1947. English.

        Bibliographies (25), document collections (29), basic
        handbooks and periodicals on the United Nations (17),
        official national reports on the General Assembly (5).
        Appended address list of noncommercial organizations that
        published cited materials.

    889 <   Z6464.I6D6

    Turner, Robert K. and Patricia S. Alexander (comps.).

    Documents of International Organizations: A selected
    bibliography, Vols. 1-3.
    Boston: World Peace Foundation, 1947 to 1950. [xcv] + 188
    + 128 + 107 pp.
    Cumulative table of contents, 31 pp., published separately
    [1950].

    890 <

    [United Nations].

    Selected bibliography of the United Nations.
    In its Yearbook of the United Nations 1946-1947.
    New York: [United Nations], 1947. pp. 879-913.

International Organization

891   JX1977.A37Y4,1947/48

International Court of Justice.

"The Court´s publications; Bibliography of the International
Court of Justice."
In its Yearbook, 1947-1948.
[Leiden: A. W. Sijthoff, for the Registry of the Court], 1948.
pp. 69-71, 79-118.

   369 items, 1945 - 1948. English, French; also Spanish, German,
   Norwegian, Dutch (9), Polish (2), other Western European
   languages. Some items have brief descriptive annotations;
   introduction (1 p.); table of contents; author index; subject
   index.

   Court´s publications (15), bibliographies concerning the
   Court (6), Conference of San Francisco (73), ratification of
   the Charter (23), accession to the statute of nonmember
   states (11), conditions under which Court shall be open to
   states not parties to the statute (2), organs of the U.N.
   other than the Court (42), International Court of Justice
   (46), cases brought before the Court (37), proposed
   references to the Court (7), works and review articles on the
   Court in general (23), settlement of international disputes
   (5), law of nations and international law (68), dissolution
   of the Permanent Court of International Justice (11).

892   JX1977.A37Y4,1948/49

International Court of Justice.

"The court´s publications; Bibliography of the International
Court of Justice."
In its Yearbook, 1948-1949.
[Leiden: A. W. Sijthoff, for the Registry of the Court], 1949.
pp. 81-84, 89-130.

   405 items, 1945 - 1949. English, French; also Polish, Spanish,
   German, Dutch, Russian (8), other Western and Eastern
   European languages. A few items have brief descriptive
   annotations; introduction (1 p.); table of contents; author
   index; subject index. Items do not repeat those in the
   bibliography of the ICJ Yearbook, 1947-1948.

   Court publications (20); bibliographies concerning the Court
   (7), Conference of San Francisco (53), accession to the
   statutes of nonmember states (1), organs of U.N. (43),
   International Court of Justice (44); cases brought before the
   Court (61), references to the Court (6); works and review
   articles on the Court in general (27), settlement of

International Organization

international disputes (15), law of nations and international
relations (121), dissolution of the Permanent Court of
International Justice (7).

893 <

Harrison, Maxine (comp.).

International Understanding: Catalogue of 16mm films dealing
with the United Nations, its member states and related
subjects.
New York: Carnegie Endowment for International Peace/National
Education Association, Committee on International Relations.
1950 (3rd ed.).

894 <

Aufricht, Hans.

Guide to League of Nations Publications: A bibliographical
survey of the work of the League, 1920-1947.
New York: Columbia University Press, 1951.

895 <

Cormack, Margaret.

Selected Pamphlets on the United Nations and International
Relations: An annotated guide.
New York: Carnegie Endowment for International Peace, 1951.

896   LC6301.N43,v.32

Rankin, E. R. (comp.).

Bibliography.
In his special issue, Building World Peace: What have been the
achievements and what are the prospects of the United Nations
(High School World Peace Study and Speaking Program, Peace
Handbook 1952-53).
University of North Carolina Extension Bulletin, 32, 2
(November, 1952): [61]-63.

    61 items, 1945 - 1952. English. Introduction (2 pp.).

    Books, articles, and films on the United Nations, world
    government, U.S. foreign policy, NATO.

International Organization

897   LC6301.N43,v.33

Rankin, E. R. (comp.).

Bibliography.
In his special issue, Building World Peace: How can the United
Nations prevent Communist aggression and preparation for
aggression? (High School World Peace Study and Speaking
Program, Peace Handbook 1953-54).
University of North Carolina Extension Bulletin, 33, 2
(November, 1953): [53]-55.

   67 items, 1945 - 1953 (most items published in 1953). English.
   Introduction (2 pp.).

   Books, articles, and films on the United Nations, U.S.
   foreign policy, conditions of peace, world government.

898 <

Rudzinski, Aleksander Witold.

Selected Bibliography on International Organization (based on
the bibliography appearing in Leland Matthew Goodrich and
Edvardisak Hambro´s Charter of the United Nations--Commentary
and Documents).
New York: Carnegie Endowment for International Peace, 1953.

899   Z6464.I6S68

Speeckaert, G. P. (comp.).

International Institutions and International Organization: A
select bibliography.
Brussels: Union of International Associations, with assistance
from UNESCO and in collaboration with the International
Federation for Documentation (FID Publication No. 292/UIA
Publication No. 151), 1956. 116 pp.

   783 items, 1824 - 1956. French, English; also German, Spanish,
   Italian (6), Dutch (5), Portuguese (2), Scandinavian
   languages (4). Introduction (2 pp.); table of contents;
   author index.

   Books, journal articles, pamphlets, reports, dissertations,
   and official documents on international organization (122),
   the League of Nations, the United Nations, and specialized
   agencies (180), supranational organizations (33), intergovernmental organizations (136), relations between

International Organization

   intergovernmental organizations and nongovernmental
   organizations (58), international nongovernmental
   organizations (119), special problems (78); yearbooks and
   directories (45), periodicals (12).

   900 <

   Wall, Linwood and Brenda Brimmer.

   Guide to the Use of United Nations Documents.
   Dobbs Ferry, N.Y.: Oceana, 1962.

   901   Z6481.A65

   American Association for the United Nations.

   Read Your Way to World Understanding: A selected annotated
   reading guide of books about the United Nations and the world
   in which it works for peace and human welfare.
   New York: Scarecrow Press, 1963.

   902 <

   Frydenberg, Per (ed.).

   Bibliography.
   In his Peace-keeping: Experience and evaluation.
   Oslo: Norwegian Institute of International Affairs, 1964.

   903 <

   Doums, J.

   Bibliography of the International Court of Justice, 1918-1964.
   Leiden: A. W. Sijthoff, 1965.

   904   Z6464.I6S68,1965

   Speeckaert, G. P.

   Bibliographie sélective sur l'organisation
   internationale/Select Bibliography on International
   Organization, 1885-1964.
   Brussels: Union des Associations Internationales/Union of
   International Associations, 1965. 150 pp.

International Organization

1098 items, 1885 - 1964. French, English; also German, Italian,
Spanish, Dutch (7), Norwegian (6), Russian (6), other Western
and Eastern European languages. Introduction (4 pp.); table
of contents; subject index; author index.

Works on international organization including the history of
international relations (26), theory and general studies
(224), legal states, immunities, administration, and civil
service (57), yearbooks, directories, periodicals, and
bibliographies (62), and works on individual international
organizations (729).

905   JX1977.R594

Ross, Alf.

References [11 lists].
In his The United Nations: Peace and Progress.
Totowa, N.J.: Bedminster Press, 1966. pp. 27-28, 53, 83-84,
105, 156-158, 184-185, 226-227, 276-277, 308, 371, 393.

136 items, 1908 - 1964. English; also French (6), German (3),
Norwegian (2). A few items have brief critical annotations.

Works on the background, organization, and activities of the
United Nations.

906 <   UA600.C28,no.66/R14

Smith, Gordon S.

A Selected Bibliography on Peacekeeping.
Ottawa: Canada, Department of National Defence, Operational
Research Division (ORD Report No. 66/R14), 1966. 35 pp.

907   JX5136.K5

Knitel, Hans G.

Bibliographie.
In his Les Délégations du Comité International de la Croix-
Rouge [The Delegations of the International Committee of the
Red Cross].
Geneva: Institut Universitaire de Hautes Etudes Internationales
(Etudes et Travaux, No. 5), 1967. pp. 119-129.
Also in: Oesterreichische Zeitschrift für öffentliches Recht,
Vol. 16, No. 3-4.

International Organization

214 items, 1863 - 1964. French; also German, English (8).
Table of contents; list of abbreviations.

Reports, studies, and other publications of the International
Committee of the Red Cross; official documents and
publications; periodicals, manuals, articles, and books
relating to the Red Cross; various relief operations and
international crises; prisoners of war; international law;
and humanitarian activities.

908 <

Legault, Albert.

Peace-keeping Operations: A bibliography.
Paris: World Veterans Federation, 1967. 200 pp.

Annotated; index.

909 <

[National Council of the Churches of Christ in the U.S.A.].

A Selected Bibliography for the Observance of the International
Year for Human Rights, 1968.
[New York: National Council of the Churches of Christ in the
U.S.A., 1968]. 4 pp.

910   JX1981.P7T37

Taylor, Alastair [MacDonald], David Cox, and J. L. Granatstein.

Bibliography.
In their Peacekeeping: International challenge and Canadian
response.
[Toronto]: Canadian Institute of International Affairs
(Contemporary Affairs, No. 39), 1968. pp. 205-211.

84 items, 1945 - 1967. English. Introduction (1 paragraph).

Books (31) and journal articles (53) on peacekeeping; U.N.
military forces for various crisis areas including West
Irian, the Congo, Lebanon, Cyprus, and Gaza; the role and
problems of the U.N. in international peacekeeping; Canadian
foreign policy and Canada's role in peacekeeping and U.N.
peacekeeping forces.

International Organization

911 <

Hüfner, Klaus and Jens Naumann.

Zwanzig Jahre Vereinte Nationen [Twenty years of the United
Nations]: Internationale Bibliographie 1945-1965 . . .
Berlin: Walter de Gruyter (Beiträge zur auswärtigen und
internationalen Politik, Vol. 2), 1969.

912 <

Johnson, Harold S. and Baljit Singh.

International Organization: A classified bibliography.
East Lansing: Michigan State University, Asian Studies Center
(South Asia Series, Occasional Paper No. 11), 1969. 261 pp.

913   Z6481.M3

McConaughy, John Bothwell and Hazel Janet Blanks.

A Student's Guide to United Nations Documents and Their Use,
with a preface by Joseph Groesbeck.
New York: Council on International Relations and United Nations
Affairs, 1969. 17 pp.

  58 items, 1928 - 1968. English. All items have brief
  descriptive annotations; introduction (2 pp.); table of
  contents.

  Publications of the United Nations (32), other sources of
  information on activity of the United Nations (6),
  documentation by the International Court of Justice (5),
  guide for researchers on U.N. (7), locating U.N. voting
  records (8).

914 <

Schlüter, Hilmar Werner.

[Bibliography].
In his Die Politische Funktion des Sicherheitsrates der
Vereinigten Nationen von 1945-1950 [The Political Function of
the United Nations Security Council from 1945 to 1950].
Bonn: H. Bouvier (Schriften zur Rechtslehre und Politik, Vol.
65), 1970. pp. 245-257.

International Organization

915 <

Haas, Michael.

International Organization: An interdisciplinary bibliography.
Stanford: Hoover Institution Press, Spring, 1974. 944 pp.

916   Z6464.I6A74

Atherton, Alexine L.

International Organizations: A guide to information sources.
Detroit: Gale Research (Gale Information Guide Library;
International Relations Information Guide Series, Vol. 1),
1976. xxviii + 350 pp.

  Chapter 2, "Bibliographies," lists 130 items including
  bibliographies of bibliographies (11), sources in social
  science, political science and international relations (10),
  and bibliographies on international organization,
  disarmament, and peace studies (84).

Peace Education

917 <

Friends Peace Committee.

Educating the Young for Peace.
Society of Friends, Peace Committee, [1924]. 8 pp.

   Apparently unavailable; not located through interlibrary
   loan.

918 <

[Carnegie Endowment for International Peace, Library].

Teaching of History, International Law and International
Relations.
Washington, D.C.: Carnegie Endowment for International Peace,
Library (Miscellaneous Reading List No. 28), 1925.

919 <

Matthews, M[ary] Alice (comp.).

History in School Text-books.
Washington, D.C.: Carnegie Endowment for International Peace,
Library (Reading List No. 3), 1926. (mimeo).

920 <

Matthews, M[ary] Alice (comp.).

Education and International Peace.
Washington, D.C.: Carnegie Endowment for International Peace,
Library (Reading List No. 15), May 17, 1927. (mimeo).

921   IaU: T1928H24

Hansen, Sylva Therese.

Bibliography.

Peace Education

In her Educational Policies of Some Prominent Peace and
Religious Organizations, 1918-1927. Unpublished M.A. thesis,
History,
State University of Iowa [Iowa City], June, 1928. pp. 163-189.

   275 items, 1908 - 1928. English.

   Books (primary sources--20, secondary sources--16), magazine
   articles (127), bulletins and pamphlets (92), newspapers
   (14), and letters (6) on peace education, religious
   education, the peace movement, the youth movement, and
   general problems of peace and war.

922 <

King, A. K.

Bibliography in "The place of history in improving
international relations."
High School Journal (Chapel Hill, N.C.), 13 (January, 1930).

923   JX1953.L6

Lobingier, Elizabeth [Erwin] Miller and John Leslie Lobingier.

"Peace plays and pageants; Source material."
In their Educating for Peace.
Boston/Chicago: Pilgrim Press, 1930. pp. 164-180, 181-209.

   254 items, 1899 - 1930 (no dates given for plays). English.
   All items have brief descriptive and/or critical annotations;
   introduction to section on peace plays and pageants (1
   paragraph) and source material (1 p.).

   Peace plays and pageants (23), collections of stories that
   tend to promote world friendship (14), stories and source
   material about other peoples (33), series of stories dealing
   with the life of children in various lands (52), geographical
   and historical readers (17), fairy tales of other lands (16),
   general nonfictional readings on war and peace for adults
   (29), courses of study (40), leaders' helps (13), magazines
   that promote peace (17).

Peace Education

924   Z5814.H58C2

Matthews, Mary Alice (comp.).

History Teaching and School Text-books in Relation to
International Understanding: Select list of books, pamphlets,
and periodical articles.
Washington, D.C.: Carnegie Endowment for International Peace,
Library (Reading List No. 29), March 4, 1931. 14 pp.

   163 items, 1887 - 1931. English; also French, German (7),
   Norwegian (1). Some items have brief descriptive annotations.

   Books and pamphlets (73) and periodical articles (90) on the
   effects of history texts on nationalist vs. internationalist
   attitudes, critical studies of texts, history teaching and
   world peace, and proposals for educational reform in the
   interests of peace.

925 <

Murphy, Albert J.

Bibliography.
In his Education for World-mindedness.
New York: Abingdon Press (Abingdon Religious Education Texts,
College Series), [1931]. pp. 341-354.

926 <

Brunauer, Esther C.

Bibliography.
In her International Attitudes of Children.
Washington, D.C.: American Association of University Women,
International Relations Office, September, 1932.

927 <

Committee on World Friendship Among Children.

Helpful literature and films.
In its Creating a World of Friendly Children: Suggestions for
children's activities and programs.
New York: Committee on World Friendship Among Children, [1932].
pp. 78-83.

Peace Education

928 <

International Bureau of Education, Geneva.

Children's Books and International Goodwill: Book list and
report of an inquiry.
Geneva: Bureau International d'Education, 1932 (2nd ed.).
243 pp.
First edition, 1929, 80 pp.

929 <

Barns, Florence E[lberta].

Study courses and bibliographies.
In her Literature and the International Mind.
Washington, D.C.: American Association of University Women,
International Relations Office, 1933. 34 pp. (mimeo).

930 <

Stoker, Spencer.

Bibliography.
In his The Schools and International Understanding.
Chapel Hill: University of North Carolina Press, 1933.
pp. [221]-238.

931 <

Redefer, Frederick L.

[Bibliography].
In his Child Education: A corrective of the adult's war spirit.
New York: World Peaceways, 1934. [16 pp.].

932 <

Smithells, Philip.

Bibliography.
In his World without War: A book for children.
London: J. M. Dent and Sons, [1934]. pp. 91-92.

Peace Education

933 <

Jones, Amy Heminway.

International Mind Alcove Booklist.
New York: Carnegie Endowment for International Peace, Division
of Intercourse and Education, 1935 (5th ed.). 19 pp.
First edition, 1928, 13 pp.; second edition, 1932, 15 pp.;
third edition, 1933, 18 pp.

934   Z7164.I8k5

King, Gertrude E[lizabeth] N[elson].

World Friendship: A bibliography; Sources of educational
material.
Boston: Chapman and Grimes, 1935. 81 pp.

  251 items, 1825 - 1934. English. Most items have brief to
  abstract-length descriptive and/or critical annotations;
  preface (1 paragraph); table of contents; title index.

  Books and articles (139), efforts and materials (112) on
  education for friendly international relations, or materials
  useful in such education. Also lists more general works on
  education or on the psychology of attitude change. Numerous
  reports of research are listed.

935

Piaget, Jean.

[Bibliography] in "Some suggestions concerning League teaching."
Bulletin of League of Nations Teaching   (Geneva), 2 (1935): 193.

936 <

Smith, Henry Lester (comp.).

Bibliography.
In Smith, Henry Lester and Peyton Henry Canary, Some Practical
Efforts to Teach Good Will.
[Bloomington: Indiana University, Bureau of Cooperative
Research] (Bulletin of the School of Education, Vol. 2, No. 4),
[1935]. pp. 165-166.

Peace Education

937   Z6464.C35,1936

Matthews, Mary Alice (comp.).

Education for World Peace: The study and teaching of
international relations; select list of books, pamphlets, and
periodical articles, with annotations.
Washington, D.C.: Carnegie Endowment for International Peace,
Library (Reading List No. 33), June 30, 1936 (rev. ed.). 37 pp.
First edition, 1932.

   371 items, 1912 - 1936. English. Many items have brief to
   medium-length descriptive annotations; table of contents;
   author/subject index; addresses of organizations mentioned.

   General works (97), books and reading--biography, drama,
   poetry, etc. (26), church, home, kindergarten (17), courses
   of study, handbooks, programs, plays, etc. (42), fellowships
   and scholarships (9), moving pictures, posters, etc. (21),
   press and radio (12), societies, institutes, and other
   agencies studying international relations (49), student
   activities, correspondence, summer schools, camps, travel,
   etc. (22), teachers and training of teachers (10),
   universities and colleges (19), world peace and social
   studies--general (15), geography and history (13), League of
   Nations (15), Paris Pact [Kellogg Peace Pact] (4).

938   JX1936.5.M25

McPherson, Imogene M[cCrary].

Sources.
In her Educating Children for Peace.
New York/Cincinnati/Chicago: Abingdon Press, 1936. pp. 187-190.

   128 items (most items undated). English.

   Bible stories and passages (31), peace story books (9),
   magazine articles (15), peace education programs (9), helpful
   materials (18), plays and pageants (7), books for study by
   teachers and pupils (25), and peace organizations (14).

939   BV1460.I63,v.12

Wilson, E[dward] Raymond.

"Resources for peace education [bibliographic essay]."

Peace Education

International Journal of Religious Education, 12, 5 (January,
1936): 13-14, 20.

   41 items (no dates given). English. Most items are critically
   discussed in the text.

   Lists organizations, books, and pamphlets that could be used
   as resource material for peace studies. Deals with
   organizations like World Peace Foundation and League of Nations.

940 <

[Carnegie Endowment for International Peace, Divison of
Intercourse and Education].

International Mind Alcove Booklist: Books selected January,
1934-May, 1937.
New York: Carnegie Endowment for International Peace, 1937.
4 pp.

941 <

Graham, [Gladys (Murphy)].

A Selected List of Books, Building for International Attitudes
in Children.
Washington, D.C.: [American Association of University Women],
1937 (3rd ed.). 10 pp.
An earlier edition, entitled "A Selected List of Fifty Books
for Building International Attitudes in Children," was
published in Santa Monica by the California branch of the
American Association of University Women, 1933.

942   LB5.N25,v.36,2

Kiely, Margaret.

"Teaching aids and materials."
In Kandel, I. L. and Guy Montrose Whipple (eds.), Thirty-sixth
Yearbook of the National Society for the Study of Education:
Part II, International understanding through the public-school
curriculum (prepared by the Society's Committee on
International Understanding).
Bloomington, Ill.: Public School Publishing, 1937. pp. 311-363.

   Several hundred items, 1925 - 1936. English. Bibliographic
   essay with brief introductions to numerous unannotated lists.

Peace Education

Surveys, books, articles, pamphlets, and other teaching
materials designed to aid in the promotion of international
good will. Covers background materials on relevant
organizations, international correspondence, teachers'
readings, readings in periodicals, and reports of
investigations. Treats instructional materials under the
headings of general sources, courses of study, syllabi,
teaching plans, discussion outlines, projects, units of work,
plays, pageants, and other materials for school assemblies
and special-day observances, sources of materials (toys,
games, folk songs, dances), exhibits, motion pictures, radio,
and the press.

943   JX1953.M335

McPherson, Imogene M[cCrary].

Book lists.
In her Learning about War and Peace: A text book for juniors in
vacation church schools.
St. Louis, Mo.: Bethany Press, for the Interdenominational
Committee on Co-operative Publication of Vacation Church School
Curriculum (Co-operative Series of Church School Texts,
Junior), 1937. pp. 179-183.

79 items (no dates given). English. A few items have brief
descriptive annotations.

Books for children (24), reference material (14), source
books of stories (11), plays and pageants (15), slide
lectures (2), peace units (2), suggested reading for teachers
(9), newspapers (2).

944   Z6464.Z9W6

Wilson, E[dward] Raymond with the assistance of Frances M.
Williams and Foreign Policy Association Staff.

Provisional Bibliography on Materials for Peace Education: For
use in institutes of international relations and summer
conferences.
Philadelphia: American Friends Service Committee, June, 1937.
16 pp. (mimeo).

334 items, 1918 - 1937 (most items published after 1934).
English. A few items have brief descriptive annotations;
table of contents.

American foreign policy (19), disarmament (36), economics and
peace (66), Europe (34), the Far East (25), international

Peace Education

organization (15), Latin America (14), spiritual aspects of
world peace (55), the World War (11), youth and peace (8),
drama (4), peace organizations and the peace movement (11),
study outlines (36).

945 <

Hyde, Marguerite R.

Good References on Educating for International Understanding.
Washington, D.C.: U.S. Government Printing Office, (United
States Office of Education, Bibliography No. 56), 1938. 16 pp.

946   Z6464.Z9C45

Matthews, Mary Alice (comp.).

Peace Education: Select list of references on international
friendship, for the use of teachers, students, and study
groups; with information regarding source material for teachers
and goodwill books for children.
Washington, D.C.: Carnegie Endowment for International Peace,
Library (Reading List No. 38), May 22, 1939. 24 pp.

269 items, 1893 - 1939. English; also French (2), Spanish (2).
Some items have brief descriptive annotations; table of
contents; author index.

General works (139), bibliographies, programs and source
material (59), special subjects, special days, etc. (34),
goodwill books and plays (19), periodicals useful to teachers
(18).

947   CSt: 370.874V269,Education

Van Norman, C[arrie] Elta.

Reference bibliography.
In her An Investigation of the Concept of War in Historical
Fiction Written for Children. Unpublished Ph.D. dissertation,
School of Education, Stanford University.
[Stanford University], October, 1941. pp. 343-347.
(typescript).

59 items, 1915 - 1941. English.

Books, pamphlets, journal articles, and unpublished materials
on peace education, appropriate teaching materials, analyses
of children's books and school texts, and empirical studies

Peace Education

    of attitudes toward war, militarism, and pacifism.

948   Z1007.B94,v.18

White, John Browning.

"Bibliography of materials on education for peace in the public
schools of the United States during the 1920s: [Part I]; Part
II."
Bulletin of Bibliography, 18, 3 (January-April, 1944): 66-68;
4 (May-August, 1944): 87-91.

   408 items, 1919 - 1941. English. Introduction (1 paragraph).

   Books, articles, syllabi, teaching materials, reports, and
   periodicals on peace education, international education, the
   teaching of history and geography in relation to peace, the
   peace movement, causes and prevention of war, military
   training in schools and colleges, militarism, citizenship,
   pacifism, social attitudes of children, and the World
   Federation of Education Associations.

949   JX1905.R6

Rosenhaupt, Hans W.

"Books for young people; Teachers and peace; How to read up on
the United Nations; Aids in waging peace."
In his How to Wage Peace: A handbook for action.
New York/Toronto: John Day/Longmans, Green, 1949. pp. 97-102,
103-106, 203-211, 214-242.

   195 items, 1945 - 1949. English. Most items have brief to
   abstract-length descriptive and/or critical annotations;
   introductions (1 paragraph to 1 p.) to each section.

   Books for young people (47), teachers and peace (10), United
   Nations (37), aids in waging peace (101).

950

UNESCO (United Nations Educational, Scientific and Cultural
Organization).

Bibliography: "The improvement of textbooks as aids to
international understanding."
In its A Handbook for the Improvement of Textbooks and Teaching
Materials as Aids to International Understanding.

Peace Education

Paris: UNESCO (Publication No. 368), 1949. pp. 136-155.

164 items, 1885 - 1949. English, French; also German, Spanish
(5), Dutch (3), Portuguese (2), Hungarian (1), other Western
European languages. Many items have brief to medium-length
descriptive annotations; introduction (1 paragraph).

Books, pamphlets, reports, and articles on the historical
development of efforts to improve textbooks and teaching
materials as aids to international understanding and on the
various approaches that have been used.

951   LB2842.G28

Garber, Joseph H.

Bibliography.
In his Our Educational Dilemma--Peace Education and Teacher
Salaries: Research papers on educational problems facing
America and the world, with forewords by Roy S. Koch and F.
James Schrag and an introduction by Albertina A. Weinlander.
New York: Exposition Press (An Exposition-Banner Book), 1959.
pp. 83-86.

55 items, 1915 - 1958. English. Appended list of peace
organizations.

Books, articles, and publications of governmental and private
organizations on war, peace, international organization,
peace education, educational administration, and teachers'
salaries.

952 <

American Friends Service Committee.

Books for Friendship: A list of books recommended for children.
Philadelphia: American Friends Service Committee, 1965. 53 pp.
Originally published under the title Books Are Bridges, 1953.
Third edition, 1962, 63 pp.

953

Flynn, Alice H. (comp. and ed.).

World Understanding: A selected bibliography, with a foreword
by Asdrubal Salsamendi and a preface by Frank W. Cyr.

Peace Education

   Dobbs Ferry, N.Y.: Oceana, for the United Nations Association,
   1965. xv + 263 pp.

      1207 items, 1890 - 1965. English; also Spanish, French, other
      western and eastern languages. Most items have brief to
      abstract-length descriptive and critical annotations;
      foreword (1 p.); preface (2 pp.); introduction (3 pp.); table
      of contents; list of publishers and sources; author/subject
      index.

      Books, pamphlets, and resource materials "for teaching and
      learning about the United Nations and the world in which it
      works for peace and human welfare." The United Nations, the
      family of nations dedicated to world peace (204); the
      United Nations in a changing world--people and places (407),
      a world of political diversity (37), communications and
      interdependence (206), science (136), the quest for
      understanding "the infinite lands of thought and prayer"
      (30); the United Nations, a challenge to individual and group
      participation--program suggestions for schools, clubs, and
      community groups (100), visual aids for programs (48), group
      and individual participation in international service
      projects (28), membership in groups (6), additional sources
      for information (5).

   954 <

   Röhrs, Hermann (ed.).

   [Bibliography].
   In his Friedenspädagogik [Peace Pedagogy].
   Frankfurt am Main: Akademische Verlagsgesellschaft
   (Erziehungswissenschaftliche Reihe, Vol. 1), 1970. pp. 177-181.

   955 <

   [Rest, H. O. Franco (ed.)].

   [Bibliography].
   In his Waffenlos zwischen den Fronten [Weaponless between the
   Fronts]: Die Friedenserziehung auf dem Weg zur Verwirklichung
   [Peace education in process of realization].
   Cologne: Styria, 1971. pp. 299-311.

Peace Education

956 <

Vasquez, J. A.

[Bibliography] in "Toward a unified strategy for peace
education: Resolving the two cultures problem in the classroom."
Journal of Conflict Resolution, 20, 4 (December, 1976):
724-728.

957

Fink, Clinton F[rederick].

[References] in "Peace education and the peace movement since
1815."
Peace and Change 6, 1 and 2 (Winter, 1980): 71-73.

   55 items, 1815 - 1976. English; also French (1), Italian (1),
   German (1).

   Books and articles on the history and philosophy of peace
   education, peace studies, international education,
   international understanding, school textbook revision, and
   the history of the peace movement.

Peace Research

958 <

Wright, Quincy.

"Cooperative research on war [bibliographic essay]."
In his A Study of War, Vol. I.
Chicago: University of Chicago Press, 1942. pp. 414-422.

959

[Gladstone, Arthur (ed.)].

"Current bibliography."
Bulletin of the Research Exchange on the Prevention of War, 2,
1 (September 20, 1953): 5-6; 2 (November 1, 1953): 6; 3 (January
1, 1954): 5; 4 (March 1, 1954): 14; 3, 1 (October 1, 1954): 3-4;
2 (November 20, 1954): 4-5; 3 (January, 1955): 21-22; 4 (March,
1955): 41; 5 (May, 1955): 64; 4, 1 (January, 1956): 16; 3-4
(May-July, 1956): 61-66.

960

Blum, Richard H.

References in "Research projects in international tensions I:
UNESCO and M.I.T."
Bulletin of the Research Exchange on the Prevention of War, 3,
5 (May, 1955): 47-50.

961

Blum, Richard H.

References in "Research projects in international tensions II:
Hoover Institute studies, Center for Research on World
Political Institutions, and the Commission to Study the
Organization of Peace."
Bulletin of the Research Exchange on the Prevention of War, 3,
6 (July, 1955): 70-73.

Peace Research

962 <

Deutsch, Morton and Richard Flacks.

"Psychologists and peace: Guide to sources of information."
SPSSI [Society for the Psychological Study of Social Issues]
Newsletter (June, 1962).

963

Engel, Trudie (comp.).

Bibliography on Peace Research in History.
Washington, D.C.: Committee on Peace Research in History,
[1964]. 24 pp. (mimeo).

   152 items, 1945 - 1964. English; also Dutch (1). Many items
   have brief descriptive annotations; introduction
   (1 paragraph).

   Works in progress, completed, or published on governmental
   policies toward peace (103), internal changes bringing
   changes in governmental policy on peace (30), effects of
   governmental war/peace policy on internal political and
   social development (7), and theories of conflict (12).

964

[Galtung, Johan and Mari Holmboe Ruge (comps. and eds.)].

International Repertory of Institutions Specializing in
Research on Peace and Disarmament.
Paris: UNESCO (Reports and Papers in the Social Sciences,
No. 23), 1966. 77 pp.

   Contains lists of works relating to the study of peace and
   disarmament published or sponsored by the U.N. and by the
   research organizations surveyed.

965 <

Metzger, W. O., K. F. Schade, and Helga Boss-Steuner.

[Documentation and bibliography of peace research--in German].
Offene Welt, No. 95-96 (September, 1967).

Peace Research

966   JX1904.5.G7

Gray, Charles H., Leslie B. Gray, and Glenn W. Gregory.

A Bibliography of Peace Research Indexed by Key Words.
Eugene, Ore.: General Research Analysis Methods, 1968.
[xxiii] + 164 pp.

   Approximately 1300 items, 1942 - 1967. English. Introduction
   (10 pp.).

   Books and journal articles, most of which were published
   between 1957 and 1967, on a wide range of topics including
   the study of war and peace, international relations, foreign
   policy, international trade, armament, arms control,
   disarmament, deterrence, nuclear weapons and war, the Cold
   War, conflict resolution, bargaining, international
   cooperation, international law, international organization,
   alliances, national security, the military, world order,
   United Nations, violence, revolutions, and the Vietnam War.

967 <

Knobloch, Eva and Dieter Senghaas.

"Ausgewählte Bibliographie zur Friedensforschung [Selected
bibliography on peace research]."
In Krippendorff, Ekkehart (ed.), Friedensforschung [Peace
Research].
Cologne/Berlin: Kiepenheuer und Witsch (Neue Wissenschaftliche
Bibliothek, 29), 1968. pp. 559-589.

968   JX1961.I5M33

Kumar, Mahendra.

[Footnote references].
In his Current Peace Research and India.
Rajghat, Varanasi: Gandhian Institute of Studies, 1968. 147 pp.

   Approximately 218 items, 1921 - 1965. English. All items
   contained in footnotes; appendices list and describe
   institutes directly conducting peace research (60),
   institutes that have part of their research program devoted
   to peace research (70), journals (39), and peace conferences
   (25).

   Books and articles on peace research, peace theory,
   methodology and philosophy of social science, international

Peace Research

relations, pacifism, nonviolence, Gandhi and Gandhism,
conflict, violence, war, arms races, armament and
disarmament, and nonviolent civil defense.

969 <

[Pax Christi].

"[Die] Wissenschaft vom Frieden [The Science of peace]."
Info-Heft der Pax-Christi-Bewegung, 3, 1-2 (1968): 37-52.

970

Newcombe, Hanna and Alan [G.] Newcombe.

References.
In their Peace Research Around the World.
Oakville, Ontario: Canadian Peace Research Institute, 1969.
pp. 204-275.

626 items, 1946 - 1967. English. All items are summarized
briefly in the text, based on Peace Research Abstracts.

Text includes chapters on international systems, crisis
research, conflict studies, attitudes, research on the
future, integration studies, economic studies, international
law, disarmament studies, protest actions, nonviolence,
theoretical conclusions, policy recommendations, and research
recommendations.

971 <

Bredow, W. v.

"Von ´realistischen´ und ´utopistischen´ Luftschlössern in der
Friedensforschung [On ´realistic´ and ´utopian´ air castles in
peace research]: Ein Literaturbericht [A review of literature]."
Blätter für Deutsche und Internationale Politik, 11 (1970):
1176.

972 <

Kaiser, Karl, in collaboration with Reinhard Meyers.

Bibliographie.
In their Friedensforschung in der Bundesrepublik [Peace
Research in the Federal Republic of Germany]: Gegenstand und
Aufgaben der Friedensforschung, ihre Lage in der Bundesrepublik

Peace Research

sowie Möglichkeiten und Probleme ihrer Förderung; mit einem
unter Mitarbeit von Reinhard Meyers ausgearbeiteten Verzeichnis
von Forschungsinstitutionen und Gesellschaften sowie einer
Bibliographie [Subject matter and tasks of peace research, its
status in the Federal Republic as well as possibilities and
problems of its development; with a list of research institutes
and societies, as well as a bibliography compiled in
collaboration with Reinhard Meyers].
Göttingen: Vandenhoeck and Ruprecht (Wissenschaft und Frieden:
Studie im Auftrag der Stiftung Volkswagenwerk), 1970. pp. 188-
241.

973 <

Noack, Paul.

[Bibliography].
In his Friedensforschung, ein Signal der Hoffnung? [Peace
Research, a Sign of Hope?]
Freudenstadt: Eurobuch/A. Lutzeyer (Bonn-actuell, 1), 1970.
pp. 128-139.

974   JX1901.J6,v.14

Singer, J[oel] David.

References in "From ´A Study of War´ to peace research: Some
criteria and strategies."
Journal of Conflict Resolution, 14, 4 (December, 1970):
540-542.

   78 items, 1903 - 1971. English; also French (2).

   Books and articles on causes and effects of war, theories of
   international relations, and quantitative approaches to the
   study of war and international conflict.

975   D1.Z37,v.20

Fricke, Dieter.

[Bibliographic footnotes] in "Neuere Literatur zur
´Friedensforschung´ in der BRD [Recent literature on ´peace
research´ in the Federal Republic of Germany]."
Zeitschrift für Geschichtswissenschaft, 20, 1 (1972): 82-92.

   31 items, 1967 - 1971. German. Bibliographic essay; footnotes
   cite items discussed.

Peace Research

Books, articles, and conference reports concerning peace
research, the idea of peace, conflict theory, peace
education, and specific topics such as aggression, armaments,
capitalism, socialism, etc.

976   DT1.A285,1973(3)

Matthies, Volker.

"Afrika als Gegenstand der Friedens- und Konfliktforschung
[Africa as subject of peace and conflict research]: einige
bibliographische Notizen [Some bibliographical notes]."
Afrika Spectrum [8], 3 (1973): 315-327.

    121 items, 1956 - 1973. German, English; also French (5). All
    items are discussed in text with some comments and quotes in
    footnotes.

    Books and articles on political sociology, African studies,
    and peace and conflict research.

977   Z6464.Z9S32,1973

Scharffenorth, Gerta and Wolfgang Huber, et al. (eds.).

Neue Bibliographie zur Friedensforschung [New Bibliography of
Peace Research], mit einer Einführung von Gerta Scharffenorth
[with an introduction by Gerta Scharffenorth].
Stuttgart/Munich: Ernst Klett/Kösel (Studien zur
Friedensforschung, Vol. 12), 1973. 327 pp.
First published as Bibliographie zur Friedensforschung,
Stuttgart/Munich: Ernst Klett/Kösel (Studien zur
Friedensforschung, Vol. 6), 1970, 188 pp.

    3778 items, 1897 - 1973. German, English, French; also Spanish,
    Dutch, Portuguese. Introduction (43 pp.), plus introductions
    (1-3 pp.) to each section; table of contents; author index.

    Peace research institutes (60), periodicals (76),
    bibliographic aids (73); peace theory and problematics (178),
    historical peace research (180), peace and conflict research
    (301), theories of international relations (85), strategic
    studies and disarmament (343), international law and
    international organization (262), imperialism, international
    dependency structures, and development politics (281), peace
    activities and strategies of social change (716), peace
    education (142), psychology of conflict, war, and peace
    (208), human ecology and peace (193), contributions of
    theology and church to peace problems (680).

Peace Research

978   JX1903.J6,v.10

Senghaas, Dieter (ed.).

Bibliography: "Recent peace research books in the Federal
Republic of Germany by German authors."
In his special issue, Peace Research in the Federal Republic of
Germany.
Journal of Peace Research, 10, 3 (1973): 317-318.

   64 items, 1960 - 1973. German; also English (1).

   Works on peace theory, peace research, disarmament, peace
   education, aggression, and social conflict.

979

UNESCO (United Nations Educational, Scientific and Cultural
Organization).

"Selective list of periodicals in the field of peace and
conflict research."
In its International Repertory of Institutions for Peace and
Conflict Research.
Paris: UNESCO (Reports and Papers in the Social Sciences, No.
28), 1973. pp. 90-91.

   46 items (no dates given; all current in 1973). English; also
   German (5), French (4), Spanish (1), Russian (1), Italian (1).

980   Z6464.Z9A37

Aggarwal, Lalit K.

Peace Science: A bibliography.
Philadelphia: University of Pennsylvania, Department of Peace
Science, 1974. 58 pp.

   651 items, 1923 - 1973. English. Preface (1 p.), plus
   introductions (1 paragraph) to each section; subject index.

   Suggested readings and references for a perspective on peace
   science (205), methodology of peace science (137), current
   research and issues in peace science (267), bibliographies
   and data sources (42).

Peace Research

981 <

Dedring, Juergen.

[Bibliography].
In his Recent Advances in Peace and Conflict Research, with a
foreword by Elise Boulding and a preface by J. David Singer.
Beverly Hills: Sage (Sage Library of Social Research, Vol. 27),
1976. pp. 219-244.

982   IU: 016.3411D93p

Durkee, Kinde (comp.).

Peace Research: Definitions and objectives; A bibliography.
Los Angeles: California State University at Los Angeles, Center
for the Study of Armament and Disarmament (Political Issues
Series, Vol. 4, No. 1), 1976. 28 pp.

   293 items, 1936 - 1975. English; also German, French (5),
   Italian (1), Polish (1), Russian (1). Introduction (5 pp.);
   table of contents.

   Defining peace research (136), peace research topics (69),
   peace research centers and projects (38), analysis of peace
   research (51), reference materials (9).

983

Van Den Dungen, Peter.

References in "Varieties of peace science: An historical
perspective."
Journal of Peace Science, 2, 2 (Spring, 1977): 256-257.

   38 items, 1815 - 1967. English, German; also French (6).

   Books and journal articles on peace science, peace theory,
   pacifism, and the history of peace and the peace movement.

Part III: War

Part III: War

PART III: WAR

INTRODUCTION

    Part III comprises bibliographies focusing mainly on war.
It is divided into 11 sections covering general works, history of
war, world wars, causes and effects of war, war and children,
psychological, economic, social, political, and legal aspects of
war, war crimes, and war crimes trials.

    The first section (24. War--General) contains 40 items, of
which the majority (24) were published since World War II. The
bibliographies included in this section are of broad scope,
usually containing materials which cross the boundaries of other
subsections in Part III of this guide or comprising works of a
general, theoretical, or cross-disciplinary character on war.
Some items are of such broad scope as to include also works on
peace (e.g., Wells, No. 1015; Stockton, No. 990), and thus
overlap to some extent with Part I, Section 1 (Peace and
War--General); however, the main emphasis of bibliographies in
this section is works concerning war.

    The bibliographies described in Section 24 are less massive
than a number of items in other sections described below.
Several of the more comprehensive and recent items are Clarke
(No. 1011) and Coats (No. 1012); two others which are
comprehensive in nature but shorter and of earlier publication
date are Nickerson (No. 996) and Nearing (No. 1000). Two which
are notable for their cross-disciplinary character are Bramson
and Goethals (No. 1016) and Divale (No. 1022). A number of
bibliographies included in this section deal with selected types
of war, such as limited war (e.g., Halperin, No. 1008),
revolutionary war (Cosyns-Verhaegen, No. 1013), or various types
of conflicts (Barringer, No. 1021). Some items deal with
specific theories of war, e.g., the ideas of Francisco Suarez
(Pereña Vicente, No. 1003) or Karl von Klausewitz (Paret, No.
1009).

    Next, Section 25 lists 25 bibliographies (the majority
published after 1945) focusing primarily on the history of war,
though some also contain more general material (e.g., Matthews,
No. 1031; Coblentz, No. 1034). For a recent, fairly
comprehensive bibliography (listing 442 works published from 1758
to 1972), see Singer and Small (No. 1040); for an earlier
bibliography, listing 242 works dating back to to 1597, see

Spaulding, Nickerson, and Wright (No. 1026). Many of the items listed here are specialized for specific periods, places, topics, or wars, such as Dikshitar's bibliography on wars in ancient India (No. 1033); Higham's guide to sources of British military history (No. 1039); or Leitenberg and Burns' guide to materials on the Vietnam conflict (No. 1042). Works on specific wars or conflicts contained in bibliographies listed in other sections may be located through the subject index. Other listings of works on the history of war may also be found in Section 1 (Peace and War--General) and Section 24, (War--General).

In Section 26 (World Wars) we include 47 bibliographies focusing on the two world wars of the twentieth century. Most of the items deal with World War I; some of them are very extensive. The most comprehensive of those focusing on World War I is Prothero (No. 1063), listing about 8000 items published between 1879 and 1922 (see also No. 1052); Bulkley (No. 1060) also lists approximately 8200 items, mainly on social and economic aspects of the war in the United Kingdom; and Vic (Nos. 1057 and 1065) lists a total of some 10,800 works in his two bibliographies of French publications from 1914 to 1918. A useful shorter bibliography dealing with World War I, the interwar period, and the beginning of World War II, is Waller (No. 1077). The most recent bibliography on World War I listed here is Schaffer (No. 1095). Recent bibliographies on World War II (primarily works in English) include Morton (No. 1088), Wright (No. 1089), Ziegler (No. 1090), Bloomberg and Weber (No. 1091), and Funk et al. (No. 1092). Both world wars are covered by De Launay et al. (No. 1085) and by Bayliss (No. 1093).

Lists of general works on the two world wars may also be found in bibliographies described in other sections of this guide, such as Peace and War--General, War--General, History of War, etc. Moreover, many bibliographies dealing with selected aspects of the world wars have been classified in other sections appropriate to their topical focus, such as Effects of War, Psychological Aspects of War, Legal Aspects of War, etc. Thus, for example, works on labor mobilization, labor relations, and the labor movement during World War I will be found in Section 31 (Economic Aspects of War).

Section 27 lists only 10 bibliographies whose primary focus is the causes of war. Six of these were published in the period between the two World Wars; the most comprehensive, however, appeared during and after World War II (Bernard, No. 1103; Pruitt and Snyder, No. 1104). Many bibliographies containing lists of works dealing with the causes of war are described in other sections of this guide. For example, Cook et al. (No. 114) list 72 works on the character, causes, and political economy of war; Johnsen (No. 26) lists 95 works on the causes of war; and Prothero (No. 1052) lists 183 works relating to the causes and issues of World War I (see also No. 1063). Works on such topics as the psychological or economic causes of war may be found in other sections appropriate to those topics, e.g., Stagner (No. 1167), under "Psychological Aspects of War." For works on causes of war appearing in other sections, consult the subject index.

In Section 28 we include 29 bibliographies on the effects of war. It may be of interest to note that the majority of these were published prior to World War II (1906-1937), and only 3 appeared after 1935. Among the more comprehensive bibliographies described here are Matthews (No. 1120), published in 1931; Sorokin (No. 1128), published in 1942; and Nelson (No. 1133), published in 1971 (but limited mainly to the United States). Many of the bibliographies focus on specific types of effects, such as the costs of war or economic effects, losses of life, or medical effects such as diseases. Two bibliographies list works on the benefits or alleged benefits of war (Nos. 1108 and 1121). Here again, many relevant lists may be found in bibliographies classified in other sections (e.g., War and Children, Psychological Aspects of War, Economic Aspects of War, Social and Political Aspects of War, War Crimes, etc.); such lists may be located through the subject index.

Section 29 (War and Children) includes 20 items, of which 17 date from the period of World War II, mainly dealing with the social and psychological effects of war on children. The most comprehensive is Conover (No. 1147), listing 609 items published from 1915 to 1943. One recent item, Tolley (No. 1154) deals with political socialization of children to war. For other relevant materials, consult the subject index under headings for children, juvenile deliquency, youth, students, etc.

Section 30 (Psychological Aspects of War) contains 38 bibliographies, only six published prior to World War II, which appears to have stimulated a great expansion of interest in this area. The bibliographies cover a variety of topics including attitude studies, military psychology and war psychiatry, psychological warfare, aggression, conflict, psychological causes and effects of war, and reactions to catastrophe. There is no bibliography comprehensive over these areas; the broadest-ranging is Meier (No. 1177), whose emphasis, however, is on military psychology and psychological warfare. On attitudes and aggression, see for example Eysenck (No. 1183); on psychological causes and effects of war, see e.g., Stagner (No. 1167), Cohen (No. 1181), and Frank (No. 1188).

Section 31 (Economic Aspects of War) is the longest in Part III, comprising 121 bibliographies, over half of which were published during the years of World War II. Surprisingly, the proportion published after 1945 is rather small (less than one sixth). The bibliographies range widely in topical focus. The most frequently appearing subjects are: war finance and debts; economic causes, costs and effects of war; economic mobilization for war (especially industrial mobilization); war economy and economic potential; economic warfare; and labor problems in wartime. Other subjects treated in one or more bibliographies include food and agriculture (e.g., Nos. 1224 and 1262); conscription of labor and wealth (e.g., Nos. 1214 and 1243); political economy (e.g., No. 1296); total war (e.g., Nos. 1271 and 1311); capitalism and war (e.g., No. 1194); and numerous more specific topics such as transportation, raw materials, taxation, price control, war profits and war contracts. The entries include an unusually high proportion of German bibliographies, especially for the years preceding and during World War II; noteworthy also are a number of Polish bibliographies (No. 1303, containing 1110 items; also Nos. 1306, 1308, and 1309). Among the more comprehensive bibliographies described are U.S. Library of Congress (No. 1274, 1009 items published between 1776 and 1942), Lauterbach (No. 1279, 776 items published between 1918 and 1942), Spiegel (No. 1271, 523 items published between 1919 and 1941), Rosenbaum (No. 1270, 518 items published between 1591 and 1941), and Salzman (No. 1294, 406 items published between 1919 and 1944). Two more recent but less extensive bibliographies are Carroll (No. 1311, 250 items published between 1902 and 1966) and Kaechele (No. 1312, 195 items published between 1850 and 1967). A useful shorter bibliography is Widger (No. 1304, 93 items, 1915 to 1958).

Section 32 (Social and Political Aspects of War) is a somewhat disparate collection of 26 bibliographies on diverse topics ranging from social welfare in wartime (e.g., No. 1315) to the 1930s debate on declaration of war by popular referendum (Nos. 1317-1323 and 1325). A considerable number of items are concerned with the relationship between war and crime (Nos. 1327, 1328 and 1332), migration or population changes (Nos. 1316, 1333, and 1337), and war memorials (Nos. 1334-1336). Other topics include minorities (e.g., No. 1316), racial violence (No. 1339), ethnological studies (No. 1338), the family (No. 1326), internal political violence (No. 1340), propaganda (No. 1324), and censorship (No. 1330). Two somewhat more general entries are Roucek (No. 1329) and Baer (No. 1331). Many listings of materials on social and political aspects of war are to be found in bibliographies classified in other sections of this guide, including Peace and War--General, War--General, Miscellaneous Political Topics, Economic Aspects of War, etc.; such listings may be located by consulting the subject index.

Section 33 (Legal Aspects of War) contains 34 entries, approximately half of which were published after 1945. They deal with a considerable range of subjects, mainly in the general categories of the laws of war, neutrality, and aggression. Other topics treated include emergency powers (Nos. 1355 and 1366), conquest (No. 1349), sanctions (No. 1356), contraband (No. 1341), renunciation of war (No. 1343), demilitarized zones (No. 1342), war damages (No. 1357), alien property (No. 1353), etc. Two of the more comprehensive bibliographies on the laws of war are Leguey-Feilleux (No. 1363, including 1680 items published between 1945 and 1958) and Greenspan (No. 1361, listing 243 items,

1851-1958). Others focus on more specific applications of the laws of war, e.g., the legality of guerrilla forces (No. 1358), laws of war in the Middle Ages (No. 1364), the United Nations in the Congo (No. 1365), the Vietnam War (Nos. 1367 and 1371), air warfare (No. 1373), and "dubious weapons" (No. 1374). Two bibliographies on aggression are Pompe (No. 1359) and Théry (No. 1344); see also González Castro (No. 1351) on legal responsibility for World War II. Most of the bibliographies on neutrality focus on maritime law and sea warfare (Nos. 1345-1348 and 1354); the most recent (1945), more general but quite brief, is Woolbert (No. 1356, 32 items published between 1932 and 1942). A recent short bibliography of fairly broad scope is Greenspan (No. 1368, 79 items published from 1909 to 1966). Other listings of works on legal aspects of war will be found in the sections on International Law, Peace and War--General, War--General, War Crimes, Atrocities, War Crimes Trials. Some may be found also in other sections (e.g., Matthews, No. 140 and No. 149); these may be located through the subject index.

Section 34 (War Crimes, Atrocities, and War Crimes Trials) contains 24 bibliographies of which 20 were published after 1945; most deal with the European war crimes trials following World War II. Only one (No. 1395) focuses on the Tokyo war crimes trial. Bibliographies of a general nature on war crimes include Conover (No. 1377, listing 1084 items, 1897-1945) and Scanlon (No. 1378, listing 182 items, 1914-1945). The largest bibliography on the European war crimes trials focuses on Poland (No. 1388, listing 2296 items, 1944-1953); three which are more general in character but considerably less extensive are Neumann and Rosenbaum (No. 1381), Bruch (No. 1383) and Davidson (No. 1391). A useful short bibliography is Harris (No. 1386). The most recent and comprehensive entry is Lewis (No. 1398).

984   Z6464.Z9N5

Seaver, W[illiam] N. (comp.), [with the assistance of George S. Maynard].

Economic and Social Aspects of War: A selected list of references.
New York: New York Public Library, April, 1915. 14 pp.
Reprinted from the Bulletin of the New York Public Library, February, 1915.

   246 items, 1824 - 1914. English; also German, French, Italian
   (1). Some items have brief descriptive and/or critical
   annotations; introduction (1 paragraph); table of contents.

   Bibliographies (5), army and navy maintenance (25), general
   economic aspects of war (76), losses of life in war (10),
   individual wars, except American (72), the United States and
   war (58).

985   D445.B28

Bakeless, John [E.].

[Bibliographical] Notes.
In his The Origin of the Next War: A study in the tensions of
the modern world.
New York: Viking Press, 1926. pp. 299-308.

   120 items, 1887 - 1925. English, French; also German (8).

   Books and articles on causes of war, role of air power in
   war, international politics relating to war, history of war,
   economic consequences of war.

986   H69.J6,1927

Johnsen, Julia E. (comp.).

"Problems of national defense."
In her Questions of the Hour.
New York: H. W. Wilson (The Reference Shelf, Vol. 4, No. 10),
April, 1927 [3rd ed.]. pp. 32-34.

War--General

34 items, 1922 - 1926 (most items undated). English.

Nature and future trend of war (6), underlying causes of war
(6), America´s naval and military strength and burden of
armaments (5), case for continued preparedness (5),
limitation of armaments (6), military training of youth (6).

987

Sorokin, Pitirim [Aleksandrovich].

Bibliographic footnotes in "Sociological interpretation of the
´struggle for existence´ and the sociology of war."
In his Contemporary Sociological Theories: Through the first
quarter of the twentieth century.
New York/Evanston/London: Harper and Row (Harper Torchbooks,
The University Library), 1928. pp. 309-356.

988   U21.D3

Davie, Maurice R[ea].

Bibliography.
In his The Evolution of War: A study of its role in early
societies.
New Haven/London: Yale University Press/Oxford University
Press, 1929. pp. [369]-385.
Reprinted, Port Washington, N.Y.: Kennikat Press, 1968.

539 items, 1807 - 1928. English; also German, French.

Books and journal articles mainly on ethnography and
ethnology with some general works on war and peace.

989   JX1952.N32

Nearing, Scott.

Bibliography.
In his War: Organized destruction and mass murder by civilized
nations.
New York: Vanguard Press, 1931. pp. 273-285.
Reprinted, with a new introduction by Scott Nearing, New
York/London: Garland (Library of War and Peace), 1971.

230 items, 1872 - 1928. English; also French, German.

Books and articles on the history, causes, costs, economics,

War--General

    and sociology of war, militarism, warfare, and general
    theories of war, peace, and politics.

990   UA23.S7

Stockton, Richard, 6th.

Selected bibliography.
In his Inevitable War.
New York: Perth, 1932. pp. 777-794.

    456 items, 1898 - 1932. English.

    Books, articles, pamphlets, and periodicals on the history of
    various wars in which the U.S. was involved, the economic and
    political aspects of war, causes and effects of war, warfare,
    military policy and operations, military history, war
    resistance, disarmament and arms limitation, U.S. foreign
    policy, international relations, and theories of war and
    peace. Memoirs and biographies of military and political
    leaders constitute approximately one-third of the
    bibliography.

991 <

Burns, Cecil Delisle.

Bibliography.
In his War and a Changing Civilisation.
London: John Lane, [1934]. pp. 151-152.

992   JX1308.S77

Steiner, H[arold] Arthur.

Bibliography in "War and force in international life."
In his Principles and Problems of International Relations.
New York/London: Harper and Brothers, 1940. pp. 326-328.

    52 items, 1906 - 1940. English.

    Books on the causes and effects of war, military science and
    technology, and the history of war and militarism.

War--General

993   U27.M3,1941

McKinley, Silas Bent.

Bibliography.
In his Democracy and Military Power, with an introduction by
Charles A. Beard.
New York: Vanguard Press, 1941 (new and enl. ed.). pp. 345-350.

   81 items, 1883 - 1941. English; also German (2), French (1).
   Introduction (1 paragraph).

   Mostly books on ancient, medieval, and modern history,
   warfare, and theories of war and politics.

994 <

Willems, Emilio.

"Subsídios bibliográficos para uma sociologia da guerra
(aspectos gerais, tecnológicos, econômicos, psicológicos e
biológicos) [Bibliographic aids for a sociology of war
(general, technological, economic, psychological and biological
aspects)]."
Sociologia, 3, 3 (August, 1941): 227-233.

995   UA10.K5

Kirk, Grayson [Louis] and Richard Poate Stebbins (eds.).

Bibliography.
In their War and National Policy: A syllabus.
New York: Farrar and Rinehart, 1942. pp. 107-131.

   757 items, 1767 - 1941. English.

   Books and pamphlets (567), periodicals and special articles
   (190) on military policy, the armed forces, military
   strategy, and various aspects of warfare and preparedness.

996   U27.N63,1942

Nickerson, Hoffman.

Bibliography; Notes on sources.
In his The Armed Horde, 1783-1939: A study of the rise,
survival and decline of the mass army.

War--General

New York: G. P. Putnam's Sons, 1942 (2nd ed.). pp. 401-407,
409-418.
First edition, 1940, same pagination.

   203 items, 1737 - 1940. English, French.

   Books on histories of war, theory of war, military history,
   moral aspects of war, defense policy, peace treaties,
   national defense systems, militarism and its history, warfare
   in general.

997   JA1.R4,v.4

Shanahan, William O.

"The literature on war: [Part I]; Part II"
[bibliographic essays].
Review of Politics, 4, 2 (April, 1942): 206-222; 3 (July,
1942): 327-346.

   222 items, 400 B.C. - 1942. English, German; also French,
   Italian (3), Latin (2), Danish (1), Dutch (1). All items are
   discussed in the text.

   Bibliographical essays dealing with classics of military
   literature, bibliographies and surveys of the history of war,
   the French Revolution and Napoleon, armies and warfare in the
   nineteenth century, national armies, World War I, sociology
   of war, propaganda in modern war, naval warfare, the United
   States in World War II, and the philosophy of war.

998   H31.P7

Friedrich, Carl J[oachim] and Ronald B. Edgerton.

Bibliography; Reading materials for pupils; List of films;
Transcriptions; Professional bibliography.
In their War: The causes, effects, and control of international
violence.
Washington, D.C.: National Council for the Social Studies and
National Association of Secondary-School Principals (Problems
in American Life, Unit No. 11), 1943. pp. 61-62, 78-80, 80-81,
81, 81-83.

   123 items, 1902 - 1943 (one item from 1842). English. Some
   items have brief descriptive or critical annotations.

   Books and articles on the nature, history, causes, effects,
   and prevention of war (60); reading materials for pupils
   (20); films on the background and events of World War II

War--General

(17); phonodisc recordings of U.S. war/defense propaganda available for loan to schools (6); pamphlets, periodicals, and books for teachers on problems of war and peace, wartime education (20).

999   U162.S53,1943a

Sikorski, Władysław.

References [8 lists].
In his Modern Warfare, with a note by George C. Marshall. New York/London: Roy/Hutchinson, 1943. pp. 25-29, 68-79, 109-112, 164-167, 203-207, 219-221, 232, 276-277.

Footnotes at the end of each chapter.

1000   U21.N36

Nearing, Scott.

Bibliography.
In his War or Peace?
New York: Island Press (Social Science Handbook, No. 4), 1946. pp. 90-94.

85 items, 1795 - 1944. English; also French (7), German (1).

Books on causes of war, economics of war, social and political aspects of war, history of militarism and warfare, and peace theory.

1001   JA83.R7

Portner, Stuart.

Bibliography in "Militarism and politics."
In Roucek, Joseph S[labey] (ed.), Twentieth Century Political Thought.
New York: Philosophical Library, 1946. p. 287.

15 items, 1923 - 1944. English. All items have brief critical and/or descriptive annotations.

Books on causes, history, and theory of war.

War--General

1002   BF1.P86,v.13

Richardson, Lewis F.

References in "War-moods: [Part] I; [Part] II."
Psychometrika, 13, 3 (September, 1948): 173-174; 4 (December,
1948): 230-232.

   42 items, 1891 - 1948. English; also French (1).

   Books and articles on the causes and effects of war,
   mathematical analyses of war, and source material from a
   variety of fields.

1003   JX4508.P46

Pereña Vicente, Luciano.

Bibliografía sistemática.
In his Teoría de la Guerra en Francisco Suárez [Theory of War
in Francisco Suárez]: I, guerra y estado [I, war and the
state].
Madrid: Consejo Superior de Investigaciones Científicas,
Instituto "Francisco de Vitoria," 1954. pp. 32-48.

   428 items, 1483 - 1949. Spanish, Latin; also French, Portuguese
   (9), English (7), German (6), Italian (4).

   List of Suarez's political, juridical, theological, and moral
   treatises, the sources Suarez used in developing his ideas on
   theological, moral, and economic issues, and his philosophy
   of war in the sixteenth century; critical works on Suarez,
   Spanish and Portuguese history, doctrines of war,
   international laws governing war, and the effects of war.

1004   JX4511.K6

Kotzsch, Lothar.

Bibliography.
In his The Concept of War in Contemporary History and
International Law.
Geneva: E. Droz (Etudes d´Histoire Economique, Politique et
Sociale, 18), 1956. pp. 299-310.

   432 items. 1752 - 1955. English, French, German; also Spanish
   (9), Italian (2).

   Books and articles on international law, jurisprudence,
   international arbitration, intervention, neutrality, concepts

War--General

and definitions of war, functions of war, termination of war,
blockades, collective security, League of Nations, and the
United Nations.

1005 <   U15.U64,no.20-60

United States Department of the Army, Army Library.

Bibliography on Limited War.
Washington, D.C.: U.S. Department of the Army (Pamphlet No. PAM
20-60), 1958. 53 pp.

1006 <

Librand, Miller W. A., et al.

Bibliographie Choisie sur la Guerre Non Conventionnelle.
Washington, D.C.: The American University (Special Operations
Research Office), 1961. 123 pp.

1007   GN1.A5

Vayda, Andrew P.

References cited in "Expansion and warfare among swidden
agriculturalists."
American Anthropologist, 63, 2, Part 1 (April, 1961): 356-358.

   50 items, 1838 - 1960. English.

   Books and articles on the nature and social functions of
   warfare among preliterate peoples, military organization, and
   cultural evolution.

1008 <

Halperin, Morton.

Annotated bibliography.
In his Limited War: An essay in the development and the theory.
New York: Wiley, 1962.

War--General

1009 <

Paret, Peter.

"Clausewitz: A bibliographical note."
World Politics, 17 (1965): 272-285.

1010 <   DU80.A947,v.19

Schaffer, Bernard.

"Recent writings on war."
Australian Outlook, 19 (August, 1965): 213-217.

1011   D445.C6

Clarke, I[gnatius] F[rederick].

Bibliographies.
In his Voices Prophesying War, 1763-1984.
London/New York/Toronto: Oxford University Press, 1966. pp.
213-249.

    1095 items, 1763 - 1965. English; also French, German, Italian
    (5), Spanish (2), Dutch (1).

    Principal works consulted (130) with emphasis on the history
    of war and peace; select list of war studies, 1770 to
    1964 (259) covering such topics as the causes, prevention,
    and effects of war, air and naval warfare, national defense,
    deterrence, military strategy and techniques, nuclear
    weapons, and national security; list of works depicting
    imaginary wars, 1763 to 1965 (706).

1012   U104.C6

Coats, Wendell J.

Bibliography.
In his Armed Force as Power: The theory of war reconsidered.
New York: Exposition Press (An Exposition-University Book),
1966. pp. 383-413.

    473 items, 1815 - 1965. English; also French (9), German (1).

    Public documents (11), books (338), articles and periodicals
    (118), and other sources (6) on warfare, the history of war,
    political theory, jurisprudence, military history, military
    policy, military strategy and tactics, militarism, civil-

War--General

   military relations, the memoirs and biographies of various
   military leaders, foreign policy, natural law, guerrilla
   warfare, arms control, disarmament, the control of atomic
   energy, strategic analysis, propaganda, conflict theory,
   mathematical theory of war, revolutions, violence, and
   aggression.

   1013   Z6721.C67

   Cosyns-Verhaegen, Roger.

   Guerres Révolutionnaires et Subversives [Revolutionary and
   Subversive Wars]: Sélection bibliographique [Selected
   bibliography].
   Brussels: "Les Ours," 1967. 41 pp. (mimeo).

      352 items, 1871 - 1966. French; also English, Italian,
      Spanish (5), German (4), Turkish (1). Many items have brief
      descriptive and/or critical annotations; introduction
      (2 pp.); table of contents; author index.

      General works on war (4), studies on revolutionary war and
      subversives (47), coups and putschs (12) guerrilla warfare
      (16), military history (11), political and social history
      (14), ideology (15), psychological warfare (25), clandestine
      organizations (23), espionage and counterespionage (24),
      techniques (14), terrorism (6), revolutionary efforts in
      Africa (38), Latin America and the Caribbean (26), Asia (40),
      Europe (33), and miscellaneous subjects (4).

   1014   JX4541.T35

   Tamkoç, Metin.

   A selected bibliography.
   In his International Civil War.
   Ankara, [Turkey]: Orta Doğu Teknik Üniversitesi/Middle East
   Technical University (Idari Ilimler Fakültesi/Faculty of
   Administrative Sciences, Publication No. 8), 1967. pp. 189-201.

      155 items, 1926 - 1967. English; also French (1), Turkish (1).

      Books (110) and articles (45) on war theory, moral aspects of
      war, international law, political aspects of war,
      international relations, foreign policy, comparative
      politics, revolutionary movements, guerrilla warfare,
      international intervention in internal wars.

War--General

1015   U21.2.W4

Wells, Donald A.

Bibliography.
In his The War Myth.
New York: Pegasus, 1967. pp. 267-279.

   249 items, 1765 - 1966. English.

   Books on the definition of war (12), just war (23),
   inevitability of war (26), patriotism and the military spirit
   (15), attacks on the war system (14), conscientious objection
   and pacifism (12), humane and inhumane war practices (12),
   religion and war (9), war is unchristian (10), can Christians
   be soldiers (15), psychological causes of war (19), military
   causes of war (26), economic causes of war (18), disarmament
   and the arms race (19), world political federation (19).

1016   U21.B637,1968

Bramson, Leon and George W. Goethals (eds.).

Selected bibliography.
In their War: Studies from psychology, sociology, anthropology.
New York/London: Basic Books, 1968 (rev. ed.). pp. 429-434.
First published in 1964.

   156 items, 1869 - 1968. English.

   General studies (10), instinct theory and comparative
   psychology (7), psychiatric perspectives (9), social learning
   and intergroup relations (20), selected studies in sociology
   and anthropology (40), studies on war, liberal democracy, and
   industrial society (50), selected literary studies of war
   (20).

1017   HM36.5.B8

Buchan, Alastair.

Select bibliography.
In his War in Modern Society: An introduction.
New York/Evanston: Harper and Row (Harper Colophon Books),
1968. pp. 199-202.
Original edition, London: C. A. Watts, 1966.

   43 items, 1941 - 1966. English; also French (1). Introduction
   (1 paragraph).

War--General

    Books on war and international relations (15), strategy (14),
    western alliances (5), and control of war and arms (9).

    1018   HM36.5.A25

Fried, Morton, Marvin Harris, and Robert Murphy (eds.).

Bibliography.
In their War: The anthropology of armed conflict and
aggression.
Garden City, N.Y.: Natural History Press, for the American
Museum of Natural History, 1968. pp. 239-254.

    276 items, 1871 - 1967. English; also German (2), Italian (2),
    Dutch (1), French (1), Spanish (1).

    Books and articles on social, biological, psychological, and
    anthropological studies of warfare and conflict, general
    ethnological studies, sociopolitical and cultural history,
    particularly of Africa.

    1019   U21.2.088

Otterbein, Keith F.

References; Ethnographic bibliography.
In his The Evolution of War: A cross-cultural study.
New Haven: HRAF [Human Relations Area Files] Press, 1970.
pp. 150-156; 157-165.

    138 items, 1822 - 1968. English; also French (2), German (2).

    References on cultural and sociopolitical history, social
    psychology, sociology of war, and the history of war and
    warfare (65); ethnographic studies (73).

    1020 <

Wette, Wolfram.

[Bibliography].
In his Kriegstheorien deutscher Sozialisten [War Theories of
German Socialists]; Marx, Engels, Lassalle, Bernstein, Kautsky,
Luxemburg: Ein Beitrag zur Friedensforschung [A contribution to
peace research].
Stuttgart: W. Kolhammer, 1971. pp. 241-251.

War--General

1021   U21.2.B36

Barringer, Richard E., with the collaboration of Robert K.
Ramers.

Selected bibliography.
In their <u>War: Patterns of conflict,</u> with a foreword by Quincy
Wright.
Cambridge, Mass./London: MIT Press, 1972. pp. 269-287.

  388 items, 1864 - 1970. English; also Spanish, French (3).

  Substantive and methodological sources (105), selected data
  sources (36), Algeria-Morocco conflict, 1962-63 (11), Angolan
  insurgency, 1961 (13), Cuba, Little War of August 1906 (18),
  Cuba, Bay of Pigs, 1961 (14), Cyprus, war of independence and
  internal conflict, 1952-1964 (21), Ethiopian resistance,
  1937-1941 (7), Ethiopia-Somalia conflict, 1960-64 (14), Greek
  insurgency, 1944-49 (13), India-China conflict, 1962 (11),
  Indonesia, war of independence, 1945-49 (16), Indonesia-
  Malaysia conflict, 1963-65 (11), Israel-Egypt conflict, 1956
  (15), Kashmir conflict, 1947-65 (24), Malayan insurgency,
  1948-60 (21), Spanish Civil War, 1936-39 (12), U.S.S.R.-Iran
  conflict, 1941-47 (12), Venezuelan insurgency, 1959-63 (14).

1022   Z5118.W3D57

Divale, William Tulio.

<u>Warfare in Primitive Societies: A bibliography.</u>
Santa Barbara, Calif./Oxford: ABC-Clio, (War/Peace Bibliography
Series, [No. 2]), 1973 (rev. ed.). xxx + 123 pp.
First edition, Los Angeles: California State College, Center
for the Study of Armament and Disarmament (Bibliography Series,
No. 2), xiv + 55 pp., 1971.

  1655 items, 1651 - 1974. English; also French, German, Spanish,
  Russian (4), Dutch (3), Portuguese (3), other western and
  oriental languages. Introductions and explanatory material
  (21 pp.); table of contents; author index; tribal name index.

  Primitive warfare (146), anthropologists on modern warfare
  (39), demographic factors (17), biological aspects (27),
  territorial and economic factors (18), psychological factors
  (77), feuding (40), peace and peacemaking (40), colonial
  pacification (39), law and order (26), head hunting (41),
  cannibalism (40), scalping and war trophies (38), war
  ceremonies (42), military organization, defense, costumes
  (66), weapons (214), North America (251), South America (96),

War--General

    Africa (78), Middle East, including North Africa (58), Europe
    and Soviet Union (33), Asia and India (70), Oceania (159).

1023   Z7161.B65IU: 016.3232B56m

Blackey, Robert.

Modern Revolutions and Revolutionists: A bibliography.
Santa Barbara, Calif./Oxford: Clio Books (War/Peace
Bibliography Series, No. 5), 1976. xxvii + 257 pp.

History of War

1024 <

Scharfenort, L[ouis] von.

Quellenkunde der Kriegswissenschaften für den Zeitraum, 1740-
1912 [Information sources of Military Science for the Period
1740-1912]: Nebst einem Verfasser und Schlagwortverzeichnis
[Including an author and subject index].
Berlin: E. S. Mittler, 1910 to 1913.

1025 <

[Carnegie Endowment for International Peace, Library].

Diplomatic History of European War.
Washington, D.C.: Carnegie Endowment for International Peace,
Library (Miscellaneous Reading List No. 9), 1921. (mimeo).

1026   U27.S6

Spaulding, Oliver Lyman, Jr., Hoffman Nickerson, and John
Womack Wright.

Bibliography: Part I; Part II; Part III.
In their Warfare: A study of military methods from the earliest
times, with a preface by General Tasker H. Bliss.
New York: Harcourt, Brace, 1925. pp. 185-187, 408-411, 573-587.
Reprinted, Washington, D.C.: The Infantry Journal, 1937.

   242 items, 1597 - 1924. English, French; also German, Spanish,
   Latin (7), Italian (3). Most items have brief descriptive and
   critical annotations.

   Books on ancient warfare to the death of Julius Caesar (35),
   warfare in the Roman Empire, the Dark and Middle Ages to 1494
   (42), warfare in modern times to the death of Frederick the
   Great [d. 1786] (165).

History of War

1027 <

Stein, Rose M.

Selected bibliography.
In her M-Day, the First Day of War.
New York: Harcourt, Brace, [1936]. pp. 383-386.

1028 <   D25.5.S35

Schmitthener, Paul.

[Bibliography].
In his Politik und Kriegführung in der neueren Geschichte
[Politics and warfare in modern history].
Hamburg: Hanseatische Verlagsanstalt, 1937. pp. 313-316.

1029   R11.B93,v.6

Hume, Edgar Erskine.

Sources in "Medical work of the Knights Hospitallers of Saint
John of Jerusalem: Third period (1798-1938)."
Bulletin of the Institute of the History of Medicine, 6, 7
(July, 1938): 816-819.

   35 items, 1581 - 1935. English, French, German; also Italian
   (3), Latin (1). Introduction (2 pp.).

   Books, documents, and memoirs on the history of the Order of
   St. John of Jerusalem, their medical work from the period of
   the Crusades to the twentieth century, and the history of the
   island of Malta.

1030   U35.W54

Westington, Mars McClelland.

Bibliography.
In his Atrocities in Roman Warfare to 133 B.C. (Ph.D.
dissertation, Latin Language and Literature, University of
Chicago, 1938).
Chicago: University of Chicago Libraries, 1938 (private ed.).
pp. 136-139.

   70 items, 1612 - 1935. English; also German (9), French (8),
   Latin (5), Italian (1).

History of War

    Books and articles on general history of ancient Rome and
    Greece, international law, military history, and the history
    and nature of international relations.

1031   JX1906.A35,no.1a

Matthews, M[ary] Alice (comp.).

"References to books on the history of war."
In her Wars of the World: Quotations on comparative war and
peace years; list of wars; and references to books on the
history of war.
Washington, D.C.: Carnegie Endowment for International Peace,
Library (Memoranda Series, No. 1), February 1, 1940 (rev.ed.).
pp. 9-11.
Original edition, Nov. 10, 1939.

    32 items, 1899 - 1939. English. Most items have brief
    descriptive and/or critical annotations.

    Books on causes, effects, and prevention of wars, with
    special attention to the history of war and lists of wars
    for various time periods.

1032   U21.C24

Calahan, H[arold] A[ugustin].

Bibliography.
In his What Makes a War End?
New York: Vanguard Press, 1944. pp. 257-260.

    86 items, 1794 - 1942. English.

    Books on European and American history, history of various
    wars, theories concerning war and its termination, and
    memoirs and biographies of political and military leaders.

1033   U43.I5D5,1948

Dikshitar, V. R. Ramachandra.

Books consulted.
In his War in Ancient India, with a foreword by
A. Lakshmanaswami Mudaliar.
Madras/Bombay/Calcutta/London: Macmillan, 1948 (2nd ed.).
pp. 393-401.

History of War

First edition, 1944, pp. 389-397.

   231 items, 1900 - 1940 (most items undated). Indian
   languages, English; also French (3).

   Original sources (83), Tamil sources (11), journals and
   commemoration volumes (27), and modern works (110) on Indian
   history and anthropology, with emphasis on the political and
   military culture. Most entries give only the title or author
   and title.

1034   U21.C57

Coblentz, Stanton A[rthur].

Bibliography.
In his From Arrow to Atom Bomb: The psychological history of
war.
New York: Beechhurst Press, 1953. pp. 487-502.

   395 items, 1789 - 1950. English.

   Books and some articles on cultural, political and social
   history and anthropology, divided chronologically to
   correspond to the chapters of the book. A substantial
   proportion of the works cited (but not the majority) deal
   specifically with the history of warfare and arms races from
   prehistoric times to the Cold War.

1035   U27.M6,1960

Montross, Lynn.

Acknowledgments and sources.
In his War through the Ages.
New York: Harper and Brothers, 1960 (3rd ed., rev. and enl.).
pp. 1017-1032.
First edition, 1944; second edition, 1946.

1036 <   Z1719.525

Santiago de Chile, Biblioteca Nacional.

Exposición Bibliográfica sobre la Guerra del Pacífico
[Bibliographic Exposition on the War of the Pacific] (1879-
1884).
Santiago: Editorial Universitaria, 1961. 56 pp.

History of War

1037 <

Higham, Robin (ed.).

A Guide to the Sources of British Military History.
Berkeley: University of California Press, 1971. 630 pp.

1038   D422.W25

Waitley, Douglas.

Bibliography.
In his The War Makers.
Washington/New York: Robert B. Luce, 1971. pp. 289-295.

   152 items, 1919 - 1970. English.

   Books on European, U.S., and Far Eastern history, the history
   of various wars, diplomatic history; memoirs and biographies
   of political leaders.

1039 <   D431.H54

Higham, Robin (comp.).

Bibliography.
In Civil Wars in the Twentieth Century.
Lexington: University Press of Kentucky, 1972. pp. 229-257.

1040   U21.2.S57

Singer, J[oel] David and Melvin Small.

References.
In their The Wages of War, 1816-1965: A statistical handbook.
New York/London/Sydney/Toronto: John Wiley and Sons, 1972. pp.
405-419.

   442 items, 1758 - 1972. English, French; also Spanish, German,
   Italian (2), Dutch (1), Russian (1). Introduction (2
   paragraphs).

   Books, reports, and articles on political and military
   history used as data sources for a statistical analysis of
   wars.

History of War

1041   U310.F388

Featherstone, Donald [F.].

Bibliography.
In his Battle Notes for Wargamers.
Newton Abbot, Devon: David and Charles, 1973. pp. 163-167.

   72 items, 1896 - 1972. English.

   Books on various battles and wars from the Roman Civil War of
   48 B.C. to the Korean War, military strategy and tactics, and
   wargaming periodicals.

1042   Z3228.V5L44

Leitenberg, Milton and Richard Dean Burns (comps.), assisted by
Janice Roswell, Judith Roswell, and Lillemor Lindh.

The Vietnam Conflict: Its geographical dimensions, political
traumas, and military developments.
Santa Barbara, Calif./Oxford: ABC-Clio (War/Peace Bibliography
Series, No. 3), 1973. xxv + 164 pp.

   2367 items, 1902 - 1973. English; also French, German (8),
   Italian (1). Introduction (11 pp.); table of contents;
   subject/author index.

   General references (93); area dimensions (298); Vietnam:
   history and politics (424); U.S. involvement (640); military
   operations (716); domestic impact of war (196).

1043 <

Beer, Francis A.

[Bibliography].
In his How Much War in History: Definitions, estimates,
extrapolations and trends.
Beverly Hills: Sage (Sage Professional Papers in International
Studies, Series No. 02-030), 1974. pp. 35-37.

History of War

1044 <   Z1249.M5G83,1975

Higham, Robin (ed.).

A Guide to the Sources of United States Military History.
Hamden, Conn.: Archon, 1975. xiii + 559 pp.

1045 <

Knightley, Phillip.

[References].
In his First Casualty; from the Crimea to Vietnam: The war
correspondent as hero, propagandist, and myth maker.
New York: Harcourt, Brace, Jovanovich, 1975. pp. 443-445.

1046   Z3479.R4D48IU: 016.
                                               95694D49a

DeVore, Ronald M.

The Arab-Israeli Conflict: A historical, political, social, and
military bibliography.
Santa Barbara, Calif./Oxford: Clio Books (War/Peace
Bibliography Series, No. 4), 1976. xxxiv + 273 pp.

1047 <

Howard, Michael Eliot.

[Bibliography].
In his War in European History.
London: Oxford University Press, 1976. pp. 147-151.

1048 <

Smaldone, Joseph P.

[Bibliography].
In his Warfare in the Sokoto Caliphate: Historical and
sociological perspectives.
Cambridge: Cambridge University Press (African Studies Series,
[No.] 19), 1977. pp. 212-215.

World Wars

1049 <   Z6207.E8L21

Lange, F[rederick] W[illiam] T[heodore] and W[illiam] T[urner] Berry.

Books on the Great War: An annotated bibliography of literature issued during the European conflict, Vols. [1]-4, with prefaces by R. A. Peddie.
London: Grafton, 1915 to 1916.

   Annotated; author index; title index.

1050   Z6466.Z9W83,v.1

Blakeslee, George H. (ed.).

"Selected list of books on the present war."
A League of Nations, 1, 1 (October, 1917): 43-50.
Reprinted from the Journal of Race Development, Vol. 8, No. 1, July, 1917.

   81 items, 1907 - 1917. English; also French (10), German (4).
   Most items have brief descriptive and/or critical
   annotations; introduction (1 paragraph).

   Books on the historical background of World War I (10), the
   outbreak of the war (4), military history (4), national and
   international legal aspects (4), descriptions and narratives
   of the war (19), conflicting national viewpoints on the war
   (16), the psychology of the war (7), war as a world problem
   (9), the peace settlements and the future (8).

1051   D511.M27

Marti, Oscar Albert.

Bibliography.
In his The Anglo-German Commercial and Colonial Rivalry as a Cause of the Great War (A thesis presented to the Department of History, University of Southern California, Los Angeles).
Boston: Stratford, 1917. pp. 79-83.

   49 items, 1897 - 1915. English.

World Wars

   Books and articles on the causes of World War I, European
   history, foreign policy, and international relations in
   Europe and the Middle East.

   1052   Z6207.E8P6

   Prothero, G[eorge] W. (comp.), with the assistance of Alex. J.
   Philip.

   Catalogue of War Publications Comprising Works Published to
   June, 1916.
   London: John Murray, for the Central Committee for National
   Patriotic Organizations, 1917. vi + 259 pp.
   Includes two previous lists compiled by G. W. Prothero and
   issued in 1914 and 1915.

      3572 items, 1879 - 1916 (most items published after 1913).
      English; also French, German, Italian, Dutch (2), Swedish (1).
      Introduction (1 p.); table of contents; subject/author index.

      Bibliographies and courses of study (10), general
      introductory and historical works (74), general references by
      countries (251), documents of World War I (13), documents
      arranged by countries (109), British speeches and addresses
      (27), speeches other than British (4), works relating to
      World War I arranged by countries (494), causes and issues of
      the war (183), maps (68), general narratives of the war (64),
      special narratives of the war (307), breaches of
      international law (58), biographies (83), prisoners (17),
      international and military law (66), economics and finance
      (80), social, commercial, and industrial (146), science and
      methods of war (385), naval and military forces (152),
      science, medicine, and nursing (122), philosophy and theology
      (271), cartoons and other humorous works (40), poetry and
      drama (168), literature (9), languages, dictionaries, etc.
      (95), essays and other miscellaneous works (152), peace and
      reconstruction (124). See also No. 1063, below.

   1053   D509.M3

   Dutcher, George Matthew, in cooperation with National Board for
   Historical Service.

   "A selected critical bibliography of publications in English
   relating to the World War."
   In McKinley, Albert E. (comp.), Collected Materials for the
   Study of the War.
   Philadelphia: McKinley, 1918. pp. 105-136.
   Reprinted from The History Teacher´s Magazine, April, 1918.

World Wars

Approximately 700 items, 1914 - 1917 (a few items published
before 1914). English. Most items have brief to abstract-
length descriptive and/or critical annotations; introduction
(1 p.); table of contents.

Mostly books on the causes, problems, and issues of World War I
on general questions of war and peace, and on the history,
conditions, problems, and foreign policies of various countries
in Europe, Asia, Africa, and North and South America.

1054 <   DLC-DB

Meyer, Herman H. B. (comp.).

A Check List of the Literature and Other Material in the
Library of Congress on the European War.
Washington, D.C.: Library of Congress, Division of
Bibliography, 1918.

1055   Z1007.B94,v.10

Smith, Robert L.

"Some bibliographies of the European war and its causes."
Bulletin of Bibliography, 10, 3 (July-September, 1918):
[49]-52.

165 items, 1914 - 1918. English; also French (5), German (3),
Dutch (1), Norwegian (1). Many items have brief descriptive
annotations.

Bibliographies on World War I including brief sections on
casualties, causes, costs, diplomatic history, social and
economic aspects, settlement of the war, U.S. participation,
and the role of women in the war.

1056   DLC-DB

[United States Library of Congress, Division of Bibliography].

A List of Bibliographies on the European War.
[Washington, D.C.]: Library of Congress, Division of
Bibliography, August 12, 1918. 8 pp. (mimeo).

103 items, 1914 - 1918. English; also French (8), Italian (2),
German (1), Norwegian (1), Russian (1).

Bibliographies in book and article form on World War I.

World Wars

1057   Z6207.E8V4

Vic, Jean.

La Littérature de Guerre [War Literature]: Manuel méthodique et
critiques des publications de langue française (Août 1914-Août
1916), Tome I, II [Systematic and critical handbook of
publications in French (August 1914 to August 1916), Volume I,
II], avec une préface de Gustave Lanson.
Paris: Payot, 1918. xxxvi + 816 pp.

    Approximately 3000 items, 1914 - 1916. French. Many items
    have critical and/or descriptive annotations; introduction
    (17 pp.) plus introductions to each section and subdivision;
    table of contents; author index; subject index.

    Books, periodicals, offical publications, pamphlets,
    almanacs, articles, documents, memoirs, and reference works
    representing the whole range of French literature on World
    War I. It is divided into three major sections: the causes of
    the war and preparations for it, the events of the war, and
    the consequences of the war. Each section has detailed
    subdivisions. Among the topics covered are Pan-Germanism,
    imperialism, diplomatic negotiations, narratives of the war
    in individual countries, colonial campaigns, socialism and
    war, women and war, religion and war, economic and social
    consequences of war, peace plans, and numerous others. See
    also Vic's subsequent three-volume work covering the period
    August 1916-November 1918 (No. 1065, below).

1058   Z881.N6B,v.24

[New York Public Library].

"The war and after"
(continuation of "The European war").
Bulletin of the New York Public Library, 24, 1 (January, 1920):
25-41; 3 (March): 196-198; 5 (May): 306-313; 6 (June): 356-366;
7 (July): 414-422; 8 (August): 461-468; 9 (September): 520-523;
10 (October): 560-572; 11 (November): 642-657; 12 (December):
737-742.

    2300 items (number of items estimated from a sample of
    pages), 1914 - 1920. English, French, German; also Italian,
    Dutch, Spanish, Swedish, Danish, other Western and Eastern
    European languages. A few items have brief descriptive
    annotations.

World Wars

> Books, articles, periodicals, and documents relating to
> effects of World War I, economic, social, and political
> aspects of war, causes of war, history of World War I,
> international relations, international law, Paris Peace
> Conference of 1919, international organization, arbitration,
> women and war, League of Nations, foreign policy, philosophy,
> religion, and literature.

1059 <

[British Museum].

Subject Index of the Books Relating to the European War, 1914-
1918, Acquired by the British Museum, 1914-1920.
London: Longmans, 1922.

1060   HC56.C35,no.6

Bulkley, M[ildred] E.

Bibliographical Survey of Contemporary Sources for the Economic
and Social History of the War.
Oxford/London/Edinburgh/New York/Toronto/Melbourne/Bombay:
Clarendon Press/Humphrey Milford, for the Carnegie Endowment
for International Peace, Division of Economics and History
(Economic and Social History of the World War, British Series),
1922. xix pp. + 628 col. + pp. 629-648 + 9 pp.

> Approximately 8200 items, 1915 - 1920. English. Most items
> have brief to abstract-length descriptive annotations;
> introduction (4 pp.); table of contents; subject/author
> index.

> Books, official publications, annual reports, acts of
> Parliament, articles, pamphlets, journals, and committee
> reports dealing with the economic and social history of the
> United Kingdom during World War I and the reconstruction
> period. Bibliography is divided into the following major
> sections: social conditions, administration, industry and
> commerce, transport, labor, army and navy, finance, prices
> and cost of living, miscellaneous.

1061 <

[Carnegie Endowment for International Peace, Library].

Prisoners of War in the European War.

World Wars

Washington, D.C.: Carnegie Endowment for International Peace,
Library (Miscellaneous Reading List No. 22), 1922. (mimeo).

1062   DLC-DB

[United States Library of Congress, Division of Bibliography].

Brief List of References on the European War.
[Washington, D.C.]: Library of Congress, Division of
Bibliography, December 13, 1922. 4 pp. (typescript).

  44 items, 1915 - 1922. English.

  Books on the military history of World War I (28) and the
  economic effects of the war (16).

1063   Z6207.E8P6,1923

Prothero, George W.

A Select Analytical List of Books Concerning the Great War,
with prefatory note by Stephen Gaselee.
London: His Majesty's Stationery Office, 1923. x + 431 pp.

  Approximately 8000 items, 1879 - 1922. English; also French,
  German, Italian, Spanish, Dutch (5), Swedish (3). Prefatory
  note (3 pp.); table of contents; author index.

  A much expanded version of his 1917 "Catalogue of War
  Publications" (see No. 1052, above), rearranged in 25
  major subject categories.

1064   HC56.C34,no.1

Spann, Othmar.

Bibliographie der Wirtschafts- und Sozialgeschichte des
Weltkrieges [Bibliography of the Economic and Social History of
the World War]: Umfassend die Erscheinungen in deutscher
Sprache über die gemeinsame Kriegswirtschaft der
österreichisch-ungarischen Monarchie, die besondere
Kriegswirtschaft Österreichs 1914-1918 und die
Nachkriegswirtschaft der Republik Österreich 1918-1920
[Including German-language works on the joint war economy of
the Austro-Hungarian Empire, the separate Austrian war economy
1914-1918 and the postwar economy of the Austrian Republic
1918-1920].

World Wars

Vienna: Holder-Pichler-Tempsky (Carnegie-Stiftung für
internationalen Frieden, Abteilung für Volkswirtschaft und
Geschichte, Wirtschafts- und Sozialgeschichte des Weltkriegs,
österreichische und ungarische Serie), 1923. xiv + 167 pp.

   1118 items, 1914 - 1920. German. Some items have brief
   descriptive annotations; introduction (2 pp.); table of
   contents; author index; subject index.

   General works, collections, books, articles, reports,
   bibliographies, and periodicals on economic theory, political
   economy, and sociology of war (81); economic policy and war
   economy--general (225), agriculture, forestry, mining (80),
   commerce, trade, transportation, tariff systems (58),
   business and industry (37), money, credit, banking, stock
   exchange, insurance (34); social policy (169); finance and
   taxation (78); government and politics (191); statistics
   (39); periodicals and newsletters (40); miscellaneous (86).
   The emphasis throughout is on the economic problems of
   Germany, Austria, Hungary, and other Central and Eastern
   European countries.

1065   Z6207.E8V,v.3-5

Vic, Jean.

La Littérature de Guerre [War Literature]: Manuel méthodique et
critique des publications de langue française (Août 1916-
Novembre 1918), Tome I, II, III [Systematic and critical
handbook of publications in French (August 1916 to November
1918), Volume I, II, III].
Paris: Les Presses Françaises, 1923. xxii + 1231 pp.

   Approximately 7800 items, 1916 - 1918. French. Many items
   have brief to abstract-length descriptive and/or critical
   annotations; foreword (7 pp.) plus brief introductions to
   each section; table of contents; author index; subject index.

   Continuation of Vic´s earlier bibliography (see item No. 1057
   above) covers French literature on World War I through the
   end of hostilities; follows the same topical outline as the
   earlier work.

1066 <

[Carnegie Endowment for International Peace, Library].

Responsibility for the World War.

World Wars

Washington, D.C.: Carnegie Endowment for International Peace,
Library (Miscellaneous Reading List No. 25), 1925. (mimeo).

1067 <

Hall, Hubert.

British Archives and the Sources for the History of the World
War.
London/New Haven: H. Milford, Oxford University Press/Yale
University Press, for the Carnegie Endowment for International
Peace, Division of Economics and History (Economic and Social
History of the World War, British Series), 1925.

1068 <

Leland, Waldo G. and Newton D. Mereness (comps.).

Bibliography.
In their Introduction to the American Official Sources for the
Economic and Social History of the World War.
New Haven: Yale University Press, for the Carnegie Endowment
for International Peace, Division of Economics and History,
1926.

1069 <

Fester, Richard (ed.).

Katalog der Weltkriegsbibliothek des historischen Seminars der
Universität Halle-Wittenberg [Catalogue of the World War
Library of the Halle-Wittenberg University Historical Seminar].
Halle/Saale: Mitteldeutsche Verlag, 1928. 165 pp.

1070   Z6207.E8F2

Falls, Cyril.

War Books: A critical guide.
London: Peter Davies, May, 1930. xiv + 318 pp.

   715 items, 1916 - 1930. English; also French, German. All
   items have medium to abstract-length descriptive and critical
   annotations; preface (8 pp.).

   Books on the general military history of World War I (224)
   and the history of specific formations and units (171);

World Wars

   personal accounts of experiences during World War I (208);
   war novels (112).

   1071 <

   [United States Library of Congress, Division of Bibliography].

   The World War: A list of books (supplementary to mimeographed
   list, April 2, 1934).
   Washington, D.C.: [Library of Congress, Division of
   Bibliography], June 28, 1936.

   1072   D521.M14

   McEntee, Girard Lindsley.

   Bibliography.
   In his Military History of the World War: A complete account of
   the campaigns on all fronts accompanied by 456 maps and
   diagrams.
   New York: Charles Scribner's Sons, 1937. pp. 567-576.

      383 items, 1914 - 1937. English; also French, German, Italian
      (1).

      Books, reports, and memoirs relating to the history of the
      First World War, primarily from the military perspective.

   1073   L11.S2,v.28

   Baird, R. F. S.

   "The literature of the World War in the school library"
   [bibliographic essay].
   The School: Secondary edition (Toronto), 28, 5 (January, 1940):
   416-420.

      71 items (no dates given). English. All items are critically
      discussed in the text.

      Books, memoirs, and biographies (38) concerning World War I,
      military history, and espionage; World War I fiction and
      poetry (33) appropriate for school libraries.

World Wars

1074   Z6464.Z9H56

Hartz, Louis et al.

Bibliographical notes [5 lists].
In Herring, [Edward] Pendleton (ed.), Civil-Military Relations:
Bibliographical notes on administrative problems of civilian
mobilization.
Chicago: Public Administration Service, for the Committee on
Public Administration of the Social Science Research Council,
1940. pp. 10-35, 39-47, 48-49, 54-66, 69-77.

   482 items, 1914 - 1940. English; also German, French. All
   items have brief to abstract-length descriptive and/or
   critical annotations; preface (2 pp.) plus an introduction to
   each list (1 paragraph to 9 pp.); table of contents.

   Separate lists for United States (212), Great Britain (84),
   Canada (48), Germany (76), and France (62) on mobilization
   during World War I.

1075   Z6207.W8H4

Heindel, Richard H[eathcote] (comp.), with the assistance
of Arthur B[enedict] Berthold and Marion G[race] Miller.

War Check List: A working guide to the background and early
months of the war (chiefly, September 1938 to January 31,
1940)--Part 1, The background; Part 2, Five months of war.
Philadelphia: War Documentation Service (Bulletin No. 4), Part 1,
March, 1940, iii + 47 pp.; Part 2, April, 1940, iv + 79 pp.
(mimeo).

   2405 items, 1937 - 1940. English, German, French; also Italian,
   Swedish, Russian, Dutch, Spanish, other European languages. A
   few items have brief critical and/or descriptive annotations;
   prefaces (2 pp. each); table of contents (for Part 1);
   subject index (for Part 2).

   Part 1: bibliographies, annuals and chronologies, books and
   articles on the political and economic background of World
   War II, the Munich crisis, domestic history, leaders and
   foreign policy of Germany and Great Britain, information on
   Western and Eastern Europe and the Americas, and U.S. foreign
   policy (910 items mainly organized geographically). Part 2:
   bibliographies (18), maps and atlases (13), international
   relations (15), biographies (28), histories and chronologies
   of the war (9), causes (28), aims and issues of the war (33),
   diplomatic documents (33), science and methods of war (67),
   militarism and philosophy of war (33), combined armed forces
   (46), air raid precautions and civilian defense (102), air

World Wars

    raids (4), specific countries and regions (429), economic
    aspects (30), food stuffs and food economy (23), colonial
    questions (34), legal aspects (84), neutrality (24), language
    manuals and slang (14), addresses (24), literature (48),
    songs and music (10), radio and motion pictures (4),
    entertainment and sports (7), educational aspects (2),
    propaganda and censorship (36), espionage, secret service, and
    sabotage (20), religious aspects, sermons, and prayers (57),
    medical aspects (19), psychological aspects (5), animals (2),
    population questions and the war (25), refugees (20), prisons
    and prisoners (3), atrocities (10), peace (104), federation
    proposals (21), League of Nations and international
    organization (10), war work (1).

1076   D635.G83

[Shotwell, James Thomson (ed.)].

[Publisher´s list of titles in the series] "Economic and social
history of the world war."
In Grebler, Leo and Wilhelm Winkler, The Cost of the World War
to Germany and to Austria-Hungary.
New Haven/London: Yale University Press/Oxford University
Press, for the Carnegie Endowment for International Peace,
Division of Economics and History, 1940. Five unnumbered pages
at end of volume.

    145 items (no dates are given). English, French; also German,
    Italian (7), Norwegian (2), Danish (2).

1077   D443.W25

Waller, Willard [Walter] (ed.).

Suggested readings [12 lists by various authors].
In his War in the Twentieth Century.
New York: Dryden Press, 1940. pp. 34-35, 98-99, 131-132, 190-
191, 253, 310-311, 335, 360, 407-408, 428, 473-477, 531-532.

    358 items, 1916 - 1939. English; also French (9), German (9).
    A few items have medium-length descriptive and critical
    annotations.

    Books, articles, pamphlets, and essays on war in the
    twentieth century (22), World War I (46), the Paris Peace
    Conference and Europe between the two wars (36), economics in
    the interwar period (28), the rise of the Soviet state (18),
    the rise of fascism (38), treaty diplomacy following World
    War I (4), the origins of World War II (9), war economy (13),
    the state in wartime (13), propaganda and public opinion
    (117), war and social institutions (19).

World Wars

1078 <

War Documentation Service.

Notes on War Documentation and Research Activities.
Philadelphia: War Documentation Service (Bulletin No. 2), 1940.
6 pp. (mimeo).

1079

War Documentation Service.

Selective List of Periodicals and Newsletters, with Other Notes
on Documentation and Films.
Philadelphia: War Documentation Service (Bulletin No. 3),
February 20, 1940. 8 pp. (mimeo).

1080   Z6207.E85S7

Spier, H. O. (comp.).

World War II in Our Magazines and Books: A bibliography.
[New York: H. O. Spier], 1941. 31 pp.

   639 items, 1939 - 1941. English. Introduction (1 p.); table
   of contents.

   Magazine articles and books published in the United States
   dealing with World War II, wartime socioeconomic and
   political conditions in various countries, foreign policy,
   and international relations.

1081   NN: *GAA

[Consumers' Book Cooperative, Inc].

"The war" [a bibliography].
Reader's Observer, 5, 4 (July-August, 1942): [1-2].

   39 items, [1942]. English. Most items have brief descriptive
   annotations; introduction (1 paragraph).

   Mostly technical and semitechnical manuals for use in the
   armed forces and civil defense and a few books on warfare and
   the immediate causes of World War II.

World Wars

1082   Z1035.A49,v.39

Melinat, Carl H.

"U.S. government publications and the war: A selected list."
The Booklist, 39, 7, Part 2 (December 15, 1942): [151]-175.

   369 items, 1940 - 1942. English. All items have brief
   descriptive annotations; introduction (3 paragraphs); table
   of contents.

   Books and pamphlets on the armed services (84), civil defense
   (59), wartime industry (49), national defense (23),
   reconstruction (8), wartime technical training (77), wartime
   living (61), World War II (8).

1083 <

Michel, H.

"Les principales sources françaises de l´histoire de la
Deuxième Guerre Mondiale [The principal French sources for the
history of the Second World War]."
Revue Historique (Paris), 200 (October-December, 1948):
206-219.

1084   D637.H6

Hoover, Herbert [Clark].

Bibliography.
In his An American Epic, Volume II; Famine in Forty-five
Nations: Organization behind the front, 1914-1923.
Chicago: Henry Regnery, 1960. pp. 469-473.

   75 items, 1904 - 1959. English.

   Books, reports, minutes, yearbooks, and articles on the
   history and work of organizations engaged in famine relief
   during and after World War I, including American Friends
   Service Committee (11), American Red Cross (16), the
   Christian Scientists (1), the Church of Jesus Christ of
   Latter-day Saints (5), Daughters of the American Revolution
   (1), the Jewish Joint Distribution Committee (26), the Near
   East Relief Committee (11), the Salvation Army (4).

World Wars

1085

De Launay, Jacques, Ettore Anchieri, and Henri Michel.

"1914-1918; Histoire des origines de la deuxième guerre
mondiale/History of the origins of the Second World War, 1919-
1939; Histoire de la deuxième guerre mondiale/History of the
Second World War, 1939-1945: Bibliographie[s] sélective[s]/
Selective bibliograph[ies]."
In Commission Internationale pour l'Enseignement de l'Histoire/
International Commission for the Teaching of History, Les
Deux Guerres Mondiales/The Two World Wars: Bibliographie
sélective/Selective bibliography.
Oxford/Brussels: Pergamon Press/Editions Brepols, 1964.
pp.89-243.

1086 <

Marwick, Arthur.

Bibliography.
In his The Deluge: British society and the First World War.
London: Bodley Head, 1965.

1087   Z674.I52,no.79

Hendricks, Donald [Duane].

Pamphlets on the First World War: An annotated bibliography.
Urbana: University of Illinois, Graduate School of Library
Science (Occasional Paper No. 79), September, 1966. 58 pp.

   461 items, 1907 - 1929. English. Many items have brief
   descriptive annotations; introduction (2 pp.); subject index.

   Guide to the collection of World War I pamphlets in the
   library of Millikin University, Decatur, Illinois.

1088   Z6207.W8M58

Morton, Louis.

Writings on World War II.
Washington, D.C.: American Historical Association, Service
Center for Teachers of History (Publication No. 66), 1967.
iv + 54 pp.

   122 items, 1946 - 1966. English. Bibliographic essay
   (49 pp.), followed by a list of selected readings (pp. 50-54).

World Wars

Most items in the list are discussed in the essay. Table of
contents; preface (1 p.).

Histories, memoirs, and other works on World War II discussed
in an extended bibliographic essay divided into sections on
bibliography and reference; general histories; memoirs and
biographies; fiction and journalism; official publications;
diplomacy and policy; organization and grand strategy;
economics, mobilization, and supply; the home front; Pearl
Harbor and the origins of the war; the debate over strategy;
and the decision to use the A-bomb. The list of selected
readings is divided under the following headings: general
histories of the war (7), origins of the war (12), diplomacy,
policy, strategy (35), military operations (44),
mobilization, supply, the home front (11), the A-bomb and the
end of the war (13).

1089   D744.W7

Wright, Gordon.

Bibliographical essay.
In his The Ordeal of Total War, 1939-1945.
New York: Harper and Row, 1968. pp. 269-305.

975 items, 1939 - 1967. English, German; also French, Russian,
other Eastern and Western European languages. Essay format.

Published or microfilmed source materials (30), periodicals
(7), general accounts (11), immediate background (14), the
problem of Hitler's war aims (8), general military aspects
(50), Polish campaign (5), Norwegian campaign (4), western
campaign (13), battle of Britain (11), Mediterranean and
North African campaigns (13), the war in Russia (57), the
campaign in Italy (8), Normandy and the invasion of Germany
(25), war in the air (22), war on the sea (18), espionage and
intelligence operations (16), civil-military relations in
wartime (13), economic aspects of the war years (39), science
and technology (31), psychological warfare (25),
psychological impact of the war (13), German occupation
policies (56), Nazi persecution of "racial" and political
enemies (67), resistance movements (116), wartime diplomacy
(100), intellectual and cultural aspects of the war period
(32), domestic events in the nations of Europe (171).

World Wars

1090 <   Z6207.W8Z5

Ziegler, Janet.

World War II: A bibliography of books in English, 1945-1965.
Stanford: Stanford University, Hoover Institution (Hoover
Bibliography Series, No. 45), 1971. 194 pp.

1091 <   Z6207.W8B58

Bloomberg, Marty and Hans H. Weber.

World War II and Its Origins: A select annotated bibliography
of books in English.
Littleton, Colo.: Libraries Unlimited, 1975. xiv + 311 pp.

1092 <   Z6207.W8F78

Funk, Arthur L[ayton], et al. (comps.), with the assistance of
Janet Ziegler.

A Select Bibliography of Books on the Second World War in
English Published in the United States, 1966-1975 (produced by
the American Committee on the History of the Second World War
on the occasion of the 14th International Congress of the
Historical Sciences, San Francisco, August 1975).
Gainesville, Fla.: American Committee on the History of the
Second World War, 1976 (2nd ed.). 33 pp.
First edition by Arthur L. Funk, entitled The Second World War:
A bibliography (A select list of publications appearing since
1968), 1972, 32 pp.

1093 <

Bayliss, Gwyn M.

Bibliographic Guide to the Two World Wars: An annotated survey
of English-language reference materials.
London/New York: Bowker, 1977. xv + 578 pp.

World Wars

    1094   Z6207.W8E57

    Enser, A. G. S.

    A Subject Bibliography of the Second World War: Books in
    English, 1939-1974.
    London/Boulder, Colo.: Andre Deutsch/Westview Press, 1977.
    592 pp.

    1095 <   Z6207.E8S31

    Schaffer, Ronald.

    The United States in World War I: A selected bibliography.
    Santa Barbara, Calif.: Clio Books (War/Peace Bibliography
    Series, No. 7), 1978. xxix + 224 pp.

Causes of War

1096   JX1252.L65

Loria, Achille.

Bibliography.
In his The Economic Causes of War, translated by John Leslie
Garner.
Chicago: Charles H. Kerr, 1917. pp. [183]-188.

   92 items, 1615 - 1916. French, English; also German, Italian
   (1).

   Works on political economy, social and economic history of
   Europe, causes and effects of war, and international law.

1097   JX1952.D53

Dickinson, G[oldsworthy] Lowes.

A short bibliography.
In his Causes of International War.
London/New York: Swarthmore Press/Harcourt, Brace and Howe,
1920. pp. 109-110.

   15 items, 1913 - 1919. English.

   Books and articles on the origin of war, treaties, and peace
   theory.

1098 <   D523.S875

Swindler, Robert Earl.

Bibliography.
In his The Causes of War, Including an Outline and Study of the
World War and Official Peace Negotiations.
Boston: R. G. Badger, [1920]. pp. 263-264.

Causes of War

1099   HB195.B3

Bakeless, John [E.].

Bibliography.
In his The Economic Causes of Modern War: A study of the period
1878-1918.
New York: Moffat, Yard, for Williams College, Department of
Political Science (David A. Wells Prize Essays, No. 6), 1921.
pp. [231]-249.

  195 items, 1879 - 1920. English; also French, German (2), Greek
  (1). Most items have brief descriptive and/or critical
  annotations; introduction (1 paragraph).

  Books, journal articles, and official documents on European
  history (5), wars from 1878 to 1918 (132), causes of war (5),
  League of Nations (22), and general studies of war (31).

1100 <   D6235.S6,1925

Spaeth, John W.

Bibliography.
In his A Study of the Causes of Rome´s Wars from 342 to
265 B.C.
Princeton: Princeton University Press, 1926. pp. 66-69.

1101 <

[Matthews, Mary Alice (comp.)].

The Causes of War.
Washington, D.C.: Carnegie Endowment for International Peace,
Library (Reading List No. 13), 1927. 7 pp. (mimeo).

1102   DLC-DB

[United States Library of Congress, Division of Bibliography].

Economic Causes of War: A bibliographical list.
[Washington, D.C.]: Library of Congress, Division of
Bibliography, January 9, 1929. 7 pp. (typescript).

  62 items, 1903 - 1928. English; also German (3), French (1).
  Some items have brief descriptive annotations.

  Books and articles dealing with economic and other causes of
  war, effects of war, commercial and economic aspects of war,

Causes of War

international politics, imperialism, international trade, oil
politics, and colonial rivalries.

1103   U21.1.B4

Bernard, L[uther] L[ee].

General bibliography.
In his War and Its Causes.
New York: Henry Holt, 1944. pp. 459-468.
Reprinted, with a new introduction by Israel W. Charny, New
York: Garland (Library of War and Peace), 1972.

330 items, 1754 - 1944. English; also French (4), German (1).

Books (260) and articles (90) on the nature, history, and
causes of war (encompassing psychological, economic,
political, geopolitical, social, biological, and cultural
aspects), war as a social institution, militarism,
imperialism, fascism, predictions of war, international
relations, and the peace movement.

1104   JX1291.T45

Pruitt, Dean G[arner] and Richard C[arlton] Snyder (eds.).

References [18 lists by various authors].
In their Theory and Research on the Causes of War.
Englewood Cliffs, N.J.: Prentice-Hall, 1969. pp. 13-14, 32-34,
38, 42, 58-59, 78-79, 93-94, 112-113, 163-164, 174-175, 186-
188, 211-212, 218, 227-228, 231, 244, 279-283, 296-300.

544 items, 1920 - 1969. English; also French (1).

Books and journal articles arranged under the following
section and chapter titles: the study of war (27), motives
and perceptions underlying entry into war (76), movement
toward war (32), the management of international crises (47),
search under crisis in political gaming and simulation (31),
restraints against the use of violence and military
preparation (36), deterrence in history (28), nuclear weapons
and alliance cohesion (27), nonmilitary restraints and
peaceful resolution of controversy (33), nonresolution
consequences of the United Nations (14), the incidence of
war, statistical evidence (6), dimensions of foreign and
domestic conflict behavior (22), frequency of wars and
geographical opportunity (1), toward an integrated theory and
cumulative research (14), intellectual history of a research
program (81), simulations in the consolidation and
utilization of knowledge (69).

Causes of War

1105

Divale, W[illiam] T[ulio] and M[arvin] Harris.

[Bibliography] in "Population, warfare, and the male
supremacist complex."
American Anthropologist, 78, 3 (September, 1976): 536-538.

   48 items, 1933 - 1974. English.

   Books, articles, and statistics on population growth,
   fertility control, female infanticide, origins and history of
   warfare, male dominance, and ethonological studies of warfare
   and female status.

Effects of War

1106   JX1953.W3

Walsh, Walter.

References [12 lists].
In his The Moral Damage of War.
Boston: Ginn, 1906. pp. 37-38, 72-78, 104-106, 149-165, 192-
198, 227-232, 265-269, 302-304, 341-343, 371-378, 407-410,
447-450.

   625 items, 1790 - 1904. English. Endnote citations for each
   chapter, some of which have lengthy extracts from the
   material cited.

   Books, newspaper and journal articles, and pamphlets on the
   moral damage of war to the nation, child, soldier,
   politician, journalist, preacher, missionary, trader,
   citizen, patriot, and reformer.

1107 <

Serrigny, Bernard.

Bibliographie.
In his Les Conséquences Economiques et Sociales de la Prochaine
Guerre, d´Après les Enseignements des Campagnes de 1870-71 et
de 1904-1905 [Economic and Social Consequences of the Next War,
in Light of the Lessons of the Campaigns of 1870-71 and 1904-
1905].
Paris: Giard et Brière, 1909. pp. 469-476.

1108   DLC-DB

[United States Library of Congress, Division of Bibliography].

List of References on the Benefits of War.
[Washington, D.C.]: Library of Congress, Division of
Bibliography, December 18, 1914. 2 pp. (typescript).

   25 items, 1891 - 1914. English.

   Books and articles on the social, political, economic, moral,
   and other benefits of war; disadvantages of peace.

Effects of War

1109   DLC-DB

[United States Library of Congress, Division of Bibliography].

List of References on the Economic Effects of War Especially
on Neutrals.
[Washington, D.C.]: Library of Congress, Division of
Bibliography, September 22, 1914. 3 pp. (typescript).

  29 items, 1870 - 1914. English. A few items have brief
  descriptive annotations.

  Books and articles on commercial and financial aspects of
  war, mainly the impact of the early stages of World War I on
  the U.S.

1110   DLC-DB

[United States Library of Congress, Division of Bibliography].

List of References on the Financial Influence of the European
War, Especially on the United States.
[Washington, D.C.]: Library of Congress, Division of
Bibliography, September 8, 1915. 4 pp.

  46 items, 1912 - 1915. English.

  Books (8) and articles (38) mainly written by economists.

1111   DLC-DB

[United States Library of Congress, Division of Bibliography].

Brief List of References on the Effect of the European War on
Religion.
[Washington, D.C.]: Library of Congress, Division of
Bibliography, June 21, 1916. 3 pp. (typescript).

  28 items, 1914 - 1916. English.

  Books, pamphlets, and articles on the effects of World War I
  on religion and the Christian churches, especially in
  Britain, France, and Germany.

Effects of War

1112   DLC-DB

[United States Library of Congress, Division of Bibliography].

List of References on the Cost of the European War.
[Washington, D.C.]: Library of Congress, Division of
Bibliography, January 17, 1918. 12 pp. (mimeo).

   154 items, 1914 - 1918. English; also French. A few items
   have brief descriptive annotations.

   Books (26), articles and periodicals (128) on war finance and
   the economic costs of World War I.

1113   HJ236.B55

Bogart, Ernest L.

Bibliography.
In his Direct and Indirect Costs of the Great World War.
New York/London/Toronto/Melbourne/Bombay: Oxford University
Press, for the Carnegie Endowment for International Peace,
Division of Economics and History (Preliminary Economic Studies
of the War, No. 24), 1920 (2nd rev. ed.). pp. [301]-330.
First edition, 1919.

   757 items, 1913 - 1918. English; also French, German, Italian
   (5).

   Yearbooks, statistical publications, books, magazine,
   newspaper, and journal articles on the effects of World War I
   on business, finance, banking, currency, loans, national
   budgets and expenditures, taxation, property, shipping, and
   human life, primarily in the U.S., Great Britain, France,
   Germany, Russia, and Italy.

1114   DLC-DB

[United States Library of Congress, Division of Bibliography].

Brief List of Recent References on the Cost of War and
Armaments.
[Washington, D.C.]: Library of Congress, Division of
Bibliography, February 12, 1921. 3 pp. (typescript).

   35 items, 1898 - 1920. English.

   Books and articles concentrating mainly on the financial
   costs of World War I.

Effects of War

1115   DLC-DB

[United States Library of Congress, Division of Bibliography].

List of Recent References on the Effect of the European War on
Religion.
[Washington, D.C.]: Library of Congress, Division of
Bibliography, June 16, 1922. 10 pp. (typescript).

   136 items, 1915 - 1922. English; also French, German.

   Books, articles, pamphlets, and reports on the effects of
   World War I on religion, the churches, Christian ethics, and
   soldiers' religious beliefs.

1116 <

[Carnegie Endowment for International Peace, Library].

Cost of War.
Washington, D.C.: Carnegie Endowment for International Peace,
Library (Miscellaneous Reading List No. 8), 1923. (mimeo).
Reprinted in Advocate of Peace, Vol. 85, April 1923, pp. 156-
159.

1117   D25.5.D8

Dumas, Samuel (ed.).

Bibliography in "Losses of life caused by war: Part I--up to
1913."
In Dumas, Samuel and [Knud Otto Vedel-Petersen,] Losses of
Life Caused by War, edited by Harald Westergaard.
Oxford/London/etc.: Clarendon Press/Humphrey Milford, 1923.
pp. [7]-13.

   164 items, 1812 - 1916. German, French; also English.

   Books, articles, and reports on military history, medical
   aspects of war, causes and effects of war, and casualty
   statistics from various wars.

Effects of War

1118   DLC-DB

[United States Library of Congress, Division of Bibliography].

Brief List of References on the Moral Effects of the European
War.
[Washington, D.C.]: Library of Congress, Division of
Bibliography, January 29, 1923. 3 pp. (typescript).

   39 items, 1915 - 1922. English; also French (4), German (1).
   Some items have brief descriptive annotations.

   Books and journal articles on ethical and religious problems
   and the moral and social effects of World War I.

1119   QL1.C15,v.25

Holmes, Samuel J[ackson].

"Selective influence of war."
In his Bibliography of Eugenics.
Berkeley: University of California Press (University of
California Publications in Zoology, Vol. 25), January, 1924.
pp. 393-408.

   325 items, 1829 - 1922. German, English; also French, Italian,
   Dutch (1). A few items have brief descriptive and/or critical
   annotations; introduction (1 paragraph).

   Books and articles dealing with medical, demographic, and
   social effects of war.

1120   Z6464.Z9C33

Matthews, M[ary] Alice (comp.).

The Cost of War and Preparedness for War: Select list of books,
pamphlets, and periodical articles on the direct and indirect
costs of war.
Washington, D.C.: Carnegie Endowment for International Peace,
Library (Reading List No. 31), March 24, 1931. 20 pp.

   244 items, 1799 - 1931. English; also French, German (2).
   Many items have brief descriptive annotations; list of other
   bibliographies prepared by CEIP Library (4).

   Books and pamphlets (244) and articles (116) on war
   casualties, naval power of nations, disarmament, peace
   theory, theory of war, social and political aspects of war,
   medical aspects of war, psychological aspects of war, war

Effects of War

    finance, world economy, statistical data on armaments,
    economic losses due to war.

1121 <

[Carnegie Endowment for International Peace, Library].

War and Its Alleged Benefits: The moral and economic case for
war.
Washington, D.C.: Carnegie Endowment for International Peace,
Library (Miscellaneous Reading List No. 54), 1934. (mimeo).

1122 <

Matthews, M[ary] Alice (comp.).

The Effect of War on Criminal Tendencies of the Race.
Washington, D.C.: Carnegie Endowment for International Peace,
Library (Brief Reference List No. 1), September, 1935 (rev.
ed.). 5 pp.
First edition, August 16, 1934.

1123   U21.S45

Shapiro, Harold Roland.

References.
In his What Every Young Man Should Know about War.
New York: Knight, 1937. pp. 131-146.

    44 items, 1915 - 1935. English. References contained in 255
    endnotes without comments.

    Contains mostly books and articles on the medical aspects of
    war, with a few items on economic aspects of war.

1124   HV6001.J63,v.30

Rosenbaum, Betty B.

Bibliography in "The relationship between war and crime in the
United States."
Journal of Criminal Law and Criminology, 30, 5
(January-February, 1940): 738-740.

    33 items, 1866 - 1937. English.

Effects of War

> Books and articles on the impact of war on crime, juvenile
> delinquency, and law enforcement practices.

1125   Z6207.W8T65

Tompkins, Dorothy [Louise] Campbell [Culver] (comp.).

Social and Economic Problems Arising Out of World War II: A
bibliography, with a foreword by Samuel C. May.
Chicago: Public Administration Service (Publication No. 80),
1941. vii + 114 pp.

> 922 items, 1939 - 1941. English. Many items have brief
> descriptive and/or critical annotations; preface (1 p.);
> table of contents; author index; subject index.

> Books, articles, and documents covering the whole range of
> social and economic problems arising in many countries during
> the Second World War, including civil defense, commodity
> supply and control, conscription, finance, health, industrial
> relations, public services, and numerous other matters.

1126   D410.U7,no.215

DeVinney, Leland C., William F. Ogburn, and Alan Valentine.

Suggested readings in "War and the family."
University of Chicago Round Table, No. 215 (April 26, 1942):
21-22.

> 18 items, 1918 - 1942. English. Many items have brief
> descriptive annotations.

> Magazine articles and books on the effects of war on the
> family unit, children, and women in the United States and
> Great Britain.

1127   R11.A85,ser.3,v.4

Roemer, Milton I.

References in "History of the effects of war on medicine."
Annals of Medical History 4 (Third Series), 3 (May, 1942):
197-198.

> 43 items, 1917 - 1941. English.

> Books and articles on the history of medicine, social forces

Effects of War

behind medical discoveries, the costs of medical care,
socialized medicine, and health care.

1128   HM299.S6

Sorokin, Pitirim A[leksandrovich].

Notes.
In his Man and Society in Calamity: The effects of war,
revolution, famine, pestilence upon human mind, behavior,
social organization and cultural life.
New York: E. P. Dutton, 1942. pp. 321-347.

280 items, 1480 - 1942. English, Russian; also French, German.
Many items have brief descriptive and/or critical comments.

References cited in 419 notes, arranged according to the 18
chapters of the text, dealing with the effects of war,
revolution, and other calamities on psychological processes,
behavior, birthrates, death rates, marriage rates, migration,
mobility, social institutions, political, economic, and
social organization, standard of living, religious and
ethical life of society, ethico-religious progress, science
and technology, fine arts, and ideologies.

1129   Z1009.U57

Grinnell, Mary E. and Ina L. Hawes (comps.).

Bibliography on Lice and Man with Particular Reference to
Wartime Conditions.
Washington, D.C.: U.S. Government Printing Office (U.S.
Department of Agriculture, Bibliographical Bulletin No. 1),
July, 1943. 106 pp.

961 items, 1758 - 1942 (only 16 items published before 1912).
English, German; also French (9), Latin (1), Italian (1),
Norwegian (1). Many items have brief descriptive annotations;
items are arranged chronologically; preface (1 p.);
introduction (1 p.); author/subject index.

Mostly zoological and medical research on lice and on
diseases transmitted by lice, but includes a considerable
number of references on the effect of wartime conditions in
the epidemiology of these problems.

Effects of War

1130   HV2350.V7,v.45

[Volta Bureau].

"War deafness: An annotated bibliography of material in the
Volta Bureau files."
Volta Review, 45, 1 (January, 1943): 27-29, 50; 2 (February,
1943): 100-102, 124; 4 (April, 1943): 224-226, 250-251.

  16 items, 1888 - 1923. English. All items have descriptive
  abstract-length annotations; introductions (1-2 paragraphs)
  to each part.

  Scrap books and personal histories of soldiers who lost their
  hearing from the Civil War to the present, bills before
  Congress on war-related deafness, medical studies on the
  effects of war on hearing, and reports of rehabilitation
  efforts.

1131 <

Duvall, E. M.

"Soldier come home: A listing of current books, pamphlets,
reprints and articles pertaining to readjustment of returning
servicemen."
Marriage and Family Living, 7 (1945): 61-63, 72.

1132 <   Z6724.C6H8

Human Sciences Research, Inc.

Civil Defense Bibliography, January 1966: A compilation of
references relevant to the study of societal recovery from
nuclear attack.
[McLean, Va.: Human Sciences Research], [1966]. 75 pp.

1133   E169.12.N4

Nelson, Keith L. (ed.).

Bibliography: "Important works on the impact of war."
In his The Impact of War on American Life: The twentieth-
century experience.
New York/Chicago/etc.: Holt, Rinehart, and Winston, 1971.
pp. 371-395.

  946 items, 1690 - 1971. English.

Effects of War

    Books and articles on conflict, disaster, and social change
    (65), war (41), non-American wars (36), American wars
    generally (37), American wars before 1914 (174), World War I
    (128), World War II (135), Cold War (135), and the problem of
    the warfare state (195).

1134 <

Archer, D. and R. Gartner.

[Bibliography] in "Violent acts and violent times: A comparative
approach to postwar homicide rates."
American Sociological Review, 41 (December, 1976): 961-963.

War and Children

1135   RA790.AIA5,v.12

Bender, Lauretta and John Frosch.

Bibliography in "Children's reactions to the war."
American Journal of Orthopsychiatry, 12 (1942): 586.

   10 items, 1935 - 1942. English.

   Reports on the psychological effects of war on children.

1136   HQ784.W3C48,1942a

[Chicago Institute for Psychoanalysis, Committee on
Psychological Problems of Children in Wartime].

Selected reading.
In its Growing Up in a World at War.
Chicago: Institute for Psychoanalysis, June, 1942. pp. [20-21].

   25 items, 1940 - 1942. English.

   Books (3), articles (17), and pamphlets (5) on psychological
   effects of war on children.

1137   L11.H5,v.25

Coleman, Martha Page and T. Ross Fink.

"A partial bibliography on juvenile delinquency in its relation
to the school and in war-time."
High School Journal, 25, 7 (November-December, 1942): 320-322.

   56 items, 1928 - 1942. English. Introduction (1 paragraph).

   Books and articles on juvenile delinquency in the war period.

War and Children

    1138 <

    Cotton, Elizabeth Storrs.

    Children's Morale in Wartime: A bibliography (Term thesis,
    Library Science, Simmons College).
    Boston: Simmons College, School of Library Science, 1942.
    42 pp. (typewritten).

        Apparently unavailable; not located through interlibrary
        loan.

    1139   IU: 136.7D46p

    Despert, J[uliette] Louise.

    Bibliography.
    In her Preliminary Report on Children's Reactions to the War,
    Including a Critical Survey of the Literature.
    [New York: New York Hospital and Cornell University Medical
    College, Department of Psychiatry], 1942. 10 pp. following
    p. 92.

        111 items, 1939 - 1942. English; also German (1).

        Clinical and statistical studies on various effects of war,
        especially on children.

    1140   D410.U7,no.219

    Eliot, Martha [M.], Daniel Prescott, and T. V. Smith.

    Suggested readings in "Children and the war."
    University of Chicago Round Table, No. 219 ([May 24], 1942):
    13.

        10 items, 1942. English. Some items have brief descriptive
        and/or critical annotations.

        Psychological effects of war on children, care and feeding of
        children in wartime.

    1141   D810.C4E5;also HV741.A32,
                                           no.279

    Eliot, Martha M.

    List of references.

War and Children

In her Civil Defense Measures for the Protection of Children:
Report of observations in Great Britain, February 1941.
Washington, D.C.: U.S. Government Printing Office (U.S.
Department of Labor, Children's Bureau Publication No. 279),
1942. pp. 179-186.

   180 items, 1938 - 1941. English.

   Mostly pamphlet and leaflet material on civil defense
   measures for the protection of children; some items on the
   physical effects of war on children.

1142   RA790.A1A5,v.12

Geleerd, Elisabeth R.

Bibliography in "Psychiatric care of children in wartime."
American Journal of Orthopsychiatry, 12 (October, 1942): 593.

   16 items, 1940 - 1941. English; also German (1).

   Works on children's psychological problems resulting from
   evacuation, separation from mother, and general wartime
   conditions.

1143 <

National Commission for Young Children.

Suggested References on Children in Wartime.
Washington, D.C.: [National Commission for Young Children],
1942. 7 pp.

1144   BF723.W3P74

Preston, Ralph C[lausius].

Bibliography.
In his Children's Reactions to a Contemporary War Situation
(Ph.D. dissertation, Columbia University, 1941), with a preface
by Arthur T. Jersild.
New York: Columbia University, Teacher's College, Bureau of
Publications (Child Development Monographs, No. 28), 1942.
pp. 93-96.

   69 items, 1893 - 1940. English; also French (3), German (3).

War and Children

General works on attitude change and child development and
empirical studies on children's attitudes toward war, peace,
and other social issues.

1145   HV851.N3

[Taylor, Mary Waldo (comp.)].

"Bibliography: War and the young child."
In Alschuler, Rose H. (ed.), Children's Centers: A guide for
those who care for and about young children.
New York: William Morrow, for the National Commission for Young
Children, 1942. pp. 163-165.

   25 items, 1933 - 1942. English. All items have brief
   descriptive annotations; introduction (1 paragraph).

   Books, government publications, and other materials on
   childhood education and problems of children and war, under
   the headings: nursery schools (6), child management and
   training (8), war and the young child (11).

1146 <

Wolf, Anna M. W.

Reading Lists.
In her Our Children Face War.
Boston: Houghton Mifflin, 1942. pp. 203-214.

1147   DLC-DB

Conover, Helen F. (comp.), under the direction of Florence S.
Hellman.

Children and War: A selected list of references.
[Washington, D.C.]: Library of Congress, Division of
Bibliography, February 19, 1943 (rev. ed.). 56 pp.
First edition, April 21, 1942, 21 pp. (mimeo).

   609 items, 1915 - 1943. English; also French (2), German (1).
   A few items have brief descriptive annotations; introduction
   (1 paragraph); table of contents; subject index.

   Impact of war on children, including child labor, day care,
   evacuation, education, health, juvenile delinquency, morale,
   nutrition, refugees, and welfare in World War I (41), Spanish
   Civil War (23), and World War II (545). Mainly periodical

War and Children

   articles; also some books, pamphlets, and government
   publications.

1148   L11.R35,v.13

Jersild, Arthur T.

Bibliography in "Mental health of children and families in
wartime."
Review of Educational Research, 13, 5 (December, 1943):
474-477.

   98 items, 1915 - 1943. English; also German (1).

   Books and articles on the physical and psychological effects
   of war on children, wartime protection and care of children,
   and juvenile delinquency in wartime.

1149 <   D810.C4Z6

Zoff, Otto.

A note on sources.
In his They Shall Inherit the Earth, translated by Anne
Garrison.
New York: John Day, 1943. pp. 249-258.

1150   DLC-DB

[Conover, Helen F. (comp.), under the direction of Florence S.
Hellman].

Memorandum on Children and War.
[Washington, D.C.]: Library of Congress, Division of
Bibliography, January 28, 1944. 5 pp. (typescript).

   43 items, 1942 - 1943. English. Many items have brief
   descriptive annotations; introduction (1 paragraph).

   Official publications (7), unofficial public organizations'
   publications (12), radio programs (3), periodicals (6), books
   and articles (15) on the impact of war on child welfare:
   educational, psychological, economic, and other aspects.

War and Children

1151   BF1.J575,v.8

Despert, J[uliette] Louise.

References in "Effects of war on children's mental health."
Journal of Consulting Psychology, 8, 4 (July-August, 1944):
218.

   25 items, 1919 - 1943. English. All items are discussed in
   the text.

   Articles and papers on the sociological and psychological
   effects of war on children, juvenile delinquency in wartime,
   and security measures for the protection of children.

1152   RA790.A1A5,v.17

Young, Florene M.

Bibliography in "Psychological effects of war on young
children."
American Journal of Orthopsychiatry, 17, 3 (July, 1947):
509-510.

   13 items, 1940 - 1945. English.

   Journal articles and a few monographs on children's reactions
   to World War II.

1153   L11.E6,v.54

Ridgway, James M.

Bibliography in "School civil defense measures."
Elementary School Journal, 54, 9 (May, 1954): 506-508.

   41 items, 1939 - 1952. English.

   Books, articles, and government reports on effects of war on
   children, air warfare, civil defense, and effects of atomic
   bombs.

1154

Tolley, Howard, Jr.

Annotated bibliography; References.

War and Children

In his Children and War: Political socialization to international conflict.
New York/London: Teachers College Press, 1973. pp. 178-183, 184-194.

Psychological Aspects of War

1155 <

Birnbaum, K.

[Current German literature on war neuro-psychiatry].
Zeitschrift für die gesamte Neurologie und Psychiatrie, 11 to 18
[1914 to 1918].

1156 <

Fenton, N. and D. E. Morrison.

"A bibliography of American contributions to war
neuropsychiatry."
American Journal of Psychiatry, 6 (1927): 507-517.

1157

Fenton, N.

"A bibliography of American contributions to war
neuropsychiatry."
In The Medical Department of the U.S. Army in the World War:
Vol. X, Neuropsychiatry.
Washington, D.C.: U.S. Government Printing Office, 1929.
pp. 477-487.

1158   Z6464.W3N4

[Netherlands Medical Association, Committee for War-Prophylaxis].

Bibliography on War-problem, War-psychology, War-psychiatry,
No. I.
[Haarlem]: Netherlands Medical Association, Committee for War-
Prophylaxis, [1935]. 24 pp.

   365 items, 1910 - 1933. German; also French, English, Italian.
   Introduction (1 p.).

   War problems (23), war psychology (124), and war psychiatry
   (208).

Psychological Aspects of War

1159 <

[Carnegie Endowment for International Peace, Library].

Propaganda and War.
Washington, D.C.: Carnegie Endowment for International Peace,
Library (Miscellaneous Reading List No. 56), 1938. (mimeo).

1160   Z720.1.G3

Gasiorowski, Janusz [Tadeusz].

Bibliografia Psychologii Woskowej [Bibliography of Military
Psychology].
Warsaw: Ksiegarnia Wojskowa, 1938. xxvi + 779 pp.

   See H. L. Ansbacher (1941, pp. 505-508), No. 1164, below,
   for a description of this bibliography.

1161   HM251.B475

Bird, Charles.

Bibliography in "Psychological aspects of war."
In his Social Psychology.
New York: D. Appleton-Century (The Century Psychology Series),
1940. pp. 544-546.

   44 items, 1911 - 1938. English.

   Books and articles on attitude studies of war, pacifism,
   militarism, and attitude change.

1162   DLC-DB

Fuller, Grace Hadley (comp.), under the direction of Florence S.
Hellman.

Propaganda: A list of bibliographies.
Washington, D.C.: Library of Congress, Division of
Bibliography, November 22, 1940. 6 pp. (mimeo).

   41 items, 1928 - 1940. English.

   Bibliographies on propaganda, public opinion, and
   psychological warfare.

Psychological Aspects of War

1163   RC343.M47,1940a

Miller, Emanuel (ed.).

Bibliography.
In his The Neuroses in War, with a concluding chapter by
H. Crichton-Miller.
New York: Macmillan, 1940. pp. 239-246.

    228 items, 1864 - 1939. English, German; also French (5).
    Introduction (1 paragraph).

    Psychiatric and psychological works on mental and emotional
    disorders produced by war, psychological adjustment to
    combat, and the psychology of war and peace.

1164   BF1.P75,v.38

Ansbacher, H. L.

"The Gasiorowski bibliography of military psychology."
Psychological Bulletin, 38, 6 (June, 1941): 505-508.

    A bibliographic essay describing J. Gasiorowski's 6,381 item
    "Bibliografia psychologii wojskowej," published in 1938.
    Details the number of items, format, distribution of items
    according to language and publication date, and analyzes the
    subject scope of the Gasiorowski bibliography in terms of the
    main section headings of the bibliography of the Emergency
    Committee in Psychology.

1165   BF1.P75,v.38

Ansbacher, H. L.

Bibliography in "German military psychology."
Psychological Bulletin, 38, 6 (June, 1941): 385-392.

    148 items, 1921 - 1940. German; also English (2), Italian (1).
    Introduction (15 pp.) in English consists of a critical
    review of the literature included in the bibliography.

    Books and articles on German military psychology (primarily
    works published during the Third Reich) including works on
    military leaders and leadership, military life, conscription,
    propaganda, mass psychology, psychological methods and tests,
    personality and characterological studies, research on race
    and psychology, national character, and other topics.

Psychological Aspects of War

1166   U21.H3

Harding, D[enys Clement] W[yatt].

References.
In his The Impulse to Dominate.
London: George Allen and Unwin, 1941. pp. 249-251.

   45 items, 1916 - 1940. English.

   Books and journal articles on individual aggression,
   neuroses, and the psychological and social development of
   children; memoirs of war participants.

1167   BF1.P75,v.38

Stagner, Ross.

Bibliography in "Psychological causes of war."
Psychological Bulletin, 38, 6 (June, 1941): 487-488.

   24 items, 1915 - 1941. English. Introduction (4 pp.).

   Books and articles on psychiatric and psychological aspects
   of war.

1168   RC321.J7,v.36

Vernon, P. E.

References in "Psychological effects of air-raids."
Journal of Abnormal and Social Psychology, 36 (1941): 476.

   20 items, 1938 - 1941. English.

   Books and journal articles on the manifestations and
   treatment of the psychological effects of air raids.

1169   HM251.A1J6

Day, Daniel Droba and O. F. Quackenbush.

References in "Attitudes toward defensive, cooperative, and
aggressive war."
Journal of Social Psychology, 16, first half (August, 1942):
20.

Psychological Aspects of War

   12 items, 1931 - 1938. English.

   Journal articles on attitude change and measuring attitudes
   toward war and pacifism.

1170   HM251.A1J6,v.15

Dudycha, George J.

References in "The attitude of college students toward war."
Journal of Social Psychology, 15, first half (February, 1942):
88-89.

   20 items, 1926 - 1940. English.

   Empirical studies of student attitudes toward war, peace,
   militarism, pacifism, and fascism; works on attitude
   measurement.

1171   BF1.P75,v.39

Dudycha, George J.

Bibliography in "Attitudes toward war."
Psychological Bulletin, 39, 10 (December, 1942): 858-860.

   35 items, 1926 - 1942. English. All items are discussed in
   the text.

   Empirical studies of attitudes toward war, peace, militarism,
   pacifism, and various social issues; works on attitude
   measurement.

1172   U21.F25,1942

Farago, Ladislas and Lewis Frederick Gittler (eds.), with the
cooperation of Gordon W. Allport and Edwin G. Boring.

Bibliography.
In their German Psychological Warfare, with interpretative
summary by Kimball Young.
New York: G. P. Putnam's Sons, 1942 (1st definitive ed.).
pp. 181-296.
First and second editions, New York: Committee for National
Morale, 1941, pp. 90-155; 63-129.

   561 items, 1877 - 1940. German. All items have brief to
   abstract-length descriptive annotations in English;
   introduction (2 pp.).

Psychological Aspects of War

    Examination and critique of past wars (49), mobilization of
German psychology (18), psychological problems of leadership
(22), selection and testing of personnel (89), psychology of
military life (69), psychology of combat (91), strategy and
tactics of psychological warfare (29), fields of
psychological campaigns (17), national psychology (26),
weapons of psychological warfare (151).

1173   D443.K2,1942

Kalijarvi, Thorsten V.

Bibliography in "Psychological aspects of warfare."
In Kalijarvi, Thorsten V. et al., Modern World Politics.
New York: Crowell, 1942. pp. 256-258.

    30 items, 1918 - 1942. English; also French (1), German (1).
Many items have brief descriptive and/or critical
annotations.

    Books (15), articles, booklets, and pamphlets (15) on
psychological warfare, war propaganda, and public opinion.

1174   BF1.J575,v.6

Watkins, John G.

References in "Offensive psychological warfare."
Journal of Consulting Psychology, 6, 3 (May-June, 1942):
121-122.

    15 items, 1920 - 1942. English; also German (1).

    Articles and books on military and industrial psychology,
morale, and psychological warfare.

1175 <

Hirschberg, C.

"Military psychiatry: A summary of some of the literature."
American Journal of Medical Science, 206 (1943): 112-127.

Psychological Aspects of War

1176

Louttit, C. M.

Bibliography in "Mental hygiene problems and programs related
to service in the armed forces."
Review of Educational Research, 13, 5 (December, 1943):
482-484.

   59 items, 1940 - 1943. English.

   Journal articles on psychiatric and psychological services in
   the U.S. military, including personnel selection,
   postinduction adjustment, morale, and special training units
   for the handicapped.

1177   U21.M35

Meier, Norman C.

Bibliography [8 lists].
In his Military Psychology, with a foreword by Ben Lear.
New York/London: Harper and Brothers, 1943. pp. 18-21, 46-50,
82-84, 149-154, 176, 219-221, 250-252, 284-285.

   251 items, 1913 - 1943. English; also German. All German
   items have abstract-length descriptive and/or critical
   annotations.

   Books and articles on causes and effects of war, military
   science, theory of military leadership and military training
   for adjustment to combat, propaganda, psychological warfare,
   and military psychology.

1178   RC343.M49

Mira [y López], Emilio.

Bibliography.
In his Psychiatry in War.
New York: W. W. Norton, 1943. pp.197-198.

   26 items, 1927 - 1942. English; also German (2), French (1),
   Italian (1).

   Books and articles on the psychological effects of war on
   civilians and soldiers, war neuroses, military psychology,
   and the role of psychiatry in war.

Psychological Aspects of War

1179   RC321.J7,v.39

Strauss, Anselm L.

Bibliography in "The literature on panic."
Journal of Abnormal and Social Psychology, 39, 3 (July, 1944):
327-328.

   18 items, 1914 - 1941. English, French. All items are
   discussed in the text.

   Books and articles on the psychological effects of war and
   the causes and prophylactic methods of treating panic among
   troops.

1180   HM1.A75,v.10

Carter, Hugh.

References in "Recent American studies in attitudes toward war:
A summary and evaluation."
American Sociological Review, 10, 3 (June, 1945): 350-352.

   58 items, 1929 - 1944. English. All items are discussed in
   the text.

   Journal articles and a few books on methods of measuring
   attitudes and empirical studies of attitudes toward war and
   the psychological effects of war, particularly among
   students.

1181   U21.C67

Cohen, John.

Bibliography.
In his Human Nature, War, and Society, with a foreword by Lord
Raglan.
London: Watts (The Thinker's Library, No. 112), 1946. pp. 180-
186.

   162 items, 1643 - 1944. English; also German (5).

   Books and articles on psychological causes and effects of
   war, race relations, social psychology, and psychology in
   general.

Psychological Aspects of War

        1182   RA790.A1P75,v.20

Weinberg, Jack.

References in "Group psychotherapy as developed in a military
setting: Its application to civilian therapy."
Psychiatric Quarterly, 20, 3 (July, 1946): 484.

    16 items, 1942 - 1945. English.

    Books and articles on the effects of war and the
    psychological and medical aspects of war.

        1183   JX1952.P35

Eysenck, H. J.

References in "War and aggressiveness: A survey of social
attitude studies."
In Pear, Tom Hatherly (ed.), Psychological Factors of Peace and
War.
London/New York: Hutchinson/Philosophical Library, 1950.
pp. 75-81.
Reprinted, Freeport, New York: Books for Libraries Press (Essay
Index Reprint Series), 1971.

    116 items, 1926 - 1948. English.

    Books and articles on political and social attitudes, social
    psychology, militarism, aggression, pacifism, attitudes of
    students and clergy toward war, public opinion, stereotypes,
    sex differences in attitudes, and the influence of films on
    children.

        1184   JX1952.P35

Himmelweit, Hilde.

References in "Frustration and aggression: A review of recent
experimental work."
In Pear, Tom Hatherly (ed.), Psychological Factors of Peace and
War.
London/New York: Hutchinson/Philosophical Library, 1950.
pp. 189-191.
Reprinted, Freeport, New York: Books for Libraries Press (Essay
Index Reprint Series), 1971.

    42 items, 1901 - 1948. English.

Psychological Aspects of War

Articles and books on experimental studies of frustration, aggression and regression, personality theory, and attitudes toward war.

1185

Cooper, Joseph B.

References in "Psychological literature on the prevention of war."
Bulletin of the Research Exchange on the Prevention of War, 3, 3 (January, 1955): 10-15.

85 items, 1939 - 1954. English.

A list of books and articles derived from a search in Psychological Abstracts, 1941-1953, which yielded over 1100 entries under the headings of conflict, hostility, international, peace, tension, war, and aggression; includes works on the problem of human nature, psychological causes of war, decision-making agencies, national character, stereotypes, nationalism, national policy, war as a symptom, research needs, and prospects for effective world organization.

1186   IU: 016.355Sp31b,no.17-17B

Baldwin, Jacqueline W. (comp.).

Psychological Warfare (Ten titles for a small library; twenty-five titles for college or public library; 100 titles for large public or academic library).
[Washington, D.C.]: Special Libraries Association (Military Librarians Division, Bibliography No. 17; 17A; 17B), June, 1959. 1 p.; 2 pp.; 8 pp.

100 items, 1930 - 1959. English.

Books dealing with modern psychological warfare, image formation, propaganda, brainwashing, Communism, public opinion, mind control, and international communication.

1187   U22.3.G713

Greyerz, Walo von.

Bibliography.

Psychological Aspects of War

In his Psychology of Survival: Human reactions to the
catastrophes of war, translated by Claude Stephenson; preface
by Tage Erlander.
Amsterdam/New York: Elsevier (Elsevier Monographs, Medicine
Section), 1962. pp. 93-96.

  75 items, 1895 - 1958. English, German; also French (2), Danish
  (1), Dutch (1). Introduction (1 paragraph).

  Reactions during bombing attacks (10), anxiety (10), fear and
  terror (3), psychosomatic reactions (6), hysteria (4),
  wartime reactions in children (4), Hiroshima and Nagasaki
  (8), catastrophe and panic (11), society during wartime (11),
  general and miscellaneous (8).

1188

Frank, Jerome D.

References.
In his Sanity and Survival: Psychological aspects of war and
peace, with a preface by J. William Fulbright.
New York: Vintage, 1967. pp. [293]-313.

  Books and articles arranged in endnote format for the
  following chapters: genocidal weapons, no more war, the
  biological roots of why men kill, unintentional or
  unauthorized destructiveness, the psychosocial determinants
  of why men fight, why nations fight, the image of the enemy,
  preparation for nuclear war, psychological aspects of prewar
  crises and war, psychological aspects of disarmament and
  international negotiations, toward a world community, and
  conflict without violence.

1189 <

Reid, Ruth.

War Toys and T.V. Violence: Their effect on children--a
bibliographical survey.
[Berkeley, Calif.]: World Without War Council, 1967. 6 pp.

1190 <

Atkin, S.

[References] in "Notes on motivation for war: Toward a
psychoanalytic social psychology."
Psychoanalytic Quarterly, 40, 4 (October, 1971): 581-583.

Psychological Aspects of War

1191   U21.2.L67

Lopez-Reyes, Ramon.

Bibliography [15 lists]; Suggested readings.
In his Power and Immortality: Essays on strategy, war
psychology, and war control.
New York: Exposition Press (An Exposition-University Book),
1971. pp. 97-99, 109, 116-117, 128-129, 139-140, 171-172, 182,
193, 206-207, 216, 237, 245, 257, 274-275, 287-288, 303-307.

   363 items, 1928 - 1970. English.

   Books under chapter headings: toward mass psychology (54),
   explorations in power (16), explorations in immortality (10),
   the hero and the final synthesis (10), on history (17), on
   war and military order (33), airborne training and group
   dynamics (7), airborne rituals, symbols and behavior (15),
   the military as a system of control (11), image of the
   military (3), on nationalism (19), alternative to sovereignty
   (5), U.N. forces (33), toward understanding war (12);
   suggested readings--on civilization and history (10),
   evolutionary analysis (4), symbolic analysis (31), Buddhism
   (6), war, military and hostility (36), and the social
   condition (31).

1192 <

Fornari, Franco.

[Bibliography].
In his Psychoanalysis of War, translated from the Italian by
Alenka Pfeifer.
New York: Doubleday, 1974. pp. 265-270.

Economic Aspects of War

1193   HJ8645.O5

O´Farrell, Horace Handley.

Bibliography.
In his The Franco-German War Indemnity and Its Economic
Results, with an introduction by Viscount Esher.
London: Harrison and Sons, 1913. pp. 67-76.

   142 items, 1816 - 1912. French, English; also German, Italian
   (1). A few items have brief descriptive annotations.

   Books and articles on national finance, war indemnity,
   comparative and international economic statistics, costs of
   war, and the economic effects of war, with special reference
   to Germany and France and the Franco-Prussian War of 1870.

1194   IU: 330.19355So52k

Sombart, Werner.

Literatur und Quellen [Literature and sources].
In his Krieg und Kapitalismus [War and Capitalism].
Munich/Leipzig: Duncker und Humblot, 1913. pp. 211-232.

   74 items plus additional citations, 1545 - 1911. German,
   French; also English, Italian (6), Spanish (5), Dutch (1).
   Bibliographic essay (74 items), with critical comments
   followed by chapter footnotes (15 pp.) containing additional
   references.

   Reference works, books, and official papers, bibliographies,
   handbooks, articles on military history, military ordnance,
   and economic history.

1195   H5.W4,v.3

Blaustein, Arthur.

"Versuch einer Bibliographie zur Kriegswirtschaftslehre
[Preliminary bibliography of war economics]."
Weltwirtschaftliches Archiv (Jena), 3, 2 (April, 1914):
506-519.

Economic Aspects of War

   407 items, 1870 - 1913. German; also French, English (5).
   Introduction (2 pp.).

   Books, articles, periodicals, and laws on war economy and
   military economy. General (59), population and military
   strength (22), industry and war (11), food supply (30),
   transportation (23), finance (162), war loan banks (12),
   insurance and war (9), Franco-Prussian War 1870-71 (28),
   Balkan War 1912-13 and related issues (10), laws and decrees
   (35), Swiss laws on war economy (6).

1196 <   D635.L38

Lenz, Friedrich.

Literaturangabe.
In his Ist Deutschlands Krieg ein Wirtschaftskrieg? [Is
Germany's war an economic war?]: Über die ökonomischen
Grundlagen des deutsch-britischen Konflikts [On the economic
bases of the German-British conflict].
Berlin: Gebrüder Pastel, 1915 (2nd ed.). pp. 113-119.

1197 <

Pratt, Edwin A.

Bibliography.
In his The Rise of Rail-power in War and Conquest, 1833-1914.
London: P. S. King and Son, 1915. pp. 376-397.

1198 <

Kolchin, Morris.

"War taxation, 1914-1917: List of references to material in the
New York Public Library."
Bulletin of the New York Public Library, 21, 7 (July, 1917):
459-470.
Also published as a pamphlet, New York Public Library Reference
Department, 1917, 14 pp.

1199   HD8051.A62

[United States Department of Labor, Bureau of Labor Statistics].

"Additional material relating to labor in foreign countries as
affected by the war."

Economic Aspects of War

In special issue, Industrial Efficiency and Fatigue in British
Munition Factories.
Bulletin of the U.S. Bureau of Labor Statistics, No. 230 (July,
1917): 196-200.
Also appears in Bulletin No. 122 (Welfare Work in British
Munition Factories) and No. 123 (Employment of Women and
Juveniles in Great Britain during the war), 1917.

   55 items, 1914 - 1917. English.

   Books, articles, bulletins on women in industry (3), labor
   conditions and legislation (25), government regulation of
   industries and commodities (6), wages (3), prices (5),
   employment (3), industrial diseases (1), industrial fatigue
   (4), welfare work (1), coal mining industry (4).

1200 <

United States Department of Labor, Bureau of Labor Statistics.

"List of official documents relating to labor and war in Great
Britain."
Monthly Labor Review, 5 (July, 1917): 172-175.

1201   DLC-DB

[United States Library of Congress, Division of Bibliography].

Brief List on the Mobilization of Labor in the United States
for the War.
[Washington, D.C.]: Library of Congress, Division of
Bibliography, November 17, 1917. 2 pp. (typescript).

   10 items, 1916 - 1917. English. A few items have brief
   descriptive annotations.

   Mostly articles on the conscription of labor.

1202   DLC-DB

[United States Library of Congress, Division of Bibliography].

List of Recent References on Railroads in War.
[Washington, D.C.]: Library of Congress, Division of
Bibliography, June 5, 1917. 14 pp. (mimeo).

Economic Aspects of War

   183 items, 1914 - 1917. English; also French (7), German (1).
   A few items have brief descriptive annotations.

   Bibliographies (5), general references (38), articles in
   periodicals (140).

   1203 <

Lauck, W. Jett.

Bibliography.
In his Cost of Living and the War: An analysis of recent
changes.
Cleveland: Doyle and Waltz, 1918. pp. 179-196.

   1204   DLC-DB

[United States Library of Congress, Division of Bibliography].

List of References on the Financing of Private Enterprises by
the Government in War Time.
[Washington, D.C.]: Library of Congress, Division of
Bibliography, May 13, 1918. 6 pp. (typescript).

   52 items, 1914 - 1917. English; also French (3).

   Articles and official publications from France (3), Great
   Britain (21); additional references from U.S. sources (9),
   speeches in U.S. Congress (19).

   1205   DLC-DB

[United States Library of Congress, Division of Bibliography].

List of References on War-saving, Thrift and Business as Usual
(with Reference to the European War).
[Washington, D.C.]: Library of Congress, Division of
Bibliography, April 22, 1918. 18 pp. (typescript).

   208 items, 1915 - 1918. English. Some items have brief
   descriptive annotations.

   Magazine and journal articles, addresses, and pamphlets on
   war economy, war finance, and specific plans to encourage
   thrift and savings on the part of individuals during World
   War I.

Economic Aspects of War

1206   HB195.S4

Śećerov, Slavko.

Bibliography.
In his Economic Phenomena before and after War: A statistical
theory of modern wars (M.S. thesis, Economics, University of
London).
London/New York: George Routledge and Sons/E. P. Dutton (London
School of Economics and Political Science, Studies in Economics
and Political Science, No. 53), 1919. pp. 193-198.

   116 items, 1863 - 1916. English; also French, German, Italian
   (2).

   Books and journal articles on trade statistics, imports and
   exports, capital, agriculture, war economics, war finance,
   prospects of food suppliers after the war, and raw materials.

1207 <

Watkins, Gordon S.

Bibliography.
In his Labor Problems and Labor Administration in the United
States during the War.
Urbana: University of Illinois (University of Illinois Studies
in the Social Sciences, Vol. 8, No. 4), December, 1919.
pp. 241-244.

1208   HC56.P7,no.18

Baker, Charles Whiting.

Bibliography.
In his Government Control and Operation of Industry in Great
Britain and the United States during the World War.
New York/London/Toronto/Melbourne/Bombay: Oxford University
Press, for the Carnegie Endowment for International Peace,
Division of Economics and History (Preliminary Economic Studies
of the War, No. 18), 1921. p. 135.

   19 items, 1917 - 1919 (some items undated). English.
   Introduction (1 paragraph).

   Books and official documents on industrial mobilization, food
   and transportation administration during World War I.

Economic Aspects of War

1209 <   HC256.2M3

Mendelsohn, Charlotte.

[Bibliography].
In her Wandlungen des liberalen England durch die
Kriegswirtschaft [Changes in Liberal England through the
Wartime Economy].
Tubingen: Mohr, 1921. pp. 127-128.

1210 <

United States Congress, House Committee on Military Affairs.

List of references on profiteering.
In its Universal Mobilization for War Purposes: Hearings . . .
68th Congress, 1st Session on H.J. Res. 128, H.R. 194, H.R.
4841 and H.R. 8111 [Texts included] March 11, 13, and 20, 1924.
Washington, D.C.: U.S. Government Printing Office, 1924.
pp. 152-158.

1211 <

[Matthews, M[ary] Alice (comp.)].

War Debt Problems, with Special Reference to France.
Washington, D.C.: Carnegie Endowment for International Peace,
Library (Reading List No. 10), February 17, 1927. (mimeo).

1212   HB195.T5,1927

Thomas, Norman [M.].

Bibliography.
In his The Challenge of War: An economic interpretation.
New York: League for Industrial Democracy, 1927 (3rd ed., rev.
and enl.). p. 55.
First edition, LID Pamphlet No. 4, April, 1923, pp. 36-[37];
second edition, 1924 (rev.), pp. 43-44.

    16 items, 1913 - 1926. English. Introduction (1 paragraph).

    Books on causes of war, economic and political theory,
    capitalism, and imperialism.

Economic Aspects of War

1213 <

McSwain, John J.

"Universal draft for war--taking the profits out of war [with
select list of references on speculation, extortion, and
fraudulent dealings during certain wars of the United States]."
Congressional Record, 69 (April 26, 1928).

1214   HB195.J6

Johnsen, Julia E. (comp.).

Bibliography.
In her Conscription of Wealth in Time of War.
New York: H. W. Wilson (The Reference Shelf, Vol. 7, No. 5),
September, 1931. pp. [31]-52.

   304 items, 1911 - 1931. English. A few items have brief
   descriptive annotations.

   Bibliographies (3), general references (183), affirmative
   references (55), and negative references (63) directed to the
   debate question "Conscripted wealth should only be used to
   pay war expenses in the event of another war."

1215   DLC-DB

[United States Library of Congress, Division of Bibliography].

The War Industries Board: A bibliographical list.
[Washington, D.C.]: Library of Congress, Division of
Bibliography, January 12, 1932. 14 pp. (typescript).

   132 items, 1917 - 1931 (most items published 1917-1919).
   English. A few items have brief descriptive annotations.

   Bulletins, executive orders, addresses, books, journal and
   magazine articles on the functions of the War Industries
   Board in the areas of price control, resources, and the
   regulation, conversion, and mobilization of industry.

1216   Z6464.A1C3,no.3

Matthews, M[ary] Alice (comp.).

Munitions of War and Embargo on Arms.

Economic Aspects of War

Washington, D.C.: Carnegie Endowment for International Peace,
Library (Brief Reference List No. 3), October 22, 1934. 9 pp.
(mimeo).

   114 items, 1912 - 1934. English. Some items have brief
   descriptive annotations.

   Articles, reports, addresses, and a few books on the
   munitions industry, arms trade, arms limitation, and arms
   embargo.

1217 <

Friedensburg, Ferdinand.

[Bibliography].
In his Die mineralischen Bodenschätze als weltpolitische und
militärische Machtfaktoren [Mineral resources as factors of
world political and military power].
Stuttgart, 1936. pp. 224-253.

1218 <

Institut für Konjunkturforschung, Berlin.

[Bibliography].
In its Industrielle Mobilmachung [Industrial Mobilization]:
Statistische Untersuchungen [Statistical Studies].
Berlin: Institut für Konjunkturforschung, 1936. pp. 94-96.

1219 <

United States Army and Navy Munitions Board.

Industrial Mobilization Plan (with bibliography).
Washington, D.C.: [U.S. Army and Navy Munitions Board], 1936
(rev. ed.).

1220   HB195.A1K7

Hesse, Kurt (ed.).

"Materialien."
In his Kriegswirtschaftliche Jahresberichte [Annual Review of
War Economics], 1937 and 1938.
Hamburg: Hanseatische Verlagsanstalt, 1937 and 1938.
pp. 209-270; 135-203.

Economic Aspects of War

465 and 427 items, 1934 - 1937. German, French, English; also
Italian, Spanish (5), Polish (2), Swedish (2), Dutch (2).
Most items have brief to abstract-length descriptive
annotations; subject indexes; lists of abbreviations.

Periodical literature concerning military economy, raw
materials and fuels, food supply, industrial mobilization,
finance, state control of industry, military technology, etc.
Lists and describes articles from about 20 military and
economic periodicals published in Germany and about 50
periodicals from other countries. The German literature is
listed by publication; the foreign literature is subdivided
topically and by countries (Germany, Austria, Belgium,
France, Great Britain, Italy, Japan, the Netherlands, Poland,
Russia, Sweden, Switzerland, Spain, Czechoslovakia, Turkey,
and U.S.A.). The 1938 volume includes a section with
abstracts of 24 pertinent books published 1936-1938.

1221   HB195.M26

Matthias, Werner.

Benutzte Literatur [Literature cited].
In his Die staatliche Organisation der Kriegswirtschaft
[Government Organization of the War Economy]: In Frankreich,
Grossbritannien, Italien, Tschechoslowakei und den Vereinigten
Staaten von Amerika.
Berlin: Junker und Dünnhaupt (Neue Deutsche Forschungen,
Abteilung Staats-, Verwaltungs-, Kirchen-, Völkerrecht und
Staatstheorie, Band 143), 1937. pp. 218-220.

66 items, 1917 - 1936. German, English, French; also Italian
(3), Polish (1).

Books, articles, and official publications on state control
and defense economy, economic mobilization for war, legal and
administrative aspects of war mobilization and war economy,
particularly in Germany, France, Great Britain, Italy,
Czechoslovakia and the U.S.A.

1222   HB195.M28

Mayer, [Johannes].

Schrifttum [Literature].
In his Preisbildung und Preisprüfung in der Kriegswirtschaft
[Price Control and Price Verification in the War Economy].
Hamburg: Hanseatische Verlagsanstalt (Schriften zur
kriegswirtschaftlichen Forschung und Schulung), 1937.
pp. 62-64.

Economic Aspects of War

85 items, 1900 - 1937. German; also English (1).

Books and articles on war economy and finance, price and wage
control, war profits, and economic planning.

1223   HC57.H9

Hyman, Sonia Zunser.

Bibliography; Sources; Footnotes.
In her Economic Security and World Peace.
New York: League for Industrial Democracy, 1938. pp. 27-29.

67 items, 1921 - 1938. English. Appended list of publications
of the League for Industrial Democracy.

Books (33), sources (14), and footnotes (20) on economic
aspects of war, world economy, economic statistics, and
armament statistics.

1224   HD9013.5.L6

Lorz, F[lorian].

Literaturverzeichnis [Literature list].
In his Kriegsernährungswirtschaft und Nährungsmittelversorgung
[Wartime Food Economy and Food Supply]: Vom Weltkrieg bis Heute
[From the world war until today].
Hannover: M. and H. Schaper, 1938. pp. 222-224.

57 items, 1915 - 1938. German.

Books, articles, statistics, and official publications on
agriculture and war, food supply and production, and war
economy.

1225 <

Muths, Margarete.

Bibliography.
In her Die deutsche Fettlücke und die Möglichkeit ihrer
Schliessung durch die Rückgewinnung der ehemaligen deutschen
Kolonien [The German fat shortage and the possibility of
overcoming it through recapture of the former German colonies].
Berlin: Bohme, 1938. pp. 76-77.

Economic Aspects of War

1226   HB195.P63

Possony, Stefan Th[omas].

[Bibliographic footnotes].
In his Die Wehrwirtschaft des Totalen Krieges [The Military
Economics of Total War].
Vienna: Gerold, 1938. 155 pp.

   Footnote format.

   References for chapters on land war, air war, air defense,
   supplies, transport, and raw materials, a look at the future,
   war economy, resources for military economy, conversion of
   the peace economy, and an outline of a rational military
   economy.

1227   HB195.R5

Richarz, Hugo.

Literaturverzeichnis [Literature list].
In his Wehrhafte Wirtschaft [Economic Preparedness]: Ein
Beitrag zur Begriffsklärung und Methode der
Wehrwirtschaftslehre [A contribution to the conceptual
clarification and method of defense economics].
Hamburg: Hanseatische Verlagsanstalt (Veröffentlichungen des
Instituts für Allgemeine Wehrlehre der Friedrich-Wilhelms-
Universität Berlin, No. 3), 1938. p. 93.

   26 items, 1907 - 1937. German; also English.

   General books on economics and military economy.

1228   HB195.S25

Scherbening, Eberhard.

Literaturverzeichnis [Literature list].
In his Wirtschaftsorganisation im Kriege [Economic Organization
in Wartime]: Mit einer Uebersicht über vorbereitende Massnahmen
im Ausland [With a survey of preparatory measures abroad].
Jena: Gustav Fischer, 1938. pp. 253-258.

   133 items, 1912 - 1937. German; also English, French, Dutch
   (1), Italian (1), Polish (1).

   Books, articles, official publications, and periodicals
   dealing with economic mobilization for war, economic warfare,

Economic Aspects of War

   military administration, and related topics.

   1229   NNC: 338.03W636

   Wiel, Paul.

   [Bibliographic footnotes].
   In his Krieg und Wirtschaft [War and Economy]:
   Wirtschaftskrieg, Kriegswirtschaft, Wehrwirtschaft [Economic
   Warfare, Wartime Economy, Military Economy].
   Berlin: Walter de Gruyter, 1938. xii + 145 pp.

      Approximately 70 items, 1914 - 1938. Some items are discussed
      in footnotes.

      Works on economic war potential, economic aspects of military
      strategy, structure and dynamics of war economy, economic
      mobilization for war, and military economy.

   1230   HF5381.A4

   Bowerman, Charles E. (ed.).

   Bibliography.
   In his The War and American Jobs.
   Chicago: Science Research Associates (Occupational Monograph
   No. 10), 1939. p. [49].

      26 items, 1914 - 1939. English. All of the books have brief
      descriptive annotations.

      Periodicals (15) and books (11) on U.S. economic history and
      economic aspects of U.S. participation in World War I.

   1231 <

   Friedensburg, Ferdinand.

   [Bibliographies in each main chapter].
   In his Das Erdöl im Weltkrieg . . ., mit 4 Karten [Petroleum
   in the World War . . ., with 4 maps].
   Stuttgart, 1939. vi + 131 pp.

Economic Aspects of War

1232 <

League of Nations, Library.

Documentation Relating to the Economic Aspects of War.
Geneva: [League of Nations Library] (Miscellaneous
Bibliographies, No. 9), September, 1939. 74 pp.

1233   HD1536.G3S27

Schröer, Bernard.

Literaturverzeichnis [literature list].
In his Der landwirtschaftliche Arbeitseinsatz als
wehrwirtschaftliches Problem [The Agricultural Labor Force as a
Problem of Military Economy]. (Inaugural-Dissertation . . . ,
Rechts- und Staatswissenschaftlichen Fakultät der Friedrich-
Wilhelms-Universität, Berlin).
Emsdetten: H. and J. Lechte, 1939. pp. 78-81.

   63 items, 1909 - 1938. German; also English (3).

   Books, articles, official publications, and periodicals
   dealing with agricultural labor, war economy, economic
   mobilization, and related topics.

1234 <

Stein, Herbert.

Bibliography.
In his Government Price Policy in the United States during the
World War.
Williamstown, Mass.: Williams College (David A. Wells Prize
Essays, No. 8), 1939. pp. 129-132.

1235   H69.T6,v.5

[Town Hall].

Selected bibliography.
In Carmody, J. et al., special issue, How Will the War
Situation Affect Unemployment?
Town Meeting, 5 (November 13, 1939): 30.

   10 items, 1938 - 1939. English. All items have brief
   descriptive or critical annotations; introduction
   (1 paragraph).

Economic Aspects of War

Current articles, pamphlets, and books on the effects of war
on industry, industrial conditions, and unemployment.

1236   D410.F65,v.15

Wilde, John C. de, with the aid of James Frederick Green and
Howard T. Trueblood.

[Bibliographic footnotes] in "Europe's economic war potential."
Foreign Policy Reports, 15 (October 15, 1939): 178-192.

   Approximately 65 items distributed among 104 footnotes.

   Article compares Britain, France, Germany, Italy, and U.S.S.R.
   on industrial capacity, raw materials, import potential,
   labor reserves, and preparedness in 1939 as compared to 1914.

1237   Z7164.L1P73,1940

Baker, Helen (comp.).

Problems and Policies in Industrial Relations in a War Economy:
A selected, annotated bibliography, with a foreword by J.
Douglas Brown.
Princeton: Princeton University, Industrial Relations Section
(Report No. 60), May, 1940 (rev. ed.). 30 pp.
First edition, December, 1939, 23 pp. (mimeo).

   223 items, 1916 - 1940. English. Most items have brief or
   medium-length descriptive and/or critical annotations;
   foreword (1 p.); table of contents; author index.

   Industrial mobilization and problems during World War I and
   the reconstruction period in the U.S. (110) and Great Britain
   (36), U.S. legislation during the 1930s concerning
   adjustments to war economy (18), current economic problems
   (46), periodicals and news sheets (13).

1238   HC601.E4

Butlin, S. J.

"The political economy of war" [book review essay].
Economic Record, 16, 30 (June, 1940): 96-108.

   16 items, 1939 - 1940. English. All items are critically
   discussed in the text.

Economic Aspects of War

    Books and pamphlets on political economy and the economic
    aspects of war.

    1239   Z1361.D4T6

    Culver [Tompkins], Dorothy [Louise] Campbell (comp.).

    Administration and Organization in Wartime in the United
    States: A bibliography.
    Chicago: Public Administration Service (Publication No. 71),
    1940. 17 pp.

       395 items, 1915 - 1940. English. Some items have brief
       descriptive annotations; table of contents.

       Bibliographies (50), national defense (24), agriculture (14),
       conscription (12), conservation (2), contracts (1), councils
       of defense (2), economic aspects (27), education (4), finance
       (11), food (17), governmental units (6), health (5), housing
       (8), industry (33), labor (31), materials (24), mobilization
       plans (18), the Negro (3), prices and profits (22),
       propaganda (9), subversive activities (20), supply (4), trade
       (11), training (8), transportation (12), utilities (3), War
       Policies Commission (3), postwar conditions (11).

    1240   DLC-DB

    Fuller, Grace Hadley (comp.), under the direction of Florence
    S. Hellman.

    A List of References on Priorities.
    Washington, D.C.: Library of Congress, Division of
    Bibliography, October 26, 1940. 16 pp. (mimeo).

       158 items, 1917 - 1940. English. Some items have brief
       descriptive annotations.

       Articles, books, and pamphlets on economic planning and
       national defense in the United States, with a heavy
       concentration on materials relating to World War I.

    1241   D635.G83

    Grebler, Leo.

    Key to literature.
    In Grebler, Leo and Wilhelm Winkler, The Cost of the World War
    to Germany and to Austria-Hungary, with an introduction by
    James T. Shotwell.

Economic Aspects of War

New Haven/London: Yale University Press/Oxford University
Press, for the Carnegie Endowment for International Peace,
Division of Economics and History, 1940. pp. 108-110.

   61 items, 1912 - 1937. German; also English (8), French (3).

   Books and articles on economic aspects of war, German
   economic war potential, economy during World War I, social
   and economic impact of World War I on Germany.

1242   HC256.4.H67,1940

Horsefield, J[ohn] Keith.

Acknowledgments and bibliography.
In his The Real Cost of the War.
Harmondsworth, England/New York: Penguin Books (Penguin
Special, S76), 1940. pp. 154-155.

   23 items, 1926 - 1940. English. Essay format, with both
   critical and descriptive comments on the works cited.

   Books and articles (mostly British) on war finance, national
   income, economic effects of war, population trends, and
   postwar problems.

1243   Z6464.Z9C25,1940

Matthews, Mary Alice (comp.).

Conscription of Men, Material Resources and Wealth in Time of
War; With Select References on War Profiteering.
Washington, D.C.: Carnegie Endowment for International Peace,
Library (Reading List No. 22), January 4, 1940 (rev. ed.).
15 pp. (mimeo).
Original edition, 1928.

   161 items, 1917 - 1940. English; also French (1). Many items
   have brief descriptive annotations.

   Books, articles, and reports on economic mobilization for war
   and its social and political implications.

Economic Aspects of War

1244   JX1906.A35,no.2

Matthews, Mary Alice (comp.).

[Books, pamphlets and periodical articles . . .]
In her The Cost of War: Quotations on the direct and indirect
cost of war; with select, annotated references on the cost of
war.
Washington, D.C.: Carnegie Endowment for International Peace,
Library (Memoranda Series, No. 2), March 30, 1940. pp. 11-25.
(mimeo).

   149 items, 1899 - 1940. English; also French (3). Most items
   have brief to medium-length descriptive annotations or
   excerpts.

   Books and pamphlets (89) and periodical articles (60).
   Emphasizes economic costs and consequences of war, but also
   includes materials on losses of life, other human and social
   costs of war, the social and economic impact of armaments and
   military expenditures, and some general works on war.

1245   HB195.M43

Mendershausen, Horst.

"Literature on the economics of war: A selected bibliography."
In his Four Lectures on the Economics of War.
Colorado Springs: Colorado College (General Series, No. 225;
Studies Series, No. 29), March, 1940. pp. 46-47.

   52 items, 1899 - 1939. English; also German (8).

   Books and articles on war profits, costs of World War I, war
   economy, and economic effects of war.

1246   HD6961.P7

Princeton University, Industrial Relations Section.

Selected bibliography.
In its Outline of Industrial Relations Policies in Defense
Industries.
Princeton: Princeton University (Industrial Relations Section,
Department of Economics and Social Institutions, Research
Report Series, No. 62), June, 1940. pp. 44-47.

   17 items, 1939 - 1940. English. All items have brief
   descriptive annotations; Introduction (1 paragraph).

Economic Aspects of War

   Recruitment of skilled labor (2), training of skilled and
   semiskilled labor (10), union attitude toward the defense
   program (5).

1247   Z7164.L1P732,1st suppl.

[Princeton University, Industrial Relations Section].

Problems and Policies in Industrial Relations in a War Economy:
Selected references; Supplement, November 15, 1940.
Princeton: Princeton University, Industrial Relations Section
(Bibliographical Series, No. 62), November 15, 1940. 11 pp.

   83 items, 1939 - 1940. English. Most items have brief
   descriptive annotations; table of contents.

   Works on labor supply, employment, training, hours, health,
   production, wage problems, leave of absence provisions, group
   relations, legislation, and government coordination for the
   U.S. and other countries.

1248   HD4811.I65, v.42

Riches, E[dward] J.

[Footnotes] in "Relative wages in wartime."
International Labour Review, 42, 4-5 (October-November, 1940):
214-237.

   43 items, 1921 - 1940. English; also French (2), German (2).
   Some items are discussed in the text.

1249   HJ4653.E8T3

Tax Foundation.

"Bibliography on war profits and excess profits tax."
In its Excess Profits Taxation: A compilation of materials
. . . and a bibliography . . .
New York: Tax Foundation, August 15, 1940. pp. 20-25. (mimeo).

   114 items, 1916 - 1940. English. Foreword (1 paragraph).

   Articles and books on war profits, war finance, economic
   mobilization, and excess profits taxes especially in the
   United States.

Economic Aspects of War

1250   UA23.T6

Tobin, Harold J[ames] and Percy W[ells] Bidwell.

Bibliography.
In their Mobilizing Civilian America.
New York: Council on Foreign Relations, 1940. pp. 259-268.

   129 items, 1916 - 1940. English.

   Books (50), U.S. government publications (63), and periodical
   articles (16) on excess profits taxes, prevention of war
   profiteering, economic mobilization, and war finance.

1251   HG4485.T7,v.71

[Trusts and Estates].

"Bibliography on war and wealth."
Trusts and Estates, 71, 2 (August, 1940): 206-208.

   34 items (no dates given). English. All items have brief
   critical annotations.

   Books on various national economic and monetary policies,
   inflation, and conscription of wealth during wartime.

1252   KF855.G7,1941

Graske, Theodore Wesley.

Bibliography.
In his The Law of Government Defense Contracts.
New York: Baker, Voorhis, 1941. pp. 369-374.

   114 items, 1898 - 1941. English.

   Books (17), handbooks, reports, monographs and miscellaneous
   (21), and law review articles and notes (76) concerning
   contracts for war production, industrial mobilization, and
   legal aspects of defense contracts and production.

Economic Aspects of War

1253   HD4813.I4,ser.B,no.33

International Labor Office [Geneva].

[Bibliographic footnotes].
In its Studies in War Economics.
Montreal/London: P. S. King and Son (Studies and Reports,
Series B--Economic Conditions--No. 33), 1941. 199 pp.

   221 items, 1917 - 1940. English. Some items are discussed in
   the text.

   Economic organization for total war with special reference to
   the workers (7), who shall pay for the war (20), relative
   wages in wartime (43), control of food prices (32), the place
   of housing policy in war economy (52), the effect of war on
   the relative importance of producing centers with special
   reference to the textile industry (67).

1254   Z7164.L1P732,2nd suppl.

[Princeton University, Industrial Relations Section].

Problems and Policies in Industrial Relations in a War Economy:
Selected references; Second supplement, March 1, 1941.
Princeton: Princeton University, Industrial Relations Section
(Bibliographic Series, No. 63), March 1, 1941. 14 pp.

   94 items, 1940 - 1941. English. Most items have brief
   descriptive annotations; table of contents.

   Pamphlets, magazine and journal articles, memoranda, and
   reports on economic mobilization (13), supply of labor,
   employment, and training (25), hours, health, and
   productivity (10), provisions for leave of absence (6), group
   relations (12), proposals concerning production programs in
   defense industries (5), housing (5), legislation and
   government coordination (17), and wage problems (1) in U.S.
   and Britain.

1255   Z7164.L1P732,3rd suppl.

[Princeton University, Industrial Relations Section].

Problems and Policies in Industrial Relations in a War Economy:
Selected references; Third supplement, August 1, 1941.
Princeton: Princeton University, Industrial Relations Section
(Bibliographical Series, No. 64), August 1, 1941. 28 pp.

Economic Aspects of War

182 items, 1940 - 1941. English. Most items have brief
descriptive annotations; table of contents.

Pamphlets, magazine and journal articles, memoranda and
reports on defense economy (29), supply of labor, employment,
and training (63), hours, health, and productivity (11),
accident prevention and industrial hygiene (6), wage problems
and the cost of living (12), group relations (30), provisions
for leave of absence (1), labor proposals concerning defense
production (1), housing (6), legislation and government
coordination (21), additional sources of information (2).

1256   HJ257.S5

Shoup, Carl [Sumner].

Bibliography.
In his Federal Finances in the Coming Decade: Some cumulative
possibilities, 1941-1951.
New York: Columbia University Press, 1941. pp. [111]-113.

41 items, 1939 - 1941. English. Introduction (1 paragraph).

Books and articles on war finance and defense spending.

1257   HB195.S787

Stewart, Maxwell S.

For further reading.
In his How Shall We Pay for Defense?
New York: Public Affairs Committee, Inc. (Public Affairs
Pamphlets, No. 52), 1941. p. 31.

15 items, 1932 - 1940. English.

Books and pamphlets on war finance and economic mobilization.

1258   D410.U7,no.214

Arnold, Thurman, Leo M. Cherne, and Neil H. Jacoby.

Suggested readings in "War profits."
University of Chicago Round Table, 214 (April 19, 1942): 21.

11 items, 1941 - 1942. English. Many items have brief
descriptive annotations.

Economic Aspects of War

   Magazine articles and a few books on war profits and war
   finance.

   1259   HJ258.B3

   Babcock, Chester D., Eber Jeffery, and Archie W. Troelstrup.

   "Films for classroom use; Transcribed radio programs;
   Bibliography."
   In their Paying for the War: A resource unit for teachers of
   the social studies, with a foreword by Roy A. Price.
   Washington, D.C.: National Council for the Social Studies
   (Bulletin No. 18), November, 1942. pp. 60-61, 61-62, 62-69.

     140 items, 1886 - 1942. English. Some items have brief
     descriptive and/or critical annotations.

     Films (7), radio programs (24), books (29), pamphlets (42),
     magazine articles (38) on war economy, the costs of war,
     defense economics, and U.S. financial mobilization for World
     War II.

   1260   H1.A4,v.224

   Baker, Helen.

   "Labor and the war: A selected bibliography."
   Annals of the American Academy of Political and Social Science,
   No. 224 (November, 1942): 190-195.

     63 items, 1940 - 1942. English. Most items have brief
     descriptive annotations; introduction (1 paragraph).

     Articles, reports, government periodicals, and trade union
     journals on labor conditions, industrial relations, and
     governmental and union policies and plans concerning
     production, wages, and hours during and after World War II.

   1261   HD9560.5.B38

   Belo Redondo, [Ernesto].

   Bibliografia.
   In his A Batalha do Petróleo [The Battle for Petroleum].
   Lisbon: A. M. Pereira (Colecção "As grandes batalhas da guerra,"
   Vol. 2), 1942. pp. 289-297.

     175 items (no dates given). French, Portuguese; also English,
     Italian, Spanish, German (6).

Economic Aspects of War

Technical, economic, and political works on the role of oil
and the petroleum industry in the world economy and modern
war.

1262   Z5074.E3U35,no.93

Borg, Walter T. (comp.).

War and Agriculture in the United States, 1914-1941: Selected
references.
Washington, D.C.: U.S. Department of Agriculture, Bureau of
Agricultural Economics (Agricultural Economics Bibliography
No. 93), January, 1942. iv + 43 pp.

   230 items, 1917 - 1941. English. Most items have brief
   descriptive annotations; foreword (1 p.); author/subject
   index.

   Books, pamphlets, journal articles, and official documents
   focusing on agriculture, wartime agricultural policies, and
   the economic effects of war.

1263   DLC-DB

Brown, Ann Duncan (comp.), under the direction of Florence
S. Hellman.

The Effect of War on the Cost of Living: A selected list of
references.
Washington, D.C.: Library of Congress, Division of
Bibliography, June 22, 1942 (rev. ed.). 32 pp. (mimeo).
First edition, June 28, 1941, 17 pp. (mimeo).

   352 items, 1939 - 1942. English; also French (1). Some items
   have brief descriptive annotations; table of contents.

   Books, pamphlets, and journal articles on standards of
   living, wages and wage policies, war economics, famine and
   food supplies, jobs and housing in U.S. (206), Great Britain
   (53), Canada (25), Russia (4), other European countries (14),
   China (11), Japan (3), Latin America (9); general (27).

1264   HJ135.C7

Crum, William Leonard, John F. Fennelly, and Lawrence Howard
Seltzer.

Economic Aspects of War

[Citations in] notes [12 lists].
In their Fiscal Planning for Total War.
New York: National Bureau of Economic Research, 1942. pp. 25-
27, 49-50, 67-68, 100-101, 125-126, 166-167, 214-215, 285-288,
302-304, 315, 336, 351.

   57 items, 1931 - 1942. English. Some items are discussed in
   the footnotes.

1265   Z6207.W8M3

Marketing Laws Survey.

Bibliography of Defense Production Associations and Community
Pools.
[Washington, D.C.]: Marketing Laws Survey (A project of the
Bureau of Foreign and Domestic Commerce, U.S. Department of
Commerce), 1942. 13 pp.

   74 items, 1940 - 1942. English. All items have brief
   descriptive annotations.

   Articles outlining specific plans for industrial mobilization
   and war production in the U.S.

1266   HB195.N4

Neal, Alfred C[larence], et al.

Background references; Sources of current information [10
lists].
In Neal, Alfred C[larence] (ed.), Introduction to War
Economics: By Brown University economists.
Chicago: Richard D. Irwin, 1942. pp. 15, 39, 61, 87, 107,
134-135, 163-164, 196, 217, 236-237.

   84 items, 1918 - 1941. English.

   Books, articles, reports, and journals on the economic
   aspects of war including monetary and banking policies,
   taxation, wages and price controls, labor, industrial
   mobilization, international trade, economic warfare, and the
   costs of war.

Economic Aspects of War

1267   HJ8019.P7

Preiswerk, Susanne.

Literatur.
In her Geschichtlicher Überblick über die Theorien der
Staatsverschuldung [Historical Survey of Theories of National
Debt]: Mit besonderer Berücksichtigung der
volkswirtschaftlichen Zusammenhänge [With special attention to
related economic factors] (Inaugural-Dissertation zur Erlangung
der Würde eines Doktors der Staatswissenschaften der höhen
philosophisch-historischen Fakultät der Universität Basel).
Basel: Universität Basel, 1942. pp. 100-103.

   91 items, 1820 - 1942. German, English; also French (1).

   Books and articles on war economy, war finance, national
   finance, national debt, and general economic policies.

1268   Z7164.L1P732,4th suppl.

Princeton University, Industrial Relations Section.

Problems and Policies in Industrial Relations in a War Economy:
Selected references; Fourth supplement, January 2, 1942.
Princeton: Princeton University, Industrial Relations Section
(Bibliographical Series, No. 66), January 2, 1942. 27 pp.

   175 items, 1941 - 1942. English. Most items have brief
   descriptive annotations; table of contents.

   General (31), supply of labor (44), hours of work (9),
   accident prevention and industrial hygiene (5), wage problems
   (31), group relations (21), provisions for leave of absence
   (2), labor force and defense production (5), housing (5),
   legislation (8), federal administrative agencies (4), social
   insurance (4), additional sources of information (6).

1269   Z7164.L1P732,5th suppl.

Princeton University, Industrial Relations Section.

Problems and Policies in Industrial Relations in a War Economy:
Selected references; Fifth supplement, August 15, 1942.
Princeton: Princeton University, Industrial Relations Section
(Bibliographical Series, No. 69), August 15, 1942. 38 pp.

   241 items, 1940 - 1942. English. Most items have brief
   descriptive annotations; table of contents.

Economic Aspects of War

General (30), supply of labor (70), hours of work (20),
accident prevention and industrial hygiene (16), wage
problems and policies (21), group relations (32), provisions
for leave of absence (9), housing (11), legislation (7),
federal administrative agencies (14), social insurance (3),
labor and postwar problems (6), additional sources of
information (2).

1270   HB1.E5

Rosenbaum, E. M.

"War economics: A bibliographical approach."
Economica, 9 (New Series), 33 (February, 1942): 64-94.

518 items, 1591 - 1941. English, German; also French, Italian.
Ninety-two items are discussed in the text and footnotes
while the rest are merely listed; introduction (1 p.).

Bibliographies (13), general works and articles (107), raw
materials and problems of economic independence (83),
production and control of labor (53), distribution and
control of prices (12), economic mobilization (120), finance
(26), transport (12), other (92).

1271   HB195.S65

Spiegel, Henry William.

Bibliography.
In his The Economics of Total War.
New York/London: D. Appleton-Century (The Century Studies in
Economics), 1942. pp. 359-389.

523 items, 1919 - 1941. English. Some items have brief
descriptive or critical annotations.

Books, journal articles, official documents, and reports on
war economics (28), economic causes of war (51), the nature
of total war (64), labor requirements for total war (28), the
war effort in real economic terms (39), the price system
under the impact of war (47), labor problems in wartime (46),
wartime control of production and consumption (24), the
supply of strategic materials (29), foodstuffs in the
military economy (30), international economic relations in
wartime (77), war finance (46), and the economic effects of
war (14).

Economic Aspects of War

1272   HB195.S78

Stein, Emanuel and Jules Backman (eds.).

Suggested readings [at the end of each chapter].
In their War Economics.
New York: Farrar and Rinehart, 1942. pp. 27, 60, 91, 115, 145,
166, 192-193, 224, 251-252, 284, 310, 335, 364-365, 381, 401,
416, 442-443.

   163 items, 1919 - 1942. English.

   Books and articles on economics of defense policy,
   mobilization of industry, labor, agriculture, and resources,
   war finance, price controls, banking regulations, fiscal
   policies, control of railways and transportation, electrical
   power requirements, wartime housing and rent, foreign trade,
   and consumption primarily in the U.S. prior to and during
   World War II.

1273 <

United States Library of Congress, Legislative Reference
Service.

Economics of War (April 1941-March 1942): Selected and
annotated bibliography of economic problems and policies in
wartime.
Washington, D.C.: [Library of Congress, Legislative Reference
Service] (Bibliographies of the World at War, No. 4), 1942.
120 pp.

1274   HB195.G4

United States Library of Congress, Legislative Reference
Service.

Syllabus for Two Courses of Study of One Term Each on the
Political Economy of Total War, Including an Essay on
Geopolitics.
Washington, D.C.: Georgetown University School of Foreign
Service, 1942. 121 pp.

   1009 items, 1776 - 1942. English. Most items have brief
   descriptive and/or critical annotations; foreword (2 pp.);
   bibliographic note (1 p.); introductions (1-2 pp.) for each
   section; table of contents.

Economic Aspects of War

Peacetime economics (25), wartime economics (35), arms,
equipment, munitions, and implements of war (33), raw
materials (16), agriculture in wartime (59), domestic mining
(23), priorities, rationing, and requisitions in World War I
and II (47), production for war (43), industrial and military
mobilization (47), World War I price control policies (34),
war finance during World War I and II (52), trade and finance
of instruments of economic warfare (63), wartime control of
exports, imports, and funds (47), Lend-Lease Act and
operations (16), warships (75), techniques of economic
warfare (40), oil and war (29), air power (37), economic
demobilization (74), political economy (214). Items include
books, pamphlets, articles, statistics, periodicals, and
government publications.

1275 <

United States Library of Congress, Legislative Reference
Service.

The War Production Program: A bibliography.
Washington, D.C.: [Library of Congress, Legislative Reference
Service], July, 1942.

1276   HD5724.P7

Baker, Helen and Rita B. Friedman.

Selected bibliography.
In their The Use of Part-time Workers in the War Effort.
Princeton: Princeton University, Industrial Relations Section,
Department of Economics and Social Institutions (Research
Report Series, No. 67), June, 1943. pp. 46-48.

19 items, 1941 - 1943. English. All items have brief
descriptive annotations.

United States (6), Great Britain (13).

1277

Browning, Albert J.

[Bibliographic footnotes] in "Price control in war procurement."
Cornell Law Quarterly, 29, 2 (November, 1943): 145-175.

Economic Aspects of War

1278   KF862.Z9G7(Law)

Graske, Theodore Wesley.

Bibliography.
In his Renegotiations of War Contracts.
New York: Baker, Voorhis, 1943. pp. 28-29.

   24 items, 1934 - 1943. English.

   Books (2), law review articles, reports, and notes (16),
   official U.S. government publications (6) on war contracts.

1279   HB195.L36

Lauterbach, Albert T.

"Bibliography on social and economic aspects of modern warfare."
In his Economics in Uniform: Military economy and social
structure.
Princeton/London: Princeton University Press/Oxford University
Press, 1943. pp. 247-278.
An expanded, partially annotated edition was compiled in
collaboration with Robert A. Kann and Deborah A. Hubbard,
"Modern war--its economic and social aspects: A bibliography,"
Princeton: Institute for Advanced Study, 52 pp. (mimeo), 1942.

   776 items, 1918 - 1942. English; also German, French, Italian,
   Spanish (1). Introduction (1 paragraph).

   Books, articles, reports, statistics, and other materials on
   the economic causes and consequences of war, economic
   warfare, economic mobilization for war, and related topics.
   Section divisions are: general (261), the United States
   (107), Great Britain and the Empire (99), the Soviet Union
   (29), Germany (155), Italy (45), France (34), Japan and the
   Far East (46).

1280   HB195.M4,1943

Mendershausen, Horst.

Suggested references.
In his The Economics of War.
New York: Prentice-Hall, 1943 (rev. ed.). pp. 363-380.
First edition, 1940.

Economic Aspects of War

215 items, 1913 - 1942. English; also German (1). All items
have brief descriptive annotations.

Introductory works (12), manpower (8), raw materials (19),
planned economy (12), war production (9), war mobilization
(14), allocations (8), price control (27), labor and war
production (17), war finance (19), civilian sector (15),
foreign trade, shipping and international cooperation (12),
economic warfare and war economy of neutral countries (8),
postwar population (9), economic demobilization and
reconstruction (17), postwar finance (9).

1281

[New York Public Library, Readers´ Advisers].

"The consumer in the war [bibliography]."
New York Public Library, Branch Library Book News, 20, 2
(February, 1943): 44-46.

43 items, 1940 - 1943. English. All items have brief
descriptive and/or critical annotations.

Adapting the budget to wartime (12), marketing and rationing
(8), food and nutrition (14), the consumer movement (9).

1282

Parker, Norman C.

[Bibliographic footnotes] in "Renegotiation of war contracts."
Missouri Bar Journal, 14, 6 (June, 1943): 136-138, 141.

17 items, 1941 - 1943. English.

Journal articles, official reports, U.S. congressional acts,
and executive orders dealing with government war contracts
and their renegotiation.

1283 <

[United States Library of Congress, Legislative Reference
Service].

Selected and Annotated Bibliography on Raw Materials in a
Wartime Economy.
Washington, D.C.: Library of Congress, Legislative Reference
Service, 1943.

Economic Aspects of War

1284   JK1108.A35,no.27

Allen, Julius W. (comp.).

"Termination of war contracts, 1943-1944: A selected list of
references."
In United States Library of Congress, Legislative Reference
Service, Termination of War Contracts.
Washington, D.C.: Library of Congress, Legislative Reference
Service (Public Affairs Bulletin No. 27), February, 1944.
pp. 17-26. (mimeo).

   64 items, 1943 - 1944. English. All items have brief
   descriptive annotations.

   Articles, governmental and nongovernmental committee reports
   and hearings on the termination of war contracts and
   industrial reconversion in the postwar period.

1285 <

Cleveland Public Library, Business Information Bureau.

Contract Termination: A list of references.
Cleveland: Cleveland Public Library, Business Information
Bureau, 1944. 5 pp. (mimeo).

   Apparently unavailable. Not located through interlibrary
   loan.

1286   DLC-DB

Fuller, Grace Hadley (comp.).

Renegotiation of War Contracts: A selected list of references.
Washington, D.C.: Library of Congress, General Reference and
Bibliography Division, August 12, 1944. 18 pp. (mimeo).

   176 items, 1942 - 1944. English. Some items have brief
   descriptive annotations.

   Association papers, congressional reports, research
   bulletins, and articles on renegotiation of contracts and
   other problems of war contracts, war profits, and government
   regulation.

Economic Aspects of War

1287   HJ8011.L37

Laufenburger, Henry.

Bibliographie sommaire.
In his Crédit Public et Finances de Guerre, 1914-1944
(Allemagne, France, Grande-Bretagne) [Public Credit and War
Finance, 1914-1944 (Germany, France, Great Britain)].
Paris: Librairie de Médicis, 1944. pp. 261-262.

  46 items, 1914 - 1944. French; also English (3), German (2).

  Books (34), journals and reports (12), on public finance,
  political economy, monetary policies, and war finance.

1288   HF5601.A6,v.19

Prickett, A. L.

Bibliography in "General principles of cost accounting."
Accounting Review, 19, 2 (April, 1944): 179-180.

  37 items, 1936 - 1943. English.

  Committee reports and articles relating to war finance, war
  contracts and their termination, and accounting problems
  during World War II.

1289   HG8055.S3

Schwandt, Johannes.

Schrifttumverzeichnis [Literature list].
In his Das Deutsche Kriegssachschädenrecht [The German Law of
War Damage Compensation].
Berlin/Potsdam/Vienna: Spaeth und Linde (Bücherei des
Steuerrechts, Bd. 53), 1944. pp. 13-15.

  44 items, 1915 - 1944. German.

  Books on compensations for war damages, taxation, modes of
  payment, and laws governing indemnities.

Economic Aspects of War

1290   Z675.F5S7,v.6

[Special Libraries Association, Financial Group].

"Bibliography on contract termination and reconversion of
industry."
SLA Financial Group Bulletin, 6, 3 (March, 1944): 9-10.

   26 items, 1943 - 1944. English. Introduction (1 paragraph).

   U.S. government documents and private organizations´ reports
   on termination of war contracts, postwar economic policy,
   postwar employment, reconversion of war industry, and postwar
   readjustments.

1291   KF862.M52X

University of Michigan, Law School.

[Bibliographic footnotes].
In its Renegotiation and Termination of War Contracts, 1942-
1944.
Ann Arbor: University of Michigan (Official Publication, Vol.
45, No. 122), April 8, 1944. 152 pp.

   Some items are discussed in the text.

1292   KF855.G7,1945

Graske, Theodore W[esley].

Bibliography.
In his The Law Governing War Contract Claims.
New York: Baker, Voorhis, 1945. pp. 637-642.

   88 items, 1909 - 1945. English.

   Books on war contracts (9), articles, reports, and notes on
   contract cancellation (41), renegotiation and repricing (15),
   arbitration and administrative appeals (8), and contract
   claims generally (15).

1293   HA1.A6,v.40

Parkin, Norman C.

[Bibliographic footnotes] in "Management statistics in war
contract renegotiation."

Economic Aspects of War

Journal of the American Statistical Association, 40, 232,
Part 1 (December, 1945): 504-515.

19 items, 1921 - 1945. English. Some items are discussed in
the footnotes.

Articles and congressional acts on war contracts, pricing,
and management control.

1294   HB195.S22,1945

Salzmann, Juan Jorge.

Bibliografía [11 lists]; Bibliografía general.
In his Economia de Guerra [War Economy].
Buenos Aires: Guillermo Kraft, 1945. pp. 41, 92, 112, 133, 145,
211, 232, 257, 277, 314, 354, 355-367.

406 items, 1919 - 1944. English; also German, Spanish, French
(2).

Books and articles on economic aspects of war and peace,
causes of war, economic warfare, war economy, economic
mobilization for war, total war, political economy, war
finance, modern warfare, international trade, and
international relations.

1295   HG2307.V7

Vredegoor, H. W. J. A.

Literatuurlijst [Literature list].
In his Monetaire Vraagstukken [Monetary Problems]: Tijdens en
na den oorlog [During and after the war].
Amsterdam/Brussels: Elsevier (Elseviers Economische
Bibliotheek), 1945. pp. 341-342.

45 items, 1937 - 1942. Dutch, German, English.

Books and periodicals on the costs of war, war finance, and
war economy.

1296

Silberner, Edmund.

Bibliography.

Economic Aspects of War

In his The Problem of War in Nineteenth Century Economic
Thought, translated by Alexander H. Krappe.
Princeton: Princeton University Press, 1946. pp. 299-324.
Reprinted, with a new introduction by Dennis Sherman, New
York/London: Garland (Garland Library of War and Peace), 1972.

   489 items, 1707 - 1943. French, English; also German, Italian,
   Spanish. Introduction (2 pp.).

   Primary works by classical (liberal) economists,
   protectionists, and socialists (411) and auxiliary works on
   the history of economic thought (78) dealing with the
   economic causes and effects of war and with the possibility
   and means of war prevention; many items listed are general
   works on political economy.

1297   HD3858.U58,1947

United States Office of Contract Settlement.

Bibliography.
In its A History of War Contract Terminations and Settlements.
Washington, D.C.: U.S. Government Printing Office, July, 1947.
pp. 66-84.

   437 items, 1915 - 1947. English.

   World War I (46), World War I legislative acts (13), World
   War II (339), World War II legislative acts (39).

1298   HD3616.U46W6

Worsley, Thomas Blanchard.

Bibliography.
In his Wartime Economic Stabilization and the Efficiency of
Government Procurement: A critical analysis of certain
experience of the United States in World War II (Ph.D.
dissertation, Economics, University of Virginia, June, 1948).
Washington, D.C.: National Security Resources Board, 1949.
pp. 398-422.

   418 items, 1918 - 1949. English.

   Public documents (189), books (67), private journals,
   articles, pamphlets, and bulletins (162) on various agency
   and departmental policies and regulations concerning wages
   and prices, economic mobilization, inflation, fiscal
   planning, war contracts and renegotiation, war finance, food

Economic Aspects of War

    supply, the Office of Price Administration, rationing, war
    economy, war profits, and war taxation.

    1299   HJ135.L3

    Lanter, Max.

    Literatur.
    In his Die Finanzierung des Krieges [The Financing of War]:
    Quellen, Methoden und Lösungen seit dem Mittelalter bis Ende
    des zweiten Weltkrieges 1939 bis 1945 [Sources, methods, and
    solutions from the Middle Ages to the end of the second World
    War 1939 to 1945].
    Lucerne: Eugen Haag, 1950. pp. 211-217.

    220 items, 1630 - 1948. German, English; also French, Italian,
    Latin (1).

    Official publications, statistics, reference works,
    periodicals, books, and some articles on war costs, war
    finance, political economy, public finance, war and
    capitalism, reparations, inflation, economic effects of war,
    and economic mobilization for war.

    1300   HB195.C43

    Chandler, Lester V[ernon] and Donald H[olmes] Wallace (eds.).

    Selected bibliography.
    In their Economic Mobilization and Stabilization: Selected
    materials on the economics of war and defense.
    New York: Henry Holt, 1951. pp. 595-605.

    156 items, 1918 - 1951. English. Introduction (1 p.).

    Government publications, books, pamphlets, and articles on
    the economics of war and defense (57), wartime controls on
    the use of economic resources (27), war finance and economic
    stabilization (17), direct stabilization controls in wartime
    (36), economics of a limited defense program (15);
    bibliographies (4).

    1301   HC106.5.H318

    Harris, Seymour E[dwin].

    A bibliographical note.
    In his The Economics of Mobilization and Inflation.

Economic Aspects of War

  New York: W. W. Norton, 1951. pp. 288-291.

    29 items, 1903 - 1950. English. All items have brief critical
    annotations; introduction (1 paragraph) plus introductory and
    concluding comments to some sections.

    General books on war economics (11), books relating to
    particular episodes (5), and special aspects of war economics
    (5); official documents (8).

  1302   HC106.5.B28

  Backman, Jules, et al.

  Suggested readings [15 lists].
  In their War and Defense Economics: Containing text of Defense
  Production Act incorporating 1951 amendments.
  New York: Rinehart, 1952. pp. 17-18, 44-45, 73, 111-112, 138,
  161, 187, 213, 239, 276, 301, 333-334, 346, 367, 402.

    132 items, 1918 - 1951. English.

    Books and articles on economics of war and American defense,
    political economy of war, economic mobilization, raw
    materials for war effort, agricultural output during war,
    labor, wages, and management during wartime, rationing and
    price control.

  1303   Z7164.E2W33

  Chęciński, M[ichał], P. Jurgaś, and Zb. Skibiński (comps.).

  Bibliografia Ekonomiki Wojennej [Bibliography of War
  Economics]: Zesyt I-próbny [No. 1--provisional].
  Warsaw: Wojskowa Academia Polityczna (Zakład Ekonomiki
  Wojennej), 1959. vii + 122 pp. (mimeo.)

    1110 items, 1900 - 1959. German, Polish; also English, French,
    Italian, Dutch (2), Spanish (2), Portuguese (1). Introduction
    (7 pp.); main bibliography (97 pp.) contains chiefly works in
    German, 1912-1940; a supplementary bibliography (19 pp.)
    contains chiefly works in Polish, published after 1945, with
    a small number of items extending back to 1900; provisional
    subject index lists some authors according to their principal
    interests.

    Books and articles on military economy, industrial
    mobilization for war, armaments, and related topics.

Economic Aspects of War

1304   IU: 016.355Sp31b,no.15b

Widger, Clara J. (comp.).

Economics of War and Economic Warfare: One hundred titles for
the large public or academic library.
[Washington, D. C.]: Special Libraries Association, Military
Librarians Division (Bibliography No. 15B), May, 1959. 7 pp.
Bibliography No. 15 contains 10 titles for a small library.

  93 items, 1915 - 1958. English. A few items have brief
  descriptive annotations.

  Books, pamphlets, and reports on economic warfare, economic
  mobilization for war, and military economy.

1305   UA929.6.A85

American Society of Corporate Secretaries.

"Selected sources of references and guidance in preparing for
industrial civil defense."
In its Continuity of Corporate Management in Event of Nuclear
Attack: A special report to corporate secretaries.
Washington, D.C.: U.S. Department of Defense, Office of Civil
Defense, Directorate for Industrial Participation, 1963. pp.
83-89.

  63 items, 1951 - 1962. English. Most items have brief to
  medium-length descriptive annotations; introduction (1 p.).

  Monographs, pamphlets, handbooks, and articles on emergency
  planning in the areas of industry, business, and banking in
  case of natural disasters or nuclear attack.

1306   HB195.L5

Libicki, Bolesław.

Literatura.
In his Ekonomiczne Aspekty Wojny [Economic Aspects of War].
Warsaw: Wydawnictwo Ministerstwa Obrony Narodowej (Biblioteka
Polskiej Myśli Woskowej), 1964. pp. 341-348.

  168 items, 1899 - 1963. Polish, English; also German, Russian,
  French (5). Introduction (1 paragraph).

  Books and articles on military history, military strategy,
  war economy, economic and industrial mobilization, nuclear
  weapons, and economic effects of war.

Economic Aspects of War

1307   HC65.C55

Clark, John J.

Suggestions for further reading [6 lists].
In his The New Economics of National Defense.
New York: Random House, 1966. pp. 36-38, 72-73, 116-117,
143-144, 186-190, 229-233.

   220 items, 1929 - 1964. English.

   Books and articles on the economist and the military (28),
   management and systems analysis (22), game theory (29),
   economic theory and theory of conflict (17), economic warfare
   (64), war and economic progress (60).

1308   HB195.S775

Stankiewicz, Wacław.

Bibliografia.
In his Rozwoj Angielskiej Myśli Wojenno-Ekonomicznej [The
Development of English Thought on War Economy].
Warsaw: Wydawnictwo Ministerstwa Obrony Narodowej, 1966.
pp. 361-371.

   254 items, 1601 - 1963. English; also Polish, German (4),
   French (1).

   Books, lectures, and documents on general economic history,
   war economy, wartime economic planning, monetary policies,
   inflation, war finance, rationing, price controls, food
   supply, the economic effects of war, economic reconstruction,
   political economy, and the costs of war.

1309   HD9000.5.C5

Chęciński, Michał.

Wykaz cytowanej bibliografii [List of references cited].
In his Rolnictwo I Wyżywienie w Wojnie Współczesnej
[Agriculture and Food Supply in Contemporary War]: Zarys
problemów [Sketch of the problems].
Warsaw: Wydawnictwo Ministerstwa Obrony Narodowej, 1967.
pp. 277-287.

Economic Aspects of War

   193 items, 1901 - 1967. German, Polish; also English, Russian,
   French (5).

   Books and articles on agriculture, the effects of war on
   agriculture, wartime agricultural policies, economic
   mobilization for war, and economic war potential.

1310   HB195.G68,1967

Grand-Jean, Paul.

Bibliographie.
In his Guerres, Fluctuations et Croissance [Wars, Fluctuations
and Growth], with a preface by A. Cotta.
Paris: Société d´Edition d´Enseignement Supérieur (Observation
Economique), 1967. pp. vii-xi.

   114 items, 1915 - 1963. English, French; also Italian (1).
   Introduction (1 paragraph).

   Books and articles (71) on economic problems during and after
   World Wars I and II; general works (43) on economic history
   and theories of economic growth and stability.

1311   HC286.4.C3

Carroll, Berenice A[nita].

Bibliography.
In her Design for Total War: Arms and economics in the Third
Reich.
The Hague/Paris: Mouton (Studies in European History, 17),
1968. pp. [273]-280.

   250 items, 1902 - 1966. English, German; also French.

   Books and articles on total war in the twentieth century, war
   economics, German rearmament and economic mobilization for
   World War II, and biographies of German military and
   political leaders.

1312   HC110.D4J3

[Kaechele, Carol (comp.)].

Bibliography.
In Janeway, Eliot, The Economics of Crisis: War, politics and
the dollar.

Economic Aspects of War

  New York: Weybright and Talley, 1968. pp. 303-311.

    195 items, 1850 - 1967. English.

    Books and articles on economic history, monetary policies,
    economic planning and theories of economic growth, finance,
    economic mobilization, imperialism, diplomacy, histories of
    specific wars, and biographies of various political and
    economic leaders.

  1313 <

  Winter, J. M. (ed.).

  "Select bibliography of works on war and economic development."
  In his War and Economic Development: Essays in memory of David
  Joslin.
  Cambridge: Cambridge University Press, 1975. pp. 257-292.

  1314

  Milward, Alan S.

  Bibliography.
  In his War, Economy and Society: 1939-1945.
  Berkeley/Los Angeles: University of California Press, 1977.
  pp. 366-388.

Social and Political Aspects of War

1315   HV1.S8,v.39

McBride, Christine and Susan M. Kingsbury.

"Social welfare in time of war and disaster: A bibliography."
Survey, 39, 4 (October 27, 1917): 94-96, 100-101; 10 (December
18, 1917): 287-289, 301; 16 (January 19, 1918): 441-443; 21
(February 23, 1918): 570-572; 25 (March 23, 1918): 682-684.

690 items, 1906 - 1918 (most items published in 1917).
English. Many items have brief descriptive and/or critical
annotations.

Articles, reports, and handbooks on women's services in
wartime (16), civilian relief in wartime (137), relief work
in time of disaster (15), child welfare (54), social hygiene
and moral prophylaxis in wartime (102), the problem of
disabled soldiers and sailors (142), industrial adjustment in
wartime (213), employment (8), and general subjects (3).

1316 <

Scott, Emmett J.

Bibliography.
In his Negro Migration during the War.
Washington, D.C.: Carnegie Endowment for International Peace
(Preliminary Economic Studies of the War, No. 16), 1920. pp.
175-183.

1317   DLC-DB

[United States Library of Congress, Division of Bibliography].

List of References on the Declaration of War by Popular Vote.
[Washington, D.C.]: Library of Congress, Division of
Bibliography, January 26, 1922. 2 pp. (typescript).

19 items, 1871 - 1921. English. A few items have brief
descriptive annotations.

Mostly magazine articles for or against the establishment of
a war referendum as a means of preventing war.

Social and Political Aspects of War

1318   PN4181.U5,1925/26

[Ball, Eleanor B. (comp.)].

Bibliography: "Popular referendum on war."
In Phelps, Edith M. (ed.), University Debaters´ Annual:
Constructice and rebuttal speeches delivered in debates of
American colleges and universities during the college year,
1925-1926 [Vol.XII].
New York: H. W. Wilson, 1926. pp. 279-281.

    37 items, 1897 - 1924. English.

    Books, pamphlets, and documents (10), magazine and newspaper
articles (27) directed to the debate resolution "That war,
except in cases of invasion or internal rebellion, should be
declared by direct vote of the people."

1319   H35.I6,v.8

Nichols, Egbert Ray (ed.).

"List of references on declaration of war by direct vote of the
people."
In his Intercollegiate Debates: A year book of college
debating, Vol. VIII.
New York: Noble and Noble, 1927. pp. 385-387.

    35 items, 1908 - 1924. English. Introduction (1 paragraph).

    Books and pamphlets (9), magazine and newspaper articles (26)
relating to the debate resolution "That the people should
have the right to declare war by direct vote except in case
of rebellion or invasion."

1320   DLC-DB

[United States Library of Congress, Division of Bibliography].

List of References on the Declaration of War by Popular Vote.
Washington, D.C.: Library of Congress, Division of
Bibliography, March 15, 1934 [2nd ed.]. 4 pp. (typescript).

    36 items, 1897 - 1932. English; also French (1). Some items
have brief descriptive annotations.

    Books, articles, pamphlets, and congressional hearings on
conscription referendum and war referendum proposals in
Australia and the U.S.

Social and Political Aspects of War

1321 <

[Debaters´ Digest].

Selected references in "Should a war-referendum amendment be
adopted?"
Debaters´ Digest, 12 (January, 1938).

1322   Z6464.Z9C53,1938

Matthews, M[ary] Alice (comp.).

Referendum on War.
Washington, D.C.: Carnegie Endowment for International Peace,
Library (Reading List No. 2), November 14, 1938 (rev. ed.).
8 pp. (mimeo).
Originally appeared in 1926. An earlier four-page revised
edition is dated October 24, 1935.

   120 items, 1915 - 1938. English; also French (1). A few items
   have brief annotations and excerpts; introduction (1
   paragraph).

   Magazine articles, speeches, and hearings on the Ludlow war
   referendum amendment, a proposed peace amendment to the U.S.
   Constitution, introduced in the U.S. House of Representatives
   in February, 1935, by Louis Ludlow of Indiana.

1323   H35.I6,v.19

Nichols, Egbert Ray (ed.).

"Bibliography on war referendum."
In his Intercollegiate Debates: A year book of college
debating, Vol. XIX.
New York: Noble and Noble, 1938. p. 245.

   24 items, 1936 - 1938. English.

   Magazine articles and speeches dealing with the pros and
   cons of the Ludlow amendment.

Social and Political Aspects of War

1324 <

Mock, J. R. and Cedric Larson.

[Bibliography of the informational and propaganda problem
during the last war].
In their Words That Won the War.
Princeton: Princeton University Press, 1939.

1325   H69.T6,v.4

[New York Public Library, Readers´ Advisers].

Selected bibliography.
In Thomas, Norman M. et al., special issue, Should We Have a
War Referendum?
Town Meeting, 4, 25 (May 1, 1939): 33.

  9 items, 1935 - 1939. English. All items have brief
  descriptive annotations; introduction (1 paragraph).

  Books and articles on American foreign policy, the war
  referendum, and U.S. isolationism.

1326   HQ728.W33

Waller, Willard [Walter].

Selected bibliography.
In his War and the Family.
New York: Dryden Press, 1940. pp. 50-51.

  20 items, 1916 - 1939. English.

  Books and articles on the social and human costs of war.

1327   H1.A4,no.217

Mannheim, Hermann.

[Bibliographic footnotes] in "Crime in wartime England."
Annals of the American Academy of Political and Social Science,
No. 217 (September, 1941): 128-137.

  30 items, 1940 - 1941. English.

  Books and articles on the relationship between war and crime
  and the treatment of juvenile delinquents.

Social and Political Aspects of War

1328   HV6189.M3

Mannheim, Hermann.

[Footnote references].
In his War and Crime.
London: Watts, 1941. ix + 208 pp.

  Approximately 230 items, 1833 - 1940. English; also German,
  French (6).

  References to chapters on the relationship between war and
  crime (27), the causes of war and the causes of crime (68),
  the influence of war on crime prior to 1914 (29), during
  World War I (40), the outlook for World War II (23), just
  wars and war crimes (35), and war as punishment (25). Some
  items cited more than once.

1329   D443.K2

Roucek, Joseph Slabey.

Bibliography in "War as a symptom of our social crisis."
In Kalijarvi, Thorsten V., et al., Modern World Politics.
New York: Crowell, 1942. pp. 606-608.

  32 items, 1936 - 1941. English. Some items have brief
  critical annotations.

  Books (14), articles and pamphlets (18) on war and the causes
  of war, particularly from a sociological perspective.

1330   Z6461.C29,no.12

Scanlon, Helen Lawrence (comp.).

Freedom of Communication in Wartime: Select list of references
on censorship in time of war.
Washington, D.C.: Carnegie Endowment for International Peace,
Library (Select Bibliographies, No. 12), April 27, 1942. 11 pp.
(mimeo).

  134 items, 1906 - 1942. English; also French (2). Some items
  have brief descriptive annotations.

  Books, pamphlets, articles, and official documents on freedom
  of speech and of the press, civil liberties, censorship, and
  espionage during wartime.

Social and Political Aspects of War

1331 <

Baer, K. A.

"The war and social problems: A selected bibliography (material
to April 1, 1943)."
Russell Sage Foundation Library Bulletin, No. 160 (1943): 15.

1332   HV9261.F4,v.7-10

[Federal Probation].

"Reviews of professional periodicals [16 lists]; Your bookshelf
on review [16 lists]."
Federal Probation, 7-10 (1943 to 1946).

   Each quarterly issue contains extensive abstracts of about
   20-25 articles from several of the following journals:
   American Journal of Sociology, American Journal of
   Orthopsychiatry, The Family, Journal of Criminal Law and
   Criminology, Journal of Criminal Psychopathology, Mental
   Hygiene, Prison World, Probation, Social Service Digest,
   Social Service Review, and Survey Midmonthly. Each issue
   also contains reviews of 10-15 books. Although most items
   deal with general problems in criminology, a substantial
   number deal with social and psychological effects of war or
   with the relationship between war and crime, criminals and
   the war effort, etc.

1333   D802.A2K8

Kulischer, Eugene M.

[Footnote references].
In his The Displacement of Population in Europe.
Montreal/London: International Labour Office/P. S. King and
Staples, 1943. iv + 171 pp.

   Approximately 315 items, 1940 - 1943. German, English; also
   French, Russian, Eastern and Western European languages,
   Yiddish (1).

   Statistical works and reports on migration movements of
   German people, movements of non-German populations (Jewish
   and non-Jewish), and the mobilization of foreign labor by
   Germany during the early years of World War II.

Social and Political Aspects of War

1334   SB469.L3,v.34

McNamara, Katherine (comp.).

"War memorials: A selected bibliography."
Landscape Architecture, 34, 4 (July, 1944): 127-130.

   79 items, 1916 - 1944. English. A few items have brief
   descriptive annotations; introductory note (1 paragraph).

   Articles, pamphlets, and reports on war memorials, mostly
   from the architect's perspective.

1335   Z7164.C84D3

Dahir, James (comp.).

Community Centers as Living War Memorials: A selected
bibliography with interpretative comments, with a foreword by
Russell H. Kurtz.
New York: Russell Sage Foundation, 1946. 63 pp.

   204 items, 1897 - 1946. English. 102 items are grouped and
   discussed by topics, the rest are merely listed by topics
   under additional reading references; foreword (1 p.).

   Articles, reports, bulletins, pamphlets, and a few books on
   community centers (27), living war memorials (30), aids in
   establishing community centers (8), types of community
   centers (64), neighborhood organization (15), programs (15),
   buildings and facilities (10), school community centers (16);
   British references (11), Canadian references (8).

1336   NA9325.W5

Whittick, Arnold.

Bibliography.
In his War Memorials.
London: Country Life, 1946. pp. 163-166.

   87 items, 1631 - 1939. English; also German (3), French (2).
   Some items have brief descriptive and/or critical
   annotations; introduction (1 paragraph).

   Books and articles on war memorials throughout history (53);
   books on related subjects including architecture (9),
   lettering (7), sculpture (12), and symbolism (6).

Social and Political Aspects of War

1337   HB3593.I2

Ibarrola, Jésus.

Bibliographie.
In his Les Incidences des Deux Conflits Mondiaux sur
l´Evolution Démographique Française [The Effects of the Two
World Wars on French Demographic Evolution], with a preface by
Jean Maillet.
Paris: Dalloz (Essais et Travaux, l´Université de Grenoble,
20), 1964. pp. 271-274.

  56 items, 1923 - 1961. French; also Italian (1).

  Some general works on the French economy, French
  civilization, and historical and contemporary social and
  political conditions; mostly works on armament, demographic
  characteristics of France, and the effects of war on the
  French populace.

1338   F2520.1.T94F38,1970

Fernandes, Florestan.

Lista de estudos sôbre a guerra entre "povos primitivos";
Bibliografia [List of studies on war among "primitive peoples";
bibliography].
In his A Função Social da Guerra na Sociedade Tupinambá [The
Social Function of War in Tupinamba Society].
Sao Paulo, Brazil: Livraria Pioneira Editôra da Universidade de
São Paulo (Biblioteca Pioneira de Ciências Sociais), 1970
(2nd ed.). pp. 398-401, 402-423.

  339 items, 1575 - 1951. English, French; also Portuguese,
  German, Spanish, Italian (7).

  Studies on wars between "primitive peoples" (32), primary
  sources (35), ethnologies and histories of the Tupinamba
  (18), historical method and functionalism (44), works on war
  in general (80), partial contributions to the study of war as
  a social phenomenon (57), sociological and anthropological
  theory (73).

Social and Political Aspects of War

1339 <

Schaich, W.

[References] in "Relationship between collective racial
violence and war."
Journal of Black Studies, 5 (June, 1975): 392-394.

1340 <

Stohl, Michael.

[References] in "War and domestic political violence: The case
of the U.S., 1890-1970."
Journal of Conflict Resolution, 19, 3 (September, 1975):
412-415.

Legal Aspects of War

1341   DLC-DB

[United States Library of Congress, Division of Bibliography].

List of Works on Contraband of War.
[Washington, D.C.]: Library of Congress, Division of
Bibliography, [1904]. 6 pp. (typescript).

   36 items, 1859 - 1904. English, French.

   Historical and legal works on contraband of war and
   international law.

1342   Z6464.A1C3,no.6

Matthews, Mary Alice (comp.).

Demilitarized Zones.
Washington, D.C.: Carnegie Endowment for International Peace,
Library (Brief Reference List No. 6), April 3, 1935. 4 pp.
(mimeo).

   40 items, 1875 - 1935. English, French; also German (2). Many
   items have brief descriptive annotations.

   General articles (14), treaties containing provisions for
   demilitarized zones (14), definition of aggression in
   international law (7), other Carnegie Endowment brief
   reference lists (5).

1343   JA1.A6

Gonsiorowski, Miroslas.

[Footnotes] in "The legal meaning of the pact for the
renunciation of war."
American Political Science Review, 30, 4 (August, 1936):
653-680.

   French, English, German.

   Works on international law and the Kellogg Peace Pact.

Legal Aspects of War

1344   JX4003.T5

Théry, René.

Bibliography.
In his La Notion d´Agression en Droit International [The Idea
of Aggression in International Law] (Doctoral thesis, Droit,
Université de Lille, June 14, 1937).
Paris: A. Pedone, 1937. pp. 249-254.

   96 items, 1913 - 1937. French; also English (3).

   Works on international law, definitions of aggression,
   nonaggression treaties; League of Nations documents on arms
   reduction and international arbitration.

1345   JX74.H3,v.64

Boye, Thorvald.

Bibliography in "Quelques aspects du développement des règles
de la neutralité [Some aspects of the development of rules of
neutrality]."
Recueil des Cours, Académie de Droit International de la Haye,
64 (1938): 229.

   26 items, 1810 - 1938. French, Norwegian; also English (4),
   German (3), Danish (1). Introduction (2 pp.).

   Books on maritime law, international law, and neutrality.

1346   JX5244.S7B7,1938a

Bruneau, Jacques.

Bibliographie.
In his La Ruse dans la Guerre sur Mer [The Ruse in Naval
Warfare] (Thèse pour le doctorat en droit, Université de
Paris).
Paris: Librairie Générale de Droit et de Jurisprudence, 1938.
pp. 209-220.

   228 items, 1607 - 1937. French; also English, German, Latin
   (6).

   Official documents and instructions, handbooks, books, and
   theses on international law, natural law, maritime law, naval
   warfare, various international conferences (including the
   London Naval Conference, 1908-1909), and jurisprudence.

Legal Aspects of War

    1347   JX5212.G4,v.2

    Genet, Raoul.

    [Bibliographic footnotes] in "Historique et généralités
    [History and generalities]."
    In his Précis de Droit Maritime pour le Temps de Guerre
    [Summary of Maritime Law for Wartime, Vol. 2].
    Paris: Marchal et Billard (Collection de la Revue
    Internationale Française du Droit des Gens, No. 2), [1938].
    pp. 9-16.

        232 items, 1782 - 1937. French, English; also Italian, German,
        Dutch, Spanish (9), Russian (2), Latin (1), Portuguese (1).

        Books and articles on neutrality, international law, and
        diplomacy in wartime situations.

    1348   JX74.H3,v.63

    Smith, Herbert Arthur.

    Bibliography in "Le développement moderne des lois de la guerre
    maritime [Modern development of the laws of naval warfare]."
    Recueil des Cours, Académie de Droit International de la Haye,
    63 (1938): 689-690.

        35 items, 1904 - 1937. English, French; also German (5),
        Italian (2). Introduction (1 paragraph).

        Yearbooks, journals and works on international law
        (especially prize law) and naval warfare.

    1349   JX4093.M2

    McMahon, Matthew M[ark].

    Bibliography.
    In his Conquest and Modern International Law: The legal
    limitations on the acquisition of territory by conquest (Ph.D.
    dissertation, Social Science, Catholic University of America).
    Washington, D.C.: Catholic University of America Press, 1940.
    pp. 215-226.

        246 items, 1621 - 1939. English; also French, Latin (7), German
        (5), Portuguese (3), Spanish (1). Introduction (1 paragraph).

        Books, journal articles, and reports on the legal aspects of
        war, the renunciation of war, nonrecognition, inter-American

Legal Aspects of War

   relations, U.S. foreign policy, international law, the League
   of Nations, and the Paris Peace Pact.

   1350   D410.F65,v.15

   Popper, David H., with the aid of the Research Staff of the
   Foreign Policy Association.

   [Bibliographic footnotes] in "American neutrality and maritime
   rights."
   Foreign Policy Reports. 15, 20 (January 1, 1940): 242-252.

      76 items, 1910 - 1939. English.

      Books, articles, and government publications on international
      law, U.S. foreign policy, neutrality, and treaties.

   1351 <   D741.G66

   González Castro, Francisco.

   Bibliografía.
   In his Ensayo sobre la Responsabilidad Jurídica de la Guerra
   Mundial de 1939 [Essay on the legal responsibility for the
   world war of 1939].
   Mexico City: Talleres Gráficos de la Nación, 1941. pp. 243-244.

   1352   JX514.F54

   Flory, William E. S.

   A selected bibliography.
   In his Prisoners of War: A study in the development of
   international law, with an introduction by Norman H. Davis.
   Washington, D.C.: American Council on Public Affairs, 1942.
   pp. 163-177.

      250 items, 1695 - 1940. English; also French, German, Italian
      (3), Latin (2), Spanish (1).

      Documents (150) and secondary materials (100) on prisoners of
      war from legal, historical, political, social, and economic
      perspectives.

Legal Aspects of War

1353   Z6461.C29,no.13

Scanlon, Helen Lawrence (comp.).

Enemy Property in World War I: A selective bibliography on the
treatment of alien enemy property in France, Germany, Great
Britain, and the United States.
Washington, D.C.: Carnegie Endowment for International Peace,
Library (Select Bibliographies, No. 13), December 15, 1944.
18 pp. (mimeo).

   149 items, 1906 - 1944. English; also French, German (7).
   Some items have brief descriptive annotations; table of
   contents.

   Bibliography (1), official and unofficial publications on
   enemy property prior to 1914 (7), enemy property 1914-1918
   (36), enemy property after World War I (105).

1354   JX5213.D8

Duttwyler, Herbert E.

Literaturverzeichnis [Literature list].
In his Der Seekrieg und die Wirtschaftspolitik des neutralen
Staates [Naval Warfare and the Economic Policy of Neutral
States]: Eine Betrachtung des Wirtschaftskrieges zur See und
seiner Auswirkungen auf die Neutralen von 1939 bis zur
Kapitulation Italiens; mit Nachträgen bis zur Kapitulation
Deutschlands; mit besonderer Berücksichtigung der Lage der
Schweiz und ihrer Hochseeschiffahrt [A view of naval economic
warfare and its effects on neutrals from 1939 until the Italian
surrender; with supplements through the German surrender; with
special attention to the situation of Switzerland and its ocean
shipping].
Zurich: Polygraphischer Verlag (Zürcher Studien zum
Internationalen Recht, Hft. 11), 1945. pp. 6-9.

   87 items, 1906 - 1943. German; also English, French, Italian
   (2).

   Books, articles, and periodicals on international law,
   maritime law, economic warfare, and neutrality.

Legal Aspects of War

1355   JF256.E7

Errázuriz Edwards, Rafael.

Bibliografía.
In his Los Regímenes Jurídicos de Emergencia en las
Constituciónes Americanas [Emergency Powers in American
Constitutions].
Santiago: Universidad de Chile (Colección de Estudios sobre
Derecho Constitucional Comparado Americano, Vol. 3), 1945. pp.
107-109.

   50 items, 1817 - 1944. Spanish; also French (5), Portuguese
   (1).

   Books and documents on constitutional law (28), journals (1),
   and a list of constitutions of North and South American
   countries (21) relevant to emergency powers and protection of
   individual liberties.

1356   Z6463.F73

Woolbert, Robert Gale.

Special topics: "Neutrality, aggression, sanctions; Law of
war."
In his Foreign Affairs Bibliography: A selected and annotated
list of books on international relations, 1932-1942.
New York/London: Harper and Brothers, for the Council on
Foreign Relations, 1945. pp. 82-83, 83-85.

   39 items, 1932 - 1942. French, German, English; also Spanish
   (1), Chinese (1), Dutch (1). All items have brief descriptive
   and/or critical annotations; introduction to whole work;
   table of contents.

   Neutrality, aggression, and sanctions (21), law of war (18).

1357   JX4505.C3

Cahn, Hans Joseph.

Literaturverzeichnis [Literature list].
In his Wesen und Grundbegriffe des Kriegsschadenrechts [Nature
and Fundamentals of the Law of War Damages] (Doctoral thesis,
Political Science, University of Geneva).
Geneva: University of Geneva, Institut Universitaire de Hautes
Etudes Internationales (Thèse No. 53), 1946. pp. xi-civ.

Legal Aspects of War

  1358   JX1.A6,v.40

  Nurick, Lester and Roger W. Barrett.

  [Footnotes] in "Legality of guerrilla forces under the laws of
  war."
  American Journal of International Law, 40, 3 (July, 1946):
  563-583.

     35 items, 1847 - 1945. English; also German (3), French (2),
     Latin (1).

     Books, reports, and official documents on military and
     international law, guerrilla warfare, and legal aspects of
     war.

  1359   JX4511.P6

  Pompe, C[ornelius] A[rnold].

  Bibliography.
  In his Aggressive War: An international crime.
  The Hague: Martinus Nijhoff, 1953. pp. 367-374.

     188 items, 1517 - 1952. English, French; also German, Dutch,
     Latin (7), Italian (2), Spanish (1).

     Books and articles on international law, war crimes, the
     Nuremberg trials, and concepts of war and aggression (157),
     relevant documents including treaties, conventions, World
     Court judgments, reports and documents of the League of
     Nations, United Nations, International Military Tribunals,
     and the International Law Commission (31).

  1360   JX4513.W38

  Wehberg, Hans.

  Bibliographie.
  In his Krieg und Eroberung im Wandel des Völkerrechts [War and
  Conquest in the Practice of International Law].
  Frankfurt am Main/Berlin: Alfred Metzner (Völkerrecht und
  Politik, Vol. 1), 1953. pp. 121-126.

     116 items, 1871 - 1951. French, English, German; also Dutch
     (1), Italian (1).

     Books and journal articles on the theory and practice of
     international law, the foundation, general rules and

Legal Aspects of War

   recognition of international law, nonrecognition, the laws of
   war and peace, doctrines of just war, the United Nations, and
   the Paris Peace Pact.

1361   JX4511.G67

Greenspan, Morris.

Bibliography of works referred to in the text and footnotes.
In his The Modern Law of Land Warfare.
Berkeley/Los Angeles: University of California Press, 1959.
pp. 684-695.

   243 items, 1851 - 1958. English; also French, German (4),
   Russian (3), Dutch (2), Latin (2), Italian (1).

   Government documents (69), books (103), articles and
   periodicals (54), and serial publications (17) on
   international relations, international law, military law, war
   crimes trials, military government, the effects of nuclear
   weapons, Hague conferences and conventions, laws and
   regulations governing warfare, and other topics.

1362   JX5136.A482

[Deutsches Roten Kreuz].

Literaturverzeichnis [Literature list].
In its Die Genfer Rotkreuz Abkommen vom 12. August 1949 [The
Geneva Red-Cross Convention of August 12, 1949] . . ., mit
einer Einführung von Rechtsanwalt Dr. Anton Schlögel,
Generalsekretär des Deutschen Roten Kreuzes.
Mainz/Heidelberg: Huthig und Dreyer, 1960 (4th rev. ed.).
pp. 80-89.
The first edition appeared in 1953. A fifth revised edition
appeared in 1965.

1363   JX68.W6

Leguey-Feilleux, Jean-Robert.

"The law of War: A bibliography 1945-1958."
In Georgetown University, Institute of World Polity, World
Polity: A yearbook of studies in international law and
organization, Volume II.
Utrecht/Antwerp: Spectrum, 1960. pp. 319-414.

   1680 items, 1945 - 1958. English, German, French; also
   Italian, Spanish, Portuguese (2). Table of contents.

Legal Aspects of War

   Books and journal articles on law and war in general (120),
   the legal existence of war (88), legal effects of war (155),
   the law of military operations (825), war crimes (380), and
   neutrality (112).

1364   JX4508.K4

Keen, M[aurice] H[ugh].

Bibliography.
In his The Laws of War in the Late Middle Ages.
London/Toronto: Routledge and Kegan Paul/University of Toronto
Press (Studies in Political History), 1965. pp. 270-280.

   192 items, 1490 - 1960. French, Latin, English; also Italian,
   Spanish (4), German (1). The manuscript sources are
   critically discussed in an essay format, the rest are merely
   listed; introduction (1 paragraph) plus introductions (1
   paragraph) to some of the subsections.

   Manuscript sources (39), printed sources (90), and secondary
   works (63) on the "law of arms."

1365   JX5136.K5

Bothe, Michael.

Bibliographie.
In his Le Droit de la Guerre et les Nations Unies [The Law of
War and the United Nations]: A propos des incidents armés au
Congo [Concerning armed incidents in the Congo].
Geneva: Institut Universitaire de Hautes Etudes Internationales
(Etudes et Travaux, No. 5), 1967. pp. 231-239.

   186 items, 1931 - 1963 (one item dated 1758). English,
   French, German; also Italian (7), Spanish (5), Dutch (5),
   Scandinavian languages (5), Czech (1).

   Official documents (15), general works (22), reports (6),
   monographs (36), articles (77), miscellaneous works (8), and
   court decisions (22) relating to international law, the legal
   aspects of war, the United Nations, and U.N. action in the
   Congo.

Legal Aspects of War

1366   KA677.G4B91

[Brinkers, Helmut (comp.)].

Notstandsrecht [Emergency Legislation]: Auswahlbibliographie
[Selected bibliography].
Bonn: Bundestag (Wissenschaftliche Abteilung des Deutschen
Bundestages, Bibliographien, No. 12), September, 1967.
[v] + 108 pp.

   Over 700 items, 1860 - 1967. German; also other western
   languages. Foreword (1 p.); table of contents; author index.

   This is a revised edition of bibliographies No. 1 (December
   1962) and No. 5 (May 1964) in the same series. Includes
   legal and political writings on constitutional law, emergency
   powers, and martial law in the German Reich, the Federal
   Republic, the German states (including the Democratic
   Republic), and in foreign countries.

1367   JX1573.H8

Hull, Roger H. and John C. Novogrod.

Bibliography.
In their Law and Vietnam, with a foreword by Myres S. McDougal.
Dobbs Ferry, N.Y.: Oceana, 1968. pp. 193-206.

   361 items, 1792 - 1967. English; also French.

   Books (328), cases (6), miscellaneous documents (20), United
   Nations materials (3), and newspapers (4) on Vietnam and the
   Vietnam War, international law, U.S. foreign policy,
   collective security, and intervention.

1368   JX4521.G68

Greenspan, Morris.

Select bibliography.
In his The Soldier's Guide to the Laws of War.
Washington, D.C.: Public Affairs Press, 1969. pp. 81-87.

   79 items, 1909 - 1966. English; also Russian (2), French (2).

   Miscellaneous official documents (9), U.N. documents (6),
   U.S. government documents (10), books (33), articles and
   periodicals (21) on international law and the legal aspects
   of war, war crimes, nuclear weapons, Nuremberg trials,
   prisoners of war; land warfare, military occupation,
   neutrality, and the Geneva Conventions of 1949.

Legal Aspects of War

1369 <

Bretton, Philippe.

[Bibliography].
In his Le Droit de la Guerre [The Law of War].
Paris: A. Colin, 1970. pp. 88-95.

1370 <

Grech, Anthony P.

"Selected bibliography on the laws of war as they affect the
individual."
In Carey, John (ed.) When Battle Rages, How Can Law Protect?
Working paper [by Howard S. Levie] and proceedings of the
fourteenth Hammarskjöld Forum, March 16, 1970.
Dobbs Ferry, N.Y.: Oceana, for the Association of the Bar of
the City of New York, 1971. pp. 89-115.

1371   JX1573.Z7U53

Moore, John Norton.

"A selected bibliography of writings on Indo-China and the
legal order."
In his Law and the Indo-China War.
Princeton: Princeton University Press, 1972. pp. 743-761.

   233 items, 1939 - 1973. English. Some items have brief
   descriptive and/or critical annotations; introduction
   (1 paragraph); table of contents.

   Books, journal articles, reports, and memoranda on the role
   of law in management of international conflict (21), world
   order perspectives (42), background and perspective on the
   Indo-China War (30), international law and the Indo-China War
   (94), the Indo-China War and the constitution (46).

1372 <

Stone, Dennis J.

Emergency Economic Control Programs, 1940-1973: An annotated
bibliography.
Sacramento: California State Library, Law Library, 1973. 14 pp.

Legal Aspects of War

1373 <

Erickson, R. J.

"Selected bibliography concerning the laws of war including the
law applicable to air operations."
Air Force Law Review, 16 (Summer, 1974): 75-95.

1374 <

[Stockholm International Peace Research Institute (SIPRI)].

[Bibliography].
In its Law of War and Dubious Weapons.
Stockholm: SIPRI/Almqvist and Wiksell International, 1976.
pp. 76-78.

War Crimes, Atrocities, War Crimes Trials

1375   JX31.G7,v.26

Cohn, Ernst J.

[Footnotes] in "The problem of war crimes to-day."
In special issue, Problems of Peace and War.
Transactions of the Grotius Society, 26 (1940): 125-151.

   70 items, 1875 - 1940. English, German; also French (9).
   Footnote format, items discussed in text and notes.

   Books, articles, and reports on international law, peace
   treaties, war crimes, and war crimes trials.

1376 <   D639.P6R37

Read, James Morgan.

Bibliography.
In his Atrocity Propaganda, 1914-1919.
New Haven: Yale University Press, for the University of
Louisville, 1941. pp. 297-310.

1377   Z2240.U6

Conover, Helen F. (comp.).

The Nazi State, War Crimes and War Criminals: A bibliography.
Washington, D.C.: Library of Congress, General Reference and
Bibliography Division, for the U.S. Chief of Counsel for the
Prosecution of Axis Criminality, August, 1945. 132 pp. (mimeo).

   1084 items, 1898 - 1945. English, German; also French,
   Norwegian (8), Polish (8), other Western and Eastern European
   languages. A few items have brief descriptive annotations;
   introduction (1 p.); table of contents; subject/author index.

   Theory of war crimes (22); the National Socialist State--
   general surveys (93), leaders (74), doctrine of race (111),
   economic and social system (208), repressive measures (45),
   foreign policy (163), World War II (71); causes of war and
   legal responsibility (32); atrocities--general (119) and by
   country (136).

War Crimes, Atrocities, War Crimes Trials

1378   Z6461.C29,no.14

Scanlon, Helen Lawrence (comp.).

War Crimes: A selected list of books and articles defining war
crimes under international law and discussing their trial and
punishment, including works on an international criminal court.
Washington, D.C.: Carnegie Endowment for International Peace,
Library (Select Bibliographies, No. 14), May 21, 1945. 16 pp.
(mimeo).

   182 items, 1914 - 1945. English; also French, Russian (1).
   Some items have brief descriptive annotations.

1379 <

Wiener Library (London).

Books on Persecution, Terror and Resistance in Nazi Germany.
London: [Wiener Library] (Catalogue Series, No. 1), 1949.
51 pp.

1380   Law. Cuba 7 "Galb"

Galbe, José Luis.

Bibliografía.
In his Crímenes y Justicia de Guerra [War Crimes and
Punishment] (Notas sobre patología del derecho penal [A
critique of the pathology of penal law]).
Havana: Jesús Montero (Biblioteca Jurídica de Autores Cubanos
y Extranjeros, Vol. 138), 1950. pp. 311-315.

   59 items, 1929 - 1949. Spanish, English; also French (8).
   Introduction (2 pp.).

   Books and official documents on Nazi war crimes and political
   repression in Spain, the Nuremberg trials, and Spanish
   history.

1381   JX1906.A43

Neumann, Inge S. and Robert A. Rosenbaum (comps. and eds.),
with additional material furnished by Wiener Library (London).

European War Crimes Trials: A bibliography, with a preface by
Telford Taylor.

War Crimes, Atrocities, War Crimes Trials

New York: Carnegie Endowment for International Peace, 1951.
113 pp. (mimeo).

  746 items, 1941 - 1950. English, French, German; also Italian,
  Dutch, Russian, and other Eastern and Western European
  languages. Many items have brief to abstract-length
  descriptive and/or critical annotations; preface (1 p.);
  author index.

  Bibliographies, document collections, official records,
  reports, declarations, books, and journal articles on Nazi
  war crimes and criminals, the Nuremberg trials, international
  law, and jurisprudence; the materials cover such subjects as
  crimes against peace and against humanity, hostages,
  genocide, quislings, extradition, guerrilla warfare,
  international penal codes, the moral aspects of war, and the
  U.N.´s role in the war crimes trials.

1382   JX1977.A2,no.19 or Z6482.
                                        45,no.19

United Nations, Secretariat, Archives Section, Communications
and Records Division.

Guide to the Records of the United Nations War Crimes
Commission, London, 1943-1948.
[New York: U.N. Department of Conference and General Services]
(United Nations Archives Reference Guide No. 19, ST/CGS/Ser.
A/19), August 27, 1951. 13 pp.

1383   JX6731.W3H4

[Bruch, Elsa aus dem (comp.)].

"Bibliographie zu den Nürnberger Prozessen und ihrer
Problematik [Bibliography on the Nuremberg trials and their
problems]."
In Heinze, Kurt, Karl Schilling, and Herman Maschke (eds.), Die
Rechtsprechung der Nürnberger Militärtribunale [The Judgments
of the Nuremberg Military Tribunal]: Sammlung der Rechtsthesen
der Urteile und gesonderten Urteilsbegründungen der dreizehn
Nürnberger Prozesse [Compilation of legal principles of the
judgments and separate judicial opinions of the thirteen
Nuremberg trials].
Bonn: Girardet, 1952. pp. 333-343.

  271 items, 1944 - 1952. German, English; also French, Italian
  (3), Spanish (1).

War Crimes, Atrocities, War Crimes Trials

Reports, memoranda, articles, and monographs on the
background, proceedings, and decisions of the Nuremberg
trials, international law, the legal basis of war crimes
trials, and the treatment of war criminals.

1384   JX6714.J4

Jescheck, Hans-Heinrich.

Schrifttum (abgeschlossen März 1952) [Literature (through March
1952)]; Quellen [Sources].
In his Die Verantwortlichkeit der Staatsorgane nach
Völkerstrafrecht [The Responsibility of State Agencies
According to International Criminal Law]: Eine Studie zu den
Nürnberger Prozessen [A study of the Nuremberg trials].
Bonn: Ludwig Röhrscheid (Rechtsvergleichende Untersuchungen zur
Gesamten Strafrechtswissenschaft, Neue Folge, Vol. 6), 1952.
pp. ix-xxi.

   389 items, 1594 - 1952. German, English; also French, Italian
   (5), Latin (5), Dutch (1), Portuguese (1), Spanish (1).

   Books, official publications, and documents on international
   criminal law, war crimes, the Nuremberg trials, criminal and
   constitutional law of Germany, England, France, and the U.S.
   S.R., accountability of states under international law, and
   related topics.

1385   JX6731.I5C3

Carjeu, P. M.

Bibliographie.
In his Projet d´une Juridiction Pénale Internationale [Plan of
an International Penal Jurisdiction].
Paris: A. Pedone, 1953. pp. 326-332.

   119 items, 1890 - 1951. French; also English (1).

   Official documents and texts (28), journal articles and a few
   books (91) on international law, war crimes, Nazi crimes
   against humanity, the Permanent Court of International
   Justice, the Nuremberg trials, political repression, and
   political and international terrorism.

War Crimes, Atrocities, War Crimes Trials

1386   IU: JX6731.W3H37x

Harris, Whitney R.

"Select bibliography relating to the proceedings of the
International Military Tribunal."
In his Tyranny on Trial: The evidence at Nuremberg, with an
introduction by Robert H. Jackson and a foreword by Robert G.
Storey.
Dallas: Southern Methodist University Press, 1954. pp. 583-592.

   171 items, 1941 - 1953. English, French; also German, Italian
   (5), Dutch (3), Spanish (2), Danish (1).

   Bibliographies (4), documentary materials (10), books and
   pamphlets (53), and periodical articles (104) on the
   Nuremberg trials and their legal basis, German war crimes,
   and the development of international criminal law.

1387   IU: D804.G42B45x

Benton, Wilbourn E. and Georg Grimm (eds.).

Select bibliography.
In their Nuremberg: German views of the war trials.
Dallas: Southern Methodist University Press, 1955. pp. 231-232.

   17 items, 1924 - 1953. German, English. Some items have brief
   descriptive annotations.

   Books, pamphlets, and articles on war crimes and the
   Nuremberg trials.

1388   Z6207.W8K6

Kosicki, Jerzy and Wacław Kozłowski.

Bibliografia Piśmiennictwa Polskiego za Lata 1944-1953 o
Hitlerowskich Zbrodniach Wojennych [Bibliography of Polish
Literature for the Years 1944-1953 on Hitlerian War Crimes],
with a foreword by Jerzy Sawicki.
Warsaw: Wydawnictwo Prawnicze, 1955. 179 pp.

   2296 items, 1944 - 1953. Polish; also French, English, German.
   Some items have brief descriptive annotations; introduction
   (1 p.); table of contents; subject index (14 categories),
   with authors and titles listed under each category; list of
   periodicals consulted.

War Crimes, Atrocities, War Crimes Trials

Books and articles on the German aggression against Poland,
the German occupation government (Généralgouvernement); legal
aspects of the Nazi occupation, persecution of the
population, extermination of the Jewish population, death
camps and concentration camps, prisoners of war, German
attacks on Polish culture, persecution of the church and
clergy, destruction and plunder of economy and property, the
armed forces, the Nuremberg war crimes trials, and legal
problems.

1389   JX6731.W3F8,1963

Fuhrmann, Peter.

Literaturverzeichnis [Literature list].
In his Der höhere Befehl als Rechtfertigung im Völkerrecht
[Higher Command as Justification in Public Law].
Munich/Berlin: C. H. Beck, 1963. pp. xi-xviv.
Originally appeared as Inaugural-Dissertation zur Erlangung der
Doktorwürde einer Hohen Juristischen Fakultät der Ludwig-
Maximilians-Universität zu München, Munich: A. Schubert, 1960.

246 items, 1563 - 1961. German, English; also French, Latin
(9), Spanish (1).

Books, articles, and documentary sources on responsibility
for war crimes under international law and penal law in
numerous countries (mainly countries of Eastern and Western
Europe, also Asia, the Near East, and Latin America).

1390   DD256.5.B366,1966

Bednarek, Irena and Stanisław Sokołowski.

Bibliografia.
In their Fanfary i Werble [Fanfares and Whirlpools].
Katowice, Poland: "Śląsk," 1966 (2nd ed.). pp. 537-538.
Third edition, 1972, pp. 550-552.

71 items, 1935 - 1963. German, Polish; also English (3), French
(1).

Books, documents, and periodicals on World War II, the Nazi
leaders, German war crimes, and the Nuremberg trials.

War Crimes, Atrocities, War Crimes Trials

1391   D804.G42D3

Davidson, Eugene.

Bibliography.
In his The Trial of the Germans: An account of the twenty-two
defendants before the International Military Tribunal at
Nuremberg.
New York: Macmillan, 1966. pp. 595-615.

    514 items, 1920 - 1966. German, English; also French, Italian
    (1), Polish (1).

    Books, articles, biographies, published documents, and trial
    records on National Socialist Germany, the defendants at the
    Nuremberg trials, the trials, legal aspects of war and war
    crimes, military law, German youth, concentration camps, war
    economy, religion and war, and related topics.

1392   D804.G42B67

Bosch, William J.

Bibliography.
In his Judgment on Nuremberg: American attitudes toward the
major German war-crimes trials.
Chapel Hill: University of North Carolina Press, 1970.
pp. 241-266.

    577 items, 1925 - 1968. English.

    Public or official documents (13), letters (14), newspapers
    (57), periodical articles (287), special studies and general
    works (206).

1393 <

Brennecke, Gerhard.

[Bibliography].
In his Die nürnberger Geschichtsentstellung [The Historical
Setting of Nuremberg]: Quellen zur Vorgeschichte und Geschichte
des 2. Weltkrieges aus den Akten der deutschen Verteidigung
[Sources on the background and history of the Second World War
from the documents of the German defense].
Tubingen: Verlag der Deutschen Hochschullehrer Zeitung
(Veröffentlichungen des Instituts für Deutsche
Nachkriegsgeschichte, Vol. 5), 1970. pp. 401-412.

War Crimes, Atrocities, War Crimes Trials

1394 <

Van Garsse, Yvan.

A Bibliography of Genocide, Crimes against Humanity and War
Crimes, Vol. I.
High Wycombe, Buckinghamshire, U.K./Sint Niklaas Wass, Belgium:
University Microfilm/Studiecentrum voor Kriminologie en
Gerechtelijke Geneeskunde, 1970. 155 pp.

1395   JX6731.W3M5

Minear, Richard H.

Bibliographical note.
In his Victors' Justice: The Tokyo war crimes trial.
Princeton: Princeton University Press, 1971. pp. 213-215.

   28 items, 1948 - 1971. English, Japanese. Essay format, most
   items are discussed in the text.

   Proceedings, library holdings, and materials on the Tokyo war
   crimes trial and international law.

1396   D843.D27

Davidson, Eugene.

Bibliography.
In his The Nuremberg Fallacy: Wars and war crimes since World
War II.
New York/London: Macmillan/Collier-Macmillan, 1973.
pp. 301-315.

   402 items, 1867 - 1972. English, French; also German, Italian
   (2), Latin (1).

   Mostly books on military, diplomatic, and political history
   since 1945, international law, war crimes, atrocities, and
   terrorism.

War Crimes, Atrocities, War Crimes Trials

1397 <

Miale, Florence R. and Michael Selzer.

[Bibliography].

In their Nuremberg Mind: The psychology of the Nazi leaders,
with an introduction and Rorschach records by Gustave M.
Gilbert.
Chicago: Quadrangle (Brooklyn College, Research Center for
Interdisciplinary Applications of Psychoanalysis, Monograph 1),
1975. pp. 299-302.

1398 <   Z6464.W33L48

Lewis, John R[odney] (comp.).

Uncertain Judgment: A bibliography of war crimes trials.
Santa Barbara, Calif.: ABC-Clio (War/Peace Bibliography Series,
No. 8), 1979. xxxiii + 251 pp.

Indexes

Abraham, Herbert J., 881
Academia Republicii Populare Romîne, Biblioteca, 678
Acts for Peace, 634-635
Aggarwal, Lalit K., 980
Aichinger, Peter, 541
Akhavi, (Ali Akbar), 593
Albers, D., 23
Albrecht-Carrié, René, 796
Alexander, Patricia S., 889
Allen, Devere, 659
Allen, Julius W., 1284
Allport, Gordon W., 1172
Almond, Nina Elizabeth, 61, 795
Alschuler, Rose H., 1145
American Association for International Conciliation, 544
American Association for the United Nations, 901
American Friends Service Committee, 952
American Friends Service Committee, Peace Section, 674,
    759
American Friends Service Committee, Peace Section, Joint
    Committee on The Conscientious Objector, 762
American Historical Association, Historical Service
    Board, 882
American Library Association, 579
American Library Institute, 811, 859
American Pax Association, 701
American Peace Society, 695
American Society of Corporate Secretaries, 1305
Anchieri, Ettore, 1085
Anderson, Martin, 425
Angell, Norman, 665
Angell, Robert C., 221
Ansbacher, H. L., 1164-1165
Archer, D., 1134
Armstrong, Hamilton Fish, 35
Arnold, Joseph Irvin, 62
Arnold, Thurman, 1258
Association de la Paix par le Droit, 646
Atherton, Alexine L., 916
Atkin, S., 1190
Atkinson, Henry Avery, 41
Atomic Bomb Casualty Commission, 704
Atwater, Elton, 327
Aufricht, Hans, 74, 883, 894
Augspurg, Anita, 469
Babcock, Chester D., 1259
Backman, Jules, 1272, 1302
Baden, Anne L., 150, 831
Baer, K. A., 1331
Bailey, Thomas Andrew, 170
Bainton, Roland H., 434, 443
Baird, R. F. S., 1073
Bakeless, John E., 985, 1099
Baker, Charles Whiting, 1208
Baker, Helen, 1237, 1260, 1276

Community service and peace, 674, 784
Concentration camps, 1063, 1377, 1382, 1388, 1391
Conciliation. See International conciliation.
Condottiere, 501
Confiscations, 1353, 1377, 1388
Conflict, Algerian-Moroccan, 1021
Conflict, Arab-Israeli, 113, 1046, 1396
Conflict, Ethiopian-Somalian, 1021
Conflict, family, 90, 128, 130
Conflict, Greco-Bulgarian, 866
Conflict, Greco-Italian, 866
Conflict, history of, 788, 963, 970, 1046
Conflict, Indian-Chinese, 1021
Conflict, Indonesian-Malaysian, 1021
Conflict, internal, 104, 128, 130, 970
Conflict, international, 52, 99, 104, 111, 122, 128, 130,
      221, 230, 361, 552-553, 737, 970, 980, 982, 1104, 1188,
      1367, 1371
Conflict, Israeli-Egyptian, 1021, 1046
Conflict, Kashmir, 1021
Conflict, social. See Social conflict.
Conflict, Soviet-Iranian, 1021
Conflict, theory of, 90, 93-96, 106-107, 111-112,
      117-118, 122, 125, 128-130, 221, 230, 361, 420, 471, 509,
      553, 638, 702, 737, 768, 781, 785, 788, 963-964, 966,
      968, 970, 974-977, 980-982, 1012, 1018, 1021-1023, 1104,
      1133, 1188, 1307
Conflict management, 128-130, 980, 1104. See also
      Peacekeeping.
Conflict research, 90, 95, 106, 222, 509, 553, 702, 964,
      970, 979, 981, 1104, 1188
Conflict resolution, 51, 89, 104, 106, 118, 122, 128-130,
      221, 230, 553, 555, 702, 737, 781, 809, 966, 970, 980,
      982, 1021-1022. See also International conciliation;
      International disputes, settlement of; Pacific
      settlement of disputes.
Congo. See Belgian Congo; French Congo.
Congo Crisis, 910, 1365
Congress of nations, 661, 666
Congress of the Peoples for Peace (Vienna, 1952), 752
Conscientious objection, 27, 85, 97, 102, 109, 113-114,
      117, 425, 448, 452, 454, 458, 619, 623, 628, 634,
      659-660, 672, 677, 680, 688, 753, 755, 766, 770, 774-775,
      779-783, 785-787, 977, 1015, 1042, 1214, 1243. See also
      Pacifism, nonviolence, conscientious objection.
Conscientious objectors, 43, 76, 109, 113, 117, 634, 659,
      674, 687-688, 753, 755, 759, 761-762, 764, 767, 769-770,
      775, 779, 782, 784, 786, 1063, 1125
Conscription, 43, 59, 67, 70, 85, 113-114, 117, 230, 385,
      387, 390, 425, 444, 458, 463, 466, 549, 566, 568,
      619-620, 625, 628-629, 631, 634, 649, 659, 676, 684, 753,
      755, 759, 761, 764-765, 767, 775, 784, 786, 995, 1042,
      1063, 1074, 1082, 1125, 1165, 1201, 1214, 1239, 1243,
      1250, 1274, 1320. See also Military training, compulsory.
Conscription of wealth, 390, 1113, 1213-1214, 1251.

Military administration, 1026, 1060, 1065, 1074, 1194,
    1228, 1311, 1363
Military and politics. See Civil-military relations.
Military and society, 377, 408, 415, 422
Military coup. See Coup d'état.
Military economy, 151, 362-363, 369, 377, 418, 423,
    1194-1195, 1220, 1226-1229, 1271, 1274, 1303, 1307, 1311,
    1391. See also Defense Economy; Economic mobilization
    for war; Industrial mobilization for war; War economy.
Military expenditures, 9, 85, 151, 361, 369, 377,
    381-382, 385, 411, 419, 423, 622, 649, 966, 984, 1113,
    1120, 1256, 1307
Military games, 403, 1041
Military government, 377, 404, 412, 1106, 1361, 1363, 1388
Military history, 7-9, 38, 61, 78, 86, 126, 230, 310,
    313, 383-385, 397-398, 400, 425, 436, 532, 536, 556, 639,
    990, 993, 995-997, 1011-1013, 1026, 1030, 1033,
    1037-1042, 1044, 1052, 1057-1058, 1062-1063, 1065, 1070,
    1072-1074, 1103, 1117, 1165, 1172, 1194, 1364, 1396.
    See also World War I, military history of.
Military-industrial complex, 124-125, 130, 230, 362, 369,
    374, 377, 411, 418-420, 423, 634, 977, 1133
Military language manuals, 1052
Military law, 230, 318, 384, 1052, 1063, 1075, 1082,
    1358, 1361, 1363-1364, 1368, 1381, 1389. See also
    War, legal aspects.
Military leaders, memoirs and biographies of, 22, 29, 53,
    57, 61, 78, 86, 352, 384, 393, 397-398, 400-401, 681,
    801, 985, 990, 997, 1011-1012, 1026, 1032, 1053,
    1057-1058, 1063, 1065, 1070, 1072-1074, 1106, 1117,
    1165-1166, 1172, 1311, 1364, 1377, 1391-1392
Military leadership, 230, 384, 801, 1026, 1172
Military leadership, psychological aspects, 404, 1165,
    1172
Military life, 1082
Military life, psychology of, 1057, 1065, 1158, 1165,
    1172, 1176, 1182
Military life, social and political aspects, 384, 404,
    412, 425, 1063, 1106
Military medicine, 384, 1029, 1082, 1117, 1127, 1164,
    1176, 1363
Military mobilization, 85, 230, 365, 387, 397, 425, 999,
    1226
Military morale, 1158, 1176-1177
Military occupation, 23, 61, 276, 394, 698, 705, 1004,
    1053, 1057-1058, 1063, 1065, 1080, 1147, 1241, 1363,
    1365, 1368, 1384, 1388, 1392
Military ordnance, 1352. See also War materials and
    supplies.
Military organization, 151, 310, 397, 404, 408, 412, 552,
    644, 1016, 1022, 1026, 1057, 1063, 1074-1075, 1082, 1304
Military organization, sociology of, 86, 130, 997, 1063,
    1191
Military periodicals, 410, 414, 1041
Military personnel, 384, 1042

Mott, John Raleigh, 738
Mozambique, 479
Multinational corporations, 130
Mundialization, 853. See also World citizenship.
Munitions, 318, 374, 377, 1274
Munitions industry, 43, 78, 140, 294, 300-301, 310, 312,
    314-318, 377, 423, 463, 590, 688, 1060, 1063, 1133, 1216,
    1219, 1221, 1237, 1239, 1243
Music, 27, 528-529, 540, 671, 1065. See also Creative
    literature, drama, arts.
Music, American Revolution, 529
Music, Mexican War, 529
Music, military, 528, 540, 1063
Music, patriotic, 528, 540
Music, peace, 648, 949
Music, peace songs, 537, 540, 549, 645
Music, protest songs, 540
Music, Spanish-American War, 529
Music, U.S. Civil War, 528-529, 535
Music, war, 1057
Music, War of 1812, 529
Music, war songs, 529, 535, 540, 1052, 1075
Music, World War I, 529, 1063
Mussolini, Benito, 501
Mutual aid, 176
Nagasaki. See Hiroshima and Nagasaki.
Nansen, Fridtjof, 738
Napoleon, 1034
Napoleonic Wars, 984
National character, 89-90, 96
National Council Against Conscription, publications, 85
National Council for Prevention of War, publications, 673
National Council of American-Soviet Friendship,
    publications, 85
National debt, 984, 1060, 1267, 1295
National defense, 27, 43, 54, 59, 69, 94, 99, 130, 144,
    146, 150-151, 153, 158, 160, 162, 166-167, 230, 263,
    293-294, 300, 304, 309-310, 313, 318, 321, 340, 348,
    353, 361, 370, 383, 390, 397, 399, 419, 423, 463, 466,
    472, 492, 590, 622, 660, 771, 775, 966, 986, 990,
    995-996, 999, 1011, 1074, 1080, 1082, 1125, 1132-1133,
    1202, 1214, 1240, 1252-1253, 1255-1257, 1260, 1262,
    1268-1269, 1271-1272, 1294, 1298, 1300, 1302, 1306-1307.
    See also Security, national.
National development, 515
National finance, 492, 1267
National interest, 87, 91, 122
National minorities, 22, 30, 87, 170, 195, 478, 489, 491,
    799, 866, 874, 1053, 1058, 1065, 1333
National Peace Council (London), 673; publications, 12-13,
    17, 19-20, 53, 59, 73, 566, 568, 649
National psychology, 489, 501, 1103, 1165, 1172. See also
    Psychology, social; War, psychological aspects.
National security. See Security, national.
National self-determination. See Self-determination.

Political prisoners, 786
Political repression, 501, 787, 1377, 1379-1381, 1385
Political socialization, 1154
Political theory, 5, 7, 23, 38, 42, 45, 71, 73, 76,
    81-82, 86, 90-92, 94, 102, 109, 111, 113-114, 119,
    124-126, 192, 195, 228, 411, 419, 436, 443, 445, 448-449,
    480, 486, 489, 492, 496-498, 501, 507, 509-510, 513, 604,
    612, 617, 620, 623, 625, 628, 638-640, 642, 659, 661,
    666, 711, 717-718, 720, 726, 730, 737, 739, 784-786, 811,
    813-814, 821, 834, 859, 865, 968, 976-977, 989, 993, 995,
    1003, 1012-1013, 1015, 1053, 1063, 1065, 1104, 1133,
    1191, 1312, 1328, 1364
Population, 89, 113, 125, 230, 420, 483, 501, 622, 964,
    990, 1057, 1060, 1105, 1195, 1206, 1271. See also War,
    demographic aspects.
Population and peace, 680
Portugal, 194, 1003, 1057, 1065. See also Foreign policy,
    Portugal.
Positive law, 233-234
Posters, 61, 949. See also Peace posters.
Postwar planning, 22, 72-73, 76, 87, 166-169, 444, 601,
    605-606, 608-611, 615, 698, 817-820, 823-824, 836-837,
    840-843, 881, 998, 1060, 1065, 1082, 1260, 1274, 1279,
    1284, 1290, 1294
Power, naval. See Naval power.
Power, political, 81, 99, 104, 117, 230, 411, 501, 640,
    788
Power, sea. See Sea power.
Power, social, 95, 396, 788
Prehistory, 1034
Presidential powers, 179, 1371. See also Warmaking,
    presidential powers.
Press, propaganda function of, 1106. See also Media,
    Propaganda function of.
Press, role of, 11, 22, 54, 800, 1013, 1042, 1172. See
    also War correspondents.
Press and peace, 11, 27, 645, 671, 690, 710, 937, 942
Price control, 1064, 1082, 1222, 1240, 1274
Price control and war, 1125, 1215, 1234, 1262, 1264,
    1266, 1270-1272, 1277, 1280-1281, 1293-1294, 1298, 1300,
    1302, 1308. See also War, economic aspects.
Price policies, 492, 1271, 1303. See also Price control;
    Price control and war.
Primitive weapons. See Weapons, primitive.
Principe. See São Tomé and Principe.
Prisoners of war, 23, 30, 61, 212, 513, 907, 995, 1042,
    1052, 1057-1058, 1061, 1063, 1065, 1070, 1075, 1087,
    1106, 1165, 1352, 1356, 1363, 1368, 1371, 1377
Prize law, 23, 30, 270, 858, 995, 1052, 1063, 1348, 1363.
    See also Maritime law.
Prizes. See Peace essay contests and prizes; Peace prizes.
Propaganda, 22, 99, 117, 180, 492, 501, 505, 791, 948, 998,
    1012-1013, 1075, 1077, 1080, 1159, 1162, 1165, 1172-1173,
    1177, 1186, 1279, 1377. See also Cartoons, war; Films;
    Media, propaganda function of; Peace propaganda;

Social change.
Social reformers and peace, 102, 640, 688-690, 784
Social revolution, 680
Social science and peace, 89, 94, 96, 109, 219, 226, 645,
    681, 968, 980, 982
Social science and war, 89, 94, 109, 111, 219, 226, 420,
    974, 1016
Social security, 76, 169, 492, 549, 611, 614, 1060, 1254
Social studies and peace, 518, 937, 950
Socialism, 22, 125, 468, 481, 484-485, 492, 498-499, 501,
    506-507, 510, 539, 640, 779, 784, 975, 977, 1023, 1058,
    1063
Socialism, history of, 30, 61, 329, 485, 506, 684, 690
Socialism, theories of, 30, 45, 61, 86, 102, 485, 489,
    506-507, 684, 690, 717, 1013, 1077
Socialism and peace, 39, 85, 91, 102, 476, 506, 571, 645,
    648, 671, 677, 681-683, 688, 690, 748, 752, 770, 859,
    1296
Socialism and war, 30, 39, 91, 114, 392, 506-507,
    683-684, 688-689, 770, 987, 1020, 1052-1053, 1057, 1065,
    1133, 1296
Socialist International, 507
Société de la Paix de Genève, 708
Société Française des Amis de la Paix (Paris), 557
Society and war, 66, 424, 501, 989, 1016, 1103, 1128,
    1134, 1190, 1314, 1339-1340
Society of Friends, 102, 427, 587, 659, 662-663, 673,
    688, 755, 757, 765, 775, 778, 782, 784, 786. See also
    Quakerism; Quakers and peace.
Söderblom, Lars Olof Nathan, 738
Somalia, 1021. See also Conflict, Ethiopian-Somalian.
Somaliland, 209
South Africa, 97, 125, 194, 209, 212, 375, 502, 629,
    631-633, 781, 1022
South African (Boer) War (1900-1901), 7, 30, 644, 775,
    984, 1099, 1106
South America, 69, 109, 132, 159-160, 194, 583, 988,
    1022, 1063, 1065, 1080
Southeast Asia, 611, 1042. See also Cambodia; Indonesia;
    Laos; Malaya; Malaysia; Philippines; Singapore;
    Thailand; Vietnam.
Southeast Asia Treaty Organization (SEATO), 1042
South-West Africa, 549, 866
Sovereignty, 30, 81, 199, 834, 858-859
Soviet Union. See Russia; U.S.S.R.
Space, outer. See Outer space.
Spain, 53, 59, 61, 65, 194, 212, 489, 583, 1003, 1057,
    1063, 1065, 1075, 1147, 1220, 1380. See also
    Foreign policy, Spain.
Spanish-American War, 1099, 1133. See also Music,
    Spanish-American War; United States, wars of.
Spanish Civil War, 47, 59, 61, 204, 1013, 1021
Spanish Succession, War of, 808
Spheres of influence and interest, 189
Sports and peace, 671

1018-1019, 1022, 1024-1048, 1051-1053, 1055,
1057-1058, 1062-1063, 1065, 1067-1077, 1083, 1085-1086,
1088, 1090-1095, 1099-1100, 1102-1103, 1117, 1120,
1127-1128, 1133, 1172, 1194-1195, 1240, 1274, 1279, 1296,
1311-1312, 1328-1329, 1337-1338, 1340, 1347, 1352, 1364,
1377, 1380
War, inevitability of, 43, 55, 59, 990, 1015, 1103
War, justifications for, 7, 18, 1108, 1172. See also Just
    war; Peace, disadvantages of.
War, labor opposition, 571
War, legal aspects, 7, 9, 14, 16, 23, 30, 43, 48, 68, 84,
    96, 179, 182, 184, 212, 236, 244, 249, 268, 270-272,
    277-279, 286-287, 374, 429, 448, 454, 557-558, 564, 566,
    568, 646, 649, 659, 666, 755, 786, 789, 821, 873, 995,
    1003-1004, 1014, 1050, 1053, 1057, 1063, 1065, 1075,
    1080, 1103, 1195, 1221, 1228, 1237, 1243, 1252, 1265,
    1268-1269, 1278, 1284, 1286, 1289, 1291-1292, 1297, 1303,
    1318, 1320, 1328, 1330, 1341-1374, 1377-1378, 1381-1384,
    1386-1389, 1391-1394, 1396
War, mathematical theory of, 60, 122, 420, 736, 974,
    1002, 1012, 1021, 1104, 1307
War, medical aspects, 9, 43, 61, 319-320, 325, 370, 372,
    384, 386, 463, 1002, 1029, 1042, 1052, 1057-1058, 1060,
    1063, 1065, 1075, 1080, 1106, 1117, 1119-1120, 1123,
    1125, 1127-1130, 1141, 1147, 1156-1158, 1163, 1167-1168,
    1182, 1239, 1315, 1326, 1362-1363. See also
    Disease; Health; Military medicine; War and deafness.
War, methods of studying, 553, 737, 958, 974, 982, 1104.
    See also Peace research.
War, moral aspects, 7, 9, 11, 14, 18, 26, 38, 45, 47, 103,
    109-110, 113, 117, 124, 125, 230, 385, 419, 429, 432,
    434, 436, 440, 442-443, 447-449, 452-455, 458, 527, 564,
    567, 571, 612, 645-646, 648-649, 658-659, 666, 688, 695,
    765, 770, 778, 782, 784, 786, 838, 996, 1003, 1015, 1031,
    1052, 1057-1058, 1063, 1065, 1106, 1108, 1111, 1115,
    1118, 1121, 1128, 1139, 1371, 1381, 1396
War, morale, 69, 1174, 1176
War, outlawry of, 26-27, 31, 35, 91, 114, 287, 309-310,
    374, 436, 549, 577, 581, 613, 655, 657, 660, 662, 671,
    691, 722, 729, 743, 813, 873, 1004, 1343, 1349. See
    also War, abolition of.
War, political aspects, 5, 22, 61, 82, 91, 108, 114, 179,
    184, 202, 222, 397, 436, 478, 542, 611, 686, 841, 1000,
    1014, 1028, 1042, 1046, 1053, 1057-1058, 1063, 1065,
    1070, 1074-1075, 1077, 1080, 1106, 1108, 1133, 1214,
    1239, 1243, 1250, 1304, 1311, 1317-1323, 1325, 1329-1330,
    1361, 1366, 1371, 1387-1388. See also Social and
    political aspects of war.
War, political economy of, 1226, 1298, 1302, 1309, 1311.
    See also War, economic aspects.
War, political effects of, 1128, 1133
War, popular fallacies, 571
War, preparations for, 151, 153, 300, 377, 381, 385, 390,
    722, 986, 1053, 1057, 1125, 1201-1202, 1226, 1236-1237,
    1252, 1311, 1377. See also Economic mobilization for
    war.

War, prevention of, 9-10, 15, 18, 26, 28-29, 35, 38-39,
    41, 44, 46, 52, 56, 62, 68, 78, 80, 94, 98, 101, 111,
    118, 129-130, 142, 150, 153, 156, 161-162, 180, 194, 279,
    295, 302, 309, 311, 318, 321, 348, 353, 389, 447, 557,
    564, 572, 587, 614, 622, 645, 648, 655-656, 659-660, 662,
    666, 671-672, 681, 687-688, 703, 722, 736-737, 743, 768,
    779, 781, 783-784, 813, 821, 845, 855, 857-859, 865-866,
    879, 931, 942, 958-959, 966, 998, 1011, 1014, 1016-1017,
    1031, 1053, 1063, 1185, 1296, 1317-1319. See also War
    referendum.
War, principles of, 989-990, 1015. See also War, theory of.
War, propaganda against, 644. See also Peace propaganda.
War, prophecies and predictions, 646
War, psychological aspects, 38, 43, 51, 70-71, 90-91, 93,
    99, 104, 110-114, 117-118, 122, 124, 222, 370, 396, 420,
    500, 527-528, 686, 765, 977, 994, 1012, 1015-1016, 1018,
    1022, 1031, 1053, 1060, 1065, 1089, 1103-1104, 1106,
    1119, 1123-1124, 1126, 1128, 1135-1137, 1139, 1142, 1145,
    1148, 1151-1152, 1154-1192, 1279, 1328, 1332, 1381, 1392,
    1397. See also Military psychology; National
    psychology; Psychiatry and war; Psychology and war;
    War, psychology of; Warfare, psychological.
War, psychological effects, 1168. See also Children,
    psychological effects of war on; Neuroses; War
    neuroses.
War, psychology of, 1050, 1338
War, quantitative approaches to the study of, 38, 96,
    111, 122, 125, 130, 221, 420, 553, 966, 974, 982, 1021,
    1104. See also War, methods of studying; War,
    mathematical theory of; Peace science.
War, renunciation of. See Renunciation of war.
War, social aspects, 5, 30, 43, 61, 91, 110, 114, 122,
    166, 397, 422, 436, 478, 527, 542, 556, 611, 648, 696,
    698, 722, 729, 765, 801, 984, 987, 991, 994, 998, 1000,
    1002, 1015-1016, 1031, 1046, 1052-1053, 1055, 1057-1058,
    1060, 1063, 1065, 1068, 1070, 1074-1077, 1080, 1082,
    1086, 1089, 1106-1108, 1118-1120, 1124-1126, 1128, 1133,
    1149, 1158, 1168, 1181, 1187, 1239, 1241-1242, 1250-1251,
    1268-1269, 1274, 1279, 1304-1305, 1314-1316, 1326-1329,
    1331-1335, 1363, 1387-1388. See also Social and
    political aspects of war.
War, socialist opposition, 571, 684, 689, 752, 770
War, sociology of, 18, 22, 35, 38, 66, 72, 86, 90-91, 96,
    106, 110, 122, 128, 130, 221, 419, 422, 648-650, 964,
    966, 974, 982, 987-989, 994, 997, 1000, 1012, 1016, 1019,
    1021, 1048, 1053, 1060, 1065, 1074, 1077, 1103-1104,
    1106, 1119, 1128, 1133-1134, 1164, 1188, 1190-1191,
    1328-1329, 1338
War, theory of, 5, 7-8, 11, 14, 18, 25-27, 29, 35, 38,
    41, 45, 54, 59, 66, 71, 78, 86, 90, 99, 103-104, 109-111,
    113-114, 118-119, 122, 124, 128, 130, 230, 315, 384, 398,
    403, 419-420, 426, 436, 453, 471, 507, 532, 572, 582,
    629-630, 639, 644-645, 648-651, 658-661, 666, 690, 729,
    736-737, 740, 784, 789, 865, 923, 951, 958, 966, 968,
    974, 982, 987-990, 993, 996-997, 1000-1001, 1003-1004,

War guilt, 22, 1363, 1377-1378, 1381, 1392
War Industries Board, 397, 1074, 1208, 1215, 1260
War loans, 1113
War materials and supplies, 1226, 1239, 1243, 1250.
    See also Military ordnance.
War memorials, 675, 1334-1336
War neuroses, 1002, 1015-1016, 1123, 1128, 1139, 1148,
    1151-1152, 1155, 1158, 1163-1164, 1168, 1176-1178,
    1181-1182, 1187-1188. See also Neuroses; War,
    psychological aspects.
War of the Pacific (1879-1884), 30, 214, 808, 1036
War of 1812, 808, 1133. See also Music, war of 1812;
    United States, Wars of.
War poetry. See Poetry, war.
War Policies Commission, 1239
War potential, economic, 409, 1217, 1229, 1236, 1241,
    1303, 1309. See also Economic mobilization
    for war.
War powers, 133
War production, 463, 1060, 1125, 1201, 1254, 1259-1260,
    1262, 1265, 1268-1271, 1275, 1280, 1298, 1300, 1302,
    1310. See also War, economic aspects.
War profits, 26, 78, 150, 314-316, 318, 390, 423, 1060,
    1074, 1210, 1213-1214, 1216, 1222, 1228, 1239-1240, 1243,
    1245, 1249-1250, 1252, 1258, 1270, 1274, 1278, 1282,
    1286, 1298. See also War, economic aspects.
War propaganda, 43, 61, 69, 78, 114, 157, 505, 536, 997,
    1057, 1063, 1065, 1074-1075, 1077, 1080, 1103, 1106,
    1125, 1159, 1162, 1177, 1183, 1239, 1250, 1324,
    1376-1377. See also Propaganda.
War referendum, 26, 153, 180, 1239, 1317-1323, 1325. See
    also War, prevention of.
War relief, 61, 73-74, 76, 463, 611, 619, 646, 795, 907,
    1060, 1065, 1315
War resistance, 43, 102, 113, 125, 659, 662, 673-674,
    681, 688, 754, 756, 760-761, 775, 779-780, 784, 786, 990,
    1239, 1311, 1371. See also Pacifism, nonviolence,
    conscientious objection; War tax resistance.
War Resisters League, publications, 85, 767
War Resisters' International, 673, 784; publications, 767
War savings, 1205
War scares, 9, 571
War sermons, 666, 1063
War statistics, 9, 122, 622, 646, 648, 974, 1040, 1043,
    1058, 1104-1105, 1113, 1119-1120, 1193, 1244, 1333
War tax resistance, 452. See also War resistance.
War termination, 23, 84, 170, 268, 287, 353, 561, 792,
    795, 800-801, 803-804, 806-808, 859, 865, 1004, 1032,
    1058, 1063, 1077, 1098, 1361, 1363
War toys, 43, 1189. See also Children's games.
War Trade Board, 1208
War trophies, 1022
Warfare, 8-9, 14, 35, 38, 43, 53, 61, 66, 78, 81, 86, 99,
    103, 109, 310, 384, 396-397, 400, 409, 436, 501, 532,
    541, 966, 989-990, 993, 995-997, 1000, 1007, 1012,

Y0-BCC-512

This volume
published by the
Mercer University Press
is given to the
Neva Lomason Memorial Library
by the University
in memory of

Thomas Sewell Plunkett

loyal Mercer alumnus,
member of the
Mercer University Board of Trustees,
and president of the
Mercer Alumni Association,
as a tribute to
his enduring support
and love of his alma mater.

September 1991   ᴍᴘ

NEVA LOMASON MEMORIAL LIBRARY

"A MAN OF BOOKS AND A MAN OF THE PEOPLE"

"A MAN OF BOOKS AND A MAN OF THE PEOPLE"

E. Y. Mullins and the Crisis
of Moderate Southern Baptist Leadership

by
William E. Ellis

MERCER

ISBN 0-86554-175-2

"*A Man of Books and a Man of the People*"
Copyright © 1985
Mercer University Press, Macon GA 31207
All rights reserved
Printed in the United States of America

All books published by Mercer University Press are produced
on acid-free paper that exceeds the minimum standards set by the
National Historical Publications and Records Commission.

Library of Congress Cataloging in Publication Data
Ellis, William E. (William Elliott), 1940–   .
    "A man of books and a man of the people."
Bibliography: p. 223.
Includes index.
    1. Mullins, Edgar Young, 1860–1928.   2. Southern
Baptist Convention—Clergy—Biography.   3. Baptists—
United States—Clergy—Biography.   4. Modernist-
fundamentalist controversy—History.   5. Southern
Baptist Theological Seminary (Louisville, Ky.)—History.
6. Southern Baptist Convention—History—19th century.
7. Southern Baptist Convention—History—20th century.
8. Baptists—History—19th century.   9. Baptists—
History—20th century.   I. Title.
BX6495.M8E45   1985   286'.132'0924 [B]   85-13738
ISBN 0-86554-175-2 (alk. paper)

Contents

PREFACE

More than a half century after the death of Edgar Young Mullins, why publish a full-length biography of this Southern Baptist leader? What could be relevant about the life of a man whose influence apparently ended so long ago? Mullins was at the center of the evolution/modernist controversy in the 1920s. As president of Southern Baptist Theological Seminary in Louisville, Kentucky, from 1899 to 1928, he came under scathing attack from Southern Baptist fundamentalists. For almost three decades Mullins helped guide his denomination through troubled doctrinal waters. Moreover, his life reflected most of the major issues and questions with which American Protestants struggled in the late nineteenth and and early twentieth centuries.[1]

---

[1]There exists only one published study of Mullins, that of his wife, Isla May Mullins, *Edgar Young Mullins: An Intimate Biography* (Nashville: Sunday School Board of the Southern Baptist Convention, 1929). Other studies include: Russell Hooper Dilday, Jr., "The Apologetic Method of E. Y. Mullins" (Th.D. diss., Southwestern Baptist Theological Seminary, 1960); Charles J. Ferris, "Southern Baptists and Evolution in the 1920s: The Roles of Edgar Young Mul-

In addition to the evolution/modernist controversy, Mullins's term as president of Southern Seminary saw the denomination make its final rush for full independence from Northern Baptist influence and the establishment of a separate identity. As a consequence, the Southern Baptist Convention grew in numbers and territory during his lifetime.

Even more far-reaching changes were afoot in American Protestantism and in American culture in general. American Protestantism lost its hegemony over the culture of the nation. The presidential election of 1928 foreshadowed this loss of definitive Protestant control over American institutions. Mullins died just a few days after this critical election, one in which he joined with fundamentalists to oppose the candidacy of Governor Alfred E. Smith. Finally, higher criticism, evolution, and modernism had divided most mainline Protestant denominations into fundamentalist and modernist wings. On the other hand, Southern Baptists survived as a denominational unit and remained true to their evangelical ethos. Only moderates and fundamentalists contended for control of the generally conservative Southern Baptist denomination.

After years of neglect or abuse by scholars of American history and American religion, evangelicalism and fundamentalism have begun to receive serious treatment once again.[2] Contrary to the theses of many

---

lins, J. Frank Norris, and William Louis Poteat" (M.A. thesis, University of Louisville, 1973); James Howell Perry, "Edgar Young Mullins" (M.A. thesis, Southern Baptist Theological Seminary, 1951); Julius H. Spears, "The Christology of Edgar Young Mullins" (M.A. thesis, Duke University, 1945); and Bill Clark Thomas, "Edgar Young Mullins: A Baptist Exponent of Theological Restatement" (Th.D. diss., Southern Baptist Theological Seminary, 1963).

Several recent books provide excellent introductions to Protestant history in Mullins's era. See especially Norman H. Clark, *Deliver Us from Evil: An Interpretation of American Prohibition* (New York: W. W. Norton, 1976); George M. Marsden, *Fundamentalism and American Culture: The Shaping of Twentieth-Century Evangelicalism, 1870-1925* (New York: Oxford University Press, 1980); Ferenc Morton Szasz, *The Divided Mind of Protestant America, 1880-1930* (University AL: University of Alabama Press, 1982); and James J. Thompson, Jr., *Tried as by Fire: Southern Baptists and the Religious Controversies of the 1920s* (Macon GA: Mercer University Press, 1982). For a more complete list, see the appended bibliographical essay.

[2]See Leonard I. Sweet, ed., *The Evangelical Tradition in America* (Macon GA: Mercer University Press, 1984), particularly the opening historiographical essay by Sweet. See also William E. Ellis, "Evolution, Fundamentalism, and the Historians: An Historiographical Review," *The Historian* 44 (November 1981): 15-27.

liberal critics, neither evangelicalism nor fundamentalism has faded in the modern era. As a matter of fact, both have grown in numbers since World War II, outstripping more liberal movements.

Evangelicalism, never an entirely American phenomenon, broke from the constraints of Calvinism in the earliest days of the Great Awakening. Fueled by the revival fires of the Great Revival era, Wesleyanism, and the exuberance of a young nation, the movement struck at the heart of nearly every American denomination in the early nineteenth century. The Southern environment appeared particularly fertile, and mainline denominations there, such as Baptists, Methodists, Presbyterians, and Disciples of Christ, evidenced a more evangelical thrust than their Northern counterparts. Stressing the annual revival while retaining the free grace, born-again conversion experience added immeasurably to the growth of such denominations as the Southern Baptists in the twentieth century.

Fundamentalism is a predominantly twentieth-century variation of evangelicalism, in effect, becoming the most conservative wing of the larger movement. The characteristics of fundamentalism are generally more pronounced than those of evangelicalism. From the variety of definitions offered by recent scholars, we can extract a number of characteristics of fundamentalism: an emphasis on the inerrancy of the Bible; a strong tendency toward dispensational premillennialism, a stress on revivalistic techniques to secure its central goal of saving souls; a belief in personal moral purity; strong hostility to modern theology; and a belief that those who do not share its convictions are not true Christians. Most of these characteristics contribute to alienation from modern religion, society, and culture.[3]

Southern Baptists have remained firmly within the bounds of American evangelicalism, with a probable majority of that denomination at any one time tending toward the conservative wing of evangelicalism: fundamentalism. Southern Baptists are evangelical in the sense that they place a near complete dependence on the born-again witnessing of the conversion experience of each individual member of the local church. The dictum "once saved, always saved" is indeed a vestige of the Calvinist heritage of Southern Baptists, but the evangelical, Arminian strain

---

[3]Sweet, *The Evangelical Tradition in America*, 20, 36, 42, 72-86; James Barr, *Fundamentalism* (Philadelphia: The Westminster Press, 1978) 1-5, 338-39, 342.

has been stronger since the turn of the century. One cannot be a Southern Baptist in spirit without being an evangelical Christian.[4]

The Southern Baptist Convention has placed its own distinctive stamp on evangelicalism/fundamentalism, just as it has been uniquely shaped by each movement. Unlike the other mainline denominations in the South, the Southern Baptist Convention has retained the evangelical thrust that has been largely responsible for its numerical success. A liberal or modernist faction has been virtually absent from the Southern Baptist fold; those whom fundamentalists identified as modernists, in Mullins's time and since, were actually moderates. Although the moderates may have represented more of the laity than is commonly assumed, fundamentalists have nearly always been able to marshal a majority of votes at the Convention's annual meetings on critical issues—whether a test of the evolution issue in the 1920s or the presidency of the Convention in the 1980s. Furthermore, moderates have never been as well known nor as colorful as fundamentalists such as J. Frank Norris, the self-proclaimed leader of Southern Baptist fundamentalists well into the 1950s.[5]

Mullins personified the dilemma of moderate Southern Baptists and, more generally, moderate evangelicals in America. His theological position remained consistently stable between that of modernism, which eventually disavowed supernaturalism, and fundamentalism, which relied almost entirely on its nineteenth-century antecedents. His devotion to evangelicalism never wavered, but he desired something more than old-fashioned camp meeting religious fervor for his denomination. In his multiple roles as theologian, administrator, and denominational leader, he tried to intellectualize evangelicalism as it came in contact with the newest and most revolutionary ideas of the late nineteenth and early twentieth centuries. For a while he apparently succeeded, but in the end he failed to develop a moderate evangelical synthesis that would mollify both fundamentalists and modernists. His failure was due in part to the diversity within the Southern Baptist Con-

---

[4]James Leo Garrett, Jr., E. Glenn Hinson, and James E. Tull, *Are Southern Baptists "Evangelicals"?* (Macon GA: Mercer University Press, 1983) 126, 174.

[5]William E. Ellis, "Edgar Young Mullins and the Crisis of Moderate Southern Baptist Leadership," *Foundations* 19 (April-June 1976): 171-85.

vention, the growing strength of fundamentalism within the Convention, the theological intransigence of both left and right, and his own innate conservatism. Perhaps the effort was doomed from the start.[6]

I wish to thank many people who have contributed to this book. Richard Lowitt, George Robinson, Ferenc M. Szasz, James J. Thompson, Jr., and Dixie Mylum have offered the intellectual stimulation so necessary to finishing such a project. Eastern Kentucky University made generous grants for research and publication. Finally, my parents, my wife Charlotte, and Bill, Eva, Greg, and Andrew have provided more inspiration than they can ever imagine.

---

[6]Ibid.

1   FROM THE OLD SOUTH TO THE NEW SOUTH

In the antebellum South, slavery predetermined the lives of both master and slave. Even the non-slaveowner came under the direct influence of a culture, mindset, and ethos that became increasingly defensive in the 1850s. The tensions that had divided North and South for generations accelerated in that decade. The political schism that rent the nation in 1860 presaged the violence and heartbreak that would soon erupt in the American Civil War. Into that milieu Edgar Young Mullins was born. His heritage was Southern to the core and conservative in most matters political, social, and theological.

Edgar Young Mullins was born on 5 January 1860 in Franklin County, Mississippi. He was the fourth of eleven children born to Seth Granberry Mullins and Sarah Cornelia Barnes Tillman Mullins. Both parents were natives of Mississippi and of English and Irish ancestry. Small landholders owning a few slaves were predominant on both sides of the family.[1]

---

[1]Isla May Mullins, *Edgar Young Mullins: An Intimate Biography* (Nashville: Sunday School Board of the Southern Baptist Convention, 1929) 10; Kate Mullins to the author, 4 January 1973.

Seth Mullins, like his father, William, was a Baptist preacher. Edgar's parents were married in 1853 at Pine Bluff, Copiah County, Mississippi. The older girls were also born in that county.[2] Seth pastored small churches in the area and attended Mississippi College in Clinton, the state Baptist college. After graduation in 1857, he accepted the call of the Hopewell Baptist Church, a rural sanctuary near Bude in Franklin County, Mississippi.[3] Although Hopewell was one of the oldest churches in the state, it did not offer enough compensation to support the growing Mullins family, so Seth supplemented his income by operating a farm near the church.[4] Census records for 1860 show that he owned $1,600 in real estate and $5,500 in personal property.[5] The latter consisted of four slaves, all rather young, but at least two of whom were old enough to be field hands.[6]

Franklin County was one of the first areas settled in the state and part of the old "black belt" or brown loam area east of Natchez. By 1860 the area was experiencing economic difficulty because of erosion and loss of soil fertility. Land declined precipitously in value. More than fifty percent of the population was slaves, but most of their owners were small farmers much like the Mullins family. The county continued to empha-

---

[2]Hawley-Mullins Family Bible (located at the Southern Baptist Theological Seminary Library); Enclosure from Allyn Gordon, 8 January 1974.

[3]Lorena Dean, Circuit Clerk of Franklin County, Mississippi, to the author, 21 November 1972; Howard E. Spell, dean, Mississippi College, to Duke McCall, president of Southern Seminary, 4 May 1959 (located in the Hawley-Mullins Family Bible).

[4]Z. T. Leavell and T. J. Bailey, *A Complete History of Mississippi Baptists From the Earliest Times* (Jackson MS: Mississippi Baptist Publishing Company, 1904) 1:42, 57.

[5]*1860 Census,* Schedule 1, Franklin County, Mississippi, 86 (Enclosure from the Department of Archives and History, Jackson, Mississippi, 24 November 1972).

[6]*1860 Census,* Schedule 2, Franklin County, Mississippi, 178 (Enclosure from the National Archives, 13 December 1972).

size the cultivation of cotton as the major cash crop.[7] In this environment the younger Mullins lived the first years of his life.

The Civil War struck hard in Mississippi, disrupting all institutions and ending the Mullinses' bucolic life. It is not known specifically how Seth reacted to the conflict that led to war, but most of his ministerial colleagues, particularly the Baptists, contributed to the war fever.[8] The 1861 Mississippi Baptist State Association enthusiastically supported secession.[9] Ministers were exempt from military service. Because of serious economic problems, most ministers had to support themselves in any way possible.[10] Baptist churches in the state lost vitality during the war due to the men being away fighting and the loss of donations. During the last part of the war the state experienced a revival movement as a result of the physical and psychological havoc caused by the war.[11]

The war directly touched the Mullins family. Seth's only adult brother, Hardy Franklin, a graduate of Mississippi College in 1859, served in the 12th Mississippi Volunteer Regiment. He died in combat near Richmond, Virginia, in the summer of 1864. While the war never reached Seth's household, the family suffered some economic privation during Sherman's siege of nearby Vicksburg in the winter and spring of 1863. A short while later Seth took his family back to Copiah County.[12]

During the Civil War a general breakdown of law and order occurred in Mississippi. Economic problems coupled with Union occu-

---

[7]John K. Buttersworth, *Confederate Mississippi* (Baton Rouge: Louisiana State University Press, 1943) v; Herbert Weaver, *Mississippi Farmers, 1850-1860* (Nashville: Vanderbilt University Press, 1945) 118-19; Percy Lee Rainwater, *Mississippi: Storm Center of Secession* (Baton Rouge: Otto Claitor, 1938) 6, 201, 206.

[8]James W. Silver, *Confederate Morale and Church Propaganda* (Gloucester MA: Peter Smith, 1964) 93-101.

[9]Bettersworth, *Confederate Mississippi*, 286.

[10]Bettersworth, *Mississippi: A History* (Austin TX: The Steck Co., 1959) 307.

[11]Leavell and Bailey, *A Complete History of Mississippi Baptists From the Earliest Times,* 1:61, 97-98.

[12]Spell to McCall, 4 May 1959; Enclosure from Allyn Gordon, 8 January 1974.

pation of the Mississippi River Valley created widespread despair.[13] These conditions did not improve during the early phases of Reconstruction. Many Mississippians moved to Texas, a state that presented new opportunities. In addition, the yellow fever epidemic of the late 1860s drove many to seek relief from this scourge in the West.[14]

Other than the general reasons mentioned, it is not known why Seth moved to Texas. The family, having grown to seven children with the youngest only a little over a year old, began the trek westward on 16 November 1869. They traveled by train to New Orleans and then by boat to Galveston. After visiting Sarah's relatives in Houston for a few weeks, they moved on to Chappell Hill, a small settlement in Washington County. Sarah's parents also left Mississippi at about the same time, settling in Corsicana, Texas. Seth remained in Chappell Hill for eighteen months, preaching regularly at the Providence Baptist Church, before moving to Corsicana, where he helped reorganize a Baptist church and establish a school.[15]

Corsicana, in Navarro County, was still a frontier town during the Reconstruction era. One resident reported "disorders" because of "outlaws" and "pillaging soldiers" in 1871, but in that same year the first railroad, the Houston and Texas Central, penetrated the area and the next year connected Corsicana with Dallas.[16] Indian problems contin-

---

[13]Bettersworth, *Confederate Mississippi*, 5-36, 40-44, 90-92.

[14]Bettersworth, *Mississippi: A History*, 318-21; William C. Harris, *Presidential Reconstruction in Mississippi* (Baton Rouge: Louisiana State University Press, 1967) 3-36; T. R. Fehrenbach, *Lone Star: A History of Texas and the Texans* (New York: The Macmillan Company, 1968) 597; Kate Mullins to the author, 4 January 1973; Enclosure from Allyn Gordon, 8 January 1974.

[15]Robert J. Potts, pastor of the First Baptist Church, Corsicana, Texas, to the author, 12 December 1972 (citation from a manuscript history of the church); Kenneth Trinkle, *This Heritage Is Ours* (Corsicana TX: First Baptist Church, 1964) 2; Jesse L. Boyd, *A Popular History of the Baptists in Mississippi* (Jackson MS: Baptist Press, 1930) 264; Enclosure from Allyn Gordon, 8 January 1974.

[16]Frank W. Johnson and Eugene C. Barker, *A History of Texas and Texans* (New York: The American Historical Society, 1914) 762-63; Rupert Norval Richardson, *Texas: The Lone Star State* (New York: Prentice-Hall, 1944) 348.

ued to create havoc on the nearby Northwest Texas frontier until 1875.[17] Corsicana also suffered through some of the political disruption of Reconstruction. In 1869 and 1871, for example, election voting lists and ballot boxes were stolen, adding to the turmoil of those years.[18]

Edgar received a grammar school education in his father's school, as well as educational and moral instruction at home. The elder Mullins's reading tastes went beyond those typical of a small town Baptist preacher. When Edgar was fourteen, he began to read his father's copy of a volume by Herbert Spencer. Seth admonished his son, saying that Edgar was too young to read the book profitably, but he could do so when he became more mature. Upon later finding his son reading a cheap pulp novel, Seth gave the boy a multivolume set of Jared Sparks's *Library of American Biography* on the condition that each volume be read carefully. Edgar later stated that this "event marked a new era in my life and a transformation in my literary ideals." Seth subsequently encouraged him to read Henry George's *Progress and Poverty* "as a masterful argument and a model of pure English."[19]

Edgar's parents did not "coerce" him into accepting their specific Baptist beliefs but did inculcate "the principle of right living."[20] The religious, pietistic view of life permeated every teaching of the elder Mullins. Later in life Edgar determined that the "best thing" his father had ever done "was to make me believe that results are always possible to honest effort." Though a "peaceful man," the elder Mullins was not op-

---

[17]Fehrenbach, *Lone Star: A History of Texas and the Texans*, 522-51, 571, 587.

[18]Ibid., 415; W. C. Nunn, *Texas Under the Carpetbaggers* (Austin TX: University of Texas Press, 1962) 18, 58.

[19]Louisville *Baptist World*, 19 September 1912.

[20]Edgar Young Mullins, "Why I Am a Baptist," *Forum* 75 (May 1926): 725. After reading the article, Broadus Mitchell, economics professor at The Johns Hopkins University, said that he had had an opposite experience as a boy and urged that Mullins implore his students to "refrain from evangelistic bludgeoning." Mitchell to Mullins, 18 May 1926 (Unless otherwise noted, Mullins's correspondence is located at Southern Seminary, Presidential Correspondence, 1899-1928). Mullins agreed that sometimes over-zealous evangelists were dangerous. He declared that his parents had never exerted undue "pressure." Mullins to Mitchell, 22 May 1926.

posed to using the "rod" in his schoolroom when he thought it necessary. His racial pronouncements were of a paternalistic nature. During Reconstruction, for example, "he discouraged all discussion of the race question" after hearing some disparaging remarks about Negroes from the older children. Seth declared that the children were not yet mature enough to make decisions on such serious topics.[21]

Due to the low family income and his fundamental belief in the value of hard work, Seth encouraged Edgar to take part-time jobs. Edgar's three older sisters attended Baylor Female College, and his work contributed to the total economic benefit of the family.[22] During his adolescent years Mullins had numerous work experiences. His first job, at the age of eleven, was as a newsboy for the local weekly paper, the *Bugle*. He later held part-time jobs as a printer's devil and a typesetter for the same paper.[23]

A few years later he left the *Bugle* and went to work as a telegraph messenger. Within a few months he had learned the Morse code and began working as a part-time telegraph operator. Edgar finished his grammar school education and continued to study and read at home under his father's direction. By the age of fifteen he had charge of the local telegraph office at the regular wage normally paid the adult operators.[24] The young Texan enjoyed the wild prairies of Navarro County and found time for hunting, fishing, trapping, and swimming. As a rather "adventurous" young man, he suffered near misses with death on several occasions when he almost drowned, was in a serious railroad accident, and received a slight facial wound in a hunting mishap.[25]

---

[21]*Baptist World*, 19 September 1912; Walter Brownlow Posey, *The Baptist Church in the Lower Mississippi Valley, 1776-1845* (Lexington: University of Kentucky Press, 1957) 155-56.

[22]Mullins, *Mullins*, 11; Perry, "Edgar Young Mullins," 2.

[23]*Courier-Journal*, 24 November 1928.

[24]Mullins, *Mullins*, 11.

[25]A. T. Robertson, "A Sketch of the Life of President Mullins," *Review and Expositor* 22 (January 1925): 7. Mrs. Mullins wrote a fictionalized account of her husband's early life entitled *Captain Pluck* (New York: George H. Doran Co., 1923). *Courier-Journal*, 24 November 1928.

In his adolescent years Mullins demonstrated a proclivity toward much activity and an impatience to reach maturity as soon as possible. He was active in school, work, and play, but did not take an active part in his father's church. When it was determined that he needed a formal education, Mullins already had experience that belied his years.

At the age of sixteen Edgar entered college. He never explained his reasons for attending the Agricultural and Mechanical College of Texas instead of Baylor College, the state Baptist school for men. A partial explanation might be the fact that he had never experienced a religious conversion and was not an official member of his father's church. He had no compulsion, therefore, to go to a denominational school. Moreover, A. and M. also offered an inexpensive education, a factor of considerable importance to a young man of modest means. In addition, the possibility of a technical education probably intrigued the young telegraph operator.[26]

Mullins entered with the first class at the school in 1876.[27] A. and M. displayed two dominant characteristics during these early years of existence: a pervading Southern "Lost Cause" atmosphere and a lack of clear direction for its chartered purpose, the training of young men in the mechanical and agricultural arts. Governor Richard Coke, a former Confederate captain, pushed the chartering of the Brazos County institution and first offered the presidency to Jefferson Davis. Davis gracefully declined, but he recommended Thomas S. Gathright, the State Superintendent of Public Instruction in Mississippi. Coke and the Board of Trustees took this advice and appointed Gathright.[28] The school demonstrated a decided Confederate milieu. Several of the faculty and staff were former Confederate officers. One faculty member personally outfitted a regiment, and Hamilton P. Bee, a former general, served as the first steward in charge of the college commissary.[29]

---

[26]Perry, "Edgar Young Mullins," 62.

[27]R. A. Lacey, Registrar, Texas A. and M. University, to the author, 30 August 1972, 14 September 1972. The records were destroyed in a fire in 1912.

[28]Clarence Ousley, "History of the Agricultural and Mechanical College of Texas," *Bulletin of the Agricultural and Mechanical College of Texas* (1 December 1935) 42; George Sessions Perry, *The Story of Texas A. and M.* (New York: McGraw-Hill, 1951) 57, 59.

[29]Perry, *The Story of Texas A. and M.*, 60, 64.

Gathright emphasized the study of literature over training in agriculture, mechanics, and engineering. He also opposed the military discipline and training and often clashed with Major Page Morris, the Commandant of the A. and M. regiment. The curriculum changed abruptly with the dismissal of Gathright in 1879.[30]

A. and M. presented a rather harsh environment for a sixteen year old away from home for the first time. One student remembered the prairie "swarming with grasshoppers" upon his arrival at the campus, which consisted of only two isolated buildings. The military drill was "very strict," and near the end of the first semester many students came down with measles.[31] Another of the original students recalled that the school did not open on the scheduled date because only six students had arrived by that time. Mullins was not among the original number, but he enrolled by the date of the delayed opening, 4 October 1876.[32]

The young cadet received a literary or liberal arts course within a military atmosphere.[33] Military discipline broke down on at least one occasion "when the Corps marched away in a body to the Brazos River bottom" for a swim on a hot April Fool's Day.[34] Though there are no academic records for Mullins available, one professor remembered him as "a fine student and a fine fellow."[35] A classmate referred to him as "the unforgettable" member of the student body at the Texas institution.[36]

Mullins took part in most of the school's activities. By the end of his stay at A. and M. he had risen to the rank of Second Lieutenant of Com-

---

[30]Ibid., 65-66; Ousley, "History of the Agricultural and Mechanical College of Texas," 45-51, 88.

[31]David Brooks Cofer, *Early History of Texas A. and M. College through Letters and Papers* (College Station: The Association of Former Students of Texas A. and M. College, 1952) 130-31.

[32]Ousley, "History of the Agricultural and Mechanical College of Texas," 46.

[33]Ibid., 45, 88.

[34]E. B. Cushing to Mullins, 1 April 1916.

[35]Cofer, *Early History of Texas A. and M. College,* 76.

[36]Ibid., 112.

pany C. In his last year he served as an associate editor of the school newspaper, *The Texas Collegian*.[37] As a charter member of the first campus organization, the Stephen F. Austin Literary Society, Mullins participated in numerous debates, including one on the eve of his graduation in 1879. This experience contributed to his general education and enlivened his years in College Station by offering "some diversion and recreation."[38]

Unsure about the future course of his life, Mullins returned to telegraphy full-time, obtaining a good position at Galveston. He intended to become a lawyer and began reading law in his spare time.[39] According to Baptist doctrine and polity, he had "no connection" with the church of his parents, never having experienced a conversion and publicly making a profession of faith. Baptists, in particular, maintained that such an individual spiritual upheaval was necessary for admittance to the fellowship of their church.[40]

On a trip to Dallas a few months after graduation, Mullins's life took an abrupt turn while attending a revival meeting at the First Baptist Church led by Major W. E. Penn, a lay evangelist. He experienced what he considered to be an "old fashioned" conversion. "Without any emotional cataclysm," he reported, "I yielded my will to Christ." Later in life he declared that his strong religious inclinations had been overshadowed by "intellectual doubt." This skepticism had been particularly evident during his college days. "The moral and spiritual reenforcement which followed this act," Mullins contended, "completely transformed my purposes and plans."[41] On 7 November 1880 Seth baptized his son at Corsicana, the last of nine surviving children to be converted to the Baptist faith.[42]

---

[37]Larry D. Hill, Department of History, Texas A. and M. University, to the author, 11 October 1972.

[38]Cofer, *Fragments of Early History of Texas A. and M. College* (College Station: The Association of Former Students of Texas A. and M. College, 1953) 5, 7-8.

[39]Robertson, "A Sketch of the Life of President Mullins," 7.

[40]Mullins, "Why I Am a Baptist," 725.

[41]Ibid.

[42]Mullins, *Mullins*, 12.

Edgar returned to telegraphy, but very soon decided to begin study for the Baptist ministry.[43] Southern Baptists believe that a minister is "called" to the ministry of God. Education is considered secondary to one's fulfillment of God's will.[44] Mullins was thoroughly convinced that a man must receive such a "call," but was also sure that to be truly effective a minister must be educated. The elder Mullins encouraged his son to obtain formal seminary training. As a Southern Baptist with an undergraduate degree, the logical school to enter was the Southern Baptist Theological Seminary, which offered the equivalent of postgraduate theological training.[45]

Mullins entered Southern Seminary in the autumn of 1881.[46] As a result of the Baptist schism over the slavery issue in 1845, Southern Seminary had grown very slowly. Even before this break in Baptist cooperation, because of the slavery issue, some Southerners had asked for their own seminary.[47] With the formation of the Southern Baptist Convention it became "highly imperative" that Southern Baptists "develop their own theological school."[48] After much financial difficulty, Southern Seminary was founded in 1859 at Greenville, South Carolina.[49] During the Civil War the school suspended operations. The entire period of 1865 to 1877 was a period of unending financial struggle for the school. Salaries were often in arrears, and professors had to preach regularly

---

[43]Perry, "Edgar Young Mullins," 2.

[44]Samuel S. Hill, Jr., and Robert G. Torbet, *Baptists—North and South* (Valley Forge PA: The Judson Press, 1964) 55.

[45]Thomas, "Edgar Young Mullins: A Baptist Exponent of Theological Restatement," 80-81; Mullins, *Mullins,* 12.

[46]Mullins, *Mullins,* 13.

[47]Robert A. Baker, *Relations Between Northern and Southern Baptists* (Fort Worth TX: Seminary Hill Press, 1948) 43-87; William A. Mueller, *A History of Southern Baptist Theological Seminary* (Nashville: Broadman Press, 1959) 5-6, 8.

[48]Mueller, *A History of Southern Baptist Theological Seminary,* 9.

[49]Ibid., 13-15.

in order to make a living.[50] In 1877 the school moved to Louisville after Kentucky Baptists pledged an enlarged endowment.[51]

Just two years before Mullins entered the Seminary, the Louisville school experienced its first major theological controversy. C. H. Toy, a professor for ten years, resigned in 1879 because he could not "reconcile Scripture and science" to his own satisfaction or that of his colleagues and the Southern Baptist constituency. Two years of study at the University of Berlin had convinced Toy that evolution explained theological as well as biological processes. He also doubted the orthodox views of biblical inspiration.[52] The denominational debate over Toy's alleged heresy accentuated an already difficult financial situation at Southern Seminary. In 1879, for example, funds intended for endowment investment had to be diverted for operating expenses. Chairman of the faculty James P. Boyce declared that Toy's ideas threatened the future of the Seminary. Toy decided not to fight and resigned. Basil Manly, Jr., a conservative on the question of biblical inspiration, replaced him. After Toy left, no other professor considered teaching the theological and teleological implications of Darwinism.[53]

The faculty, during Mullins's matriculation, consisted of Boyce, John A. Broadus, Manly, William H. Whitsitt, and George W. Riggan. Boyce served as chairman of the faculty without the designation of president. These men were adequate scholars, adamant Baptists, and generally

---

[50]John R. Sampey, *Southern Baptist Theological Seminary: The First Thirty Years, 1859-1889* (Baltimore: Wharton, Barron, 1890) 14.

[51]Leo T. Crismon, "Southern Baptist Theological Seminary," *Encyclopedia of Southern Baptists* (Nashville: Broadman Press, 1958) 2:1269-73; Sampey, *Southern Baptist Theological Seminary*, 16; Mueller, *A History of Southern Baptist Theological Seminary*, 39-43.

[52]Billy Grey Hurt, "Crawford Howell Toy: Interpreter of the Old Testament" (Th.D. diss., Southern Baptist Theological Seminary, 1965) 41-50, 177, 184, 260; William R. Hutchison, *The Modernist Impulse in American Protestantism* (Cambridge MA: Harvard University Press, 1976) 77.

[53]Ibid., 176, 186, 197; Marjorie May Dysart, "Darwinism versus Southern Orthodoxy: A Survey of Southern Thought About Evolution as Reflected in Periodicals of Four Protestant Churches, 1865-1900" (M.A. thesis, University of Kentucky, 1954) 73; Kenneth K. Bailey, *Southern White Protestantism in the Twentieth Century* (New York: Harper and Row, 1964) 12.

conservative. All had accommodated themselves to the "New South" ideology of Southern Bourbonism and the corresponding civil religion of the "Lost Cause."[54] They were Southern to the core, even if they had studied outside the South or in Europe. Southern Seminary retained its Southernness although having moved from a Deep South state to a border state of the upper South. Whitsitt was the most liberal teacher, though hardly subversive to Baptist doctrine. The faculty followed the traditional recitation method with few exceptions.[55]

Mullins participated in the "full course," a four-year curriculum. The Seminary offered no formal degrees except awards as "Full Graduates" or, on a lower level, "English Graduates."[56] It did not offer masters and doctoral degrees until after Mullins's graduation. Courses were called "electives" but, in effect, were prescribed. There were no definite entrance requirements, and students of varying levels of academic achievement attended the same classes. The "core course" was the study of the English Bible rather than the Hebrew and Greek Bible as was common in the older seminaries of the Northeast.[57] Those who chose the path toward the "Full Graduate" award took extra courses in the Hebrew, Greek, and German languages. A student of poorer educational background took any course except those in the languages.[58] Usually only about one-half of the student body was made up of college graduates. This trend prevailed until around the turn of the century.[59]

---

[54]Bailey, *Southern White Protestantism in the Twentieth Century*, 9; Mueller, *A History of Southern Baptist Theological Seminary*, 16-134.

[55]William O. Carver, "Recollections and Information from Other Sources Concerning the Southern Baptist Theological Seminary" (unpublished manuscript, Southern Baptist Theological Seminary Library, 1954) 18-22 (hereinafter cited as Carver, "Recollections").

For a description of the role of religion in the development of the Lost Cause see Charles Reagan Wilson, *Baptized in Blood: The Religion of the Lost Cause, 1865-1920* (Athens: University of Georgia Press, 1980) 35, 119-38, 161-82.

[56]*Catalogue of the Southern Baptist Theological Seminary, 1881-1882*, 7, 22.

[57]Mueller, *A History of Southern Baptist Theological Seminary*, 113-14.

[58]Ibid., 114-17; Carver, "Recollections," 77.

[59]Carver, "Recollections," 17.

Southern Seminary charged no tuition, but estimated expenses for room, board, and incidentals were approximately $120 for an eight-month term. Grants and loans were available, but a student usually received only partial aid.[60] When Edgar entered the Seminary in 1881, the school continually struggled for endowment and was in so precarious a financial condition that it was forced to use uninvested endowment money for current expenses. The Seminary administration used endowment increments to pay salaries, and special donations supplemented the Student Aid Fund. Increased endowment money, especially a gift of $50,000 by former Governor Joseph E. Brown of Georgia in 1880, started Southern Seminary toward greater financial stability and growth.[61]

Mullins successfully negotiated his first-year classes in Old Testament Interpretation, English; Old Testament Hebrew, Junior Class; New Testament Interpretation, English; and New Testament Greek, Junior Class. College graduates normally took these courses in their first session at Southern.[62] Permanent grade records were not kept during Mullins's matriculation, since the faculty discouraged student competition. Each individual course was called a "school." After passing one course, or school, a student was permitted to take the next course in the sequence. The academic year was not divided into semesters. A course continued for the entire eight-month term.[63] Difficult and lengthy examinations, nine to ten hours long, were given for each course at the middle and end of the session.[64]

The young Texas theolog paid his first year's expenses from his savings. At the end of the session his fellow students elected him manager of Waverly Hall, the dormitory. This responsibility included planning meals, purchasing food, and arranging housing. As manager he did not have to pay any fees. A successful administrator, he was reelected to the

---

[60]*Catalogue of the Southern Baptist Theological Seminary, 1881-1882*, 22.

[61]Mueller, *A History of Southern Baptist Theological Seminary*, 45-47.

[62]Diplomas, 6 May 1882, signed by Boyce, Manly, and Broadus (Southern Baptist Theological Seminary Library).

[63]Isla May Mullins, "Dr. Mullins as a Student," *Review and Expositor* 26 (April 1929): 144.

[64]Mueller, *A History of Southern Baptist Theological Seminary*, 115-16.

same post for his remaining two years at the Seminary. He earned money in the summers as a telegrapher and supplied the pulpits of various churches during the school term.[65]

In his second year at Southern Seminary Mullins completed courses in New Testament, Senior Greek; Systematic Theology, English; Homiletics; and German.[66] During the third year he studied Church Government and Pastoral Duties; Old Testament Hebrew, Senior Class; Biblical Introduction; and Ecclesiastical History.[67] In 1884-1885 he passed Polemic Theology and Systematic Theology, Latin and was awarded the "Full Graduate" degree "having obtained Degrees in all the schools."[68]

His class elected him as one of the five student graduation speakers, the only honor bestowed on a graduating student. Mullins chose as his topic "Manliness in the Ministry." He viewed the ministry as any other profession, entailing responsibilities of public trust. A minister should ask for no special favors nor accept "small charities" like a "pauper," but should be adequately rewarded for his ministrations. Only then could a minister hold up his head as a proud and integral part of his community.[69]

The life of the young theolog was not limited to work and study. Early in his third year of study, Mullins met Isla May Hawley at a student reception at the Walnut Street Baptist Church in Louisville. Her family had recently come to the city from Selma, Alabama. The young couple began dating and enjoyed attending lectures, band concerts, and art ex-

[65]Mullins, *Mullins,* 13-14. While a student, Mullins preached for several months at Colesburg, Kentucky. Sam N. Hurst to Mullins, 26 February 1910. A classmate and, later, colleague of Mullins at Southern Seminary praised his planning and efficiency in that position. Years later, he still recalled with amazement Mullins's ability to serve turkey and oysters on Christmas Day 1883 and turkey and ice cream on New Year's Day 1884 on such a limited budget. Sampey, *Memoirs* (Nashville: Broadman Press, 1947) 29.

[66]Diplomas, 5 May 1883, signed by Boyce and Broadus.

[67]Diplomas, 2 June 1884, signed by Boyce, Manly, Whitsitt, and Riggan.

[68]Diplomas, 1 June 1885, signed by Boyce and Whitsitt. Mullins was also granted the "Full Graduate" diploma.

[69]Louisville *Western Recorder,* 4 June 1885.

hibits together. Edgar shared with Isla May his ambition to go to Brazil as a missionary upon graduation.[70]

Mullins graduation picture shows him as a rather boyish twenty-five year old with a full though sparse beard. Standing a little over six feet tall, his thin stature accentuated his height.[71] The picture belies the fact that the young man had worked hard to obtain his education and had had numerous experiences that matured him beyond his years. He believed, like most middle-class Americans of the late nineteenth century, that hard and diligent work guaranteed success. Though late in coming, his evangelical faith was firm and sincere. His theological education had been orthodox by the standards of the day, but he had a predilection for inquiry into all realms of thought and a great store of energy. Mullins's background prepared him for the sometimes turbulent world of the Southern Baptist minister.

---

[70]Mullins, *Mullins,* 15-19.

[71]This composite picture of his graduating class is located in the Southern Seminary Library.

2

"A MAN OF BOOKS
AND A MAN
OF THE PEOPLE"

Mullins's first years in the Baptist ministry gave him a broad range of experiences and prepared him for more important posts. Each position offered more opportunity than the previous one and also provided a larger income, no small matter to one who had been raised to accept the tenets of the Protestant work ethic. He was a young man on his way up and, displaying confidence in his ability, would not be content with minor pastorates.

While Mullins concluded his seminary training, he considered the options open to a young, relatively well-trained Southern Baptist minister. He supplied the pulpit of the Harrodsburg, Kentucky, First Baptist Church for a few weeks prior to graduation from seminary. His first ambition was to go to Brazil as a missionary. He asked the Foreign Mission Board of the Southern Baptist Convention for an appointment, but "received no response" since there was a lack of funds. Shortly afterward a Harrodsburg physician advised him to forgo his desire to go to the tropics, because the climate would seriously impair his health. The precise nature of his illness at this time is not known, though later in life he suffered from chronic respiratory ailments.[1]

When the Harrodsburg church extended a call to him, Mullins accepted the offer in May 1885. At the time, he was only licensed to preach. According to usual Southern Baptist procedure of that day the regular minister had to be "ordained" to his task. They considered a licensed minister to be undergoing a period of testing and preparation, while the ordained minister was considered to be officially appointed.[2] The church invited a visiting presbytery consisting of nine Baptist ministers to examine Mullins closely on the doctrine of the denomination on 6 June 1885. The group questioned him about his beliefs on Christianity and his views of the Bible, and they agreed that he showed sincerity as well as knowledge and should be accepted. The church then voted to ordain Mullins properly. The presbytery and deacons of the church performed the necessary ceremonies, officially ordaining Mullins into the Baptist ministry.[3]

After a few months in his new post, Mullins reflected on his initial experiences of ministering to his small-town, mostly middle-class parishioners. He believed the work to be progressing, but he felt hampered in sermon selection. Moreover, sermons had to be popularized to suit the nonintellectual climate of his church. Some sermons that he laboriously developed could not be used; however, one possible outlet was publication. If a young pastor wanted to broaden his ministry, he mused, "Why can he not be a man of books and a man of the people both?" Mullins maintained that he intended to study and write as well as minister to the needs of his congregation. One ministerial responsibility he did not relish; his parishioners expected far too much visitation and this was a "source of considerable annoyance."[4]

---

[1]Mullins, *Mullins*, 21.

[2]*Harrodsburg Baptist Church* (Harrodsburg: First Baptist Church, 1961) 17; Winthrop Still Hudson, *Baptist Convictions* (Valley Forge PA: Judson Press, 1963) 18-19; Norman H. Maring and Winthrop Still Hudson, *A Baptist Manual of Polity and Practice* (Valley Forge PA: Judson Press, 1963) 101-104.

[3]*Western Recorder*, 18 June 1885.

[4]Mullins to E. M. Poteat, 16 November 1885.

In response to the young minister's efforts the church spent $1,500 renovating the main auditorium and reported that it was quite satisfied with Mullins's ministry.[5] Mullins entered into state Baptist organizational activities serving as a "messenger" (delegate) from his church to the 1886 General Association of Kentucky Baptists meeting.[6]

Edgar and Isla May continued their courtship from a distance, with all the proprieties of the Victorian Era.[7] They agreed to wait for a year before marrying, having decided that Mullins needed time to start his ministry and save enough money to pay for initial housekeeping expenses. Isla May bided her time traveling in the South visiting relatives and cultivating her tastes for art and music. Whenever possible, Edgar traveled to Louisville to see her.[8] On 2 June 1886 they were married in the Hawley home in Louisville, with Professor Manly of the Seminary performing the ceremony.[9] The couple immediately left for Harrodsburg by train, where they were met by a number of well-wishers from the church who escorted them to their apartment with all the light-heartedness of the old-fashioned chivaree.[10]

An easy pace characterized Mullins's remaining two years in Harrodsburg. He usually studied from eight in the morning until noon during the week, while his wife wrote poetry. In the afternoons Mullins attended to his ministerial duties, including the unpleasant task of visiting church members. At least two nights each week the young minister devoted to church duties or services. On other occasions the Mullinses enjoyed a quiet evening at home reading together and memorizing poetry. But life was not always this pleasant. Isla May later recalled that her husband told her soon after their marriage that they could not have "intimate friends" in the congregation because this would cause "jeal-

---

[5]*Western Recorder*, 26 August 1885.

[6]Frank M. Masters, *A History of Baptists in Kentucky* (Louisville: Kentucky Baptist Historical Society, 1953) 385.

[7]Mullins to E. M. Poteat, 16 November 1885.

[8]Mullins, *Mullins*, 22-25.

[9]Hawley-Mullins Family Bible.

[10]Mullins, *Mullins*, 25-26.

ousies." Social relations with parishioners, therefore, existed on a rather businesslike level.[11]

The Harrodsburg church grew in membership under Mullins's direction. An evangelical Christian, Mullins decided the church needed a revival in the autumn of 1886. He invited an evangelist, Fred D. Hale, to lead the effort. As a result of their combined efforts, the church added nearly one hundred members to the rolls.[12] Mullins also found time to publish a sermon in a state Baptist paper, displaying his evangelicalism as well as exercising his desire to write. "Brotherly love," he vowed, was one "evidence of conversion." A Christian should always show concern for both the "temporal" and "spiritual" welfare of his neighbor.[13]

The church displayed various evidences of satisfaction with Mullins's leadership. In Mullins's last year the congregation spent $3,000 to build a parsonage for the young couple, a considerable expense for such a small church.[14] In addition, the church raised travel funds for their pastor. In the summer of 1887, Mullins and a ministerial companion from nearby Danville traveled to Europe, but because of his small salary and savings, Mullins was unable to take his wife. The two-month trip through England, France, and Germany afforded him the opportunity to broaden his understanding of the world.[15]

Before long new opportunities opened the doors for a move from Harrodsburg. Mullins first accepted a call to the San Antonio, Texas, First Baptist Church, but then declined after Isla May became ill because of some problems in the early stages of pregnancy. The family doctor advised Mullins that Isla May should not travel for several weeks. In December he began to consider a call to the Lee Street Church in Baltimore. E. M. Poteat, a former classmate at Southern Seminary, resigned this charge, intending either to study in Europe or accept a pastorate in New Haven, Connecticut, and suggested that Mullins be chosen as his successor. "Agreeably surprised" about this possibility, Mullins de-

---

[11]Ibid., 26-42.

[12]*Western Recorder*, 30 September 1886.

[13]Ibid., 12 January 1888.

[14]*Baltimore Baptist*, 4 October 1888; *Harrodsburg Baptist Church*, 17.

[15]Mullins, *Mullins*, 43-46.

clared he would accept if offered the position. He urged Poteat to inquire about the specific salary. Did this church, moreover, pay "promptly" and "allow a summer vacation?"[16] Poteat accepted the New Haven position, and his former charge officially invited Mullins.[17] When Isla May's condition improved, Mullins accepted the new post. The Mullinses moved to Baltimore in the fall of 1888.[18]

The Lee Street Church offered the young pastor a larger congregation and salary than Harrodsburg, while the city of Baltimore presented cultural opportunities. Mullins attended The Johns Hopkins University part-time in the 1888-1889 session, taking graduate courses in Logic and Ethics.[19] He later took speech courses to improve his pulpit delivery, with all this effort indicating his desire to become a more proficient minister.[20] Isla May also took advantage of the opportunities of living in an urban area and became a member of the Women's Missionary Union Executive Committee, an auxiliary of the Southern Baptist Convention housed in Baltimore.[21]

Only a few weeks after arriving in the new pastorate, the couple became the proud parents of a son, Edgar Wheeler.[22] The father doted on his son and always set aside some time each day to play with the boy.[23] Personal tragedy struck the family three years later when their second

---

[16]Ibid.; Mullins to E. M. Poteat, 19 December 1887.

[17]*Baltimore Baptist*, 2 August 1888.

[18]Mullins, *Mullins*, 47.

[19]Enclosure from David A. Warren, Director of Registration and Records, The Johns Hopkins University, to the author, 15 May 1972. Mullins probably studied under George Henry Emmott, associate professor of logic and ethics and lecturer in Roman Law, an undistinguished instructor. Hugh Hawkins, *Pioneer: A History of The Johns Hopkins University, 1874-1889* (Ithaca NY: Cornell University Press, 1960) 205.

[20]Inman Johnson, *Of Parsons and Profs* (Nashville: Broadman Press, 1959) 31.

[21]Mullins, *Mullins*, 5.

[22]Hawley-Mullins Family Bible.

[23]Mullins, *Mullins*, 50-52.

son, Roy Granberry, died four weeks after birth because of a druggist's mistake in filling a prescription.[24]

The Lee Street charge presented a considerably different environment from the rural-oriented county seat of Harrodsburg, since it was located in South Baltimore, a complex residential and industrial area with the highest population density in the city. Part of the area had a high concentration of German and Italian immigrants and Negroes. Most of the members of the church were from the working class. The church was medium-sized and one of the poorer among Baltimore's Baptist churches. Only two blocks away was the harbor.[25]

Mullins energetically accepted the challenge of an urban church. The local Baptist paper reported that he worked hard making pastoral calls and that the community responded with an increase in attendance. In only one year the Sunday school doubled in size. The young minister taught a regular Monday evening Bible class for young people in addition to his regular duties. When hot weather threatened to cut the size of the Sunday evening crowds, Mullins began holding open-air meetings on the church lawn.[26]

As active as he appeared to be with his church, he still found time to publish some sermons similar to the one previously published by the *Western Recorder* on 12 January 1888. Though evangelical, the young minister urged his audience to prove its conversion by living the "Godly Life." The trials and tribulations of life, moreover, fitted one to move toward "perfection." He was optimistic about the role of Christianity and the good works it could accomplish in the world.[27]

The Baltimore pastorate afforded Mullins the opportunity to meet such important local Baptists as Curtis Lee Laws, A. C. Dixon, Joshua

---

[24]Ibid., 58; Hawley-Mullins Family Bible.

[25]Barry Click, pastor, Lee Street Memorial Baptist Church, Baltimore, to the author, 8 December 1972 (enclosed manuscript from Rev. Click that described the area extensively, 14-15, 18-19, 24, 61, 70); James B. Crooks, *Politics and Progress: The Rise of Urban Progressivism in Baltimore, 1895-1911* (Baton Rouge: Louisiana State University Press, 1968) 3-8.

[26]*Baltimore Baptist*, 31 January, 11 April 1889; 9 January, 6 February, 10 April, 10 July, 7 August 1890.

[27]Ibid., 4 July, 12 September, 1889; 21 August 1890.

Levering, A. J. Rowland, and W. E. Hatcher. In May 1890 Mullins attended his first meeting of the Southern Baptist Convention at Fort Worth, in the company of Rowland and Levering.[28] He presented a brief report on "Pagan Missions," which the Convention accepted.[29]

In Baltimore he participated in the Monday morning Baptist Ministers Conference and soon became a leading member.[30] A chance meeting on a train introduced him to E. Nelson Blake, a prominent member of the Arlington, Massachusetts, Baptist Church, who persuaded his church to hire Mullins for summer ministerial supply work.[31] For several summers during the Baltimore pastorate, Isla May and young Edgar Wheeler stayed in New England, avoiding the city's heat.[32] Mullins also supplied the pulpits of churches near Boston occasionally, spending most of the week with his family. In 1894 the faculty of Crozer Seminary in Chester, Pennsylvania, invited him to be on a judging committee for student examinations.[33]

Mullins was popular with his parishioners. On three occasions before 1895, rumors spread that he had received calls to higher paying positions. At one time the Lee Street Church became so concerned over

---

[28]Laws, Dixon, Rowland, and Hatcher were Baltimore ministers at one time or another during Mullins's stay in that city. Laws later edited the New York *Watchman-Examiner*. He and Dixon became fundamentalist leaders in the 1920s. Rowland was corresponding secretary of the American Baptist Publication Society for a number of years. Hatcher and Levering were trustees of Southern Seminary. Levering was a wealthy Baltimore layman and president of the Board of Trustees of Southern Seminary. *Baltimore Baptist*, 8 May 1890.

[29]*Baltimore Baptist*, 22 May 1890; *Proceedings of the Southern Baptist Convention, 1890*, 32.

[30]*Baltimore Baptist*, 17 January, 7 February 1889; 9 October 1890; 18 November 1891; *Baptist*, 12 October 1892; 22 March, 26 April, 11 October 1893.

[31]E. Nelson Blake to Mullins, 11 April 1914; *Evangel*, 6 February 1895. The *Baptist* and later the *Evangel* were successors of the *Baltimore Baptist*.

[32]Mullins, *Mullins*, 52.

[33]*Baltimore Baptist*, 6 August, 10 September 1891; *Baptist*, 31 August, 7 September 1892; 19 July 1893; 6 June, 22 August 1894.

losing his services that they urged him to remain with a "rising unanimous vote."[34]

The Southern Seminary graduate played a more important role in Maryland Baptist affairs during the last year and a half of his Baltimore ministry. In January 1894 he assumed responsibility for a weekly column for the *Baptist* entitled "Our Signal Station."[35] He participated in the 1895 meeting of the Southern Baptist Convention, serving as Maryland vice-president on the Home Mission Board and member of a committee on youth work, entering into discussions of various reports. The Convention appointed him as a "Fraternal Messenger," or observer, to the meeting of the Northern Baptist Anniversaries.[36]

Throughout his seven-year ministry in Baltimore Mullins never wavered in his devotion to evangelicalism. He continually kindled a revivalistic spirit in his church. Using the revival method at least once yearly, he invited visiting pastors to deliver evangelistic sermons. All churches, he maintained, needed periodic spiritual revivals.[37]

The weekly column gave him an opportunity to voice opinions on current issues and whetted his appetite for more writing. Soon after he began writing "Our Signal Station," Mullins explained the causes for poverty. Poverty, he argued, was only partly due to "intemperance," a reason many conservatives claimed was the only cause for such a plight. He believed that only about twenty-five percent of this malady was due to "immoral" causation. Most poverty resulted from accidents, environment, or disability. By far the most despicable laboring conditions existed in sweatshops that employed young children. He supported a Maryland Child Labor Bill, noting that he had personally witnessed "over-worked" children in Baltimore who worked for "pitiably small"

[34]*Baltimore Baptist,* 22 January 1891; *Baptist,* 14 June 1893; 22 August 1894.

[35]*Baptist,* 17 January 1894.

[36]*Proceedings of the Southern Baptist Convention, 1895,* 5, 17, 28, 51-52, 59.

[37]*Baltimore Baptist,* 23 April 1891; *Baptist,* 13 April, 16 November, 23 November 1892; 18 October, 5 November 1893; 14 February, 25 April 1894.

wages. The "greedy employers," Mullins charged, were to blame for these conditions.[38]

During the labor upheavals of 1894-1895 Mullins usually took the side of the strikers. When a western miners' strike erupted, he proposed that only enforced arbitration would lead both employers and employees to an appreciation of the "spirit of the golden rule."[39] Reacting to the Pullman strike, Mullins accepted at face value a statement by a Methodist minister from Chicago who found George Pullman at fault for that dispute.[40] Though Mullins supported President Cleveland's actions as justified, he maintained that the violence was evidence of a "class" struggle that went deeper than most people were willing to admit. When all the "facts" were in, Mullins contended, the workers would be exonerated of the "lawlessness" that characterized only a minority.[41] Later in the year he scored the Managers' Association for not arbitrating the Pullman strike, and he favored federal studies of labor conditions.[42] Early in 1895 he found that troops "provoked" a crowd during a Brooklyn street railway strike. Behind the troops, he believed, stood a "greedy, grasping, insolent and heartless corporation."[43]

In Mullins's own city, streetcar owners contributed to the "slaughter" of children by not having fenders on their cars and by forcing their drivers to race at impossible speeds to keep up with a demanding schedule. Mullins said that the cause was "greed," and he accused the city administration of being controlled by the traction interests.[44]

------

[38]*Baptist*, 24 January, 31 January 1894. Henry M. Wharton, pastor of the Brantly Baptist Church, the largest Baptist church in the city, edited and owned the *Baptist.* He took a vivid interest in fighting boss rule in the city, the machine of Isaac Freeman Rasin, and probably encouraged Mullins to take a liberal tack in his column. Crooks, *Politics and Progress*, 13-49.

[39]*Baptist*, 20 June 1894.

[40]Ibid., 25 July 1894.

[41]Ibid., 18 July 1894.

[42]Ibid., 28 November 1894.

[43]*Evangel*, 30 January 1895.

[44]*Baptist*, 26 September, 17 October 1894.

In his critique of the urban labor crisis Mullins proposed that something other than soul-saving evangelism was needed as a cure for the ills of the city. One possible remedy was the use of arbitration to settle the issues dividing labor and management. Corrupt politicians exacerbated an already difficult situation, and Mullins applauded whenever they were turned out at the polls.[45] Mullins characterized slums as a "cancer on the social organism." Christians could do no other than support slum clearance.[46] As an expedient measure, charity should be carefully planned and administered. Mullins, consequently, supported the work of the Baltimore Charity Organization Society, a group that attempted to centralize the work of several charitable groups.[47] He also supported moralist reforms such as Prohibition. Local option statutes, he maintained, made it possible for Christian people to oppose this social problem.[48] True to his older evangelical inclination, Mullins opened a church mission at Locust Point in the poorest section of South Baltimore. This mission was mostly frequented by immigrants.[49]

Mullins's view of Negroes was a mixture of prejudice, paternalism, and genuine Christian concern for their welfare. In no uncertain terms he voiced opposition to lynching in the South. This development was "far too common," but attributable primarily to the "hoodlum element," not the "best people." Though Mullins deplored all mob violence, he declared that some "colored people" worsened the problem by demanding social equality.[50] Several months later a lynching in Maryland caused him to demand that the culprits be brought to immediate justice.[51] After a visit to the state prison, Mullins exposed the unlawful killing of black

---

[45]Ibid., 7 February, 7 March, 11 July, 10 October, 14 November 1894; *Evangel*, 3 July 1895.

[46]*Baptist*, 21 November 1894; *Evangel*, 1 May, 29 May 1895.

[47]*Baptist*, 18 November 1891; 31 January, 22 August 1894.

[48]Ibid., 31 January, 21 February, 28 February, 25 April, 11 July, 31 October 1894; 2 January 1895; *Evangel*, 17 April 1895.

[49]*Baptist*, 5 April 1893; *Evangel*, 28 August 1895.

[50]*Baptist*, 19 September 1894.

[51]Ibid., 5 June 1895.

prisoners by the "unsanitary" conditions of living in a "pesthouse." This disgrace represented, he vowed, an "unauthorized form of capital punishment."[52]

The urban experience shocked his moral sensitivity and broadened his views of the problems of the urban poor and Negroes. He developed a Social Gospel that was quite liberal for his time, particularly for a Southern Baptist. Though he sometimes showed evidence of racial prejudices, he more often than not rose above his milieu to voice somewhat more liberal sentiments.

Mullins's reaction to Catholicism was less commendable. He equated Catholicism with the liquor "interests" and condemned both as being part of a conspiracy to keep the cities wet.[53] However, he found the "methods" of the anti-Catholic American Protective Association to be just as objectionable. "In contending for religious liberty," he maintained, "let us guard against flagrant violations of it." When a Baptist editor in Texas criticized Governor W. J. Northen of Georgia, a Baptist, for appointing a Catholic to fill out a term in the United States Senate, Mullins defended the governor's action and maintained that any Catholic who upheld the Constitution could hold public office.[54] His prejudice toward Catholicism came to the fore again, however, when he concurred with a proposal to send Baptist missionaries to Catholic-dominated countries.[55]

Mullins held to his strong evangelical proclivities while accommodating his ideals of social responsibility to the exigencies of an inner-city pastorate. Already his moderate predilection had taken hold. He made every effort to reshape his form of Southern Baptist evangelical Christianity to meet the exigencies of the modern world. A few of his sermons and the only book he published during the Baltimore experience demonstrate his continued concern for evangelicalism. He emphatically upheld the virgin birth and divinity of Christ. Higher criticism that attacked

---

[52]Ibid., 28 February 1894.

[53]Ibid., 29 August, 5 September, 31 October 1894; *Evangel,* 1 May, 15 May 1895.

[54]*Baptist,* 2 May, 16 May 1894.

[55]*Evangel,* 15 May 1895.

these dictums claimed "too much," but was relevant for textual examination. Some things, however, were "obviously supernatural."[56] The regenerate were part, furthermore, of a "Kingdom Built on a Cross." The command to evangelize the world was God's commandment.[57] A Christian also had to live in this world. He should be thoroughly trained in biblical doctrine. The destiny of the Christian, Mullins believed, was to control the "Ship of State" and all facets of world affairs.[58]

Mullins's first book, *Christ's Coming and His Kingdom*, contained a compilation of several carefully prepared sermons on the millennium. He revealed a mild dispensational premillennialism, vowing that "Christ will return literally" and will not find a completely regenerate world.[59] The missions movement, however, would redeem many people before that event.[60] Mullins's attitude was one of cheerful expectancy. While he scored Roman Catholicism as an "apostate church," he did not propose that the pope was the anti-Christ as did many of his more conservative brethren.[61] Again displaying moderation, he maintained that man would reform the world "radically," but Christ would make the final, decisive changes in the world order. Service, moreover, was not limited to winning souls. Ministering to human needs was important, but evangelism should always remain in the forefront.[62] During the Baltimore ministry, Mullins demonstrated that evangelicalism was compatible with a moderate Social Gospel.[63]

---

[56]*Baptist*, 26 April 1893.

[57]Mullins, "A Kingdom Built on a Cross," in *The Southern Baptist Pulpit*, ed. J. F. Love (Philadelphia: American Baptist Publication Society, 1895) 248-52.

[58]*Baptist*, 19 July 1893; 24 January 1894.

[59]Ibid., 13 April 1892; Mullins, *Christ's Coming and His Kingdom* (Baltimore: C. W. Schneidereith, 1894) 8; Timothy P. Weber, *Living in the Shadow of the Second Coming* (New York: Oxford University Press, 1979) 11.

[60]Mullins, *Christ's Coming and His Kingdom*, 13.

[61]Ibid., 16, 38-39.

[62]Ibid., 45.

[63]Rufus B. Spain, *At Ease in Zion: Social History of Southern Baptists, 1865-*

In the summer of 1895 Mullins considered leaving the Lee Street Church for a more lucrative position. The larger churches in New England became aware of Mullins's abilities after he had completed several years of summer ministerial supply work there. In July he received two offers: one as pastor of the North Avenue Baptist Church, Cambridge, Massachusetts, and the other as an administrator with the Foreign Mission Board in Richmond, Virginia. Mullins chose the latter position, believing that it offered greater "usefulness."[64] He insisted that he be designated associate rather than assistant secretary, desiring "an opportunity to exercise whatever initiative might be his."[65] Soon after taking up the new post he published a series of three articles in the Richmond *Religious Herald* recommending a missions-oriented educational program in Southern Baptist colleges. Special lectures or courses should be developed, he maintained, in order to train leaders in mission work. "Men of means" could make their contribution and should be educated as to the virtues of endowing missions.[66]

In effect, Mullins thought of his duties as promotion and public relations, rather than administration. R. H. Willingham, longtime corresponding secretary of the Board, misunderstanding Mullins's intentions, believed the younger man overstepped his authority, and friction soon developed between the two men. Sensing Willingham's opposition,

---

1900 (Nashville: Vanderbilt University Press, 1961) 209-14; Bailey, *Southern White Protestantism*, 4; John L. Eighmy, "The Social Conscience of Southern Baptists from 1900 to the Present as Reflected in Their Organized Life" (Ph.D. diss., University of Missouri, 1959) 8. Henry F. May, *Protestant Churches and Industrial America* (New York: Harper and Brothers, 1959), in a study of the development of the Social Gospel through 1895, found that labor crises caused a serious shift in Protestant sentiment toward the plight of labor (91). Mullins would qualify as an adherent of "Progressive Social Christianity" during his Baltimore years. May determined that his group represented the typical Social Gospeler of the progressive era (see part 4). Mullins turned more conservative and less interested in progressive reform after he left Baltimore. Ferenc M. Szasz, in "The Progressive Clergy and the Kingdom of God," *Mid-America* 55 (January 1973): 3-20, develops the thesis that liberals and conservatives cooperated in a Social Gospel effort that lasted until after World War I.

[64]*Evangel*, 10 July, 17 July, 21 August 1895.

[65]Mullins, *Mullins*, 73.

[66]*Religious Herald*, 17 October, 14 November, 28 November 1895.

Mullins curtailed his lecturing trips and concentrated on office work. He was unhappy, but silent. After a few weeks of this impasse, he casually revealed to his wife a letter from the Newton Centre, Massachusetts, Baptist Church, asking that he consider a call as their pastor. Recognizing how upset her husband was, Isla May did not press him to accept, but encouraged him indirectly by asking friends to talk to him. Mullins still hoped to settle his differences with Willingham, but he agreed to preach a trial sermon at the Newton Centre church. After a trip to Newton Centre, he decided to send a telegram asking not to be considered for the post. His cable "miscarried," however, and did not arrive until after the church had voted to issue an invitation.[67] The offer included a salary of $3,000, six weeks' annual vacation, a parsonage, and $500, immediately upon his acceptance, for moving and incidental expenses. One deacon, urging him to accept, reported that the congregation voted ninety-nine for and eight against extending the call.[68] After much soul-searching, Mullins accepted the position. Isla May later admitted that she was elated by the decision to leave Richmond.[69]

While Mullins was in Texas on his last lecture and promotional trip for the Board, tragedy struck the family. Edgar Wheeler, only seven years old, died after a brief illness on 20 February 1896. His father rushed back when he heard of the illness but arrived too late. Isla May was too distraught to attend the funeral, so a broken-hearted father took his son's remains to Baltimore for burial. Edgar Wheeler was buried beside the baby, Roy Granberry, and a young friend who had died two years earlier.[70] Both parents reacted stoically to the tragic loss. Mullins sorrowfully commented, "Our prayer is that this sorrow which has come to us may better fit us for our duties as laborers in His vineyard."[71] Isla May

---

[67]Mullins, *Mullins,* 75-82.

[68]Dwight Chester to Mullins, 1 February, 3 February 1896; Frank W. Pevear to Mullins, 3 February 1896.

[69]Mullins, *Mullins,* 82.

[70]Ibid., 84-86; Hawley-Mullins Family Bible.

[71]Mullins to Mrs. J. I. Compere, 13 March 1896 (located in the E. L. Compere Collection, Dargan-Carver Library, Nashville).

consoled herself by writing a romantic novel about her son two years later.[72]

Less than a month after the boy's death, Edgar and Isla May moved to Newton Centre, "Boston's Best Bedroom."[73] The move dispelled some of the gloom associated with the death of their only son. The new pastorate contrasted with the Lee Street environment as it was located in an upper-class suburb, with Newton Theological Institution, the oldest Baptist seminary in the country, only two blocks from the church.[74]

Alvah Hovey, president of Newton during Mullins's tenure at the Newton Centre Church, exemplified the moderate evangelical position of most of his colleagues.[75] He showed a "spirit of investigation" about the newer liberal theology, but remained evangelical.[76] During the late 1890s Newton was basically a conservative institution with an evangelical and biblical emphasis. Hovey's son, George, of Richmond, had encouraged Edgar to take the Newton Centre Church.[77]

Most of the Newton faculty attended Mullins's church, thus affording him an opportunity to develop his homiletical style before an educated audience. Though he came in contact with a number of strong premillennialists in the Boston area, he did not join their small and militant movement.[78] The environment of Newton Centre offered material

---

[72]*Side by Side* (Philadelphia: Judson Press, 1898). The grieved mother presented an idealized account of her son's life. She revealed no bitterness, rather a faith that his death had been part of a divine plan.

[73]Mullins, *Mullins*, 88-92.

[74]*Blue Book of Newton, 1899* (Newton MA: Edward A. Jones, 1898) 248; Mullins, *Mullins*, 86-92.

[75]*Newton Theological Institution Historical Catalogue, 1925,* 8; George Rice Hovey, *Alvah Hovey: His Life and Letters* (Philadelphia: Judson Press, 1928) 206-208.

[76]Norman Maring, "Baptists and Changing Views of the Bible, 1865-1918," *Foundations* 1 (July 1958): 56.

[77]Henry Melville King, *Newton Theological Institution in the Last Fifty Years* (n.p., 1899) 5-14; Mullins, *Mullins*, 76.

[78]Ernest R. Sandeen, "The Baptists and Millenarianism: Suggestions for Further Research," *Foundations* 13 (January-March 1970): 24; Sandeen, *The Roots of Fundamentalism: British and American Millenarianism, 1800-1930* (Chicago: University of Chicago Press, 1970) 166, 244.

benefits as well as intellectual stimulation. The charge paid well, and Mellon Bray, "a millionaire member," built the Mullinses a new parsonage.[79]

After his first year in Newton Centre, Mullins vacationed in Europe. In 1895 Carson-Newman College of Tennessee conferred an honorary Doctor of Divinity degree on Mullins.[80] He remained true to his belief in revivalism even though the Newton Centre Church usually followed a more Calvinistic course in church doctrine. When he tried to encourage a revival in the church, the deacons only agreed to allow special meetings with the young people. The addition of forty young converts satisfied his craving for a more evangelical emphasis in the church without an open clash with the deacons.[81]

The four-year tenure in Newton Centre represented a pleasant and healing experience for Edgar and Isla May in contrast to the excitement of the Baltimore ministry, the tensions of the Richmond interlude, and the tragic deaths of two young sons. The intellectualism of the congregation was rewarding, yet Mullins missed the evangelical thrust of his Southern brethren. Isla May, moreover, enjoyed the Newton Centre environment, free from the poverty and social problems of the Lee Street Church.[82]

While Mullins enjoyed the advantages of a prestigious Northeastern church, controversy beset his alma mater, Southern Seminary in Louisville. William Heth Whitsitt, professor of church history for twenty-two years, succeeded John A. Broadus as president in 1895. Before long Whitsitt clashed with a conservative wing of Southern Baptists known as Landmarkists, who maintained that the individual Baptist church was the successor of the original primitive Christian church.[83] They believed

---

[79]Mullins, *Mullins*, 92-96.

[80]Ibid., 98.

[81]Ibid., 100-101; James Leo Garrett, Jr., E. Glenn Hinson, and James E. Tull, *Are Southern Baptists "Evangelicals"?* (Macon GA: Mercer University Press, 1983) 214.

[82]Mullins, *Mullins*, 90.

[83]William Wright Barnes, *The Southern Baptist Convention, 1845-1953* (Nashville: Broadman Press, 1954) 136-38; O. K. Armstrong and Marjorie Armstrong, *The Indomitable Baptists* (Garden City NY: Doubleday and Company, 1967) 282.

that since the time of Christ there had been an unbroken line of Baptist churches and tended to be anti-mission and anti-institutional.[84]

Whitsitt was a devout evangelical Christian. After two years of study in Germany, however, he had accepted the newer inductive approach to church history, which maintained that modern denominations evolved from primitive origins without any godly sanction.[85] As early as 1880 Whitsitt published three unsigned articles in the *Independent*, in which he proposed that Baptist histories were inaccurate. An article by him in the 1895 *Johnson's Cyclopedia* touched off an immediate controversy.[86] The next year he defended his views in a monograph.[87] In contrast to the Landmarkists, he claimed that English Baptists did not accept "believer's baptism" until 1641 and that Roger Williams had probably been sprinkled rather than totally immersed. Whitsitt's inductive methods contrasted with the deductive or fiat tradition of his conservative brethren. Many ill-educated Southern Baptists followed the tenets of Landmarkism, and they believed that Whitsitt's scholarly efforts struck at the foundations of their faith. They glorified the "Baptist distinctives" that gave them their separate identity and that Whitsitt seemed to attack.[88]

---

[84]Charles Basil Bugg, "The Whitsitt Controversy: A Study in Denominational Conflict" (Th.D. diss., Southern Baptist Theological Seminary, 1972) 10-11; Lynn E. May, Jr., "Southern Baptist Crises," *Encyclopedia of Southern Baptists*, 1:333-36; W. Morgan Patterson, "Landmarkism," *Encyclopedia of Southern Baptists*, 2:757; Patterson, "The Development of the Baptist Successionist Formula," *Foundations* 5 (October 1962): 343.

[85]Patterson, "The Development of the Baptist Successionist Formula," 343; William Owen Carver, "William Heth Whitsitt," *Review and Expositor* 51 (October 1954): 449-57.

[86]E. B. Pollard, "The Life and Work of William Heth Whitsitt," *Review and Expositor* 9 (April 1912): 173.

[87]William H. Whitsitt, *A Question of Baptist History* (Louisville: n.p., 1896); Gaines S. Dobbins, "William Heth Whitsitt," *Encyclopedia of Southern Baptists*, 2:1496.

[88]Mueller, *A History of Southern Baptist Theological Seminary*, 156. "Believers' Baptism" literally means "for believers only" and is symbolic of "death, burial, and resurrection" of the believer. Hudson, *Baptist Convictions*, 22; James E. Tull, *A History of Southern Baptist Landmarkism in the Light of Historical Baptist Ecclesiology* (New York: Arno Press, 1980) 577-618.

Two strategically placed Landmarkists, B. H. Carroll, dean of the theology department of Baylor University, and T. T. Eaton, pastor of the Walnut Street Baptist Church, Louisville, and editor of the powerful *Western Recorder,* led the assault on Whitsitt.[89] Eaton published a long series of articles and editorials in the spring of 1896 refuting Whitsitt's claims. He became more embittered as the conflict wore on and finally demanded Whitsitt's resignation.[90] A trustee of Southern Seminary, Eaton lamented that the "heretic" had more freedom than the "heresy-hunter." An "honest" Baptist, Eaton sarcastically contended, would voluntarily remove himself from denominational leadership if his views changed.[91]

Though outside the Southern Baptist Convention, Mullins kept in touch with the affairs of his Southern brethren by writing occasional articles, as a correspondent for New England Baptist news, for the *Religious Herald.* He could not refrain from taking notices of the attacks on Whitsitt, his former professor, and defended him without reservation in a series of four articles.[92] Noting that Whitsitt's enemies misused the true details of the life of Roger Williams, Mullins claimed that the freedom-loving Williams "would scorn and repudiate" such assaults on religious freedom. A few weeks later Mullins scorned the Landmarkist faction as "a Roman Catholic Party Among the Baptists" bent on the destruction of free inquiry. In later articles he continued the defense of Whitsitt.[93]

---

[89]Davis C. Woolley, "Major Convention Crises over a Century and a Quarter," *Review and Expositor* 67 (Spring 1970): 173-75; George Raleigh Jewell, "Western Recorder," *Encyclopedia of Southern Baptists,* 2:1489; Leo T. Crismon, "Thomas Treadwell Eaton," *Encyclopedia of Southern Baptists,* 1:385; C. Ferris Jordan, "Thomas Treadwell Eaton: Pastor, Editor, Controversialist, and Denominational Servant" (Th.D. diss., New Orleans Baptist Theological Seminary, 1965) 9, 67, 81.

[90]Mueller, *A History of Southern Baptist Theological Seminary,* 160-61; *Western Recorder,* 26 January 1899; Jordan, "Thomas Treadwell Eaton," 37-38, 98.

[91]*Western Recorder,* 26 January, 6 April, 13 April, 4 May 1899.

[92]William Owen Carver, "Edgar Young Mullins—Leader and Builder," *Review and Expositor* 26 (April 1929): 131; Sampey, *Memoirs,* 101.

[93]*Religious Herald,* 21 May, 16 July, 8 October 1896; 14 April 1898.

Mullins published his articles in a relatively "friendly" area of the South, and, surprisingly, "he was not identified with either side of the controversy."[94]

Although the faculty of Southern Seminary went on record in defense of Whitsitt, only A. T. Robertson and John R. Sampey independently defended the much maligned president in the denominational press.[95] The conflict terrified at least two professors. "What is going to become of us?" F. H. Kerfoot asked in desperation. He implied that the heretical "*Chicago University*" was behind Whitsitt's machinations.[96] W. J. McGlothlin proposed to take a year of study in Germany hoping that the "seminary situation" would "be solved and quiet" by the time he returned.[97]

Whitsitt's refusal to recant forced the issue into a conventionwide test of strength. Carroll pushed through a resolution at the 1898 Southern Baptist Convention asking for a dissolution of "the slight and remote bond of connection between this body and the Seminary." By amend-

---

[94]Mueller, *A History of Southern Baptist Theological Seminary,* 180; Carver, "Edgar Young Mullins—Leader and Builder," 131. R. H. Pitt, editor of the *Religious Herald,* defended Whitsitt, carrying on a running controversy with Eaton. For example, see the *Religious Herald,* 21 April 1898. Whitsitt was popular in Virginia and later found refuge for the remaining years of his life at the University of Richmond, a Baptist institution.

No mention was made of Mullins's defense of Whitsitt when he was offered the presidency of Southern Seminary. In later years Mullins and Eaton often clashed over doctrinal matters, but Eaton never referred to Mullins's defense of Whitsitt in the late 1890s. Eaton's biographer maintains that Eaton's opposition to Whitsitt was mostly a "personal battle." Jordan, "Thomas Treadwell Eaton," 212-13.

[95]Carver, "Recollections," 51; Mueller, *A History of Southern Baptist Theological Seminary,* 162-64, 205; *Baptist Argus,* 19 January 1899; *Western Recorder,* 30 April 1896.

[96]Kerfoot to J. M. Frost, 26 January 1899 (Frost-Bell Letters, Dargan-Carver Library). The University of Chicago Divinity School gained a reputation in the 1890s as being a "liberal" school, and conservatives often vilified that institution. Norman H. Maring, "Baptists and Changing Views of the Bible, 1865-1918," *Foundations* 1 (October 1958): 45.

[97]McGlothlin to Frost, 2 February 1899 (Frost-Bell Letters, Dargan-Carver Library).

ment the Convention appointed a committee to undertake an investigation, a step that was nothing less than an attempt to force Whitsitt to resign.[98] The Seminary's trustees, however, did not ask for his resignation.[99] Prior to the 1899 Convention in Louisville the trustees met for their annual session. Whitsitt, weary of the incessant attacks, submitted his resignation. While the board debated the issue, Whitsitt sent word that it should be accepted, and the trustees concurred.[100] When the Convention met a few days later, Carroll withdrew his resolution, and an uneasy peace settled over the Southern Baptist denomination.[101]

An immediate and important task now faced the board: to select a new president acceptable to all factions in the Southern Baptist Convention. Meeting soon after the Convention adjourned, the board elected J. P. Greene, then chief administrator of William Jewell College in Missouri, who promptly declined the offer.[102]

Though aware of the turmoil in Southern Baptist ecclesiastical politics, Mullins had no idea that he would be suggested as Whitsitt's successor.[103] After Greene declined the presidency, Henry W. Battle, a Richmond pastor, suggested Mullins's name to close associates, including Seminary trustee W. E. Hatcher. Mullins's initial support came from trustees in the Richmond area. During his brief stay in that city, Mullins joined "The Club," an association of prominent Richmond Baptist ministers and laymen that included most of the Richmond trustees. This vital contact kept Mullins's name before these trustees as they sought a man untouched by the recent controversy over Whitsitt.[104]

---

[98]*Annual of the Southern Baptist Convention, 1898,* 22-23; Carver, "William Heth Whitsitt," 466.

[99]Pollard, "The Life and Work of William Heth Whitsitt," 177.

[100]Carver, "William Heth Whitsitt," 466.

[101]*Annual of the Southern Baptist Convention, 1899,* 18. Whitsitt bowed out graciously, claiming he held "charity for all." *Baptist Argus,* 8 June 1899.

[102]*Baptist Argus,* 18 May 1899. By coincidence Kerfoot was visiting Mullins in Newton Centre at the time. Mrs. Mullins reported that they had "warm" debates over the Whitsitt resignation. Mullins, *Mullins,* 105.

[103]Mullins, *Mullins,* 105.

[104]R. E. Gaines to Mullins, 13 January 1919.

At the 29 June 1899 meeting of the Board in Atlanta two names were placed in nomination: F. H. Kerfoot, by those who opposed Whitsitt, and Mullins. Hatcher did not publicly mention his desire to nominate Mullins until the Board convened, believing that electioneering would produce a united front of opposition from the Eaton faction. This proved to be a sensible strategy. During a lengthy discussion Mullins gained support, while Kerfoot lost it. One trustee mentioned that he had read something that Mullins had written about Whitsitt, but he could not remember which side the Newton Centre minister took in the Whitsitt debate. Mullins's supporters kept silent. The Eaton group finally withdrew the Kerfoot nomination and the Board unanimously elected Mullins as president of Southern Seminary.[105]

In Newton Centre, Mullins received a premature message of congratulations from J. N. Prestridge, editor of the Louisville *Baptist Argus*, before the official message arrived from the Board of Trustees. At his wife's insistence, Mullins went to the telegraph office, and sitting at the key, took the Board's dispatch himself.[106]

Mullins took his time in making such a crucial decision. The presidency of Southern Seminary offered only turmoil compared with the tranquil pastorate at Newton Centre. W. J. Northen, ex-governor of Georgia and a Seminary trustee, made a personal plea by visiting the Mullins household. Mullins agreed only to go to Louisville to confer with the faculty.[107] He returned to Newton Centre ill with a high fever, but reported to his distressed wife that he had accepted.[108] In his letter of acceptance Mullins made no specific promises to any faction; rather, he asked for support from the entire "Baptist Brotherhood of the South."[109]

---

[105]Carver, "Edgar Young Mullins—Leader and Builder," 139; Carver, "The Nomination of Dr. Mullins for the Seminary Presidency," *Review and Expositor* 26 (July 1929): 302-303; *Courier-Journal*, 30 June 1899; *Religious Herald*, 6 July 1899; Sampey, *Memoirs*, 101.

[106]Mullins, *Mullins*, 106-107.

[107]The *Courier-Journal* (6, 7, and 9 July 1899) kept up with the trustees' effort to secure the services of Mullins. Mullins, *Mullins*, 111-13.

[108]Mullins, *Mullins*, 115; *Courier-Journal*, 9 July 1899.

[109]*Baptist Argus*, 20 July 1899. Mullins probably took a salary cut to come to Southern Seminary. *Baptist Argus*, 6 July 1899.

Mullins received immediate expressions of support from both sides of the Whitsitt conflict.[110] Eaton warned Mullins, however, not to serve "partisan" interests and continued his attacks on Whitsitt, an implicit warning to the new president.[111] With the possible exception of Kerfoot, the president-elect had the support of the faculty. Kerfoot resigned before the opening of the Seminary for the 1899-1900 session, forcing Mullins to prepare to teach theology instead of church history.[112]

The new president received advice from friends that made him more cognizant of continued doctrinal conflict.[113] Equally important was the critical fact that Southern Seminary faced financial difficulties as well. Contributions and enrollment had declined abruptly during the last two years of the Whitsitt administration.[114] Though Mullins had little ad-

---

[110]Eaton to Mullins, 31 July 1899; *Religious Herald*, 13 July 1899; *Baptist Argus*, 13 July 1899.

[111]*Western Recorder*, 13 July 1899.

[112]Carver maintained that Kerfoot thought "he would succeed Dr. Boyce in the presidency," but Broadus became the next chief executive. When Broadus died, Whitsitt, Kerfoot, and Eaton were all nominated in 1895. Kerfoot and Eaton were both unhappy that Whitsitt had been appointed over them. Carver, "William Heth Whitsitt," 462-63; Kerfoot to Frost, 3 July 1899 (Frost-Bell Letters, Dargan-Carver Library); Mullins, *Mullins,* 120. One professor reported that Kerfoot had disclosed a divided loyalty to the Seminary and his conservatism. Kerfoot refused to write an article showing his unqualified support of Mullins, fearing that the new president would not be any different than Whitsitt. McGlothlin to Mullins, 14 August 1899.

[113]W. B. Crumpton to Mullins, 22 August 1899; Pitt to Mullins, 21 August 1899. Sampey also revealed that Eaton had tried to "temporarily" house a diphtheria-ridden student family in New York Hall, the only student dormitory. This was dangerous for other students and would certainly have led to some type of "misunderstanding." "Our good matron stoutly resisted," he replied. This indicated his fear that Eaton was searching for any reason to attack the Seminary. Sampey to Mullins, 8 September 1899.

[114]Crismon, "Southern Baptist Theological Seminary," 1270. In the 1888-1889 session only large donations by John D. Rockefeller, W. J. Northen, and George W. Norton saved Southern Seminary from having a large deficit. Bugg, "The Whitsitt Controversy," 190. Whitsitt blamed the continued decline in endowment interest rates as the chief cause for lessened revenues. Whitsitt, "Finances

ministrative experience, he immediately grasped the gravity of the financial crisis. He decided to reshuffle the course load instead of replacing Kerfoot, and he promised an early campaign to enlarge the endowment. He hired B. Pressley Smith, a South Carolina layman and businessman, to administer the important Student Aid Fund, which paid for the room and board of many students.[115]

Mullins's inaugural address was rather oblique, offering nothing specific, but promising "consecrated" scholarship. Southern Seminary, moreover, would project an "irenic spirit."[116] He returned to an enlarged institution in Louisville. New York Hall served as the men's dormitory, and Norton Hall replaced an old frame structure on Fourth Street as the classroom and administrative center. By 1899 the Master in Theology degree replaced the Full Graduate award. This degree, plus five special classes and a thesis, afforded the student the opportunity to be awarded the doctorate in theology, the Th.D. Not long after Mullins returned to Southern Seminary, the faculty raised the grading standards in an attempt to upgrade the theological training of Southern Seminary students.[117]

Mullins understood the direct relationship between doctrinal and financial problems. The Southern Baptist Convention did not directly contribute to the finances of the Seminary at this time; instead, the

---

of the Seminary," *Seminary Magazine* 12 (April 1899): 346-47.

Other seminaries suffered from much the same problems in the 1890s. Newton Seminary had difficulty making ends meet because of general economic problems. Ernest D. Burton, "Ministerial Education," in *Papers on Newton Theological Institution* (Boston: The Watchman, 1891) 16. At Hamilton Seminary of Colgate University, the school had difficulty collecting funds because many considered a professor, Nathaniel Schmidt, to be subversive owing to his modernistic views of the Bible. This situation was similar to the repercussions of the Whitsitt controversy. Roland Tenus Nelson, "Fundamentalism and the Northern Baptist Convention" (Ph.D. diss., University of Chicago Divinity School, 1964) 112.

[115]*Baptist Argus*, 17 August 1899.

[116]Ibid., 12 October 1899.

[117]Everett Gill, *A. T. Robertson: A Biography* (New York: The Macmillan Company, 1943) 53; Sampey, *Memoirs*, 65; Mueller, *A History of Southern Baptist Theological Seminary*, 183.

Louisville institution depended on the support of individual Baptists and state and local Baptist associations. Doctrinal suspicion would lead to withdrawal of support. A man with personal and institutional ambition, Mullins knew he would have to walk a doctrinal tightrope to build much needed financial support.

3

"TO FURNISH
A THOROUGHLY TRAINED
AND WELL-EQUIPPED MINISTRY"

Mullins reentered the Southern Baptist Convention at a critical time. Evolution, higher criticism of the Bible, and the social implications of Christianity agitated theological discussion of the day. Fundamentalist editors, ministers, and laymen often dominated these debates among Southern Baptists. This same group, moreover, moved the denomination to the right in doctrine compared with their Northern counterparts. The University of Chicago, in particular, became the focal point of fundamentalist Baptist diatribes. Fundamentalists accepted no variations in views. In the North, liberal, moderate, and fundamentalist factions existed among Baptists, while in the South only fundamentalists and moderates contended for control of the denominational machinery. Mullins became a leader of the moderate faction. His position as Southern Seminary president demanded that he accept a leadership role.[1]

---

[1]Although the term *fundamentalist* is not normally used to identify reli-

The Southern Baptist Convention moved toward centralization in the early part of the twentieth century.[2] The Landmarkist-moderate conflict eventually led to a schism, but only a small group of Landmarkists left the Convention. Landmarkist philosophy, however, continued to influence the thinking of many fundamentalists, particularly when they looked for excuses to oppose centralization of denominational polity.[3] Mullins faced the problem of building support for Southern Seminary in this difficult atmosphere, and he often clashed with fundamentalists.

In his role as chief executive of Southern Seminary, Mullins attempted to fulfill three functions: administrator, theologian, and denominational leader. His duties as chief administrator necessitated that he also accept a role as a denominational leader. Furthermore, he also wrote books, pamphlets, and articles fulfilling his desire to be a "man of books" and to defend himself and the Seminary. He assumed more responsibilities than any previous president, and the faculty took its lead from him.[4]

Mullins faced a financial crisis when he became president in 1899. At this time Southern Seminary received no regular sustaining funds from the Convention except as special offerings.[5] The bonds between the

---

gious conservatives until the era after World War I, the characteristics ascribed to this group were clearly evident among conservative Southern Baptists at the turn of the century. James J. Thompson, Jr., *Tried as by Fire: Southern Baptists and the Religious Controversies of the 1920s* (Macon GA: Mercer University Press, 1982) 3-14, 43-47; Norman F. Furniss, *The Fundamentalist Controversy* (New Haven: Yale University Press, 1954) 35-45.

[2]Samuel S. Hill, Jr., and Robert C. Torbet, *Baptists—North and South* (Valley Forge PA: Judson Press, 1964) 55-56; Barnes, *The Southern Baptist Convention,* 32.

[3]Nelson, "Fundamentalism and the Northern Baptist Convention," 90-91.

[4]Gill, *Robertson,* 90-91; F. M. Powell, "The Southern Baptist Theological Seminary Completes Seventy-Five Years of Struggle and Achievement," *Review and Expositor* 31 (July 1934): 343.

[5]The results of appeals to the annual Convention meetings showed a sharp decline during the Whitsitt controversy. In 1894 the delegates gave nearly $1,500 for the student fund. Four years later, during the height of the conflict, the special offering fell off to only $428. After the resignation of Whitsitt, the amount collected rose to nearly $1,200. These amounts, though small, are indicative of the tenuous nature of Seminary finances. *Proceedings of the Southern Baptist Convention, 1894,* 17; *Annual of the Southern Baptist Convention, 1898,* 20; *Annual of the Southern Baptist Convention, 1899,* 16.

Convention and the Seminary were slight in a technical, financial sense though quite close in a practical, doctrinal sense. Mullins realized that the Whitsitt controversy cast an aura of suspicion over the Seminary that endangered the financial viability of the institution. Increments from endowment investments, individual gifts, and donations from churches and associations were the only sources of income. The school did not charge a tuition fee, only room and board.[6] As the number of Southern Baptists increased and as the Southern economy slowly improved, more money became available for denominational activities. During the early part of the century numerous Southern Baptist institutions clamored for funds: colleges, academies, orphanages, hospitals, and Southern Seminary among others. There was no central direction, and each institution campaigned independently. Mullins took the lead in a movement to weld the solicitations of these institutions for financial support into a single cooperative program.[7]

In his attempts to secure a strong financial base for the Seminary, Mullins encouraged promotional activities and sponsored fund drives. Promotional efforts were primarily aimed at securing funds and students. The same activities, moreover, were needed to allay the fears of the fundamentalists. Mullins had no single source upon which he could rely for funds for expansion of the physical plant and student body. Continuous deficits made it impossible to plan for the future. Just before Mullins took office, for example, Southern Seminary had overdrawn its endowment account by nearly $5,400; therefore, he had to raise $1,600 quickly in order to pay faculty salaries for October 1899.[8]

Desiring, above all, "to furnish a thoroughly trained and well-equipped ministry," Mullins energetically accepted the promotional role of administration. The results, while encouraging, were hard won.[9] Promotion took several forms. Most important was the necessity of creating good relations with Southern Baptist denominational leaders, including editors of the state papers, executives of the state associations,

---

[6]*Baptist Argus,* 17 July 1902.

[7]Gill, *Robertson,* 90-91; Porter Routh, "The Southern Baptist Convention Presidency, 1845-1970," *Review and Expositor* 67 (Spring 1970): 157-64.

[8]W. J. McGlothlin to Mullins, 23 August 1899.

[9]*Baptist Argus,* 9 May 1901.

and Southern Baptist Convention officials. Mullins corresponded frequently with editors of the leading state denominational papers urging their support for the Seminary program.[10] Faculty members also played a role. At the end of the first session of school Mullins assigned a faculty member to represent the interests of Southern Seminary at each of seventeen state associations that met in the summer of 1900.[11] In addition, he encouraged the faculty to travel, supply pulpits, and write articles during the summer months, thereby supplementing their salaries.[12] Mullins, himself, usually spent the summers supplying pulpits in the larger churches in Chicago, Detroit, and Elgin, Illinois.[13] Pastors of key urban churches were important because of their comparatively wealthy congregations, especially if these men were Southern Seminary graduates. Mullins developed the habit of periodically visiting these churches to preach and solicit funds.[14]

J. N. Prestridge, the moderate editor of the Louisville *Baptist Argus*, became one of Mullins's closest allies. During the Whitsitt controversy the *Argus* openly supported the moderate faction. Professor A. T. Robertson played a "prominent part" in the organization of this journal in 1897 and contributed frequent articles.[15] Indeed, some charged that the

---

[10]The following editors solicited articles about Southern Seminary for their papers: J. B. Cranfill, editor of the Dallas *Baptist Standard*, 17 May 1901; J. C. Armstrong, St. Louis *Central Baptist*, 10 June 1903; A. J. Barton, Little Rock *Baptist Advance*, 6 December 1902; R. H. Pitt, Richmond *Religious Herald*, 17 February 1904; T. P. Bell, Atlanta *Christian Index*, 2 October 1903.

[11]A list dated 11 June 1900 found in the Presidential Correspondence.

[12]Robertson to Mullins, 4 July, 14 July 1902; Dargan to Mullins, 9 July 1902; Carver, "Recollections," 41-43; Carver to Mullins, 1 July 1902.

[13]J. L. Martin to Mullins, 11 February 1904; McGlothlin to Mullins, 21 September 1903; Sampey to Mullins, 14 August 1900.

[14]W. W. Landrum, Atlanta First Baptist Church, to Mullins, 13 October 1903; J. L. White, Macon First Baptist Church, to Mullins, 10 February 1904; John T. M. Johnson, St. Louis Delmar Avenue Baptist Church, to Mullins, 13 October 1903; Leonard Doolan, Henderson, Kentucky, First Baptist Church, to Mullins, 29 February 1904.

[15]Gill, *Robertson*, 92.

Argus was the "mouthpiece of the Seminary."[16] As the chief competitor of the *Western Recorder,* edited by T. T. Eaton, the *Argus* always supported Mullins and the Seminary in denominational debates. In turn Seminary professors contributed numerous articles to the *Argus.* The *Argus* enthusiastically championed the Seminary's financial campaigns, while the *Recorder* made only grudging mention of these activities.

Developing a rapport with J. M. Frost, the powerful corresponding secretary of the leading Southern Baptist Convention agency, the Sunday School Board, was crucial to Mullins's success. During his tenure Frost led the Board from a small printing house for denominational Sunday school literature to a powerful publishing house that controlled almost all of the printed matter used in Southern Baptist churches.[17] Mullins often asked advice and support from this elder statesman of Southern Baptists and kept Frost informed of Seminary plans.[18]

Mullins did not limit his promotional activities to the South. He kept in contact with the executives of the Northern Baptist societies. A few Northern Baptist ministers annually attended Southern Seminary. Southern-born trainees of the Louisville institution often supplied small churches in southern Indiana, which was then nominally Northern Baptist territory.[19]

Promotional efforts also included recruitment of students. Southern Seminary advertised in the denominational press, particularly during the summer months. The curriculum was aimed at two levels: the language course for college-trained men that would culminate in the doc-

---

[16]T. P. Bell to Mullins, 2 October 1903.

[17]James L. Sullivan, "James Marion Frost," *Encyclopedia of Southern Baptists,* 1:512-13.

[18]Mullins to Frost, 19, 22, 26, and 29 October 1900; 7 June, 25 June, 11 August, 10 September 1901; 8 February 1902 (Frost-Bell Letters, Dargan-Carver Library); Frost to Mullins, 29 December 1903; 5, 9, 19, 22, and 28 January, 1 February 1904.

[19]Carver, "Recollections," 127. Territorial disputes between Northern and Southern Baptists continued throughout Mullins's years in office. Marvin E. Hall, "The Problem of Comity Between American and Southern Baptists" (Th.D. diss., Southern Baptist Theological Seminary, 1956) 18-57.

tor of theology degree and the "pastors" or English course meant for those without college training. Though Mullins attempted to upgrade the student body, the number of college-trained Southern Baptist ministers continued to lag behind that of the better-established Northern seminaries and forced Mullins to maintain a dual program. When Mullins took office, only half of the student body had bachelor degrees, with some lacking even a high school diploma.[20] Mullins constantly tried to improve methods of recruiting. To facilitate correspondence he adopted modern office procedures and developed a system of form paragraphs in answering student inquiries.[21]

During Mullins's first five years as president, enrollment rose slowly from 256 in 1899-1900 to 273 in 1903-1904.[22] Most students were poor and had families to support.[23] Men who aspired to enter Southern Seminary usually were already licensed or ordained ministers, though some preached only on a part-time basis. One prospective student bemoaned the fact that he was forty years old and married with two children. "Of course I'm 'poor and needy,' " he affirmed, asking for extensive aid from the student fund.[24] A mill worker from far-away Lawrence, Massachusetts, declared his fleeting hope of attending Southern Seminary since "I

[20]Carver, "Recollections," 17, 32, 77; Sampey, *Memoirs*, 65.

[21]Mullins encouraged the younger men to go to college first and implied that the Pastor's Course was for the older, untrained men. *Baptist Argus*, 25 April 1901. His system of numbered form sentences and paragraphs included such answers as "2. Our Seminary will furnish you exactly the opportunity you need for theological training," and form answers about expenses, courses, and living facilities. (The above found as part of a list with no date.) After Mullins read a student letter he placed numbers at the bottom of the page, and his secretary transcribed the appropriate form letter. Another example of Mullins's attempts to create efficiency in the student correspondence urged those prospective students who had not yet enrolled for the school term to write him about their problems. Mullins to "Dear Brother," 4 October 1904.

[22]Sampey, *Memoirs*, 103, 105, 107, 108, 111; *Annual Report of the Faculty of the Southern Baptist Theological Seminary, May 12, 1904*.

[23]Gill, *Robertson*, 72.

[24]A. B. Carson to Mullins, 28 June 1904.

work in a mill and as you know mills do not pay a large wage."[25] Most students needed aid at some time during their stay at the Seminary.

The close association with student ministers gave Mullins the opportunity to benefit the Seminary in other ways. He received numerous requests from churches asking for the president to suggest names of pastors; the number increased as Mullins became better known throughout the country. Though the emphasis was supposedly on the "call" of the congregation, Mullins, in effect, acted in the capacity of coordinating the needs of churches without pastors. One congregation asked for a "hustling pastor" to pay off the church debt, while another declared that they did not want a "slow fellow" but one "who will preach more 'Hellfire and brimstone' to the people."[26] After a number of pastors had been placed by Mullins, he gained a strong source of support within the Convention. Though Mullins ridiculed a central ministerial supply bureau as contrary to Baptist ecclesiology, in effect, he fulfilled this role.[27]

Mullins realized the need for an increased endowment when he took office in 1899, and after a brief period of delay, he declared the immediate need for an endowment drive of $200,000.[28] In early 1902 the Board of Trustees accepted his recommendation that Southern Seminary launch a Twentieth Century Endowment Campaign.[29] The next year John H. Eager, a former Louisville minister, took the position of financial agent with the responsibility of adding to the endowment and Student Aid Fund.[30] In addition to hiring Eager, Mullins urged the adoption of a special alumni drive, informing one denominational leader that he

---

[25]Ernest E. Heald to Mullins, 8 October 1904.

[26]Mrs. Della Boaz to Mullins, 26 January 1904; O. R. Sholars to Mullins, 5 February 1904.

[27]*Baptist Argus*, 17 July 1902.

[28]Mullins, "The Seminary Outlook at the Opening of the Year," *Seminary Magazine* 13 (January 1900): 207; *Baptist Argus*, 25 April 1901; Mullins, "The Seminary and the Outlook for the New Century," *Seminary Magazine* 14 (February 1901): 205-206.

[29]Mueller, *A History of Southern Baptist Theological Seminary*, 190.

[30]*Courier-Journal*, 12 July 1899; A. J. S. Thomas to Mullins, 18 March 1903.

would use the next annual alumni meeting at the Southern Baptist Convention to "stir up interest in our endowment."[31] He soon asked the alumni to raise part of the money needed to endow a professorship.[32]

Mullins threatened to move the Seminary to Atlanta to encourage more endowment effort from Louisville Baptists. During a meeting with Atlanta Baptist pastors and laymen, a millionaire layman offered to guarantee a $1,000,000 addition to the endowment if the Seminary would move to that central Southern city. A Louisville paper reported that the Seminary leadership seriously considered the offer.[33] Robertson believed that the article benefited the Seminary, because it stirred Kentucky Baptists to renewed efforts in the endowment campaign. He denied, however, the practicality of a move since the school already had $1,000,000 invested in property, and he further recognized that the Seminary would lose its influence over the Midwest, becoming instead a "sectional" institution.[34] The threatened move to Atlanta, therefore, aided Mullins in his pleas for support. Soon thereafter, the 1904 meeting of the Southern Baptist Convention adopted a resolution sanctioning a conventionwide drive.[35]

To promote the Twentieth Century Endowment campaign, Mullins persuaded several Southern Baptist leaders to write articles or letters for the denominational press.[36] One important Texas minister urged Mullins to "Command me, unreservedly, whenever you will."[37] Mullins adopted a policy of dividing the total pledge into a five-year commitment, thereby making it easier on the donor's finances. Of course, this

---

[31]Mullins to I. J. Van Ness, 15 April 1902.

[32]Mullins, "The Alumni Endowment Movement," *Seminary Magazine* 17 (January 1904): 141-43.

[33]*Courier-Journal*, 16 April 1903.

[34]Robertson to Mullins, 17 April 1903.

[35]Mullins, *Mullins*, 129; Mueller, *A History of Southern Baptist Theological Seminary*, 190.

[36]William H. Smith to Mullins, 11 June 1903; Thomas S. Potts to Mullins, 12 June 1903; Eldridge B. Hatcher to Mullins, 25 June 1903; Leonard Doolan to Mullins, 10 June 1903; R. H. Pitt to Mullins, 17 May 1904.

[37]George W. Truett to Mullins, 23 December 1903.

long-term pledge limited an individual's ability to give to other denominational purposes. In effect, the plan offered the advantage of being better able to anticipate annual revenues of Southern Seminary. Mullins and his faculty believed that they should initiate the procedure as soon as possible or "somebody will get ahead of us."[38]

Mullins and the faculty periodically took fund raising trips, while Eager worked full-time at that task. From his base in Baltimore, Eager labored throughout the South. He received a salary of $118 per month, plus expenses while on the road, from his cash collections, with the pledges going to the Student Aid Fund or endowment.[39] Mullins and Eager carefully planned the subscription trips.[40] Eager's success often depended on the status of the Southern economy, the whims of the weather, other denominational campaigns, and even epidemics. On one occasion, for example, he was caught in the midst of a smallpox epidemic in Griffin, Georgia, which curtailed his progress for several weeks.[41]

Most important was the competition with other denominational enterprises. For example, a South Carolina Baptist leader bluntly told Mullins to keep Eager out of that state until Furman University completed a fund drive.[42] The pastor of a large church in Macon, Georgia, warned Mullins to forego a canvass since some of his "moneyed" deacons expressed the need to regroup their fortunes after a fund drive by Monroe College.[43] On another occasion, Eager declared that North Carolina Baptist organizations and schools had "buttonholed nearly every man of means" and this explained his poor showing.[44]

Campaign workers encouraged donors to sign five notes, which were cashed annually. They tried for the large individual contributions. George W. Norton, a wealthy trustee from Louisville, contributed as

---

[38]Sampey to Mullins, 20 July 1900.

[39]Robertson to Mullins, 14 July 1902; Eager to Mullins, 2 October 1903.

[40]Eager to Mullins, 27 May 1903.

[41]Ibid., 13 February 1904.

[42]A. J. S. Thomas to Mullins, 18 March 1903.

[43]J. L. White to Mullins, 10 February 1904.

[44]Eager to Mullins, 5 September, 9 September 1904.

much as $1,000 at a time.[45] Since donations reflected the health of the
Southern economy, sometimes wealthy Baptists found themselves unable to fulfill their subscriptions.[46] On the other hand, Samuel G. B. Cook,
a Baltimore merchant, paid $600 per quarter for five years to partially
endow a chair.[47] Southern Seminary successfully concluded its drive for
$200,000 in endowment but its needs continued to outrun available
funds. Endowment income paid faculty salaries, whereas the Student
Aid Fund generally met operating expenses. Needy students were always seeking funds. M. C. Treat, a Pennsylvania benefactor, contributed to students individually by doling out from $25 to $50 at a time to
needy scholars.[48]

Mullins requested help for the Student Aid Fund from outside
Southern Baptist Convention territory with little initial success. Northern Baptist leaders from Ohio, Illinois, Kansas, Michigan, and Minnesota expressed concern for the plight of Southern Seminary, but proved
unwilling to give financial aid directly to the school.[49] Ignoring the
warnings of Southern fundamentalists, Mullins tried to obtain funds in
the North, understanding that this had been one of the major criticisms
made of his predecessor. A close friend from Newton Centre days urged
Mullins not to "be sensitive about asking for a good cause," but to go
straight to Rockefeller with a request, avoiding the bureaucratic pitfalls
of working through the American Baptist Education Society.[50] Mullins

[45]Norton to Mullins, 25 July 1904.

[46]John T. M. Johnson to Mullins, 13 October 1903.

[47]Eager to Mullins, 17 November 1904; Joshua Levering to Mullins, 9 January 1905; Samuel G. B. Cook to Mullins, 7 April 1905; 13 January 1906.

[48]Treat to Mullins, 15 October, 24 December 1903; 7 June, 21 November
1905.

[49]Augustine S. Carman to Mullins, 6 May 1903; E. P. Brand to Mullins, 21
May 1903; E. B. Merridith to Mullins, 4 May 1903; C. H. Irving to Mullins, 5
May 1903; E. R. Pope to Mullins, 5 May 1903.

[50]The financial success of the University of Chicago was a glowing example
to Mullins and others of what Rockefeller, through the American Baptist Education Society, could do for educational institutions. Robert L. Harvey, "Baptists and the University of Chicago, 1890-1894," *Foundations* 14 (July-September
1971): 240; Kerfoot to Mullins, 10 February 1910; C. W. Kingsley to Mullins,
10 January 1900.

approached the New York millionaire about developing a $100,000 matching fund for Southern Seminary, pleading that this was only an attempt to fulfill the "King's business." Rockefeller's secretary brusquely replied that the magnate refused to consider such a proposal.[51] Mullins let the matter rest for nearly two years and then appealed to Rockefeller again with the beginning of the Twentieth Century Drive. He asked for a personal interview, but received no encouragement.[52] Eager tried to approach through Rockefeller's son, whom he knew personally, but he was no more successful than Mullins.[53]

The publication of a theological journal played a prominent role in Mullins's promotional plans. In late 1903 he announced the founding of a new theological quarterly supplanting the student edited *Seminary Magazine*.[54] He declared that there was no "distinctively Baptist Theological Review." In particular, the new journal, *The Baptist Review and Expositor*, would offer a medium for a scholarly expression of views.[55] He urged all interested alumni and friends of Southern Seminary to contribute time and money in support of the new journal.[56] Mullins, seeking representatives from all Baptist factions, persuaded two editors of the defunct *Southwestern Theological Review*, B. H. Carroll and A. H. Newman, to become associate editors while he assumed the position of editor-in-chief. In addition, all members of Southern's faculty became associate editors, as did selected Baptists from England, Canada, and

---

[51]Mullins to John D. Rockefeller, 10 January 1901; F. T. Gates to Mullins, 26 January 1901. Gates acted as "principal aide" for Rockefeller's philanthropic agencies and controlled much of the direction over distributing that fortune. Allan Nevins, *John D. Rockefeller: The Heroic Age of American Enterprise* (New York: Charles Scribner's Sons, 1940) 2:269.

[52]Gates to Mullins, 12 January, 17 January 1903.

[53]Eager to Mullins, 4 November, 3 December 1903; Gates to Mullins, 9 May 1904.

[54]Thomas, "Edgar Young Mullins," 107.

[55]Mullins, "The Need for a High Class Theological Journal," *Seminary Magazine* 17 (December 1903): 61-63.

[56]Mullins, Circular Letter, 18 December 1903.

the Northern Baptist constituencies.[57]

In the first issue Mullins declared that the editors would labor to avoid the "extremes" of "indifference" on one hand, and of "narrow traditionalism, sectarianism, or sectionalism," on the other. He promised a "diversity of opinion," including those of non-Baptist sources. The journal, furthermore, would wage war against those who attempted to tear down the tenets of evangelicalism.[58]

The initial reactions of Southern Baptists to the publication were favorable. E. M. Poteat, a classmate of Mullins who had become president of Furman University, offered his full support. Editor R. H. Pitt of the *Religious Herald* echoed these sentiments, while J. M. Frost declared that the journal would "make a great hit."[59]

Mullins used the publication to publicize Southern Seminary and its work. The inclusion of Baptist leaders from varying constituencies as associates gave him important contacts with men whose influence could help the Seminary. The journal became, for several years, the only scholarly forum in the Southern Baptist Convention. Mullins hoped that he could control doctrinal debate among his brethren through the new journal. It also fulfilled his desire to intellectualize conservative Christian thought.

In spite of Mullins's diligent efforts in promotion of Seminary activities and finances, revenue for the school remained an endemic problem. This crisis forced him to spend much valuable time seeking sources of income for the Seminary, setting patterns for the years ahead. On one occasion Mullins and McGlothlin had to borrow money on personal notes to supply a deficit in the budget.[60] Loans from the Student Fund

---

[57]H. C. Goerner, "Review and Expositor," *Encyclopedia of Southern Baptists,* 2:1158-59. D. F. Estes of Colgate and H. C. Vedder of Crozer represented Northern Baptists. J. H. Farmer of Toronto and W. T. Whitley of Preston, England, represented their brethren. J. P. Greene, president of William Jewell College in Liberty, Missouri, was another associate editor. Mullins, "Introductory," *Review and Expositor* 1 (April 1904): 3-4.

[58]Mullins, "Introductory," 1-3.

[59]Poteat to Mullins, 2 February, 3 March 1904; Pitt to Mullins, 5 April 1904; Frost to Mullins, 1 April 1904.

[60]C. S. Gilbert to Mullins, 19 September 1903; McGlothlin to Mullins, 21 September 1903.

were to be repaid by alumni when they took full-time pastorates; but many neglected their obligations, even some "who attained high position and ample income."[61] The faculty and staff, moreover, were not always happy with their salaries and nagged Mullins for increased compensation. Mullins's secretary, C. S. Gilbert, threatened to resign at one time arguing that he was rarely paid promptly.[62] Professor McGlothlin complained that he did not receive the same salary as Sampey and Robertson, yet he had the same responsibilities and qualifications.[63] Mullins did little, however, to raise salaries, and faculty members continued to supply church pulpits to supplement their income.

Mullins's first years as president of Southern Seminary were devoted to efforts to hold the institution together. Carping criticisms by fundamentalists within the denominational leadership added to Mullins's financial woes. The competition between Eaton's paper, the *Western Recorder*, and the *Baptist Argus*, edited by Prestridge, intensified, with the Seminary faction adhering to the *Argus*.

Eaton had great appeal to his unlettered brethren and dominated the anti-intellectual majority among Southern Baptists.[64] He gave only grudging support to the Seminary. While he found that the school did a creditable job in training ministers, he urged that it not be forgotten that "some" good ministers had no formal seminary training.[65] Like most of the editors of Baptist papers of the time, Eaton mirrored the "opinions and prejudices of the rank and file of Southern Baptists." He never cast new light on a subject, only rehashing old, mostly Landmarkist-fundamentalist, doctrines.[66]

---

[61]B. Pressley Smith to Mullins, 30 July 1902; Carver, "Recollections," 134-35.

[62]Gilbert to Mullins, 22 September 1902.

[63]McGlothlin to Mullins, 25 September 1901.

[64]Duke K. McCall, "The Role of Southern Seminary in Southern Baptist Life," *Review and Expositor* 67 (Spring 1970): 183; Jordan, "Thomas Treadwell Eaton," xiii, 117, 122; S. M. Provence, "Our Seminary," *Review and Expositor* 14 (April 1917): 251.

[65]*Western Recorder*, 14 May 1903.

[66]Jordan, "Thomas Treadwell Eaton," 211-12; Carl Dean English, "The Ethical Emphases of the Editors of Baptist Journals Published in the Southeastern Region of the United States, 1865-1915" (Th.D. diss., Southern Baptist Theological Seminary, 1948) 287-88.

Mullins thus inevitably clashed with Eaton's intense personal desire for power. Eaton intended to keep up the same pressures he had applied on Whitsitt.[67] Though Mullins probably knew about Eaton's vituperative nature, the professors of the Seminary urged Mullins not to join Eaton's Walnut Street Church as Whitsitt had, but instead to attend the Broadway Baptist Church. They warned Mullins to avoid a confrontation with Eaton if at all possible.[68]

As a longtime trustee, Eaton led a group of trustees, known as the "smelling committee" to the faculty, who periodically visited the Seminary searching for heresy. Eaton had earlier crossed swords with Robertson and Sampey in the Whitsitt controversy. He continued his intermittent attacks trying to lure the young president into debate.[69]

The cleavage between Eaton, who led the fundamentalists, and Mullins, who led the moderates, finally surfaced in a debate over an old Landmark tenet. Landmarkists claimed "the virtual identification of the kingdom of God and the visible church." In addition, they opposed alien immersion, the acceptance of a member into a Baptist church without baptism, and open communion, allowing any Christian to participate in the Lord's Supper.[70] While not an entirely consistent Landmarkist, Eaton voiced its doctrines when he wanted evidence of Southern Seminary's heresy and a defense against centralization of the denominational machinery.[71] Eaton's doctrinal conservatism led him to renew his full attacks on the Seminary in 1901 after only a two-year respite.[72]

In particular, Eaton aimed his attacks at Mullins, who should have taken notice of a cooling attitude by the irascible Eaton when the latter commented upon the death of F. H. Kerfoot, a former professor at

---

[67]Jordan, "Thomas Treadwell Eaton," 123, 125, 129, 189, 212.

[68]Robertson to Sampey, 6 September 1899.

[69]Carver, "Recollections," 51.

[70]John E. Steeley, "The Landmark Movement in the Southern Baptist Convention," in *What is the Church? A Symposium of Baptist Thought,* ed. Duke K. McCall (Nashville: Broadman Press, 1958) 143.

[71]Jordan, "Thomas Treadwell Eaton," 41-50.

[72]Eaton to Mullins, 8 August 1900; 25 March, 30 September, 19 November 1901.

Southern Seminary. Eaton publicly declared that Kerfoot "would have been elected President" in 1899 if he had not withdrawn his name, and he attacked a New York *Evening Post* editorial that viewed Kerfoot as one of the "bitterest" opponents of Whitsitt.[73] Eaton declared that someone had misinformed the *Post* about Southern Baptist affairs. He demanded to know the identity of the culprit, obtaining written "denials" from fifty-five of the sixty-two members of the board of trustees of the Seminary. He charged the *Argus* and *Religious Herald* with harboring the "guilty man."[74] Finally he stigmatized Whitsitt as the guilty party. If not, he demanded, his brethren should "uncover the guilty."[75] These charges showed the tenor of Eaton's vituperations. Mullins chose not to answer Eaton's charges and simply allowed the matter to die.

In late 1902 Eaton touched off a new controversy that lasted for several years. He charged that the Seminary now held adherents of the invisible church dictum, a belief foreign to the Seminary until Whitsitt took charge of that school.[76] Prestridge asked Mullins to make an immediate reply in behalf of the Seminary.[77] Previous to this dispute Mullins refused to antagonize Eaton by joining in a doctrinal debate, but now he accepted the challenge. Mullins replied that the Seminary did teach the doctrine of the universal spiritual (invisible) church. He explained that all Christians past, present, and future formed a spiritual union. Landmarkists like Eaton restricted the regenerate to a more exclusive grouping, demonstrating a strong Calvinist tendency. Mullins further claimed that the Seminary faculty of the nineteenth century had accepted this belief.[78] Eaton challenged Mullins on all counts and pushed him toward further public debate.[79]

---

[73]*Western Recorder*, 27 June 1901; 9 January 1902.

[74]Ibid., 28 January 1902.

[75]Ibid., 13 February 1902.

[76]Ibid., 18 December 1902; 15 January 1903.

[77]Prestridge to Mullins, 16 January 1903.

[78]*Baptist Argus*, 22 January 1903.

[79]*Western Recorder*, 14 March, 9 April 1903.

With the lines of battle drawn, Eaton kept on the offensive by printing editorials and articles that made incessant attacks on the orthodoxy
of Southern Seminary teaching. He took any opportunity to vary the attack. For example, after a few weeks he refocused the controversy on
some pronouncements made by McGlothlin in a speech. Eaton claimed
that the Seminary professor had revived the issues in Baptist ecclesiology and polity that had led to the Whitsitt controversy.[80]

While the debate continued over doctrine, a more important practical denominational matter arose. The presidency of Georgetown College became vacant, and the election of a new chief executive developed
into a denominational test of strength between the Eaton and Mullins
factions. As chairman of the Georgetown trustees, Eaton led the old anti-
Whitsitt faction and proposed the appointment of J. J. Taylor as the new
president.[81] Taylor was pastor of the Norfolk, Virginia, Freemason Street
Baptist Church and had supported Eaton in the visible-invisible church
controversy by occasionally attacking Mullins.[82] Eaton strengthened his
position when he gained control of the Kentucky General Association of
Baptists in June.[83] When the Georgetown trustees met, they elected Taylor by a one vote margin.[84] The Seminary faction recognized the potential danger of this development. An anti-Seminary president of
Georgetown could turn potential ministerial students toward other seminaries.

This last episode frightened Sampey, who saw in Taylor's election
"a walking of the Whitsitt ghost."[85] A few days after Taylor's election,
Mullins stated that the doctrinal controversy was more a matter of nuances in interpretation than substance. He found that some Baptists ex-

---

[80]Ibid., 12 February, 26 February, 26 March, 16 April, 7 May, 21 May, 4
June, 18 June 1903.

[81]Prestridge to Mullins, 20 August, 21 August 1903.

[82]*Western Recorder,* 4 June 1903; Taylor to Mullins, 8, 17, 26, and 31 January, 7 February 1903.

[83]Carver to Mullins, 23 June 1903.

[84]Prestridge to Mullins, 5 September 1903; *Courier-Journal,* 5 September
1903.

[85]Sampey to Mullins, 5 September 1903.

pected too much, demanding that one could be nothing other than a "twin brother" on doctrinal matters.[86] The pastor of the Georgetown First Baptist Church acted as the peacemaker and pleaded with Mullins to speak at Taylor's inauguration. Mullins finally accepted, but the fundamentalist faction continued to make spasmodic attacks on the Seminary.[87]

Fundamentalists continually forced Mullins into meaningless doctrinal debates, because he believed he had to defend himself to ensure that necessary funds would flow toward the school. A. H. Strong, president of the Rochester Seminary, and other moderates did not worry as much about financial support because their institutions were well-endowed. The University of Chicago faculty could be independent of other Baptist sources because of the Rockefeller fortune. Mullins, however, never had the financial means that could have led Southern Seminary toward a more independent course in doctrinal and denominational matters. Thus, in his first five years as president Mullins had little time to devote to expounding his theology. Compared with promotional articles, he contributed only a few essays directly concerned with theology to the denominational press.

Mullins exhibited great faith in the future of Christianity and his denomination. He flirted with the currents of premillennialism around the turn of the century, but, like most moderate evangelicals, did not emphasize it because he was not interested in the dire predictions of the radical premillennialists.[88] In a special article for the Louisville *Courier-Journal* Mullins displayed an optimistic disposition toward the new century, but he vowed that the great increase in material wealth had to

---

[86]*Baptist Argus*, 10 September 1903.

[87]E. B. Pollard to Mullins, 22, 26, and 30 September 1903.

[88]He corresponded with the leaders of the Boston Prophetic Conference, but never took a prominent part, despite their urgings. Robert Cameron to Mullins, 9 September, 5 November 1901; J. D. Herr to Mullins, 20 September, 16 October, 22 October 1901; Sandeen, *The Roots of Fundamentalism*, 166, 214; Sandeen, "The Baptists and Millenarianism," 24; George M. Marsden, *Fundamentalism and American Culture: The Shaping of Twentieth Century American Evangelicalism, 1870-1925* (New York: Oxford University Press, 1980) 241 n. 17.

be tempered by moral growth.[89] Christianity, he asserted, appealed to the better educated people of the world, and the growth of Christianity was concomitant with the development of a better educated world population. This gave the missionary more opportunity than ever before, and Mullins concluded that there was no greater task in the world than that of the minister.[90]

Mullins remained true to his evangelical heritage, "frankly" accepting "the substitutionary sacrifice of Christ [the Atonement]." In an eight-part series entitled "The Atonement," Mullins demonstrated a restrained evangelicalism. His approach was unhurried compared with the radical premillennialists. He continued, however, to emphasize the nineteenth-century teaching of the value of personalism, or individualism, in religious experience.[91]

One of the most debated topics of the day was the controversy created by the theological implications of evolution. Among Southern Baptists, W. L. Poteat, professor and later president of Wake Forest College, openly avowed his belief in evolution. In the spring of 1900 Poteat accepted Mullins's invitation to deliver the Gay Lectures, an endowed series. In these lectures Poteat tried to reconcile his evangelical faith and the new teachings of science.[92] Mullins came under fire from fundamentalists for sanctioning Poteat's appearance at the Seminary. While he did not completely agree with Poteat's ideas of Christianity and evolution, he maintained that the full rights of academic freedom belonged to lecturers invited to the Southern Seminary campus.[93] A few months later an ominous sign developed when a donor sent a check to Mullins with the admonition that he did not believe young preachers should be exposed to "infidel works" like Darwinism. He implied that further do-

---

[89]*Courier-Journal,* 30 December 1900.

[90]*Baptist Argus,* 1 January 1903; Mullins, "The Importance of Work for Men," *Seminary Magazine* 14 (April 1901): 281-83.

[91]*Baptist Argus,* 13, 20, and 27 February, 6 March, 20 March, 3 April, 10 April, 1 May 1902.

[92]Suzanne Cameron Linder, *William Louis Poteat: Prophet of Progress* (Chapel Hill: University of North Carolina Press, 1966) 72-73; Poteat to Mullins, 7 November 1899.

[93]Mullins to Charles E. Taylor, 9 April 1900.

nations might not be forthcoming if such teaching continued at Southern Seminary.[94] Mullins took the opportunity to briefly expound his own views on evolution later in the year. He maintained that law applied to both science and religion. Denying the validity of atheistic evolution, he asserted that "Christian evolution" was tenable for evangelical Christians.[95]

The incessant attacks by the fundamentalists, the financial pressures of the presidency, and the ill health of Isla May caused Mullins to consider leaving the Louisville institution for a more sedate post at one of the Northern seminaries. His wife became ill soon after moving to Louisville, and the climate aggravated her respiratory ailments. The smoke-laden atmosphere of downtown Louisville's winters, in particular, contributed to a breakdown of her health.[96] The old house near the Seminary that served as the president's home had an antiquated heating system that added to her health problems. Upon the advice of her physician she spent several months in Chicago for special treatments. Mullins visited in the Chicago area on weekends, supplying the more lucrative pulpits in the area.[97]

In the summer of 1903 Chancellor Harper of the University of Chicago offered Mullins a position in the Divinity School.[98] Several of Mullins's friends assumed that he had been offered the deanship of the Divinity School. At the time Eri Hulbert and Shailer Mathews were codeans. Not long afterward, Mathews became sole dean of the school. It is not known specifically if Mullins was offered the deanship, but a vacancy existed in the chair of Systematic Theology, the field Mullins taught at Southern Seminary, and he spent part of the summer of 1903 in Chicago, meeting at least once with Harper.[99]

---

[94]W. W. Jones to Mullins, 18 February 1901.

[95]*Western Recorder*, 9 May 1901; Mullins, *The Task of the Theologian Today* (Louisville: Southern Baptist Theological Seminary, 1901) 9-10.

[96]Sampey, *Memoirs*, 109-10.

[97]Mullins, *Mullins*, 122-25.

[98]Sampey, *Memoirs*, 109-11.

[99]William Rainey Harper to S. A. McKay, 9 November 1904 (University Presidents' Papers, 1889-1925, University of Chicago Archives); Harper to Mullins, 9, 14, and 22 May, 22 June 1903.

Mullins's friends and colleagues reacted immediately to rumors emanating from Chicago. Prestridge, Dargan, Sampey, and Robertson implored Mullins to refuse any offers from Chicago. Sampey recognized that the "old barn on Fourth Street" injured Isla May's health, but "ought not to be taken as proof that she cannot enjoy health in Louisville." Dargan, in London on sabbatical leave, added that Chicago could not possibly be any healthier for residence than Louisville. Prestridge maintained that his "heart was crushed" when he heard the news. Robertson could not believe that Mullins "would join forces with the radicalism of Harper any more than the reactionary traditionalism of Eaton."[100] All argued that Mullins had a greater area of service at Southern Seminary than he would ever have at Chicago. Mrs. Mullins's health would improve, Sampey maintained, when the "modern new house in the Highlands" was completed. He admitted, furthermore, that while Mullins's salary was inadequate, future prospects for the Seminary were bright.[101] Owing to Isla May's poor health, his low salary, and the incessant administrative problems, Mullins might have considered leaving Louisville. When the Chicago rumor spread in the North, other positions opened for Mullins: a professorship at Colgate and the pastorate of the prestigious Memorial Baptist Church in Philadelphia.[102] Though Mullins refused all offers to leave Louisville, it is clear that Northern Baptists favored him both personally and doctrinally at this time. Soon the Southern Seminary trustees accelerated plans for the new house in the exclusive Highlands area in the east end of Louisville.[103] Mullins lost all qualms about his future plans. His decision to stay in Louisville demonstrated his full commitment to the Southern Seminary presidency.

---

[100]Sampey to Mullins, 30 June 1903; Dargan to Mullins, 28 July 1903; Prestridge to Mullins, no date, Box 3A; Robertson to Mullins, 30 June 1903.

[101]Sampey to Mullins, 30 June 1903.

[102]George E. Merrill, president of Colgate University, to Mullins, 11 November 1903; A. J. Rowland, corresponding secretary of the American Baptist Publication Society, to Mullins, 2 January 1904.

[103]Mullins, *Mullins,* 122-25; Sampey to Mullins, 2 August 1905; Sampey, *Memoirs,* 110.

4   THE WIDER INFLUENCE: DENOMINATIONAL AND INTERDENOMINATIONAL LEADERSHIP

During his first decade as president of Southern Seminary, Mullins participated in denominational and interdenominational organizations and activities outside the Southern Baptist Convention. To most Southern Baptists, influenced by Landmarkism and Southern culture, cooperation even with Northern Baptists was impossible. These fundamentalists considered dialogue with other denominations to be disloyal and heretical. Moderates like Mullins did not find their denominational integrity endangered by contact with other Christian groups.

In the early twentieth century Mullins served as a viable link between Southern and Northern Baptists. While at Baltimore and Newton Centre he developed numerous contacts with Northern Baptists that were useful during his years in Louisville. He participated in more denominational and interdenominational activities than any other Southern Baptist leader. Though he had contact with Chicago liberals such as

William Rainey Harper, Shailer Mathews, and Ernest D. Burton, he had an even closer rapport with Northern Baptist moderates.[1]

Some midwestern Northern Baptist moderate leaders, in fact, preferred Southern Seminary's leadership to that of the University of Chicago. Leaders of the Ohio Baptist Education Society and the Ohio Baptist Convention, for example, regularly urged Mullins to attend meetings at Denison University in Granville, Ohio, to offset the influence of the Chicago Divinity School. They particularly found Burton, Eri Hulbert, and Mathews to be too liberal and desired a "sound" influence from Southern Seminary.[2] At least one moderate evangelical Chicago minister found that the university nearby rightfully did not dominate Chicago Baptists, and he voiced his faith in the orthodoxy of the Louisville faculty.[3]

Other Northern Baptists also feared the development of liberalism in their denomination. The moderate treasurer of the Northern Baptist Education Society warned that "an insidious Universalism and Unitarianism is getting into our pulpits," and he praised Southern Seminary for adhering to the old teachings.[4] Northern Baptist moderates often asked Mullins for advice about ministerial appointments and reciprocated by recommending prospective students to Southern Seminary.[5]

Mullins also had close contact with leaders of the American Baptist Home Mission Society and the American Baptist Publication Society. The Publication Society published several of his early books and used his editorial skills.[6] Home Mission Society executives admitted that they wanted

---

[1]Norman H. Maring, "Baptists and Changing Views of the Bible, 1865-1918," *Foundations* 1 (July 1958): 72-73; Maring, "Baptists and Changing Views of the Bible, 1865-1918," *Foundations* 1 (October 1958): 30-31.

[2]Augustine S. Carman to Mullins, 14 February, 18 March 1904; 6 March, 31 March 1906; C. J. Rose to Mullins, 10 August 1907.

[3]David Heagle to Mullins, 1 July 1908.

[4]R. J. Adams to Mullins, 20 January 1904.

[5]Henry C. Mabie to Mullins, 9 March 1900; J. S. Kirtley to Mullins, 18 January 1904; H. E. Tralle to Mullins, 9 July 1904; Alexander Blackburn to Mullins, 17 January 1905; F. P. Haggard to Mullins, 14 April 1905; Kittredge Wheeler to Mullins, 17 May 1905; H. L. Morehouse to Mullins, 23 November 1907.

[6]C. R. Blackall to Mullins, 29 September 1908; Charles M. Roe to Mullins, 30 October 1908.

Southern Seminary graduates, often finding them superior to the graduates of other seminaries.[7]

During his early years as president, Mullins also had a rapport with the executives and faculties of the Northern Baptist seminaries, particularly with the Chicago Divinity School and Newton Theological Institution. Most of the early correspondence concerned publications.[8] In 1902 the Chicago faculty initiated a movement to form a cooperative union of the Northern and Southern Baptist seminaries. Mathews, in particular, wanted to join these institutions into a "federated seminaries" union.[9] After preliminary meetings between the Northern seminaries, Chicago issued an invitation to Louisville to join the Baptist Theological Faculties' Union.[10]

Remembering that Whitsitt's connections with Chicago had been used against him by the Landmarkists, Mullins was wary of joining such a group. At first he promised only to present the matter to the Southern faculty for their consideration.[11] After several delays Mullins admitted that the Southern Seminary faculty was afraid of being placed in an "awkward position" if the Union endorsed a "particular policy" that they could not support. He implied that this would immediately lead to repercussions in the Southern Baptist Convention that would injure his institution.[12]

---

[7]Judson B. Thomas to Mullins, 20 August 1904; L. C. Barnes to Mullins, 23 December 1908; D. D. Proper to Mullins, 16 January 1909.

[8]A. H. Strong to Mullins, 7 March 1900; J. W. English to Mullins, 8 November 1899; Alvah Hovey to Mullins, 14 April, 5 October, 8 November 1900; 29 March 1901; W. R. Harper to Mullins, 23 November 1901; Shailer Mathews to Mullins, 15 February, 3 March 1901; Mullins to Mathews, 13 February 1901.

[9]Shailer Mathews to W. R. Harper, 14 May 1902 (Divinity School Correspondence, University of Chicago Archives).

[10]Ernest Dewitt Burton to Mullins, 12 February, 8 March 1904.

[11]Mullins to Burton, 29 February 1904 (Divinity School Correspondence, University of Chicago Archives).

[12]Mullins to Burton, 5 March 1904 (Divinity School Correspondence, University of Chicago Archives).

The Chicago and Rochester faculties continued to pressure Mullins to make a decision and join the Union.[13] After much discussion the Union agreed that any member institution could suspend an action by the Union for three months. This provision mollified the Southern faculty's apprehensions, and they voted to join in the fall of 1904.[14] Southern Seminary did not commit itself, however, to any united efforts, only promising to participate in an annual conference and continue dialogue with the Union. These conditions satisfied the other members of the Union who understood Mullins's predicament. They rejoiced in Southern Seminary's participation under any circumstances.[15]

Before the Union had time to develop a close relationship between the seminaries, a controversy erupted that severely limited its effectiveness. Competition for students was to blame, reviving Baptist sectionalism. Southern Seminary claimed that "other seminaries" were actively recruiting ministerial students in Southern colleges and offering financial aid to young men as an inducement to leave Southern Baptist territory. Mullins stated that Southern Seminary "[could not] and would not compete" with Northern seminaries.[16] Specifically, Mullins accused Colgate, Newton, and Rochester of offering "injuriously large sums of money" to potential seminarians in the South. Leaders of these institutions denied the charge.[17] President Merrill of Colgate compounded the confusing situation by insisting that only Rochester committed such acts and had sent recruiting circulars to his own school.[18] Several Southern

---

[13]Burton to Mullins, 4 March, 12 March 1904; Mullins to Burton, 21 March 1904 (Divinity School Correspondence, University of Chicago Archives); A. H. Strong to Mullins, 23 April 1904.

[14]Burton to Mullins, 13 August, 5 November 1904; George E. Merrill to Mullins, 19 November 1904.

[15]Mullins to the Baptist Theological Faculties' Union, 24 December 1904 (Divinity School Correspondence, University of Chicago Archives).

[16]Mullins to Burton, 9 December 1904 (Divinity School Correspondence, University of Chicago Archives); *Faculty Report to the Trustees of Southern Baptist Theological Seminary, 1905-1906* (a pamphlet).

[17]George E. Merrill to Mullins, 28 April 1905; Nathan E. Wood to Mullins, 29 June 1905; Walter R. Betteridge to Mullins, 4 January 1906.

[18]Merrill to Mullins, 30 March 1906.

Baptist leaders entered the fray, including the presidents of Wake Forest and Furman universities, who supported Mullins's contention, declaring that a representative of Rochester made unusually large offers to their students.[19] Merrill continued to defend the actions of his school and laid the blame entirely on Rochester.[20] There is some evidence that Southern Seminary tried to retaliate by offering aid that could not then be fulfilled. Professor Sampey, for example, was caught off guard when he matched a Colgate offer to two Southern college students and they accepted. When he tried to lower the sum to a more reasonable figure, the students decided to go North for their theological education.[21] Milton G. Evans, president of Crozer Theological Seminary, finally acted as peacemaker and urged all concerned to use the Union as a meeting ground for a settlement on financial aid to students.[22]

The controversy over aid to prospective students continued to stir debate among Baptist seminarians for several more months. Mullins, president of the 1906 meeting of the Union in Louisville, introduced a resolution asking that member schools not use "paid agents" to recruit students, which passed after a "lively discussion."[23] This arrangement seemingly reassured the Louisville faculty that they would not continually be placed at a financial disadvantage in their own home territory.

The Union successfully united the seminaries in cooperative promotional and advertising efforts. Mullins became a member of the "Committee on the Effect of Beneficiary Aid," which produced nothing substantial, but the dialogue did bring tacit agreements on the territory to be recruited by the seminaries and the amount of aid that could be offered to prospective students.[24] The Louisville president also served on

---

[19]C. E. Taylor to Mullins, 10 February 1906; E. M. Poteat to Mullins, 2 March 1906; J. H. Spaulding to Mullins, 14 March 1906; Livingston Johnson to Mullins, 24 April 1906.

[20]Merrill to Mullins, 14, 15, and 28 April 1906.

[21]Sampey to Mullins, 14 August 1906.

[22]Evans to Mullins, 2 July 1906.

[23]*Courier-Journal*, 29 December 1906.

[24]Burton to Mullins, 24 January, 13 November, 21 November 1905; 6 January, 1 March 1906; Mullins to Burton, 20 December 1905 (Divinity School Correspondence, University of Chicago Archives).

a committee to encourage young men to enter the ministry. Ernest D. Burton, secretary of the Union, contracted Mullins to write a tract, which was soon expanded into a sixteen-page publication entitled *Choosing a Life Calling: An Address to Christian Young Men.*[25] Within a year of publication the Union sent 40,000 copies to college students throughout the United States and Canada. The members of the Union warmly praised Mullins's effort.[26] Mullins continued to cooperate, remembering however that his fundamentalist Southern Baptist brethren considered any union with Northern Baptists to be destructive. The precarious financial base of Southern Seminary always tempered Mullins's cooperative predilections with caution.

Participation in the Union was not the only evidence of Mullins's interest in dialogue with Northern Baptists. Mullins and the moderate Southern Baptist leadership represented by Southern Seminary participated in other associations that tried to build a bridge between Northern and Southern Baptists, namely, the General Convention of Baptists in North America and the Baptist Young People's Union of America.[27] Fundamentalist Southern Baptists opposed the creation of these groups. J. M. Frost, corresponding secretary of the Sunday School Board, displaying the ultimate Southern Baptist sectionalism, declared that he wanted nothing whatsoever to do with any Northern Baptist organizations.[28] Mullins, in addition, cooperated with the Baptist Congress, an annual meeting of Baptist intellectuals who gathered to present papers on questions of church polity and doctrine.[29]

---

[25]*Courier-Journal*, 28 December 1906; Burton to Mullins, 5, 7, 12, 14, 23, and 29 January, 4 March, 9 March, 5, 6, and 23 April 1907.

[26]Burton to Mullins, 7 May, 11 May 1907; Mullins to Burton, 27 December, 28 December 1906; 28 June 1907 (Divinity School Correspondence, University of Chicago Archives). A copy of the pamphlet is contained in the University of Chicago Archives.

[27]Donnell R. Harris, "The Gradual Separation of Southern and Northern Baptists, 1845-1907," *Foundations* 7 (April 1964): 143.

[28]Frost to Mullins, 1 June 1901; Harris, "The Gradual Separation of Southern and Northern Baptists," 139.

[29]W. C. Bitting to Mullins, 7 December 1901; W. B. Matteson to Mullins, 15 January 1907; Theodore A. K. Gessler to Mullins, 25 July 1900, 7 July 1907, 30 July 1909; Shailer Mathews, *New Faith for Old: An Autobiography* (New York: The Macmillan Company, 1936) 109.

In many respects Mullins functioned as the major point of contact between Northern and Southern Baptists. Mullins defended his activities in the North as necessary for the successful operation of Southern Seminary, owing to the fact that twenty percent of the student body came from Northern Baptist territory. A large donation to the Student Aid Fund, moreover, came from a Pennsylvania layman. Though he admitted that his institution was "in the strict sense of the word . . . a Southern institution," Mullins insisted that Southern Seminary's continued influence over the Midwest demanded participation in such groups.[30]

In 1906-1907, in particular, Mullins acted as liaison in coordinating the meeting dates for the Northern and Southern conventions and the General Convention. Just before the 1906 meetings of the above groups, H. L. Morehouse, corresponding secretary of the American Baptist Home Mission Society, claimed that Southern Baptist leaders were trying to sabotage the meeting of the General Convention by scheduling Southern Baptist Convention sessions so that no Southern Baptist could attend the General Convention. He asked Mullins's help in scheduling the 1907 meetings so that representatives of both Baptist constituencies could attend the General Convention.[31] In addition, Morehouse urged Mullins to use his influence to coordinate the meetings of the three groups. In particular, Morehouse wanted the Baptists of Richmond, Virginia, to invite the General Convention to meet in that city as soon as the Southern Baptist Convention adjourned.[32] When this invitation did not come, Mullins and the Northern Baptist leadership met and decided to change the meeting of the Northern Baptist anniversaries (meetings of the three societies) to Washington, D.C., and the meeting of the General Convention to the neutral ground of Jamestown, Virginia.[33]

This plan would not work, however, unless Mullins could persuade the Southern Baptist leadership to change the dates for the meetings of

---

[30]Mullins to Frost, 7 March 1906 (Frost-Bell Letters, Dargan-Carver Library).

[31]Morehouse to Mullins, 23 March 1906.

[32]Ibid., 16 August, 8 November, 24 November 1906.

[33]Ibid., 10 November, 4, 13, and 19 December 1906.

the Southern Baptist Convention.[34] Mullins contacted the leaders of the Convention urging that they influence the president to change these dates to correspond with the requests of their Northern brethren. R. J. Willingham, corresponding secretary of the Foreign Mission Board, O. F. Gregory, secretary of the Convention, and B. D. Gray, corresponding secretary of the Home Mission Board, agreed to encourage President E. W. Stephens of the Southern Baptist Convention to comply with Mullins's request.[35] Stephens agreed to change the meeting date after the urgings of such a prestigious group.[36] Frost bitterly complained about the changed dates and openly admitted that he never wanted to witness such a development again, charging that the General Convention worked only to the benefit of Northern Baptists who increasingly tried to lure Southern Baptists into union meetings.[37]

Mullins participated in planning the meeting of the General Convention as a member of the Executive Committee.[38] He took advantage of the meeting by advertising the work of Southern Seminary through an exhibit and by presenting an address entitled "The Contribution of Baptists to American Civilization."[39]

The Louisville seminary president's efforts on behalf of the Baptist Young People's Union of America is another example of his earnest cooperation with his Northern brethren. The Young People's Union originated as a national movement separate from the two conventions. It sought to develop programs for young people through the local churches. This organization infuriated most fundamentalist Southern Baptists. Frost, for example, felt disadvantaged because of the larger resources of the American Baptist Publication Society, which administered the Northern half of the Young People's Union. This rivalry resulted in an

---

[34]Ibid., 16 January, 30 January 1907.

[35]Willingham to Mullins, 9 January 1907; Gregory to Mullins, 9 January 1907; Gray to Mullins, 11 January 1907.

[36]Stephens to Mullins, 9 January 1907.

[37]Frost to Mullins, 12 January, 18 January 1907.

[38]E. M. Thresher to Mullins, 10 April 1907.

[39]Morehouse to Mullins, 28 May 1907; C. H. Spaulding to Mullins, 3 June 1907; Mullins, *Mullins*, 138, 141.

intense competition between the Sunday School Board and the Publication Society for control of literature to be used by the Union in the South.[40]

Mullins actively cooperated with the national organization throughout the first decade of his presidency.[41] He so impressed the 1906 meeting with a speech that the Union elected him president at its next annual session and made him chairman of the Educational Commission.[42] As part of its aggressive policies, the Sunday School Board, under the direction of Frost and Van Ness, decided to take over the publication of all materials used in the South. They charged that the materials published by Northern agencies did not fit the Southern environment.[43]

George T. Webb, general secretary of the Union, and A. J. Rowland, secretary of the American Baptist Publication Society, depended on Mullins to allay the fears of his Southern brethren. Rowland charged that Frost and Van Ness were "simply desiring to make trouble" and would continually search for opportunities to strike at the Young People's Union.[44] After the Publication Society purchased *Service*, the official journal of the Union, they offered free publication services to the South.[45] Frost immediately viewed this as a conspiracy to take over all functions of his Board. He charged that the Publication Society paid Webb's salary and therefore dictated policy to the national organiza-

---

[40]J. E. Lambdin, "Baptist Young People's Union of America," *Encyclopedia of Southern Baptists*, 1:134-35; Robert Andrew Baker, *Relations Between Northern and Southern Baptists* (New York: Arno Press, 1980) 144-200.

[41]Walter Calley to Mullins, 17 November 1904; George T. Webb to Mullins, 16 March 1906; E. M. Thresher to Mullins, 28 November 1906.

[42]H. C. Lyman to Mullins, 18 July 1907; Webb to Mullins, 9 August, 10 October, 27 September, 30 September, 30 October 1907; H. G. Baldwin to Mullins, 14 November 1907.

[43]Frost to Mullins, 2 December 1907; Van Ness to Mullins, 26 November 1907. For a fuller account of the development of the Sunday School Board see Robert A. Baker, *The Story of the Sunday School Board* (Nashville: Broadman Press, 1966) 74-92.

[44]Webb to Mullins, 26 December 1907; Rowland to Mullins, 26 December 1907.

[45]Rowland to Mullins, 4 January 1908; Webb to Mullins, 9 January 1908.

tion.[46] Webb denied these allegations imploring Mullins to negotiate peace with Frost so that the Union could function as a national organization.[47]

The impasse between the Sunday School Board and the Publication Society continued, with Mullins caught between the contending forces. The competition between these two agencies exacerbated the conditions necessary for the cooperative effort of the Union. Webb finally suggested that the Sunday School Board be allowed to control the Union work in the South if they would allow national educational materials to circulate freely in the South.[48] Frost agreed to cooperate but only on his own terms, which meant only temporary acceptance of Publication Society materials in the South, while Van Ness claimed that the Publication Society always discriminated in favor of its own interests.[49] Mullins's efforts to bring the two groups together finally failed. Frost continued to spurn anything but complete Sunday School Board control over young people's groups in the South.[50] Webb and Rowland, realizing that the situation was hopeless, tried only to persuade the Sunday School Board to use *Service* along with their own materials.[51] Mullins finally gave up all hope of peace between the two publishing agencies. He decided to sever his own relationship with the Baptist Young People's Union of America in 1909, asking to be relieved of his duties as president of that body. The growing power of Frost and the Sunday School Board in Southern Baptist affairs discouraged Mullins's interest in influencing national Baptist affairs by direct participation. He began to adhere more closely to the polity developing within the Southern Baptist Convention.

---

[46]Frost to Mullins, 25 March 1908.

[47]Webb to Mullins, 7 April, 11 April 1908.

[48]Webb to Mullins, 7 May 1908. He enclosed a "Basis of Agreement" proposed to the Sunday School Board.

[49]Van Ness to Mullins, 2 April 1909; Frost to Mullins, 12 June 1908.

[50]Frost to Mullins, 5, 11, and 22 February 1909.

[51]Webb to Mullins, 16 January, 16 February 1909; Rowland to Mullins, 11 February 1909.

This change was not sudden, but it is evident in the breakup of the national Young People's Union.[52]

Mullins found it increasingly difficult to participate enthusiastically in denominational activities outside the Southern Baptist Convention without incurring the suspicions of the fundamentalists. The moderate Southern Seminary faction, particularly Professor Robertson and Editor Prestridge, pushed the idea of developing an international organization of Baptists, the Baptist World Congress, later known as the Baptist World Alliance. After some initial promotion, the Congress met in London in 1905 with Mullins, Carver, Gardner, and Robertson in attendance.[53]

Neither the leaders of the Northern Baptists nor fundamentalist Southern Baptists took much interest in the formation of the Congress.[54] Mullins, however, assumed a dominant role in the Congress when he delivered a major address at the London meeting.[55] He extolled the virtues of "a free church in a free state" and a church in which all believers had equal rights.[56] The Seminary contingent was elated with the initial success of the Congress, with Mullins expressing the conviction that the Congress represented the hope for a "conception of world-wide unity and co-operation" among Baptists.[57] Mullins, desiring unity beyond the confines of the Southern Baptist Convention, understood that the opposition of fundamentalist Southern Baptists limited his opportunities for such activity. He hoped, however, that fundamentalist Southern

---

[52]Webb to Mullins, 11 December, 27 December 1909; Mullins, *Mullins*, 142.

[53]Mueller, *A History of Southern Baptist Theological Seminary*, 188-89.

[54]Rowland to Mullins, 9 September 1904; *Western Recorder*, 28 September 1905.

[55]"Suggestions Toward a New Baptist Apologetic," *Literary Digest* 31 (14 October 1905): 537-38.

[56]*Baptist World Congress, Proceedings, 1905*, 152; Torbet, *A History of Baptists*, 425. Mullins took the opportunity in attending the Congress to expand his trip into a six-month leave of absence for travel and study on the Continent. He particularly was impressed by the beauty of the art museums of Europe and the municipal administration of Berlin. *Baptist Argus*, 31 August, 14 September, 19 October 1905; *Courier-Journal*, 26 January 1906.

[57]*Baptist Argus*, 17 August 1905.

Baptists possibly would support, or at least not violently oppose, a Baptist organization that was not dominated by Northern Baptists.

Mullins's contacts with interdenominational groups offered further evidence of his willingness to work with other Christians, particularly those of a moderate bent. The Southern Seminary faculty cooperated with the International Sunday School Association. Sampey, for example, wrote lessons and served on committees before Mullins came to Southern Seminary. Mullins soon became a member of the Education Committee of the Association.[58] The Sunday School Board, on the other hand, only half-heartedly cooperated with the Association. Early in Mullins's tenure Frost declared his disdain of any interdenominational work with the Association.[59] Van Ness later noted Mullins's participation on the Education Committee and voiced his dislike for the International Sunday School diploma that Mullins had helped design. He declared, furthermore, that numerous Southern brethren had voiced similar complaints.[60] In 1909 when Mullins asked to be relieved of his duties on the committee because of a Southern Seminary fund drive, the leaders of the Association pleaded that he remain lest they lose all influence in the Southern Baptist Convention.[61] This is another example of Mullins's growing concern with stronger Southern Baptist denominationalism and adherence to the dictates of the Sunday School Board.

The Southern Seminary president joined the American Bible League, later becoming a member of its board of directors.[62] In addition, he cooperated with the Kentucky Anti-Saloon League, participating in panel discussions and preaching anti-alcohol sermons.[63]

---

[58]Marion Lawrence to Mullins, 9, 11, 18, and 26 July, 6 August, 23 September 1904; H. M. Hamill to Mullins, 3 December 1903.

[59]Frost to Mullins, 29 December 1902.

[60]Van Ness to Mullins, 19 February 1909.

[61]William N. Hartshorn to Mullins, 15 March 1909; Lawrence to Mullins, 23 March 1909.

[62]John Lewis Clark to Mullins, 20 May, 25 May 1904; Daniel Gregory to Mullins, 2 December 1904, 24 May 1907; Oliver C. Morse to Mullins, 18 April 1907.

[63]F. S. Buckingham to Mullins, 7 February 1907; J. W. West to Mullins, 22 December 1908.

Mullins's reactions to the liberal interdenominational movements of the twentieth century offer further examples of his moderation. The leaders of these organizations were always interested in obtaining his cooperation, knowing that without it they would have little influence in the Southern Baptist Convention. The Council of Seventy, a Chicago-based group, tried to lure him into helping them liberalize the publications of the International Sunday School Association. Realizing that the already tenuous hold of the Association on the South would be irrevocably broken if the Sunday School Board got wind of the liberal movement, he refused to join their efforts.[64]

The organizers of the Federal Council of Churches of Christ in America also wanted his participation in their union and urged him to use his influence to obtain the cooperation of the Southern Baptist Convention.[65] Mullins cautiously cooperated with the Federal Council. He understood that most Southern Baptists opposed interdenominationalism because of the influence of Landmarkism. The corresponding secretary of the Federal Council was able to enlist his participation at a meeting in Louisville, but knowing that violent repercussions could erupt, Mullins did not push for Southern Baptist Convention cooperation in the work of the Federal Council.[66] The fear of fundamentalist reprisals against Southern Seminary always moderated Mullins's interdenominational tendencies.

Publication was also a major part of Mullins's wider influence in the early years of his presidency. Throughout his years in Louisville he was the intellectual leader at the Seminary though he did not publish his first book until he entered his seventh year as president.[67] During his first decade there, he published *Why Is Christianity True?* and *The Axioms of Religion: A New Interpretation of the Baptist Faith.* The Publication Society issued both volumes and, actively seeking more books from

---

[64]C. W. Votaw to Mullins, 18 October, 21 October, 18 December 1902.

[65]E. B. Sanford to Mullins, 28 March 1905; 6 May 1907; 21 April, 5 May, 16 September 1908.

[66]Sanford to Mullins, 9 November, 19 November, 16 December, 22 December 1909.

[67]Carver, "Recollections," 76-77.

Mullins, guaranteed to print anything he wrote.[68] His books, therefore, connected him with his Baptist brethren outside the confines of the Southern Baptist Convention. He also reacted to contemporary ideas that stirred debate, such as pragmatism, higher criticism, and evolution. In his publications he commented on these topics. His writings further exemplified his moderate evangelical inclination.

Through the Publication Society the Baptist Young People's Union of America contracted Mullins to write *Why Is Christianity True?* as part of its Christian Culture Series. Using a nondenominational approach, he never once mentioned the Baptist denomination. He used the apologetic method, in effect, an attempt to use empirical and philosophical proof in defending the place of Christianity in the modern world.[69] In addition, as a Christian apologist he attempted to prove that Christianity was the only "true religion," one that was "compatible with reason."[70]

In his book Mullins declared his intention to prove that Christianity was compatible with modern culture. To be the most effective, the Christian apologist should use the "principles employed by the opposition, so far as those principles are valid."[71] To facilitate his method, he divided the book into four parts: "The Christian View of the World," "Jesus Christ the Evidence of Christianity," "The Evidence of Christian Experience," and "The Evidence from Christian History."[72]

In analyzing Mullins's views, content from some of his articles published near the same time will be used to clarify his position on the ma-

---

[68]Mullins, *Why Is Christianity True?* (Philadelphia: American Baptist Publication Society, 1905); Mullins, *The Axioms of Religion: A New Interpretation of the Baptist Faith* (Philadelphia: Judson Press, 1908).

[69]Bernard Ramm, "Apologetics," *Encyclopedia of Southern Baptists*, 1:55; Spears, "The Christology of Edgar Young Mullins," 13; Dilday, "The Apologetic Method of E. Y. Mullins," iii; Herbert W. Schneider, *Religion in 20th Century America* (Cambridge: Harvard University Press, 1952) 133.

[70]Dilday, "The Apologetic Method of E. Y. Mullins," 1. The most complete exposition of Mullins's theology is in Bill Clark Thomas, "Edgar Young Mullins," which emphasizes Mullins's attempt to develop a "restatement" of the Christian faith (1-14).

[71]Mullins, *Why Is Christianity True?* 4.

[72]Ibid., 16-19.

jor theological issues in *Why Is Christianity True?* These further illuminate his theology in the first decade of the twentieth century.

One area of emphasis was Mullins's continued adherence to evangelical faith. Crediting his father's evangelical influence with turning him from a life of sin, he dedicated the book to his parents. Admitting that he was an evangelical Christian, he declared that "Christianity stands or falls with the resurrection of Jesus," the theme always most apparent among evangelicals. "Conversion" was central to the experience.[73]

Foremost in Mullins's defense of Christianity was the belief that "Christian experience" was evidence of the working of God in the world.[74] Believing that each individual was given the opportunity at some time for an intensely personal religious experience, he propounded the evangelical dependence on the efficacy of revivals.[75]

While Mullins did not extensively document his remarks, he did criticize the ideas of other scholars in the text of his books and articles.[76] The influences of William James, Borden Parker Bowne, and F. E. D. Schleiermacher are particularly evident in *Why Is Christianity True?* and his articles of this period.[77]

James's work had a special attraction for Mullins and influenced the Louisville seminarian's ideas about experience and belief. Mullins directly referred to James at least fifteen times in *Why Is Christianity True?* James's philosophy impressed Mullins as "a stage midway between agnosticism and Christianity."[78] He credited the Harvard philosopher with

---

[73]Ibid., v, 3, 203, 266-67.

[74]*Baptist Argus,* 12 April 1906; Mullins, "The Theological Trend," *Review and Expositor* 2 (October 1905): 507, 512-13, 517-18; Spears, "The Christology of Edgar Young Mullins," 153; Thomas, "Edgar Young Mullins," 200.

[75]*Baptist Argus,* 16 March 1905.

[76]Harold W. Tribble, "Edgar Young Mullins," *Review and Expositor* 49 (April 1952): 125.

[77]Dilday, "The Apologetic Method of E. Y. Mullins," 46; Mueller, *A History of Southern Baptist Theological Seminary,* 192; Gaines S. Dobbins, "Men Who Have Made Seminary History," *Quarterly Review* 18 (July, August, September 1958): 31; Thomas, "Edgar Young Mullins," 163.

[78]Mullins, "Is Jesus Christ the Author of Religious Experience?" *Review and Expositor* 1 (April 1904): 55-56.

freeing many people from the materialistic dogma of Darwinism and giving credulity to religious experience.[79] James limited the "practical need" for religion, however, to a certain time and place. Mullins proposed that this need was constant and could only be fulfilled through submission to Christ.[80] Likewise Mullins believed that James's emphasis on "will" was shallow because he did not pinpoint the "First Cause" as God. Christianity, Mullins found, changed the conduct of the regenerate individual, proving that it "works in practical life."[81]

The theological implications of modern philosophy, particularly pragmatism, intrigued Mullins. He found that Christianity passed the "pragmatic test of success" because it continued to influence the world for good since its founding, that is, the end in view was good.[82] While pragmatism offered solace for the philosophically minded, Mullins found that it did not offer enough for most people. The humanistic tendency of pragmatism did not answer, moreover, the eternal questions about the end of time or purpose for the world. He did not fault, however, the pragmatic emphases on purpose, progressive discovery of truth, and faith. If pragmatists would only accept the validity of Christianity, he declared, they would change the world of philosophy into a potent world force for good.[83]

Schleiermacher and Bowne also influenced his ideas about personality, experience, and the individual.[84] Though he disapproved of Schleiermacher's pantheistic tendencies, he supported the nineteenth-century German theologian's emphasis on the "experience of the individual" in combating the rationalistic dogmatism of the Enlighten-

---

[79]Mullins, *Why Is Christianity True?* 241, 264-65, 275-77, 280, 306-308.

[80]Ibid., 75.

[81]Ibid., 77-78; Mullins, "Is Jesus Christ the Author of Religious Experience?" 69.

[82]Mullins, *Why Is Christianity True?* 325-42; Mullins, "Pragmatism, Humanism, and Personalism—The New Philosophic Movement," *Review and Expositor* 5 (October 1908): 501-15.

[83]Mullins, "Pragmatism, Humanism, and Personalism—The New Philosophic Movement," 505, 515; *Baptist World*, 9 September 1909.

[84]Tribble, "Edgar Young Mullins" (1952), 134; Carver, "Recollections," 81.

ment.[85] However, he believed that Schleiermacher did not go far enough and identify Christ as the cause of the experience.[86]

Mullins considered the "personalism" of Bowne to be a midpoint between atheism and Christianity, but, nevertheless, a valid argument for the Christian apologist. Bowne proposed that the individual was not self-sufficient; he needed communion with "the Infinite and Absolute Being." Personalism led inevitably, Mullins believed, to theism.[87] Schleiermacher and Bowne gravitated toward pantheism, which Mullins found particularly distasteful because this denied the "personality" of God. Without personality, God could not demand that man adhere to a code of conduct or command his regeneration.[88]

Mullins selectively used the pragmatism of James, the experientialism of Schleiermacher, and the personalism of Bowne in developing his apologetic style while disagreeing with their conclusions. He tried to clothe the continued dependence on individual regeneration in the intellectual rhetoric of the early twentieth century.[89] This again is an example of Mullins's moderate approach, that is, maintaining the eternal truths of Christianity while accepting newer methods of study.

No theologian of the early twentieth century could ignore the implications of evolution; therefore, Mullins had to grapple with Darwinism. He admitted that science had much to offer in explanation of phenom-

---

[85]Mullins, "The Theological Trend," *Review and Expositor* 2 (October 1905): 508; *Baptist Argus,* 25 April 1901.

[86]Dilday, "The Apologetic Method of E. Y. Mullins," 45-46.

[87]Thomas, "Edgar Young Mullins," 138-51; Mullins, "Pragmatism, Humanism, and Personalism—The New Philosophic Movement," 510; Mullins, Review of *Theism* by Borden P. Bowne, in *Review and Expositor* 1 (July 1904): 247.

[88]Mullins, *Why Is Christianity True?* 29-30.

[89]Winthrop S. Hudson, "Shifting Patterns of Church Order in the Twentieth Century," in *Baptist Concepts of the Church,* ed. Winthrop S. Hudson (Philadelphia: Judson Press, 1959) 215; Schneider, *Religion in 20th Century America,* 133; Sydney E. Ahlstrom, "Theology in America: A Historical Survey," in *The Shaping of American Religion,* vol. 1 of *Religion of American Life,* ed. James Ward Smith and A. Leland Jamison (Princeton: Princeton University Press, 1961) 303-309.

ena, but it did not extend beyond its special realm. He divided the "physical sphere," or "world of matter," from the "spiritual sphere," or "world of spirit."[90] He chided Thomas Huxley for admitting that "faith" was needed to believe the great truths of science while denying the validity of faith in the religious realm.[91] Mullins became the first Southern Baptist leader to accept the concept of progressive revelation, which taught that God progressively revealed his plans for the world as man became both willing and intelligent enough to receive such knowledge. This development was predicated on the evolutionary implication that life progressed from lower to higher forms.[92] Mullins, however, scorned the evolutionists' proclivity of developing a monist position. He accepted the usage of the term *evolution* as valid, but maintained that all the evidence was not in, so the theory should not be taught as fact.[93] Some evolutionists drifted toward theism, while others found the theory compatible with evangelical Christianity. Though Mullins did not specifically state his belief in Christian theistic evolution, he left the strong implication that this form suited his tastes.[94]

Mullins's reaction to biblical criticism is further evidence of his moderation. Higher criticism represented the use of an inductive or scientific approach to the study of the Bible.[95] He favored "sober, sane, and reverent criticism," maintaining that no "true Baptist" could oppose the casting of new light on the Bible. Mullins accepted, moreover, the new discipline of the psychology of religion, an influence of William James on theological education.[96]

Baptists and non-Baptists alike credited *Why Is Christianity True?* with a valuable contribution to the Christian apologetic. The presidents

---

[90]Mullins, *Why Is Christianity True?* 21, 46.

[91]Ibid., 16.

[92]Dale Moody, "Progressive Revelation," *Encyclopedia of Southern Baptists*, 2:1115.

[93]Mullins, *Why Is Christianity True?* 61-66, 90.

[94]Ibid., 69, 71, 89-90; Mullins, "The Theological Trend," 517.

[95]*Baptist Argus,* 3 October, 10 October 1901.

[96]Mullins, "The Theological Trend," 512; Mullins, *Why Is Christianity True?* 177, 241, 264-66.

of Colgate and Rochester, George E. Merrill and A. H. Strong, praised the volume, as did Professor William Newton Clarke of Colgate.[97] Shailer Mathews recommended the book as a text for college Bible courses.[98] Leaders of the Baptist Young People's Union of America rejoiced over the initial success of the book.[99] Among Southern Baptists, Frost and Sampey voiced their approval, while Eaton ignored its publication.[100]

While *Why Is Christianity True?* radiated a nondenominational character, *The Axioms of Religion* glorified the Baptist denomination. For several years before the publication of the book, Mullins refined the axioms of Christianity as they related to the Baptist denomination. However, unlike the Landmark-fundamentalist faction, while he praised his own denominational roots, he did not automatically "disenfranchise" others from the Christian fold. He displayed a strong inclination to systematize his faith, with the *Axioms* being a prime example.[101]

The officials of the Publication Society encouraged Mullins's writing and hoped to issue the book in conjunction with the 1907 meetings of the Northern and Southern conventions.[102] Several chapters appeared in the religious press prior to publication or had been drafted previously, but Mullins had difficulty working the material into the form that he desired.[103] There is some indication that he delayed because he desired

---

[97]Merrill to Mullins, 31 August 1905; Strong to Mullins, 9 September 1905; Clarke to Mullins, 18 September 1905.

[98]Mathews to S. E. Price, 5 November 1906 (Divinity School Correspondence, University of Chicago Archives).

[99]H. C. Lyman to Mullins, 21 December 1905; George T. Webb to Mullins, 15 February 1907.

[100]Mullins to Frost, 27 December 1905 (Frost-Bell Letters, Dargan-Carver Library); Sampey to Mullins, 1 November 1905; Tribble, "Edgar Young Mullins," *Review and Expositor* 26 (July 1929): 416; Wilbur F. Tillett to Mullins, 9 February 1906.

[101]*Western Recorder*, 24 September 1903; Mullins, "The Theological Trend," 520; Garrett, Hinson, and Tull, *Are Southern Baptists "Evangelicals"?* 136.

[102]A. J. Rowland to Mullins, 8 November, 26 December 1906; 9 January, 29 January, 4 February 1907.

[103]Rowland to Mullins, 7 May, 28 May, 3 June 1907; *Religious Herald*, 6 December, 13 December 1906, 13 June 1907; *Baptist Argus*, 29 August, 17 October 1907.

a larger return in the form of royalties. Rowland finally agreed to send a $300 advance on royalties and guaranteed that the Publication Society would push sales of the book.[104] The sales of *Axioms* proved so successful that the business manager of the Publication Society implored Mullins to let them have a new book for the press as soon as possible. Jealous of Mullins's connection with Northern Baptist agencies, Frost inquired about the arrangements he had with the Publication Society, asking him to write a major book for the Sunday School Board.[105]

Axioms did not have the continuity of *Why Is Christianity True?* because it was written in piecemeal fashion.[106] Mullins declared that his intention was to inspire Baptists to greater work as well as to record the unique features of the denomination.[107] Taking his normal moderate evangelical tack, Mullins faulted both conservatives and liberals for their extremism that resulted in a lack of communication. He declared, "The really safe leaders of thought, however, are between the extremes. They are men who have sympathy on the one hand with those who are perplexed by the difficulties to faith occasioned by modern science and philosophy, and on the other are resolved to be loyal to Christ and his gospel."[108] This summed up not only the moderate evangelical dilemma, but also Mullins's approach as a denominational moderate.

After preliminary chapters on the necessity of denominationalism and the historical importance of Baptists, Mullins presented the axioms as follows:

1. The theological axiom: The holy and loving God has a right to be sovereign.
2. The religious axiom: All souls have an equal right to direct access to God.

---

[104]Rowland to Mullins, 3, 9, and 16 September, 2 October, 7 October 1907; Charles M. Roe to Mullins, 18 January, 23 January, 11 February, 5 April 1908.

[105]Roe to Mullins, 5 June, 6 June 1908; Frost to Mullins, 30 July, 13 September 1909.

[106]Mullins, *The Axioms of Religion*, 7. The *Axioms* were presented as a series of speeches before the American Baptist Publication Society, Richmond College, and the Baptist Convention of North America.

[107]Mullins, *The Axioms of Religion*, 8.

[108]Ibid., 14.

3. The ecclesiastical axiom: All believers have a right to equal privileges in the church.
4. The moral axiom: To be responsible man must be free.
5. The religio-civic axiom: A free Church in a free State.
6. The social axiom: Love your neighbor as yourself.[109]

Several of Mullins's ideas offer an interesting contrast, some of which will be explained in a later chapter. *Axioms* is in many ways a self-glorification of the Baptist denomination in contrast to *Why Is Christianity True?* Specifically, Mullins, identifying Baptists as the major source for the ideas of religious liberty, claimed too much importance for Baptists in the founding and sustaining of American church-state relations. He displayed great optimism not only for the denomination but for the role of Christianity in the world.[110] Also evident is the paradox created by the Baptist free church tradition in conflict with the growing institutionalization of the denomination. Mullins tried to blend what he saw as the best of both of these trends. "The church," he maintained, "is the institutional embodiment of the kingdom of God," but a "repressive" hierarchy, on the other hand, could stifle the spirituality of the church.[111] In the last sentence of *Axioms* Mullins continued to reflect his moderation and optimism. He asserted that the world was being led toward a "progressive civilization" by the practice of the axioms.[112]

Mullins received glowing recommendations for *Axioms* from his Southern, Northern, and English Baptist colleagues. His publications spread his influence throughout the Baptist constituency. By the end of the first decade of his tenure at Southern Seminary, he had emerged as an outstanding religious leader. His denominational and interdenominational activities, along with the publication of two major books and numerous articles, marked him as a rising leader among the religious

---

[109]Ibid., 73-74.

[110]Ibid., 255-308; Garrett, Hinson, and Tull, *Are Southern Baptists "Evangelicals"?* 179.

[111]Mullins, *The Axioms of Religion*, 37.

[112]Ibid., 307.

moderates. In addition, his political, social, and economic ideals corresponded with those of moderate urban progressivism in the early twentieth century.[113]

---

[113]Carver, "Recollections," 82; A. H. Strong to Mullins, 20 March 1908; J. H. Shakespeare to Mullins, 1 June 1908; *Watchman,* 19 March 1908; Ferenc M. Szasz, *The Divided Mind of Protestant America, 1880-1930* (University AL: University of Alabama Press, 1982) 62-63.

5   THE WIDENING BREACH BETWEEN MODERATES AND FUNDAMENTALISTS

Mullins set the tone for the Seminary, and he attempted to do the same for Kentucky Baptists. While he could dominate the destiny of Southern Seminary, fundamentalists continued to block his control of Kentucky Baptist affairs. A power struggle ensued, with Mullins leading the moderate side in denominational battles. This conflict mirrored the broader division taking place throughout the Southern Baptist Convention.

Southern Seminary could not help being influenced by the intellectual and social crosscurrents affecting the nation during the first decade of the twentieth century. For example, Mullins and the Seminary faculty displayed a moderate reaction to the Social Gospel. The entire faculty was Southern born and raised. Though most had traveled or attended institutions of higher learning in the North, they all were Southern-oriented and identified themselves as Southerners. Their immediate background, both educationally and culturally, had been the "Lost Cause"

South of the late nineteenth century.[1] Fundamentalists dominated Southern Baptist opinion of the nascent Social Gospel; the denomination continued to emphasize individual regeneration over social or political reform. Baptists generally supported only those moral reforms that touched personal behavior, such as gambling and drinking of alcoholic beverages.[2]

Southern Seminary took a moderate tack on the Social Gospel in the early twentieth century, with Mullins providing the leadership. The Southern Baptist Convention, moreover, moved ever so slowly toward a social consciousness, urged in great measure by the influence of Southern Seminary.[3] The strong premillennialism of fundamentalist Southern

---

[1]The Civil War influence remained quite strong for Mullins. For example, he delivered an address entitled "The Battle of Gettysburg" before the Robert E. Lee Camp of Confederate Veterans at Richmond, Virginia, in the fall of 1910. *Courier-Journal*, 16 September 1910. The anti-carpetbagger view of Reconstruction also permeated the thinking of the Seminary faculty. When Robertson reviewed *The Clansman* by Thomas Dixon, Jr., he found that the author had exaggerated somewhat but concluded that the period was "the shameful era in American history." Review by Robertson of *The Clansman*, in *Review and Expositor* 2 (October 1905): 589. See Wilson, *Baptized in Blood*, 95.

[2]Bailey, *Southern White Protestantism*, 4; Spain, *At Ease in Zion*, 153, 209-14; Charles Price Johnson, "Southern Baptists and the Social Gospel Movement" (Th.D. diss., Southwestern Baptist Theological Seminary, 1948) 28-29.

[3]A recent historiography has developed reinterpreting the origins and extent of Social Gospel sentiment among Southern Baptists. Several authors view Southern Baptists as slightly readjusting their attitudes toward the Social Gospel after the turn of the century. All carefully qualify their interpretations, because the shift is very small. John L. Eighmy, "The Social Conscience of Southern Baptists from 1900 to the Present as Reflected in Their Organized Life," 14, 38-39; Eighmy, *Churches in Cultural Captivity: A History of the Social Attitudes of Southern Baptists* (Knoxville: University of Tennessee Press, 1972) 57-108; Foy Dan Valentine, "A Historical Study of Southern Baptists and Race Relations, 1917-1947" (Th.D. diss., Southwestern Baptist Theological Seminary, 1949) 215; Bailey, *Southern White Protestantism*, 41-42; Henry Y. Warnock, "Moderate Racial Thought and Attitudes of Southern Baptists and Methodists, 1900-1921" (Ph.D. diss., Northwestern University, 1963) 261, 275. The main exception to this interpretation is in Wayne Flynt, "Dissent in Zion: Alabama Baptists and Social Issues," *Journal of Southern History* 35 (November 1969): 523-42. Flynt sees much more movement toward a Social Gospel.

Baptists, the majority of that denomination, blunted any rapid trend toward liberalization. Their major concern continued to be the evangelization of the world.[4] Ruralism, combined with individualistic religion, kept the denomination from proposing any substantive social change.[5]

The faculty of Southern Seminary represented the only facet of Southern Baptist leadership that accommodated itself to the Social Gospel. The average, rural Southern Baptist pastor was uneducated and had no seminary training, while the urban minister was more apt to have a college and seminary education. The latter group generally supported Southern Seminary's moderate Social Gospel.[6]

The experiences at the Lee Street Church in Baltimore gave Mullins some understanding of the problems developing in urban life. Even then, however, evangelicalism tempered his Social Gospel inclinations. The pastorate in the upper-middle-class church in Newton Centre and the exigencies of the Louisville seminary presidency severely moderated whatever Social Gospel tendencies Mullins might have had. When compared with an active Southern Progressive, Edgar Gardner Murphy, for example, Mullins never directly influenced the trends of political, social, and economic reforms in the early twentieth century. Murphy, a Birmingham Episcopal priest, epitomized moderate Southern progressivism in the first decade of the century. While an "aristocratic bias" limited Murphy's reformism, Mullins's evangelicalism militated against any rapid move toward liberalism. Walter Rauschenbusch, professor at Rochester Theological Seminary, went through the same shocking experiences in an urban church as Mullins, but he developed a stronger Social Gospel passion than the president of Southern Seminary.[7]

The Social Gospel never became a major part of Mullins's overall concerns about the Christian ministry to the world. In his first major book, for example, he declared that Christianity served the world by en-

---

[4]Johnson, "Southern Baptists and the Social Gospel Movement," 107-109.

[5]Ibid., 4-5, 89, 91-92.

[6]Ibid., 96.

[7]Armstrong, *The Indomitable Baptists*, 192-206; Hugh C. Bailey, *Edgar Gardner Murphy: Gentle Progressive* (Coral Gables FL: University of Florida Press, 1968) 62-63.

couraging political and economic discontent. The cause, he maintained, was the Christian emphasis on the worth of the individual. He offered, however, no answers to specific social problems.[8] On the other hand, in a speech delivered about the time he wrote *Axioms of Religion,* Mullins declared, "We are our brother's keeper in spite of ourselves." America had to choose between moral and materialistic emphases.[9] Concerning the social axiom, the shortest chapter of *Axioms,* Mullins especially condemned corruption in business and politics. The church could not be "indifferent or callous to moral conditions." Though Mullins followed the Social Gospel, only individual regeneration, he believed, would solve the problems of the world in a final sense.[10]

In his personal life Mullins exemplified the same moderate approach in politics. He publicly demanded the very highest moral standards in political life, regarding such "service" as a calling equal to that of the ministry.[11] During the critical Louisville elections in the first decade of the century, however, he lent only moral support to the reformers who battled a corrupt Democratic political machine. The leaders of the Citizens' League, a progressive political organization, urged him to join in their efforts, but he never became deeply involved.[12] He maintained his undying faith in the necessity for "civic righteousness," but took no active role in fighting the city machine in 1905.[13] He did, however, oppose the attempt of this group to control the Board of Trustees of the Louisville Free Public Library. Appointed to the board in 1904,

---

[8]Mullins, *Why Is Christianity True?* 348-49.

[9]*Baptist Argus,* 12 March 1908.

[10]Mullins, *The Axioms of Religion,* 17, 202-10.

[11]Mullins, "Christ's Law of Service," in *History of Southern Oratory,* ed. Thomas E. Watson (Richmond: The Southern Historical Publication Society, 1909) 9:495.

[12]Lafon Allen to Mullins, 16 February, 9, 11, and 23 March, 15 April 1904; Charles C. Stoll to Mullins, Circular Letter, no date.

[13]Thomas D. Clark, *Helm Bruce, Public Defender: Breaking Louisville's Gothic Political Ring, 1905* (Louisville: The Filson Club, 1973) 94.

Mullins jealously guarded his position.[14] He also took an interest in other public affairs, cooperating with the American Conference on International Arbitration, the Congo Reform Association, and the National Civic Federation. Leaders of these groups sought his participation because of his growing prestige throughout the nation.[15]

Mullins's reactions to American capitalism also offered a moderate approach. He invested in Mississippi real estate and in the Motzorongo Company, a Chicago-based firm that operated coffee and sugar plantations in Mexico.[16] Committed to capitalism, he admitted that business, particularly the trust, posed "a great ethical problem" for the American public. Though "concrete conditions" might change, he proposed, "moral principles" never varied.[17]

The Seminary faculty followed Mullins's lead in adopting a moderate Social Gospel. This conclusion is warranted by articles and book reviews in the *Review and Expositor,* the Seminary organ. For example, books by Walter Rauschenbusch, Washington Gladden, and Edmund A. Ross were given positive reviews, and Shailer Mathews published an article urging Baptist seminarians to study sociology. The *Review and Expositor* lent a "voice generally friendly to liberalism," if not fully accepting a primary Social Gospel thrust.[18]

---

[14]*Courier-Journal,* 20 April 1904; John Stites to Mullins, 13 November 1906; Paul C. Barth to Mullins, March (no day) 1907.

[15]Robert Lansing to Mullins, 17 December 1904; Hugh P. McCormich to Mullins, 21 February 1906; John Daniels to Mullins, 1 June 1906; R. M. Easley to Mullins, 28 October 1909.

[16]Dwight Chester to Mullins, 1 April 1901; A. D. McRaven to Mullins, 27 March 1901; A. E. Merrifield to Mullins, 26 August 1902; James Parkyn to Mullins, 15 September 1904, 24 October 1906, 5 March 1908.

[17]Mullins, "Baptists in the Modern World," *Review and Expositor* 8 (July 1911): 346.

[18]George Kesler, Review of *Christianity and the Social Crisis* by Rauschenbusch, in *Review and Expositor* 4 (October 1907): 669-70; George B. Eager, Review of *The Church and Modern Life* by Washington Gladden, in *Review and Expositor* 5 (July 1908): 446-48; Eager, Review of *Sin and Society* by Ross, in *Review and Expositor* 5 (July 1908): 448; Mathews, "The Preacher and Study of Sociology," *Review and Expositor* 7 (January 1910): 49-56; Hutchison, *The Modernist Impulse in American Protestantism,* 195.

In particular, one professor, Charles S. Gardner, became the social conscience of Southern Seminary.[19] Gardner declared his intention to emphasize social concern in his classes even before accepting a faculty position. He tried to blend the newer ideas of sociology and psychology with evangelicalism. Eventually, he developed courses in Christian Sociology. Like most moderate adherents of the Social Gospel, Gardner was more philosophical than practical.[20]

Southern Social Gospel advocates, like their more liberal counterparts in the North, timidly confronted the race issue.[21] Mullins and the Southern Seminary faculty were stringently paternalistic in their racial attitudes and often had contact with Negroes. Fundamentalists, on the other hand, took a hard line against any change in Southern mores. The Southern Seminary faculty was always less racist than the average Southern Baptist.[22] Mullins cooperated with black religious leaders and others in the South who had an interest in improving race relations.[23] In

---

[19]Gardner, "The Christian View of the Inequalities of Men," *Seminary Magazine* 12 (April 1899): 327-29; Mueller, *A History of Southern Baptist Theological Seminary,* 206-207; Hugh Alexander Brimm, "The Social Consciousness of Southern Baptists in Relation to Some Regional Problems, 1910-1935" (Th.D. diss., Southern Baptist Theological Seminary, 1944) 6; Eighmy, "Religious Liberalism in the South During the Progressive Era," *Church History* 38 (September 1969): 369.

[20]Gardner to Mullins, 7 April 1907; Earl R. Whaley, "The Ethical Contribution of Charles S. Gardner" (Th.M. thesis, Southern Baptist Theological Seminary, 1953) 15, 16, 58-59.

[21]David M. Reimers, *White Protestantism and the Negro* (New York: Oxford University Press, 1965) 54; Flynt, "Dissent in Zion: Alabama Baptists and Social Issues, 1900-1914," 537.

[22]Spain, *At East in Zion,* 84; Valentine, "A Historical Study of Southern Baptists and Race Relations, 1917-1947," 55-56.

[23]Blacks with whom Mullins had contact included the following: Frank L. Williams to Mullins, 12 November 1903; T. T. Timberlake to Mullins, 2 May 1905; L. G. Jordan to Mullins, 6 June 1905; J. E. Cox to Mullins, 1 December 1905; John H. Frank to Mullins, 6 November 1909. White leaders who showed interest in improving the plight of Negroes included the following: Alfred Struck to Mullins, 22 May 1908; L. L. Henson to Mullins, 21 November 1906; B. D. Gray to Mullins, 6 April 1905.

particular, he developed a working relationship with C. H. Parrish, Sr., principal of the Eckstein Norton Institute in Bullitt County. Parrish later became president of Simmons University, a black Baptist college and seminary in Louisville.[24] Their contact, predicated on a common interest in education, lasted until Mullins's death in 1928.[25] They served together on a Baptist World Alliance Committee, and Mullins chaired a Simmons University building fund committee for several years.[26]

Mullins's contact with blacks and his moderate position on racial matters contrasted with the more adamant positions assumed by the fundamentalists. T. T. Eaton espoused violent racial views, openly applauding the action of the 1904 Kentucky General Assembly outlawing racial integration in public education.[27] He opposed any connection at all between the races.[28] When the Baptist World Congress met in London in 1905 under the leadership of the Seminary faculty, Eaton took the opportunity to attack the meeting on the grounds that the color barrier had been broken.[29] Prestridge answered for the Seminary faction, claiming that the whites and blacks acted discreetly by never mixing socially but only in their official capacities as representatives of Baptist bodies throughout the world. He also maintained that nearly one-third of the Baptists in the world who were black had "a right to be heard and to be honored for their work's sake." These arguments did not deter Eaton, who thereafter launched a tirade of anti-Negro editorials.[30]

When the General Convention met in Jamestown in 1907 the integration of facilities again plagued the Baptist conscience. Mullins and Morehouse agreed that Negroes could not be prohibited from the ex-

---

[24]*Kentucky's Black Heritage* (Frankford KY: Kentucky Commission on Human Rights, 1971) 41-42; *Courier-Journal*, 24 November 1928.

[25]Parrish to Mullins, 5 May, 15 May, 6 June 1905; *Courier-Journal*, 24 November 1928.

[26]W. L. Holmes to the author, 15 September 1972; C. H. Parrish, Jr., to the author, 10 June 1972; *Kentucky's Black Heritage*, 58.

[27]*Western Recorder*, 3 March 1904.

[28]Ibid., 13 April 1905.

[29]Ibid., 10 August, 31 August, 19 October 1905.

[30]*Baptist Argus*, 31 August 1905.

hibit or social gatherings of the conference.[31] One Southern Baptist leader warned Mullins of the dire consequences of mixing the races and urged that Mullins strictly adhere to Southern racial mores.[32] Eaton later took notice that a few Negroes attended the Jamestown meetings, but stated that his agitation had kept the number from being very large.[33]

As a result of Mullins's contacts with black religious leaders, white leaders often depended upon him to be their liaison with their black counterparts. Northern and Southern Baptist leaders of the Young People's Union asked him to write a book on race relations and Christianity. He negotiated for several weeks but declined, claiming that he was overburdened with work.[34] However, he wrote two articles for the denominational press in which he admitted that "the Negro problem" was exceedingly difficult. While he offered no social panaceas, Mullins maintained that "the Negro ought to be improved mentally, morally and spiritually." White Baptists, he claimed, should be "constructive" in dealing with their black brethren.[35] The paternalistic approach of Mullins and his moderate colleagues, while not offering a viable solution to racial tension in the early twentieth century, did not feed the fires of racial antipathy as did the fundamentalism of Eaton.[36]

---

[31]Morehouse to Mullins, 8 April, 13 April 1907.

[32]C. H. Ryland to Mullins, 5 March 1907.

[33]*Western Recorder,* 30 May 1907.

[34]T. B. Ray to Mullins, 23 March, 3 April, 30 May 1908; 20 February 1909; J. M. Frost to Mullins, 15 April 1908; Mullins to Frost, 18 April 1908 (Frost-Bell Letters, Dargan-Carver Library); Morris W. Ehnes to Mullins, 15 February 1909.

[35]*Baptist World,* 8 July, 19 August 1909.

[36]Robert Moats Miller contends that for all the bad aspects of Southern paternalism in the deplorable racial atmosphere, "things might have been worse." He claims, moreover, that the church's "message . . . is always superior to its practice." Mullins and his faction fit Miller's definition of the paternalist. Miller, "Southern White Protestantism and the Negro, 1865-1965," in *The Negro in the South Since 1865,* ed. Charles E. Wynes (University AL: University of Alabama Press, 1965) 233, 235-36, 238, 240, 244. Even Edgar Gardner Murphy never moved so far to the left that he advocated a complete end to racial segregation. Bailey, *Edgar Gardner Murphy,* 192; Bailey, *Liberalism in the New South: Southern Social Reformers and the Progressive Movement* (Coral Gables FL: University of Florida Press, 1969) 130.

In other areas Mullins led the trend toward change at Southern Seminary. He aimed at improving the quality of the student body. During the 1907-1908 school year the school changed from a two-term calendar to a quarter system. Examination time for each course was reduced from five to two hours. About twenty percent of the student body continued to fail their examinations.[37] The Seminary continued to admit ministers with no college training, but they were limited to a one-year course of study and were not allowed to take language courses.[38] The percentage of students with at least some college experience, meanwhile, rose to eighty-five to ninety percent of the total enrollment.[39] While all courses continued to be "electives," a student had to take a prescribed curriculum to obtain a degree.[40]

An innovation favored by Mullins was the admission of women. Beginning in 1902 women were allowed to audit regular classes. Thereafter, W. O. Carver began teaching special classes for them. Most of the women were wives of ministerial students.[41] By the spring of 1904 forty-five women were in attendance, and three years later the trustees allowed the Women's Missionary Union Training School to be organized as an adjunct to Southern Seminary.[42]

To expand the offerings of the Seminary, Mullins sought closer connections with the boards of the Southern Baptist Convention. In particular, he asked the Sunday School Board and the Foreign Mission Board to finance two professorships. The Foreign Mission Board refused, claiming a lack of funds, but the Sunday School Board complied with the request.[43]

---

[37]Sampey, *Memoirs*, 123.

[38]Mullins, "The Contribution of Southern Baptist Theological Seminary to Theological Education," *Review and Expositor* 7 (January 1910) 163-65.

[39]*Baptist World*, 27 January 1910.

[40]Ibid., 1 September 1910.

[41]Mueller, *A History of Southern Baptist Theological Seminary*, 184.

[42]*Baptist Argus*, 7 April 1904; Carrie U. Littlejohn, *History of Carver School of Missions and Social Work* (Nashville: Broadman Press, 1958) 71; Joshua Levering to Mullins, 21 March, 12 April 1906.

[43]R. J. Willingham to Mullins, 9 September, 19 December 1908.

The Sunday School Board-Publication Society conflict now caught Mullins in a dilemma: if he adhered too closely to either, he stood the chance of losing valuable revenue from the other. He finally chose the Sunday School Board. Frost, corresponding secretary of that agency, continuously badgered Mullins about connections with the Publication Society.[44] After several years of negotiations, Frost agreed to pay $1,500 annually toward the endowment of a "Chair of Sunday School Pedagogy," the equivalent of present-day religious education. This action obligated Mullins to Frost. The Sunday School Board-Southern Seminary connection tightened.[45]

In his desire to improve church "efficiency" Mullins publicized the necessity for religious education in the church and in seminary education. The Sunday school concept served as a vehicle for that form of educational experience. Mullins, emphasizing the need for trained personnel, now accepted a broader role in denominational and interdenominational Sunday school work. He wrote articles urging all denominations to adopt aggressive programs.[46] Mullins often used the word "efficiency" in a context usually ascribed to the business world. "Pastoral efficiency," he maintained, should promote "pedagogical efficiency" through the Sunday school.[47] When Southern Seminary established the first full-time professorship in educational work of this

---

[44]Frost to Mullins, 5 March 1906.

[45]Thomas, "Edgar Young Mullins," 106; Frost to Mullins, 12 December 1904, 6 March 1906, 18 November 1907, 12 April 1909; Mullins to Frost, 25 January, 17 February, 28 February 1906 (Frost-Bell Letters, Dargan-Carver Library).

[46]Thomas, "Edgar Young Mullins," 106; Mullins, "The Seminaries' Opportunity in the Sunday-School," in *The Pastors, the Seminaries, and the Sunday-School* (Philadelphia: Sunday School Times Co., 1903) 7-12; Mullins, "The Actual Relation of the Pastor to the Sunday-School," *Homiletic Review* 51 (February 1906): 122-23; Mullins, "Ideal Relation of the Pastor to the Sunday-School," *Homiletic Review* 51 (March 1906): 205-206; Mullins, "The Pastor's Best Point of Contact with the Sunday-School," *Homiletic Review* 51 (April 1906): 283-84; Mullins, "A New Chair of Sunday School Pedagogy," *Religious Education* 2 (June 1907): 56-57.

[47]Mullins, "The Pastor's Best Point of Contact with the Sunday-School," 283-84.

type, numerous leaders looked to it for leadership and guidance.[48] Byron H. DeMent became the first occupant of the new chair at Southern Seminary.[49] Thus, the progressive impulse for competent management even influenced the areas of theological education and church organization. The development of modern business practices at Southern Seminary also gave evidence of this influence. The trend toward specialization and professionalization in business and education encouraged a similar movement in theological circles. Like most Southerners, the Southern Seminary leadership accepted the "business progressive philosophy" because of the influence of the New South economic philosophy and the progressive movement.[50]

Though internal problems within the faculty were never serious, Mullins was not free of them. Salaries did not offer enough compensation for men with families to support. Carver, for example, claimed he had to preach twice monthly just "to make ends meet."[51] Raises for all faculty members were rare. In 1907 the Seminary lost one faculty member, E. C. Dargan, reputedly because his wife did not enjoy living in Louisville. This loss actually benefited the Seminary because it opened the way for Gardner to join the faculty.[52]

Mullins's reactions to denominational realities in Kentucky evidenced a belief in the consolidation and organization trend taking place

---

[48]Marion Lawrence to Mullins, 18 December 1906; W. C. Everett to Mullins, 16 May 1908; A. C. Crews to Mullins, 17 October 1903.

[49]Mullins, "A New Chair of Sunday School Pedagogy," 56-57.

[50]Eric F. Goldman, *Rendezvous with Destiny* (New York: Alfred A. Knopf, 1952) 64; Robert H. Wiebe, *The Search for Order, 1877-1920,* in *The Making of America,* gen. ed., David Donald (New York: Hill and Wang, 1967) 111-95; George B. Tindall, *The Emergence of the New South, 1913-1945,* vol. 10 of *A History of the South,* ed. Wendell H. Stephenson and E. Merton Coulter (Baton Rouge: Louisiana State University Press, 1967) 233. For more information, see Paul M. Gaston, *The New South Creed: A Study in Southern Mythmaking* (New York: Alfred A. Knopf, 1970).

[51]Carver, "Recollections," 64.

[52]Mueller, *A History of Southern Baptist Theological Seminary,* 192; Sampey to Mullins, 18 March 1907; Sampey, "Brief History of the Southern Baptist Theological Seminary," *Review and Expositor* 7 (January 1910): 3-21.

in the contemporary business world. His desire for coordination and consolidation of denominational resources and institutions led to connections with other facets of Baptist education in Kentucky. He helped organize the Education Society of Kentucky Baptists and became its first president.[53] Its ostensible objective was to raise money. Basically, however, it offered a vigorous leader such as Mullins an opportunity to exert some control over all Baptist institutions in the state.[54] It also afforded the added advantage of ending cutthroat competition for funds among these institutions. Mullins could be assured, therefore, of a steady flow of money from Kentucky Baptists to Southern Seminary, and it was not long before Mullins began a campaign among the Baptist leadership aimed at creating a major denominational university in Louisville. Even Eaton and Taylor publicly supported the idea.[55] Mullins never publicly presented all of his ideas about such a university, but he did think about its organization. The university would have several colleges, directed by a single board of trustees. Visualizing an institution like the University of Chicago, he implied that Southern Seminary trustees would assume this function.[56]

Working through the auspices of the Education Society, Mullins tried to obtain funds for this proposal from the General Education Board. Just before the Society organized, Georgetown College lost a large grant from the Rockefeller agency when it could not raise matching funds.[57] Mullins broached the subject with Wallace Buttrick, secretary of the G. E. B., and other Rockefeller aides. Negotiations lasted for several months. Buttrick finally declined Mullins's propositions for Board financing of

---

[53]Lewis C. Ray, "Education Society of Kentucky Baptists," *Encyclopedia of Southern Baptists,* 1:395; P. T. Hale to Mullins, 2 May 1907.

[54]*Courier-Journal,* 29 December 1905.

[55]Arthur Yager to Mullins, 14 November 1906; J. W. Hedden to Mullins, 12 December 1906; J. J. Taylor to Mullins, 12 November 1906; *Western Recorder,* 15 November 1906.

[56]A Mullins manuscript contained in Box 16 A.

[57]*Baptist Argus,* 5 July 1906.

a new university.[58] However, the Board did give $50,000 to Williamsburg Institute, saving that school from financial ruin.[59] After the failure to develop a major university with Southern Seminary as its center, Mullins took less interest in the welfare of other Kentucky Baptist institutions.

Theological controversy never abated during these years as the Mullins and Eaton factions contended for control of Kentucky Baptist affairs. Eaton continually sought the slightest opportunity to attack Mullins and the Seminary. When Mullins gave a favorable reaction to a book by A. H. Strong, Eaton challenged him to a public debate over the 1640 thesis of Baptist origins, attempting to revive the Whitsitt-Landmarkist controversy.[60] Failing to lure Mullins into open debate, Eaton retaliated by challenging McGlothlin, who had recently made a speech on the origins of Baptists before a meeting of the state Baptist historical society.[61]

Mullins tried to evade doctrinal debate, but Eaton pressed the attack in the *Western Recorder.* Eaton blatantly argued that seminaries should teach preachers to preach. A diligent theological teacher, he contended, would not have time for research.[62] A few weeks later Eaton scorned a recently published book by Robertson on biblical theology, and he arrogantly offered "a handsome chroma [chromolithograph]" to anyone who would produce anything new from biblical study.[63] Drawing no immediate response, Eaton renewed the attack on McGlothlin's heresy.[64] Mullins tried an indirect defense without answering Eaton's charges. He condemned alike the "Baptist and a half," or the conservative who overreacted to doctrinal differences, and the "half Baptist,"

---

[58]Wallace Buttrick to Mullins, 21 June 1906; 3 January, 26 February, 5 June, 11 July, 8 October 1907; Stanley Murphey to Mullins, 4 November 1907; P. T. Hale to Mullins, 14 September, 18 October 1907.

[59]John H. Chandler to Mullins, 15 July 1908.

[60]*Western Recorder,* 26 October, 10 November 1904.

[61]Eaton to Mullins, 12 October, 28 October, 7 November 1904.

[62]*Western Recorder,* 1 December 1904.

[63]Ibid., 23 February 1905.

[64]Ibid., 1 June 1905.

or liberal who never emphasized creedal belief.[65] Eaton replied that he gloried in being called "a Baptist and a half."[66] After giving Southern Seminary a brief respite, Eaton revived his suspicions about Seminary loyalty to the Baptist creed. When Seminary librarian Edgar Allen Forbes resigned, Eaton claimed that he had done so because the school destroyed his "faith." In addition, he raised the old alien immersion issue, claiming that Carver held to that anti-Baptist doctrine.[67]

Within a short time another opportunity for attack came to Eaton, and he made another frontal assault on Southern Seminary, implying editorially that the institution followed the dictates of higher criticism.[68] This time Mullins took up the challenge and replied that Southern Seminary "has not a single man in it who belongs to the higher critics in the bad sense."[69] He received his usual support from friends of the Seminary in this dispute. A former classmate and pastor of the Louisville Broadway Baptist Church, Mullins's home church, replied that it was only another prank by the "Western Discorder" and should be ignored.[70] After the immediate crisis lessened somewhat, Mullins told Frost that the Landmarkists had been very "unkind" to the Seminary, wasting the time and energy of the denomination on divisive quarrels.[71]

---

[65]*Baptist Argus,* 1 June 1905.

[66]*Western Recorder,* 15 June 1905.

[67]Jordan, "Thomas Treadwell Eaton," 189.

[68]The *Word and Way,* state Baptist paper for Missouri, misquoted a speech made by J. P. Greene, president of William Jewell College, inferring that Southern Seminary was unorthodox in its teachings. Greene immediately notified Mullins and apologized. He implied that the editor of the *Word and Way* may have manufactured the crisis. Whether by design or not, Eaton jumped at the opportunity to attack the Seminary. Greene to Mullins, 9, 22, and 26 February 1906; *Western Recorder,* 22 February, 1 March, 22 March 1906.

[69]*Western Recorder,* 8 March 1906.

[70]B. F. Proctor to Mullins, 11 July 1906; Carter Helm Jones to Mullins, 12 July 1906.

[71]Mullins to Frost, 20 September 1906 (Frost-Bell Letters, Dargan-Carver Library).

Toward the end of 1906 these debates cooled. Mullins and Eaton personally became more friendly.[72] Though Eaton continued to oppose alien immersion or any concession that might be considered liberal, he did not pull the Seminary into his *Recorder* editorials as a source of attack.[73] When Southern Seminary celebrated its first Founder's Day in 1907, ex-president Whitsitt made one of the principal addresses, and Eaton lauded the speech of his old adversary.[74] A few months later Eaton died suddenly, suffering a stroke, temporarily leaving a power vacuum among Baptist fundamentalists in Kentucky.[75]

There is little doubt that Mullins grew tired of Eaton's continuous "heresy" hunts.[76] Eaton's sincerity is doubtful because of his jealousy of denominational leaders. His chief biographer claimed that "to his credit" the *Recorder* editor always allowed those whom he attacked "to speak for themselves."[77] It seems obvious, however, that Eaton simply enjoyed debate and needed an adversary. In effect, he was always trying to lure someone into debate. With the debate written up in the *Recorder*, Eaton held the upper hand, because in his editorial position he always had the last word.

After the death of Eaton, other fundamentalists rushed to assume his dominant position while the denominational war of words continued between the *Argus* and *Recorder*. A few weeks after Eaton's death, W. P. Harvey resigned as business manager, president, and treasurer of the Baptist Book Concern, a joint stock company that owned and operated the *Recorder*.[78] Harvey and Mullins joined forces and reorganized the

---

[72]Eaton's letters became more jovial in his relations with Mullins. He even refused to publish some very critical letters from a Denver Landmarkist who rebuked Mullins's leadership at the Seminary. Eaton to Mullins, 6 October 1906; 27 March, 3, 15, and 29 April 1907.

[73]*Western Recorder*, 7 March, 14 March, 18 April, 16 May, 30 May, 6 June 1907.

[74]Ibid., 17 January 1907.

[75]Ibid., 4 July 1907.

[76]Jordan, "Thomas Treadwell Eaton," 189.

[77]Ibid., 54.

[78]*Western Recorder*, 5 September 1907.

Argus. They were interested in becoming part of the "contemplated enterprise" for two reasons: one, Harvey maintained that they would reap personal financial profits, and, two, the *Argus* could become the organ of the Seminary.[79]

Mullins had considered the possibility of directing a "newspaper enterprise" for several years and unsuccessfully tried to interest George W. Norton, a wealthy Louisvillian and chief creditor of the *Argus,* in the new venture.[80] Mullins, Harvey, and members of the Southern faculty sold stock in the new corporation, and Prestridge continued as editor of the reorganized paper. As the price for his defection to the *Argus* and his organizational abilities, Harvey demanded the positions of president and business manager.[81] The Seminary faculty guaranteed to raise $5,900 of the total of $30,000 needed for capitalization of the new company. Mullins, Sampey, Robertson, DeMent, McGlothlin, and Gardner signed personal notes promising to raise this amount for Harvey.[82] After much effort and a few anxious moments, they succeeded.[83]

Even before the money was raised for capitalization of the new corporation, the *Baptist World* supplanted the *Baptist Argus* on 7 May 1908. Prestridge remained as editor and declared that the approach of the new journal would be worldwide but "strongly and loyally Baptist." As planned, Harvey became president and business manager of the new firm.[84] He almost became involved in a lawsuit over his abrupt departure from the *Recorder,* but the matter was settled out of court.[85]

Southern Seminary's participation in the *Argus* had been quite evident for several years and a source of conflict between that paper and

---

[79]Harvey to Mullins, 4 February, 11 February 1908.

[80]Mullins to Norton, 22 September 1906.

[81]A. T. Robertson to Mullins, 25 March, 9 May 1908; B. F. Proctor to Mullins, 13 March 1908; Harvey to Mullins, 27 February, 7 March, 13 March 1908; Box 15 A contains a list of those who promised to purchase stock.

[82]The note was signed by the faculty and dated 13 April 1908.

[83]Boyce Watkins to Mullins, 25 November 1908; B. F. Proctor to Mullins, 28 January 1909.

[84]*Baptist World,* 7 May 1908.

[85]Prestridge to Mullins, 9 May 1908; McGlothlin to Mullins, 11 May 1908.

the *Recorder*. Now the faculty cast their lot fully with the *World* by becoming financially involved in its direction. Mullins appointed the Baptist World Publishing Company as the "Official Book Seller" to the Seminary's students, guaranteeing a regular source of income for the company of which he was a director.[86]

It was not long until J. H. Eaton, son of the late *Recorder* editor, began to make vicious charges against Mullins and Harvey by sending circular letters to numerous Southern Baptist leaders. Mullins replied by sending a circular letter of his own to all those who notified him that they had received a letter from Eaton. He denied all charges, including one that he and Harvey had tried to pool the stock of the Baptist Book Concern to gain control over the editorial policy of the *Western Recorder*. In particular, Mullins took exception to the claim by the younger Eaton that his father had never made friends with Mullins in his last years. Mullins issued the countercharge that the younger Eaton was only using the occasion of his father's death as a ploy in attacking organized Baptist work, the Seminary in particular. Numerous leaders relayed to Mullins the widespread nature of Eaton's circular letters and their unaltered confidence in Southern Seminary and its president.[87]

After the death of the elder Eaton, the *Recorder* continued its role as the bastion of Baptist fundamentalism. The reorganization of the *Baptist World* exacerbated relations between the *Recorder* and Seminary factions. Mullins's position on dialogue with the Disciples of Christ denomination gave the *Recorder* and fundamentalist Baptists another opportunity to attack the Seminary faction.

Mullins never took a hard stand against his Disciples brethren. Fundamentalist Baptists, however, could not forget the epic battles of the

---

[86]Charles T. Dearing to Mullins, 1 June 1908; Thomas A. Johnson to Mullins, 19 February 1909. This arrangement continued to be a source of conflict between the *Recorder* and *World* factions. J. W. Porter to Mullins, 27 December 1913.

[87]Eaton to J. T. Christian, 30 December 1908. This letter contained all of Eaton's charges. Christian sent the letter on to Mullins. Mullins answered in a circular letter on 12 September 1908, implying he knew of the charges long before he received the letter from Christian. At least fifteen other Southern Baptist leaders who received letters from Eaton notified Mullins that they had written rebuttals to Eaton.

mid-nineteenth century that in part spawned the Landmarkist Baptist movement as a counterattack on the church created by Barton W. Stone and the Campbells. As seen in the previous chapter, Mullins proposed a moderate approach to interdenominational cooperation.[88] He did not believe, for example, that Baptists should move toward a total commitment to interdenominationalism, but he believed they should continue dialogue with other denominations.[89]

In the spring of 1906 Mullins spoke to a Disciples meeting in Indianapolis. He called for further discussion and an end to the hostility that had marked Disciples-Baptist relations since the early nineteenth century. At the same time he did not foresee the possibility of union of the denominations.[90] Though Mullins received words of praise from such moderate Disciples leaders as J. H. Garrison, editor of the St. Louis *Christian-Evangelist*, and Herbert L. Willett, dean of the Disciples Divinity House of the University of Chicago, fundamentalist Baptists scorned his efforts.[91]

The *Western Recorder* continued to provide leadership for the fundamentalist, anti-Seminary faction. J. M. Weaver and C. M. Thompson, successively, directed the editorial policies of that paper until J. W. Porter became editor with the 1 July 1909 issue.[92] All three took hard stands against any cooperation with the Disciples church. These fundamentalists, moreover, complicated the issues by combining this issue with alien immersion, claiming that Disciples, though baptized, should never be allowed into the Baptist fellowship without being rebaptized.[93]

---

[88]See chapter 4.

[89]*Baptist Argus*, 11 February 1904.

[90]J. H. Garrison to Mullins, 9 April, 25 June 1906; *Baptist Argus*, 3 May 1906.

[91]Garrison to Mullins, 24 September 1906; Willett to Mullins, 12 July 1906; Charles R. Brock to Mullins, 22 January, 29 March, 10 April, 16 April, 1 May 1907.

[92]*Western Recorder*, 7 November, 21 November 1907; 8 April, 15 April, 17 June 1909.

[93]Ibid., 30 July, 13 August, 3, 10, and 17 September, 15, 22, and 29 October, 12 November, 31 December 1908.

Mullins defended his remarks calling for further dialogue with Disciples, but claimed that union would never be possible as long as both groups maintained their distinctive doctrines. On the alien immersion issue he defended the right of each individual church to do as it pleased, but he personally favored the immediate acceptance of anyone into the Baptist brotherhood if they had already been baptized. Baptism, he claimed, should never be a test of orthodoxy.[94]

Weaver, Thompson, and Porter appeared to have accepted Mullins's explanations, though they disagreed with his faith in the honesty of the Disciples.[95] A letter published by a fundamentalist Disciples paper caused the problem to flare up again. In what became known as the Lewis Letter, E. R. Lewis extolled the efforts of Mullins in his dialogue with the Disciples and found that he was the only Baptist who could lead his denomination into union with the Disciples.[96]

Fundamentalist Baptists now intensified their efforts to ward off any hint of union with the Disciples. H. Boyce Taylor, editor of the Murray *News and Truths*, enjoyed printing the Lewis Letter and scored Mullins for liberalizing Seminary doctrine.[97] Weaver, Thompson, and Porter questioned the intent of the Seminary in encouraging dialogue with the Disciples.[98] Mullins corresponded with the editor of the *Christian Standard*, and they discovered that the Lewis Letter was a fake. Repeated inquiries failed to turn up a Disciples leader by the name of E. R. Lewis. The editor of the *Standard* admitted he had published the letter without checking on the identity of the author. Mullins developed the theory that an enemy of the Seminary, a Baptist, sent the letter to the *Standard*.[99]

---

[94]Ibid., 11 April, 10 October 1907; 20 August 1908; *Baptist Argus*, 3 October 1907; *Baptist World*, 20 August 1908.

[95]*Western Recorder*, 10 September, 24 September 1908; Porter to Mullins, 17 September 1908.

[96]Cincinnati *Christian Standard*, 26 September 1908.

[97]*News and Truths*, 23 October 1908.

[98]Porter to Mullins, 3 November, 22 December, 28 December 1908; *Western Recorder*, 24 December 1908, 7 January 1909.

[99]*Baptist World*, 10 December 1908. Privately, Mullins declared his frustration in dealing with such opponents, but hoped the conflict served some good purpose. Mullins to Frost, 4 January 1909 (Frost-Bell Letters, Dargan-Carver Library).

Mullins thought the controversy had now ended, but fundamentalists would not let the issue die. Taylor continued to make absurd charges from his base in western Kentucky at Murray. He charged that "Mullinsism" was worse than "Whitsittism" because Mullins promised union with the "Campbellites."[100] Thompson and Porter prolonged the controversy by asking that Mullins make public statements about his intentions. The alien immersion issue was never far removed from the conflict over union with the Disciples.[101] Mullins faced the issue squarely and preached two sermons on the union issue at Porter's church, Lexington Calvary Baptist Church, reiterating the same themes he had been using all along.[102] He also directly challenged Thompson to cease printing "insinuations" and use proof, if he had any, of Mullins's heresy.[103]

After Porter became editor of the *Western Recorder* in the middle of 1909, Weaver and Thompson contributed less to the intensity of the conflict. Porter abruptly withdrew his earlier conciliatory position and promised to wage unremitting war on any "heresy" against the tenets of Landmarkism, implicitly warning Mullins and Southern Seminary of unending conflict.[104] Even before he became editor, Porter ominously reported that his church had passed a resolution against receiving anyone into the congregation by alien immersion.[105] Other foreboding signs also presented themselves, giving the flavor of the Whitsitt controversy. A contributor to the *Recorder* predicted a "split" if Mullins continued to be anti-Landmarkist and in favor of alien immersion.[106] Even more frightening must have been the letter from a regular contributor who voiced his opposition to the Seminary stance on union with Disciples and

[100]*News and Truths,* 8 January 1909.

[101]*Western Recorder,* 21 January, 28 January 1909; Porter to Mullins, 25 January 1909.

[102]G. R. Elliott to Mullins, 14 January 1909.

[103]*Western Recorder,* 1 January, 21 January 1909; *Baptist World,* 21 January, 4 February 1909.

[104]*Western Recorder,* 8 July, 15 July, 5, 12, and 26 August, 30 September, 7, 14, and 28 October, 4 November, 2, 9, 16, and 30 December 1909.

[105]Ibid., 22 April 1909.

[106]Ibid., 23 September 1909.

immersion, ending with the admonition that he would no longer "contribute to a school that possibly has a Campbellite as its president."[107]

Mullins had the complete support of the faculty during the Lewis Letter controversy. From outside the state of Kentucky, Mullins also received support. J. B. Cranfill of Dallas, Texas, for example, offered his services as intermediary between the *Recorder-World* factions by corresponding with Thompson when he was editor of the *Recorder*.[108] Fundamentalists tired of the conflict after a few more months. Such controversies as that of the Lewis Letter illustrate the pressures that Mullins periodically faced. Some of the strongest opposition to the Seminary came from Kentucky fundamentalist Baptists. As an administrator Mullins had to keep a tight control over finances. The threat of curtailed revenues because of fundamentalist suspicions about the orthodoxy of Southern Seminary continually faced the school. Fundamentalists forced Mullins into useless and petty controversies. The debates were philosophical and doctrinal and demonstrated the fundamentalists' fear of any change. Long before the crucial evolution controversy of the 1920s, fundamentalists displayed an intransigence that foretold their reaction to the issues of the later decade.

---

[107]T. E. Pinegar to Mullins, 15 February 1909.

[108]Cranfill to Mullins, 8 February, 18 February 1909; Cranfill to C. M. Thompson, 8 February 1909; *Baptist World*, 11 February 1909; S. S. Lappin to Mullins, 2 November 1908; Edgar E. Folk to Mullins, 7 December 1908; William E. Hatcher to Mullins, 11 December 1908.

6   THE JUBILEE YEARS: BUILDING THE LARGEST SEMINARY IN THE WORLD

The Twentieth Century Endowment Drive had no sooner ended than Mullins began to think about a new effort to coincide with the fiftieth anniversary of the Seminary. Finances of the school continued to be one of the major problems that Mullins faced as president. The Student Aid Fund, in particular, caused persistent problems. By the beginning of the 1907 school term the Fund was in debt nearly $4,000, a situation that forced Mullins to search continually for some means of establishing dependable sources of funds.[1]

Until regular sources of funds could be derived from steady Southern Baptist Convention contributions, Mullins tried for large personal donations. He and Levering sought from Samuel G. B. Cook, an international businessman from Baltimore, an increase in his $2,400 annual

---

[1]*Baptist Argus,* 14 February 1907. Southern Seminary's charter limited its investments to federal, state, and corporation bonds. George W. Norton to Mullins, 11 May 1911.

donation to Southern Seminary, but with no apparent success.[2] Mullins repeatedly and unsuccessfully tried to interest John D. Rockefeller in funding a large contribution to Southern Seminary.[3] The same was true of Andrew Carnegie, who refused to contribute to a Seminary building fund.[4] In answer to an inquiry from Mullins, a New York City Baptist pledged to encourage his fellow big-city Baptists to contribute $5,000 each to Southern Seminary, but doubted that he could interest them in giving to an institution outside the Northern Baptist Convention. All of Mullins's efforts to interest wealthy Baptists in contributing to Southern Seminary failed.[5]

After the official end of the Twentieth Century Drive, John H. Eager continued his work as a full-time fund raiser. His salary, as before, came from cash collections. Like Mullins, he tended to go after the donations from "men of large means."[6] At times Eager's efforts were so unfruitful that he received no monthly salary.[7] One problem Eager constantly encountered was the lack of coordination between the fund drives of state Baptist institutions and Southern Seminary. In particular, he ran into difficulties in Georgia and Virginia, where Baptist leaders literally told him to leave the state and not solicit for Southern Seminary until they had finished their own fund drives.[8] Mullins attempted to gain official Southern Baptist Convention endorsement of the endowment drive in order to forestall such opposition.

---

[2] Joshua Levering to Mullins, 2 July, 5 October 1908.

[3] F. T. Gates to Mullins, 12 June 1905; 3 March, 12 November 1906. Mullins finally confronted Rockefeller during a trip to Cleveland where they met by accident. Mullins and Rockefeller played golf and Mullins dined with the Rockefeller family, but the Standard Oil magnate did not commit himself to any donations to the Seminary. Mullins, *Mullins,* 158; Rockefeller to Mullins, 7 September 1909; Mullins to Rockefeller, 7 September, 10 September 1909.

[4] James Beckam to Mullins, 5 March 1906.

[5] W. J. Slayden to Mullins, 31 December 1907; 14 July, 16 August 1909.

[6] Eager to Mullins, 30 March 1905.

[7] Olive May Eager to Mullins, 15 December 1906; Eager to Mullins, 19 February, 3 March, 16 December 1906.

[8] Eager to Mullins, 5 October, 15 October, 14 December 1906; 19 September 1907.

Mullins used his earlier experiences in the Twentieth Century Endowment Drive to build plans for the anniversary fund drive. He first secured approval from editors of state denominational papers, then sent letters to several thousand ministers asking support for the drive, offering them promotional literature, and urging that they make suggestions for the campaign.[9] At the 1908 meeting of the Southern Baptist Convention he received the endorsement of the Convention, but even this sanction did not guarantee success.[10] This approval could, however, keep the agents of the Seminary from being "shut-out" of the Southern states. Mullins also sought the support of each state association, and by the beginning of the next year he reported that all states had endorsed the endowment drive.[11] Only a well-coordinated fund-raising campaign could be successful. This time Mullins aimed to increase the the endowment by at least $500,000.[12]

Mullins scheduled the drive to coincide with the Seminary Jubilee, the fiftieth anniversary celebration in 1909. He leaned heavily on the advice of William E. Hatcher, a Virginia trustee and confidant, in planning strategy for the campaign. At Mullins's insistence Hatcher used his influence to limit a Richmond College fund drive and urged the Virginia Baptist leadership to support the Southern Seminary drive.[13] Even be-

---

[9]Mullins sent a form letter dated 30 August 1907. Those who replied included: J. C. Armstrong, editor of the St. Louis *Central Baptist,* to Mullins, 2 September 1907; Pitt to Mullins, 23 September 1907; C. W. Blanchard, editor of the Raleigh *Biblical Recorder,* to Mullins, 5 September 1907; T. J. Bailey, editor of the Jackson, Mississippi, *Baptist Record,* to Mullins, 2 September 1907; J. B. Searcey, editor of the Little Rock *Baptist Advance,* to Mullins, 24 September 1907; L. C. Thomas, editor of the Kansas City, Missouri, *Word and Way,* to Mullins, 5 September 1907; J. M. Dawson, editor of the Dallas *Baptist Standard,* to Mullins, 4 September 1907; T. P. Bell, editor of the Atlanta *Christian Index,* to Mullins, 2 September 1907. A Mullins form letter dated 6 November 1907; *Baptist Argus,* 2 January 1908.

[10]Sampey, *Memoirs,* 125.

[11]*Baptist World,* 14 January 1909.

[12]Tribble, "Edgar Young Mullins" (1952), 129-31.

[13]Hatcher to Mullins, 25 December, 31 December 1907; 7 January, 22 January, 6 April 1908.

fore the celebration of the Jubilee formally started, Mullins had three full-time agents in the field: D. Y. Quisenberry, J. W. Greathouse, and Eager. In their first year of work they collectively raised over $83,000 in pledges, approximately $6,900 of which was in cash. Quisenberry primarily worked Louisiana, Alabama, and Mississippi, while Greathouse concentrated his efforts in Kentucky and Tennessee. Eager generally worked along the coastal states. The effort in Mississippi was particularly successful with Eager and Quisenberry working together and collecting nearly $40,000 in pledges.[14]

As part of Mullins's promotional plans, the Seminary celebrated when the enrollment again reached the peak level of the Whitsitt years; more than 300 students enrolled in 1895-1896.[15] After ten years of effort, Mullins celebrated this event with a turkey dinner. He invited all the important editors and denominational leaders in the Convention to attend, and nearly 400 students, faculty, and Seminary supporters met for the festive occasion.[16]

In preparation for and promotion of the Jubilee fund drive, Mullins publicly announced the needs of the Seminary and the ends toward which he hoped to use the enlarged endowment. As the largest seminary in the world, Southern Seminary needed work on the physical plant, more books for the library, better salaries and homes for the faculty, a full-time librarian, and additional faculty. "Efficiency and scholarship," Mullins explained, "ought to go hand in hand," but only a vastly increased endowment would fulfill the destiny of Southern Seminary in the work of the Convention. In making this declaration Mullins was only

---

[14]*Financial Agent's Report, May, 1909* (contained in Box 15 A); Quisenberry to Mullins, 25 July, 5 October, 7 November, 8 December 1908; 18 February, 1 July 1909; Greathouse to Mullins, 18 January 1908; 28 January, 16 February, 1 July 1909; Eager to Mullins, 7 April, 2 May, 10 October, 16 November 1908; 18 February, 23 March, 9 October 1909; 18 January, 16 February, 10 June 1910; *Baptist World*, 18 March 1909.

[15]Sampey, *Memoirs*, 126.

[16]*Western Recorder*, 8 October 1908, 11 March 1909. The farmer who supplied the turkeys sent a personal bill to Mullins for nearly $60. Thomas J. Watts to Mullins, 8 March 1909.

following the efficiency and modernization plans that other Southern Progressives had applied to business, education, and philanthropy.[17]

During the 1909-1910 school term, Southern Seminary celebrated its Jubilee. Mullins invited a number of prominent Protestant theologians and administrators to participate in the festivities. Professors from Vanderbilt University, Presbyterian Seminary of Louisville, and Chicago, Newton, Colgate, McMaster, Drew, Princeton, and Crozer seminaries presented addresses during the two-day celebration.[18] Shailer Mathews delivered a well-received talk entitled "Sociology and the Minister." A. H. Strong of Rochester presented a major address entitled "The Present Outlook in Theology."[19] This prestigious gathering publicized Southern Seminary's important role among American religious institutions.

Mullins supplemented the efforts of Eager, Quisenberry, and Greathouse by hiring additional agents during the Jubilee year. One young Southern Seminary graduate tried to work the Texas churches, but with little success because of the overriding influence of Southwestern Seminary.[20] A young Georgian reported that the work was so hard that it had caused his health to break down, thus forcing his resignation. Several Seminary students worked during the summer months. Agents were not always satisfied with their salaries, which usually were around $150 per month plus expenses.[21] One over-zealous agent ended his efforts by angering several important leaders in Virginia and North Carolina.[22]

---

[17]*Baptist World*, 6 May 1909; Dewey W. Grantham, *Southern Progressivism* (Knoxville: University of Tennessee Press, 1983) 275-318.

[18]*Courier-Journal*, 28 September, 29 September 1909; *Baptist World*, 9 September 1909; Shailer Mathews to Mullins, 30 June 1909; A. H. Strong to Mullins, 22 June, 30 June 1909.

[19]*Courier-Journal*, 1 October 1909.

[20]L. T. Mays to Mullins, 24 February, 6 April, 19 October, 23 December 1909.

[21]F. L. Hardy to Mullins, 30 June 1909; W. S. Brooke to Mullins, 10 June, 2 October 1909; S. A. Smith to Mullins, 25 December 1909.

[22]The young man, T. Benton Hill, angered Livingston Johnson, corresponding secretary of the North Carolina convention. Johnson claimed that Hill was "rather coarse" and "too loud." Johnson to Mullins, 27 September 1909. William E. Hatcher complained that Hill's "braggadocio and other things give the black eye." Hatcher to Mullins, 30 June 1910. Hill may have resigned because Mullins cut his monthly salary by $50. Hill to Mullins, 11 June, 29 September 1910.

During the Jubilee campaign, P. T. Hale joined the endowment drive as a full-time agent, a position he kept until 1925.[23]

Good public relations with the Baptist ministry was vital to the success of the drive. Many ministers encouraged their churches to accept a quota that was pledged to the Seminary fund. The larger churches in particular asked that Mullins make a personal appearance and plead for funds.[24] Opposition to the campaign surfaced because of the fundamentalist-moderate schism. A few ministers reported that the Louisville Seminary had developed a liberal image that slowed efforts to gain pledges. Many said their parishioners opposed the Seminary because of its stance on alien immersion.[25]

Southern Seminary also competed with other Southern Baptist institutions for funds. State Baptist officials in North Carolina, Alabama, Oklahoma, Virginia, and Arkansas gave Southern Seminary a full year for its drive and then asked its agents to either leave the state or "work quietly" without the fanfare of a promotional campaign.[26] Georgia, in particular, provided setbacks because the Seminary drive coincided with a campaign staged by some Georgia Baptist institutions. Several leaders in that state asked Mullins to delay his campaign until all Georgia institutions had completed their drives. Mullins had no choice but to do

---

[23]Carver, "Recollections," 99.

[24]J. L. Rosser to Mullins, 8 October 1909; M. Ashby Jones to Mullins, 28 January 1910; J. C. Massee to Mullins, 22 April 1909.

[25]One western Kentucky leader expressed sorrow over the controversy but maintained that his association "cannot and will not" contribute to any institution that did not take a conservative stance on alien immersion. J. T. Enock to Mullins, 10 June 1909. Another pastor determined that "many queer things" occurred at Southern Seminary and warned Mullins not to attempt to collect funds at his church. W. J. Puckett to Mullins, 10 June 1909. Other pastors in Louisiana, Mississippi, St. Louis, and Alabama expressed the same sentiments. J. L. Rosser to Mullins, 6 December 1909; George C. Hawes to Mullins, 10 September 1912; I. H. Anding to Mullins, 24 October 1908; Leon W. Sloan to Mullins, 28 August 1909.

[26]Livingston Johnson to Mullins, 31 May 1911; W. J. E. Cox to Mullins, 16 January 1912; A. J. Holt to Mullins, 10 June 1911; R. H. Pitt to Mullins, 31 May 1910; R. G. Bowers to Mullins, 24 December, 31 December 1910.

as they suggested.[27] In Kentucky, Porter did not voice opposition to the Seminary endowment drive, but neither did he write editorials in favor of the movement.[28]

Nevertheless, Mullins, driving himself to exhaustion in the process, increased the Seminary endowment by nearly $600,000.[29] The method of collection was similar to that of the Twentieth Century Drive, with donors signing five notes that were annually presented to their bank for payment.[30] These notes were not always honored. One Mississippi farmer, for example, reported that he had hoped to pay his yearly pledge to Southern Seminary, but this year the "boll weevil" had wiped him out.[31] Even with the increase in endowment, financial exigency often forced Mullins to make near panic-stricken pleas for emergency funds. On one occasion he received thirty-eight prompt denials for contributions.[32] During the financial panic following the outbreak of World War I, Mullins sent a form letter to numerous former donors. One pessimistic Texas banker, for example, replied that if the situation was so bad at Southern Seminary, "it might be a good plan to let those young breth-

---

[27]C. J. Thompson to Mullins, 2 March 1909; John E. White to Mullins, 2 March, 5 July 1909; John F. Purser to Mullins, 6 March, 7 March 1909; John E. Harrison to Mullins, 6 March 1909; John W. Green to Mullins, 20 April 1909.

[28]*Western Recorder*, 7 August 1913. An agent in Arkansas told Mullins that the *Recorder* and Porter had much influence in that state, and he found it impossible to get any cooperation. R. F. Tredway to Mullins, 27 June, 29 June 1910.

[29]Mueller, *A History of Southern Baptist Theological Seminary*, 191. Just before the school term opened in 1909 Mullins spent several weeks recuperating at the Battle Creek, Michigan, Sanitarium. B. Pressley Smith to Mullins, 10 September 1909; Robert Rabb to Mullins, 29 November 1909.

[30]A form letter sent as a reminder to those who had made pledges, in this case to C. K. Henderson, 25 November 1914.

[31]J. W. Graham to Mullins, 16 December 1913.

[32]Form letter sent 27 February 1912. A list of thirty-eight leaders promptly replied no to Mullins's urgent call for donations (Box 45). To a Southern Baptist leader Mullins admitted that the Student Aid Fund was "becoming an embarrassing problem on account of the large attendance." Mullins to E. C. Dargan, 3 June 1913; *Baptist World*, 4 July 1912.

ren go home" instead of attempting to carry on with the impending school term.[33]

Throughout his tenure as president Mullins never attained financial independence for the Seminary, but the tenuous nature of its finances never deterred him from thinking about the future. He soon launched preparations for a new physical plant. In late 1910, before the Jubilee Drive was assured of success, the Seminary purchased a forty-five acre tract on the north side of Brownsboro Road. Mullins planned to build a new Seminary on that tract and went ahead with landscaping plans even though construction money was nowhere in sight. He hoped the Seminary could move from downtown Louisville to the new site within five years.[34]

The Jubilee Drive of Southern Seminary exacerbated a growing problem within the Southern Baptist Convention. The southwestern part of the Convention (Texas, Arkansas, and Oklahoma) had always been the most conservative area, with the strongest evidence of Landmarkism. B. H. Carroll, a Texas minister and faculty member of Baylor University, had been one of the leaders in the onslaught against Whitsitt. In 1901 Carroll became chairman of the theology department at Baylor University. Four years later the department adopted the title Baylor Theological Seminary.[35] Not long after Mullins came to Southern Seminary, his father warned him that Carroll's "unwarranted ambition" could cause the Louisville institution problems in the future.[36] Carroll and his faculty became more aggressive, urging that the Convention no longer recognize Southern Seminary as the only official sanctioned institution for the education of Southern Baptist ministers.[37] J. B. Gambrell, corresponding secretary of the Baptist General Convention of

---

[33]George E. Webb to Mullins, 14 November 1914.

[34]Olmstead Brothers, Brookline, Massachusetts, to Mullins, 20 April 1911; *Courier-Journal,* 19 December 1910; *Baptist World,* 12 January 1911.

[35]W. W. Barnes, "Southwestern Baptist Theological Seminary," *Encyclopedia of Southern Baptists,* 2:1277.

[36]S. G. Mullins to E. Y. Mullins, 23 March 1901.

[37]*Western Recorder,* 9 May 1901; L. T. Mays to Mullins, 8 February 1912; Leonard W. Doolan to Mullins, 8 September 1905.

Texas, kept Mullins well-informed of Carroll's machinations.[38] The conservatism of Carroll and his faculty prompted Eaton and the *Recorder* to support the progress of Baylor Seminary toward parity with Southern Seminary.[39] Carroll boasted that he already had five full-time members of his department, nearly as many as Southern Seminary.[40]

Another seminary would, of course, offer a serious threat to the economic security of Southern Seminary and precariously divide available sources of denominational funds. There was some evidence of a movement to split the southwestern area from the Southern Baptist Convention and form a new convention with Southwestern Seminary as its ministerial training school. Mullins and Southern Seminary representatives making financial forays into the Southwest realized that their intentions were always suspect to Carroll and fundamentalist Texas Baptists.[41]

In 1907 Carroll, severing connections with Baylor, named the new institution Southwestern Baptist Theological Seminary.[42] Within a short period of time, Southern and Southwestern seminaries came into direct conflict when both initiated endowment drives at the same time. Carroll demanded that Southern Seminary agents not enter Texas until his campaign ended. He denied that he was motivated by doctrinal conservatism in opposing Southern Seminary's fund drive, but did admit that he believed the Louisville seminary to be too liberal.[43] Although some Texas ministers still adhered to Southern Seminary, most seemed to favor Carroll's course of action, or else were afraid to oppose him. One prominent Texas minister implied that Carroll would make it difficult for any

---

[38]Gambrell to Mullins, 28 November 1899; 26 March, 27 April 1903.

[39]*Western Recorder*, 14 September 1905.

[40]Carroll to Mullins, 16 September 1905.

[41]Fred W. Freeman to Mullins, no date, Box 44; William E. Hatcher to Mullins, 13 April 1908; T. B. Ray to Mullins, 8 September 1908; John T. Christian to E. P. J. Garrott, 20 September 1909 (copy to Mullins from Garrott); P. C. Schilling to Mullins, 18 April 1909.

[42]Barnes, "Southwestern Baptist Theological Seminary," 1278.

[43]Carroll to Mullins, 16 March, 20 April 1909.

pro-Southern Seminary man to remain in the state.[44] The agent sent by Mullins into the state encountered numerous difficulties and finally admitted that "the door is closed upon us in Texas."[45] In nearby Arkansas the Southwestern Seminary influence was also strong. In 1909, for example, the Southwestern faction tried to get the Arkansas state convention to vote its total financial support to that institution instead of evenly dividing its aid between the two seminaries.[46] Mullins understood that Texas, if not the entire Southwest, was lost to him as a major source of revenue and students. Southwestern continued to manifest an "ultraconservative, hyper-orthodox" image until Carroll's death in 1914.[47]

With the loss of revenue from Texas and the inability to obtain funds outside the South, Mullins turned increasingly toward cementing better relations with leaders of the Southern Baptist Convention agencies. Frost, in particular, began to play a bigger role in the reactions of Mullins to denominational issues. After the Sunday School Board agreed to endow a chair, the connection became more complete.

Frost continued to oppose cooperation with the Baptist Young People's Union of America and the American Baptist Publication Society.[48] He and Van Ness pressured Mullins into writing something important for the Sunday School Board.[49] Frost and the Seminary faction debated prolonged cooperation with the International Sunday School Association, with the Sunday School Board leader consistently urging that the

[44]A. J. Barton to Mullins, 11 January 1908; A. R. Watson to Mullins, 13 December 1908; J. B. Gambrell to Mullins, 7 May 1909; Frost to Mullins, 27 November 1909; J. Frank Norris to Mullins, 18 August, 27 August 1908.

[45]L. T. Mays to Mullins, 2 July 1909.

[46]R. F. Tredway to Mullins, 20 September, 24 November 1909.

[47]J. J. Reeve to Mullins, 23 May 1913. Mullins and Professor L. R. Scarborough, later president of Southwestern Seminary, developed a rather close relationship. Scarborough to Mullins, 25 December 1909; Mullins to Scarborough, 29 December 1909, 21 November 1912 (Fleming Library, Southwestern Baptist Theological Seminary, Fort Worth, Texas).

[48]Mullins to Frost, 9 February, 12 February 1909 (Frost-Bell Letters, Dargan-Carver Library).

[49]Ibid., 31 July 1909; Van Ness to Mullins, 6 September 1910.

Southern Baptist Convention exit from interdenominational affiliation.[50] Frost and Mullins argued the merits of cooperation with the I. S. S. A. The Sunday School Board secretary became angry and asserted that Mullins's faith in the Association was obviously "wrong." To Frost the greatest danger of the Association was that it was controlled by Northern religious interests.[51]

Mullins was caught in the middle of a conflict not only between the Sunday School Board and the Association, but also between those who favored or opposed interdenominational cooperation. T. P. Bell, editor of the influential Atlanta *Christian Index,* displayed Southern Baptist chauvinism when he declared that the denomination no longer needed the materials of the Association and was now strong enough to go it alone.[52] On the other hand, moderate R. H. Pitt, editor of the Richmond *Religious Herald,* noted a "distinct reactionary spirit" on the Sunday School Board and vowed his support of Southern Baptist cooperation with the Association.[53] The leaders of the Association profusely thanked Mullins for his help in keeping Southern Baptists in the Association. W. N. Hartshorn, chairman of the executive committee of the Association, declared that Mullins's "friends in the North" realized the struggles and sacrifices he was forced to make in order to obtain Southern Baptist Convention support of the Association's graded lesson programs.[54] In these affairs Mullins represented the border state mediator who assuaged the apprehension of his Southern brethren toward participation in national groups.

Frost received a measure of revenge by grudgingly doling out the money promised to endow the Sunday school professorship in 1911.[55]

----

[50]Sampey to Mullins, 9 May 1910; Frost to Mullins, 3 May, 23 May, 18 June 1910.

[51]Frost to Mullins, 27 June, 7, 14, 22, 25, and 29 July, 2 August, 5 August 1910; Mullins to Frost, 14, 18, and 24 June, 5, 11, 16, 25, and 30 July 1910 (Frost-Bell Letters, Dargan-Carver Library).

[52]Bell to Mullins, 13 July 1910.

[53]Pitt to Mullins, 27 September, 17 October 1910.

[54]Hartshorn to Mullins, 15 June 1910, 21 February 1911.

[55]Mullins to Frost, 14 April, 25 April, 6 May, 30 June, 11 July 1911 (Frost-Bell Letters, Dargan-Carver Library).

By the next year relations between the Seminary and Sunday School Board had broken down completely. Only a conference with Frost and Van Ness brought about a "better understanding."[56] Exactly what took place at this meeting is not known, but thereafter Mullins began to write books and pamphlets for the Board. Moreover, Mullins, resuming close ties with Frost and Van Ness, no longer automatically took the side of the International Sunday School Association in their disputes with the Sunday School Board.[57]

Though Mullins continued to have much contact with his Northern brethren, both denominational and interdenominational, the nature and tone of this contact changed over the years. By the end of his first decade as president of Southern Seminary, he was more aware than ever of the importance of contacts within the Convention. He also sought a closer liaison with Northern Baptist moderates.[58]

Relations with the University of Chicago Divinity School faculty illustrated this change. During the summer of 1909 Mullins spent six weeks at the University of Chicago as "University Preacher," teaching eight hours and preaching two sermons per week for a salary of $500.[59] This assignment was his last major contact with the Chicago Divinity School faculty. As the University of Chicago became the leader of theological liberalism, Southern Seminary more obviously became the exponent of moderation. The basic difference that developed between liberals, who became known as modernists, with moderates and fundamentalists was over the question of the divinity of Christ. Though these

---

[56]Mullins to Frost, 22 May 1912 (Frost-Bell Letters, Dargan-Carver Library); Mullins to Van Ness, 22 May 1912 (Frost-Bell Letters, Dargan-Carver Library).

[57]Mullins to Frost, 10 June 1912 (Frost-Bell Letters, Dargan-Carver Library); Frost to Mullins, 6, 16, and 23 January, 3 February 1913; 22 March 1915.

[58]Contact with the following men illustrated this continuity: J. S. Dickerson to Mullins, 13 January 1914; W. S. Shallenberger to Mullins, 20 March, 18 April 1911; Frederick L. Anderson to Mullins, 9 February 1911; E. B. Pollard to Mullins, 15 July 1912; George E. Horr to Mullins, 9 July 1912; Curtis Lee Laws to Mullins, 10 July 1914.

[59]Shailer Mathews to Mullins, 25 November, 7 December 1908; 18 January, 25 January, 17 April, 14 June 1909.

groups clashed over such substantive matters, the debates before World War I were more gentlemanly than the theological imbroglio of the 1920s.[60]

An article published by Mullins in 1911 illustrated the differences between liberals and moderate evangelicals. Repeating many of his earlier findings on will, experience, and science, Mullins declared that endless debates over the scientific implications of Christianity were useless. He vowed his boundless belief in evangelical Christianity. Only through "submission," "faith," and "self-surrender" could a person find peace of mind.[61] Moderate Ira M. Price of the Chicago faculty praised Mullins's article as meeting "the issue squarely," while his liberal colleague, Gerald Birney Smith, disagreed with Mullins's "Christology." Smith affirmed his belief in a more scientific explanation of Christianity. In particular, he found that the Louisville seminarian placed too much emphasis on individual "experience." In effect, Smith proposed a philosophical approach to understanding Christ, while Mullins advocated the evangelical concept. Smith ended a lengthy letter by praising Mullins for his "catholic spirit" that dampened the ferocity of their fundamentalist brethren.[62] This discussion illustrated the widening rift

---

[60]When Professor McGlothlin spent a summer at the University of Chicago, he noted that the faculty seemed to be divided between liberals and moderates. McGlothlin to Mullins, 15 July 1907. Professor George B. Foster was the most liberal of all the Chicago faculty. After a speech by Foster in which he deprecated traditional Christian tenets, President Harper admonished Dean Hulbert to stop Foster from making shocking public statements. William R. Harper to Eri B. Hulbert, 3 October 1903 (University Presidents' Papers, 1889-1925, University of Chicago Archives). Foster later published a book that created a "theological storm," and Harper "was apparently relieved" when he could transfer Foster from the Divinity School to Arts and Sciences. This all illustrates that the Chicago faculty did not become liberal very quickly, though the general trend was in that direction. Maring, "Baptists and Changing Views of the Bible, 1865-1918," *Foundations* 1 (October 1958): 51-52. See Hutchison, *The Modernist Impulse in American Protestantism,* for a broad description of the modernist movement.

[61]Mullins, "The Modern Issue as to the Person of Christ," *Review and Expositor* 8 (January 1911): 26-27.

[62]Price to Mullins, 3 February 1911; Smith to Mullins, 21 January 1911.

between the moderate and the liberal. On the other hand, the fundamentalist violently opposed modernism.

Though Mullins continued close contact with denominational and
interdenominational leaders outside the South, his interest cooled toward participating in organizations outside the Southern Baptist domain. After 1909 the Baptist Theological Faculties' Union rapidly
deteriorated. Part of the answer lies in the rather aggressive attitude of
the Chicago faculty. Shailer Mathews, for example, constantly badgered Mullins about meetings and plans of that group. Mullins and other
seminary leaders soon lost interest in any group activity that was dictated by the Chicago Divinity School. After 1911 even the interest of the
Chicago faculty seemed to wane.[63] By early 1915 Smith reported that he
had inquired about a meeting of the Union and no one displayed any
interest in further meetings.[64]

The Baptist Congress and the Baptist Young People's Union of
America were other groups with which Mullins lost contact, thereby
lessening his opportunity to have extensive influence over his Northern
brethren. In 1914 the chairman of the executive committee of the Baptist
Congress reported that this group could no longer afford to publish the
annual proceedings because of a lack of interest and funds.[65] In 1910
Mullins had requested to be relieved of his duties as president of the
Young People's Union.[66] It is significant that these changes took place
around the time of the Jubilee Drive and the unstable relations with Frost,
who was adding considerably to the power of the Sunday School Board.
The advent of Southwestern Seminary added another dimension to Mullins's dilemma in denominational leadership. If he adhered too closely
to Northern liberal Baptist views or to money from that area, he risked
losing support in the South to Southwestern Seminary, a purely South-

---

[63]Mathews to Mullins, 17 November 1905; 14 April 1906; 29 April 1907; 12
May, 11 June, 19 June 1908; 8, 17, and 27 March 1909; Smith to Mullins, 9
September 1914; George E. Horr to Mullins, 21 September 1914.

[64]Smith to Mullins, 10 February 1915.

[65]Henry M. Sanders to Mullins, 1 October 1914.

[66]Executive Committee of B. Y. P. U. A. to Mullins, 9 May 1910. The position actually took very little time because most of the work was done by a staff
in Chicago, later in Philadelphia.

ern and Southern Baptist institution. For several years Southern Seminary displayed the border state function because of its proximity to the
Midwest and the moderation of its theology. In effect, the border state
stance of Southern Seminary began to change when Mullins took on a
more definite Southern Baptist perspective.

The moderate evangelical faction became an increasingly identifi-
able group in the seminaries. Mullins and A. H. Strong, president of
Rochester Seminary, developed a friendship that extended to a close
doctrinal compatibility. Strong gladly participated in the Jubilee celebration.[67] He praised Mullins's article "The Modern Issue as to the Person of Christ" as "the best piece of your writing."[68] As the Rochester
faculty became more liberal, Strong did not change his theological tenets and in some ways became more conservative with age.[69] Particularly
after the publication of the above mentioned article, a reaffirmation of
evangelical Christianity, Mullins and Strong began to correspond frequently and intimately.[70] When Strong retired from Rochester in 1911,
he did not want the presidency to fall into the hands of the liberals.[71] At
first he tried to persuade the trustees to appoint his son as president.
When this failed, Strong and some trustees worked for Mullins's nomination.[72] It is not known how Mullins reacted to the offer, but one is led
to believe that he was not interested in changing positions. Strong,
maintaining that only Southern Seminary among all Baptist seminaries

[67]Strong to Mullins, 20 September 1909.

[68]Ibid., 21 January 1911.

[69]Irwin Reist, "Augustus Hopkins Strong and William Newton Clarke,"
Foundations 13 (January-March 1970): 29-39; LeRoy Moore, Jr., "The Rise of
American Religious Liberalism at the Rochester Theological Seminary, 1872-
1928" (Ph.D. diss., The Claremont Graduate School, 1966) 248-49.

[70]Strong to Mullins, 4 March, 9 March, 27 April, 5 October 1911; 16 April,
26 April 1912; 3 January, 24 April, 9 October 1913.

[71]Moore, "The Rise of American Religious Liberalism at the Rochester
Theological Seminary," 165.

[72]Ibid., 165-67; Robert Stuart MacArthur to Mullins, 2 May 1912; Grant
Wacker, *Augustus H. Strong and the Dilemma of Historical Consciousness*
(Macon GA: Mercer University Press, 1985), ch. 4.

now represented moderate evangelical theology, decried the liberal takeover at Rochester.[73]

Mullins's last major effort at a liaison between his Northern and Southern Baptist brethren developed over border states' conflicts in New Mexico, Illinois, Missouri, Oklahoma, and West Virginia. Since the schism in 1845, the Northern and Southern conventions slowly formalized their separate polities and, with the creation of the Northern Baptist Convention in 1907, the break became irrevocable.[74] The Home Mission Board and the Home Mission Society competed for territorial rights in the above states. As mentioned previously, the Publication Society and the Sunday School Board battled for control of religious literature. Agreements made in the late nineteenth century about the rights of each of the above groups broke down after the reorganization of Northern Baptists in 1907.[75] To many people the name Northern Baptist Convention completed the adamant sectionalism begun by the formation of the Southern Baptist Convention and implied definite territorial boundaries for these two entities.[76]

Mullins, becoming embroiled in this denominational conflict, served as liaison between the warring parties, the only man whom both sides trusted. In 1907 a group of Baptists in southern Illinois left the regular state convention and petitioned the Southern Baptist Convention for membership.[77] From his base in Texas J. B. Gambrell encouraged the Illinois schism. He claimed that "ever since the [Civil] war the North has been projecting into the South," and now was the time to reverse the

---

[73]Strong to Mullins, 5 June 1912. A Rochester trustee later admitted that he was sorry that Mullins did not consider the position at Rochester. He stated that he voted for Mullins. It is not known, however, if Mullins's name was put into an official nomination. Albert E. Waffle to Mullins, 27 April 1914.

[74]Robert G. Torbet, "Historical Background of the Southern Baptist 'Invasion'," *Foundations* 2 (October 1959): 315.

[75]Hall, "The Problem of Comity Between American and Southern Baptists," 47-89.

[76]Baker, *Relations Between Northern and Southern Baptists,* 196.

[77]Hall, "The Problem of Comity Between American and Southern Baptists," 54, 82-83.

trends of that "war."[78] Again, Mullins found himself caught between Southern brethren like Gambrell and Frost and his Northern friends of long standing like Morehouse.

A second crisis occurred in New Mexico where Southern Baptist emigrants agitated for alignment with the Southern Baptist Convention.[79] Representatives of the Northern and Southern Baptist conventions met and agreed to make territorial adjustments, but neither convention accepted the compromise.[80] The New Mexico convention voted to continue cooperation with the Home Mission Society, but Southern Baptist sympathizers continued to opt for affiliation with the Southern wing of Baptists. Mullins met with the representatives of both groups at Old Point Comfort, Virginia, in September 1911. The corresponding secretary of the Northern Baptist Convention praised Mullins for his "positive contribution" to the conference.[81]

As chairman of a subcommittee appointed by both conventions to study the problem, Mullins made a trip to New Mexico to view the situation firsthand and develop recommendations.[82] B. D. Gray, the corresponding secretary of the Home Mission Board, pressured Mullins to influence his committee in favor of the Board, all the while protesting that his group had never been aggressive in New Mexico.[83] Frost, meanwhile, claimed that only "interference" from the North precipitated the crisis in New Mexico.[84] From the Northern Baptist view came other pressures. H. L. Morehouse urged that Mullins visit the offices of the

---

[78]Gambrell to Mullins, 22 July, 2 August 1909; 9 March 1910.

[79]Hall, "The Problem of Comity Between American and Southern Baptists," 51-52.

[80]Baker, *Relations Between Northern and Southern Baptists*, 199-200.

[81]Hall, "The Problem of Comity Between American and Southern Baptists," 53-54; W. C. Bitting to Mullins, 2 October 1911; Baker, *Relations Between Northern and Southern Baptists*, 184-86.

[82]Hall, "The Problem of Comity Between American and Southern Baptists," 55-56.

[83]Gray to Mullins, 4 November 1911; 21 March, 23 March 1912.

[84]Frost to Mullins, 30 March 1910.

Home Mission Society in New York to obtain their side of the story.[85] J. S. Dickerson, editor of the *Standard* of Chicago, was a member of the Mullins subcommittee. He took an adamant stand against Southern Baptist influence in New Mexico.[86] His Southern counterpart on the committee, A. J. Barton, a minister from Waco, Texas, took a hardline, pro-Southern Baptist stand.[87] Alvah S. Hobart, a professor at Crozer and a Northern representative on the subcommittee, asked only for an "honorable" settlement to the New Mexico situation, implying that most Northern Baptists had about given up hope of keeping their influence in New Mexico.[88]

After trips to New York, Chicago, and New Mexico, Mullins presented his report to the full committee at Hot Springs with the support of both factions. In effect, Mullins's committee recommended that the Home Mission Society taper off its work in New Mexico, implying that the state would soon join the Southern Baptist Convention. Each church in that state retained the right to join the convention of its choice.[89] This document became the "Principles of Comity" adopted by both conventions in 1912.[90]

The decision in favor of the Southern Baptist Convention led to further successes in Oklahoma, Missouri, and Arizona as the Southern faction took over work originally done by the Northern Baptist societies.[91] Gray and Gambrell were not satisfied with the conquest of New Mexico and agitated for control of other states along the periphery of Southern

---

[85]Morehouse to Mullins, 9 February 1912.

[86]Dickerson to Mullins, 2, 14, 15, and 19 December 1911; 2 February, 15 March 1912.

[87]Barton to Mullins, 30 March, 4, 6, and 13 April, 1 July 1912.

[88]Hobart to Mullins, 28 January, 20 March, 24 April 1911.

[89]Mullins to W. C. Bitting, 25 April 1912; Mullins to Walter Calley, 25 April 1912; Mullins to P. W. Longfellow, 25 April 1912; Bitting to Mullins, 27 April 1912.

[90]Hall, "The Problem of Comity Between American and Southern Baptists," 55-56.

[91]Ibid., 54-57, 83.

Baptist territory.[92] Once these states became part of Southern Baptist "territory," Mullins lost some contact with his Northern Baptist brethren. When there was no further agitation for a realignment of state associations in his lifetime, there became less need for his services as liaison between the contending conventions and their agencies.

During the Jubilee years Mullins pragmatically turned toward more dependence upon his Southern brethren for support. A number of factors encouraged Mullins's stronger adherence to Southern Baptist denominationalism. The increasing power of the Sunday School Board frightened him away from closer contact with Northern Baptist agencies. The financial viability of the Seminary became more of a Southern problem than ever before. Large donations from wealthy Northern Baptists were not forthcoming during a very critical period in the Seminary's history. Mullins retained his personal contacts with his Northern brethren, but the trend was toward a closer communion with Southerners.

---

[92]Gray to Mullins, 6 March, 28 June 1912; Gambrell to Mullins, 26 January, 28 February 1914; Joshua Levering to Mullins, 22 June 1912; W. C. Bitting to Mullins, 17, 22, and 23 January 1914.

7 THE LAST CHANCE FOR RECONCILIATION

The war years represented the last hope for resolving the tensions that were dividing conservatives, moderates, and liberals in the mainline Protestant denominations in America. Soon many of the conservatives would proudly adopt the banner of fundamentalism. Many liberals, on the other hand, would just as proudly take the name of modernist. Caught in the middle were such moderate evangelicals as Mullins. He persisted in his efforts to synthesize the old and the new. He continued to publish books widely acclaimed by friends and sometimes by foes. *The Christian Religion in Its Doctrinal Expression* represented his last, best hope for saving centrist Christian theology and, thereby, holding together the contending religious parties already clearly evident in the country. The tumultuous 1920s were just beyond the horizon.

In two major books and several articles written during his second decade as president of Southern Seminary, Mullins continued the moderate evangelical approach to religious experience and theology.[1] His

---

[1]Ahlstrom, "Theology in America: A Historical Survey," 303-309.

pronouncements on Christology, doctrine, and theology offered little that
was new, only reaffirmations of his earlier books and articles. The old
influences, moreover, were still there with Schleiermacher, Bowne, and
James prominently mentioned in Mullins's publications.[2]

Mullins began to take greater notice of evolution as a theological issue, but he did not change his earlier ideas about the religious implications of Darwinism. He adamantly maintained that science and
religion were separate "spheres."[3] God was the "first cause," Mullins
asserted, creating the world through a "gradual" process. He found too
many inconsistencies to make natural selection a viable concept for an
explanation of the slow process of creation and preferred the use of the
word *development* in place of *evolution*.[4] More important in an apologetics sense, both science and the Bible placed man at the end of the
creation cycle, proving that the Scriptures were not entirely unreliable
as a source of scientific information.[5] Mullins finally declared that man
was not an "afterthought" but a "forethought of God."[6] Mullins obviously molded his acceptance of a moderate form of evolution to suit
his moderate evangelical temperament. He tried to accept only as much
as would not endanger his belief in evangelical experience.

Though he usually wrote in language unfamiliar to his unlettered
brethren, Mullins, like them, never wavered in his maintenance of the
evangelical faith.[7] Experience continued to be the focal point of his

---

[2]Borden P. Bowne to Mullins, 26 March 1910. See, for example, Mullins,
The Christian Religion in Its Doctrinal Expression (Philadelphia: Roger Williams Press, 1917) 53, 195, 199, 231-32.

[3]Mullins, *Freedom and Authority in Religion*, 399; Mullins, *The Christian
Religion in Its Doctrinal Expression*, 83-84.

[4]*Baptist World*, 11 May 1916, 6 September 1917.

[5]Mullins, *The Christian Religion in Its Doctrinal Expression*, 225-57.

[6]Ibid., 255.

[7]*Courier-Journal*, 22 June 1914; Mullins, "The Response of Jesus Christ to
Modern Thought," *Review and Expositor* 13 (April 1916): 161-65; *Baptist
World*, 10 September 1914; 22 July 1915; 18 May, 1 June, 8 June 1916. For a
concise interpretation of the cultural milieu in which Mullins operated, see
Wayne Flynt, *Dixie's Forgotten People* (Bloomington: Indiana University Press,
1979) 33-63.

theological schema.[8] He remained entirely consistent when he contributed an article to *The Fundamentals,* a series of volumes considered by many to be the genesis of the interdenominational fundamentalist movement. Thereafter, the lines between fundamentalists and modernists were readily apparent. However, Mullins's piece was conciliatory in tone. He stressed the experiential quality of Christianity without the rabid dogmatism normally associated with fundamentalism. During this same era, Mullins replied to those who denied the existence of God with this declaration: "We experience God. He becomes actual to us in religious experience."[9] As George Marsden recently declared, Mullins's essay and other such "mediating essays" in the early *Fundamentals* demonstrated that "the trenches were not yet deeply dug for the coming fundamentalist battle" of the 1920s. There was still time left for Mullins's conciliatory efforts.[10]

Mullins's theology was a counterpoint to that of the liberals and fundamentalists. Porter, for example, editorially attacked Mullins's moderate views on progressive revelation by declaring that revelation was "fixed and permanent."[11] Unlike the moderates, Porter proudly declared his commitment to premillennialism.[12] Another prominent Baptist fundamentalist found that Southern Seminary was subversive to Christianity.[13]

The liberals, on the other hand, contrasted with Mullins's moderation. Mullins criticized the scientific bent of his liberal colleagues.[14] In

---

[8]Schneider, *Religion in 20th Century America,* 133; Mullins, *Freedom and Authority in Religion,* 156; *Baptist World,* 20 June 1918; Mullins, *The Christian Religion in Its Doctrinal Expression,* 1-34.

[9]Mullins, "The Testimony of Christian Experience," in *The Fundamentals: A Testimony to the Truth* (Los Angeles: The Bible Institute, 1917) 4:314-23; Szasz, *The Divided Mind of Protestant America,* 9, 78-80.

[10]Mullins, *Freedom and Authority in Religion,* 248; Marsden, *Fundamentalism and American Culture,* 122.

[11]*Western Recorder,* 20 September 1917.

[12]Ibid., 18 July 1918.

[13]I. N. Penick to Mullins, 28 February, 3 March 1914.

[14]Mullins, Review of *Theology as an Empirical Science* by D. C. Macintosh, in *Review and Expositor* 17 (January 1920): 96-97.

the books of liberal Shirley Jackson Case of the University of Chicago, Mullins found the denials of Christ's divinity unacceptable. Particularly frightening to Mullins was Case's open-ended world view predicated on his blind obedience to evolution. Without a goal, Mullins believed, the world would be unintelligible and without purpose.[15] Other moderates, like A. H. Strong, supported Mullins's theological stance. In effect, Mullins's theology stood still in this decade, while the liberals moved toward scientific modernism.[16]

In other areas Mullins continued his moderate approach. During the second decade of Mullins's administration, Southern Seminary exhibited a moderate Social Gospel tendency, with Gardner and Mullins leading the movement. Particularly in the *Review and Expositor* the faculty usually gave good marks to the outstanding Social Gospel books of the period. Other members of the Seminary faction contributed articles that favored a moderate Social Gospel. Carver appeared to be the least favorable, while Gardner had the more liberal outlook.[17]

Gardner developed classes in sociology as part of the curriculum. Students in his classes were won over to the sociological approach as a means of understanding the human condition. One group of young men, for example, petitioned Mullins to make sociology courses mandatory

---

[15]Mullins, "The Jesus of 'Liberal' Theology," *Review and Expositor* 12 (April 1915): 174-92.

[16]Strong to Mullins, 16 October 1917.

[17]Marshall Louis Mertins, "Is the Modern Church a Good Samaritan?" *Review and Expositor* 14 (April 1917): 223-35; Gardner, Review of *The Making of Tomorrow: The Making of the World Today* by Shailer Mathews, in *Review and Expositor* 11 (January 1914): 133; unsigned, Review of *Social Service Series* by Mathews, in *Review and Expositor* 10 (April 1913): 291; John Henry Barber, "Socializing the Christian Order," *Review and Expositor* 12 (October 1915): 545-61; George B. Eager, Review of *Christianity and the Labor Movement* by William Monroe Balch, in *Review and Expositor* 10 (January 1913): 147-48; Eager, Review of *Sin and Society* by E. A. Ross, in *Review and Expositor* 5 (July 1908): 448-49; J. L. Kesler, Review of *Christianity and the Social Crisis* by Walter Rauschenbusch, in *Review and Expositor* 4 (October 1907): 669-70; Carver, Review of *A Theology for the Social Gospel* by Walter Rauschenbusch, in *Review and Expositor* 15 (July 1918): 358-59.

for all Southern Seminary students.[18] In 1914 Gardner contributed a major article and a book on the evangelically oriented Social Gospel. In particular, he found poverty primarily due to the selfishness of the wealthy class. On the one hand, he took a Marxian approach to the "accumulation of wealth," condemning the capitalist class; on the other, he advocated the teachings of Christ through stewardship. The key to solving economic inequity, he believed, was the "diffusion of wealth."[19] Always the moderate and forever the Christian, Gardner maintained that "the evangelistic and the social aspects" of Christianity could never be isolated from each other.[20]

Though Mullins did not write as extensively about the Social Gospel as did Gardner, he often discussed the social responsibilities of his faith, optimistically predicting a "triumph of democracy," with Baptists playing a key role in evangelizing the globe.[21] Out of this development, Mullins believed, would come social betterment of the human race. Baptists working through the Baptist World Alliance should "deepen" their social commitment.[22] He challenged all seminaries to teach courses in Christian ethics and sociology. Ministers should assume the lead in "civic life."[23] Mullins, as a further indication of his social concerns, applauded the advent of the Children's Bureau and invited Samuel Z. Batten, a liberal Northern Baptist advocate of the Social Gospel, to lecture at Southern Seminary.[24] Though he gave more than lip service to the need

---

[18]J. W. Morgan, et al., to Mullins, 21 February 1910; Morgan to Mullins, 24 February 1910.

[19]Gardner, "The Accumulation of Wealth," *Review and Expositor* 11 (April 1914): 213-16; Gardner, Review of *The Social Creed of the Churches* by Harry F. Ward, ed., in *Review and Expositor* 11 (July 1914): 458; Mullins, Review of *The Ethics of Jesus and Social Progress* by Gardner, in *Review and Expositor* 11 (July 1914): 454.

[20]*Baptist World*, 27 April 1916.

[21]Ibid., 9 May 1912.

[22]Ibid., 20 April 1914.

[23]Mullins, "Training the Ministry for Civic Leadership," *Religious Education* 9 (December 1914): 559-60.

[24]*Baptist World*, 1 May 1913; Rauschenbusch to Mullins, 25 April 1912; Batten to Mullins, 27 February, 7 March, 22 March 1912.

for social responsibility, Mullins did not ask for a de-emphasis in the evangelistic effort of the denomination. Rather, he sought a balance between the Social Gospel and evangelism.[25] He never displayed the strong "ethical passion" of a Rauschenbusch but stayed moderate throughout.[26]

On specific social issues Mullins also maintained his moderation. Although he took relatively little interest in the Prohibition issue, Mullins had more practical concern for the plight of his black brethren than even the liberal Social Gospelers in the North.[27] He continued his close contacts with both whites and blacks who attempted to improve Negro education in the South.[28] In particular, he encouraged the work of B. F. Riley, the most liberal Southern Baptist on race issues in the early twentieth century. Riley declared in his first major book that the white Southerner's responsibility for his black brethren was unavoidable.[29] Mullins praised not only the book but also Riley's work among Negroes in the South.[30] Mullins also wrote an introduction for Riley's biography of

----

[25]*Baptist World,* 6 September 1917; Mullins, "Christ's Challenge to Manhood: A Sermon to Young Men," *Homiletic Review* 74 (September 1917): 233-37.

[26]Ahlstrom, "Theology in America: A Historical Survey," 307. Among Northern Baptists, Rauschenbusch and Strong represented the liberal and moderate strains in the denomination. A student of both men declared, "From Strong I learned the fear of God; from Rauschenbusch I learned the love of man," illustrating the evangelical emphasis of the moderate Strong and the Social Gospel emphasis of the liberal Rauschenbusch. S. Frazer Langford, "The Gospel of Augustus H. Strong and Walter Rauschenbusch," *Chronicle* 14 (January 1951): 3-18.

[27]H. F. Worley to Mullins, 11 February 1916; N. A. Palmer to Mullins, 22 October 1918; Thompson, *Tried as by Fire,* 44-45.

[28]William T. Amiger to Mullins, 14 December 1910, 12 January 1911, 19 October 1914, 17 November 1915, 20 November 1916; P. N. Clarke to Mullins, 29 October, 1 November 1910; James H. Dillard to Mullins, 15 May 1919; George Rice Hovey to Mullins, 2 May 1911; C. H. Parrish to Mullins, 17 March 1913; 5 August 1916; 8 June, 22 October, 23 December 1918; 23 January 1919.

[29]Riley, *The White Man's Burden* (Birmingham: B. F. Riley, 1910); Reimers, *White Protestantism and the Negro,* 49-50.

[30]Riley to Mullins, 19 June 1909, 30 April 1910; *Baptist World,* 8 July 1909, 12 August 1910.

Booker T. Washington, praising the Tuskegee mentor as "one of the most remarkable characters of his generation" and supporting Washington's economic approach to racial uplift.[31] Riley's books were surprisingly liberal for the time and for a man of Southern Baptist background. For example, he scorned the Ku Klux Klan as a detrimental force to both races and praised educational efforts made in behalf of the Negro.[32] These views suited the moderate racial tendencies of Mullins and Southern Seminary. As further proof, the *Review and Expositor,* for example, published an article by Washington in 1913 in which the Tuskegee patriarch extolled the economic and educational progress of his race since the end of the Civil War.[33]

The fundamentalists, in contrast, did not favor the work of Riley. Van Ness censored this activist approach, declaring that Riley unnecessarily stirred up trouble with his work and writings.[34] J. W. Porter, editor of the *Western Recorder,* did not often comment on racial issues, but reacted violently to any suggestion of racial mixing.[35] Similar to most editors' reactions in the Southern Baptist Convention, Porter's racial pronouncements were shallow and often inflammatory.[36]

---

[31]Riley to Mullins, 29 December 1915, 5 April 1916; Fleming H. Revell, Jr., to Mullins, 16 April, 1 May 1916; Mullins, "Introduction," in *The Life and Times of Booker T. Washington,* B. F. Riley (New York: Fleming H. Revell, 1916) 7-8.

[32]Riley, *The Life and Times of Booker T. Washington,* 83.

[33]Washington, "Fifty Years of Negro Freedom," *Review and Expositor* 10 (January 1913): 81-88.

[34]Van Ness to Mullins, 23 December 1918 (Van Ness Papers, Dargan-Carver Library).

[35]Porter believed that "we might say that the negroes [*sic*] know their best friends, and are therefore quite content to live in the South." *Western Recorder,* 25 May, 6 July 1916; 27 June 1918. Porter maintained that Riley always exaggerated the racial strictures of Southern Baptists, declaring that if he ever reviewed Riley's work he would "disprove his statements, and deprecate his work." Porter to Van Ness, 20 December 1918 (Van Ness Papers, Dargan-Carver Library).

[36]Patrick Henry Hill, "The Ethical Emphases of the Editors of Baptist Journals Published in the Southeastern Region of the United States, 1915-1940" (Th.D. diss., Southern Baptist Theological Seminary, 1949) 275-76, 291.

Mullins participated in an effort to found a Negro Baptist seminary in the South. Riley particularly strove toward this development.[37] Mullins became chairman of a racially mixed committee that discussed the problem. Not only did the Southern Baptist Convention members of the committee argue with their Northern counterparts over the site and financing of the new seminary, their black brethren divided into two factions and vied for control over the proposed institution. Mullins was again the moderating influence among these factions and worked for a quick solution to their rivalries.[38] The 1913 Southern Baptist Convention became officially committed to the support of the Negro seminary, with Mullins introducing a resolution, but the new school did not open until 1924.[39] Though Mullins did not believe in racial equality or desegregation, he had more contact with blacks than many liberal Social Gospelers. Despite Mullins's moderate racial views, he was a pioneer within the Southern Baptist context in working for improved race relations.

Mullins also pursued a moderate course in cooperation with the political reform element in Louisville. The Men's Federation was born out of the turmoil over the contested mayoral election of 1905 in Louisville. Representatives from the Baptist, Disciples of Christ, Methodist, Presbyterian, Episcopal, and Catholic churches banded together for the moral uplift of the state, and the city of Louisville in particular.[40] Mullins served as a member of the organizing committee. The group took the official title of Men's Federation of Louisville and reported that other

---

[37]Riley to Mullins, 12 March 1913.

[38]H. L. Morehouse to Mullins, 14 September 1914; Sutton E. Griggs to Mullins, 23 May, 6 June, 13 June 1913; E. C. Morris to Mullins, 5 June 1913; James T. Simpson to Mullins, 3 June 1916; O. L. Hailey to Mullins, 13 November 1917; B. F. Riley to Mullins, 4 September 1914.

[39]Reimers, *White Protestantism and the Negro,* 119; Valentine, "A Historical Study of Southern Baptists and Race Problems, 1917-1947," 80; Warnock, "Moderate Racial Thought and Attitudes of Southern Baptists and Methodists, 1900-1921," 31-40; *Annual of the Southern Baptist Convention, 1913,* 21; L. S. Sedberry, "American Baptist Theological Seminary," *Encyclopedia of Southern Baptists,* 1:42-44.

[40]Robert F. Sexton, "Kentucky Politics and Society, 1919-1932" (Ph.D. diss., University of Washington, 1970) 50-51.

cities in the country organized similar groups. Over the next few years Mullins took part in the activities of the Federation, but only on a sporadic basis.[41]

During the height of the Red Scare the Churchmen's Federation, formerly the Men's Federation, cooperated with the Interchurch World Movement in a nationwide labor survey. In particular, the Louisville study concentrated on labor relations and housing. Mullins chaired an Industrial Committee charged with the study of labor conditions in the city. Frank L. McVey, president of the University of Kentucky, and other prominent citizens also served on this committee.[42]

The committee labored throughout late 1919 and early 1920. Interchurch officials came to Louisville to aid in the effort.[43] When completed by Mullins, the report called for class peace. Though their report may have seemed ambivalent to the opposing camps in labor-management struggles, the Churchmen called for the "golden rule" to be the dictum controlling labor relations. Deploring violence, Mullins urged that arbitration be mandatory, calling it the "safest, wisest, and most just method of settling irreconcilable conflicts." Labor had the right to organize as long as it was reasonable in its demands on capital. Religious sanctions were called forth from time to time in this document, for example, the Ten Commandments, "the religion of Christ," and so forth. Mullins also called for a cooling-off period in labor-management relations since the major problems of "American Christian democracy" would work themselves out if given enough time.[44] Socialism, he be-

---

[41]J. H. Chandler to Mullins, 12 February 1913; W. N. Little to Mullins, 8 April 1913; Henry M. Johnson to Mullins, 14 September 1915; C. J. Meddis to Mullins, 22 September 1915; M. P. Hunt to Mullins, 24 May 1917; W. S. Lockhart to Mullins, 28 January, 7 September 1918.

[42]Robert K. Murray, *Red Scare: A Study in National Hysteria, 1919-1920* (Minneapolis: University of Minnesota Press, 1955) 57; Mullins to McVey, 18 October 1919; McVey to Mullins, 14 October, 18 October, 18 November 1919.

[43]H. R. Gold to Mullins, 3 February, 4 February 1920; James A. Crain to Mullins, 5 November 1919; W. S. Lockhart to Mullins, 2 February, 7 February, 9 March, 20 March, 15 May 1920; Mullins to Victor Cartwright, 14 February 1920; Mullins to Morris B. Gifford, 17 February 1920.

[44]Typed manuscript copy, n.d., in Desk in General Office to March 1926; "Resolutions Submitted to the Labor Committee of Seven of the Churchmen's Federation of Louisville," n.d., Box 84.

lieved, would "probably influence future legislation," though he deplored its political implications. Mullins called for new laws and enforcement of existing laws dealing with radicalism, but he optimistically urged labor and management to show "sympathy" for each other as an answer to the violent labor upheavals of the era.[45]

Fundamentalist Baptists, in contrast, railed against the dangers of unionism, alien population, and Bolshevism. Porter, for example, suggested a "drum-head court-martial" as a solution for slackers during the war.[46] Aliens were a danger to the security of the country, he maintained, because they were clustered in the large cities, and "as the cities go, sooner or later, the nation will go."[47] During the height of the Red Scare, Porter demanded "either death or deportation" for subversives without the formalities of trials.[48] He continued to see unionism as detrimental to the American system of free enterprise.[49]

During the war years Mullins's roles in denominational and interdenominational affairs shifted. Though he did not lose contact with Northern Baptists and the leaders of other denominations, Mullins took less interest in affairs outside of his denomination. While his activities outside the Southern Baptist Convention became more perfunctory, the denominational strife between Kentucky Baptist moderates and fundamentalists continued unabated. Much of the controversy centered around the *Baptist World-Western Recorder* rivalry, with Taylor in western Kentucky adding his divisive voice to the turmoil.[50] The Seminary adhered closely to the policies of the *World*, with Mullins and the faculty taking part in the reorganization and editorial policy. When editor Prestridge died in early 1914, Mullins, Sampey, and Robertson assumed editorial direction of the weekly journal. Mullins believed that

---

[45]Mullins, "Recent Phases of Democracy," *Review and Expositor* 17 (April 1920): 160, 166.

[46]*Western Recorder*, 14 June 1917; Marsden, *Fundamentalism and American Culture*, 153-64.

[47]*Western Recorder*, 27 September 1917.

[48]Ibid., 9 January 1919.

[49]Ibid., 10 April, 1, 8, 15, 22, and 29 May, 19 June 1919.

[50]W. L. Poteat to Mullins, 13 October 1916.

this was the only recourse as long as the fundamentalist Porter edited the *Recorder*.[51] As before, Mullins and Porter locked horns in useless theological and denominational debates. One controversy, for example, concerned the question of whether or not President Whitsitt had at one time written editorials for the *Western Recorder* before he became president of the Seminary and before Eaton assumed the editorship of the paper.[52] Periodically Mullins felt obliged to answer charges that the Seminary dictated the *World*'s editorial politics. He stated that other denominational agencies had publication outlets, so why should Southern Seminary be denied use of the *World?* More important was the "proximity" of the journal, which made it easy for the faculty to contribute to its publications.[53] Some of the tension abated when in 1918 Mullins chose E. B. Hatcher, son of his longtime friend W. E. Hatcher, to edit the *World*.[54] This move eliminated some criticism that the Seminary faculty wrote all the editorials for the *World*.

The doctrinal and political squabbles between Southern Baptist fundamentalists and moderates during the war years centered on the merits of union with other denominations or Northern Baptists. Mullins and the moderate Seminary faction took the position that some union dialogue was necessary for the ongoing work of all Christians.[55] Fundamentalists, on the other hand, opposed all thought of union either with their Northern Baptist brethren or other denominations.[56] Porter, for

---

[51]W. P. Harvey to Mullins, 3 April 1914; McGlothlin to Mullins, 9 June 1914; James A. White to Mullins, 24 September 1915; F. A. Sampson to Mullins, 5 August 1916; Thomas A. Johnson to Mullins, 20 March 1914.

[52]J. W. Porter to Mullins, 14 October, 23 October, 4 November, 18 November 1918; Robertson to Mullins, 21 August 1918; *Baptist World*, 14 November 1918.

[53]*Baptist World*, 26 September, 10 October 1918.

[54]*Baptist World*, 5 September 1918; E. B. Hatcher to Mullins, 5 August, 20 September 1918; B. D. Gray to Mullins, 11 September 1918.

[55]*Baptist World*, 22 August 1918; J. W. Porter to Mullins, 9 March 1916; Livingston Johnson to Mullins, 3 September 1918; John E. White to Mullins, 21 November 1918.

[56]J. B. Gambrell to Mullins, 13 March 1914; 5, 8, and 19 August 1918; *Western Recorder*, 12 September, 31 October 1918.

example, declared that Northern Baptists were beyond reclamation because of the subversive influence of the University of Chicago.[57]

Above all, the spectre of a schism in the Convention continued to haunt the moderates. Much of the fundamentalist opposition came out of Texas, in part due to the increasing competition between Southern and Southwestern seminaries. Southwestern Seminary usually took the fundamentalist tack and cut into Southern Seminary enrollment from Texas, Arkansas, Louisiana, and Mississippi.[58] J. B. Gambrell, a Texas Baptist leader, threatened a split if the rest of the states did not begin to pay more attention to the needs of the Southwest.[59] Professor Sampey, on a promotional and fund-raising trip to Alabama, frantically asked what would happen to Southern Seminary if Kentucky decided to go with the Southwest should a schism develop within the Southern Baptist Convention.[60] Though a geographical split always loomed, nothing ever came of it in this period.

Relations with Northern Baptists continued during the war period, but changed in intensity and purpose. Attempts by the Chicago faculty to revive the Baptist Theological Faculties' Union did little practical good except to continue dialogue in an oblique way. Mullins's attitude was one of only partial cooperation since the Union had little practical consequence anyway.[61] He continued to have contact with leaders of the

---

[57]*Western Recorder*, 27 February, 5 June 1919.

[58]Ibid., 11 July 1918; W. T. Lowrey to Mullins, 19 October 1915; Livingston Johnson to Mullins, 26 July, 6 August 1918. A native of western Kentucky reported that he had been encouraged to go to Southwestern Seminary because of the strong "prejudice" in that area against Southern Seminary. L. C. McGee to Mullins, 12 April 1916.

[59]Gambrell to Mullins, 30 August 1916.

[60]Sampey to Mullins, 11 June 1916.

[61]Gerald B. Smith to Mullins, 4 December 1915, 22 January 1916, 8 April 1919; Shailer Mathews to Mullins, 8 July 1916; Gerald B. Smith to Mullins, 16 December 1914; 10 February, 29 December 1915; 25 November 1918; 8 April, 23 April 1919 (Correspondence of the Baptist Theological Faculties' Union, University of Chicago Archives); Mullins to Smith, 11 February, 29 December 1915; 21 January 1918; 25 November, 11 December 1918; 5 April, 25 April 1919 (Correspondence of the Baptist Theological Faculties' Union, University of Chicago Archives).

Northern Baptist seminaries, but the amount of correspondence less-ened.[62] On the other hand, correspondence with Northern Baptist fun-damentalists rapidly increased, particularly with Curtis Lee Laws, editor of the New York *Watchman-Examiner.*[63]

An evident change in Mullins's relationships with the chief publish-ing agencies of the Northern and Southern conventions completed a shift already noted in an earlier chapter. In particular, Mullins more closely adhered to the Sunday School Board than ever before during his tenure at Southern Seminary. In 1913 the Board published a Bible study vol-ume by Mullins.[64] In the same year the Publication Society brought out his book *Freedom and Authority in Religion.*[65] In 1917 both groups jointly published Mullins's volume *The Christian Religion in Its Doctrinal Expression.* The Board and Society competed for printing this volume and Mullins's royalties increased because of this competition.[66] Editor Van Ness of the Sunday School Board declared that it was "very humil-iating" to have never published a major work of Mullins. He urged Mul-lins to think more of his impact in the South than in the North.[67] Mullins's relationships with Frost and Van Ness now became even more close.

---

[62]Clarence A. Barbour to Mullins, 11 September, 29 October, 18 November 1915; George E. Horr to Mullins, 11 June 1915; Shailer Mathews to Mullins, 23 November 1915, 29 June 1916, 3 January 1917, 26 January 1918, 13 May 1919.

[63]J. C. Massee to Mullins, 9 May 1917, 12 March 1919; J. Whitcomb Brougher to Mullins, 28 September 1919; John Roach Straton to Mullins, 12 September 1917; T. T. Shields to Mullins, 5 June 1917; David Heagle to Mul-lins, 22 June 1915; John W. Dean to Mullins, 11 April 1916; Laws to Mullins, 5 June, 20 June, 20 September, 27 September, 1 October 1916; 27 April 1917; 16 January, 24 January 1918; 12 March, 29 March 1919.

[64]*Studies in Ephesians and Colossians* (Nashville: Sunday School Board, 1913).

[65]A. J. Rowland to Mullins, 30 August, 6 September 1912; Philip L. Jones to Mullins, 9 January 1913.

[66]*Western Recorder*, 20 September 1917; A. J. Rowland to Mullins, 1 March, 3 March 1916; Guy Lawson to Mullins, 5 October, 16 October, 7 November 1916; 2 May 1917; Van Ness to Mullins, 14 February, 2, 10, 22, and 26 March, 23 April 1917.

[67]Van Ness to Mullins, 2 March 1917.

Complete cooperation characterized their connections during the war years.[68]

Mullins's interdenominational activities did not end, but they did lessen in intensity. He understood that it would be better for his denominational effectiveness to have less concern for interdenominational affiliation. Nevertheless, he did not completely sever his relations with the Federal Council, Religious Education Association, Interchurch World Movement, or the International Sunday School Association.[69] More than any other Southern Baptist leader of his time, Mullins cooperated with the Federal Council. The Southern Baptist Convention never joined the Council, and he realized that his unqualified participation would only stir up endless criticism from the fundamentalist faction. He chose, therefore, to cooperate cautiously with the Council.[70]

The beginning of World War I caught Mullins and Southern Seminary unprepared for the challenge. McGlothlin was vacationing in Paris when the war started and had difficulty returning home. He kept the faculty informed about the turmoil of the early days of the war.[71] In fact, the Seminary hardly took notice of the war for several months. The Seminary journal published an article in which an Englishman declared that the war was a struggle against evil, that is, Prussian militarism, which should be destroyed once and for all.[72] The Seminary did not, however, push the issue even though its sympathy was with the Allies. A close

---

[68]Mullins to Frost, 4, 15, and 27 March, 25 April 1916 (Frost-Bell Letters, Dargan-Carver Library); Frost to Mullins, 12 May, 15 June 1916 (Frost-Bell Letters, Dargan-Carver Library); Van Ness to Mullins, 23 February 1916; Mullins to Van Ness, 11 February, 17 February, 26 June 1920 (Van Ness Papers, Dargan-Carver Library).

[69]Henry F. Cope to Mullins, 25 April 1920; Marion Lawrence to Mullins, 21 June, 24 June 1915; J. Campbell White to Mullins, 12 December 1919.

[70]Roy B. Guild to Mullins, 5 October 1916; A. DeWitt Mason to Mullins, 13 October 1916; Charles S. MacFarland to Mullins, 21 April, 27 August 1917; 9 March 1918.

[71]McGlothlin felt "safe, unless 1870 should be repeated." McGlothlin to Mullins, 7 August 1914.

[72]John Clifford, "The European War as a Conflict of Ideas," *Review and Expositor* 12 (January 1915): 3-19.

ministerial associate of Mullins ardently defended the policies of the Wilson administration in 1916 declaring that the president acted only out of a concern for the nation's defense and not because of any aggressive tendencies.[73] Mullins participated in an Americanization Day rally on 4 July 1915, extolling the virtues of American liberty, but he never developed an ultranationalist tack.[74] He urged that European nations practice "Christian principles" and negotiate an immediate settlement.[75]

In the interim in 1917 between the Wilson speech to Congress and the formal declaration of war, Mullins editorially supported intervention as a correct and just measure. The Allies, he declared, fought against "evil" and "evil doers." A war against such forces would be a "righteous war"; the justness of the Allied cause would undoubtedly lead to victory and a "long stride toward permanent peace."[76]

After Congress declared war, Mullins and the Southern Seminary faction threw themselves into the war effort, as did nearly all churchmen in the country. Sampey helped minister to the needs of young soldiers at Camp Zachary Taylor on the outskirts of Louisville.[77] McGlothlin served as a representative of the Food Administration beginning in August 1917, and he remained in that position until the end of the war.[78] Mullins also became actively involved in war work, accepting a position as Y. M. C. A. religious director at Camp Taylor.[79] He worked hard to

---

[73]Len G. Broughton, "Is the Policy of President Wilson for National Defense Unchristian? Mr. Bryan Says It Is," *Review and Expositor* 13 (April 1916): 167-75.

[74]Louisville *Evening Post*, 6 July 1915.

[75]Mullins, "The Church in the Present World Crisis," *Homiletic Review* 73 (January 1917): 23.

[76]George D. Kelsey, *Social Ethics Among Southern Baptists, 1917-1969* (Metuchen NJ: Scarecrow Press, 1973) 105, 108; Hutchison, *The Modernist Impulse*, 236-37; Louisville *Evening Post*, 4 April 1917; Thompson, *Tried as by Fire*, 6.

[77]Sampey, *Memoirs*, 155.

[78]McGlothlin to Mullins, 14, 15, and 30 August, 20 September, 24 September, 15 October 1917.

[79]Charles A. Barbour to Mullins, 17 August, 24 September 1917.

supply each soldier with a copy of the New Testament and coordinated the efforts of several denominations in the camp.[80] His greatest challenge came in the terrible influenza epidemic that struck the camp in full force in October and November 1918, killing nearly 900 young men. Disregarding his own poor health he made daily trips to the camp to minister to the sick and dying.[81] At one time the authorities reported more than 4,000 cases in the camp. The epidemic reached such proportions that for several weeks churches and other social organizations nearly ceased to function because of severe restrictions on travel and public meetings.[82]

Mullins was not only active in religious work at Camp Taylor, he also supported the propaganda battle against the Central Powers. In speeches, articles, and sermons Mullins repeatedly endorsed the war policies of the Wilson administration.[83] He found theological implications in the conflict, proposing that Germany was guilty of starting the war and, therefore, had to repent of its sin against humanity. If necessary, he declared, America should be willing to "fight fifty years . . . to kill the beast" of Prussian militarism.[84] Mullins oversimplified the problems of Europe, but he did not predict apocalypse like his premillennialist-oriented fundamentalist brethren.[85] He did not give up hope for

---

[80]Mullins to Van Ness, 19 September 1917 (Van Ness Papers, Dargan-Carver Library); Guy C. Lawson to Mullins, 26 September 1917.

[81]Sampey, *Memoirs*, 156-57; Benjamin Jay Bush to Mullins, 5 December 1918.

[82]*Courier-Journal*, 1 October, 4 October 1918.

[83]For example, Mullins presented a patriotic speech in Lexington entitled "Why We Are in This War," declaring that only the United States could decide the outcome of the war and the peace. Florence Dillard to Mullins, 26 January, 1 March 1918. He later presented a paper on "German Kultur" to the prestigious Conversation Club. Temple Bodley to Mullins, 11 May 1918. A few days later he presented a high school graduation address entitled "America Fighting for a Great Idea." Minnie Kemp to Mullins, 22 May 1918.

[84]*Baptist World*, 15 August 1918.

[85]Manuscript copy of speech presented on Britain Day at Camp Taylor, 7 December 1918; Szasz, *The Divided Mind of Protestant America*, 84-91; Marsden, *Fundamentalism and American Culture*, 141-53.

a solution to the political problems of Europe.[86] Likewise, in the theological sphere he believed that the people of Germany still had the spark of humanity left and only needed the demise of a "military oligarchy" to return to their strong religious traditions. Exuberantly he declared that renewed efforts would return the world to sanity and a new day for religious activity in the world. In reply to the charge that Christianity failed to retard the causes of World War I, Mullins declared that "everything else has failed except Christianity"; the faith had never been given a full opportunity to function.[87] In contrast, fundamentalists like Porter dourly predicted that "the end of the age is at hand" and that the Second Coming of Christ was near.[88] Porter and other fundamentalists developed the critique that much of what was wrong with America had Germanic origins, particularly the insidious liberal theological ideas known as higher criticism.[89]

Richard H. Edmonds, a Seminary trustee and editor of the Baltimore *Manufacturers Record* who figured so prominently in the development of the New South Creed, took an ultranationalist position during the war. He clashed with Mullins when the seminarian used a story in one of his speeches about a young English flyer befriended by a German mother. Edmonds declared that the story was a fabrication of German propaganda intended to lure naive Americans into believing that the Germans were honorable.[90] Another fundamentalist like Edmonds advised that in the next Seminary catalog the word *Berlin* be deleted after McGlothlin's name. Even if the Seminary professor had earned his history doctorate years before at the University of Berlin, this patriot feared that

---

[86]Mullins, "The Church's Message for the Coming Time," *Homiletic Review* 75 (March 1918): 189.

[87]*Baptist World*, 31 January, 13 June 1918; Thompson, *Tried as by Fire*, 6-14.

[88]*Western Recorder*, 24 January 1918. Porter also favored the purging of German books and the language from the public schools.

[89]*Western Recorder*, 27 June 1918; 24 July, 14 August 1919; W. A. Ayres to Mullins, 29 October 1919; Mordecai F. Ham to Mullins, 2 January 1920.

[90]Richard H. Edmonds to Mullins, 13 June, 14 August, 27 September 1918; Gaston, *The New South Creed*, 50-51.

others might find Southern Seminary to be following the subversive ideas of Germany.[91] In contrast, a former student of Mullins declared that the hatred engendered by the war would lead to repercussions within the country that could only develop a "blood lust" that would destroy America if not checked by the role of Christians.[92]

The war years also presented other problems for Mullins. His participation in Y. M. C. A. work at Camp Taylor again put him in a controversial position. Fundamentalist Baptists demanded that Baptist ministers or chaplains be allowed free reign in ministering to the needs of servicemen regardless of Y. M. C. A. or U.S. Army regulations. Boyce Taylor declared that the Y. M. C. A. represented something worse than no religion at all, being an interdenominational palliative offering no salvation to young soldiers.[93] Some Southern Baptist clergymen claimed that the Y. M. C. A. discriminated against Baptists, and others saw dark plots against Christianity in it.[94] When the War Department enforced regulations limiting the number of ministers allowed in the military camps at any one time, fundamentalist Baptists claimed discrimination. Mullins explained that the Y. M. C. A. had had nothing to do with this decision, and he defended the efficacy of its interdenominational approach to work in the military camps.[95] Porter, in contrast, charged that the Y. M. C. A. portrayed a subversive influence to the Landmarkism of Southern Baptists since they had been included among all other Protestants in the war work.[96] One Y. M. C. A. executive said that only Mullins had been able to keep his unruly brethren in check.[97]

---

[91]M. L. Thomas to Mullins, 25 July 1918.

[92]Livingston Mays to Mullins, 4 January 1918.

[93]*Richmond* (Kentucky) *Daily Register,* 14 January 1918; O. O. Green to Mullins, 11 January, 15 January 1918.

[94]J. B. Gambrell to Mullins, 21 October 1916, 29 May 1919; W. L. Yarborough to Mullins, 13 March 1918; Victor I. Masters to Mullins, 10 August 1918; B. A. Copass to Mullins, 15 August 1918.

[95]John S. Johnson, Adjutant General, to Mullins, 6 September 1918; John R. Mott to Mullins, 7 September, 28 September, 29 October 1918; Clarence A. Barbour to Mullins, 9 June 1919.

[96]*Western Recorder,* 6 February, 1 May, 5 June 1919.

[97]Clarence A. Barbour to Mullins, 10 May 1919.

The war seriously disrupted the rhythm of Seminary life. Enrollment plummeted from 322 in 1916-1917 to only 239 two years later.[98] Wartime dislocations led to the Seminary's having great difficulty finding a source of coal in the winter of 1917 and paying inflated prices for what it could find. It took the resourcefulness of the entire faculty to keep the Seminary functioning.[99]

Conditions spawned by the war touched off the most serious faculty controversy during Mullins's tenure as president. Over the years he assumed more control over Seminary administration with little aid from the rest of the faculty. As demands for even larger amounts of money increased, Mullins took little counsel from his faculty. By the beginning of World War I the long established but unofficial "Faculty Club" no longer contributed to administrative decisions. Mullins also stifled the aspirations of several of his colleagues who longed for positions of denominational leadership. Robertson gave up his desire for such positions by applying his energies to numerous publications. Though friction never openly erupted, McGlothlin chafed under Mullins's domination over the leadership function of Seminary work. The "tension" between the two men worsened when McGlothlin accepted an appointment with the Food Administration.[100] Having broken from the Seminary moorings, McGlothlin found it easy to accept appointment as president of Furman University in 1919, thereby offering him an enlarged opportunity for denominational leadership.[101]

The rest of the faculty was jealous of Mullins's increasing power.[102] More particularly, they felt that Mullins had lost contact with the needs of the faculty. Inflation added to their woes since most had large families to support. Mullins did not work to raise their salaries, but accepted a $1,500 raise for himself. Moreover, the directorship at Camp Taylor paid him another $2,000 per year. Carver found this action to be

---

[98]Sampey, *Memoirs,* 153, 155, 157; Charles S. Gardner to Mullins, 6 May 1917.

[99]S. H. Newbold to Mullins, 14 December 1917.

[100]Carver, "Recollections," 8-11, 45, 57.

[101]McGlothlin to Mullins, 1 July 1918, 27 May 1919.

[102]Carver, "Recollections," 11-12.

the greatest blot on Mullins's association with the faculty, and while Sampey did not directly condemn Mullins in his *Memoirs,* he recalled that he himself gave nearly half his time to war work at Camp Taylor without remuneration while keeping up with his duties at Southern Seminary.[103] This tension never broke into the public forum, thereby saving the Seminary from a divisive issue that could have been used with telling effect by its fundamentalist enemies.

The war years closed with the League of Nations as a major political issue. Mullins supported the concept of an international peace-keeping body, as did the rest of the faculty.[104] In the *Baptist World* Hatcher decried the possibility of defeat of the treaty in the Senate and called for a presidential tour publicizing the merits of the proposed League of Nations.[105] Mullins cooperated fully with the League to Enforce Peace, speaking at rallies at the University of Kentucky and Berea College.[106] He also cooperated along these lines with interdenominational groups, such as the Committee on War and the Religious Outlook and the World Alliance for International Friendship Through the Churches. He served as a director of both groups but was unable to attend meetings, which were usually held in New York City.[107] This activity, though limited, evidenced Mullins's concern for international peace and cooperation. A Kentucky fundamentalist, Noel Gaines, on the other hand, reviled Mullins for supporting the League of Nations. Gaines proposed an inane alternative, the "Peace Plan of the Prince of Peace" and scolded the League founders for not directly mentioning God's name in the document.[108] The

---

[103]Ibid., 10-11; Sampey, *Memoirs,* 155.

[104]Robert Moats Miller, *American Protestantism and Social Issues, 1919-1939* (Chapel Hill: University of North Carolina Press, 1958) 323; Miller, "Social Attitudes of American Baptists, 1919-1929," *Chronicle* (April 1956): 74.

[105]*Baptist World,* 19 December 1918, 7 August 1919.

[106]Allan P. Ames to Mullins, 23 October, 22 November 1918; W. J. Campbell to Mullins, 22 January 1919; C. Rexford Raymond to Mullins, 10 June 1919.

[107]Angus Dun to Mullins, 23 June 1919; Samuel McCrea Cavert to Mullins, 15 July, 25 July, 29 September 1919; 30 March 1920; Henry A. Atkinson to Mullins, 11 May 1920.

[108]Noel Gaines to Mullins, 26 February, 8 April, 30 April 1919.

Western Recorder likewise did not take an interest in the League because of its apocalyptic view of the war.

The war years provided a time of severe testing for Mullins. All growth, including any expansion of Seminary endowment or the Student Fund, was precluded by the turmoil of the times. Continuing his moderate evangelical approach in the theological and denominational spheres, Mullins consolidated his personal control over the faculty and turned toward more consistent cooperation with the agencies of the Southern Baptist Convention, particularly the Sunday School Board. He continued to show an interest in denominational and interdenominational affairs outside the confines of the Convention, but the intensity of his efforts lessened throughout the war years continuing a trend that had begun several years before. By 1920 Mullins was established as the most important moderate Baptist leader in the country.

8   THE OPENING BATTLE
OF THE ANTIEVOLUTION WAR

Throughout the 1920s, Mullins maintained his roles as administrator, theologian, and denominational leader with increasing difficulty as he reacted to crucial religious and secular issues including evolution, Prohibition, and the election of 1928. These struggles tested all of his ability and experience gained through twenty years at Southern Seminary. As a result of an inordinate amount of time and energy expended on the evolution controversy and the construction of a new Seminary plant, Mullins published only one major book during the decade, *Christianity at the Crossroads*, in 1924. Though he played a key role in the fight against antievolution legislation, he became increasingly absorbed in the construction of a new Seminary during the 1920s.

In the early phases of the evolution controversy, Mullins's moderating influence dampened the impact of his fundamentalist brethren, who proposed legislation. Moreover, the fundamentalist-moderate cleavage surfaced in full public view because of the controversy over evolution. This conflict cut across denominational lines forming new interdenominational coalitions. Moderates generally opposed legislation, while fundamentalists supported restriction of the teaching of evolution. Until 1925 Mullins held a dominant position in the Southern Baptist leadership and commanded wide respect within the Southern Baptist Convention. Thereafter, his leadership posture rapidly deteriorated. In the latter part of the decade his innate conservatism won out over his progressive tendencies. In the election of 1928 he and fundamentalists cooperated in the anti-Smith campaign.

The denominational warfare between the *World* and *Recorder* exemplified the cleavage between the moderate and fundamentalist wings of Southern Baptists. These factions became openly antagonistic during the first phase of the evolution controversy. These weekly papers, moreover, continued to represent the two distinct factions among Southern Baptists, not only in Kentucky but throughout the South as well, with Mullins continually battling the fundamentalists for control of denominational interests. When the Convention initiated a denominationwide fund drive, the 75 Million Campaign, many leaders urged that old differences be forgotten in favor of a united fund drive. As part of this movement, some leaders outside the state suggested that Kentucky Baptists merge the two papers for the sake of denominational efficiency.[1]

The Seminary had, of course, close contact with the publication of the *World,* particularly since the reorganization in 1914. After E. B. Hatcher became editor, the Seminary faction continued their heavy contribution to its publication of news and doctrinal articles despite its financial struggle for existence. When the Baptist State Board of Missions urged merger with the *Recorder* in 1919, the leaders of the *World* faction jumped at the chance to ease themselves out of a financially weak publication.[2] The Board of Missions agreed to make an outright purchase of the papers to be continued under the name *Western Recorder.* The parent companies, the Baptist Book Concern for the *Recorder* and the Baptist World Publishing Company for the *World,* would continue to operate as publishing houses and bookstores. H. Boyce Taylor, however, refused to sell his rights to the *News and Truths,* a move that would have eliminated a source of trouble for the Seminary. Citing the need for the denominational unity because of the 75 Million Campaign, Corre-

---

[1]J. B. Gambrell to Mullins, 9 September 1919.

[2]Thomas A. Johnson to Mullins, 15 May 1918; E. B. Hatcher to Mullins, 7 April, 7, 9, and 14 August 1919.

sponding Secretary O. E. Bryan of the Board declared that Kentucky Baptists could only reach their financial goals through merger of the papers.[3]

As part of the arrangement, Porter became managing editor and Hatcher became news editor of the new publication, thereby giving both factions representation. Bryan admitted that "several raw edges" existed, but he hoped that the factions would keep the peace.[4] For a short time the new arrangement seemed to work. Porter and Hatcher were each given an editorial page in the first issue of the merged paper, but within two weeks Hatcher no longer had an equal amount of editorial space. The managing editor, moreover, failed to offer much support for the 75 Million drive.[5]

Both factions accepted the uneasy truce afforded by the merger. Porter and Mullins superficially developed more cordial relations, but Porter's dominance of the new *Recorder* soon stirred the conflict anew.[6] At the time this controversy was brewing, Mullins made plans to go to Europe with J. B. Gambrell to visit European Baptists.[7] When Hatcher complained about the editorial arrangements, a member of the Board of Missions denied that an anti-Seminary faction controlled the *Recorder*. He warned Mullins, furthermore, not to start another pro-Seminary paper like the old *World*.[8]

Just before Mullins left for Europe the Board worked out a new compromise, agreeing to appoint a new editor. Hatcher, however, demanded that Mullins support his side of the conflict since the *Recorder* and the Board had removed him from any responsibility on the paper.[9]

---

[3]*Baptist World*, 21 August 1919; *Western Recorder*, 28 August 1919.

[4]Bryan to Mullins, 9 September 1919; *Western Recorder*, 21 August, 4 September, 11 September 1919.

[5]*Western Recorder*, 4, 11, and 18 September, 2 October 1919.

[6]Porter to Mullins, 6, 20, and 24 May 1920.

[7]Mullins, *Mullins*, 164-72.

[8]W. W. Landrum to Mullins, 23 March 1920.

[9]W. M. Seay, secretary of the Board of Missions, to Mullins, n.d., (Box 87); Hatcher to Mullins, 2 June 1920.

Mullins refused to intervene, believing that the *Recorder* editorial situation was settled with the impending election of a new editor. He left Louisville in late June 1920.[10] Mullins thus acquiesced to the Board's decision to eliminate Hatcher from the editorship, in return for the promise that Porter would also be eased out. Hatcher reacted violently, charging that only he had been able to pay off most of the debts of the *World* from which all the stockholders benefited and now he was being sacrificed for denominational unity to placate the real enemies of the Seminary.[11] In response to urgent pleas from Mullins, Sampey and Robertson worked to appease Hatcher. Robertson soon replied that through his influence Hatcher had been "called" to a pastorate at Blue Mountain, Mississippi, thereby removing him from the scene of conflict.[12]

However, the Board procrastinated on the promise to appoint a new editor, and then offered the position to Porter, taking advantage of Mullins's absence to assume control of Kentucky denominational affairs.[13] Mullins immediately confronted the corresponding secretary of the Board with the accusation that the agreements of a few months before had been broken. He declared that the Board had not honored the "moral obligations" to the *World* since it was never fully represented in the merged paper. The only solution, Mullins contended, was to demand Porter's immediate resignation and appoint an outsider as editor.[14] By the time Mullins returned from Europe, the Board had moved toward acceding to his demands. Secretary Bryan declared that he had "been through the fire as never before," but he believed that Porter would resign and a new editor could be appointed.[15]

Within a couple of weeks Porter announced his resignation, declaring that the Board "rightfully" felt the *Recorder* needed a full-time editor. The Board considered appointment of Victor I. Masters, an editor

---

[10]Mullins, *Mullins*, 168-76.

[11]Hatcher to Mullins, 2 June, 25 June, 19 July 1920.

[12]Robertson to Mullins, 20 July 1920; Sampey to Mullins, 23 July 1920.

[13]*Western Recorder*, 14 October 1920; Sampey to Mullins, 19 October 1920.

[14]Mullins to Bryan, 30 September 1920. Mullins was in Paris at the time.

[15]Bryan to Mullins, 15 December 1920.

on the Home Mission Board in Atlanta, as chief executive of the *Recorder*, but only if Mullins approved. Mullins consented and personally urged that Masters accept the post.[16] Masters pledged his personal loyalty, asking for Mullins's "patience" and "confidence."[17] The new editor initially displayed a fawning attitude, leading Mullins to the conclusion that he could easily control the editorial policy of the *Recorder*. Mullins's confidence grew even more after the Convention elected him as president by an overwhelming majority a few months later.[18] However, if Mullins thought he could dominate Masters, he soon found that Masters was his own man and a fundamentalist nearly as conservative as Porter.[19] The addition of Masters to the ranks of Kentucky Baptist fundamentalists only compounded Mullins's problems in leading his Southern Baptist brethren.

The differences between fundamentalists, represented by Porter and Masters, and the moderates, represented by Mullins and the Seminary faction, soon became more evident as the antievolution controversy unfolded in the early 1920s. By this time premillennialism and fundamentalism had become synonymous, and the teaching of evolution had become the principal adversary of this ultraconservative movement. Kentucky was the first state where fundamentalists gathered enough strength to propose antievolution bills before a state legislature. Moderates and fundamentalists in the major Protestant denominations in the state divided over the evolution issue with the latter supporting the introduction of antievolution legislation. To fundamentalists, evolution became the focal point of their frustrations in trying to retain control over

---

[16]*Western Recorder*, 13 January 1921; Landrum to Mullins, 11 January 1921; Mullins to Masters, 11 January 1921; Thompson, *Tried as by Fire*, 37.

[17]Masters to Mullins, 13 January, 19 January 1921.

[18]Masters displayed an awe of Mullins in their correspondence before Masters came to the *Recorder*. For example, he declared Mullins to be one of the "abler men" or one of "our leaders." Masters to Mullins, 24 April 1916, 1 November 1918. To a Baptist leader Mullins gave the impression that he desired total control of the *Recorder*. Gambrell to Mullins, 20 January 1921; Mullins to W. C. Bitting, 20 May 1921.

[19]Hill, "The Ethical Emphases of the Editors of Baptist Journals Published in the Southeastern Region of the United States, 1915-1940," 10, 148, 274-95.

a rapidly changing country. World War I unleashed the latent hypersensitivity of fundamentalists to patterns of behavior that they considered to be un-American. Evolution presented a convenient target because it could be identified as a theory of foreign origin. Fundamentalists also attacked other areas, such as immigration or Prohibition, and their activity spilled over into the political arena. Kentucky fundamentalists, with Porter and Masters as prime examples, exhibited these same characteristics.[20]

Through the pages of the *Recorder,* Porter and Masters led the initial phase of the campaign for legislation.[21] Particularly in his last year as editor of that journal, Porter turned to evolution as the most pernicious issue in America. While previously he had found the influence of German Kultur on higher criticism to be the most insidious influence on the nation, he now perceived the teaching of evolution to young Americans to be the greatest danger to church and state.[22] At first, the issue was primarily a denominational matter, with Porter supporting the attacks by evangelist T. T. Martin on President William Louis Poteat of Wake Forest.[23] When Masters became editor he immediately extended the antievolution campaign to public education, characterizing evolution as part of an "American Tragedy in Education." "The way out?" he asked, "Suppose we leave that part of the subject for future consideration."[24]

---

[20]Thompson, *Tried as by Fire,* 101-36; Ellis, "Edgar Young Mullins and the Crisis of Moderate Southern Baptist Leadership," 176; Weber, *Living in the Shadow of the Second Coming,* 177.

[21]Bailey, *Southern White Protestantism,* 75.

[22]*Western Recorder,* 24 July, 14 August 1919; 22 January, 26 February, 13 May, 3 June, 17 June, 15 July 1920.

[23]Ibid., 22 January, 29 January, 5 February, 12 February 1920. Porter supported Martin in an editorial on 6 May 1920. Willard B. Gatewood, Jr., declared these articles to be the "opening volley" in the North Carolina antievolution controversy. Gatewood, *Preachers, Pedagogues, and Politicians: The Evolution Controversy in North Carolina, 1920-1927* (Chapel Hill: University of North Carolina Press, 1966) 30.

[24]*Western Recorder,* 3 February 1921.

From early 1921 through the 1922 meeting of the Kentucky General Assembly, Masters and Porter used the *Recorder* to promote the antievolution campaign with each issue including at least one article or editorial denouncing evolution.[25] There was, indeed, a purpose behind so many antievolution articles. By the middle of 1921 this trend became clear as Masters urged his readers to "Tell your state legislators that if the public schools and colleges cannot function for Christianity, you have vowed before God Almighty and his son that is [*sic*] shall not function against it."[26] A short while later another ardent fundamentalist, M. P. Hunt, declared that he had evidence that the University of Kentucky was "infected" with German rationalism and evolution. He demanded that the university assure the people of the state that it did not attempt to destroy the faith of its students or face opposition to appropriations in the 1922 meeting of the General Assembly.[27]

Other fundamentalist Baptists played key roles in the antievolution campaign. Several associations railed against evolution, passing resolutions demanding legislation outlawing the teaching of evolution in the public schools. The most ominous sign was a resolution passed by the Long Run Association, which included churches in Louisville and Jefferson County, the most heavily populated part of the state.[28] Porter added his vehement style to the campaign in the *Recorder*. While the General Association of Kentucky Baptists did not pass an antievolution resolution, the State Board of Missions "unanimously adopted" a resolution calling for the removal of the teaching of evolution by legislative act.[29] William Bell Riley, a graduate of Southern Seminary and pastor of the Minneapolis, Minnesota, First Baptist Church, made a sixty-day tour

---

[25]Authors such as William Bell Riley, J. W. Porter, T. T. Martin, John D. Freeman, J. J. Taylor, J. B. Cranfill, and William Jennings Bryan castigated evolution. Between 24 March 1921 and the end of the legislative session one year later, the *Recorder* printed at least one antievolution article or editorial each week.

[26]*Western Recorder*, 7 July 1921.

[27]Ibid., 28 July 1921.

[28]Ibid., 18 August, 22 September, 20 October 1921.

[29]Ibid., 15 December 1921; Thompson, *Tried as by Fire*, 130.

of the state just before the legislature met, proposing antievolution legislation during his evangelistic sermons. As a founder of the World's Christian Fundamentals Association, Riley gave his personal sanction for the Kentucky antievolution campaign, if not for the W. C. F. A.[30]

The *Recorder* campaign did not go unnoticed by Mullins, but he decided not to enter the fray. He found that "some of the Brethren" wanted to attack evolution directly, but he believed this to be a "great mistake."[31] When the *Recorder* attacked President Poteat of Wake Forest, Mullins defended the beleaguered executive, but only privately.[32] As the evolution controversy developed, the ill feelings of the recent *Recorder-World* merger degenerated into personal recriminations. Porter charged that Mullins misappropriated Seminary endowment funds. Mullins vehemently denied the charges and demanded an apology, which Porter privately acknowledged.[33]

The fundamentalist Baptist antievolution campaign culminated in the introduction of two bills in the Kentucky General Assembly, the Rash Bill in the state Senate and the Ellis Bill in the House of Representatives. Three men played key roles in defeating the aspirations of Kentucky fundamentalists. The efforts of Frank L. McVey, president of the University of Kentucky, E. L. Powell, pastor of the Louisville First Christian Church, and Mullins blunted the demands of the fundamentalists.[34]

---

[30]Stewart G. Cole, *The History of Fundamentalism* (Hamden CT: Archon Books, 1963) 298-317; Furniss, *The Fundamentalist Controversy*, 42; LeRoy Johnson, "The Evolution Controversy During the 1920's" (Ph.D. diss., New York University, 1954) 109.

[31]Mullins to Z. T. Cody, 15 September 1921.

[32]W. L. Poteat to Mullins, 24 February 1920.

[33]Mullins to Porter, 10 May, 19 May 1921; Porter to Mullins, 17 May 1921.

[34]William E. Ellis, "The Kentucky Evolution Controversy" (M.A. thesis, Eastern Kentucky University, 1967) 1-4, 40-94; Ellis, "Frank LeRond McVey: His Defense of Academic Freedom," *The Register of the Kentucky Historical Society* 67 (January 1969): 37-54. Willard Gatewood, Jr., reported that those who opposed antievolution legislation were "moderates" or others who supported academic freedom. Gatewood, *Preachers, Pedagogues, and Politicians*, 231. The Rash Bill provided a fine of $50 to $1,000 for teaching evolution. The

Powell and Mullins had been friends for many years prior to the evolution controversy. McVey came to the University of Kentucky as president in 1917.[35] All three were members of the prestigious Louisville Conversation Club, which gave them a point of contact before the evolution controversy started.[36] In addition, they cooperated with the Churchmen's Federation, a progressive reform organization based in Louisville that conducted an industrial survey during the Red Scare in 1919.[37]

The public response of these three leaders varied. McVey took an active role publicizing the virtues of the university, appearing before the state legislature on two occasions and organizing the opponents of anti-evolution legislation. Powell functioned in much the same role. He acted as liaison with liberal Disciples ministers and also appeared before the state legislature.[38] Mullins, on the other hand, chose a more cautious role. He encouraged the State Board of Missions to drop its legislative campaign, warning their corresponding secretary that the bills violated "our age-long Baptist principle of separation of church and state." Christians had the right to demand that atheism not be taught, but the church should not specifically prohibit a "scientific teaching" such as evolution. Furthermore, he urged the introduction of a less stringent bill that would only protect Christianity in general terms.[39] The night before a scheduled hearing on the Senate bill, Mullins met with a committee from the Board of Missions chaired by Porter. He tried to persuade them to see the "error of their way" by advocating the innocuous bill suggested

---

more stringent Ellis Bill in the House included one year in prison for the person found guilty of teaching evolution. The offending institution could also be fined and have its charter revoked for allowing evolution to be taught. *Journal of the Kentucky House of Representatives, 1922*, 2:1668; *Journal of the Kentucky Senate, 1922*, 2:1082-83.

[35]Ellis, "Frank LeRond McVey," 38.

[36]*Conversation Club, List of Members and Activities, 1879-1935* (Louisville, 1935) 6, 49-50; Frank McVey to Mullins, 19 December 1919; *The Louisville Blue Book*, 1923, 13.

[37]See chapter 7.

[38]Ellis, "Frank LeRond McVey," 37-54.

[39]Mullins to Calvin M. Thompson, 31 January 1922.

to Secretary Thompson. Though Porter and his adherents did not falter in their appeals for stringent measures, Mullins believed that his action divided the Baptist antievolutionists on the committee to the extent that they did not move with concerted action. At least one proponent of legislation, M. P. Hunt, later announced that he deferred to Mullins's judgment, a sign of Mullins's moderating influence.[40]

Mullins's first public response came with his appearance along with Powell and McVey before the Senate in opposition to the Rash Anti-Evolution Bill. All three offered substitute bills "as the best way out." Porter, however, testified to the necessity of passage of the Rash Bill. The Mullins substitute prohibited any theory that would "undermine the religious beliefs" of students in tax-supported schools. He appealed to the legislators to pass "no legislation interfering with science," even though "some science teachers had showed a lack of common sense and tact." Religious people, he said, needed assurance that their faith would not be attacked. Advocating a substitute bill, Mullins repudiated the actions of Porter and the Board of Missions who urged passage of the Rash Bill.[41]

The Seminary faction followed Mullins's lead and denounced the proposed legislation. A. T. Robertson expressed his hope that the bills would be defeated.[42] R. J. Pirkey, pastor of the Louisville Broadway Baptist Church and Mullins's minister, denied the right of a legislature to pass such "un-American" statutes.[43]

The *Courier-Journal* remonstrated against any concessions to the antievolutionists and singled out Mullins's substitute as a "compromise with wrong," asserting that the bill undermined the separation of church and state.[44] Mullins replied that his bill did not distinguish Christianity from other faiths as charged by the *Courier* and, therefore, protected all faiths or "lack of" faith. In the same issue the *Courier* attempted to de-

---

[40]Mullins to McVey, 2 March 1922; Mullins to J. H. Franklin, 24 October 1922 (a collection in the files of the American Baptist Historical Society, Rochester, New York); *Courier-Journal*, 8 February 1922.

[41]*Courier-Journal*, 3 February 1922; Thompson, *Tried as by Fire*, 130-31.

[42]Louisville *Evening Post*, 14 February 1922.

[43]*Courier-Journal*, 6 February 1922.

[44]Ibid., 4 February 1922.

termine "who would decide what is an attack on religion . . ." or even "what is religion."[45] Mullins retorted that his bill "aimed to secure, not the recognition of religious beliefs, but only of religious and nonreligious rights." "The substitutes were offered," he contended, "to prevent something much worse."[46] In effect, he maintained that the substitute bill defused an explosive legislative session that seemed bent on passing the Rash Bill. The *Courier*, however, continued to attack Mullins's conciliatory efforts.[47] Mullins hedged, but this may have been his strategy, hoping to obfuscate the issue into a meaningless debate and thereby divide the antievolutionists.

Mullins took a stronger stance against the antievolution bills after McVey published a "Statement to the people of Kentucky" and the Senate Committee on Kentucky Statutes rejected the Rash Bill.[48] Mullins now unequivocally supported McVey's statement, a defense of the university. He found that McVey's proclamation met the requirements of "any reasonable person." The Baptist leader praised McVey for recognizing the "folly of laws prescribing what is and what is not science" and sharply criticized the antievolution measures pending before the state legislature.[49]

McVey expressed "appreciation of the way in which you stated the matter for it puts us in the same team." He implored further cooperation "to allay anything that is likely to result in sectarian controversy."[50] Mullins replied that he received letters from many who disagreed with McVey's statement, but he expected this reaction from the adamant foes of evolution. He maintained personal enmity for legislation and advocated a substitute "in order to save what looked like an ugly situation . . . after laboring hard for a number of hours the night before with a committee to convince them of the error of their way in pushing the

---

[45]Ibid., 6 February 1922.

[46]Ibid., 9 February 1922.

[47]Ibid., 10 February, 14 February 1922.

[48]Ibid., 12 February 1922.

[49]Louisville *Evening Post*, 14 February 1922; Mullins to Lewis Humphrey, 13 February 1922.

[50]McVey to Mullins, 14 February 1922.

original bill [the Rash Bill]." In principle he thought the substitute was sound, "yet such laws are exceedingly difficult to interpret and to enforce and allow room for all kinds of differences and recriminations." He warned that the situation was more serious than many thought, particularly in rural areas, and claimed that the "want of common sense and tact on the part of some teachers" caused the current crisis. As a resident of Kentucky for nearly thirty years, Mullins observed that Kentuckians were "conservative" on educational topics, and sometimes "extremely determined, not to say reckless," when challenged by the newer currents of thought. "Kentucky needed a few mediators," Mullins contended, "between the people and the more progressive teachers and educated men."[51]

Mullins made every attempt to mediate between extremes in the subsequent antievolution struggle. At the end of the immediate legislative crisis in 1922 he fulfilled this pledge. McVey's public announcements gave Mullins the courage to repudiate legislation. The fact that Mullins offered a substitute, but did not push for passage, demonstrated that he trusted McVey to counteract any further suspicions of the university. Like McVey, he suggested a substitute measure, fearing passage of the Rash Bill in the Senate. As a leader of a conservative denomination, he could not go too far in opposition to legislation, but his acceptance of McVey's statement showed the means he would use to suppress what he considered "folly." At the same time Mullins realized his responsibility to his denomination and the Seminary. In his efforts he defied Porter and the fundamentalists, thereby proving his willingness to use the prestige of his position to influence the defeat of antievolution legislation. On the other hand, although he supported an anti-racetrack gambling bill, he did not choose to appear before the state legislature. In Tennessee no major religious leader testified before the state legislature against the Butler antievolution bill in 1925, as had Powell and Mullins in 1922. The courageous stand of these two men averted a fundamentalist victory in that crucial legislative session.[52]

---

[51]Mullins to McVey, 2 March 1922.

[52]This was the only time Mullins ever appeared before the state legislature in support of or in opposition to a bill, exemplifying the critical nature of the bill as he saw it. *Western Recorder*, 26 January 1922; Kenneth K. Bailey, "The Antievolution Crusade of the Nineteen-Twenties" (Ph.D. diss., Vanderbilt University, 1953) 93.

Mullins's greatest service came in sidetracking further efforts toward legislation. Privately and publicly he repudiated antievolution restriction, but at the same time he tried to reconcile the factious elements.[53] In correspondence he cautioned his fellow Baptists about the pernicious implications of antievolution legislation. To a Louisville Baptist who questioned his orthodoxy because of his opposition to the 1922 bills, Mullins replied that no legislature had the right to censor any specific idea or concept, for instance, evolution, but should only protect the liberties of free speech and religion.[54] During the two years preceding the 1924 General Assembly, Mullins continually refused to grant his sanction to those who wanted antievolution legislation. To Porter, who urged the Seminary president to join the fundamentalist forces, Mullins replied that it was "inexpedient" to continue the antievolution agitation and warned that the campaign would serve no good purpose either for the denomination or the state of Kentucky.[55] Mullins gave the same counsel to other Baptists.[56]

------

[53]Mullins to R. H. Pitt, 28 March 1922. Bryan appeared before the General Assembly on 19 January 1922. The first half of his speech concerned the adoption of a state trade commission and the problem of farm bankruptcy. In the latter part of his talk he staunchly advocated a law to prohibit the teaching of Darwinism, believing such instruction to be "anti-Bible." Bryan then traveled to Lexington and delivered his famous Chautauqua lecture entitled "The Enemies of the Bible." He warned students against the professor who taught the Darwinian theory as "the most dangerous man that could be met." A Lexington Baptist minister, Walter L. Brock, successfully introduced a resolution to the crowd that the state legislature outlaw evolution in the public school system. Bryan spent a few more days in the state, speaking against the teaching of evolution. *Courier-Journal*, 20 January 1922; Alonzo Fortune, "The Kentucky Campaign Against the Teaching of Evolution," *Journal of Religion* 2 (May 1922): 228; *Lexington Herald*, 20 January 1922; Arthur M. Miller, "Kentucky and the Theory of Evolution," *Science* 55 (17 March 1922): 178; Lawrence W. Levine, *Defender of the Faith: William Jennings Bryan; The Last Decade, 1915-1945* (New York: Oxford University Press, 1965) 228.

[54]Mullins to Josie H. Cahoe, 23 March 1922.

[55]Porter to Mullins, 18 October, 23 October 1922; Mullins to Porter, 20 October, 25 October 1922.

[56]Mullins to L. L. Gwaltney, 6 March 1923; Mullins to A. R. Evans, 7 February 1922; Mullins to Louie D. Newton, 28 March 1922.

Mullins took this stand despite the fears about teaching evolution in the public schools. He denied that science had ever disproven any of the verities of the evangelical faith. The greatest danger, however, was that a "generation of young people is very likely to grow up in some schools who will never become conscious of the existence of such a thing as evangelical Christianity, because the atmosphere in which they live is so impregnated with denials." He contended that he was not an "alarmist," but only interested in religion's receiving a fair hearing. Christianity, furthermore, was a "supernatural" faith. Moderate evangelical Christians, Mullins explained, were angry because fundamentalists and modernists forced them to the extremes.[57] During the evolution controversy of the 1920s the bifurcation of his denomination was a distinct possibility. Mullins did all he could to avert such a schism among Southern Baptists.[58]

There is strong evidence that Mullins influenced the *Recorder* into a more moderate position on the subject of legislation. As president of the Southern Baptist Convention from 1921 to 1923 and the Baptist World Alliance from 1923 to 1928, Mullins held the highest offices within the denomination. His prestige was at its zenith. The number of articles by Mullins in the *Recorder* in 1923 more than doubled the number in 1922.[59] Moreover, Mullins neutralized the influence of Porter. Prior to the evolution controversy, Mullins's contributions to the *Recorder* consisted mainly of articles about the welfare of the Seminary. Thereafter, he wrote more articles about religion and science. Mullins donated only one article on evolution throughout the remainder of 1922 to the *Recorder*, maintaining that science and religion were separate. He scored those who made excessive claims for science, since "biology in the strict sci-

---

[57]Mullins to E. B. Pollard, 14 September 1922.

[58]Eighmy, "The Social Conscience of Southern Baptists from 1900 to the Present as Reflected in Their Organized Life," 133; Blake Smith, "The Evolution Controversy: Remembrance and Reflection," in *Darwinism in Texas: The Exhibition in the Texas History Center*, ed. Thomas F. Glick (Austin: University of Texas Press, 1972) 36.

[59]*New York Times*, 27 July 1923. Mullins published seven articles in the *Recorder* in 1922 and seventeen in 1923.

entific sense of the word has not one syllable against the supernatural."[60]

The reactions of Porter and Masters offered a counterpoint to those of Mullins. After the immediate legislative crisis ended with the defeat of the Ellis Bill in the Kentucky House of Representatives in March 1922, Masters continued his vituperations against evolution and his support for legislation. He viewed with interest the controversy in South Carolina and implied that success there would influence later events in Kentucky.[61] By the middle of 1922, however, Masters made fewer editorial comments, tending to emphasize the dangers of modernism with evolution as only a concomitant evil. Porter brought out a pseudoscientific refutation of Darwinism entitled *Evolution—A Menace*.[62] Using characteristic sarcasm, he also devised a "church for the Descendants of Apes," with appropriate names for Sunday school classes, such as "Industrious Ants," "Shrewd Foxes," and "Snakes in the Grass."[63]

The number of articles by Porter in the *Recorder* steadily declined throughout 1922 though his activities continued on other fronts. At the end of the year, he gained approval from the annual General Association of Baptists in Kentucky, which voted to "withhold all financial support from any of our denominational schools, in which is taught the Darwinian or any other theory of evolution that contradicts any part of the Holy Writ," and urged the Southern Baptist Association to concur. The Association, however, did not make a public demand for antievolution legislation. For most antievolutionists the struggle now turned inward, within the denomination, while the more violent foes of evolution continued their rancorous crusade for legislation.[64]

---

[60]*Western Recorder*, 28 September 1922.

[61]Ibid., 30 March 1922.

[62]The *Recorder* advertised the book as early as 9 March 1922.

[63]*Western Recorder*, 4 May 1922.

[64]*Proceedings of the General Association of Baptists in Kentucky, 1922*, 5. Furniss reported that this group "pledged itself later in 1922 to enter the political campaign in order to elect a legislature more amenable to the Fundamen-

Porter continued to contribute articles to the *Recorder,* but he discussed evolution only once in 1923. Even then he did not mention anti-evolution legislation.[65] Losing his influence at the *Recorder,* Porter stepped outside regular denominational channels to organize and co-edit the *Baptist Monthly Magazine,* later known as the *American Baptist.* Another ardent fundamentalist, T. T. Martin, served as coeditor. First published in April 1924, the *Baptist Monthly* emphasized evolution as its primary adversary. In the first issue, Martin, seconded by Porter, proposed "through local boards of trustees and through legislatures, to drive out every evolution teacher . . . and text book."[66] Porter, with characteristic invective, thought, "Naturally, most of the evolutionists live in large cities. There's a reason. For a few cents, they can hold a family reunion in the zoo every Sunday morning."[67] Later Porter applauded Tennessee's Butler Law and commented that this would "stir up the animals. . . . Already the infidel with twitching ears, is raising the cry of academic freedom."[68]

Expanding the Anti-Evolution League of Minnesota, founded by William Bell Riley, Porter and Martin formed the Anti-Evolution League

---

talists' demands." Furniss, *The Fundamentalist Controversy,* 82. Footnotes for this paragraph do not correspond with any such statement by the General Association. Though this proposition may have been discussed, the minutes for the meeting do not mention any pledge or resolution. A "special" to the *New York Times,* 18 November 1922, mentioned that "The anti-evolution campaign will be carried into the political fights next year [1923], when members of the legislature will be elected. Candidates will be questioned as to their attitudes on the evolution theory." Perhaps Furniss drew his conclusion from this article. No real effort was made to make evolution an issue in the elections. If Baptists proposed such a campaign, the *Recorder* would have led the fight. The *Recorder* did not repeat its legislative campaign.

[65]*Western Recorder,* 25 January, 5 April, 19 April, 7 June, 30 August, 27 September, 4 October, 29 November, 20 December 1923.

[66]T. T. Martin, "Evolution and Legislation," *Baptist Monthly Magazine* 1 (April 1924): 41.

[67]J. W. Porter, "Random Remarks—Evolution," *Baptist Monthly Magazine* 1 (June 1924): 13-14.

[68]Porter, "Evolution in Tennessee," *Baptist Monthly Magazine* 2 (April 1925): 9-10.

of America.[69] Porter, as president of the League, vowed to enlist American and Canadian fundamentalist evangelists to propagandize its program, the "Bible-Christ-and-Constitution Campaign against Evolution in Tax-Supported Schools." Porter maintained that the teaching of evolution was unconstitutional. The grandiose plans of the League, however, never materialized, and it disbanded within a year.[70]

Porter's mode of agitation closely resembled that of William Jennings Bryan and other prominent antievolutionists. He often negated logic in favor of attempts to ridicule evolution through bitter humor, perhaps believing this technique had great effect on his uneducated brethren.[71] In Kentucky antievolutionists like Porter followed Bryan, whom they looked upon as their leader, seeking to "blend populistic democracy and the old-fashioned evangelistic faith."[72] Bryan proposeed the "populistic" ideal that ultimate control of education resided in the parents, that is, the taxpayers.[73] Fundamentalist leaders in Kentucky followed suit stressing the misplaced monopolistic control of education in the hands of anti-Christian forces.[74] Anti-intellectualism was a corollary to the ethos of these spokesmen. For example, Masters declared, "[T]hese unbelieving savants in their blindness are headed toward killing the goose that lays their salary egg."[75]

The crucial year in the Kentucky evolution controversy was 1923. Though Porter's influence was still strong, Mullins now held the key

---

[69]William Bell Riley, "Southern Baptist Convention and Skepticism," *Baptist Beacon* 1 (April 1924): 8.

[70]Cole, *The History of Fundamentalism*, 261.

[71]Thomas D. Clark, "A History of Baptist Involvement in Higher Education," *Review and Expositor* 64 (Winter 1967): 19-30.

[72]Gatewood, *Controversy in the Twenties: Fundamentalism, Modernism, and Evolution*, 29. See, for example, the *Western Recorder*, 23 June 1921, 19 January, 16 March, 30 March 1922, for editorials that praise Bryan's stand against evolution with the rhetoric of a political campaign.

[73]See, for example, Bryan in the *Western Recorder*, 23 June 1921; Szasz, *The Divided Mind of Protestant America*, 117-25.

[74]*Western Recorder*, 24 February 1921.

[75]Ibid.

leadership position. By this time, McVey no longer took a vital interest in the conflict. As long as legislation posed no serious threat, he saw no reason to jeopardize the future of the university by unwarranted actions. Mullins, however, became more deeply involved. His moderating influence dampened the ferocity of Masters's editorials and frustrated the legislative designs of Porter.

As president of the 1923 Southern Baptist Convention annual meeting, Mullins prepared the way for acceptance of a compromise on evolution. Owing to the antievolution campaign in other states, most religious leaders understood that evolution would be a primary doctrinal issue at the Convention.[76] In the Seminary organ Mullins condemned modernism as leading some Christians away from evangelicalism without offering any satisfactory substitute.[77] Those who attacked Christianity, he maintained, created their own "New Orthodoxy."[78] In a widely published essay entitled "Evolution and Belief in God," he answered an anonymous letter from an "Anxious Enquirer" in the *Religious Herald,* urging him to be more candid about the theory of evolution.[79] Mullins affirmed that God not only worked through natural law, but also through human freedom. "God," he proclaimed, "is creative in the sense that he rises above the law of continuity and above the resident forces of nature when the needs of His Kingdom require it." Moreover, the Genesis account of creation was true "when correctly understood." He felt it absurd to limit the creation to six, twenty-four-hour days. To Mullins the "order of creation in Genesis from lower to higher forms" constituted the order as taught by modern biology. God provided for the so-called "missing links" with special alterations. The

---

[76]Eighmy, *Churches in Cultural Captivity,* 128.

[77]Mullins, "Professor Beckwith's Idea of God," *Review and Expositor* 20 (January 1923): 67-69.

[78]Mullins, "The Present Situation in Theology," *Review and Expositor* 20 (April 1923): 132.

[79]The "Enquirer" was Professor E. B. Pollard of Crozer Seminary, an old friend of Mullins and former pastor of the Georgetown, Kentucky, First Baptist Church. *Religious Herald,* 8 February 1923; Pitt to Mullins, 17 February 1923; Mullins to Pollard, 22 February 1923 (American Baptist Historical Society, Rochester, New York).

authors of the Bible knew nothing of modern science, therefore, it was "nonsense to talk about conflict between the Bible and science." Both had totally different purposes, the "natural and the spiritual." He saw no great fault with "Christian theistic evolution," since it "presupposed the fundamental teachings of Christianity." He had only contempt, however, for the atheistic evolutionist and believed that even the theistic evolutionist negated the true place of Christ. Mullins maintained that Christian theistic evolution was "in the strict sense not a theory of evolution," but simply "development." The only requirements for a minister or professor should be his "fundamental assumptions." No proved fact of science necessarily disproved the Bible. In conclusion, he maintained that doctrine and tradition bound Baptists to two premises: "First, insist that the teacher be loyal to the Christian fundamentals; second, encourage and sympathize with the search for truth in all realms of knowledge."[80]

Masters declared that Mullins's article was "so written as to give the least possible offense without the sacrifice of truth." While Masters admitted a "penchant for plain language," he also recognized "the fitness and dignity of mild and restrained utterances on the part of our President—President at once of the largest Theological Seminary and the largest Baptist body in the world."[81] Another fervid antievolutionist, J. J. Taylor, reported that he accepted Mullins's article. He praised Mullins for concealing nothing and affirmed that this "allayed any suspicions that may have arisen concerning the soundness of the institution of which he is President."[82] Masters agreed with Taylor, but found that Mullins's style of writing would be too difficult for "the great mass of our people" to understand.[83] Other Southern Baptist leaders also sup-

---

[80]*Religious Herald,* 8 March 1923. The *Recorder* of 22 March and the *Biblical Recorder* of 28 March published substantially the same article by Mullins. Thompson in *Tried as by Fire* declared Mullins to be near the small group of "mild" evolutionists, W. L. Poteat being the major exponent of the "Baptist evolutionists" (115-16).

[81]*Western Recorder,* 22 March 1923.

[82]Ibid., 3 May 1923.

[83]Ibid., 10 May 1923.

ported Mullins's moderate approach as represented in the *Herald* article.[84]

After these major pronouncements on the evolution issue, Mullins presented pleas for unity and fulfillment of the 75 Million Campaign. To him unity represented the hope of denominational success that should "not be destroyed by any influence from within or without."[85]

Mullins's opening address to the Southern Baptist Convention in Kansas City, entitled "Science and Religion," developed the same moderate position as his earlier efforts. He urged that scientists and teachers be reasonable in their propagation of any scientific theory. More important, he did not advocate legislation and forestalled any such support from the Convention floor.[86] Masters accepted Mullins's speech as "our Baptist gauge" and endorsed the lack of "bitterness and faction" at the Convention, but could not forego one last opportunity to support the "cure." He asked that evolutionists either cease their propagation of that theory or start their own schools.[87] Fundamentalists J. J. Taylor and Porter also praised Mullins's Kansas City statement, though Porter still believed that McVey was not entirely candid about the teachings of the university.[88] For his own part, Mullins was satisfied that his speech had been "successful" in averting an open fight with the "ultra brethren."[89] He also praised the good sense of the Convention in quickly disposing of the evolution issue, since it "really had become hurtful to our work."[90]

Lewis Humphrey, editor of the Louisville *Evening Post*, supported Mullins and McVey. He thought that the Convention speech was "the way out" of further legislative turmoil over evolution in Kentucky.

---

[84]O. O. Green to Mullins, 24 March 1923; L. L. Gwaltney to Mullins, 6 February 1923; M. C. Reeves to Mullins, 23 March 1923; S. M. Brown to Mullins, 21 March 1923; A. T. Cinnamond to Mullins, 26 March 1923.

[85]*Western Recorder*, 12 April, 26 April 1923.

[86]*Annual of the Southern Baptist Convention, 1923*, 75-76; *Western Recorder*, 24 May 1923.

[87]*Western Recorder*, 24 May 1923.

[88]Porter to Mullins, 24 May 1923; Taylor to Mullins, 31 May 1923.

[89]Mullins to Pitt, 29 May 1923; Mullins to F. M. Powell, 22 December 1923.

[90]*Western Recorder*, 31 May 1923.

Teachers, in dealing with evolution, he asserted, should state that "these guesses are guesses, and guesses only." He believed that McVey and the university complied with Mullins's standards. Therefore, Kentucky could "expect the Christian people . . . to stand forward next year [1924] and smother proposed laws that can have no possible effect except to weaken the university, discredit the church, and cause unwarranted bitterness among our people."[91]

One question remained: Would the *Recorder* stage a campaign similar to that of 1921-1922? Having played an intrinsic role earlier, the *Recorder* remained silent on the subject of legislation during the remainder of 1923. Fundamentalists like Riley, Taylor, Masters, and Porter occasionally railed against the dangers of evolution in the pages of the *Recorder*, but they mounted no campaign for legislation in 1923. If anything, the *Recorder* turned more toward the anti-racetrack gambling issue, but did not develop the vehemence of the 1921-1922 antievolution campaign.[92] As president of the Convention and World Alliance, Mullins succeeded in creating a positive denominational atmosphere. He propagandized the virtues of denominational cooperation.[93] Masters and Porter followed suit and called for unity and completion of the 75 Million Campaign.[94] With no support from the two most prominent proponents of legislation in 1922, introduction of restrictive measures in 1924 became impossible. With Mullins at the height of his prestige, neither Porter nor Masters dared to clash openly with him.

Mullins's conciliatory efforts in the evolution controversy were quite successful in 1923. As president of the Convention and World Alliance, his views commanded both attention and respect. Always the moderate and peacemaker, he counseled a Southern Baptist college professor not to be too critical of the fundamentalists. "My own attitude," Mullins revealed, "is to try to find points of agreement and to harmonize and

---

[91]*Louisville Post,* 19 May 1923.

[92]Unlike in 1922, in 1923 the number of anti-racetrack gambling articles and editorials equaled the antievolution editorials and articles.

[93]*Western Recorder,* 21 June, 28 June, 4, 11, and 18 October 1923.

[94]Ibid., 29 November 1923.

unify."[95] The success of this approach was exemplified by his address to the 1923 Alliance meeting. Mullins found the quest for religious liberty to be the nexus for all freedom. If the state guaranteed religious freedom, there was no reason to fear scientific teaching.[96] Mullins's commitment to concepts of the free church emerged in the evolution controversy in Kentucky through 1924. Evolution was never again a serious legislative threat in Kentucky. His success in reconciling his denomination with evolution, however, was short-lived because the issue disrupted later Conventions. While this controversy continued to stir the souls of Southern Baptists, Mullins pushed for the completion of his obsession, the construction of a new Seminary plant.

---

[95]Mullins to T. O. Mabry, 7 June 1923.

[96]*Baptist Standard*, 6 September 1923.

9 "THE BEECHES": BUILDING A NEW SEMINARY

In the 1920s Mullins pushed for completion of his greatest dream, a new physical plant for the Seminary. After several false starts, he urged renewed efforts when the 75 Million Campaign failed to provide ample building funds. That campaign had the unforeseen result of further limiting Mullins's denominational independence. While he displayed some independence in the initial antievolution crusade in Kentucky, Mullins feared that a fundamentalist backlash would destroy the opportunity to develop a new physical plant. With his election to the Southern Baptist Convention presidency in 1921 Mullins began to adhere more closely than ever to the programs of the denomination. He now took less interest in interdenominational affairs and devoted himself more and more to Southern Baptist and Seminary business, thereby dissipating adverse reaction to his earlier cooperation with Northern Baptist and interdenominational organizations. In the 1920s Mullins also espoused a more conservative Social Gospel than during the early years at Southern Seminary.

Throughout the decade, however, Mullins maintained an ambivalent position that allowed him some independence to participate in outside affairs on a "voluntary" basis with room enough for the fullest expression of denominationalism.[1] Thus, the Seminary cautiously co-operated with the Interchurch Movement, because Mullins realized that participation in even the Baptist World Alliance was suspect to the fundamentalists, especially since he dominated the Alliance.[2] The Sunday School Board, under the direction of Van Ness, attempting to take control of the *Review and Expositor*, became a more potent denominational force by purchasing the Baptist Book Concern and the Baptist World Publishing Company. The publishing role of the Board, moreover, became one of its chief functions.[3]

As Mullins adhered more closely to Southern Baptist affairs, his relationships with Northern Baptists became more ceremonial and perfunctory. The Baptist Theological Faculties' Union disintegrated in the early 1920s with Mullins refusing to cooperate in any plans of the Chicago Divinity School faculty, which moved toward the theological left during the decade.[4] Relations with Shailer Mathews, for example, cooled from the earlier friendly correspondence to businesslike formal letters.[5]

---

[1]*Western Recorder*, 29 April 1920; Mullins and Harold W. Tribble, *The Baptist Faith* (Nashville: Sunday School Board, 1935) 14. The latter was a shorter version of *Axioms* rewritten for denominational study courses.

[2]Porter, for example, railed against the World Alliance because of affiliation with "dangerous men" as he referred to English liberal Baptists. *Western Recorder*, 21 February 1918. Mullins led the Alliance campaign to guarantee the rights of Rumanian Baptists. *New York Times*, 21 November 1926.

[3]J. W. Porter to Van Ness, 31 August 1921; 7 August, 12 October 1925; Van Ness to Mullins, 20 January 1920, 8 March 1923, 17 August 1925; Mullins to Van Ness, 15 August 1925. All of the above correspondence is located in the Van Ness Papers, Dargan-Carver Library.

[4]Gerald B. Smith to Mullins, 3 March 1923; Mullins to Smith, 4 December 1924 (Correspondence of the Baptist Theological Faculties' Union, University of Chicago Archives); Smith to Mullins, 3 March 1923, 2 December 1924; Mullins to Smith, 4 December 1924.

[5]Kenneth Cauthen, *The Impact of American Religious Liberalism* (New York: Harper and Row, 1965) 148; Mathews to Mullins, 6 February 1922, 8 March 1923, 11 May 1925; Mullins to Mathews, 24 February, 6 March 1923; 26 May, 29 May 1925. Mullins stated that he had once believed that Mathews

Mullins published no more books with the American Baptist Publication Society, although that group bought the plates of *Baptist Beliefs* from the Baptist Book Concern.[6] He participated in the Columbia Conference, a meeting of Southern and Northern Baptists in 1922, which failed to produce any closer relations between the two conventions, but thereafter he showed little inclination to renew his earlier activities as liaison between the two groups.[7]

In the early 1920s Mullins had a rapport with other denominations in Louisville. Catholic, Episcopal, Jewish, and Unitarian leaders flooded Mullins's office with requests for his services at their functions. As the decade progressed, however, he devoted less time to these ecumenical activities.[8] While Mullins realized affiliation of the Southern Baptist Convention with the Federal Council was impossible, he cautiously cooperated by participating in a session of the 1924 Quadrennial Meeting of the Council in Atlanta. He presented a sermon, at the invitation of the president of the Council, on the "Spiritual Sovereignty" of Christ over man, emphasizing prayer as a communion with Christ and stressing the ecumenical appeal of "fellowship."[9] Mullins also cooperated with the

---

was an "evangelical," but now thought the Chicago Divinity School dean had turned toward scientific modernism. Mullins to Fred W. Freeman, 2 May 1924. In a congratulatory message on Mullins's twenty-fifth anniversary at Southern Seminary, Mathews urged Mullins to "help the brethren to better appreciation of evolution." Mathews to Mullins, 21 October 1924. Mullins replied that that was exactly what he was trying to do, but Mathews should "remember, it is a long, long way to Tipperary, and some people are mighty slow learners." Mullins to Mathews, 24 October 1924.

[6]Mullins to Daniel G. Stevens, 29 May 1925; H. E. Cressman to Mullins, 10 January 1921; Samuel Z. Batten to Mullins, 9 September 1921.

[7]Mullins to Fred W. Freeman, 26 May 1922; Mullins to George E. Horr, 1 April 1922; E. B. Pollard to Mullins, 12 February 1920; Thomas, "Edgar Young Mullins," 70.

[8]P. H. Callahan to Mullins, 27 April 1920, 21 February 1921; program for the "Centennial of Christ Church Cathedral" in which Mullins spoke on the topic "Christian Education" on 29 May 1922; Louis Cohen to Mullins, 14 November 1922; R. Ernest Akin to Mullins, 11 September, 14 November 1922. Mullins spoke to the Unitarian Laymen's League. In an advertisement, the secretary of the League urged members to attend Mullins's address (Box 90).

[9]Robert E. Speer to Mullins, 29 August 1924; Mullins to Speer, 9 September 1924; Mullins to Arthur E. Hungerford, 1 December 1924.

Council in efforts to encourage American participation in the World Court and to raise funds for relief of famine in China.[10] He encouraged internationalism in the 1920s by joining the National Committee on American-Japanese Relations, the China Relief Committee, and the World Alliance for International Friendship Through the Churches. Mullins declared that the United States should not be a "hermit nation," but should take an active role in world affairs.[11] However, he did not take an active role in any of these programs, merely allowing these groups to use his name in preparing testimonials for publication.

Similarly, Mullins's Social Gospel was perfunctory, but still much more liberal than that of the majority of his Southern Baptist coreligionists. He aided the new Negro seminary in Nashville and supported Simmons University in Louisville. As a member of its advisory committee, Mullins helped raise funds to keep the struggling Louisville Negro institution functioning.[12] Paternalistic in his racial views, Mullins became aroused when the Louisville Free Public Library added a controversial book that he found to be excessively critical of Southern white attitudes. He exercised his prerogative as a member of the board of trustees, asking that the volume be "excluded" from circulation.[13] Like his limited participation in interdenominational activities, Mullins allowed his name to be used by the Child Conservation League of America, for example, without ever taking an active part in its activities.[14] He

[10]Mullins to Sidney L. Gulick, 3 November 1923, 23 April 1928; Samuel McCrea Cavert to Mullins, 30 October 1922.

[11]Gulick to Mullins, 4 December 1925; Thomas W. Lamont to Mullins, 10 December, 14 December 1920; Woodrow Wilson to Mullins, 9 December 1920; Linley V. Gordon to Mullins, 29 July 1925; Mullins to Robert W. Bingham, 14 January 1925.

[12]Henrietta P. Butler, Executive Secretary-Treasurer of the General Association of Colored Baptists in Kentucky, to the author, 12 June 1972; Mullins to C. H. Parrish, 10 January 1921; Mullins to William T. Amiger, 27 August 1924; Parrish to Mullins, 20 July 1925.

[13]Mullins to Mayor Huston Quin, 7 April 1922. The volume in question was *The Soul of John Brown* by Stephen Graham (New York: The Macmillan Co., 1920).

[14]Mary Laux Beckwith to Mullins, 25 May 1920.

also wrote less about the social function of Christianity in the 1920s as compared with his previous output.

Removing himself from the sphere of interdenominational and social concerns, Mullins became increasingly preoccupied with Seminary administration. His position as Seminary president and chief executive of the Convention gave him a strong power base from which to thrust his plans before his Southern Baptist brethren. Similar to the New Era Expansion Program of the Presbyterian Church, U.S.A. or the interdenominational financial goals of the Interchurch World Movement, the Southern Baptist Convention launched an ambitious financial program known as the 75 Million Campaign after the end of World War I. Mullins helped in organizing the campaign, a move that would further limit his maneuvering room.[15]

President L. R. Scarborough of Southwestern Seminary served as chief executive of the campaign, with Van Ness acting as treasurer. Each state received a quota to be pledged by individuals and churches and then paid over a five-year period. The funds thus derived would be distributed among denominational colleges, seminaries, orphanages, and boards.[16] Though the drive contained no building funds for Southern Seminary, Mullins cooperated because the school would receive money for the Student Aid Fund.[17]

Shortly after the campaign started, Mullins began to have doubts about the success of the drive. He and Scarborough proposed that their seminaries be given any surplus funds that might accrue or else be granted the privilege of staging their own drives outside the auspices of the 75 Million Campaign.[18] Mullins queried denominational leaders on these points and claimed that the consensus of opinion supported a sep-

---

[15]George H. Pascal, Jr., and Judith A. Benner, *One Hundred Years of Challenge and Change: A History of the Synod of Texas of the United Presbyterian Church in the U.S.A.* (San Antonio: Trinity University Press, 1968) 125-26; Thomas, "Edgar Young Mullins," 41; Thompson, *Tried as by Fire,* 15-18.

[16]Frank E. Burkhalter, "Seventy-Five Million Campaign," *Encyclopedia of Southern Baptists,* 2:1196-98; Sampey, *Memoirs,* 161.

[17]*Baptist World,* 1 May 1919; Joshua Levering to Mullins, 3 December 1919.

[18]Scarborough to Mullins, 5 November, 19 December 1919; 13 February 1920.

arate fund drive as long as it did not deter from the 75 Million Campaign. Editor Lewis Humphrey of the *Louisville Evening Post* also called upon all Louisvillians to aid the Seminary fund drive.[19]

After passing this important test, Mullins called a special meeting of the Seminary board of trustees for early January 1920. Initial correspondence with the trustees indicated their willingness to underwrite a building drive.[20] When the trustees met, Mullins presented his plans, declaring that the Seminary had been left out of the 75 Million Campaign as far as building funds were concerned and subsequent efforts to gain a share of the building funds from the campaign had failed. The dire need for new facilities, he declared, necessitated that Southern Seminary be given the right to proceed outside the confines of the denominational drive.[21] The trustees agreed and authorized the Seminary to raise $2,000,000 and to begin construction as soon as the first receipts materialized. The trustees urged Mullins to ask for over-subscriptions from the 75 Million Campaign and, if not forthcoming, to go it alone in a new fund drive.[22]

Mullins next approached other denominational leaders before the 1920 Convention met. Editor P. I. Lipsey of the Jackson, Mississippi, *Baptist Record,* a longtime Landmark-fundamentalist foe of the Seminary, warned Mullins not to tamper with the 75 Million drive.[23] Other

---

[19]J. E. Dillard to Mullins, 9 September 1919; J. B. Gambrell to Mullins, 11 March 1920; George W. McDaniel to Mullins, 9 February 1920; Dabney R. Yarborough to Mullins, 4 September 1919; George W. Truett to Mullins, 19 April 1920; Z. T. Cody to Mullins, 12 April 1920; Humphrey to Mullins, 18 December 1919.

[20]J. J. Darlington to Mullins, 16 December 1919; B. V. Ferguson to Mullins, 5 January 1920; R. M. Inlow to Mullins, 3 January 1920; Walter L. Johnson to Mullins, 20 December 1919; Leon M. Latimer to Mullins, 7 December 1919; Joshua Levering to Mullins, 22 December 1919; S. P. Brooks to Mullins, 16 December 1919.

[21]"Report of the Faculty to Special Meeting of the Board of Trustees, January 8, 1920" (Copy in file marked Desk in General Office to March, 1926); Sampey, *Memoirs,* 163.

[22]"Paper adopted by the Board of Trustees of the Southern Baptist Theological Seminary, Louisville, Jan. 9, 1920" (Copy in Box 87).

[23]Lipsey to Mullins, 5 March 1920.

leaders were more positive and urged completion of the construction campaign. Mullins also presented his pleas to the denomination, contending that the poor facilities of the downtown location precipitated this urgent request. The facilities were "too small" for the current enrollment of nearly 350 students since the present plant had been built to accommodate only about 200.[24] Not many weeks later, the recording secretary of the Education Board of the Convention reported that this group voted to supply up to $1,000,000 from the funds previously allocated to the Home Mission Board and the Foreign Mission Board. The sum would be contingent on the amount collected by the 75 Million Campaign.[25] After the annual meeting of the Convention, the Foreign Mission Board agreed to advance building loans to any of the seminaries in the denomination for construction purposes.[26]

Mullins realized this money would not be enough to construct a new plant, so he pursued plans for an independent fund drive. As the success of the 75 Million drive became more doubtful, denominational pessimism endangered the Student Fund and threatened to spread to the Seminary's drive. Many contributors to the old Jubilee Drive, moreover, asserted that their obligations to the Seminary ended with their pledges to the 75 Million Campaign. Southern Seminary, therefore, might lose over $75,000 unless these donors honored the original pledges.[27]

In the face of these obstacles, Mullins laid plans for a separate fund drive and construction of a new plant. He hoped to begin construction by the summer of 1922 despite apparent setbacks to the 75 Million Cam-

---

[24]Richard H. Edmonds to Mullins, 21 January 1920; L. L. Gwaltney to Mullins, 8 March 1920; R. H. Pitt to Mullins, 4 March 1920; *Western Recorder*, 29 April 1920.

[25]J. E. Dillard to Mullins, 26 March 1920; Joshua Levering to Mullins, 26 April 1920.

[26]The money would be in the form of loans, not grants. J. F. Love to Mullins, 11 June 1920. In 1918 the Baptist Bible Institute opened in New Orleans, adding another competitor to those with which Southern Seminary had to compete. Barnes, *The Southern Baptist Convention*, 211.

[27]*Report of the Financial Agent, May, 1920* (Copy in the file marked Desk in General Office to March ,1926); S. B. Rogers to B. Pressley Smith, 26 November 1920.

paign, which by early 1922 had failed to collect the annual quotas.[28] Undaunted by this ominous sign, Mullins persuaded the trustees to authorize purchase of "The Beeches," a thirty-four-acre estate on Lexington Road, about six miles east of the Seminary's downtown location. He then announced that the Brownsboro Road property, purchased as a future site in 1911, would be sold immediately and that more land would be added to the new Lexington Road site in the future.[29] While he protested the inadequacy of the present campus, the Seminary itself faced a deficit, indicating that it still did not receive enough revenue for its regular operating expenses.[30] His plans for a two-million-dollar campus in a rather luxurious setting were ambitious in the face of an operating deficit and growing concern for the success of the 75 Million Campaign. As these plans were being developed despite growing financial worries, Mullins and his Southern Baptist brethren were experiencing the first throes of the antievolution controversy, which heaped additional criticism on Southern Seminary. Prospective contributors maintained that the Seminary was too liberal and demanded assurance that the school would return to its orthodox moorings. Some "ultra-conservative" brethren like the Landmarkists used Mullins's role in the evolution controversy to oppose the financial campaign.[31]

Since Mullins determined it was now or never for construction of the new Seminary, he went ahead undeterred by those who counseled against any more expensive programs because of denominational economic doldrums. P. T. Hale, the chief agent for the Seminary since the Jubilee campaign began before World War I, redoubled his efforts to make collections and obtain pledges for the building fund. As in previous campaigns, Hale ran into difficulty obtaining permission to solicit

---

[28]Mullins to Joshua Levering, 29 August 1921; *Western Recorder*, 9 March 1922; *Courier-Journal*, 1 January 1922.

[29]*Courier-Journal*, 28 July 1921; Mullins to George W. Norton, 28 July 1921; Crismon, "Southern Baptist Theological Seminary," 1271.

[30]Mullins to Van Ness, 4 June 1921; *Annual of the Southern Baptist Convention, 1922*, 38-39.

[31]Davis C. Woolley, "Major Convention Crises over a Century and a Quarter," *Review and Expositor* 67 (Spring 1970): 176; E. L. Compere to Mullins, 15 December 1919; J. B. Gambrell to Mullins, 23 March 1920.

funds in some areas. On one occasion, Mullins warned Hale to "take it easily and quietly" and provide no opportunity for criticism of the Seminary.[32] As his primary defense Mullins suggested to Hale that he maintain that the Seminary could not wait five years for the completion of the 75 Million Campaign.[33] When a Mississippi Baptist official complained about one of Hale's forays into that state, Mullins retorted that the Seminary had no regular source of revenue like the boards and state colleges. Mullins insisted that until the Convention annually provided funds for the Seminary, agents like Hale were entirely necessary. Because the $1,000,000 promised from the boards never materialized, Mullins was acutely aware that Southern Seminary could not survive unless it sought every possible source of funds both within regular denominational fund drives and in its own campaigns.[34] Hale proved successful in raising funds for the Seminary. In 1922-1923, for example, he collected more than $19,000 in cash and obtained notes for an additional $55,000.[35]

Undaunted by previous failures, Mullins once again sought to tap the Rockefeller fortune. An extensive correspondence with John D. Rockefeller, Jr., and his agents, however, failed to produce any results. Mullins even named one of the proposed residence halls New York Hall, but Rockefeller could not be lured into making a commitment to the new Seminary.[36] This failure reemphasized to Mullins the fact that the bulk of building funds would have to come from the South and in competi-

---

[32]Mullins to George W. McDaniel, 10 June 1921; D. F. Green to Mullins, 27 April 1922; Mullins to Hale, 13 August 1923.

[33]Mullins to Oscar E. Sams, n.d. (Copy in Old Letters to March, 1926).

[34]*Annual of the Southern Baptist Convention, 1920,* 525; ibid., *1921,* 587-88; Mullins to R. B. Gunter, 26 April 1923; Mullins to A. R. Bond, 10 June 1922; Mullins to A. C. Cree, 10 June 1922.

[35]Hale's salary and expenses for the year were nearly $8,000, but Mullins believed that this was a good investment. A record of Hale's accomplishments in Mullins's handwriting dated from September 1909 to 10 April 1923 indicates that the agent collected a total of more than $775,000 in notes and nearly $124,000 in cash (Copy in Old Letters to March, 1926).

[36]Mullins to John D. Rockefeller, Jr., 20 December 1922; Rockefeller to Mullins, 12 January 1923; W. S. Richardson to Mullins, 4 October, 10 October 1923; 21 July, 13 October, 14 December 1925; 19 November 1926.

tion with other denominational interests. The 75 Million Campaign merely accentuated the continuing problems of denominational competition for available funds. Ever interested in efficiency, Mullins worked for the adoption of a "cooperative program" that would designate annual funds for the operation of denominational boards and institutions. Additional drives would be permitted for construction and special projects.[37]

In late 1923 the Seminary held groundbreaking ceremonies at "The Beeches." Mullins publicized his plans for a three-million-dollar plant with twenty-one buildings in the architectural style of the University of Virginia.[38] By that time the 75 Million Campaign was a dismal failure, collecting only 58 of a total of 92 million dollars pledged. The over-subscription led many denominational institutions and boards to expand their operations too rapidly for the available revenue. After 1923 most were in dire financial straits.[39]

Undismayed by these revelations, Mullins continued both the building fund drive and construction, though he reported to a colleague, "I . . . am going to kill myself, if I don't let up somewhere."[40] To reduce some of the personal pressure, Mullins reorganized the financial campaign. Charles F. Leek became publicity secretary with the primary responsibility of keeping the needs of the Seminary before the denomination.[41]

---

[37]Mullins to Pitt, 10 November 1922; Mullins to John L. Hill, 10 November 1925. Victor I. Masters later charged that Mullins and other leaders pushed Southern Baptists "into that stupid 75-million campaign. Out of it we turned fool and gave up our liberties to centralized dictation." Masters to J. Frank Norris, 8 May 1949 (J. Frank Norris Papers, Dargan-Carver Library). The Cooperative Program was the culmination of the centralization trend.

[38]*Courier-Journal*, 6 April 1923; Mueller, *A History of Southern Baptist Theological Seminary*, 208.

[39]Austin Crouch, "Debt and Southern Baptists," *Encyclopedia of Southern Baptists*, 1:356-57; James D. Bernard, "The Baptists," *American Mercury* 7 (February 1926): 136-46; B. D. Gray, "A Quarter of a Century in the Southern Baptist Convention," *Review and Expositor* 22 (January 1925): 78.

[40]Mullins to O. O. Green, 10 September 1923; Sampey, *Memoirs*, 179-80.

[41]Mullins to "The Editors of Our Baptist Papers," 12 September 1923; Sampey, *Memoirs*, 193; *Western Recorder*, 23 July, 12 November 1925.

During the summer break of 1924 a number of Seminary students worked as fund raisers following a procedure developed for the earlier Jubilee Drive.[42] Later in the year Mullins hired an associate director, Allan H. Bissell, who had much experience raising money for religious organizations.[43] Bissell expertly directed the work of several field agents, promising them appropriate raises in salary if they collected above their quotas. After a year's effort, Mullins reported satisfaction with this arrangement, praising Bissell's organizational ability.[44]

The attempt to use excess funds from the boards for construction fell through since the boards never developed surplus funds.[45] George W. Norton and his sisters offered some relief from the pressure by donating $100,000 for construction of the new Norton Hall, a combination classroom, library, and administrative center.[46] Beginning in late 1924 Mullins demanded a special collection day in denominational Sunday schools as compensation for being excluded from the 75 Million Campaign. When the educational secretary of the Convention asked that all institutions share in the same collection program, Mullins irately refused to let the matter go further. Southern Seminary received, he charged, "almost unprecedented unfavorable treatment."[47] When President Scarborough of Southwestern balked at the suggestion, Mullins implied that other Southern Baptist institutions worked to keep Southern Seminary from prospering.[48] Despite the urgings of denominational leaders not to give the Seminary a special collection day in the Sunday schools, Mul-

---

[42]Mullins to George Rice Hovey, 2 May 1924.

[43]Mullins to Bissell, 10 December 1924.

[44]Bissell to Mullins, 23 June 1925; Bissell, "TO ALL FIELD MEN," 28 September, 19 October, 26 October 1925; Mullins to Bissell, 16 December 1925.

[45]J. F. Love to Mullins, 20 June 1924; Joshua Levering to Mullins, 12 June 1925; *Western Recorder*, 7 May, 21 May 1925.

[46]Mullins to Van Ness, 12 September 1924 (Van Ness Papers, Dargan-Carver Library).

[47]Mullins to J. W. Cammack, 10 October 1924 (copy sent to Van Ness, 11 October 1924, Van Ness Papers, Dargan-Carver Library).

[48]Mullins to Scarborough, 25 April, 1 July 1924.

lins won the support of the Convention and, after nearly a year of struggle, the Seminary had its special collection day in June 1925.[49]

Mullins's 1924 report to a special meeting of the trustees detailed his "Reasons for Removal" from downtown Louisville, citing the "small," antiquated facilities built of "cheap material" as a major factor in the decision to move. In warm weather with the windows open the "noise of the streets" created an unscholarly atmosphere, while in the winter the heating plant continually threatened to break down. Mullins estimated it would take more to repair the downtown structures than they were worth. Economy would be served by constructing new buildings on the site already acquired. The estimated cost of construction changed from $2,000,000 to as much as $3,500,000 because of World War I inflation. Norton Hall would house a library, chapel, classrooms, and offices at a cost of about $850,000. Dormitory units for single and married students would cost about the same as Norton Hall. A gymnasium, heating plant, dining hall, professors' homes, and landscaping would add another $500,000 to the total. "Present Plans" called for the completion of Norton Hall and the construction of a men's dormitory and the heating plant as rapidly as possible. Other units would be added as more money became available. The present Seminary property would be held for "endowment purposes" as leased or rental property. Mullins, citing the recent construction of the Brown Hotel just across the street, believed this property would grow rapidly in value. Blaming the inflation of construction costs since World War I, he defended his decision to go ahead with an independent fund drive so persuasively that the Building Committee of the board of trustees unanimously approved his presentation.[50]

When construction commenced, the boards doled out funds slowly. These sources soon dried up as the 75 Million Campaign failed to pro-

---

[49]J. W. Cammack to Mullins, 5 December 1924; Mullins to B. H. DeMent, 16 April 1925; *Western Recorder*, 4 June 1925. The following correspondence is all located in the Van Ness Papers: Van Ness to J. W. Cammack, 1 October 1924; Mullins to Van Ness, 20 August, 14 October 1924; 20 April, 25 May 1925; Van Ness to Mullins, 4 September 1924.

[50]*Report of the Financial Agent, 1924* (Pamphlet File, Southern Seminary Library).

duce surplus funds.[51] In late December 1923 the Seminary held ground-breaking ceremonies for the new Norton Hall. Mullins announced that construction would consist of only the "vital necessities."[52] To meet these costs he plunged Southern Seminary into debt, borrowing large sums from a Louisville mortgage company.[53] At the same time Mullins worked closely with architect James Gamble Rogers of New York and the land-scape architects, the firm of Olmstead Brothers of Brookline, Massachusetts.[54] Mullins looked after the smallest details. For example, he had protective fences built around the beech trees on the building site, fearing that the construction would injure the distinctive forested atmosphere of the property. In late March 1926 the Seminary moved from Broadway to the Lexington Road site with only Norton Hall, Mullins Hall (the new men's dormitory), and the heating plant completed.[55]

Though Mullins considered the 1925 drive to be successful, he estimated that the Seminary owed nearly $1,000,000 in construction loans. To help meet these costs, Mullins sold part of the downtown property (the library at the corner of Fifth and Broadway).[56] The major papers of the city and the Louisville Board of Trade supported his efforts. As a result of this support, Louisville area non-Baptists pledged over $200,000

---

[51]Mullins to J. F. Love, 19 June 1923; Mullins to T. B. Ray, 29 June 1923; George W. McDaniel to Mullins, 14 October 1924; Van Ness to Mullins, 7 November 1924; Robert A. Baker, *The Southern Baptist Convention and Its People* (Nashville: Broadman Press, 1974) 392-94.

[52]*Courier-Journal*, 23 December 1923; Mullins to C. P. Stealey, 17 December 1923; Mullins to F. M. Powell, 22 December 1923.

[53]John Stites to Mullins, 6 February 1925; Mullins to Stites, 26 March 1925; *Western Recorder*, 13 August 1925.

[54]Rogers to Mullins, 24 March 1922; 19 April, 9 May 1923; Mullins to Rogers, 28 April 1926; Olmstead Brothers to Mullins, 8 June 1926.

[55]Mullins to Olmstead Brothers, 20 December 1923; Louisville *Sunday Herald-Post*, 11 April 1926; Mueller, *A History of Southern Baptist Theological Seminary*, 208.

[56]*Financial Agent's Report, 1925-1926* (Pamphlet File, Southern Seminary Library); *Western Recorder*, 14 July 1927.

to the fund drive.[57] Before Mullins died in 1928, he had guided the completion of other dormitories and the Levering Gymnasium.[58]

Mullins led the movement for construction without due concern for the indebtedness of the Seminary. Even before the Great Depression, the Southern economy failed to measure up to the alleged prosperity of the 1920s. The buoyant spirit of the initial 75 Million Campaign pledge drive degenerated into a bitter lesson of denominational indebtedness. When Sampey succeeded Mullins as president of the Seminary in late 1928, the school still had a mortgage debt of nearly $1,000,000. Only the most stringent economy of Sampey's administration paid off the debt in the 1940s. Mullins's obsession nearly brought financial ruin to the Seminary.[59]

While money was a continuous problem, enrollment rose steadily in the 1920s with a high of 442 in 1923-1924. During Mullins's last session, 1928-1929, the Seminary maintained a total teaching staff of ten professors with six fellowship scholars as their assistants.[60] Throughout his tenure Mullins encouraged the faculty to publish. When Robertson ran into financial difficulty publishing his Greek grammar just before the outbreak of World War I, Mullins assigned Hale to raise $10,000 to print the giant volume. Thereafter, the Seminary created a permanent faculty publishing fund.[61]

---

[57]Robert W. Bingham to Mullins, 18 December 1925; Mullins to Lewis Humphrey, 17 December 1925; Louisville *Board of Trade Journal,* November 1925, 10-11 (Pamphlet File, Southern Seminary Library).

[58]Crismon, "Southern Baptist Theological Seminary," 1271; *Courier-Journal,* 27 January 1929.

[59]Sampey, *Memoirs,* 209-10; Sampey, "Paying the Debt of the Southern Seminary" (Manuscript Copy, Southern Seminary Library); Lynn E. May, Jr., "Southern Baptist Crises," *Encyclopedia of Southern Baptists,* 1:333-36; *Annual of the Southern Baptist Convention, 1942,* 64-65.

[60]W. O. Carver, "A Forward," *Review and Expositor* 22 (January 1925): 3-4; Sampey, *Memoirs,* 180, 199. In Mullins's first year the Seminary had a total enrollment of only 256 students and a faculty of 5 members. Sampey, *Memoirs,* 103.

[61]Mueller, *A History of Southern Baptist Theological Seminary,* 204; Carver, "Recollections," 41-43. Robertson's massive volume contained more than 1,300 pages in its first edition. Robertson, *A Grammar of the Greek New Testament* (New York: George H. Doran, 1914).

Mullins's administrative and fund-raising duties in the 1920s precluded his efforts in the classroom. A teaching assistant took his place most of the time, though technically Mullins still had charge of the classes in theology. One student remembered his increasingly infrequent classroom appearances as great occasions for the young theologs. Mullins's imposing ramrod stature and his cultivated speaking manner awed the student body. A music teacher at Southern Seminary in the 1920s remembered that as a young man he had been impressed by Mullins's "thick black beard." Over the years Mullins changed styles to that of a "chic grey Vandyke" in his later years.[62] The relationship between Mullins and the faculty improved in the 1920s. In particular, faculty salaries became less a point of contention. In 1925, for example, salaries varied from $6,000 for Mullins to $4,500 to $5,000 for the other senior professors including Robertson, Carver, and Gardner. All faculty members, moreover, received rent-free use of a home.[63]

While the students at Southern Seminary usually presented no discipline problems for the faculty, periodic disruptions occurred among the seminarians. At the height of the evolution controversy and the building fund drive, a conflict developed that threatened to disrupt academic life. In April 1923 a small group of students led by J. B. Henderson attacked the administration and faculty for sanctioning literary clubs. Henderson, deploring the secrecy and "organized exclusiveness" of these groups, claimed that the faculty favored their members over other students.[64] The anti-club men circulated a newspaper, the *Pectograph*, scoring the faculty.[65] One anonymous student called the secret

---

[62]Carver, "Recollections," 95-98; Mullins to L. W. Teague, 12 December 1925; Interview with Ernest N. Perry, 25 February 1972; Johnson, *Of Parsons and Profs*, 30. Another contemporary of Mullins remembered his scholarly philosophical sermons, which were never overbearing, and his "impressive" appearance. He contended, moreover, that Mullins could also display a humorous side when the occasion demanded it. Gordon Wilson, Sr., former chairman of the English department, Western Kentucky University, to the author, 8 May 1969.

[63]Mullins to George W. Taft, 20 November 1925.

[64]J. B. Henderson, "What is the Matter at the Southern Baptist Theological Seminary?" (photostatic copy, Old Letters to March, 1926).

[65]Sampey, *Memoirs*, 176.

clubs "The Invisible Government" of the Southern Baptist Convention. Only clubmen, he asserted, became the "Big Preachers" in the large influential urban churches.[66] Mullins issued a statement urging a return to the proper business of seminarians, study, and requested a statement from each club outlining its purposes and members.[67] Henderson, however, refused to end his agitation, forcing Mullins to dismiss him and another student. The expelled students countered with a circular letter to numerous denominational officers and editors, whereupon Mullins sent an urgent request to several leaders asking that they not answer or publicize Henderson's claims. The dispute ended without developing into a public controversy.[68] Two years later ninety-one men signed a petition protesting the food served in the Seminary dining hall, but no student controversy during Mullins's tenure threatened the school as did the secret club disturbance in 1923. If fundamentalists had seized on this as an issue, they could have caused Mullins much trouble during the crucial Kentucky antievolution controversy and the building fund drive. In addition to pressing and time-consuming administrative problems, Mullins also faced the resurgence of the evolution controversy as fundamentalists in the Southern Baptist Convention developed a larger following.[69]

---

[66]Anonymous letter to Mullins (Old Letters to March, 1926).

[67]"Statement from the Faculty of the Seminary to the Student Body" (photostatic copy, Old Letters to March, 1926).

[68]Mullins to John Jeter Hurt, 24 December 1923; Cecil V. Cook to Mullins, 3 December 1923; J. W. Roberts to Mullins, 28 November 1923; W. O. Blount to Mullins, 26 November 1923; T. B. Ray to Mullins, 10 December 1923; L. L. Gwaltney to Mullins, 7 December 1923; P. I. Lipsey to Mullins, 7 December 1923.

[69]The students declared the food to be "ill-balanced and poorly prepared, thereby causing undernourishment and illness at times" (Student Petition signed by ninety-one seminarians, n.d., in file L-Z, March 10, 1925-March 15, 1927).

10   THE TRIUMPH OF FUNDAMENTALISM

Mullins's restatement of evangelical Christianity throughout the 1920s was little more than that since he offered nothing substantially new to the interpretation of that faith. He published only one important book during the decade, *Christianity at the Crossroads*, in 1924.[1] Though his theological system remained unchanged, Mullins continued to have a wide influence among religious moderates as well as his Southern Baptist brethren. He attempted to give viability to the old-time religion through the scholastic approach.

The latent evangelicalism of Mullins was never far below the surface in his theological system. Christianity, above all else, was "An In-

---

[1]Mullins, *Christianity at the Crossroads* (New York: George H. Doran Co., 1924). The *Watchman-Examiner* serialized parts of the book on 22 May, 5, 19, and 26 June 1924. Though the book was published by George H. Doran Co., the Sunday School Board held the copyright. Mullins to Van Ness, 10 July 1925 (Van Ness Papers, Dargan-Carver Library).

dividual Experience."[2] He declared himself to be an "evangelical Christian," maintaining faith in the supernatural aspects of Christianity.[3] Only a "personal faith in Jesus Christ as Lord and Savior" offered a final solution to the problems of the individual in this world.[4] Though Mullins did not claim to be a strong premillennialist, he professed belief in the literal Second Coming of Christ.[5]

In the 1920s, in particular, Mullins took more notice of the deity in his theological system than ever before. In what might be described as the fullest expression of his moderate Calvinism, he reconciled the Calvinistic enigma of the authority of God and freedom of man in his usual moderate approach.[6] God was an "omnipotent Being," the "sovereign" who always controlled the destiny of the world. The individual had the grace of God as well, meaning that individual salvation was attainable through a religious experience.[7] Mullins insisted on the immanence and transcendence of God, proposing that modernists made the same mistake as the deists. Twentieth-century rationalists made the deity only a

---

[2]Mullins "The Contribution of Baptists to the Interpretation of Christianity," *Hibbert Journal* 21 (April 1923): 536; Mullins, *Talks on Soul Winning* (Nashville: Sunday School Board, 1920) 77-84; *Western Recorder,* 12 November 1925.

[3]Mullins, "The Freedom of Faith," *Independent* 114 (25 April 1925): 473-74; Mullins, "Baptist Theology in the New World Order," *Review and Expositor* 17 (October 1920): 402.

[4]Mullins to W. W. Keen, 19 July 1924.

[5]Mullins to J. B. Bunn, 20 May 1921. J. Frank Norris violently attacked Mullins for his soft view of millennialism in *Christianity at the Crossroads.* Mullins vowed belief in a moderate premillennialism, but he admitted that this was not an important part of his theological beliefs. Norris to Mullins, 27 June 1924; Mullins to Norris, 3 July 1924.

[6]William J. McGlothlin, "Edgar Young Mullins," *Dictionary of American Biography,* 13:322; Garrett, Hinson, and Tull, *Are Southern Baptists "Evangelicals"?,* 90.

[7]Mullins, "God and the War," *Review and Expositor* 21 (October 1924): 453; Mullins, "The Father Almighty," in *My Idea of God: A Symposium of Faith,* ed. Joseph Fort Newton (Boston: Little, Brown and Co., 1926) 195-97.

part of nature, while their earlier counterparts entirely "locked him out."[8] He also affirmed the anthropomorphic qualities of the personality of God as being necessary for dialogue with the individual seeking a religious experience. Professing a belief in the Trinity, he confessed the impossibility of rationally explaining the concept.[9]

Mullins also remained optimistic about the future of the church and Christianity in the early 1920s. The world was just beginning to appreciate the importance of Christianity, and world economic and social conditions would improve as Christianity fulfilled its destiny as the dominant world religion.[10] Balanced with this optimism, however, was his fear that religious liberalism would lead to a weakening of the role of Christianity in the world. Particularly disturbing was the attendant vogue of "scientific absolutism."[11] Religious modernism became the "new radical orthodoxy," Mullins contended, without offering the hope and guidance of evangelical Christianity.[12] He also believed that science claimed too great a role in explaining phenomena, and religious people unnecessarily tried to answer every question in a rational way.[13] Religion, moreover, lost its dynamism when it turned to rationalism and sought to answer the needs of a lost world with a message that was "too

---

[8]Mullins, *Christianity at the Crossroads*, 105; Szasz, "Three Fundamentalist Leaders," 362-63.

[9]Mullins, "My Idea of God," *Women's Home Companion* 53 (February 1926): 14, 167; Mullins, "Why I Am a Baptist," 727.

[10]Mullins to Lewis Humphrey, 27 October 1924; Mullins to C. H. Parrish, 25 July 1925; *New York Times*, 1 October 1925; Mullins, "The Contribution of Baptists to the Interpretation of Christianity," *Review and Expositor* 20 (October 1923): 394-95; Mullins, "Baccalaureate Sermon," *Bulletin of the Agricultural and Mechanical College of Texas* 10 (1 July 1924): 7-9.

[11]Mullins, *Christianity at the Crossroads*, 40.

[12]Ibid., 27; *Western Recorder*, 11 September, 11 December 1924.

[13]Mullins, "Spiritual Sovereignty," *Record of Christian Work* 46 (October 1927): 794; Mullins, "Christianity in the Modern World," *Review and Expositor* 22 (October 1925): 478; Mullins, "The Modern Minister and His Task," *Record of Christian Work* 46 (October 1927): 712.

general and too abstract."[14] Especially in his last years Mullins appeared to move to the theological and political right. "What is the matter with modern society?" he asked, and then detailed a list of charges. America had "lost the road to happiness," "the incentive to effort," "our ideals," "our conviction as to righteousness," and, most important to Mullins, "we have lost our sense of sin, and the need for redemption." The old social passion of the Baltimore days was entirely lost in a posthumously published essay entitled "Social Problems of Today." One would expect at least mention of the myriad social problems of the 1920s, but Mullins launched instead into a tirade against "modern education," which he found to be teaching young people "a gospel of dirt." "A deadly philosophy is being taught" at all levels of education, Mullins uncharacteristically extolled.[15] In the end his theology and philosophy failed to offer solace even to the moderate evangelical in the face of the economic, social, and political problems of the decade. Increasingly on the defensive, Mullins's ideas lost any resemblance to his liberal positions of the late nineteenth century.

The most crucial issue of the 1920s, of course, was evolution. In *Christianity at the Crossroads,* Mullins's last contribution to apologetics, he placed major emphasis on the failures of modernism and science to answer the problems of man. Mullins assailed the "religion of biology" of Princeton zoologist Edwin Grant Conklin by insisting that there was more than one way to discover truth.[16] Evangelical Christians only asked that their religion not be judged by the methods and standards of science. On the specific topic of evolution, Mullins chose the moderate tack. He maintained that Christian theistic evolution was not, in "the strict sense of the word," evolution—apparently leaning in that direction himself. But Mullins never made a clear declaration of belief on this point. More important, he publicly denounced the antievolutionists and maintained that "Nothing could be more ill-advised than for Americans

---

[14]Mullins, "A Dynamic Ministry," *Record of Christian Work* 47 (January 1928): 33; Mullins, "What Is the Matter with Religion?" *Religious Education* 23 (July 1928): 511.

[15]*Western Recorder,* 21 April 1927; Mullins, *Faith in the Modern World* (Nashville: Sunday School Board, 1930) 130.

[16]Mullins, *Christianity at the Crossroads,* 96.

to attempt to employ legislative coercion in the realm of scientific opinion."[17]

The book proved to be Mullins's last popular contribution to Christian literature. Unfortunately, his peaceable middle approach, even in print, had become increasingly more difficult to maintain. The more vociferous fundamentalists like Norris claimed the book was a sellout to modernism. Moreover, J. Gresham Machen, the most scholarly of fundamentalists, said much the same in a widely circulated review.[18]

In 1924 violent repercussions developed in the Southern Baptist Convention over the evolution issue. J. Frank Norris, the flamboyant pastor of the Fort Worth First Baptist Church and editor of the *Searchlight,* emerged as leader of the fundamentalists, who demanded that evolution be "extracted, root and branch," even if a schism resulted.[19] From outside the Convention, William Bell Riley of Minneapolis attacked the Seminary as being "smitten" with evolution and modernism.[20] Disregarding Mullins's apparent compromise victory over the evolution issue at the 1923 Convention, fundamentalists pushed for an outright repudiation of evolution at the 1924 meeting. Mullins, however, blunted their demands by proposing that the matter be postponed until a committee could write a statement for presentation to the next convention. Mullins chaired a seven-man committee charged with writing a "Statement of Baptist Faith and Message."[21]

C. P. Stealey, editor of the Oklahoma *Baptist Messenger,* was the only avowed antievolutionist member of the committee. He immediately urged Mullins to call a meeting so that an "unmistakable and direct"

---

[17]Ibid., 13, 39-62, 230-31.

[18]Ibid., 66; Marsden, *Fundamentalism and American Culture,* 216; Thompson, *Tried as by Fire,* 137-65; Wacker, "Augustus H. Strong," Epilogue.

[19]Fort Worth *Searchlight,* 27 July 1923; Livingston Johnson to Mullins, 20 May 1924; James D. Jenkins to Mullins, 31 May 1924.

[20]Riley, "Southern Baptist Convention and Skepticism," *Baptist Beacon* 1 (April 1924): 7; Mullins to J. H. Franklin, 24 May 1924; *Watchman-Examiner,* 29 May 1924.

[21]Eighmy, *Churches in Cultural Captivity,* 128; *Annual of the Southern Baptist Convention, 1924,* 95.

pronouncement against evolution could be made.[22] Mullins tried to put off Stealey, arguing against the necessity for such statements, but Stealey called for a declaration that would be "bomb proof" with no "loophole."[23] In the meantime, several moderates had warned Mullins about a fundamentalist plot to gain control of the Convention. Norris and Riley, they proclaimed, were behind Stealey. The agitation was aimed at discrediting Mullins and Southern Seminary.[24] To the moderates on the committee Mullins urged caution. He hoped to forestall a floor fight, but realized that some pronouncement about evolution would be necessary.[25]

Increasingly poor health, the building fund drive, and overseeing construction of the new Seminary compounded Mullins's problems in chairing a committee dealing with a controversial topic. Mullins suffered from recurring attacks of pain and indigestion until he had an operation on an ulcer of the duodenum in March 1925, a few weeks before the opening of the Convention. He returned to work too quickly and suffered a physical breakdown from overexertion. Disregarding his health he attended the Convention meeting in Memphis, fearing that Stealey would take control of the committee and issue a radical statement on evolution.[26]

When the 1925 S. B. C. annual meeting convened, debate over the proposed statement, specifically the part on evolution, "almost broke up the sessions."[27] Mullins presented a lengthy document to the Convention. Part three, "The Fall of Man," failed to mention evolution. It showed

---

[22]Stealey to Mullins, 14 June 1924.

[23]Stealey to Mullins, 31 December 1924; Mullins to Stealey, 25 March 1925.

[24]Acker C. Miller to Mullins, 1 October 1924; Mrs. E. K. Caldwell to Mullins, 4 October 1924; Fred A. McCaulley to Mullins, 9 October 1924.

[25]Mullins to McGlothlin, 25 October 1924; McGlothlin to Mullins, 4 November 1924; Mullins to E. C. Dargan, 25 March 1925.

[26]Mullins to R. H. Pitt, 16 April, 27 April 1925; Mullins to F. M. Powell, 21 February 1924; Mullins to J. H. Rushbrooke, 27 May 1925; Joshua Levering to Mullins, 28 March 1925; Sampey, *Memoirs*, 179-80; *Western Recorder*, 2 April 1925.

[27]Cole, *History of Fundamentalism*, 287.

the mark of his usual moderate tack by concluding that "Man was created by the special act of God, as recorded in Genesis."[28] Immediately after Mullins's presentation, Stealey moved that part three be replaced with a direct condemnation of evolution. Mullins and Stealey debated the issue, and the Convention accepted the Mullins statement by 2,259 to 218, defeating Stealey's motion 2,103 to 950.[29]

Moderates in the Convention congratulated Mullins and voiced their continued support of all peace-making efforts.[30] Mullins overconfidently declared that "it was an open defeat of the Radicals and Extremists . . . who want to put the thumb screws on everybody who does not agree in every detail with their statements of doctrine."[31] Only a continued "strong, clear stand," he believed, would keep fundamentalist Southern Baptists from destroying the concepts of toleration.[32] Mullins intended to press the point through "educative writing" in the Baptist press.[33]

The antievolutionists in the Convention, however, did not accept Mullins's statement and renewed the attack. The debate between Mullins and Stealey continued in the religious press. Stealey claimed that the word *evolution* had been part of the original statement, but that Mullins deleted direct mention in his speech. Mullins denied this. Then Mullins and Stealey came close to calling each other liars.[34] The *Recorder* and other Baptist papers carried numerous articles from both sides during the summer and fall of 1925. As a result of his maintenance of a middle

---

[28]*Annual of the Southern Baptist Convention, 1925*, 72.

[29]Ibid., 76.

[30]Hight C. Moore to Mullins, 22 June 1925; Louie D. Newton to Mullins, 3 June 1925; *Baptist New Mexican*, 25 June 1925; Livingston Johnson to Mullins, 29 June 1925; R. H. Pitt to Mullins, 5 August 1925; S. M. Brown to Mullins, 3 August 1925.

[31]Mullins to Livingston Johnson, 3 July 1925.

[32]Ibid., 31 July 1925.

[33]Mullins to Pitt, 30 July 1925.

[34]*Western Recorder*, 16 July, 30 August, 1 October 1925; Mullins to Stealey, 26 May, 6 November 1925; 6 February 1926; Stealey to Mullins, 15 January 1926.

course, Mullins came under violent attack from fundamentalists during 1925-1926.[35]

In Kentucky, criticisms of Mullins were usually by implication. Victor I. Masters, editor of the *Western Recorder,* mentioned early in 1925 that he "felt heavy pressure from persons of influence" who wanted a halt to agitation. Masters supported Mullins's position in the conflict with Oklahoma Baptists and, more important, he urged completion of the Seminary building drive.[36] It was not long, however, until even Masters's support began to waver. In early June 1925, J. W. Porter introduced an anti-Mullins resolution before the state Board of Missions: "Resolved that we . . . hereby express our abiding conviction that man came into this world by direct creation of God as recorded in the Book of Genesis, and not by Evolution."[37] Here was a direct repudiation of Mullins's moderate course. As an employee of the Board of Missions, Masters applauded the resolution, since "no one can misunderstand." Though Masters remained an adamant foe of evolution, he never repeated the campaign for antievolution legislation, an influence of Mullins.[38]

From other fundamentalists, especially Norris, Riley, and H. Boyce Taylor, Mullins sustained stinging denunciation.[39] Riley concluded that

---

[35]Mullins claimed that "extremists on both sides are constantly making new complications and creating new difficulties." This created a difficult situation for the "friends of evangelical Christianity." Mullins determined that Riley, in particular, seemed bent on destroying Southern Seminary. "Surely, some of the hyper-orthodox brethren are lacking in common sense," Mullins declared. Mullins to Howard P. Whidden, 20 May 1924.

[36]*Western Recorder*, 14 January, 26 February, 11 June, 23 July 1925.

[37]Ibid., 24 May, 11 June 1925.

[38]For example, see Masters's editorials in the *Western Recorder,* 29 January, 12 February, 11 June, 18 June, 9, 16, and 23 July, 15 October 1925; 4 January 1926. In 1925 at least fifty-nine articles and editorials dealt with the subject of evolution. Most of the articles and editorials violently opposed evolution. Even when Masters attacked Vanderbilt University for teaching evolution and violating the Tennessee law, he did not propose a law for the state of Kentucky. *Western Recorder*, 12 November 1925.

[39]Mullins to W. B. Crumpton, 30 January 1924; Mullins to John D. Mell, 24 June 1926.

"either Dr. Mullins is absolutely in his heart an evolutionist or a man so far convinced of the theory that he dare not risk his reputation as a scholar in any pronounced position against it."[40] He continued the attack with sorties into Kentucky churches.[41] Porter believed Mullins's statement offered theistic evolutionists a "loophole," but he did not caustically criticize Mullins personally.[42]

Norris and Taylor voiced the most violent opposition to Mullins. Norris campaigned openly to repudiate Mullins's 1925 statement at the next convention. He characterized evolution as a "fly in the ointment" that should be totally eradicated from Baptist doctrine.[43] Mullins, he said, "should cease to disturb the peace of our Southern Baptist Zion."[44] Norris tried to lure Mullins into debating the issue in the *Searchlight* and condemned Mullins for opposing legislation in *Christianity at the Crossroads*.[45] One of his followers asked Mullins if he believed that God created man "practically like he is today, by an immediate act, and not by any process of evolution or development from a lower form."[46] Mullins replied that "some of you brethren who train with the radical fundamentalists are going over on Catholic ground and leaving the Baptist position. . . . A man who tries to pin his brethren down to stereotyped statements, such as your letter contains, has missed the Baptist spirit."[47] Taylor, declaring Mullins's 1925 statement to be "Sadducean," since it

---

[40]Riley, "Mullins and Evolutionary Modernism," *Baptist Beacon* 1 (June 1925): 5.

[41]Riley, "The Conflict of Christianity with Its Counterfeit in Kentucky," *Baptist Beacon* 2 (May 1926): 8; Riley, "Recent Engagement of the Editor," *Baptist Beacon* 2 (November 1925): 11.

[42]Porter, "1925 Statement of Faith," *Baptist Monthly Magazine* 2 (May 1925): 9; Fort Worth *Searchlight*, 30 May 1925.

[43]*Searchlight*, 30 May 1925.

[44]Ibid., 25 June 1925.

[45]Ibid., 24 June 1926; Mullins to Norris, 12 June, 19 June 1925.

[46]*Searchlight*, 9 June 1926.

[47]Ibid., 16 April 1926.

left out direct condemnation of evolution, commended the Board of Missions for its repudiation of "Pope" Mullins.[48]

After the 1925 Convention meeting, Mullins tried to calm the situation by distributing articles on evolution and religion to the denominational press.[49] He contributed three articles on evolution to the *Recorder* in the fall of that year. Masters probably wanted him to take a stronger stand, but Mullins tried to conciliate the factions.[50] He offered little that he had not said before, but, more important, he urged that no official condemnation of evolution be passed by the next Convention. If restrictions were placed on the teaching of evolution, Mullins contended, students would conclude that Christians were "afraid of interpretation" and assume "that if science is accepted Christianity must be rejected."[51]

Through the 1925 meeting of the Southern Baptist Convention, Mullins's prestige and power in the denomination was at its height. He denied the validity of the theory of evolution in the realm of religion, but refused to ask for legislation and continually pointed to the futility of such restriction.[52] In Baptist schools, teachers should give assurances that

---

[48]*News and Truths,* 17 June 1925.

[49]Mullins declared that he had "no hope" of influencing the fundamentalists, but only of strengthening the moderate position. Mullins to E. B. Pollard, 12 October 1925 (American Baptist Historical Society, Rochester, New York).

[50]Mullins to Fred W. Freeman, 11 August 1925.

[51]*Western Recorder,* 6 August, 3 September, 17 September 1925.

[52]Mullins to Erskine Brooks, editor of the Louisville *Civic Opinion,* 5 August 1925. In a New Orleans speech Mullins declared that the effort to pass anti-evolution laws was "a blunder and foreign to the New Testament." New Orleans *Times-Picayune,* 28 January 1927; *Courier-Journal,* 28 January 1927; Mullins to J. S. Compere, 8 February 1927; W. H. P. Faunce to Mullins, 22 March 1927; Mullins to Louie D. Newton, 28 March 1922.

After the New Orleans speech, Billy Sunday attacked Mullins for opposing legislation. In a subsequent letter of explanation, even the irascible evangelist seemed convinced by Mullins's arguments that legislation would not be helpful. The tone of his last letter changed to one of friendship. Billy Sunday to Mullins, 29 January, 4 February 1927; Mullins to Sunday, 1 February 1927.

Similarly, when a group of religious zealots proposed making Bible reading compulsory in the public schools by legislative act, Mullins proposed that the Bible could be read in the classroom if no one objected. However, the reading must be free of any form of "compulsion." Mullins to Thomas E. Boorde, 8 May 1924.

they were evangelical Christians, but not be required to take oaths about their specific beliefs in the scientific realm.[53] At the height of the controversy, for example, he refused to aid either William Jennings Bryan or Shailer Mathews during the Scopes Trial, attempting to maintain the middle ground. To Bryan, who asked for a deposition to be presented at the trial, Mullins retorted that he had always opposed antievolution legislation while disagreeing with the theory of evolution. He could be of no help to Bryan's cause. To a similar request from the modernist Mathews, Mullins replied that science and religion were becoming monistic to the detriment of both their causes. He disavowed belief in any form of evolution and maintained his unwavering evangelical faith.[54] When Mathews presented Mullins's name in an affidavit at the Scopes Trial as one who would qualify as an evolutionist, Mullins immediately claimed that he was "not a theistic, nor any other kind of evolutionist."[55] These reactions are prime examples of Mullins's moderate approach to the evolution question. A border state denominational leader, Mullins throughout his tenure at Southern Seminary tried to mediate the differences between liberals and conservatives, in both a geographical and ideological sense. For years he had been able to moderate the radical tendencies of Southern Baptist fundamentalists, but as they gained strength Mullins lost his dominant position over denominational affairs. The increasingly acerbic responses of fundamentalists struck Mullins as well as modernists, leaving him less room to maneuver without going to one extreme or the other.

By 1925 fundamentalists among Kentucky Baptists were more interested in attacking those they considered to be subversive within their denomination than in assaulting public education. Controversies at Cumberland College and at the Danville First Baptist Church preoccu-

---

[53]Mullins to Livingston Johnson, 12 September 1925; Mullins, "Christianity in the Modern World," *Review and Expositor* 22 (October 1925): 488; Mullins to E. C. Dargan, 29 July 1925.

[54]Bryan to Mullins, 1 July 1925; Mullins to Bryan, 8 July 1925; Mathews to Mullins, 31 July 1925; Mullins to Mathews, 4 August 1925.

[55]*Western Recorder*, 6 August 1925; Mathews, *New Faith for Old: An Autobiography* (New York: The Macmillan Co., 1936) 228-29; Szasz, *Divided Mind of Protestant America*, 128.

pied them for much of the time.[56] Their adherence to Landmarkism re-
tarded cooperation with other denominations in the name of conservative
causes such as the antievolution campaign.[57] Fundamentalists in Lexington, led by George Ragland, pastor of the First Baptist Church, invited leading Baptist antievolutionists, such as Norris, Riley, and T. T.
Shields, to their city for revival services, which usually degenerated into
denunciatory platforms against Mullins and the Seminary. Ragland tried
to gain control of the Elkhorn Baptist Association in central Kentucky in
order to denounce Mullins publicly. Though Ragland failed, Mullins lost
much of his support in the central Kentucky area.[58] Mullins and other
moderates in the Convention, in absorbing the antievolution vituperations of the fundamentalists, blunted attacks that might otherwise have
been aimed toward public education.[59]

Selsus E. Tull, an adherent of the Stealey-Norris faction, promised
renewed efforts to pass a resolution in direct repudiation of evolution at

---

[56]*Leonard W. Doolan and E. E. Wood, 1925* (Pamphlet File, Southern Seminary Library); Doolan, *The Facts About the Faction in the First Baptist Church,
Danville, Kentucky,* 1928 (Pamphlet File, Southern Seminary Library); Mullins
to Wood, 12 November 1924; Doolan to Mullins, 22 September 1925; Wood to
Doolan, 23 March 1925, Circular Letter.

[57]Bailey, *Southern White Protestantism,* 66-67; Roland Tenus Nelson,
"Fundamentalism and the Northern Baptist Convention" (Ph.D. diss., University of Chicago Divinity School, 1964) 90-91. Boyce Taylor, for example, was
completely anti-institutional and deplored the "uniontarian" emphasis engendered by the interdenominational fundamentalist movement. *News and Truths,*
3 February 1926.

[58]Riley, "The Conflict of Christianity with Its Counterfeit in Kentucky," 8;
Fort Worth *Searchlight,* 9 April 1926; *Lexington Leader,* 28 November 1925;
William H. Porter to Mullins, 28 November 1925; Mullins to Porter, 30 November 1925; A. J. Vining to Mullins, 25 July 1925; Mullins to Vining, 26 September 1925; Mullins to Howard Whidden, 12 December 1925, 19 January 1926.

[59]The internal conflict over the Statement of Faith within the Convention
eased the thrust against public education in several states. Poteat at Wake Forest, Mullins, and others absorbed these blows. Gatewood, *Preachers, Pedagogues, and Politicians,* 30-37, 59-76; Ellis, "The Kentucky Evolution
Controversy," 79-88; Thomas, "Edgar Young Mullins," 62-69; Thompson, *Tried
as by Fire,* 164.

the next Convention.[60] Masters, who thought the issue had been settled at the 1925 meeting, hoped this matter could be disposed of "amicably" if brought up again. More important, he continued public support of Mullins and the Seminary fund drive.[61]

The fundamentalist forces gained strength in the months preceding the 1926 meeting. Convention President George W. McDaniel decided to give up the fight, though Mullins initially counseled against a direct condemnation of evolution. Mullins found that "big 'F' fundamentalists" agitated for control of the Convention and sought to "harrass and muzzle teachers in our schools."[62] In the last months before the 1926 Convention, however, a ground swell of opinion developed favoring a quick resolution of the evolution issue. Moderates tried to hold out against the inclusion of a definitive statement against evolution. Editor Pitt of the *Religious Herald,* for example, held that the passage of such a resolution "would make us the laughing stock of the intelligent world."[63] Fundamentalists, on the other hand, urged the adoption of an antievolution pronouncement.[64] Mullins reluctantly acquiesced, declaring that all seminaries must stand together in order to keep the fundamentalists from passing a direct restriction against any of the teachings of these schools. Implicit was his fear that this would appear to be a sign of weakness on the part of the seminaries and the moderate leadership.[65]

Fundamentalists achieved their long-sought goal at the 1926 Convention. Fearful of the growing antievolutionist sentiment among his

----

[60]*Western Recorder,* 22 April 1926; Garrett, Hinson, and Tull, *Are Southern Baptists "Evangelicals"?,* 101-102.

[61]*Western Recorder,* 29 April 1926.

[62]McDaniel to Mullins, 21 July 1925, 28 April 1926; Mullins to McDaniel, 24 July 1925, 30 April 1926.

[63]Pitt to Mullins, 7 May 1926; Gwaltney to Mullins, 22 February 1926; R. L. Bolton to Mullins, 1 May 1926; Livingston Johnson to Mullins, 4 May 1926.

[64]Selsus E. Tull to Mullins, 13 April, 26 April 1926; J. J. Taylor to Mullins, 5 March 1926; Mullins to Taylor, 12 April 1926; Norris to Mullins, 5 April, 13 April 1926; Mullins to Norris, 12 April, 7 May 1926.

[65]Mullins to Z. T. Cody, 4 May 1926; Mullins to J. H. Farmer, 16 July 1926.

brethren, Mullins carefully reassured the trustees in their annual pre-Convention meeting that the Seminary abided by the "fundamental articles of faith set forth in the original establishment" of the school. He presented a homily to the standard tenets of evangelicalism, but did not directly mention evolution.[66] In an attempt to forestall debate, McDaniel, in his opening address, vowed that "this Convention accepts Genesis as teaching that man was the special creation of God, and rejects every theory, evolution or other, which teaches that man originated in, or came by way of, a lower animal ancestry."[67] The Convention accepted this statement as the "sentiment of the body" after a delegate, by prearrangement, jumped to his feet and moved for adoption.[68] Mullins did not attend because of ill health and the rush of the financial campaign, but he definitely knew of McDaniel's plans.[69] George Ragland tried to rebuke Mullins directly for his alleged evolutionist beliefs, but the Convention voted to disallow continuation of the speech.[70] A later move by the fundamentalists caught the moderates by surprise. Selsus E. Tull of Arkansas successfully introduced a resolution asking that all Convention institutions and boards "give like assurance . . . of a hearty and individual acceptance" of the McDaniel Resolution.[71]

The moderates were furious about the Tull Resolution. One editor, for example, called Tull's move "a piece of mean, dirty, ecclesiastical politics." Another moderate editor found the Tull Resolution to be a plot of the "Bible Union crowd" led by Norris.[72] The ostensible purpose was to force Mullins and Southern Seminary to conform to the wishes of the fundamentalists.[73] Southern Seminary assumed the defensive after the

---

[66]*Faculty Report, 1926* (Pamphlet File, Southern Seminary Library).

[67]*Annual of the Southern Baptist Convention, 1926*, 18.

[68]*Western Recorder*, 27 May 1926.

[69]Mullins to C. H. Parrish, 19 June 1926; Mullins to Pitt, 22 May 1926.

[70]*Western Recorder*, 20 May 1926; *Baptist Standard*, 20 May 1926.

[71]*Annual of the Southern Baptist Convention, 1926*, 98.

[72]Livingston Johnson to Mullins, 19 May 1926; *Religious Herald*, 20 May 1926; *Baptist Courier*, 3 June 1926; Gwaltney to Mullins, 15 June 1926; Mullins to Gwaltney, 17 June, 2 July 1926.

[73]*Christian Century*, 2 September 1926.

Southwestern Seminary trustees complied with the Tull pronouncement before the Convention adjourned.[74] Mullins refused to sign such a pledge.[75] Later, however, he stated that he had on numerous occasions voiced basically the same sentiment, and "now if everybody is happy let us go on with the work of Kingdom building."[76]

Stealey was not happy, and neither were other antievolutionists in Oklahoma. The Baptist General Convention of that state adopted a resolution ordering J. B. Rounds, their corresponding secretary, to withhold funds from all Southern Baptist institutions until each faculty member "signed up" in concurrence with the McDaniel and Tull resolutions.[77]

Fundamentalists applauded the efforts of Stealey and Rounds, urging full compliance from Southern Seminary.[78] Even Masters became more assertive, requesting that the Seminary adopt the Tull dictum immediately. He gleefully published the notices of Southern Baptist agencies and institutions that adopted the Tull Resolution. Masters left no doubt that he now completely supported the witch-hunt methods of the fundamentalists.[79]

Mullins questioned the right of any state to defer payments to the Seminary building fund, but Rounds continued to withhold the Oklahoma funds.[80] Later Mullins published a public acceptance of the McDaniel Resolution by the faculty and board of Southern Seminary. He included twenty "Seminary Articles of Faith" that all faculty members had signed since the inception of the institution. Part four of that doc-

---

[74]Livingston Johnson to Mullins, 19 May 1926; Mullins to Pitt, 22 May 1926.

[75]Furniss, *The Fundamentalist Controversy*, 125.

[76]*Western Recorder*, 17 June 1926.

[77]*Baptist General Convention of Oklahoma, Minutes, 1926*, 24; Elbert L. Watson, "Oklahoma and the Anti-Evolution Movement of the 1920s," *Chronicles of Oklahoma* 42 (Winter 1964-1965): 402.

[78]Mullins to W. B. Riley, 28 July 1927; Fort Worth *Searchlight*, 2 July 1926; Fort Worth *Baptist Fundamentalist*, 7 October, 4 November 1927 (the successor of Norris's *Searchlight*).

[79]*Western Recorder*, 3 June, 24 June, 22 July, 12 August 1926.

[80]Mullins to Rounds, 27 November, 10 December, 17 December 1926.

ument maintained that "God originally created man in His own image.
. . ." But again, Mullins made no direct mention of evolution.[81] Collection of funds for the building drive plummeted because of the furor created by the Oklahoma controversy. One fund-raiser in Mississippi, for example, urged adoption, believing that doubt about the orthodoxy of Southern Seminary "hurts in the country churches worse than you have any idea." A prospective donor from Texas asked for immediate compliance, implying a substantial donation was in the balance.[82] Indeed, prior to the 1927 meeting of the Convention most moderate denominational leaders urged Mullins to comply with the Tull Resolution.[83]

As this controversy wore on into 1927, Southern Seminary completed the initial phases of construction. Mullins planned to present the new buildings at the 1927 Southern Baptist Convention meeting in Louisville. A severe case of bronchitis, however, developed into bronchial pneumonia and he could not attend a single session.[84] The Southern Seminary report to the Convention concluded with an acceptance of the McDaniel statement "as to the origin of man," a partial surrender to the demands of the fundamentalists. The Convention approved this pronouncement.[85] Neither Stealey nor Rounds, however, accepted it as complying with the Tull Resolution.

Mullins countered with a pamphlet. He mentioned the previous times the Seminary faculty and board accepted the spirit of the 1926 Houston declarations. State conventions like Oklahoma had no right to "divert" funds from legitimate Southern Baptist institutions. The Seminary Articles of Faith, he maintained, covered all contingencies concerning

---

[81]*Western Recorder*, 3 February 1927.

[82]W. H. Patton to Mullins, 8 March 1927; T. W. Burleson to Mullins, 25 October, 29 November 1926; Mullins to Van Ness, 26 September 1927 (Van Ness Papers, Dargan-Carver Library).

[83]S. P. Brooks to Mullins, 4 January 1927; Carver to Mullins, 23 June 1926; Mullins to B. H. DeMent, 17 December 1926; DeMent to Mullins, 31 December 1926; Mullins to Scarborough, 4 March, 15 March 1927; Livingston Johnson to Mullins, 8 June 1926.

[84]Sampey, *Memoirs,* 184, 199; Mueller, *A History of Southern Baptist Theological Seminary,* 210.

[85]*Annual of the Southern Baptist Convention, 1927,* 105.

seminary teaching and doctrine. If Oklahoma were allowed to force the Seminary to "sign up" now, it would be possible for another Convention to ask the faculty to ascribe to a "modernistic or subversive statement." Moreover, a legal problem arose due to the inclusion of the Articles of Faith in the charter of the Seminary issued by the Commonwealth of Kentucky. Adoption of the Tull Resolution would be an illegal insertion into the charter and could possibly lead to its revocation. "In conclusion," he asserted, "the Seminary . . . should not be treated in the manner which it has suffered at the hands of Oklahoma."[86]

Despite Mullins's pamphlet, Oklahoma Baptists continued to withhold funds.[87] Stealey charged that Mullins was incapable of leading a Baptist seminary on an orthodox path. In frustration, Mullins retorted to Stealey that he was "so saturated with prejudice against me that it would be rather difficult for you to see anything good in me whatsoever."[88] A change in Oklahoma Baptist attitudes occurred in 1927 when the board of that state fired Stealey as editor of the *Baptist Messenger*.[89] In March 1928 the imbroglio ended when Mullins sent an acceptable letter to the Oklahoma Convention reiterating his earlier arguments. This time signatures of the Seminary faculty accompanied the commitment. The letter did not mention evolution directly, and Mullins made it clear that the signatures only meant that the faculty approved the previous declarations of the Southern Baptist Convention, and not those of Oklahoma Baptists. Shortly thereafter, Rounds forwarded the long withheld funds to Mullins.[90]

Mullins, fearing fundamentalist reprisals against the Seminary building drive, yielded to increased opposition and repudiated any be-

---

[86]Mullins, *The Southern Baptist Theological Seminary and the Oklahoma Resolutions* (Louisville: Southern Baptist Theological Seminary, 1927) 4, 6, 7, 8. A Louisville attorney gave the opinion that the charter could not be tampered with by demanding that professors pledge to anything other than the original document. W. Pratt Dale to Mullins, 14 December 1926, 3 January 1927; Mullins to Dale, 15 December 1926.

[87]*New York Times*, 11 November 1927.

[88]Mullins to Stealey, 1 November 1927.

[89]*Baptist Messenger*, 14 December, 21 December 1927.

[90]Ibid., 28 March 1928; Mullins to Rounds, 29 March, 6 April 1928.

lief in evolution. The Oklahoma situation was an omen that could have meant the end of all plans for completing construction of the Seminary. Mullins underestimated the strength of the fundamentalists who demanded both antievolution legislation and a direct pronouncement against evolution in the Convention. In 1922-1923 the conflict was confined to Kentucky, but later spread throughout Southern Baptist Convention territory. After 1925 Mullins lost his dominant position in the Convention and was no longer able to control Convention meetings as he had in the early 1920s. In Kentucky he could no longer dominate Masters, the editor of the *Recorder.* Though he no longer controlled Convention affairs, Mullins still refused to submit to the fundamentalists' pleas for legislation.[91] His opposition helped prevent a more successful antievolution crusade in the South in the 1920s.

A change in Mullins's attitude toward evolution occurred in the 1920s because of the constant antievolutionist barrage. His earlier adherence, or at least toleration of Christian theistic evolution, began to cool. The turmoil over evolution in 1925 was the dividing point. In 1923, for example, Mullins publicly advised that it was possible for Christians to be evolutionists, listing a number of prominent Baptist theologians who believed in Christian theistic evolution. Four years later, he denied that any earlier Baptist scholars really believed in any form of evolution.[92]

A survey of Mullins's correspondence in the 1920s reveals more questions about evolution than any other single topic. In early 1924, for example, he told an interested Alabama minister that there was nothing to fear from evolution, sending a list of liberal books on the topic.[93] After his apparent success at the 1925 Memphis Convention, Mullins pri-

---

[91]Masters demanded more independence than he had earlier in the decade. His opposition to the Baptist World Alliance became an embarrassment to Mullins. Masters declared that he did not adhere to the Norris-Shields faction, but sometimes he did agree with them on "principles." Victor I. Masters to Van Ness, 15 October 1928 (Van Ness Papers, Dargan-Carver Library); Mullins to J. H. Rushbrooke, 24 April 1928; Mullins to Masters, 3 August 1928; Masters to Mullins, 21 September 1928.

[92]*Western Recorder,* 22 March 1923, 5 May 1927; Thomas, "Edgar Young Mullins," 315.

[93]Mullins to J. M. Thomas, 19 January 1924.

vately counseled his brethren that it was possible to be both an evolutionist and a Christian. The Convention, moreover, had no right to enforce "scientific creeds upon their teachers."[94] He even suggested that when students reached a "suitable age" they should be given a "fair treatment" of evolution.[95] However, the incessant attacks by fundamentalists, ill health, and worries about the building fund drive soon wore down Mullins's resistance. Just before the fundamentalist victory at the 1926 meeting of the Convention, he denied belief in any form of evolution and continued this tack when approached by other fundamentalist brethren.[96]

Secular historians and commentators have been quite critical of Mullins's performance in the antievolution controversy. Virginius Dabney, criticizing the leadership of Mullins, asserted that he "wobbled around a great deal, and on the whole gave encouragement to the antievolutionists."[97] Norman Furniss later repeated this charge, declaring that Mullins's "deep conservatism bred a suspicion of evolution that forced him to contradict his more liberal statements."[98] Robert Moats Miller supported Dabney and Furniss, stating that Mullins was "equivocal" and "evasive" in his positions on evolution.[99] These interpretations are too harsh because they do not recognize the tenuous nature of Mullins's position. The shadow of the Whitsitt controversy militated against Mullins's becoming a controversialist.[100] Even so, Mullins took the Convention to the brink of schism, and only then did he relent.

---

[94]Mullins to J. W. R. Jenkins, 4 August, 18 August 1925; Mullins to Charles E. Dicken, 27 August 1925.

[95]Mullins to C. W. Davis, 29 July 1925.

[96]Mullins to John R. Gilpin, 7 May 1926; Mullins to Clarence C. Walker, 7 May 1926; Mullins to A. G. Melton, 3 July 1926; Mullins to J. J. Taylor, 16 June 1927.

[97]Dabney, *Liberalism in the South* (Chapel Hill: University of North Carolina Press, 1932) 301.

[98]Furniss, *The Fundamentalist Controversy*, 120.

[99]Miller, "Social Attitudes of American Baptists," 84; Miller, *American Protestantism and Social Issues*, 156.

[100]Bailey, *Southern White Protestantism*, 64.

Part of the problem in evaluating Mullins's role is the attempt, engaged in by Dabney, Furniss, and Miller, to view him as a liberal gone conservative. Mullins's basic beliefs remained constant during his lifetime. Some of his writings made him appear more liberal than he probably intended. Because they were so often reviled by fundamentalists, liberals like Mathews mistook open, friendly dialogue with Mullins and other moderate evangelicals as assent. Mullins did perhaps at one time flirt with theistic evolution or, more specifically, Christian theistic evolution. However, his deep faith in the supernatural base of evangelicalism never allowed him to ascribe to any form of naturalistic evolution. The theological flux of the 1920s, in accentuating his moderate evangelical Christianity, made him appear increasingly conservative. The surface schism of religious factions into modernists and fundamentalists heightened with the antievolution controversy and made it ever more difficult for a moderate like Mullins to keep his separate identity.[101]

Both factions, exemplified by Bryan and Mathews at the Scopes Trial, denied the availability of a middle ground. Furniss further charged that Mullins "stood between the camps of the liberals and the Fundamentalists" and failed "to guide his brethren through the obfuscations of the evolution controversy."[102] Mullins, however, could lead no further than his brethren would or could be led. He was more liberal than the majority of his coreligionists. Given his religious beliefs and the question of funds for the Seminary, Mullins chose the only path he could accept if he wished to retain his credibility in the Southern Baptist Convention as a theologian and administrator.[103]

---

[101]Szasz, *The Divided Mind of Protestant America*, 128; Thompson, *Tried as by Fire*, 114-16; Robert T. Handy, "Fundamentalism and Modernism in Perspective," *Religion in Life* 24 (Summer 1955): 392.

During the height of the antievolution conflict, Shailer Mathews indicated that Protestantism had divided into two factions, modernists and fundamentalists. His hope was that modernism would soften the biblical intransigence of the fundamentalists. Mathews, "Fundamentalism and Modernism: An Interpretation," *American Review* 2 (January-February 1924): 1-9.

[102]Furniss, *The Fundamentalist Controversy*, 120.

[103]*Christian Century*, 6 December 1928; Miller, *American Protestantism and Social Issues*, 165. Miller also incorrectly judged that Mullins did not accept the concept of academic freedom until 1927, when in fact this had been his primary defense throughout the decade.

Church historians have generally praised Mullins's scholarly attainments though never placing him in the highest rank of twentieth-century American theologians.[104] Southern Baptist writers have commended his denominational leadership, his close attention to the "middle course." To this day many consider him to be the "supreme Baptist theologian." For example, in a recent book entitled *Are Southern Baptists "Evangelicals"?*, Mullins was cited more than any other source. Old associates like Harold W. Tribble praised his defense of the Seminary against "self-propelling dogmatists" and "vociferous egotists."[105] One Southern Baptist biographer found that Mullins was "no vacillating weakling who refused to take a stand."[106] Another Southern Baptist commentator paradoxically found that Mullins and the Southern Seminary faculty "successfully countered efforts to place restrictions upon classroom instruction," but then later declared that they "could have laid a broader foundation for theological understanding among Southern Baptists."[107]

Mullins's moderate tack became more difficult to maintain in the 1920s.[108] The bitter fundamentalist attacks indicated that they consid-

---

[104]Thomas, "Edgar Young Mullins," 136; C. W. Cline, "Some Baptist Systematic Theologians," *Review and Expositor* 20 (July 1923): 315; Walter Marshall Horton, "Systematic Theology," in *Protestant Thought in the Twentieth Century*, ed. Arnold S. Nash (New York: The Macmillan Co., 1951) 112; Mueller, *A History of Southern Baptist Theological Seminary*, 192; Cauthen, *The Impact of American Religious Liberalism*, 31-32.

[105]Tribble, "Edgar Young Mullins" (1952), 129; Walter B. Shurden, *Not a Silent People* (Nashville: Broadman Press, 1972) 95; Garrett, Hinson, and Tull, *Are Southern Baptists "Evangelicals"?*, 238; Eighmy, *Churches in Cultural Captivity*, 126.

[106]Charles J. Ferris, "Southern Baptists and Evolution in the 1920s: The Roles of Edgar Young Mullins, J. Frank Norris, and William Louis Poteat" (M.A. thesis, University of Louisville, 1973) 188.

[107]Reuben E. Alley, "Southern Baptist Seminaries and Academic Freedom" (Founders' Day Address, 17 September 1963, Pamphlet File, Southern Seminary Library).

[108]In a footnote Paul A. Carter noted that Mullins represented the "dilemma" of one who maintained a "compromise position." Carter, "The Fundamentalist Defense of the Faith," in *Change and Continuity in Twentieth Century America*, ed. John Braeman, Robert H. Bremner, and David Brody (Columbus: Ohio State University Press, 1968) 210.

ered him to be a traitor to the cause of evangelical Christianity.[109] Mullins certainly does not qualify as a fundamentalist, especially in the meaning of the term as ascribed to the most conservative Protestants of the 1920s. Compared with Riley, Norris, Masters, A. C. Dixon, and Boyce Taylor, Mullins was quite liberal.[110] He fitted the definition assigned to the nonfundamentalist who is conservative, but "speaks to the issues, is aware of the problems, is well informed, and is in communication with those from whom he dissents."[111] Much is made of the alleged liberal-

---

[109]Cole, *The History of Fundamentalism,* 286; Szasz, "Three Fundamentalist Leaders," 195.

[110]Carroll E. Harrington's study of fundamentalism identified Riley, Dixon, Torrey, and Straton as church leaders who exhibited an "authoritarian personality." Harrington, "The Fundamentalist Movement in America, 1870-1920" (Ph.D. diss., University of California, Berkeley, 1959) 197.

A number of excellent biographical studies of prominent fundamentalists have appeared. The more violent fundamentalists, such as Norris and Riley, displayed strong, aggressive personalities and often attacked Mullins. For example, see the following: Szasz, "William B. Riley and the Fight Against Teaching of Evolution in Minnesota," *Minnesota History* 41 (Spring 1969): 201-16; C. Allyn Russell, "William Bell Riley, Architect of Fundamentalism," *Minnesota History* 43 (Spring 1972): 14-30; Russell, "J. Frank Norris: Violent Fundamentalist," *Southwestern Historical Quarterly* 75 (January 1972): 271-302.

Other less violent fundamentalists displayed the same theological intransigence, but they never made strong attacks on Mullins. For example, see the following articles: Joseph D. Ban, "Two Views of One Age: Fosdick and Straton," *Foundations* 14 (April-June 1971): 153-71; Brenda M. Meehan, "A. C. Dixon: An Early Fundamentalist," *Foundations* 10 (January-March 1967): 50-63. Russell has well-researched and judicious articles on the less adamant fundamentalists. J. C. Massee and J. Gresham Machen were the least combative of those already mentioned. Another article on John Roach Straton offers an interesting contrast to the scholarly Machen. Russell, "J. C. Massee: Unique Fundamentalist," *Foundations* 12 (October-December 1969): 330-56; Russell, "John Roach Straton, Accusative Case," *Foundations* 13 (January-March 1970): 44-72; Russell, "J. Gresham Machen, Scholarly Fundamentalist," *Journal of Presbyterian History* 51 (Spring 1973): 41-69. Seven of Russell's articles have been compiled in *Voices of American Fundamentalism* (Philadelphia: Westminster Press, 1976). See also Szasz, *The Divided Mind of Protestant America* for essays on Bryan (107-25), and Thompson, *Tried as by Fire,* for an essay on Norris (137-65).

[111]Sydney F. Ahlstrom, "Continental Influence on American Christian Thought Since World War I," *Church History* 27 (September 1958): 271.

ism of William L. Poteat, president of Wake Forest University in the early
1920s and an oft-attacked foe of the antievolutionists. While Poteat accepted Christian theistic evolution, in contrast, Mullins never ruled out
the possibility that the theory had some relevance. Poteat was not an active participant in the tumultuous Convention controversies. He fought
his battles in North Carolina, while Mullins was forced to fight in the
more open and chaotic Southern Baptist Convention.[112]

Though Mullins refused to condemn evolution directly in any Seminary pronouncement after the McDaniel and Tull resolutions, he could
only fight a rear guard action. The hypersensitivity of the fundamentalists finally dominated the Convention and, in the end, Mullins yielded.
Ill health, the failure of the 75 Million Campaign, the construction of the
new Seminary, and the decline of the revenues for the Seminary were
real concerns for him. Moreover, he lost his important denominational
position of leadership after 1925. More subtle, but equally important,
was the change in Southern Baptist polity in the decade. The 1920s
marked the culmination of a centralization trend in the Southern Baptist Convention, as it did in business and industry as well. The growth
of the boards, particularly the Sunday School Board, and appointment
of an Executive Committee to handle denominational affairs illustrated
the shift in polity from a democratic body to one dominated by institutionalists. By the late 1920s the development of the Cooperative Program, a comprehensive funding source, completed the centralization
trend initiated by the 75 Million Campaign. What began as a voluntary
association grew into control on a regional, and later national, basis by
the various boards, the heads of which comprised the leadership hierarchy of the Southern Baptist Convention.[113] "Institutionalists" like Mullins were forced to mute their doctrinal leadership fearing reprisals by

---

[112]Gerald W. Johnson, "Billy with the Red Necktie," *Virginia Quarterly Review* 30 (Autumn 1943): 551-61; Suzanne C. Linder, "William Louis Poteat and
the Evolution Controversy," *North Carolina Historical Review* 40 (April 1963):
135, 157; Bernard, "The Baptists," 137; Linder, *William Louis Poteat: Prophet
of Progress,* 143-72.

[113]Bailey, *Southern White Protestantism,* 59-60; Donald F. Trotter, "A Study
of Authority and Power in the Structure and Dynamics of the Southern Baptist
Convention" (D.R.E. thesis, Southern Baptist Theological Seminary, 1962) 40-
41, 56-57, 77-78, 88, 99; Duke K. McCall, "Authority of the Southern Baptist
Convention," *Encyclopedia of Southern Baptists,* 1:99.

their fundamentalist brethren.[114] This situation was accentuated by the Great Depression, which saw most moderates in the Convention acquiesce to the demands of the larger fundamentalist faction.[115] The moderates could no longer control their doctrinally fundamentalist brethren as they had up until the 1926 meeting of the Convention. Unlike their Northern Baptist brethren, who suffered schism because of the evolution controversy and thereafter limited success in growth, Southern Baptists united and expanded after the end of the evolution controversy. Moreover, no issue or controversy healed the cleavage in the Convention as did the nearly unanimous Southern Baptist anti-Smith campaign in 1928.[116]

[114]Poteat, "Religion in the South," 267; Nelson, "Fundamentalism and the Northern Baptist Convention," 166-69.

[115]Eighmy, *Churches in Cultural Captivity*, 111; Poteat, "Religion in the South," 256-57; Furniss, *The Fundamentalist Controversy*, 125; Bailey, *Southern White Protestantism*, 66-67.

[116]Edward Lassiter Clark, "Southern Baptist Reaction to the Darwinian Theory of Evolution" (Th.D. diss., Southwestern Baptist Theological Seminary, 1952) 162-67; Winthrop Hudson, "The Divergent Careers of Southern and Northern Baptists; A Study in Growth," *Foundations* 16 (April-June 1973): 178; Bailey, *Southern White Protestantism*, 101-103.

11 THE FINAL CRUSADE

Though an advocate of Prohibition, Mullins took little interest in that issue until the mid-1920s. At that time he became increasingly concerned over the fate of Prohibition. Like many mainline Southern Protestants, Mullins was spurred into political activism for one of the few times in his life by the political ambitions of Governor Alfred E. Smith. Mullins's all-out opposition to Smith and his embracing of Herbert Hoover's candidacy coincided with his apparent turn toward religious conservatism. For the first time in years, Southern Baptist moderates and fundamentalists generally agreed on a public issue: Democratic candidate Smith, if elected, would do his best to destroy one of the hallmarks of the evangelical ethos, Prohibition. It was not the first time in American history that citizens voted for or against a candidate because of his religion. Some scholars have argued that the 1928 presidential election represented a major shift in American politics, piecing together the Roosevelt Democratic coalition of the 1930s. Patrick Henry Callahan, a dry Catholic layman from Louisville and supporter of many a Progressive ideal, convincingly contended that Smith's religion drew him more votes than he lost. Nevertheless, Mullins demonstrated an atypical political reaction and entered the political fray with uncharacteristic ferocity. Perhaps the loss of Protestant hegemony actually had become apparent to him. He joined the dry forces in their crusade to retain one of the last reforms of the Progressive era.[1]

In the summer of 1926 Mullins made his first contribution to the emerging fight over Prohibition enforcement in the *Recorder*, later distributed as a tract by the Anti-Saloon League of Kentucky. Mullins declared that liquor was "evil." "As to the next President of the United States," he warned, "I am against Gov. Al Smith of New York."[2] Participating in the national convention of the Anti-Saloon League in late 1927, Mullins predicted the solid South would break if the Democratic party nominated Smith. In rhetoric more common to his antievolutionist detractors, Mullins declared, "We must provide adequate funds for the propaganda. We must be united and determined and armed with an undying faith."[3]

---

[1]Thompson, *Tried as by Fire*, 167-94; Szasz, *The Divided Mind of Protestant America*, xi; Norman H. Clark, *Deliver Us from Evil: An Interpretation of American Prohibition* (New York: W. W. Norton, 1976) 189; Allan J. Lichtman, *Prejudice and the Old Politics: The Presidential Election of 1928* (Chapel Hill: University of North Carolina Press, 1979) 240-46; Patrick Henry Callahan, "Religious Prejudice in the Election," *Current History* 29 (December 1928): 381-83; George Brown Tindall, *The Emergence of the New South, 1913-1945* (Baton Rouge: Louisiana State University Press, 1967) 219, 246; Paul A. Carter, *Another Part of the Twenties* (New York: Columbia University Press, 1977) 85-102.

[2]*Western Recorder*, 3 June 1926. Further possible evidence of Mullins's shift to the political right is given in his response to entreaties from rightist organizations. In 1922 and 1923 the "Companions of the Crested Clan" and the Ku Klux Klan tried to obtain Mullins's cooperation in their activities. Mullins ignored their pleas. State Director's Office, Companions of the Crested Clan to Mullins, 18 October, 3 November, 11 November 1922; William J. Mahoney to Mullins, 19 November 1923. By 1926, however, Mullins was willing to allow the Klan to publish his article "Prohibition To-day" in the *Kourier Magazine*. W. A. Hamlett to Mullins, 29 September 1925; 10 June, 29 June 1926; Mullins to Hamlett, 2 October 1925, 14 June 1926. The Klan paper published the article a year later. Mullins, "Prohibition To-day," *Kourier Magazine* 3 (June 1927): 10-11.

[3]*Western Recorder*, 15 December 1927, 5 January 1928.

Mullins did not attend the 1928 Southern Baptist Convention in Houston because of the press of Seminary duties and ill health. When the Convention declared its opposition to any anti-Prohibition candidate, Mullins concurred.[4] The day after the May commencement ceremonies, Mullins suffered a slight stroke. Disregarding his doctor's advice, and with only a few days' rest, he traveled to North Carolina on a fundraising tour. The strain was too great. After preaching three sermons in one day, he suffered a complete physical breakdown a day later, losing all feeling on his left side.[5]

After several weeks of recuperation in North Carolina, he returned to Louisville. At the opening meeting of the Baptist World Alliance in Toronto, a colleague read Mullins's presidential address, "Baptist Life in the World's Life." In these remarks Mullins glorified his denomination, particularly excoriating Catholicism as the antithesis of Baptist polity.[6] In a presidential election year, with a Catholic running for that office for the first time, Mullins's attack carried great weight among the more moderate evangelical element in the country.

Though his health did not improve, Mullins continued to aid the anti-Smith cause.[7] While Bishop James Cannon, Jr., desired a more active role by Mullins in the anti-Smith campaign, he realized that the Southern Baptist Theological Seminary president could add prestige to the Prohibition forces with his pen. Cannon urged Mullins to do as much as he dared, short of speaking engagements, which were out of the question.[8] Mullins responded by cooperating with both the national of-

---

[4]Bailey, *Southern White Protestantism*, 96-97; Edmund A. Moore, *A Catholic Runs for President: The Campaign of 1928* (New York: The Ronald Press Co., 1956) 168-69; *Western Recorder*, 14 June 1928.

[5]Sampey, *Memoirs*, 204-205.

[6]*Western Recorder*, 5 July 1928; Mullins, "Baptist Life in the World's Life," *Review and Expositor* 25 (July 1928): 300-14; *Fourth Baptist World Congress: 1928, Record of Proceedings*, 55, 60-62.

[7]Mullins to Van Ness, 9 July 1928 (Van Ness Papers, Dargan-Carver Library); *Western Recorder*, 19 July 1928.

[8]Cannon to Mullins, 11, 16, and 30 July 1928; Mullins to Cannon, 16 July 1928.

fices and the Kentucky Anti-Saloon League.[9] Unable to attend a meeting of the Anti-Saloon heirarchy to be held in Asheville, North Carolina, he wrote a widely disseminated tract for that convention. Mullins, reiterating the usual Prohibitionist forebodings about the candidacy of Smith, declared that the Democratic party had repudiated Jeffersonian ideals that he held dear. With uncharacteristic sarcasm Mullins scored that party for nominating a "bone-dry running mate from Arkansas for the sopping wet head of the ticket from the sidewalks of New York." As a "Christian" and a "citizen," Mullins vowed he could not be silent "when a great moral issue is at stake."[10]

Mullins continually denied that he opposed Smith because of his religion. He cautioned his brethren not to raise the Catholic issue, but realized that the topic would be implicit in the campaign.[11] When Billy Sunday came to Kentucky, Mullins urged an Anti-Saloon League official to keep the evangelist from pressing the religious issue.[12] Patrick Henry Callahan, a longtime friend of Mullins, praised his efforts to keep the religious issue out of the campaign.[13]

The Louisville seminary president received mixed opinions about his exceptional activity in the political sphere. Kentucky Republicans, including United States Senator Fred Sackett, welcomed Mullins's activity

---

[9]R. J. Grindell to Mullins, 12 December 1927; Mullins to Grindell, 14 December 1927; E. S. Shumaker to Mullins, 28 January 1928; Francis Scott McBride to Mullins, 13 February 1928; John Preston McConnell to Mullins, 16 February 1928; O. G. Christeau to Mullins, 27 February 1928; Ernest Cherrington to Mullins, 12, 18, and 23 July 1928; Mullins to Cherrington, 16, 20, and 28 July 1928; A. G. Graham to Mullins, 6 December 1927.

[10]*Western Recorder*, 12 July 1928; *Courier-Journal*, 8 July 1928; Bailey, *Southern White Protestantism*, 97-98. Shorter versions of Mullins's pronouncement appeared in the *Minneapolis Journal*, 7 July 1928, and the *Boston Evening Transcript*, 7 July 1928.

[11]Mullins to J. W. Gillon, 17 July 1928; Mullins to A. C. Graham, 9 June 1928; Mullins to M. M. Logan, 30 October 1928.

[12]Mullins to A. C. Graham, 27 September 1928.

[13]Callahan to Mullins, 5 September, 20 September 1928; Mullins to Callahan, 7 September 1928. In an article published not long after the election, Callahan played down the influence of religion on the outcome of the presidential election, emphasizing instead Prohibition as the "main issue." Callahan, "Religious Prejudice in the Election," 381-83.

in behalf of Hoover.[14] Others praised Mullins for taking a stand against Smith because of the Prohibition issue.[15] The Seminary faculty took the same tack as their president, publicly urging the defeat of the New York governor.[16] Not all people, however, agreed with Mullins's excursion into partisan politics. Judge Robert W. Bingham, owner of the *Courier-Journal*, expressed sorrow that they disagreed over the election.[17] Some of Mullins's own Baptist brethren denied his right to enter politics in such an active manner. When at least four correspondents asked Mullins how he could support the party that had not enforced Prohibition throughout the decade, Mullins ignored their logic, maintaining his unbounded faith in Hoover.[18]

The 1928 presidential campaign brought together the factious elements among Southern Baptists. Moderate and fundamentalist Baptists agreed that the danger to Prohibition outweighed any past differences over evolution or any other issue. The anti-Smith campaign completed a détente between Mullins and his fundamentalist Baptist brethren; Riley, Norris, and T. T. Martin resumed friendly relations after years of bickering over the evolution issue. Martin even claimed that one of Mullins's articles meant at least a half million votes for Hoover.[19]

---

[14]Sackett to Mullins, 5 November 1928. Earlier in the year Sackett sent a $1,000 donation in the memory of George W. Norton. Sackett to Mullins, 25 February 1928.

[15]Charles W. Powers to Mullins, 10 July 1928; Richard H. Edmonds to Mullins, 18 July 1928; A. J. Barton to Mullins, 13 July 1928; John S. Craig to Mullins, 9 July 1928; W. H. Jones to Mullins, August 1928; C. B. Vaughn to Mullins, 6 July 1928; George B. Winslow to Mullins, 14 July 1928.

[16]*Courier-Journal*, 8 October 1928; Robertson to Mullins, 7 November 1928; W. O. Carver, "Edgar Young Mullins—Leader and Builder," *Review and Expositor* 26 (April 1929): 134.

[17]Bingham to Mullins, 26 October 1928.

[18]E. B. Teague to Mullins, 1 August, 4 August 1928; John T. Duncan to Mullins, 18 October 1928; B. W. Griffith to Mullins, 1 November 1928; E. F. Holmes to Mullins, 1 November 1928; Mullins to Teague, 28 July 1928; Mullins to Duncan, 2 November 1928.

[19]Norris to Mullins, 25 August 1928; Mullins to Norris, 31 August 1928; Mullins to Riley, 7 February 1927; Riley to Mullins, 9 February 1927; Martin to Mullins, 8 August, 20 September 1927; Mullins to Martin, 22 September 1927, 11 July 1928.

The nearly unanimous Southern Baptist campaign against Smith brought together the contrasting styles of the moderates and fundamentalists. The moderates did not emphasize religion, preferring instead the Prohibition issue. Fundamentalists, however, rushed to display their virulent opposition to Catholicism.[20] In the *Recorder* numerous articles merged into an anti-Catholic and anti-Smith crusade.[21] From his stronghold in western Kentucky, Boyce Taylor even found a small word of praise for Mullins's anti-Smith pronouncements, further evidence of the détente. He assailed the New York governor as bitterly as the *Recorder*.[22]

Mullins's health only slightly improved in July and August, and his doctors placed him on a rigid schedule. By September the hope of getting back to work after rest for six more months buoyed his spirits.[23] Though he could not travel, Mullins left no doubt about his political preferences in the religious and secular press. In a caustic article, entitled "Preachers and Politics," he bristled at the thought that a minister should never enter political campaigns; a "moral issue" was at stake and ministers were supposed to lead in that sphere. He compared Prohibition to issues such as world peace, freedom of speech, press, and worship, and opposition to slavery that were above mere politics and were "non-partisan" issues.[24] Throughout the remainder of the campaign, Mullins maintained a strong anti-Smith stance.[25]

---

[20]Hill, "The Ethical Emphases of the Editors of Baptist Journals Published in the Southeastern Region of the United States, 1915-1940," 72, 117, 142-43; Thompson, *Tried as by Fire*, 167-94.

[21]See the *Western Recorder*, for example, 12 April, 31 May, 2 August, 30 August 1928 for anti-Catholic editorials. The *Recorder* printed nearly one hundred articles between 5 January and election day that would be considered pro-Prohibition, anti-Smith, anti-Catholic articles and editorials.

[22]*News and Truths*, 13 June, 20 June, 4, 11, and 18 July, 8 August, 22 August, 12 September, 3, 10, 17, 24, and 31 October 1928.

[23]Mullins to Robertson, 6 September 1928; Mullins to W. H. P. Faunce, 21 September 1928.

[24]*Courier-Journal*, 21 August 1928; *Western Recorder*, 23 August 1928.

[25]*Christian Herald*, 6 October 1928; *Western Recorder*, 18 October 1928; *Courier-Journal*, 21 October 1928.

When the returns overwhelmingly gave the election to Hoover, Mullins rejoiced and extended his congratulations to the victor. In his letter to Hoover, Mullins betrayed his Southern chauvinism by expressing the hope that the region would "play a larger role in the nation's life than has been possible since 1865." He had complete faith that Hoover would continue his "magnificent service for God and humanity" as president.[26]

A few days after the election Mullins suffered a serious stroke that permanently paralyzed his left side.[27] He lingered for about two weeks, dying at noon on Friday, 23 November 1928.[28] All of Louisville mourned Mullins's death. The *Courier*, using the idiom of the business world, declared that the country had "lost one of its recognized captains of religion" and the city its "most renowned citizen."[29] The *Herald Post* likewise eulogized Mullins as "a great and a good man."[30] Similar opinions were expressed elsewhere.[31] Professor Sampey presided at the memorial service on Sunday, 25 November. Representatives from several Louisville churches and Baptist organizations took part in the ceremonies.[32]

---

[26]Mullins to Hoover, 12 November 1928; Hoover to Mullins, 14 November 1928.

[27]*New York Times*, 15 November 1928.

[28]Louisville *Herald Post*, 23 November 1928; Isla May Mullins to Van Ness, 20 November 1928 (Van Ness Papers, Dargan-Carver Library); *Western Recorder*, 29 November 1928.

[29]*Courier-Journal*, 24 November 1928.

[30]Louisville *Herald Post*, 24 November 1928.

[31]*New York Times*, 24 November 1928; *The Baptist*, 8 December 1928; *Christian Century*, 6 December 1928; *Outlook and Independent*, 12 December 1928; *Watchman-Examiner*, 29 November 1928.

[32]"Funeral Services for Dr. E. Y. Mullins" (manuscript in Southern Seminary Library); *Courier-Journal*, 30 November 1928.

12 CONCLUSION

$\mathbf{M}$ullins's life displayed many complexities. Though a native of the South and the son of a Southern Baptist preacher, Mullins did not join that denomination until he had already reached his adult years. He studied at a "Southern" college, Texas A. and M. After a religious conversion he decided on a life in the ministry, matriculating at Southern Baptist Theological Seminary. After his thoroughly Southern and Southern Baptist background, he took ministerial charges in Baltimore and Newton Centre. There he preached before liberal Northern Baptist congregations, took classes at Northern universities and seminaries, and had time to study such current topics as labor unrest and the philosophy of pragmatism. In 1899 he came back to Southern Seminary as a compromise president after the previous administrator, William H. Whitsitt, had been forced to resign by Landmarkists.[1]

At this stage of his life Mullins could have very soon disappeared into the mainstream of mediocre Southern Baptist teachers, yet he chose to

---

[1]W. J. McGlothlin, "Edgar Young Mullins," *Dictionary of American Biography*, 13:322-23.

218 🗐 William E. Ellis

strike off on a singularly different path than one might expect. For the
next three decades he labored to fulfill the three roles of theologian, administrator, and denominational leader in his public ministry. He became the "Supreme Baptist theologian" in his attempt to formulate a
"theological restatement" of evangelical faith. He tried to intellectualize
the old-time religion of nineteenth-century evangelicalism. Never yield-
ing on the necessity of supernaturalism for a viable Christian witness,
Mullins stressed experience as the key ingredient of a religious life. Most
of his writings were an attempt to rationalize this experience in terms
of modern theology. He endeavored to synthesize the supernaturalism
of evangelicalism with modern ideas of philosophy and science. Pragmatism, particularly of the William James variety, intrigued him because of its emphasis on individualism. Even Darwinism did not pose
an immediate threat, as long as Mullins could presume God as the founder of the system unlocked by the English scientist. However, Mullins's
"Christian theistic evolution" failed to suit the temper of the 1920s. The
theological tightrope that he had so skillfully negotiated prior to World
War I became increasingly difficult to walk in the 1920s. After 1925 he
lost ground not only among his coreligionists but with other theists as
well. Assailed on the right by fundamentalists within his own denomination and abandoned on the left by modernists who no longer had
much patience with moderate evangelicals, Mullins was tormented by
a loss of prestige and position in his last years. Under tremendous administrative pressure he finally yielded to the desires of Southern Baptist
fundamentalists.[2]

Not long after beginning his ministry, Mullins told a Seminary classmate of his intention to pursue a ministry in which he would be both "a
man of books and a man of the people." Clearly, he possessed the ambition that would carry him far beyond the typical pastorate of a Southern Baptist minister. He aspired to something greater, something that
would be both challenging and rewarding. He could not have found a
better place from which to seek those goals than as president of Southern Seminary. As a man of books, he came in contact with the current

---

[2]Garrett, Hinson, and Tull, *Are Southern Baptists "Evangelicals"?*, 202; Ellis, "Edgar Young Mullins and the Crisis of Moderate Southern Baptist Leadership," 171-83.

theological, intellectual, and religious ideas of his day. Not being passive in nature, he contributed to Christian literature by attempting to accommodate modern thought in evangelicalism. In this phase of his work he rubbed shoulders with leading theologians and religious leaders, many of whom were more liberal than himself. As a man of the people, he came in contact with all types of parishioners. He witnessed poverty in Baltimore and affluence in the Boston area. After taking over the Seminary presidency, he came in touch with many fundamentalists, a group that presented just as much of a challenge as modernist thought.[3]

Several interrelated themes were repeated throughout Mullins's life. First, Mullins was an example of the moderate evangelical, particularly as he tried to synthesize evangelical faith with modernity. Second, his attempt to be "a man of books and a man of the people" was a difficult task in a denomination with such diversity as the Southern Baptist Convention. Third, throughout his career at Southern Seminary Mullins attempted to blend his roles as administrator, theologian, and denominational leader. Finally, Mullins exemplified the crisis of moderate Southern Baptist leadership, from its origins in the late nineteenth century to the time of his death.

What is the place of Mullins among early-twentieth-century American religious leaders? The difficulty of categorizing a moderate like Mullins is well illustrated by the attempts to classify his theology. He has been described as a "moderate Calvinist," "conservative progressive," "liberal fundamentalist," and "modern Positive."[4] Sydney E. Ahlstrom perhaps best depicted Mullins as "Urbane, conciliatory, and reasonable," an advocate of "Moderation" on doctrinal matters.[5] During the critical evolution controversy in the 1920s, Mullins characteristically declared, "I have no sympathy with the ultra fundamentalists who would deprive" teachers of their rights.[6] To another Baptist, he stated that the

---

[3]Mullins to Poteat, 16 November 1885.

[4]McGlothlin, "Edgar Young Mullins," 322; Cline, "Some Baptist Systematic Theologians," 315; Wayne E. Ward, professor at Southern Baptist Theological Seminary, to the author, 9 March 1967; Horton, "Systematic Theology," 212.

[5]Ahlstrom, "Theology in America: A Historical Survey," 303, 306.

[6]Mullins to Livingston Johnson, 12 September 1925.

220 🖅   William E. Ellis

clash "Between the modernists and the fogies [fundamentalists]" placed
the moderates in a precarious position.[7]

Displaying moderation on most controversial topics, including economic, political, and racial matters, Mullins never became a political
activist until the battle over Prohibition developed in the late 1920s. In
the theological sphere Mullins acted as liaison between his Southern and
Northern Baptist brethren, illustrating the moderate as border-state
conciliator. The proximity of Southern Seminary to the Midwest demanded such an effort. In addition, he tried to create a moderate synthesis combining evangelicalism with the newer trends of thought. Until
World War I he fulfilled this role with difficulty, ameliorating the factious elements in his denomination. His work with the Baptist Young
People's Union of America, the General Convention of Baptists in North
America, the Baptist Congress, and the Federal Council evidenced Mullins's strong ecumenical inclinations. His important volume *The Christian Expression in Its Doctrinal Expression* represented the last hope
for synthesis. In the tumultuous 1920s, however, fundamentalists and
modernists forced moderates to choose between them, and the middle
ground disappeared.

At the end of his career Mullins was more closely attuned than ever
to the conservatism of his Southern Baptist fundamentalist brethren. The
progressive urgings in both religious and civic affairs were no longer
clearly evident. In his attempt to fulfill the roles of administrator, theologian, and denominational leader, Mullins sought independence, but
in the end the fundamentalists wore him down. They took control of the
Convention leadership by 1926, already dominating on the local level.
Mullins abandoned the role of theologian because theological change
passed him by, and the obsession of building a new Seminary con-
sumed his time. In his last years he no longer taught, thereby losing his
moderating influence over young theological students. The evolution
controversy among Southern Baptists demanded uniformity as the price
for denominational identity and survival, while the economic difficulties of the agrarian South militated against moderation in the Southern
Baptist Convention. The conformity that emerged from the evolution
controversy was compounded by denominational centralization within

---

[7]Mullins to Walter M. Lee, 15 February 1926.

the Southern Baptist Convention owing to the impetus of the 75 Million Campaign and the advent of the Cooperative Program. More than any other single group, the moderates had urged centralization, only to lose control to the fundamentalists. Beset by these difficulties, however, Mullins helped limit the scope of antievolutionist success through legislation, continually arguing that religious people leave public education alone. By the end of his career Mullins demonstrated a growing concern for the welfare of his nation. His submission to the antievolutionist forces within the Convention signified a victory for religious fundamentalism, which also had its counterpart in the public sphere. In 1928 he took a leading role in the anti-Smith campaign, displaying uncharacteristic disdain for urban, Catholic America.

In addition, Mullins evinced other themes throughout his years at Southern Seminary. Foremost was his strong evangelical inclination. His role as theologian was that of the scholar attempting to reconcile the newer methods of scholarship and scientific knowledge with the old-time religion. Those of moderate inclinations praised his efforts; fundamentalists hardly listened at all. Moderate and fundamentalist Baptists alike held to the ethos of evangelicalism. This common trait bound their reactions toward increasing conformity. Mullins's role as theologian suffered because his evangelical predilections and the Southern Baptist atmosphere precluded any real theological innovation.

The desire for efficiency, an influence of business Progressivism, permeated his administration. His thoughts in this area often reflected quantitative terms more than quality, gauging the Seminary's growth in terms of enrollment, number of buildings, and size of the faculty. During his nearly three decades as its president, he saw the Seminary double its student body and faculty. Against nearly overwhelming odds he worked to build a new Seminary plant, an outstanding legacy to Southern Baptists. Competition with two other Southern Baptist seminaries, as well as with Northern seminaries, brought out his materialistic instincts. He did improve, however, the quality of the Southern Baptist ministry, providing a scholarly example for most of his career to his colleagues and students.

Mullins should rank as the premiere Southern Baptist theologian of this century. Successful in many ways as a theologian, administrator, and denominational leader, he was unable to break the hold of Southern culture on his denomination, and in the end the pervasive cultural configuration of that region prevailed. The victories of religious fundamentalism and political conservatism were part of that milieu.

A BIBLIOGRAPHICAL NOTE

Primary Sources. The Presidential Correspondence of Mullins for the years 1899-1928, located in the Boyce Memorial Library, Southern Baptist Theological Seminary, proved to be invaluable in piecing together Mullins's daily life. In many cases, the correspondence helped separate the private Mullins from the public Mullins. During the initial stages of this research, the Mullins collection was much as it had been when he died in 1928. An indexing system now can be used to mine this valuable collection in Southern Baptist history. Other manuscript collections at the University of Chicago, the Dargan-Carver Library in Nashville, and the American Baptist Historical Society, Rochester, New York, contain valuable Mullins correspondence with other Baptist leaders.

Baptist periodicals, particularly the *Western Recorder, Baptist Argus (World),* and *Religious Herald* provided a major source of information for gauging the thoughts and actions of Southern Baptists. Selected issues of other Baptist periodicals at crucial times in Mullins's life were viewed.

Of course, the voluminous writings of Mullins himself proved to be another valuable primary source. In ten major books, dozens of pamphlets and reports, and over one hundred articles and book reviews in the denominational press, Mullins left behind an excellent record of his theological and religious thought.

Secondary Works. The published and unpublished works listed below represent only a few of the most important secondary sources consulted in the preparation of this book.

As noted in my article, "Evolution, Fundamentalism, and the Historians: An Historiographical Review," *The Historian* 44 (November 1981): 15-27, three historiographical trends have been clearly evident since Mullins's time. The old standbys, including, of course, Norman F. Furniss, *The Fundamentalist Controversy, 1918-1931* (New Haven: Yale University Press, 1954) and Stewart G. Cole, *The History of Fundamentalism* (Hamden CT: Archon Brooks, 1963) continue to provide a somewhat biased but reliable historical base for an older generation of evangelical/fundamentalist historiography.

In the early 1960s a new generation of monographs, which treated conservative religion more sympathetically, began to reinterpret the field. Although not specifically a scholar of conservative Protestantism, Paul A. Carter questioned old shop-worn interpretations in such offerings as *The Twenties in America* (New York: Thomas Y. Crowell, 1968) and "The Fundamentalist Defense of the Faith," in *Change and Continuity in Twentieth Century America: The 1920s,* ed. John Braeman, et al. (Columbus: Ohio State University Press, 1968), and provided a counterpoise to the liberal bias of such authors as Richard Hofstadter. Willard B. Gatewood, Jr., *Preachers, Pedagogues, and Politicians: The Evolution Controversy in North Carolina, 1920-1927* (Chapel Hill: University of North Carolina Press, 1966) and Kenneth K. Bailey, *Southern White Protestantism in the Twentieth Century* (New York: Harper and Row, 1964) provided model monographs in the transitional stage of historiographical development in the mid-1960s.

Several important studies, published and unpublished, have had a profound impact on my interpretation of Mullins and his era. Some of the books below were published after the initial work was completed; however, these books represent the current state of evangelical/fundamentalist historiography and are suggested for further reading.

Ferenc Morton Szasz, *The Divided Mind of Protestant America, 1880-1930* (University AL: University of Alabama Press, 1982) separates the liberal and conservative wings of Protestantism a bit too conveniently. However, as an introduction to late-nineteenth- and early-twentieth-century history of American Protestantism there is no better starting point than Szasz's clearly written account.

Four more specialized studies should be of particular concern to those interested specifically in the history of evangelical fundamentalism. Books by Ernest R. Sandeen, Timothy P. Weber, and George M. Marsden work the fields of fundamentalism and premillennialism from different perspectives. These books, along with another by Norman H. Clark, have elevated the study of conservative religion and civil religion to an art.

In 1970 Sandeen produced *The Roots of Fundamentalism: British and American Millenarianism, 1800-1930* (Chicago: University of Chicago Press, 1970), in which he traced the ideological roots of fundamentalism to a melding of Princeton theology and dispensational premillennialism. In this and other works he declared that fundamentalism was neither a Southern phenomenon nor a rural one. Timothy P. Weber in a more recent book, *Living in the Shadow of the Second Coming: American Premillennialism, 1875-1925* (New York: Oxford University Press, 1979) was more concerned about the purely indigenous origins of the movement. He stressed nuances among premillennialists and the fact that psychological pronouncements alone will not explain the complexities of premillennialist behavior and thought. George M. Marsden's *Fundamentalism and American Culture: The Shaping of Twentieth-Century Evangelicalism, 1870-1925* (New York: Oxford University Press, 1980) found a much broader base to evangelicalism and fundamentalism than any of the commentators so far discussed, hence his cultural rubric. He claimed that fundamentalists, in particular, were never as one dimensional as usually claimed by their liberal critics. Marsden's book is so well-developed and balanced that it should replace earlier accounts of evangelical and fundamentalist theology as the standard text. Although not a book specifically about evangelicals or fundamentalists, but on a topic dear to many of them, *Deliver Us From Evil: An Interpretation of American Prohibition* (New York: W. W. Norton, 1976) by Norman H. Clark recognizes liquor restriction as a genuine reform movement and contributes to a whole library of excellent alcohol studies in the last decade.

For the more specific study of Southern Baptists, several works stand out. The dissertations of Bill Clark Thomas, "Edgar Young Mullins: A

Baptist Exponent of Theological Restatement" (Th.D. diss., Southern Baptist Theological Seminary, 1963), Hugh Alexander Brimm, "The Social Consciousness of Southern Baptists in Relation to Some Regional Problems, 1910-1935" (Th.D. diss., Southern Baptist Theological Seminary, 1944), and Russell Hooper Dilday, Jr., "The Apologetic Method of E. Y. Mullins," (Th.D. diss., Southwestern Baptist Theological Seminary, 1960) provided valuable insights, particularly of the theological variety, on Baptist thought and action. John Lee Eighmy's *Churches in Cultural Captivity: A History of the Social Attitudes of Southern Baptists* (Knoxville: University of Tennessee Press, 1972) became a model for Southern Baptist scholars when published posthumously in 1972. James J. Thompson, Jr., *Tried as by Fire: Southern Baptists and the Religious Controversies of the 1920s* (Macon GA: Mercer University Press, 1982) is an important study of a specific era of Southern Baptist history. While Thompson's classification of Southern Baptists in the 1920s may be a bit skewed, this is an excellent interpretative account of one of the most important eras in the history of that denomination. Finally, Wayne Flynt's "Dissent in Zion: Alabama Baptists and Social Issues," *Journal of Southern History* 35 (November 1969): 523-42, is a landmark in the elevation of Southern Baptist history to the realm of serious analysis.

INDEX